LECTURES

ON

METAPHYSICS AND LOGIC

BY

SIR WILLIAM HAMILTON, BART.

PROFESSOR OF LOGIC AND METAPHYSICS IN THE UNIVERSITY OF EDINBURGH;

ADVOCATE, A. M. (OXON.), ETC.; CORRESPONDING MEMBER OF THE INSTITUTE OF FRANCE; HONORARY
MEMBER OF THE AMERICAN ACADEMY OF ARTS AND SCIENCES; AND OF THE
LATIN SOCIETY OF JENA, ETC.

EDITED BY

THE REV. HENRY L. MANSEL, B. D., OXFORD,

AND

JOHN VEITCH, M. A., EDINBURGH.

IN TWO VOLUMES.

VOL. I.

METAPHYSICS.

BOSTON:

GOULD AND LINCOLN,

59 WASHINGTON STREET.

NEW YORK: SHELDON AND COMPANY.

CINCINNATI: GEORGE S. BLANCHARD.

1865.

ON EARTH, THERE IS NOTHING GREAT BUT MAN;

IN MAN, THERE IS NOTHING GREAT BUT MIND.

AUTHORIZATION.

MESSRS. GOULD AND LINCOLN, OF BOSTON, UNITED STATES, ARE EXCLUSIVELY AUTHOR-IZED BY ME TO PUBLISH IN AMERICA THE LECTURES, METAPHYSICAL AND LOGICAL, OF THE LATE SIR WILLIAM HAMILTON, BART.

HUBERT HAMILTON.

16 GREAT KING STREET,
EDINBURGH, 14 SEPT., 1858.

ELECTROTYPED AND PRINTED BY
W. F. DRAPER, ANDOVER, MASS.

PREFACE.

THE following Lectures on Metaphysics constitute the first portion of the Biennial Course which the lamented Author was in the habit of delivering during the period of his occupation of the Chair of Logic and Metaphysics, in the University of Edinburgh. The Lectures on Logic, which were delivered in the alternate years, will follow as soon as they can be prepared for publication.

In giving these Lectures to the world, it is due, both to the Author and to his readers, to acknowledge that they do not appear in that state of completeness which might have been expected, had they been prepared for publication by the Author himself. As Lectures on Metaphysics, — whether that term be taken in its wider or its stricter sense, — they are confessedly imperfect. The Author himself, adopting the Kantian division of the mental faculties into those of Knowledge, Feeling, and Conation, considers the Philosophy of Mind as comprehending, in relation to each of these, the three great subdivisions of Psychology, or the Science of the Phænomena of Mind; Nomology, or the Science of its Laws; and Ontology, or the Science of Results and Inferences.[1] The term *Metaphysics*, in its strictest sense, is synonymous with the last of these subdivisions; while, in its widest sense, it may be regarded as including the first also, — the second

[1] See below, Lecture vii., p 86 *et seq.*

B

being, in practice at least, if not in scientific accuracy, usually distributed among other departments of Philosophy. The following Lectures cannot be considered as embracing the whole province of Metaphysics in either of the above senses. Among the Phænomena of Mind, the Cognitive Faculties are discussed fully and satisfactorily; those of Feeling are treated with less detail; those of Conation receive scarcely any special consideration; while the questions of Ontology, or Metaphysics proper, are touched upon only incidentally. The omission of any special discussion of this last branch may perhaps be justified by its abstruse character, and unsuitableness for a course of elementary instruction; but it is especially to be regretted, both on account of the general neglect of this branch of study by the entire school of Scottish philosophers, and also on account of the eminent qualifications which the Author possessed for supplying this acknowledged deficiency. A treatise on Ontology from the pen of Sir William Hamilton, embodying the final results of the Philosophy of the Conditioned, would have been a boon to the philosophical world such as probably no writer now living is capable of conferring.

The circumstances under which these Lectures were written must also be taken into account in estimating their character, both as a specimen of the Author's powers, and as a contribution to philosophical literature.

Sir William Hamilton was elected to the Chair of Logic and Metaphysics in July, 1836. In the interval between his appointment and the commencement of the College Session (November of the same year), the Author was assiduously occupied in making preparation for discharging the duties of his office. The principal part of those duties consisted, according to the practice of the University, in the delivery of a Course of Lectures on the subjects assigned to the chair. On his appointment to the Professorship, Sir William Hamilton experienced considerable difficulty in deciding on the character of the course of Lectures on Philosophy, which, while doing justice to the subject, would at the same time meet the wants of his auditors, who were ordinarily composed of comparatively young students, in the second year of their university curriculum. The Author of the articles on *Cousin's Philosophy*,[1] on *Perception*,[2] and on *Logic*,[3] had already given ample proof of those speculative accomplishments, and that profound philosophical learning, which, in Britain at least, were conjoined in an equal degree by no other man of his time. But those very qualities which placed him in the front rank of speculative thinkers, joined to his love of precision and system, and his lofty ideal of philosophical composition, served but to make him the more keenly alive to the requirements of his subject, and to the difficulties that lay in the way of combining elementary instruction in Philosophy with the adequate discussion of its topics. Hence, although even at this period his methodized stores of learning were ample and pertinent, the opening of the College Session found him still reading and reflecting, and unsatisfied with even the small portion of matter which he had been able to commit to writing. His first Course of Lectures (Metaphysical) thus·fell to be written during the currency of the Session (1836–7). The Author was in the habit of delivering three Lectures each week; and each Lecture was usually written on the day, or, more properly, on the evening and night, preceding its delivery. The Course of Metaphysics, as it is now given to the world, is the result of this nightly toil, unremittingly sustained for a period of five months. These Lectures were thus designed solely for a temporary purpose — the use of the Author's own classes; they were, moreover, always regarded by the Author himself as defective as a complete Course of Metaphysics; and they never were revised by him with any view to publication, and this chiefly for the reason that he intended to make use of various portions of them which had not been incorporated in

---

[1] *Edinburgh Review*, 1829. [2] *Ibid.*, 1830. [3] *Ibid.*, 1833.

his other writings, in the promised Supplementary Dissertations to Reid's Works, — a design which his failing health did not permit him to complete.

The Lectures on Logic were not composed until the following Session (1837–8). This Course was also, in great part, written during the currency of the Session.

These circumstances will account for the repetition, in some places, of portions of the Author's previously published writings, and for the numerous and extensive quotations from other writers, which are interspersed throughout the present Course. Most of these have been ascertained by references furnished by the Author himself, either in the manuscript of the present Lectures, or in his Common Place Book. These quotations, while they detract in some degree from the originality of the work, can, however, hardly be considered as lessening its value. Many of the authors quoted are but little known in this country; and the extracts from their writings will, to the majority of readers, have all the novelty of original remarks. They also exhibit, in a remarkable degree, the Author's singular power of appreciating and making use of every available hint scattered through those obscurer regions of thought, through which his extensive reading conducted him. No part of Sir William Hamilton's writings more completely verifies the remark of his American critic, Mr. Tyler: "There seems to be not even a random thought of any value, which has been dropped along any, even obscure, path of mental activity, in any age or country, that his diligence has not recovered, his sagacity appreciated, and his judgment husbanded in the stores of his knowledge."[1] Very frequently, indeed, the thought which the Author selects and makes his own, acquires its value and significance in the very process of selection;

---

[1] *Princeton Review*, October, 1855. This article has since been republished with the Author's name, in his Essay on the *Progress of Philosophy in the Past and in the Future.* Philadelphia, 1858.

and the contribution is more enriched than the adopter; for what, in another, is but a passing reflection, seen in a faint light, isolated and fruitless, often rises, in the hands of Sir William Hamilton, to the rank of a great, permanent, and luminous principle, receives its appropriate place in the order of truths to which it belongs, and proves, in many instances, a centre of radiation over a wide expanse of the field of human knowledge.

The present volume may also appear to some disadvantage on account of the length of time which has elapsed between its composition and its publication. Other writings, particularly the *Dissertations* appended to Reid's Works,[1] and part of the new matter in the *Discussions*, though earlier in point of publication, contain later and more mature phases of the Author's thought, on some of the questions discussed in the following pages. Much that would have been new to English readers twenty years ago, has, subsequently, in a great measure by the instrumentality of the Author himself, become well known; and the familiar expositions designed for the oral instruction of beginners in philosophy, have been eclipsed by those profounder reflections which have been published for the deliberate study of the philosophical world at large.

But, when all these deductions have been made, the work before us will still remain a noble monument of the Author's philosophical genius and learning. In many respects, indeed, it is qualified to become more popular than any of his other publications. The very necessity which the Author was under, of adapting his observations, in some degree, to the needs and attainments of his hearers, has also fitted them for the instruction and gratification of a wide circle of general readers, who would have less relish for the severer style in which some of his later thoughts are conveyed. The present Lectures,

---

1 The *foot-notes* to Reid were, for the most part, written nearly contemporaneously with the present Lectures.

if in depth and exactness of thought they are, for the most part, not equal to the *Dissertations* on Reid, or to some portions of the *Discussions*, possess attractions of their own, which will probably recommend them to a more numerous class of admirers; while they retain, in no small degree, the ample learning and philosophical acumen which are identified with the Author's previous reputation.

Apart, however, from considerations of their intrinsic value, these Lectures possess a high academical and historical interest. For twenty years, — from 1836 to 1856, — the Courses of Logic and Metaphysics were the means through which Sir William Hamilton sought to discipline and imbue with his philosophical opinions, the numerous youth who gathered from Scotland and other countries to his class-room; and while, by these prelections, the Author supplemented, developed, and moulded the National Philosophy, — leaving thereon the ineffaceable impress of his genius and learning, — he, at the same time and by the same means, exercised over the intellects and feelings of his pupils an influence which, for depth, intensity, and elevation, was certainly never surpassed by that of any philosophical instructor. Among his pupils there are not a few who, having lived for a season under the constraining power of his intellect, and been led to reflect on those great questions regarding the character, origin, and bounds of human knowledge, which his teachings stirred and quickened, bear the memory of their beloved and revered Instructor inseparably blended with what is highest in their present intellectual life, as well as in their practical aims and aspirations.

The Editors, in offering these Lectures to the public, are, therefore, encouraged to express their belief, that they will not be found unworthy of the illustrious name which they bear. In the discharge of their own duties as annotators, the Editors have thought it due to the fame of the Author, to leave his opinions to be judged entirely by their own merits, without the accompaniment of criticisms, concurrent or dissentient. For the same reason, they have abstained from noticing such criticisms as have appeared on those portions of the work which have already been published in other forms. Their own annotations are, for the most part, confined to occasional explanations and verifications of the numerous references and allusions scattered through the text. The notes fall, as will be observed, into three classes:

I. Original; notes printed from the manuscript of the present Lectures. These appear without any distinctive mark. Mere Jottings or Memoranda by the Author, made on the manuscript, are generally marked as such. To these are also added a few Oral Interpolations of the Author, made in the course of reading the Lectures, which have been recovered from the note-books of students.

II. Supplied; notes extracted or compiled by the Editors from the Author's Common Place Book and fragmentary papers. These are enclosed in square brackets, and are without signature.

III. Editorial; notes added by the Editors. These always bear the signature " ED." When added as supplementary to the original or supplied notes, they are generally enclosed in square brackets, besides having the usual signature.

The Editors have been at pains to trace and examine the notes of the first and second classes with much care; and have succeeded in discovering the authorities referred to, with very few and insignificant exceptions. The Editors trust that the Original and Supplied Notes may prove of service to students of Philosophy, as indications of sources of philosophical opinions, which, in many cases, are but little, if at all, known in this country.

The Appendix embraces a few papers, chiefly fragmentary, which appeared to the Editors to be deserving of publication. Several of these are fragments of discussions which the Author had written with a view to the Memoir of Mr. Dugald Stewart, on the editorship of whose works he was engaged at the period of his death. They thus possess the melancholy interest which attaches to the latest of his compositions. To these philosophical fragments have been added a few papers on physiological subjects. These consist of an extract from the Author's Lectures on Phrenology, and communications made by him to various medical publications. Apart from the value of their results, these physiological investigations serve to exhibit, in a department of inquiry foreign to the class of subjects with which the mind of the Author was ordinarily occupied, that habit of careful, accurate, and unsparing research, by which Sir William Hamilton was so eminently characterized.

CONTENTS.

LECTURE I.

LECTURE II.

LECTURE III.

LECTURE IV.

LECTURE V.

LECTURE VI.

LECTURE VII.

LECTURE VIII.

LECTURE IX.

LECTURE X.

LECTURE XI.

LECTURE XII.

LECTURE XIII.

LECTURE XIV.

LECTURE XV.

LECTURE XVI.

LECTURE XVII.

LECTURE XVIII.

LECTURE XIX.

LECTURE XX.

LECTURE XXI.

LECTURE XXII.

LECTURE XXIII.

LECTURE XXIV.

LECTURE XXV.

LECTURE XXVI.

LECTURE XXVII.

LECTURE XXVIII.

LECTURE XXIX.

LECTURE XXX.

LECTURE XXXI.

LECTURE XXXII.

LECTURE XXXIII.

LECTURE XXXIV.

LECTURE XXXV.

LECTURE XXXVI.

LECTURE XXXVII.

LECTURE XXXVIII.

LECTURE XXXIX.

LECTURE XL.

LECTURE XLI.

LECTURE XLII.

LECTURE XLIII.

LECTURE XLIV.

LECTURE XLV.

LECTURE XLVI.

APPENDIX.

LECTURES ON METAPHYSICS.

LECTURE I.

PHILOSOPHY—ITS ABSOLUTE UTILITY.

(A.) SUBJECTIVE.

GENTLEMEN—In the commencement of a course of instruction in any department of knowledge, it is usual, be-

PHILOSOPHY: its benefits and pleasures.

fore entering on the regular consideration of the subject, to premise a general survey of the more important advantages which it affords, and this with the view of animating the student to a higher assiduity, by holding up to him, in prospect, some at least of those benefits and pleasures which he may promise to himself in reward of his exertions.

And if such a preparation be found expedient for other branches of study, it is, I think, peculiarly requisite in Phil-

The exhibition of these, why peculiarly requisite.

osophy, — Philosophy Proper, — the Science of Mind. For, in the first place, the most important advantages to be derived from the cultivation of philosophy, are not, in themselves, direct, palpable, obtrusive: they are, therefore, of their own nature, peculiarly liable to be overlooked or disparaged by the world at large; because to estimate them at their proper value requires in the judge more than a vulgar complement of information and intelligence. But, in the second place, the many are not simply by negative incompetence disqualified for an opinion; they are, moreover, by positive error, at once rendered incapable of judging right; and yet, by positive error, encouraged to a decision. For there are at present afloat, and in very general acceptation, certain superficial misconceptions in regard to the end and objects of education, which render the popular opinion of the comparative importance of its different branches, not merely false, but precisely the reverse of truth; the

1 *

studies which, in reality, are of the highest value as a mean of intellectual development, being those which, on the vulgar standard of utility, are at the very bottom of the scale; while those which, in the nomenclature of the multitude, are emphatically, — distinctively, denominated the Useful, are precisely those which, in relation to the great ends of liberal education, possess the least, and least general, utility.

In considering the utility of a branch of knowledge, it behooves us, in the first place, to estimate its value as viewed simply in itself; and, in the second, its value as viewed in relation to other branches. Considered in itself, a science is valuable in proportion as its cultivation is immediately conducive to the mental improvement of the cultivator. This may be called its Absolute utility. In relation to others, a science is valuable in proportion as its study is necessary for the prosecution of other branches of knowledge. This may be called its Relative utility. In this latter point of view, that is as relatively useful, I cannot at present enter upon the value of Philosophy, — I cannot attempt to show how it supplies either the materials or the rules to all the sciences; and how, in particular, its study is of importance to the Lawyer, the Physician, and, above all, to the Theologian. All this I must for the present pass by.

Utility of a branch of knowledge of two grand kinds — Absolute and Relative.

In the former point of view, that is, considered absolutely, or in itself, the philosophy of mind comprises two several utilities, according as it, 1°, Cultivates the mind or knowing subject, by calling its faculties into exercise; and, 2°, Furnishes the mind with a certain complement of truths or objects of knowledge. The former of these constitutes its Subjective, the latter its Objective utility. These utilities are not the same, nor do they even stand to each other in any necessary proportion. As the special consideration of both is more than I can compass in the present Lecture, I am constrained to limit myself to one alone; and as the subjective utility is that which has usually been overlooked, though not assuredly of the two the less important, while at the same time its exposition affords in part the rationale of the method of instruction which I have adopted, I shall at present only attempt an illustration of the advantages afforded by the Philosophy of Mind, regarded as the study which, of all others, best cultivates the mind or subject of knowledge, by supplying to its higher faculties the occasions of their most vigorous, and therefore their most improving, exercise.

Absolute utility of two kinds — Subjective and Objective.

There are few, I believe, disposed to question the speculative dig-

Practical utility of Philosophy.

nity of mental science; but its practical utility is not unfrequently denied. To what, it is asked, is the science of mind conducive? What are its uses?

I am not one of those who think that the importance of a study is sufficiently established when its dignity is admitted; for, holding that knowledge is for the sake of man, and not man for the sake of knowledge, it is necessary, in order to vindicate its value, that every science should be able to show what are the advantages which it promises to confer upon its student. I, therefore, profess myself a utilitarian; and it is only on the special ground of its utility that I would claim for the philosophy of mind, what I regard as

The Useful.

its peculiar and preëminent importance. But what is a utilitarian? Simply one who prefers

the Useful to the Useless — and who does not? But what is the useful? That which is prized, not on its own account, but as conducive to the acquisition of something else, — the useful is, in short, only another word for a mean towards an end; for every mean is useful, and whatever is useful is a mean. Now the value of a mean is always in proportion to the value of its end; and the useful being a mean, it follows, that, of two utilities, the one which conduces to the more valuable end will be itself the more valuable utility.

So far there is no difference of opinion. All agree that the useful is a mean towards an end; and that, *cœteris paribus*, a mean towards a higher end constitutes a higher utility than a mean towards a lower. The only dispute that has arisen, or can possibly arise, in regard to the utility of means (supposing always their relative efficiency), is founded on the various views that may be entertained in regard to the existence and comparative importance of ends.

Now the various opinions which prevail concerning the comparative utility of human sciences and studies,

Two errors in the popular estimate of the comparative utility of human sciences.

have all arisen from two errors.[1]

The first of these consists in viewing man, not as an end *unto himself*, but merely as a mean organized for the sake of something *out of himself;*

and, under this partial view of human destination, those branches of knowledge obtain exclusively the name of *useful*, which tend to qualify a human being to act the lowly part of a dexterous instrument.

[1] With the following observations may be compared the author's remarks on the distinction between a *liberal* and a *professional* education, in his article on the study of mathematics, *Edinburgh Review*, vol. lxii., p. 409, reprinted in his *Discussions*, p. 263. — ED.

The second, and the more dangerous of these errors, consists in regarding the cultivation of our faculties as subordinate to the acquisition of knowledge, instead of regarding the possession of knowledge as subordinate to the cultivation of our faculties; and, in consequence of this error, those sciences which afford a greater number of more certain facts, have been deemed superior in utility to those which bestow a higher cultivation on the higher faculties of the mind.

As to the first of these errors, the fallacy is so palpable, that we may well wonder at its prevalence. It is manifest, indeed, that man, in so far as he is a mean for the glory of God, must be an end unto himself, for it is only in the accomplishment of his own perfection, that, as a creature, he can manifest the glory of his Creator. Though therefore man, by relation to God, be but a mean, for that very reason, in relation to ,all else is he an end. Wherefore, now speaking of him exclusively in his natural capacity and temporal relations, I say it is manifest that man is by nature necessarily an end to himself,— that his perfection and happiness constitute the goal of his activity, to which he tends, and ought to tend, when not diverted from this, his general and native destination, by peculiar and accidental circumstances. But it is equally evident, that, under the condition of society, individual men are, for the most part, to a greater or less degree, actually so diverted. To live, the individual must have the means of living; and these means, (unless he already possess them,) he must procure,—he must purchase. But purchase with what? With his services, *i. e.*—he must reduce himself to an instrument,—an instrument of utility to others, and the services of this instrument he must barter for those means of subsistence of which he is in want. In other words, he must exercise some trade, calling, or profession.

Thus, in the actualities of social life, each man, instead of being solely an end to himself,— instead of being able to make everything subordinate to that full and harmonious development of his individual faculties, in which his full perfection and his true happiness consist, — is, in general, compelled to degrade himself into the mean or instrument towards the accomplishment of some end, external to himself, and for the benefit of others.

Now the perfection of man as an end, and the perfection of man as a mean or instrument, are not only not the same, they are, in reality, generally opposed.

And as these two perfections are different, so the training requisite for their acquisition is not identical, and has, accordingly, been distinguished by different names. The one is styled Liberal, the other Professional education, — the branches of knowledge cultivated for these purposes being called respectively liberal and professional, or liberal and lucrative, sciences. By the Germans, the latter are usually distinguished as the *Brodwissenschaften*, which we may translate, *The Bread and Butter Sciences*.[1] A few of the professions, indeed, as requiring a higher development of the higher faculties and involving, therefore, a greater or less amount of liberal education, have obtained the name of liberal professions. We must, however, recollect that this is only an accidental and a very partial exception. But though the full and harmonious development of our faculties be the high and natural destination of all, while the cultivation of any professional dexterity is only a contingency, though a contingency incumbent upon most, it has, however, happened that the paramount and universal end of man, — of man absolutely, — has been often ignorantly lost sight of, and the term *useful* appropriated exclusively to those acquirements which have a value only to man considered in his relative, lower, and accidental character of an instrument. But, because some have thus been led to appropriate the name of useful to those studies and objects of knowledge, which are conducive to the inferior end, it assuredly

Misapplication of the term useful. does not follow that those conducive to the higher have not a far preferable title to the name thus curiously denied to them. Even admitting, therefore, that the study of mind is of no immediate advantage in preparing the student for many of the subordinate parts in the mechanism of society, its utility cannot, on that account, be called in question, unless it be asserted that man "liveth by bread alone," and has no higher destination than that of the calling by which he earns his subsistence.

The second error to which I have adverted, reverses the relative subordination of knowledge and of intellectual cultivation. In refutation of this, I shall attempt *Knowledge and intellectual cultivation.* briefly to show, *firstly*, that knowledge and intellectual cultivation are not identical; *secondly*, that knowledge is itself principally valuable as a mean of intellectual cultivation; and, *lastly*, that intellectual cultivation is more directly and effectually accomplished by the study of mind than by any other of our rational pursuits.

But to prevent misapprehension, I may premise what I mean by knowledge, and what by intellectual cultivation. By knowledge is understood the mere possession of truths; by intellectual cultiva-

---

1 Schelling, *Vorlesungen über die Methode des Academischen Studium*, p. 67. — ED.

tion, or intellectual development, the power, acquired through exercise by the higher faculties, of a more varied, vigorous and protracted activity.

In the first place, then, it will be requisite, I conceive, to say *Not identical.* but little to show that knowledge and intellectual development are not only not the same, but stand in no necessary proportion to each other. This is manifest if we consider the very different conditions under which these two qualities are acquired. The one condition under which all powers, and consequently the intellectual faculties, are developed, is exercise. The more intense and continuous the exercise, the more vigorously developed will be the power.

But a certain quantity of knowledge,—in other words, a certain amount of possessed truths,—does not suppose, as its condition, a corresponding sum of intellectual exercise. One truth requires much, another truth requires little, effort in acquisition; and, while the original discovery of a truth evolves perhaps a maximum of the highest quality of energy, the subsequent learning of that truth elicits probably but a minimum of the very lowest.

But, as it is evident that the possession of truths, and the development of the mind in which they are deposited, *Is truth or mental exercise the superior end?* are not identical, I proceed, in the second place, to show that, considered as ends, and in relation to each other, the knowledge of truths is not supreme, but subordinate to the cultivation of the knowing mind. The question—Is Truth, or is the Mental Exercise in the pursuit of truth, the superior end?—this is perhaps the most curious theoretical, and certainly the most important practical, problem in the whole compass of philosophy. For, according to the solution at which we arrive, must we accord the higher or the lower rank to certain great departments of study; and, what is of more importance, the character of its solution, as it determines the aim, regulates from first to last the method, which an enlightened science of education must adopt.

But, however curious and important, this question has never, in so far as I am aware, been regularly discussed. *Popular solution of this question.* Nay, what is still more remarkable, the erroneous alternative has been very generally assumed as true. The consequence of this has been, that sciences of far inferior, have been elevated above sciences of far superior, utility; while education has been systematically distorted,—though truth and nature have occasionally burst the shackles which a perverse theory had imposed. The reason of this is sufficiently obvious. At first sight, it seems even absurd to doubt that truth is more valuable than its pursuit; for is this not to say that the end is less important than the mean?—and on this superficial view is the prevalent misapprehension founded. A slight consideration will, however, expose the fallacy.

Knowledge is either practical or speculative. In practical knowledge it is evident that truth is not the ultimate end; for, in that case, knowledge is, *ex hypothesi*, for the sake of application. The knowledge of a moral, of a political, of a religious truth, is of value only as it affords the preliminary or condition of its exercise.

Practical knowledge; its end.

In speculative knowledge, on the other hand, there may indeed, at first sight, seem greater difficulty; but further reflection will prove that speculative truth is only pursued, and is only held of value, for the sake of intellectual activity: "Sordet cognita veritas" is a shrewd aphorism of Seneca. A truth, once known, falls into comparative insignificance. It is now prized, less on its own account than as opening up new ways to new activity, new suspense, new hopes, new discoveries, new self-gratulation. Every votary of science is wilfully ignorant of a thousand established facts,—of a thousand which he might make his own more easily than he could attempt the discovery of even one. But it is not knowledge,—it is not truth,—that he principally seeks; he seeks the exercise of his faculties and feelings; and, as in following after the one he exerts a greater amount of pleasurable energy than in taking formal possession of the thousand, he disdains the certainty of the many, and prefers the chances of the one. Accordingly, the sciences always studied with keenest interest are those in a state of progress and uncertainty; absolute certainty and absolute completion would be the paralysis of any study; and the last worst calamity that could befall man, as he is at present constituted, would be that full and final possession of speculative truth, which he now vainly anticipates as the consummation of his intellectual happiness.

The end of speculative knowledge.

"Quæsivit cœlo lucem, ingemuitque reperta."[1]

But what is true of science is true, indeed, of all human activity. "In life," as the great Pascal observes, "we always believe that we are seeking repose, while, in reality, all that we ever seek is agitation."[2] When Pyrrhus proposed to subdue a part of the

1 Virgil, Æn. iv. 692.—Ed.
2 *Pensées*, partie i. art. vii. § 1, (vol. ii. p. 34,

ed. Faugère): "Ils croient chercher sincèrement le repos, et ne cherchent en effet que

world, and then to enjoy rest among his friends, he believed that what he sought was possession, not pursuit; and Alexander assuredly did not foresee that the conquest of one world would only leave him to weep for another world to conquer. It is ever the contest that pleases us, and not the victory. Thus it is in play; thus it is in hunting; thus it is in the search of truth;[1] thus it is in life. The past does not interest, the present does not satisfy, the future alone is the object which engages us.

> "(Nullo votorum fine beati)
> Victuros agimus semper, nec vivimus unquam."[2]

> "Man never is, but always to be, blest."[3]

The question, I said, has never been regularly discussed, — probably because it lay in too narrow a compass; but no philosopher appears to have ever seriously proposed it to himself, who did not resolve it in contradiction to the ordinary opinion. A contradiction of this opinion is even involved in the very term Philosophy; and the man who first declared that he was not a σοφὸς, or possessor, but a φιλόσοφος,[4] or seeker of truth, at once enounced the true end of human speculation, and embodied it in a significant name. Under the same conviction Plato defines man "the hunter of truth,"[5] for science is a chase, and in a chase the pursuit is always of greater value than the game.

How resolved by philosophers.

> "Our hopes, like towering falcons, aim
> At objects in an airy height,
> But all the pleasure of the game
> Is afar off to view the flight."[6]

"The intellect," says Aristotle, in one passage, "is perfected, not by knowledge but by activity;"[7] and in another, "The arts

l'agitation." "Le conseil qu'on donnait à Pyrrhus, de prendre le repos qu'il allait chercher par tant de fatigues, recevait bien des difficultés." — ED.

1 "Rien ne nous plaît que le combat, mais non pas la victoire . . . Ainsi dans le jeu, ainsi dans la recherche de la vérité. On aime à voir dans les disputes le combat des opinions; mais de contempler la vérité trouvée, point du tout . . . Nous ne cherchons jamais les choses, mais la recherche des choses."— Pascal, *Pensées*, vol. i. p. 205, ed. Faugère.—ED.

2 Manilius, *Astronomicon*, lib. iv. 4.—ED.

3 Pope, *Essay on Man*, i. 96.—ED.

4 Pythagoras, according to the ordinary account; see Cicero, *Tusc. Quæst.* v. 3. Sir

W. Hamilton, however, probably meant Socrates. See lecture III., p. 47.—ED.

5 This definition is not to be found in the Platonic Dialogues; a passage something like it occurs in the *Euthydemus*, p. 290. Cf. Diog. Laert., lib. viii. *Pythagoras*, § 8.—Ἐν τῷ βίῳ, οἱ μὲν ἀνδραποδώδεις φύονται, δόξης καὶ πλεονεξίας θηραταί· οἱ δὲ φιλόσοφοι, τῆς ἀληθείας.—ED.

6 Prior, *Lines to the Hon. C. Montague. British Poets*, vol. vii. p. 393, (Anderson's ed.)—ED.

7 Said of moral knowledge, *Eth. Nic.* i. 8: Τέλος οὐ γνῶσις, ἀλλὰ πρᾶξις. Cf. *ibid.* i. 7, 13; i 8, 9; ix. 7, 4; xi. 9, 7; x. 7, 1. *Met.*, xi. 7: Ἡ νοῦ ἐνέργεια ζωή.—ED.

and sciences are powers, but every power exists only for the sake of action; the end of philosophy, therefore, is not knowledge, but the energy conversant about knowledge."[1] Descending to the schoolmen: "The intellect," says Aquinas, "commences in operation, and in operation it ends;"[2] and Scotus even declares that a man's knowledge is measured by the amount of his mental activity — "tantum scit homo, quantum operatur."[3] The profoundest thinkers of modern times have emphatically testified to the same great principle. "If," says Malebranche, "I held truth captive in my hand, I should open my hand and let it fly, in order that I might again pursue and capture it."[4] "Did the Almighty," says Lessing, "holding in his right hand *Truth*, and in his left *Search after Truth*, deign to tender me the one I might prefer,— in all humility, but without hesitation, I should request *Search after Truth*."[5] "Truth," says Von Müller, "is the property of God, the pursuit of truth is what belongs to man;"[6] and Jean Paul Richter: "It is not the goal, but the course, which makes us happy." But there would be no end of similar quotations.[7]

But if speculative truth itself be only valuable as a mean of intellectual activity, those studies which determine the faculties to a more vigorous exertion, will, in every liberal sense, be better entitled, absolutely, to the name of useful, than those which, with a greater complement of more certain facts, awaken them to a less intense, and consequently to a less improving exercise. On this ground I would rest one of the preëminent utilities of mental philosophy. That it comprehends all the sublimest objects of our theoretical and moral interest; — that every (natural) conclusion concerning God, the soul, the present worth and the future destiny of man, is exclusively deduced from the philosophy

Philosophy best entitled to the appellation useful.

1 This sentence seems to be made up from two separate passages in the *Metaphysics*, lib. viii. c. 2. Πᾶσαι αἱ τέχναι καὶ αἱ ποιητικαὶ καὶ ἐπιστῆμαι δυνάμεις εἰσίν. Lib. viii. c. 8: Τέλος δ' ἡ ἐνέργεια, καὶ τούτου χάριν ἡ δύναμις λαμβάνεται· . . . καὶ τὴν θεωρητικὴν (ἔχουσιν) ἵνα θεωρῶσιν· ἀλλ' οὐ θεωροῦσιν ἵνα θεωρητικὴν ἔχωσιν. — ED.

2 This is perhaps the substance of *Summa*, Pars i., Q. lxxix., art. ii. and iii. — ED.

3 These words contain the substance of the doctrine of Scotus regarding science, given in his *Quæstiones in Aristotelis Logicam*, p. 318 — *Super. Lib. Post.*, Q. i. "Scire in *actu*," says the subtle doctor, "est quum aliquis cognoscit majorem et minorem, et, simul cum hoc, applicat præmissas ad conclusionem. Sic igitur patet quod actualitas scientiæ est ex applicatione causæ ad effectum." Compare Quæst. ii., "An acquisitio scientiæ sit nobis per doctrinam" — for his view of the end and means of education. — ED.

4 ["Malebranche disait avec une ingénieuse exagération, 'Si je tenais la vérité captive dans ma main, j'ouvrirais la main afin de poursuivre encore la vérité.'" — Mazure, *Cours de Philosophie*, tom. i. p. 20.]

5 *Eine Duplik*, § 1; *Schriften*, edit. Lachmann, x. p. 49. — ED.

6 ["Die Wahrheit ist in Gott, uns bleibt das Forschen."]

7 Compare *Discussions*, p. 40.

of mind, will be at once admitted. But I do not at present found the importance on the paramount dignity of the pursuit. It is as the best gymnastic of the mind, — as a mean, principally, and almost exclusively, conducive to the highest education of our noblest powers, that I would vindicate to these speculations the necessity which has too frequently been denied them. By no other intellectual application is the mind thus reflected on itself, and its faculties aroused to such independent, vigorous, unwonted, and continued energy; — by none, therefore, are its best capacities so variously and intensely evolved. "By turning," says Burke, "the soul inward on itself, its forces are concentred, and are fitted for greater and stronger flights of science; and in this pursuit, whether we take or whether we lose our game, the chase is certainly of service."[1]

These principles being established, I have only now to offer a few observations in regard to their application, that is, in regard to the mode in which I conceive that this class ought to be conducted. From what has already been said, my views on this subject may be easily anticipated. Holding that the paramount end of liberal study is the development of the student's mind, and that knowledge is principally useful as a mean of determining the faculties to that exercise, through which this development is accomplished, — it follows, that I must regard the main duty of a Professor to consist not simply in communicating information, but in doing this in such a manner, and with such an accompaniment of subsidiary means, that the information he conveys may be the occasion of awakening his pupils to a vigorous and varied exertion of their faculties. Self-activity is the indispensable condition of improvement; and education is only education, — that is, accomplishes its purpose, only by affording objects and supplying incitements to this spontaneous exertion. Strictly speaking, every one must educate himself.

Application of the foregoing principles to the conduct of a class of philosophy.

But as the end of education is thus something more than the mere communication of knowledge, the communication of knowledge ought not to be all that academical education should attempt. Before printing was invented, Universities were of primary importance as organs of publication, and as centres of literary confluence: but since that invention, their utility as media of communication is superseded; consequently, to justify the continuance of

Universities; their main end.

---

[1] *On the Sublime and Beautiful*, p. 8. — ED.

their existence and privileges, they must accomplish something that cannot be accomplished by books. But it is a remarkable circumstance that, before the invention of printing, universities viewed the activity of the pupil as the great mean of cultivation, and the communication of knowledge as only of subordinate importance; whereas, since that invention, universities, in general, have gradually allowed to fall into disuse the powerful means which they possess of rousing the pupil to exertion, and have been too often content to act as mere oral instruments of information, forgetful, it would almost seem, that Fust and Coster ever lived. It is acknowledged, indeed, that this is neither the principal nor the proper purpose of a university. Every writer on academical education from every corner of Europe proclaims the abuse, and, in this and other universities, much has been done by individual effort to correct it.[1]

But though the common duty of all academical instructors be the cultivation of the student, through the awakened exercise of his faculties, this is more especially incumbent on those to whom is intrusted the department of liberal education; for, in this department, the pupil is trained, not to any mere professional knowledge, but to the command and employment of his faculties in general.

The true end of liberal education.

But, moreover, the same obligation is specially imposed upon a professor of intellectual philosophy, by the peculiar nature of his subject, and the conditions under which alone it can be taught. The phænomena of the external world are so palpable and so easily described, that the experience of one observer suffices to render the facts he has witnessed intelligible and probable to all. The phænomena of the internal world, on the contrary, are not capable of being thus described: all that the prior observer can do, is to enable others to repeat his experience. In the science of mind, we can neither understand nor be convinced of anything at second hand. Here testimony can impose no belief; and instruction is only instruction as it enables us to teach ourselves. A fact of consciousness, however accurately observed, however clearly described, and however great may be our confidence in the observer, is for us as zero, until we have observed and recognized it ourselves. Till that be done, we cannot realize its possibility, far less admit its truth. Thus it is that, in the philosophy of mind, instruction can do little more than point out the position in which the pupil ought to place himself, in order to verify, by his own

The conditions of instruction in intellectual philosophy.

---

1 Compare *Discussions*, p. 772. — ED.

experience, the facts which his instructor proposes to him as true. The instructor, therefore, proclaims, οὐ φιλοσοφία, ἀλλὰ φιλοσοφεῖν; he does not profess to teach *philosophy, but to philosophize*.

It is this condition imposed upon the student of doing everything himself, that renders the study of the mental sciences the most improving exercise of intellect. But everything depends upon the condition being fulfilled; and, therefore, the primary duty of a teacher of philosophy is to take care that the student does actually perform for himself the necessary process. In the first place, he must discover, by examination, whether his instructions have been effective, — whether they have enabled the pupil to go through the intellectual operation; and, if not, it behooves him to supply what is wanting, — to clear up what has been misunderstood. In this view, examinations are of high importance to a professor; for without such a medium between the teacher and the taught, he can never adequately accommodate the character of his instruction to the capacity of his pupils.

Use and importance of examinations in a class of Philosophy.

But, in the scond place, besides placing his pupil in a condition to perform the necessary process, the instructor ought to do what in him lies to determine the pupil's *will* to the performance. But how is this to be effected? Only by rendering the effort more pleasurable than its omission. But every effort is at first difficult, — consequently irksome. The ultimate benefit it promises is dim and remote, while the pupil is often of an age at which present pleasure is more persuasive than future good. The pain of the exertion must, therefore, be overcome by associating with it a still higher pleasure. This can only be effected by enlisting some passion in the cause of improvement. We must awaken emulation, and allow its gratification only through a course of vigorous exertion. Some rigorists, I am aware, would proscribe, on moral and religious grounds, the employment of the passions in education; but such a view is at once false and dangerous. The affections are the work of God; they are not radically evil; they are given us for useful purposes, and are, therefore, not superfluous. It is their abuse that is alone reprehensible. In truth, however, there is no alternative. In youth passion is preponderant. There is then a redundant amount of energy which must be expended; and this, if it find not an outlet through one affection, is sure to find it through another. The aim of education is thus to employ for good those impulses which would otherwise be

The intellectual instructor must seek to influence the will of his pupils.

The place of the passions in education.

turned to evil. The passions are never neutral; they are either the best allies, or the worst opponents, of improvement. "Man's nature," says Bacon, "runs either to herbs or weeds; therefore let him seasonably water the one, and destroy the other."[1] Without the stimulus of emulation, what can education accomplish? The love of abstract knowledge, and the habit of application, are still unformed, and if emulation intervene not, the course by which these are acquired is, from a strenuous and cheerful energy, reduced to an inanimate and dreary effort; and this, too, at an age when pleasure is all-powerful, and impulse predominant over reason. The result is manifest.

These views have determined my plan of practical instruction. Regarding the communication of knowledge as a high, but not the highest, aim of academical instruction, I shall not content myself with the delivery of lectures. By all means in my power I shall endeavor to rouse you, gentlemen, to the free and vigorous exercise of your faculties; and shall deem my task accomplished, not by teaching Logic and Philosophy, but by teaching to reason and philosophize.[2]

---

1 Essay xxxviii. — "Of Nature in Men." — *Works*, ed. Montagu, volume i. p. 133. — ED.

2 For Fragment containing the Author's views on the subject of Academical Honors, see Appendix I. — ED.

LECTURE II.[1]

PHILOSOPHY—ITS ABSOLUTE UTILITY.

(B.) OBJECTIVE.

IN the perverse estimate which is often made of the end and objects of education, it is impossible that the
The value of a study. Science of Mind,—Philosophy Proper,—the Queen of Sciences, as it was denominated of old, should not be degraded in common opinion from its preëminence, as the highest branch of general education; and, therefore, before attempting to point out to you what constitutes the value of Philosophy, it becomes necessary to clear the way by establishing a correct notion of what the value of a study is.

Some things are valuable, finally, or for themselves,—these are
Ends and means. ends; other things are valuable, not on their own account, but as conducive towards certain ulterior ends,—these are means. The value of ends is absolute, —the value of means is relative. Absolute value is properly called a *good*,—relative value is properly called a *utility*.[2] Of goods, or absolute ends, there are for man but two,—perfection and happiness. By perfection is meant the full and harmonious development of all our faculties, corporeal and mental, intellectual and moral; by happiness, the complement of all the pleasures of which we are susceptible.

Now, I may state, though I cannot at present attempt to prove,
Human perfection and happiness coincide. and I am afraid many will not even understand the statement, that human perfection and human happiness coincide, and thus constitute, in reality, but a single end. For as, on the one hand, the perfection or full development of a power is in proportion to its capacity of free, vigorous, and continued action, so, on

---

1 It is to be observed, that the Lectures here printed as First and Second, were not uniformly delivered by the Author in that order. The one or other was, however, usually given as the Introductory Lecture of the Course. This circumstance accounts for the repetition of the principal doctrines of Lecture I. in the opening of Lecture II.—ED.

2 [Cf. Aristotle, *Eth. Nic.*, lib. i., c. 7, § 1.]

the other, all pleasure is the concomitant of activity; its degree being in proportion as that activity is spontaneously intense, its prolongation in proportion as that activity is spontaneously continued; whereas, pain arises either from a faculty being restrained in its spontaneous tendency to action, or from being urged to a degree, or to a continuance, of energy beyond the limit to which it of itself freely tends.

To promote our perfection is thus to promote our happiness; for to cultivate fully and harmoniously our various faculties, is simply to enable them by exercise, to energize longer and stronger without painful effort; that is, to afford us a larger amount of a higher quality of enjoyment.

Perfection (comprising happiness) being thus the one end of our existence, in so far as man is considered

Criterion of the utility of a study.

either as an end unto himself, or as a mean to the glory of his Creator; it is evident that, absolutely speaking, that is, without reference to special circumstances and relations, studies and sciences must, in common with all other pursuits, be judged useful as they contribute, and only as they contribute, to the perfection of our humanity, — that is, to our perfection simply as men. It is manifest that in this relation alone can anything distinctively, emphatically, and without qualification, be denominated useful; for as our perfection as men is the paramount and universal end proposed to the species, whatever we may style useful in any other relation, ought, as conducive only to a subordinate and special end, to be so called, not simply, but with qualifying limitation. Propriety has, however, in this case, been reversed in common usage. For the term Useful has been exclusively bestowed, in ordinary language, on those branches of instruction which, without reference to his general cultivation as a man or a gentleman, qualify an individual to earn his livelihood by a special knowledge or dexterity in some lucrative calling or profession; and it is easy to see how, after the word had been thus appropriated to what, following the Germans, we may call the *Bread and Butter* sciences, those which more proximately and obtrusively contribute to the intellectual and moral dignity of man, should, as not having been styled the useful, come, in popular opinion, to be regarded as the useless branches of instruction.

General and Particular Utility.

As it is proper to have different names for different things, we may call the higher utility, or that conducive to the perfection of a man viewed as an end in himself, by the name of Absolute or General; the inferior utility, or that conducive to the skill of an individual viewed as an instrument for some end out of himself, by the name of Special or Particular.

Now, it is evident, that in estimating the utility of any branch of education, we ought to measure it both by the one kind of utility and by the other; but it is also evident, that a neglect of the former standard will lead us further wrong in appreciating the value of any branch of common or general instruction, than a neglect of the latter.

It has been the tendency of different ages, of different countries, of different ranks and conditions of society, to measure the utility of studies rather by one of these standards, than by both. Thus it was the bias of antiquity, when the moral and intellectual cultivation of the citizen was viewed as the great end of all political institutions, to appreciate all knowledge principally by the higher standard; on the contrary, it is unfortunately the bias of our modern civilization, since the accumulation, (and not too the distribution), of riches in a country, has become the grand problem of the statesman, to appreciate it rather by the lower.

In considering, therefore, the utility of philosophy, we have, first, to determine its Absolute, and, in the second place, its Special utility—I say its special utility, for, though not itself one of the professional studies, it is mediately more or less conducive to them all.

In the present Lecture I must, of course, limit myself to one branch of this division; and even a part of the first or Absolute utility will more than occupy our hour.

Limiting myself, therefore, to the utility of philosophy as estimated by the higher standard alone, it is

Philosophy: its Absolute utility.

further to be observed, that, on this standard, a science or study is useful in two different ways, and, as these are not identical, — this pursuit being more useful in the one way, that pursuit more useful in the other, — these in reality constitute two several standards of utility, by which each branch of knowledge ought to be separately measured.

The cultivation, the intellectual perfection, of a man, may be estimated by the amount of two different elements; it may be estimated by the mere sum

Absolute utility of a science of two kinds— Objective and Subjective.

of truths which he has learned, or it may be estimated by the greater development of his faculties, as determined by their greater exercise in the pursuit and contemplation of truth. For, though this may appear a paradox, these elements are not merely not convertible, but are, in fact, very loosely connected with each other; and as an individual may possess an ample magazine of knowledge, and still be little better than an intellectual barbarian, so the utility of one science may be principally seen in affording a greater number of higher and more indisputable truths, — the utility of another in determining the faculties to a higher energy, and consequently to a higher cultivation. The former of these utilities we may call the Objective, as it regards the object-matter about which our cognitive faculties are occupied; the other Subjective, inasmuch as it regards our cognitive faculties themselves as the subject in which knowledge is inherent.

I shall not at present enter on the discussion which of these utilities is the higher. In the opening lecture of last year, I endeavored to show that all knowledge is only for the sake of energy, and that even merely speculative truth is valuable only as it determines a greater quantity of higher power into activity. In that lecture, I also endeavored to show that, on the standard of subjective utility, philosophy is of all our studies the most useful; inasmuch as more than any other it exercises, and consequently develops to a higher degree, and in a more varied manner, our noblest faculties. At present, on the contrary, I shall confine myself to certain views of the importance of philosophy, estimated by the standard of its Objective utility. The discussion, I am aware, will be found somewhat disproportioned to the age and average capacity of my hearers; but, on this occasion, and before this audience, I hope to be excused if I venture for once on matters which, to be adequately understood, require development and illustration from the matured intelligence of those to whom they are presented.

Philosophy: its Objective utility.

Considered in itself, a knowledge of the human mind, whether we regard its speculative or its practical importance, is confessedly of all studies the highest and the most interesting. "On earth," says an ancient philosopher, "there is nothing great but man; in man, there is nothing great but mind."[1] No other study fills and satisfies the soul like the study of itself. No other science presents an object to be compared in dignity, in absolute or in relative value, to that which human consciousness furnishes to its own contemplation. What is of all things the best, asked

The human mind the noblest object of speculation.

---

1 [Phavorinus, quoted by Joannes Picus Mirandulanus, *In Astrologiam*, lib. iii. p. 351, Basil. — Ed.] For notice of Phavorinus, see Vossius, *De Hist. Græc.*, lib. ii. c. 10. — Ed.

Chilon of the Oracle. "To know thyself," was the response. This is, in fact, the only science in which all are always interested; for, while each individual may have his favorite occupation, it still remains true of the species, that

"The proper study of mankind is man." [1]

Sir Thomas Browne quoted.

"Now for my life," says Sir Thomas Browne, "it is a miracle of thirty years, which to relate were not a history, but a piece of poetry, and would sound to common ears like a fable. "For the world, I count it not an inn, but an hospital; and a place not to live, but to die in. The world that I regard is myself; it is the microcosm of my own frame that I cast mine eye on; for the other, I use it but like my globe, and turn it round sometimes, for my recreation. Men that look upon my outside, perusing only my condition and fortunes, do err in my altitude; for I am above Atlas his shoulders. The earth is a point not only in respect of the heavens above us, but of that heavenly and celestial part within us. That mass of flesh that circumscribes me, limits not my mind. That surface that tells the heavens it hath an end, cannot persuade me I have any. I take my circle to be above three hundred and sixty. Though the number of the ark do measure my body, it comprehendeth not my mind. Whilst I study to find how I am a microcosm, or little world, I find myself something more than the great. There is surely a piece of divinity in us; something that was before the elements, and owes no homage unto the sun. Nature tells me, I am the image of God, as well as Scripture. He that understands not thus much hath not his introduction or first lesson, and is yet to begin the alphabet of man." [2]

Relation of Psychology to Theology.

But, though mind, considered in itself, be the noblest object of speculation which the created universe presents to the curiosity of man, it is under a certain relation that I would now attempt to illustrate its utility; for mind rises to its highest dignity when viewed as the object through which, and through which alone, our unassisted reason can ascend to the knowledge of a God. The Deity is not an object of immediate contemplation; as existing and in himself, he is beyond our reach; we can know him only mediately through his works, and are only warranted in assuming his ex-

---

[1] Pope, *Essay on Man*, ii. 2. — ED.
[2] Browne's *Religio Medici*, part ii. § 11. *Discussions*, p. 811. — ED.

istence as a certain kind of cause necessary to account for a certain state of things, of whose reality our facul-
ties are supposed to inform us. The affirmation
of a God being thus a regressive inference, from
the existence of a special class of effects to the
existence of a special character of cause, it is evident, that the
whole argument hinges on the fact, — Does a state of things really
exist such as is only possible through the agency of a Divine Cause?
For if it can be shown that such a state of things does not really
exist, then, our inference to the kind of cause requisite to account
for it, is necessarily null.

Existence of Deity an inference from a special class of effects.

This being understood, I now proceed to show you that the
class of phænomena which requires that kind of
cause we denominate a Deity, is exclusively
given in the phænomena of mind, — that the
phænomena of matter, taken by themselves (you
will observe the qualification, taken by themselves), so far from
warranting any inference to the existence of a God, would, on the
contrary, ground even an argument to his negation, — that the study
of the external world taken with, and in subordination to, that of
the internal, not only loses its atheistic tendency, but, under such
subservience, may be rendered conducive to the great conclusion,
from which, if left to itself, it would dissuade us.

These afforded exclusively by the phænomena of mind.

We must first of all then consider what kind of cause it is
which constitutes a Deity, and what kind of effects they are
which allow us to infer that a Deity must be.

The notion of a God is not contained in the notion of a mere
First Cause; for in the admission of a first cause,
Atheist and Theist are at one. Neither is this
notion completed by adding to a first cause the
attribute of Omnipotence, for the atheist who holds matter or
necessity to be the original principle of all that is, does not convert his blind force into a God, by merely affirming it to be all-
powerful. It is not until the two great attributes of Intelligence
and Virtue (and be it observed that virtue involves Liberty) —
I say, it is not until the two attributes of intelligence and virtue
or holiness, are brought in, that the belief in a primary and omnipotent cause becomes the belief in a veritable Divinity. But these
latter attributes are not more essential to the divine nature than
are the former. For as original and infinite power does not of
itself constitute a God, neither is a God constituted by intelligence
and virtue, unless intelligence and goodness be themselves conjoined with this original and infinite power. For even a crea-

The notion of a God — what.

tor, intelligent, and good, and powerful, would be no God, were he dependent for his intelligence and goodness and power on any higher principle. On this supposition, the perfections of the creator are viewed as limited and derived. He is himself, therefore, only a dependency, — only a creature; and if a God there be, he must be sought for in that higher principle, from which this subordinate principle derives its attributes. Now is this highest principle (*ex hypothesi* all-powerful), also intelligent and moral, then it is itself alone the veritable Deity; on the other hand is it, though the author of intelligence and goodness in another, itself unintelligent, — then is a blind Fate constituted the first and universal cause, and atheism is asserted.

The peculiar attributes which distinguish a Deity from the original omnipotence or blind fate of the atheist, being thus those of intelligence and holiness of will, — and the assertion of theism being only the assertion that the universe is created by intelligence, and governed not only by physical but by moral laws, we have next to consider how we are warranted in these two affirmations, 1°, That intelligence stands first in the absolute order of existence, — in other words, that final preceded efficient causes; and, 2°, That the universe is governed by moral laws.

Conditions of the proof of the existence of a God.

The proof of these two propositions is the proof of a God; and it establishes its foundation exclusively on the phænomena of mind. I shall endeavor, gentlemen, to show you this, in regard to both these propositions; but, before considering how far the phænomena of mind and of matter do and do not allow us to infer the one position or the other, I must solicit your attention to the characteristic contrasts which these two classes of phænomena in themselves exhibit.

1. Is intelligence first in the order of existence? 2. Is the universe governed by moral law?

In the compass of our experience, we distinguish two series of facts, — the facts of the external or material world, and the facts of the internal world or world of intelligence. These concomitant series of phænomena are not like streams which merely run parallel to each other; they do not, like the Alpheus and Arethusa, flow on side by side without a commingling of their waters. They cross, they combine, they are interlaced; but notwithstanding their intimate connection, their mutual action and reaction, we are able to discriminate them without difficulty, because they are marked out by characteristic differences.

Contrasts of the phænomena of matter and mind.

The phænomena of the material world are subjected to immutable laws, are produced and reproduced in the same invariable succession, and manifest only the blind force of a mechanical necessity.

The phænomena of man, are, in part, subjected to the laws of the external universe. As dependent upon a bodily organization, as actuated by sensual propensities and animal wants, he belongs to matter, and, in this respect, he is the slave of necessity. But what man holds of matter does not make up his personality. They are his, not he; man is not an organism, — he is an intelligence served by organs.[1] For in man there are tendencies, — there is a law, — which continually urge him to prove that he is more powerful than the nature by which he is surrounded and penetrated. He is conscious to himself of faculties not comprised in the chain of physical necessity, his intelligence reveals prescriptive principles of action, absolute and universal, in the Law of Duty, and a liberty capable of carrying that law into effect, in opposition to the solicitations, the impulsions of his material nature. From the coëxistence of these opposing forces in man there results a ceaseless struggle between physical necessity and moral liberty; in the language of Revelation, between the Flesh and the Spirit; and this struggle constitutes at once the distinctive character of humanity, and the essential condition of human development and virtue.

In the facts of intelligence, we thus become aware of an order of existence diametrically in contrast to that displayed to us in the facts of the material universe. There is made known to us an order of things, in which intelligence, by recognizing the unconditional law of duty and an absolute obligation to fulfil it, recognizes its own possession of a liberty incompatible with a dependence upon fate, and of a power capable of resisting and conquering the counteraction of our animal nature.

Now, it is only as man is a free intelligence, a moral power, that he is created after the image of God, and it is only as a spark of divinity glows as the life of our life in us, that we can rationally believe in an Intelligent Creator and Moral Governor of the universe. For, let us suppose, that in man intelligence is the product of organization, that our consciousness of moral liberty is itself only an illusion; in short, that acts of volition are results of the same iron necessity which determines

Consciousness of freedom, and of a law of duty, the conditions of Theology.

---

1 [" Mens cujusque, is est quisque; non ea figura, quæ digito demonstrari potest." — Cicero, *Somnium Scipionis*, c. 8 — after Plato.] Cf. Plato, *Alc. Prim.* p.130, and *infra*, p. 114. — ED.

the phænomena of matter, — on this supposition, I say, the foundations of all religion, natural and revealed, are subverted.[1]

The truth of this will be best seen by applying the supposition of the two positions of theism previously stated — viz., that the notion of God necessarily supposes, 1°, That in the absolute order of existence intelligence should be first, that is, not itself the product of an unintelligent antecedent; and, 2°, That the universe should be governed not only by physical but by moral laws.

Now, in regard to the former, how can we attempt to prove that the universe is the creation of a free original intelligence, against the counter-position of the atheist, that liberty is an illusion, and intelligence, or the adaptation of means to ends, only the product of a blind fate? As we know nothing of the absolute order of existence in itself, we can only attempt to infer its character from that of the particular order within the sphere of our experience, and as we can affirm naught of intelligence and its conditions, except what we may discover from the observation of our own minds, it is evident that we can only analogically carry out into the order of the universe the relation in which we find intelligence to stand in the order of the human constitution. If in man intelligence be a free power, — in so far as its liberty extends, intelligence must be independent of necessity and matter; and a power independent of matter necessarily implies the existence of an immaterial subject, — that is, a spirit. If, then, the original independence of intelligence on matter in the human constitution, in other words, if the spirituality of mind in man, be supposed a datum of observation, in this datum is also given both the condition and the proof of a God. For we have only to infer, what analogy entitles us to do, that intelligence holds the same relative supremacy in the universe which it holds in us, and the first positive condition of a Deity is established, in the establishment of the absolute priority of a free creative intelligence. On the other hand, let us suppose the result of our study of man to be, that intelligence is only a product of matter, only a reflex of organization, such a doctrine would not only afford no basis on which to rest any argument for a God, but, on the contrary, would positively warrant the atheist in denying his existence. For if, as the materialist maintains, the only intelligence of which we have any experience be a consequent of matter, — on this hypothesis, he not only cannot assume this

First condition of the proof of a Deity, drawn from Psychology. Analogy between our experience and the absolute order of existence.

Psychological Materialism: its issue.

1 See *Discussions*, p. 623. — ED.

order to be reversed in the relations of an intelligence beyond his observation, but, if he argue logically, he must positively conclude, that, as in man, so in the universe, the phænomena of intelligence or design are only in their last analysis the products of a brute necessity. Psychological materialism, if carried out fully and fairly to its conclusions, thus inevitably results in theological atheism; as it has been well expressed by Dr. Henry More, *nullus in microcosmo spiritus, nullus in macrocosmo Deus.*[1] I do not, of course, mean to assert that all materialists deny, or actually disbelieve, a God. For, in very many cases, this would be at once an unmerited compliment to their reasoning, and an unmerited reproach to their faith.

Such is the manifest dependence of our theology on our psychology in reference to the first condition of a Deity, — the absolute priority of a free intelligence. But this is perhaps even more conspicuous in relation to the second, that the universe is governed not merely by physical but by moral laws, for God is only God inasmuch as he is the Moral Governor of a Moral World.

Second condition of the proof of a Deity, drawn from Psychology.

Our interest also in its establishment is incomparably greater, for while a proof that the universe is the work of an omnipotent intelligence, gratifies only our speculative curiosity, — a proof that there is a holy legislator by whom goodness and felicity will be ultimately brought into accordance, is necessary to satisfy both our intellect and our heart. A God is, indeed, to us only of practical interest, inasmuch as he is the condition of our immortality.

Now, it is self-evident, in the first place, that, if there be no moral world, there can be no moral governor of such a world; and, in the second, that we have, and can have, no ground on which to believe in the reality of a moral world, except in so far as we ourselves are moral agents. This being undeniable, it is further evident, that, should we ever be convinced that we are not moral agents, we should likewise be convinced that there exists no moral order in the universe, and no supreme intelligence by which that moral order is established, sustained, and regulated.

Theology is thus again wholly dependent on Psychology; for, with the proof of the moral nature of man, stands or falls the proof of the existence of a Deity.

---

1 Cf. *Antidotus adversus Atheismum*, lib. iii. c. 16, (*Opera Omnia*, vol. ii. p. 143, Londini, 1679); and the Author's *Discussions*, p. 788. — ED.

But in what does the character of man as a moral agent consist?

Man is a moral agent only as he is accountable for his actions, — in other words, as he is the object of praise or blame; and this he is, only inasmuch as he has prescribed to him a rule of duty, and as he is able to act, or not to act, in conformity with its precepts. The possibility of morality thus depends on the possibility of liberty; for if man be not a free agent, he is not the author of his actions, and has, therefore, no responsibility, — no moral personality at all.

Wherein the moral agency of man consists.

Now the study of Philosophy, or mental science, operates in three ways to establish that assurance of human liberty, which is necessary for a rational belief in our own moral nature, in a moral world, and in a moral ruler of that world. In the first place, an attentive consideration of the phænomena of mind is requisite in order to a luminous and distinct apprehension of liberty as a fact or datum of intelligence. For though, without philosophy, a natural conviction of free agency lives and works in the recesses of every human mind, it requires a process of philosophical thought to bring this conviction to clear consciousness and scientific certainty. In the second place, a profound philosophy is necessary to obviate the difficulties which meet us when we attempt to explain the possibility of this fact, and to prove that the datum of liberty is not a mere illusion. For though an unconquerable feeling compels us to recognize ourselves as accountable, and therefore free, agents, still, when we attempt to realize in thought how the fact of our liberty can be, we soon find that this altogether transcends our understanding, and that every effort to bring the fact of liberty within the compass of our conceptions, only results in the substitution in its place of some more or less disguised form of necessity. For, — if I may be allowed to use expressions which many of you cannot be supposed at present to understand, — we are only able to conceive a thing, inasmuch as we conceive it under conditions; while the possibility of a free act supposes it to be an act which is not conditioned or determined. The tendency of a superficial philosophy is, therefore, to deny the fact of liberty, on the principle that what cannot be conceived is impossible. A deeper and more comprehensive study of the facts of mind overturns this conclusion, and disproves its foundation. It shows that, — so far from the principle being true, that what is inconceivable is impossible, — on the contrary, all that is conceivable is a mean be-

Philosophy operates in three ways, in establishing assurance of human liberty.

tween two contradictory extremes, both of which are inconceivable, but of which, as mutually repugnant, one or the other must be true. Thus philosophy, in demonstrating that the limits of thought are not to be assumed as the limits of possibility, while it admits the weakness of our discursive intellect, reëstablishes the authority of consciousness, and vindicates the veracity of our primitive convictions. It proves to us, from the very laws of mind, that while we can never understand *how* any original datum of intelligence is possible, we have no reason from this inability to doubt *that* it is true. A learned ignorance is thus the end of philosophy, as it is the beginning of theology.[1]

In the third place, the study of mind is necessary to counterbalance and correct the influence of the study of matter; and this utility of Metaphysics rises in proportion to the progress of the natural sciences, and to the greater attention which they engross.

An exclusive devotion to physical pursuits, exerts an evil influence in two ways. In the first place, it diverts from all notice of the phænomena of moral liberty, which are revealed to us in the recesses of the human mind alone; and it disqualifies from appreciating the import of these phænomena, even if presented, by leaving uncultivated the finer power of psychological reflection, in the exclusive exercise of the faculties employed in the easier and more amusing observation of the external world. In the second place, by exhibiting merely the phænomena of matter and extension, it habituates us only to the contemplation of an order in which everything is determined by the laws of a blind or mechanical necessity. Now, what is the inevitable tendency of this one-sided and exclusive study? That the student becomes a materialist, if he speculate at all. For, in the first place, he is familiar with the obtrusive facts of necessity, and is unaccustomed to develop into consciousness the more recondite facts of liberty; he is, therefore, disposed to disbelieve in the existence of phænomena whose reality he may deny, and whose possibility he cannot understand. At the same time, the love of unity, and the philosophical presumption against the multiplication of essences, determine him to reject the assumption of a second, and that an hypothetical, substance, — ignorant as he is of the reasons by which that assumption is legitimated. In the infancy of science, this tendency of

Twofold evils of exclusive physical study.

Physical study in its infancy not materializing.

---

1 See *Discussions*, p. 634. — ED.

physical study was not experienced. When men first turned their attention on the phænomena of nature, every event was viewed as a miracle, for every effect was considered as the operation of an intelligence. God was not exiled from the universe of matter; on the contrary, he was multiplied in proportion to its phænomena. As science advanced, the deities were gradually driven out; and long after the sublunary world had been disenchanted, they were left for a season in possession of the starry heavens. The movement of the celestial bodies, in which Kepler still saw the agency of a free intelligence, was at length by Newton resolved into a few mathematical principles; and at last even the irregularities which Newton was compelled to leave for the miraculous correction of the Deity, have been proved to require no supernatural interposition; for La Place has shown that all contingencies, past and future, in the heavens, find their explanation in the one fundamental law of gravitation.

But the very contemplation of an order and adaptation so astonishing, joined to the knowledge that this order and adaptation are the necessary results of a brute mechanism, — when acting upon minds which have not looked into themselves for the light of which the world without can only afford them the reflection, — far from elevating them more than any other aspect of external creation to that inscrutable Being who reigns beyond and above the universe of nature, tends, on the contrary, to impress on them, with peculiar force, the conviction, that as the mechanism of nature can explain so much, the mechanism of nature can explain all.

"Wonder," says Aristotle, "is the first cause of philosophy:"[1] but in the discovery that all existence is but mechanism, the consummation of science would be an extinction of the very interest from which it originally sprang. "Even the gorgeous majesty of the heavens," says a religious philosopher, "the object of a kneeling adoration to an infant world, subdues no more the mind of him who comprehends the one mechanical law by which the planetary systems move, maintain their motion, and even originally form themselves. He no longer wonders at the object, infinite as it always is, but at the human intellect alone which in a Copernicus, Kepler, Gassendi, Newton, and La Place, was able to transcend the object, by science to terminate the miracle, to reave the heaven of its divinities, and to

If all existence be but mechanism, philosophical interest extinguished.

---

[1] *Metaphysics*, book i. 2, 9. Compare Plato, *Theætetus*, p. 155. — ED.

exorcise the universe. But even this, the only admiration of which our intelligent faculties are now capable, would vanish, were a future Hartley, Darwin, Condillac, or Bonnet, to succeed in displaying to us a mechanical system of the human mind, as comprehensive, intelligible, and satisfactory as the Newtonian mechanism of the heavens."[1]

To this testimony I may add that, should Physiology ever succeed in reducing the facts of intelligence to Phænomena of matter, Philosophy would be subverted in the subversion of its three great objects, — God, Free-Will, and Immortality. True wisdom would then consist, not in speculation, but in repressing thought during our brief transit from nothingness to nothingness. For why? Philosophy would have become a meditation, not merely of death, but of annihilation; the precept, *Know thyself*, would have been replaced by the terrific oracle to Œdipus —

" May'st thou ne'er know the truth of what thou art;"

and the final recompense of our scientific curiosity would be wailing, deeper than Cassandra's, for the ignorance that saved us from despair.

The views which I have now taken of the respective influence of the sciences of mind and of matter in relation to our religious belief, are those which have been deliberately adopted by the profoundest thinkers, ancient and modern. Were I to quote to you the testimonies that crowd on my recollection to the effect that ignorance of Self is ignorance of God, I should make no end, for this is a truth proclaimed by Jew and Gentile, Christian and Mohammedan. I shall content myself with adducing three passages from three philosophers, which I select, both as articulately confirming all that I have now advanced, and because there are not, in the whole history of speculation, three authorities on the point in question more entitled to respect.

The first quotation is from Plato, and it corroborates the doctrine I have maintained in regard to the conditions of a God, and of our knowledge of his existence. "The cause," he says, "of all impiety and irreligion among men is, that reversing in themselves the relative subordination of mind and body, they have, in like manner, in the universe, made that to be first which is second, and that to be second

Coincidence of the views here given, with those of previous philosophers.

Plato.

1 Jacobi, *Werke*, vol. ii. p. 52-54. Quoted in *Discussions*, p. 312. — ED.

which is first; for while, in the generation of all things, intelligence and final causes precede matter and efficient causes, they, on the contrary, have viewed matter and material things as absolutely prior, in the order of existence, to intelligence and design; and thus departing from an original error in relation to themselves, they have ended in the subversion of the Godhead."[1]

The second quotation is from Kant; it finely illustrates the influences of material and mental studies by contrasting them in reference to the very noblest object of either, and the passage is worthy of your attention, not only for the soundness of its doctrine, but for the natural and unsought-for sublimity of its expression: "Two things there are, which, the oftener and the more steadfastly we consider, fill the mind with an ever new, an ever rising admiration and reverence; —*the* STARRY HEAVEN *above, the* MORAL LAW *within.* Of neither am I compelled to seek out the reality, as veiled in darkness, or only to conjecture the possibility, as beyond the hemisphere of my knowledge. Both I contemplate lying clear before me, and connect both immediately with my consciousness of existence. The one departs from the place I occupy in the outer world of sense; expands, beyond the bounds of imagination, this connection of my body with worlds rising beyond worlds, and systems blending into systems; and protends it also into the illimitable times of their periodic movement — to its commencement and perpetuity. The other departs from my invisible self, from my personality; and represents me in a world, truly infinite indeed, but whose infinity can be tracked out only by the intellect, with which also my connection, unlike the fortuitous relation I stand in to all worlds of sense, I am compelled to recognize as universal and necessary. In the former, the first view of a countless multitude of worlds annihilates, as it were, my importance as an *animal product*, which, after a brief and that incomprehensible endowment with the powers of life, is compelled to refund its constituent matter to the planet — itself an atom in the universe — on which it grew. The other, on the contrary, elevates my worth as an *intelligence* even without limit; and this through my personality, in which the moral law reveals a faculty of life independent of my animal nature, nay, of the whole material world: — at least if it be permitted to infer as much from the regulation of my being, which a conformity with that law exacts; proposing, as it does, my moral worth for

1 *De Legibus*, book x. pp. 888, 889. Quoted in *Discussions*, p. 312. Compare Cudworth, *Intell. System*, c. v. § iv. (p. 435 *et seq.* of vol. iii., Lond. ed.), and *Eternal and Immut. Morality*, book iv., c. vi. § 6, *seq.* — ED.

the absolute end of my activity, conceding no compromise of its imperative to a necessitation of nature, and spurning, in its infinity, the conditions and boundaries of my present transitory life."[1]

The third quotation is from the pious and profound Jacobi, and it states the truth boldly and without disguise in regard to the relation of Physics and Metaphysics to Religion. "But is it unreasonable to confess, that we believe in God, not by reason of the nature[2] which conceals him, but by reason of the supernatural in man, which alone reveals and proves him to exist?

Jacobi.

"*Nature conceals God:* for through her whole domain Nature reveals only fate, only an indissoluble chain of mere efficient causes without beginning and without end, excluding, with equal necessity, both providence and chance. An independent agency, a free original commencement within her sphere and proceeding from her powers, is absolutely impossible. Working without will, she takes counsel neither of the good nor of the beautiful; creating nothing, she casts up from her dark abyss only eternal transformations of herself, unconsciously and without an end; furthering, with the same ceaseless industry, decline and increase, death and life, — never producing what alone is of God and what supposes liberty, — the virtuous, the immortal.

" *Man reveals God;* for man by his intelligence rises above nature, and in virtue of this intelligence is conscious of himself as a power not only independent of, but opposed to, nature, and capable of resisting, conquering, and controlling her. As man has a living faith in this power, superior to nature, which dwells in him; so has he a belief in God, a feeling, an experience of his existence. As he does not believe in this power, so does he not believe in God; he sees, he experiences naught in existence but nature, — necessity, — fate."[3]

Such is the comparative importance of the sciences of mind and of matter in relation to the interests of religion. But it may be said, how great soever be the value of philosophy in this respect, were man left to rise to the divinity by the unaided exercise of his faculties, this value is superseded under the Christian dispensation, the Gospel now assuring us of

These uses of Psychology not superseded by the Christian revelation.

---

1 *Kritik der praktischen Vernunft.* Beschluss. Quoted in *Discussions*, p 310. — ED.

2 [In the philosophy of Germany, *Natur* and its correlatives, whether of Greek or Latin derivation, are, in general, expressive of the world of Matter, in contrast to the world of Intelligence.] — *Oral Interpolation,* supplied from *Reid's Works,* p. 216. — ED.

3 *Von den Göttlichen Dingen. Werke,* iii. p. 424-26. — ED.

all and more than all philosophy could ever warrant us in surmising. It is true, indeed, that in Revelation there is contained a great complement of truths of which natural reason could afford us no knowledge or assurance, but still the importance of mental science to theology has not become superfluous in Christianity; for whereas anterior to Revelation, religion rises out of psychology as a result, subsequently to revelation, it supposes a genuine philosophy of mind as the condition of its truth. This is at once manifest. Revelation is a revelation to man and concerning man; and man is only the object of revelation, inasmuch as he is a moral, a free, a responsible being. The Scriptures are replete with testimonies to our natural liberty; and it is the doctrine of every Christian church, that man was originally created with a will capable equally of good as of evil, though this will, subsequently to the fall, has lost much of its primitive liberty. Christianity thus, by universal confession, supposes as a condition the moral nature of its object; and if some individual theologians be found who have denied to man a higher liberty than a machine, this is only another example of the truth, that there is no opinion which has been unable to find not only its champions but its martyrs. The differences which divide the Christian churches on this question, regard only the liberty of man in certain particular relations, for fatalism, or a negation of human responsibility in general, is equally hostile to the tenets of the Calvinist and Arminian.

In these circumstances it is evident, that he who disbelieves the moral agency of man must, in consistency with that opinion, disbelieve Christianity. And therefore inasmuch as Philosophy, — the Philosophy of Mind, — scientifically establishes the proof of human liberty, philosophy, in this, as in many other relations not now to be considered, is the true preparative and best aid of an enlightened Christian Theology.

LECTURE III.

THE NATURE AND COMPREHENSION OF PHILOSOPHY.

I HAVE been in the custom of delivering sometimes together, more frequently in alternate years, two systematic courses of lectures, — the one on PSYCHOLOGY, that is, the science which is conversant about the phænomena of mind in general, — the other on LOGIC, that is, the science of the laws regulating the manifestation and legitimacy of the highest faculty of Cognition, — Thought, strictly so denominated — the faculty of Relations, — the Understanding proper. As first, or initiative, courses of philosophy, — each has its peculiar advantages; and I know not, in truth, which I should recommend a student to commence with. What, however, I find it expedient to premise to each is an *Introduction*, in which the nature and general relations of philosophy are explained, and a summary view taken of the faculties (particularly the Cognitive faculties), of mind.

In the ensuing course, we shall be occupied with the General Philosophy of Mind.

You are, then, about to commence a course of philosophical discipline, — for Psychology is preëminently a philosophical science. It is therefore proper, before proceeding to a consideration of the special objects of our course, that you should obtain at least a general notion of what philosophy is. But in affording you this information, it is evident that there lie considerable difficulties in the way. For the definition, and the divisions of philosophy are the results of a lofty generalization from particulars, of which particulars you are, or must be presumed to be, still ignorant. You cannot, therefore, it is manifest, be made adequately to comprehend, in the commencement of your philosophical studies, notions which these studies themselves are intended to enable you to understand. But although you cannot at once obtain a full knowledge of the nature of philosophy, it is desirable that you should be enabled to form at least some vague conception of the road you are about to travel, and of the point to which it will conduct you. I must, therefore, beg that you will, for

What Philosophy is.

the present, hypothetically believe,—believe upon authority,— what you may not now adequately understand; but this only to the end that you may not hereafter be under the necessity of taking any conclusion upon trust. Nor is this temporary exaction of credit peculiar to philosophical education. In the order of nature, belief always precedes knowledge,—it is the condition of instruction. The child (as observed by Aristotle) must believe, in order that he may learn;[1] and even the primary facts of intelligence,— the facts which precede, as they afford the conditions of, all knowledge,—would not be original were they revealed to us under any other form than that of natural or necessary beliefs. Without further preamble, therefore, I shall now endeavor to afford you some general notion of what philosophy is.[2]

In doing this, there are two questions to be answered:—1st, What is the meaning of the *name?* and, 2d, What is the meaning of the *thing?* An answer to the former question is afforded in a nominal definition of the term *philosophy*, and in a history of its employment and application.

Two questions regarding Philosophy.

In regard to the etymological signification of the word, you are aware that Philosophy is a term of Greek origin —that it is a compound of φίλος, a *lover* or *friend*, and σοφία,[3] *wisdom*—speculative wisdom. Philosophy is thus, literally, *a love of wisdom.* But if the grammatical meaning of the word be unambiguous, the history of its application is, I think, involved in considerable doubt. According to the commonly received account, the designation of philosopher (*lover or suitor of wisdom*) was first assumed and applied by Pythagoras; whilst of the occasion and circumstances of its assumption, we have a story by Cicero,[4] on the authority of Heraclides Ponticus;[5] and by Diogenes Laertius, in one place,[6] on the authority

Philosophy — the name.

Commonly referred to Pythagoras.

---

1 *Soph. Elench.* c. 2. — ED.

2 On comprehension of Philosophy *inter Antiquos*, see Brandis, *Geschichte der Philosophie*, etc., vol. i. § 6, p. 7, *seq.*

3 Σοφία in Greek, though sometimes used in a wide sense, like the term *wise* applied to skill in handicraft, yet properly denoted speculative, not practical wisdom or prudence. See Aristotle, *Eth. Nic.* lib. vi. c. 7, with the commentary of Eustratius. [Διὸ Ἀναξαγόρον, καὶ Θαλῆν καὶ τοὺς τοιούτους, σοφοὺς μὲν, φρονίμους δ' οὔ φασιν εἶναι, ὅταν ἴδωσιν ἀγνοοῦντας τὰ συμφέροντ' ἐαυτοῖς· καὶ περιττὰ μὲν, καὶ θαυμαστὰ, καὶ χαλεπὰ, καὶ δαιμόνια εἰδέναι αὐτούς φασιν, ἀχρηστα δ',

ὅτι οὐ τὰ ανθρώπινα, ἀγαθὰ ζητοῦσιν. Ἡ δὲ φρόνησις περὶ τὰ ανθρώπινα, καὶ περὶ, ὧν ἔστι βουλεύσασθαι. From the long commentary of Eustratius, the following extract will be sufficient: Ἀλλὰ τὸ τέλος τοῦ σοφοῦ ἡ θεορία τῆς ἀληθείας ἐστὶ, καὶ ἡ τοῦ ὄντος κατάληψις· οὐχὶ δέ τι πρακτὸν ἀγαθόν. Πρακτὸν γάρ ἐστιν ἀγαθὸν τὸ διὰ πράξεως κατορθούμενον, θεωρία δὲ πράξεως ἑτέρα.— ED.

4 *Tusc. Quæst.* lib. v. c. 3.

5 Heraclides Ponticus — scholar both of Plato and of Aristotle.

6 Lib. 1. 12.

of Heraclides, and in another,[1] on that of Sosicrates, — although it is doubtful whether the word Sosicrates be not in the second passage a corrupted lection for Heraclides;[2] in which case the whole probability of the story will depend upon the trustworthiness of Heraclides alone, for the comparatively recent testimony of Iamblichus, in his Life of Pythagoras, must go for

The interview of Pythagoras and Leon.

nothing. As told by Cicero, it is as follows: —

Pythagoras once upon a time (says the Roman orator), having come to Phlius, a city of Peloponnesus, displayed, in a conversation which he had with Leon, who then governed that city, a range of knowledge so extensive, that the prince, admiring his eloquence and ability, inquired to what art he had principally devoted himself. Pythagoras answered, that he professed no art, and was simply a *philosopher*. Leon, struck by the novelty of the name, again inquired who were the philosophers, and in what they differed from other men. Pythagoras replied, that human life seemed to resemble the great fair, held on occasion of those solemn games which all Greece met to celebrate. For some, exercised in athletic contests, resorted thither in quest of glory and the crown of victory; while a greater number flocked to them in order to buy and sell, attracted by the love of gain. There were a few, however, — and they were those distinguished by their liberality and intelligence, — who came from no motive of glory or of gain, but simply to look about them, and to take note of what was done, and in what manner. So likewise, continued Pythagoras, we men all make our entrance into this life on our departure from another. Some are here occupied in the pursuit of honors, others in the search of riches; a few there are who, indifferent to all else, devote themselves to an inquiry into the nature of things. These, then, are they whom I call students of wisdom, for such is meant by philosopher.

Pythagoras was a native of Samos, and flourished about 560 years before the advent of Christ,[3] — about 130 years

Rests on doubtful authority.

before the birth of Plato. Heraclides and Sosicrates, the two vouchers of this story, — if Sosicrates be indeed a voucher, — lived long subsequently to the age of Pythagoras; and the former is, moreover, confessed to have been an egregious fabulist. From the principal circumstances of

---

1 Lib. viii. 8.

2 See Menage, *Commentary on Laertius*, viii. 8.

3 The exact dates of the birth and death of Pythagoras are uncertain. Nearly all authorities, however, are agreed that he "flourished"

B. C. 540–510, in the times of Polycrates and Tarquinius Superbus (Clinton, *F. H*, 510.) His birth is usually placed in the 49th Olympiad (B. C. 584). See Brandis, *Gesch. der Phil.* vol. i. p. 422; Zeller, *Phil. der Griechen.*, vol. i. p. 217, 2d ed. — ED.

his life, mentioned by Laertius after older authors, and from the fragments we possess of the works of Heraclides, — in short, from all opinions, ancient and modern, we learn that he[1] was at once credulous and deceitful, — a dupe and an impostor. The anecdote, therefore, rests on very slender authority. It is probable, I think, that Socrates was the first who adopted, or, at least, the first who familiarized, the expression.[2] It was natural that

Socrates pobably the first to familiarize the term.

he should be anxious to contradistinguish himself from the Sophists, (οἱ σοφοὶ, οἱ σοφισταὶ, sophistæ), literally, the *wise* men ;[3] and no term could more appropriately ridicule the arrogance of these pretenders, or afford a happier contrast to their haughty designation, than that of philosopher (*i. e.*, the *lover* of wisdom); and, at the same time, it is certain that the substantives φιλοσοφία and φιλόσοφος, first appear in the writings of the Socratic school.[4] It is true, indeed, that the verb φιλοσοφεῖν is found in Hero-

Φιλοσοφεῖν found in Herodotus.

dotus, in the address by Crœsus to Solon ;[5] and that too in a participial form, to designate the latter as a man who had travelled abroad for the purpose of acquiring knowledge, (ὡς φιλοσοφέων γῆν πολλὴν θεωρίης εἵνεκεν ἐπελήλυθας). It is, therefore, not impossible that, before the time of Socrates, those who devoted themselves to the pursuit of the higher branches of knowledge, were occasionally designated philosophers: but it is far more probable that Socrates and his school first appropriated the term as a distinctive appellation; and that the word *philosophy*, in consequence of this appropriation, came to be employed for the complement of all higher knowledge, and, more especially, to denote the science conversant about the principles or causes of existence. The term *philosophy*, I may notice, which was originally assumed in modesty, soon lost its Socratic and etymological signification, and returned to the meaning of σοφία, or wisdom. Quintilian[6] calls it *nomen insolentissimum ;* Seneca,[7] *nomen invidiosum ;* Epictetus[8]

1 Compare Meiners, *Geschichte der Wissenschaften in Griechenland und Rom*, vol. i. p. 118; and Krug. *Lexikon*, vol. iii. p. 211. — Ed.

2 There is, however, the ἰητρὸς φιλόσοφος ἰσόθεος of Hippocrates. But this occurs in one of the Hippocratic writings which is manifestly spurious, and of date subsequent to the father of medicine. Hippocrates was an early contemporary of Socrates. [The expression occurs in the Περὶ Εὐσχημοσύνης, *Opera — Quarta Classis*, p. 41, ed. Venice, 1588.—Ed.]

3 Perhaps rather " the Professors of Wisdom," See an able paper by Mr. Cope in the

Journal of Classical and Sacred Philology, vol. i. p. 182. — Ed.

4 See especially Plato, *Phædrus*, p. 278 :— Τὸ μὲν σοφόν, ὦ Φαῖδρε, καλεῖν ἔμοιγε μέγα εἶναι δοκεῖ καὶ θεῷ μόνῳ πρέπειν· τὸ δὲ ἢ φιλόσοφον ἢ τοιοῦτόν τι μᾶλλόν τε ἂν αὐτῷ ἁρμόττοι καὶ ἐμμελεστέρως, ἔχοι. Compare also the description of the philosopher in the *Symposium*, p. 204, as μεταξὺ σοφοῦ καὶ ἀμαθοῦς. — Ed.

5 Lib. i. 30.

6 *Inst. Orat.* Prœm.

7 *Epist.* v.

8 *Ench.* c. 63, ed. Wolf; 46 ed. Schweigh.

counsels his scholars not to call themselves "Philosophers;" and *proud* is one of the most ordinary epithets with which philosophy is now associated. Thus Campbell, in his Address to the Rainbow, says:

"I ask not *proud* philosophy
To tell me what thou art."

So much for the name signifying; we proceed now to the thing signified. Were I to detail to you the various definitions[1] of philosophy which philosophers have promulgated — far more, were I to explain the grounds on which the author of each maintains the exclusive adequacy of his peculiar definition — I should, in the present stage of your progress, only perplex and confuse you. Philosophy, for example, — and I select only a few specimens of the more illustrious definitions, — philosophy has been defined: — The science of things divine and human, and of the causes in which they are contained;[2] — The science of effects by their causes;[3] — The science of sufficient reasons;[4] — The science of things possible, inasmuch as they are possible;[5] — The science of things, evidently deduced from first principles;[6] — The science of truths, sensible and abstract;[7] — The application of reason to its legitimate objects;[8] — The science of the relations of all knowledge to the necessary ends of human reason;[9] — The science of the original form of the ego or mental self;[10] — The science of science;[11] — The science of the

Philosophy — the thing — its definitions.

---

1 Vide *Gassendi*, i. p. 1, *seq.*; Denzinger, *Instit. Log.* i. p. 40: Scheidler's *Encyclop.* pp. 56, 75; Weiss, *Log.* p. 8; Scheiblerus, *Op. Log.* i. p. 1, *seq.*

2 Cicero, *De Officiis*, ii. 2. Nec quidquam aliud est philosophia, si interpretari velis, quam studium sapientiæ. Sapientia autem est, (ut a veteribus philosophis definitum est), rerum divinarum et humanarum, causarumque quibus hæ res continentur, scientia. Cf. *Tusc. Quæst.* iv. 26, v. 3. *De Fin.* ii. 12; Seneca, *Epist.* 89; Pseudo-Plutarch, *De Plac. Philos.* Prooem.: οἱ μὲν οὖν Στωϊκοὶ ἔφασαν τὴν μὲν σοφίαν εἶναι θείων τε καὶ ἀνθρωπίνων ἐπιστήμην· τὴν δὲ φιλοσοφίαν, ἄσκησιν τέχνης ἐπιτηδείου. Cf. Plato, *Phædrus*, p. 259; *Rep.* vi. p. 486. — ED.

3 Hobbes, *Computatio sive Logica*, c. 1; Philosophia est effectuum sive Phænomenων ex conceptis eorum causis seu generationibus, et rursus generationum quæ esse possunt, ex cognitis effectibus per rectam ratiocinationem acquisita cognitio. Cf. Arist. *Metaph.* i. 1. τὴν ὀνομαζομένην σοφίαν περὶ τὰ πρῶτα αἴτια καὶ τὰς ἀρχὰς ὑπολαμβάνουσι πάντες. — ED.

4 Leibnitz, quoted by Mazure, *Cours de Philosophie*, tom. i. p. 2; see also Wenzel, *Elementa Philosophiæ*, tom. i. § 7. Cf. Leibnitz, *Lettres entre Leibnitz et Clarke, Opera*, p. 778, (ed. Erd.) — ED.

5 Wolf, *Philosophia Rationalis*, § 29. — ED.

6 Descartes, *Principia*, Epistola Authoris. Cf. Wolf. *Phil. Rat.* § 33. — ED.

7 Condillac, *L'Art de Raisonner, Cours*, tom. iii. p. 3, (ed. 1780). Cf. Clemens Alex., *Strom.* viii. 8, p. 782. ἡ δὲ τῶν φιλοσόφων πραγματεία περί τε τὰ νοήματα καὶ τὰ ὑποκείμενα καταγίνεται. — ED.

8 Compare Tennemann, *Geschichte der Philosophie*, Einleitung, § 13. — ED.

9 Kant, *Kritik der reinen Vernunft*, Methodenlehre, c. 8; Krug, *Philosophisches Lexikon*, iii. p. 213. — ED.

10 Krug, *Philosophisches Lexikon*, iii. p. 213. The definition is substantially Fichte's. See his *Grundlage der Gesammten Wissenschaftslehren*, (*Werke*, i p. 283); and his *Zweite Einleitung in die Wissenschaftslehre*, (*Werke*, i. p. 515.) — ED.

11 Fichte, *Über den Begriff der Wissenchaftslehre*, § 1 (*Werke*, i. 45.) — ED.

absolute; — The science of the absolute indifference of the ideal and real [2] — or, The identity of identity and non-identity, etc., etc.[3] All such definitions are (if not positively erroneous), either so vague that they afford no precise knowledge of their object; or they are so partial, that they exclude what they ought to comprehend; or they are of such a nature that they supply no preliminary information, and are only to be understood, (if ever,) after a knowledge has been acquired of that which they profess to explain. It is, indeed, perhaps impossible, adequately to define philosophy. For what is to be defined comprises what cannot be included in a single definition. For philosophy is not regarded from a single point of view, — it is sometimes considered as theoretical, — that is, in relation to man as a thinking and cognitive intelligence; sometimes as practical, — that is, in relation to man as a moral agent; — and sometimes, as comprehending both theory and practice. Again, philosophy may either be regarded objectively, that is, as a complement of truths known; or subjectively, — that is, as a habit or quality of the mind knowing. In these circumstances, I shall not attempt a definition of philosophy, but shall endeavor to accomplish the end which every definition proposes, — make you understand, as precisely as the unprecise nature of the object-matter permits, what is meant by philosophy, and what are the sciences it properly comprehends within its sphere.

As a matter of history I may here, however, parenthetically mention, that in Greek antiquity there were in all

Definitions in Greek antiquity.

six definitions of philosophy which obtained celebrity. On these collectively there are extant various treatises. Among the commentators of Aristotle, that of Ammonius Hermiæ[4] is the oldest; and the fullest is one by an anonymous author, lately published by Dr. Cramer in the fourth volume of his *Anecdota Græca Parisiensia*.[5] Of the six, the first and second define philosophy from its object matter, — that which it is about; the third and fourth, from its end, — that for the sake of which it is; the fifth, from its relative preëminence; and the sixth, from its etymology.

---

1 Schelling, *Vom Ich als Princip der Philosophie*, §§ 6, 9; Krug, *Lexikon*, iii. p. 213. — ED.

2 Schelling, *Bruno*, p. 205 (2d ed.) Cf. *Philosophie der Natur*, Einleitung, p. 64, and Zusatz zur Einleitung, p. 65 — 88 (2d ed.) — ED.

3 Hegel, *Logik*, (*Werke*, iii. p. 64.) — ED.

4 *Ammonii in quinque voces Porphyrii Commentarius*, p. 1. (ed. Ald.) Given in part by Brandis, *Scholia in Aristotelem*, p. 9. — ED.

5 P. 389. Extracted also in part by Brandis, *Scholia in Aristotelem*, p. 6. This commentary is conjectured by Val. Rose (*De Aristotelis Librorum Ordine et Auctoritate*, p. 243) to be the work of Olympiodorus. The definitions quoted in the text are given by Tzetzes, *Chiliads*, x. 600. — ED.

The first of these definitions of philosophy is, — "the knowledge of things existent as existent," —(γνῶσις τῶν ὄντων ᾗ ὄντα.)[1]

The second is — "the knowledge of things divine and human,—" (γνῶσις θείων καὶ ἀνθρωπίνων πραγμάτων.)[2] These are both from the object-matter; and both were referred to Pythagoras.

The third and fourth, the two definitions of philosophy from its end, are, again, both taken from Plato. Of these the third is,— "philosophy is a meditation of death," (μελέτη θανάτου;)[3] the fourth — "philosophy is a resembling of the Deity in so far as that is competent to man, (ὁμοίωσις θεῷ κατὰ τὸ δυνατὸν ἀνθρώπῳ.)[4]

The fifth, that from its preëminence, was borrowed from Aristotle, and defined philosophy "the art of arts, and science of sciences," (τέχνη τεχνῶν καὶ ἐπιστήμη ἐπιστημῶν.)[5]

Finally, the sixth, that from the etymology, was like the first and second, carried up to Pythagoras — it defined philosophy "the love of wisdom," (φιλία σοφίας.)[6]

To these a seventh and even an eighth were sometimes added,— but the seventh was that by the physicians who defined medicine the philosophy of bodies, (ἰατρική ἐστι φιλοσοφία σωμάτων); and philosophy, the medicine of souls, (φιλοσοφία ἐστὶν ἰατρικὴ ψυχῶν).[7] This was derided by the philosophers; as, to speak with Homer, being an exchange of brass for gold, and of gold for brass, (χρύσεα χαλκείων); and as defining the more known by the less known.

The eighth is from an expression of Plato, who, in the Theætetus,[8] calls philosophy "the greatest music," (μεγίστη μουσικὴ,) meaning thereby the harmony of the rational, irascible, and appetent, parts of the soul, (λόγος, θυμός, ἐπιθυμία).

But to return: All philosophy is knowledge, but all knowledge is not philosophy. Philosophy is, therefore, a kind of knowledge.

---

1 Cf. Arist. Metaph. iii. 1. — ED.

2 See ante, p. 35, note 2. — ED.

3 Phædo, p. 80: τοῦτο δὲ οὐδὲν ἄλλο ἐστὶν ἢ ὀρθῶς φιλοσοφοῦσα καὶ τῷ ὄντι τεθνάναι μελετῶσα ῥᾳδίως· ἢ οὐ τοῦτ' ἂν εἴη μελέτη θανάτου; Cf. Cicero Tusc. Quæst. i. 30; Macrobius, In Som. Scipionis, i. 13; Damascenus, Dialectica, c. 3. — ED.

4 Theætetus, p. 176: διὸ καὶ πειρᾶσθαι χρὴ ἐνθένδε ἐκεῖσε φεύγειν ὅτι τάχιστα· φυγὴ δὲ ὁμοίωσις θεῷ κατὰ τὸ δυνατόν. — ED.

5 The anonymous commentator quotes this as a passage from the Metaphysics. It does not occur literally, but the sense is substantially that expressed in Book i. c 2. Ἀκριβέσταται δὲ τῶν ἐπιστημῶν αἱ μάλιστα τῶν πρώτων εἰσίν . . . Ἀλλὰ μὴν καὶ διδασκαλική γε ἡ τῶν αἰτιῶν θεωρητικὴ μᾶλλον. . . . οὔτε τῆς τοιαύτης ἄλλην χρὴ νομίζειν τιμιωτέραν· ἡ γὰρ θειοτάτη καὶ τιμιωτάτη. Cf. Eth. Nic. vi. 7: δῆλον ὅτι ἡ ἀκριβεστάτη ἂν τῶν ἐπιστημῶν εἴη ἡ σοφία. The nearest approach to a definition of Philosophy in the Metaphysics is in A minor, c. 1. Ὀρθῶς δ' ἔχει καὶ τὸ καλεῖσθαι τὴν φιλοσοφίαν ἐπιστήμην τῆς ἀληθείας. — ED.

6 See ante, p. 45. — ED.

7 Anon. apud Cramer, Anecdota, iv. p. 318; Brandis, Scholia, p. 7. — ED.

8 So quoted by the commentator; but the passage occurs in the Phædo, p. 61. Καὶ ἐμοὶ οὕτω τὸ ἐνύπνιον ὅπερ ἔπραττον, τοῦτο ἐπικελεύειν, μουσικὴν ποιεῖν, ὡς φιλοσοφίας μὲν οὔσης μεγίστης μουσικῆς. — ED.

What, then, is philosophical knowledge, and how is it discriminated
from knowledge in general? We are endowed

Philosophical and empirical knowledge.

by our Creator with certain faculties of observation, which enable us to become aware of cer-
tain appearances or phænomena. These faculties may be stated,
as two, — Sense, or External Perception, and Self-Consciousness
or Internal Perception; and these faculties severally afford us the
knowledge of a different series of phænomena. Through our
senses, we apprehend what exists, or what occurs, in the external
or material world; by our self-consciousness,[1] we apprehend what
is, or what occurs, in the internal world, or world of thought.
What is the extent, and what the certainty, of the knowledge
acquired through sense and self-consciousness, we do not at present
consider. It is now sufficient that the simple fact be admitted, that
we do actually thus know; and that fact is so manifest, that it
requires, I presume, at my hands, neither proof nor illustration.

The information which we thus receive,—that certain phænomena
are, or have been, is called Historical, or Empir-

*Empirical knowl-
edge—what.*

ical knowledge.[2] It is called historical, because,
in this knowledge, we know only the fact, only
that the phænomenon is; for history is properly only the narration
of a consecutive series of phænomena in time, or the description of
a coëxistent series of phænomena in space. Civil history is an example of the one; natural history, of the other. It is called empirical or experiential, if we might use that term, because it is given
us by experience or observation, and not obtained as the result of
inference or reasoning. I may notice, by paren-

*By-meaning of the
term empirical.*

thesis, that you must discharge from your minds
the by-meaning accidentally associated with the
word *empiric* or *empirical*, in common English. This term is with
us more familiarly used in reference to medicine, and from its fortuitous employment in that science, in a certain sense, the word empirical has unfortunately acquired, in our language, a one-sided and an
unfavorable meaning. Of the origin of this meaning many of you
may not be aware. You are aware, however, that ἐμπειρία is the
Greek term for experience, and ἐμπειρικὸς an epithet applied to one
who uses experience. Now, among the Greek physicians, there arose
a sect who, professing to employ experience alone to the exclusion
of generalization, analogy, and reasoning, denominated themselves
distinctively οἱ ἐμπειρικοί — the Empirics. The opposite extreme was
adopted by another sect, who, rejecting observation, founded their

---

1 On the place and sphere of Consciousness, see *Discussions*, p. 47.— ED.

2 Brandis, *Geschichte der Philosophie*, vol. i. p. 2. [Cf. Wolf, *Phil. Rat.* § 3.— ED.]

doctrine exclusively on reasoning and theory;—and these called themselves οἱ μεθοδικοί—or Methodists. A third school, of whom Galen was the head, opposed equally to the two extreme sects of the Empirics and of the Methodists, and, availing themselves both of experience and reasoning, were styled οἱ δογματικοί—the Dogmatists, or rational physicians.[1] A keen controversy arose; the Empirics were defeated; they gradually died out; and their doctrine, of which nothing is known to us, except through the writings of their adversaries,[2] has probably been painted in blacker colors than it deserved. Be this, however, as it may, the word was first naturalized in English, at a time when the Galenic works were of paramount authority in medicine, as a term of medical import—of medical reproach; and the collateral meaning, which it had accidentally obtained in that science, was associated with an unfavorable signification, so that an Empiric, in common English, has been long a synonym for a charlatan or quack-doctor, and, by a very natural extension, in general, for any ignorant pretender in science. In philosophical language, the term *empirical* means simply what belongs to, or is the product of, experience or observation, and, in contrast to another term afterwards to be explained, is now technically in general use through every other country of Europe. Were there any other word to be found of a corresponding signification in English, it would perhaps, in consequence of the by-meaning attached to empirical, be expedient not to employ this latter. But there is not. *Experiential* is not in common use, and *experimental* only designates a certain kind of experience—viz. that in which the fact observed has been brought about by a certain intentional prearrangement of its coëfficients. But this by the way.

Returning, then, from our digression: Historical or empirical knowledge is simply the knowledge that something is. Were we to use the expression, *the knowledge that*, it would sound awkward and unusual in our modern languages. In Greek, the most philosophical of all tongues, its parallel, however, was familiarly employed, more especially in the Aristotelic philosophy,[3] in contrast to another knowledge of which we are about to speak. It was called the τὸ ὅτι, that is, ἡ γνῶσις ὅτι ἔστιν.[4] I should notice, that

---

1 See Galen, *De Sectis*, c. 1, and the *Definitiones Medicæ* and *Introductio seu Medicus*, ascribed to the same author; Celsus, *De Re Medica*, Præf.; Dan. Le Clerc, *Histoire de la Médecine*, part ii., lib. ii., ch. 1—lib. iv., ch. 1.—ED.

2 Le Clerc, *Histoire de la Médecine*, part ii., lib. ii., ch. 1.—ED.

3 See *Anal. Post.* ii. 1. Τὰ ζητούμενά ἐστιν

ἴσα τὸν ἀριθμὸν ὅσαπερ ἐπιστάμεθα. Ζητοῦμεν δὲ τέτταρα, τὸ ὅτι, τὸ διότι, εἰ ἔστι, τί ἐστιν. These were distinguished by the Latin logicians as the *quæstiones scibiles* and were usually rendered *quod sit, cur sit, an sit, quid sit.*—ED.

4 This expression in Latin, at least in Latin not absolutely barbarous, can only be translated vaguely by an accusative and an infini-

with us, *the knowledge that*, is commonly called the knowledge of the *fact*.[1]　As examples of empirical knowledge, take the facts, whether known on our own experience or on the testified experience of others, — that a stone falls, — that smoke ascends, — that the leaves bud in spring and fall in autumn, — that such a book contains such a passage, — that such a passage contains such an opinion, — that Cæsar, that Charlemagne, that Napoleon, existed.[2]

But things do not exist, events do not occur, isolated, — apart —

Philosophical knowledge — what.

by themselves, — they exist, they occur, and are by us conceived, only in connection.　Our observation affords us no example of a phænomenon which is not an effect; nay, our thought cannot even realize to itself the possibility of a phænomenon without a cause.　We do not at present inquire into the nature of the connection of effect and cause,[3] — either in reality, or in thought.　It is sufficient for our present purpose to observe that, while, by the constitution of our nature, we are unable to conceive anything to begin to be, without referring it to some cause, — still the knowledge of its particular cause is not involved in the knowledge of any particular effect.　By this necessity which we are under of thinking some cause for every phænomenon; and by our original ignorance of what particular causes belong to what particular effects, — it is rendered impossible for us to acquiesce in the mere knowledge of the fact of a phænomenon: on the contrary, we are determined, — we are necessitated, to regard each phænomenon as only partially known, until we discover the causes on which it depends for its existence.　For example, we are struck with the appearance in the heavens called a rainbow.　Think we cannot that this phænomenon has no cause, though we may be wholly ignorant of what that cause is.　Now, our knowledge of the phænomenon as a mere fact, — as a mere isolated event, — does not content us; we therefore set about an inquiry into the cause, — which the constitution of our mind com-

---

tive, for you are probably aware that the conjunctive *quod*, by which the Greek ὅτι is often translated, has always a *causal* signification in genuine Latinity.　Thus, we cannot say, *scio quod res sit, credo quod tu sis doctus :*— this is barbarous.　We must say, *scio rem esse, credo te esse doctum.*

1 [Empirical is also used in contrast with Necessary knowledge; the former signifying the knowledge simply of what is, the latter of what must be.]— *Oral Interpolation.*

2 The terms historical and empirical are used as synonymous by Aristotle, as both de-

noting a knowledge of the ὅτι.　(Compare the *De Incessu Animalium*, c. 1; *Metaph.* i. 1.) Aristotle, therefore, calls his empirical work on animals, *History of Animals ;* — Theophrastus, his empirical work on plants, *History of Plants ;* — Pliny, his empirical book on nature in general, *Natural History.*　Pliny says: " nobis propositum est *naturas* rerum indicare *manifestas*, non *causas* indagare *dubias.*" See Brandis, *Geschichte der Philosophie*, i. p. 2.

3 See on this point the Author's *Discussions*, p. 609. — ED.

pels us to suppose, — and at length discover that the rainbow is the effect of the refraction of the solar rays by the watery particles of a cloud. Having ascertained the cause, but not till then, we are satisfied that we fully know the effect.

Now, this knowledge of the cause of a phænomenon is different from, is something more than, the knowledge of that phænomenon simply as a fact; and these two cognitions or knowledges[1] have, accordingly, received different names. The latter, we have seen, is called *historical*, or *empirical* knowledge; the former is called *philosophical*, or *scientific*, or *rational* knowledge.[2] Historical, is the knowledge that a thing is — philosophical, is the knowledge why or how it is. And as the Greek language, with peculiar felicity, expresses historical knowledge by the ὅτι — the γνῶσις ὅτι ἔστι: so, it well expresses philosophical knowledge by the διότι[3] — the γνῶσις διότι ἔστι, though here its relative superiority is not the same. To recapitulate what has now been stated : — There are two kinds or degrees of knowledge. The first is the knowledge that a thing is — ὅτι χρῆμα ἔστι, *rem esse ;* — and it is called the knowledge of the fact, historical, or empirical knowledge. The second is the knowledge why or how a thing is, διότι χρῆμα ἔστι, *cur res sit ;* — and is termed the knowledge of the cause, philosophical, scientific, rational knowledge.

Philosophical knowledge, in the widest acceptation of the term, and as synonymous with science, is thus the knowledge of effects as dependent on their causes. Now, what does this imply? In the first place, as every cause to which we can ascend is itself also an effect, — it follows that it is the scope, that is, the aim of philosophy, to trace up the series of effects and causes, until we arrive at causes which are not also themselves effects. These first causes do not indeed lie within the reach of philosophy, nor even within the sphere of our comprehension; nor, consequently, on the actual reaching them does the existence of philosophy depend. But as philosophy is the knowledge of effects in their causes, the tendency of philosophy is ever upwards; and philosophy can, in thought, in theory, only be viewed as accomplished, — which in reality it never can be, — when the ultimate causes, — the causes

Philosophy implies a search after first causes.

---

1 *Knowledges* is a term in frequent use by Bacon, and though now obsolete, should be revived, as, without it, we are compelled to borrow *cognitions* to express its import.] — *Oral Interpolation.* [See Bacon's *Advancement of Learning*, p. 176, (*Works*, vol. ii., ed. Mont.);

and Sergeant's *Method to Science*, Preface, p. 25, p. 166 *et passim.* — ED.

2 Wolf, *Philosophia Rationalis*, § 6; Kant, *Kritik der reinen Vernunft*, Methodenlehre, c. 3. — ED.

3 Arist. *Anal. Post.* ii. 1. — ED.

on which all other causes depend, — have been attained and understood.[1]

But, in the second place, as every effect is only produced by the concurrence of at least two causes, (and by cause, be it observed, I mean everything without which the effect could not be realized), and as these concurring or coëfficient causes, in fact, constitute the effect, it follows, that the lower we descend in the series of causes, the more complex will be the product; and that the higher we ascend, it will be the more simple. Let us take, for example, a neutral salt. This, as you probably know, is the product — the combination of an alkali and an acid. Now, considering the salt as an effect, what are the concurrent causes, — the co-efficients, — which constitute it what it is? These are, *first*, the acid, with its affinity to the alkali; *secondly*, the alkali, with its affinity to the acid; and *thirdly*, the translating force (perhaps the human hand) which made their affinities available, by bringing the two bodies within the sphere of mutual attraction. Each of these three concurrents must be considered as a partial cause; for, abstract any one, and the effect is not produced. Now, these three partial causes are each of them again effects; but effects evidently less complex than the effect which· they, by their concurrence, constituted. But each of these three constituents is an effect; and therefore to be analyzed into its causes; and these causes again into others, until the procedure is checked by our inability to resolve the last constituent into simpler elements. But, though thus unable to carry our analysis beyond a limited extent, we neither conceive, nor are we able to conceive, the constituent in which our analysis is arrested, as itself anything but an effect. We therefore carry on the analysis in imagination; and as each step in the procedure carries us from the more complex to the more simple, and, consequently, nearer to unity, we at last arrive at that unity itself, — at that ultimate cause which, as ultimate, cannot again be conceived as an effect.[2]

Philosophy thus, as the knowledge of effects in their causes, necessarily tends, not towards a plurality of ultimate or first causes, but towards one alone. This first cause, — the Creator, — it can

---

1 Arist. *Anal. Post.* i. 24. Ἔτι μέχρι τούτου ζητοῦμεν τὸ διὰ τί, καὶ τότε οἰόμεθα εἰδέναι, ὅταν μὴ ᾖ ὅτι τι ἄλλο τοῦτο ἢ γινόμενον ἢ ὂν· τέλος γὰρ καὶ πέρας τὸ ἔσχατον ἤδη οὕτως ἐστίν. Cf. *Metaph.* i. 2: δεῖ γὰρ ταύτην τῶν πρώτων ἀρχῶν καὶ αἰτίων εἶναι θεωρητικήν. — Ed.

2 I may notice that an ultimate cause, and a first cause, are the same, but viewed in different relations. What is called the ultimate cause in ascending from effects to causes, — that is, in the regressive order, is called the first cause in descending from causes to effects, — that is, in the progressive order. This synonymous meaning of the terms ultimate and primary it is important to recollect, for these words are in very common use in philosophy.

indeed never reach, as an object of immediate knowledge; but, as

Philosophy necessarily tends towards a first cause.

the convergence towards unity in the ascending series is manifest, in so far as that series is within our view, and as it is even impossible for the mind to suppose the convergence not continuous and complete, it follows, — unless all analogy be rejected, — unless our intelligence be declared a lie, — that we must, philosophically, believe in that ultimate or primary unity which, in our present existence, we are not destined in itself to apprehend.

Such is philosophical knowledge in its most extensive signification; and, in this signification, all the sciences, occupied in the research of causes, may be viewed as so many branches of philosophy.

There is, however, one section of these sciences which is denom-

Sciences denominated philosophical by preëminence.

inated philosophical by preëminence; — sciences, which the term philosophy exclusively denotes, when employed in propriety and rigor. What these sciences are, and why the term philosophy has been specially limited to them, I shall now endeavor to make you understand.

"Man," says Protagoras, "is the measure of the universe;"[1] and,

Man's knowledge relative.

in so far as the universe is an object of human knowledge, the paradox is a truth. Whatever we know, or endeavor to know, God or the world, — mind or matter, — the distant or the near, — we know, and can know, only in so far as we possess a faculty of knowing in general; and we can only exercise that faculty under the laws which control and limit its operations. However great, and infinite, and various, therefore, may be the universe and its contents, — these are known to us, not as they exist, but as our mind is capable of knowing them. Hence the brocard — "Quicquid recipitur, recipitur ad modum recipientis."[2]

In the first place, therefore, as philosophy is a

The primary problem of philosophy.

knowledge, and as all knowledge is only possible under the conditions to which our faculties are subjected, — the grand, — the primary problem of philosophy

1 See Plato, *Theætetus*, p. 152; Arist. *Metaph.* x. 6. — ED.

2 Boethius, *De Consol. Phil.* v. Prosa iv. Omne enim quod cognoscitur, non secundum sui vim, sed secundem agnoscentium potius comprehenditur facultatem. Proclus in *Plat. Parm.* p. 748, ed. Stallbaum, τὸ γιγνῶσκον κατὰ τὴν ἑαυτοῦ γιγνώσκει φύσιν. Aquinas, *Summa*, part i. Q. 79, art. 3. Similitudo agen-

tis recipitur in patientem secundum modum patientis. *Ibid.* part i. Q. 14, art. 1. Scientia est secundum modum cognoscentis. Scitum enim est in sciente secundum modum scientis. Chauvin gives the words of the text. See *Lexicon Philosophicum*, art. *Finitas*. See also other authorities to the same effect quoted in the Author's *Discussions*, p. 644. — ED.

must be to investigate and determine these conditions, as the necessary conditions of its own possibility.

In the second place, as philosophy is not merely a knowledge, but a knowledge of causes, and as the mind itself is the universal and principal concurrent cause in every act of knowledge; philosophy is, consequently, bound to make the mind its first and paramount object of consideration. The study of mind is thus the philosophical study by preëminence. There is no branch of philosophy which does not suppose this as its preliminary, which does not borrow from this its light. A considerable number, indeed, are only the science of mind viewed in particular aspects, or considered in certain special applications. Logic, for example, or the science of the laws of thought, is only a fragment of the general science of mind, and presupposes a certain knowledge of the operations which are regulated by these laws. Ethics is the science of the laws which govern our actions as moral agents; and a knowledge of these laws is only possible through a knowledge of the moral agent himself. Political science, in like manner, supposes a knowledge of man in his natural constitution, in order to appreciate the modifications which he receives, and of which he is susceptible, in social and civil life. The Fine Arts have all their foundation in the theory of the beautiful; and this theory is afforded by that part of the philosophy of mind, which is conversant with the phænomena of feeling. Religion, Theology, in fine, is not independent of the same philosophy. For as God only exists for us as we have faculties capable of apprehending his existence, and of fulfilling his behests, nay, as the phænomena from which we are warranted to infer his being are wholly mental, the examination of these faculties and of these phænomena is, consequently, the primary condition of every sound theology. In short, the science of mind, whether considered in itself, or in relation to the other branches of our knowledge, constitutes the principal and most important object of philosophy, — constitutes in propriety, with its suit of dependent sciences, philosophy itself.[1]

The limitation of the term Philosophy to the sciences of mind,

The study of mind the philosophical study.

Branches of this study.

Logic.

Ethics.

Politics.

The Fine Arts.

Theology dependent on study of mind.

---

1 Cf. Cousin, *Cours de l' Histoire de la Phil. Mod.*, Prem. Ser. tom. ii.; Programme de la Première Partie du Cours. — ED.

when not expressly extended to the other branches of science, has been always that generally prevalent; — yet it must be confessed that, in this country, the word is applied to sub-

Misapplication of the term Philosophy in this country.

jects with which, on the continent of Europe, it is rarely, if ever, associated. With us the word philosophy, taken by itself, does not call up the precise and limited notion which it does to a German, a Hollander, a Dane, an Italian, or a Frenchman; and we are obliged to say the philosophy of mind, if we do not wish it to be vaguely extended to the sciences conversant with the phænomena of matter. We not only call Physics by the name of Natural Philosophy, but every mechanical process has with us its philosophy. We have books on the philosophy of Manufactures, the philosophy of Agriculture, the philosophy of Cookery, etc. In all this we are the ridicule of other nations. Socrates, it is said, brought down philosophy from the clouds, — the English have degraded her to the kitchen; and this, our prostitution of the term, is, by foreigners, alleged as a significant indication of the low state of the mental sciences in Britain.[1]

From what has been said, you will, without a definition, be able to form at least a general notion of what is meant by philosophy. In its more extensive signification, it is equivalent to a knowledge of things by their causes, — and this is, in fact, Aristotle's definition;[2] while, in its stricter meaning, it is confined to the sciences which constitute, or hold immediately of, the science of mind.

---

1 See Hegel, *Werke*, vi. 13; xiii. 72; Scheidler, *Encyclop. der Philosophie*, i. p. 27. — ED.

2 *Metaph.* v. 1: πᾶσα ἐπιστήμη διανοητικὴ περὶ αἰτίας καὶ ἀρχάς ἐστιν ἢ ἀκριβεστέρας ἢ ἁπλουστέρας. I. 1: τὴν ὀνομαζομένην σοφίαν περὶ τὰ πρῶτα αἴτια καὶ τὰς ἀρχὰς ὑπολαμβάνουσι πάντες . . . ὅτι μὲν οὖν ἡ σοφία περὶ τινας αἰτίας καὶ ἀρχάς ἐστιν ἐπιστήμη, δῆλον. *Eth. Nic.* vi. 7: δεῖ ἄρα τὸν σοφὸν μὴ μόνον τὰ ἐκ τῶν ἀρχῶν εἰδέναι, ἀλλὰ καὶ περὶ τὰς ἀρχὰς ἀληθεύειν. — ED.

LECTURE IV.

THE CAUSES OF PHILOSOPHY.

HAVING thus endeavored to make you vaguely apprehend what
cannot be precisely understood, — the Nature
and Comprehension of Philosophy, — I now
proceed to another question, — What are the
Causes of Philosophy? The causes of philoso-
phy lie in the original elements of our constitution. We are
created with the faculty of knowledge, and, consequently, created
with the tendency to exert it. Man philosophizes as he lives. He
may philosophize well or ill, but philosophize he must. Philosophy
can, indeed, only be assailed through philosophy itself. "If," says
Aristotle, in a passage preserved to us by Olympiodorus,[1] "we must
philosophize, we must philosophize; if we must not philosophize, we
must philosophize; — in any case, therefore, we must philosophize."
"Were philosophy," says Clement of Alexandria,[2] "an evil, still
philosophy is to be studied, in order that it may be scientifically
contemned." And Averroes,[3] — "Philosophi solum est spernere philosophiam." Of the causes of philosophy some are, therefore, contained in man's very capacity for knowledge;
these are essential and necessary. But there
are others, again, which lie in certain feelings
with which he is endowed; these are comple-
mentary and assistant.

Of the former class, — that is, of the essential causes, — there are
in all two: the one is, the necessity we feel
to connect Causes with Effects; the other, to
carry up our knowledge into Unity. These
tendencies, however, if not identical in their origin, coincide in

*The causes of phil-
osophy in the elements
of our constitution.*

*These causes either
essential or comple-
mentary.*

*The first class appa-
rently two-fold.*

1 *Olympiodori in Platonis Alcibiadem Priorem
Commentarii*, ed. Creuzer, p. 144. Καὶ Ἀρισ-
τοτέλης ἐν τῷ Προτρεπτικῷ ἔλεγεν ὅτι
εἴτε φιλοσοφητέον, φιλοσοφητέον· εἴτε μὴ
φιλοσοφητέον, φιλοσοφητέον· πάντως δὲ φιλοσοφητέον. Quoted also by the anonymous
commentator in Cramer's *Anecdota*, iv. p. 391.
—ED.

2 Εἰ καὶ ἄχρηστος εἴη φιλοσοφία, εἰ εὔχ-
ρηστος ἡ τῆς ἀχρηστίας βεβαίωσις, εὔχρησ-
τος. *Stromata*, i. 2.—ED.

3 See *Discussions*, p. 786.—ED. ["Se mo-
quer de la philosophie, c'est vraiment philosopher." Pascal, *Pensées*, part i. art. xi. §
36. Compare Montaigne, *Essais*, lib. ii. c. xii.
—tom. ii. p. 216, ed. 1725.]

their result; for, as I have previously explained to you, in ascending from cause to cause, we necessarily, (could we carry our analysis to its issue,) arrive at absolute unity. Indeed, were it not a discussion for which you are not as yet prepared, it might be shown, that both principles originate in the same condition;—that both emanate, not from any original power, but from the same original powerlessness of mind.[1] Of the former,—namely, the

1. The principle of Cause and Effect. tendency, or rather the necessity, which we feel to connect the objects of our experience with others which afford the reasons of their existence,—it is needful to say but little. The nature of this tendency is not a matter on which we can at present enter; and the fact of its existence is too notorious to require either proof or illustration. It is sufficient to say, or rather to repeat what we have already stated, that the mind is unable to realize in thought the possibility of any absolute commencement; it cannot conceive that anything which begins to be is anything more than a new modification of preëxistent elements; it is unable to view any individual thing as other than a link in the mighty chain of being; and every isolated object is viewed by it only as a fragment which, to be known, must be known in connection with the whole of which it constitutes a part. It is thus that we are unable to rest satisfied with a mere historical knowledge of existence; and that even our happiness is interested in discovering causes, hypothetical at least, if not real, for the various phænomena of the existence of which our experience informs us.

"*Felix qui potuit rerum cognoscere causas.*"[2]

The second tendency of our nature, of which philosophy is the result, is the desire of Unity. On this, which

2. The love of Unity. indeed involves the other, it is necessary to be somewhat more explicit. This tendency is one of the most prominent characteristics of the human mind. It, in part, originates in the imbecility of our faculties. We are lost in the multitude of the objects presented to our observation, and it is only by assorting them in classes that we can reduce the infinity of nature to the finitude of mind. The conscious Ego, the conscious Self, by its nature one, seems also constrained to require that unity by which it is distinguished, in everything which it receives, and in everything which it produces. I regret that I can illustrate this only by examples which cannot, I am aware, as yet be fully intelligible

---

[1] This is partially argued in the *Discussions*, p. 609.—ED.   [2] Virgil, *Georgics*, ii. 490.

to all. We are conscious of a scene presented to our senses only by uniting its parts into a perceived whole. Perception is thus a unifying act. The Imagination cannot represent an object without uniting, in a single combination, the various elements of which it is composed. Generalization is only the apprehension of the one in the many, and language little else than a registry of the factitious unities of thought. The Judgment cannot affirm or deny one notion of another, except by uniting the two in one indivisible act of comparison. Syllogism is simply the union of two judgments in a third. Reason, Intellect, νοῦς, in fine, concatenating thoughts and objects into system, and tending always upwards from particular facts to general laws, from general laws to universal principles, is never satisfied in its ascent till it comprehend, (what, however, it can never do), all laws in a single formula, and consummate all conditional knowledge in the unity of unconditional existence. Nor is it only in science that the mind desiderates the one. We seek it equally in works of art. A work of art is only deserving of the name, inasmuch as an idea of the work has preceded its execution, and inasmuch as it is itself a realization of the ideal model in sensible forms. All languages express the mental operations by words which denote a reduction of the many to the one. Σύνεσις, περίληψις, συναίσθησις, συνεπιγνῶσις, etc. in Greek; — in Latin, *cogere*, (*co-agere*), *cogitare*, (*co-agitare*), *concipere*, *cognoscere*, *comprehendere*, *conscire*, with their derivatives, may serve for examples.

The history of philosophy is only the history of this tendency; and philosophers have amply testified to its reality. "The mind," says Anaxagoras,[1] "only knows when it subdues its objects, when it reduces the many to the one." "All knowledge," say the Platonists,[2] "is the gathering up into one, and the indivisible apprehension of this unity by the knowing mind." Leibnitz[3] and Kant[4] have, in like manner, defined knowledge by the representation of multitude in unity. "The end of philosophy," says Plato,[5] "is the intuition

Testimonies to the love of unity.

1 Arist. *De Anima*, iii 4: Ἀνάγκη ἄρα, ἐπεὶ πάντα νοεῖ, ἀμιγῆ εἶναι, ὥσπερ φησὶν 'Αναξαγόρας, ἵνα κρατῇ, τοῦτο δ' ἐστὶν ἵνα γνωρίζῃ. The passage of Anaxagoras is given at length in the Commentary of Simplicius, and quoted in part by Trendelenburg on the *De Anima*, p. 466. — ED.

2 Priscianus Lydus: Κατὰ τὴν εἰς ἐν συναίρεσιν, καὶ τὴν ἀμέριστον τοῦ γνωστοῦ παντὸς περίληψιν, ἀπάσης ἱσταμένης γνώσεως. (Μετάφρασις τῶν Θεοφράστου Περὶ Αἰσθήσεως — *Opera Theoph.* ed. Basil p. 273).

Thus rendered in the Latin version of Ficinus: "Cognitio omnis constat secundum quandam in unum congregationem, atque secundem impartibilem cognoscibilis totius comprehensionem. — ED.

3 *Monadologie*, § 14. — ED.

4 *Kritik der reinen Vernunft*, p. 359, ed. 1799. — ED.

Cf. *Philebus*, sub init., especially p. 16: Δεῖν ἡμᾶς ἀεὶ μίαν ἰδέαν περὶ παντὸς ἑκάστοτε θεμένους ζητεῖν; and *Republic*, v. p. 475, *et. seq.* — ED.

of unity;" and Plotinus, among many others,[1] observes that our knowledge is perfect as it is one. The love of unity is by Aristotle applied to solve a multitude of psychological phænomena.[2] St. Augustin even analyzes pain into a feeling of the frustration of unity. "Quid est enim aliud dolor, nisi quidam sensus divisionis vel corruptionis impatiens? Unde luce clarius apparet, quam sit illa anima in sui corporis universitate avida unitatis et tenax."[3]

This love of unity, this tendency of mind to generalize its knowledge, leads us to anticipate in nature a corresponding uniformity; and as this anticipation is found in harmony with experience, it not only affords the efficient cause of philosophy, but the guiding principle to its discoveries. "Thus, for instance, when it is observed that solid bodies are compressible, we are induced to expect that liquids will be found to be so likewise; we subject them, consequently, to a series of experiments; nor do we rest satisfied until it be proved that this quality is common to both classes of substances. Compressibility is then proclaimed a physical law, — a law of nature in general; and we experience a vivid gratification in this recognition of unconditioned universality." Another example; Kant,[4] reflecting on the differences among the planets, or rather among the stars revolving round the sun, and having discovered that these differences betrayed a uniform progress and proportion, — a proportion which was no longer to be found between Saturn and the first of the comets, — the law of unity and the analogy of nature, led him to conjecture that, in the intervening space, there existed a star, the discovery of which would vindicate the universality of the law. This anticipation was verified. Uranus was discovered by Herschel, and our dissatisfac-

Love of unity a guiding principle in philosophy.

1 *Enn.* iii. lib. viii. c. 2, on which Ficinus says: "Cognoscendi potentia in ipso actu cognitionis unum quodammodo sit cum objecto, et quo magis sit unum, eo perfectior est cognitio, atque vicissim — ED.

Enn. vi. lib. ix. c. 1: Ἀρετὴ δὲ ψυχῆς ὅταν εἰς ἓν, καὶ εἰς μίαν ὁμολογίαν ἐνωθῇ. . . . Ἐπειδὴ τὰ πάντα εἰς ἓν ἄγει, δημιουργοῦσα καὶ πλάττουσα καὶ μορφοῦσα καὶ συντάττουσα. Proclus, — Γνῶσις οὐδενὸς ἔσται τῶν ὄντων, εἴπως μὴ ἔστι τὸ ἕν . . . Οὐδὲ λόγος ἔσται· καὶ γὰρ ὁ λόγος ἐκ πολλῶν εἷς, εἴπερ τέλειος· καὶ ἡ γνῶσις, ὅταν τὸ γινῶσκον ἐν γίνηται πρὸς τὸ γνωστόν. *In Platonis Theologiam*, p. 76 (ed. 1618). — ED.

2 See *De Memoria*, § 5, for application of this principle to the problem of Reminiscence. Cf. *Reid's Works*, p. 900. See also *Problems*, xviii. 9, where it is used to explain the higher pleasure we derive from those narratives that relate to a single subject. — ED.

3 *De Libero Arbitrio*, lib. iii. 23. [St. Augustin applied the principle of Unity to solve the theory of the Beautiful: "Omnis pulchritudinis forma unitas est." *Epist.* xviii.] — *Oral Interp.*

4 *Allgemeine Naturgeschichte und Theorie des Himmels*, 1755; *Werke*, vol. vi. p. 88. Kant's conjecture was founded on a supposed progressive increase in the eccentricities of the planetary orbits. This progression, however, is only true of Venus, the Earth, Jupiter, and Saturn. The eccentricity diminishes again in Uranus, and still more in Neptune. Subsequent discoveries have thus rather weakened than confirmed the theory. — ED.

tion at the anomaly appeased. Franklin, in like manner, surmised that lightning and the electric spark were identical; and when he succeeded in verifying this conjecture, our love of unity was gratified. From the moment an isolated fact is discovered, we endeavor to refer it to other facts which it resembles. Until this be accomplished, we do not view it as understood. This is the case, for example, with sulphur, which, in a certain degree of temperature melts like other bodies, but at a higher degree of heat, instead of evaporating, again consolidates. When a fact is generalized, our discontent is quieted, and we consider the generality itself as tantamount to an explanation. Why does this apple fall to the ground? Because all bodies gravitate towards each other. Arrived at this general fact, we inquire no more, although ignorant now as previously of the cause of gravitation; for gravitation is nothing more than a name for a general fact, the *why* of which we know not. A mystery, if recognized as universal, would no longer appear mysterious.

"But this thirst of unity,—this tendency of mind to generalize its knowledge, and our concomitant belief in the uniformity of natural phænomena, is not only an effective mean of discovery, but likewise an abundant source of error. Hardly is there a similarity detected between two or three facts, than men hasten to extend it to all others; and if, perchance, the similarity has been detected by ourselves, self-love closes our eyes to the contradictions which our theory may encounter from experience."[1] "I have heard," says Condillac, "of a philosopher who had the happiness of thinking that he had discovered a principle which was to explain all the wonderful phænomena of chemistry, and who, in the ardor of his self-gratulation, hastened to communicate his discovery to a skilful chemist. The chemist had the kindness to listen to him, and then calmly told him that there was but one unfortunate circumstance for his discovery,—that the chemical facts were precisely the converse of what he had supposed them to be. 'Well, then, said the philosopher, 'have the goodness to tell me what they are, that I may explain them on my system.'"[2] We are naturally disposed to refer everything we do not know to principles with which we are familiar. As Aristotle observes,[3] the early Pythagoreans, who first studied arithmetic, were induced, by their scientific predilections, to explain the problem of the universe by the properties of

Love of unity a source of error.

1 Garnier, *Cours de Psychologie*, p. 192–94. [Cf. Ancillon, *Nouv. Mélanges*, i. p. 1, *et seq.*]

2 *Traité des Systèmes*, chap. xii. *Œuvres Philos.* tom. iv. p. 146 (ed. 1795).

3 *Metaph.* i. 5. — ED.

number; and he notices also that a certain musical philosopher was, in like manner, led to suppose that the soul was but a kind of harmony.[1] The musician suggests to my recollection a passage of Dr. Reid. "Mr. Locke," says he, "mentions an eminent musician who believed that God created the world in six days, and rested the seventh, because there are but seven notes in music. I myself," he continues, "knew one of that profession who thought that there could be only three parts in harmony — to wit, bass, tenor and treble; because there are but three persons in the Trinity."[2] The alchemists would see in nature only a single metal, clothed with the different appearances which we denominate gold, silver, copper, iron, mercury, etc., and they confidently explained the mysteries, not only of nature, but of religion, by salt, sulphur, and mercury.[3] Some of our modern zoölogists recoil from the possibility of nature working on two different plans, and rather than renounce the unity which delights them, they insist on recognizing the wings of insects in the gills of fishes, and the sternum of quadrupeds in the antennæ of butterflies, — and all this that they may prove that man is only the evolution of a molluscum. Descartes saw in the physical world only matter and motion;[4] and, more recently, it has been maintained that thought itself is only a movement of matter.[5] Of all the faculties of the mind, Condillac recognized only one, which transformed itself like the Protean metal of the alchemists; and he maintains that our belief in the rising of to-morrow's sun is a sensation.[6] It is this tendency, indeed, which has principally determined philosophers, as we shall hereafter see, to neglect or violate the original duality of consciousness; in which, as an ultimate fact, — a self and not-self, — mind knowing and matter known, — are given in counterpoise and mutual opposition; and hence the three Unitarian schemes of Materialism, Idealism, and Absolute Identity.[7] In fine, Pantheism, or the doctrine which identifies mind and matter, — the Creator and the creature, God and the universe, — how are we to explain the prevalence of this modification of atheism in the most ancient and in the most recent times? Simply because it carries our love of unity to its highest fruition. To sum up what

---

1 *De Anima*, i. 4; Plato, *Phædo*, p. 86. The same theory was afterwards adopted by Aristotle's own pupil, Aristoxenus. See Cicero, *Tusc. Quæst.* i. 10. — ED.

2 *Intellectual Powers*, Ess. vi. chap. viii.; *Coll. Works*, p. 473.

3 See Brucker, *Hist. Philosophiæ*, vol. iv. p. 677, *et. seq.*— ED.

4 *Principia*, pars ii. 23. — ED.

5 Priestley, *Disquisitions relating to Matter and Spirit*, sect. iii. p. 24, *et. seq.; Free Discussions of Materialism and Necessity*, pp. 258, 267, *et. seq.* — ED.

6 The preceding illustrations are borrowed from Garnier, *Psychologie*, p. 194. — ED.

7 See the Author's Supplementary Dissertations to Reid, note C. —ED.

has just been said in the words of Sir John Davies, a highly philosophic poet of the Elizabethan age : —

> " Musicians think our souls are harmonies;
>   Physicians hold that they complexions be;
> Epicures make them swarms of atomies:
>   Which do by chance into our bodies flee.
>
> One thinks the soul is air; another fire;
>   Another blood, diffus'd about the heart;
> Another saith the elements conspire,
>   And to her essence each doth yield a part.
>
> Some think one gen'ral soul fills every brain,
>   As the bright sun sheds light in every star;
> And others think the name of soul is vain,
>   And that we only well-mix'd bodies are.
>
> Thus these great clerks their little wisdom show,
>   While with their doctrines they at hazard play;
> Tossing their light opinions to and fro,
>   To mock the lewd,[1] as learn'd in this as they;
>
> For no craz'd brain could ever yet propound,
>   Touching the soul so vain and fond a thought;
> But some among these masters have been found,
>   Which, in their schools, the self-same thought have taught."[2]

To this love of unity — to this desire of reducing the objects of our knowledge to harmony and system — a source of truth and discovery if subservient to observation, but of error and delusion if allowed to dictate to observation what phænomena are to be perceived; to this principle, I say, we may refer the influence which preconceived opinions exercise upon our perceptions and our judgments, by inducing us to see and require only what is in unison with them. What we wish, says Demosthenes, that we believe;[3] what we expect, says Aristotle, that we find[4] — truths which have been reëchoed, by a thousand confessors, and confirmed by ten thousand examples. Opinions once adopted become part of the

Influence of preconceived opinion reducible to love of unity.

---

[1] *Lewd*, according to Tooke, from Anglo-Saxon, *Læwed*, past participle of *Lawan*, to *mislead*. It was formerly applied to the (*lay*) people in contradistinction from the clergy. See Richardson, *Eng. Dict.*, v. *Lewd*. — ED.

[2] *On the Immortality of the Soul*, stanza 9, *et seq.*

[3] Βούλεται τοῦθ' ἕκαστος καὶ οἴεται, Demosth. *Olynth.* iii. p. 68. — ED.

[4] *Rhet.* ii. 1. Τῷ μὲν ἐπιθυμοῦντι καὶ εὐέλπιδι ὄντι, ἐὰν ᾖ τὸ ἐσόμενον ἡδύ, καὶ ἔσεσθαι καὶ ἀγαθὸν ἔσεσθαι φαίνεται, τῷ δ' ἀπαθεῖ, καὶ δυσχεραίνοντι, τοὐναντίον. — ED.

intellectual system of their holders. If opposed to prevalent doctrines, self-love defends them as a point of honor, exaggerates whatever may confirm, overlooks or extenuates whatever may contradict. Again, if accepted as a general doctrine, they are too often recognized, in consequence of their prevalence, as indisputable truths, and all counter appearances peremptorily overruled as manifest illusions. Thus it is that men will not see in the phænomena what alone is to be seen; in their observations, they interpolate and they expunge; and this mutilated and adulterated product they call a fact. And why? Because the real phænomena, if admitted, would spoil the pleasant music of their thoughts, and convert its factitious harmony into discord. "Quæ volunt sapiunt, et nolunt sapere quæ vera sunt."[1] In consequence of this, many a system, professing to be reared exclusively on observation and fact, rests in reality mainly upon hypothesis and fiction. A pretended experience is, indeed, the screen behind which every illusive doctrine regularly retires. "There are more false facts," says Cullen,[2] "current in the world, than false theories;" — and the livery of Lord Bacon has been most ostentatiously paraded by many who were no members of his household. Fact, — observation, — induction, have always been the watchwords of those who have dealt most extensively in fancy. It is now above three centuries since Agrippa, in his *Vanity of the Sciences*, observed of Astrology, Physiognomy, and Metoposcopy, (the Phrenology of those days), that experience was professedly their only foundation and their only defence: "Solent omnes illæ divinationum prodigiosæ artes non, nisi experientiæ titulo, se defendere et se objectionum vinculis extricare."[3] It was on this ground, too, that, at a later period, the great Kepler vindicated the first of these arts, Astrology. For, said he, how could the principle of a science be false where experience showed that its predictions were uniformly fulfilled."[4] Now, truth was with Kepler even as a passion; and his, too, was one of the most powerful intellects that ever cultivated and promoted a science. To him, astronomy, indeed, owes perhaps even more than to Newton. And yet, even his great mind, preöccupied with a certain prevalent belief, could observe and judge only in conformity with that belief. This tendency to look at realities only through the spectacles of an hypothesis, is perhaps seen most conspicuously in the fortunes of medicine. The history

---

1 [St. Hilarii, lib. vii., *De Trinitate*, sub init.]

2 For Cullen's illustrations of the influence of a pretended experience in Medicine, see his *Materia Medica*, vol. i. c. ii. art. iv., second edition. — ED.

3 *Opera*, vol. ii. c. 33, p. 64:

4 *De Stella Nova*, c. 8, 10; *Harmonice Mundi*, lib. iv. c. 7. — ED.

of that science is, in truth, little else than an incredible narrative of the substitution of fictions for facts; the converts to an hypothesis, (and every, the most contradictory, doctrine has had its day), regularly seeing and reporting only in conformity with its dictates.[1] The same is also true of the philosophy of mind; and the variations and alternations in this science, which are perhaps only surpassed by those in medicine, are to be traced to a refusal of the real phænomenon revealed in consciousness, and to the substitution of another, more in unison with preconceived opinions of what it ought to be. Nor, in this commutation of fact with fiction, should we suspect that there is any *mala fides*. Prejudice, imagination, and passion, sufficiently explain the illusion. "Fingunt simul creduntque."[2] "When," says Kant, "we have once heard a bad report of this or that individual, we incontinently think that we read the rogue in his countenance; fancy here mingles with observation, which is still farther vitiated when affection or passion interferes."

"The passions," says Helvetius,[3] "not only concentrate our attention on certain exclusive aspects of the objects which they present, but they likewise often deceive us in showing these same objects where they do not exist. The story is well known of a parson and a gay lady. They had both heard that the moon was peopled, — believed it, — and, telescope in hand, were attempting to discover the inhabitants. If I am not mistaken, says the lady, who looked first, I perceive two shadows; they bend toward each other, and, I have no doubt, are two happy lovers. Lovers, madam, says the divine, who looked second; oh fie! the two shadows you saw are the two steeples of a cathedral. This story is the history of man. In general, we perceive only in things what we are desirous of finding: on the earth as in the moon, various prepossessions make us always recognize either lovers or cathedrals."

Such are the two intellectual necessities which afford the two principal sources of philosophy: — the intellectual necessity of refunding effects into their causes;[4] — and the intellectual necessity of carrying up our knowledge into unity or system. But, besides these intellectual necessities, which are involved in the very existence of our faculties of knowledge, there is another powerful subsidiary to the same effect, — in a certain affection of our capacities of feeling. This feeling, according to circumstances, is denominated *surprise, astonishment, admiration, wonder,* and, when blended with the

Auxiliary cause of philosophy—Wonder.

---

1 See the Author's Article "On the Revolutions of Medicine," *Discussions*, p. 242. — ED.

2 Tacitus, *Hist.* lib. ii. c. 8. — ED.

3 *De l' Esprit*, Discours i. chap. ii.

4 [This expression is employed by Sergeant. See *Method to Science*, p. 222. Cf. pp. 144, 145.]

intellectual tendencies we have considered, it obtains the name of *curiosity.* This feeling, though it cannot, as some have held, be allowed to be the principal, far less the only, cause of philosophy, is, however, a powerful auxiliary to speculation; and, though inadequate to account for the existence of philosophy absolutely, it adequately explains the preference with which certain parts of philosophy have been cultivated, and the order in which philosophy in general has been developed. We may err both in exaggerating, and in extenuating, its influence. Wonder has been contemptuously called the daughter of ignorance; true, but wonder, we should add, is the mother of knowledge. Among others, Plato, Aristotle, Plutarch, and Bacon, have all concurred in testifying to the influence of this principle. "Admiration," says the Platonic Socrates in the *Theætetus,*[1] — "admiration is a highly philosophical affection; indeed, there is no other principle of philosophy but this." — "That philosophy," says Aristotle, "was not originally studied for any practical end, is manifest from those who first began to philosophize. It was, in fact, wonder which then, as now, determined men to philosophical researches. Among the phænomena presented to them, their admiration was first directed to those more proximate and more on a level with their powers, and then rising by degrees, they came at length to demand an explanation of the higher phænomena, — as the different states of the moon, sun, and stars, — and the origin of the universe. Now, to doubt and to be astonished, is to recognize our ignorance. Hence it is that the lover of wisdom is in a certain sort a lover of mythi, (φιλόμυθός πως), for the subject of mythi is the astonishing and marvellous. If then, men philosophize to escape ignorance, it is clear that they pursue knowledge on its own account, and not for the sake of any foreign utility. This is proved by the fact; for it was only after all that pertained to the wants, welfare, and conveniences of life had been discovered, that men commenced their philosophical researches. It is, therefore, manifest that we do not study philosophy for the sake of anything ulterior; and, as we call him a free man who belongs to himself and not to another, so philosophy is of all sciences the only free or liberal study, for it alone is unto itself an end."[2] — "It is the business of philosophy," says Plutarch, "to investigate, to admire, and to doubt."[3] You will find in the first book of the *De Augmentis* of Bacon,[4] a recognition of the principle "admiratio

1 P. 155. — ED.

2 *Metaph.* lib. i. c. 2. See also for a passage to a similar effect, *Rhetoric,* lib. i. c. 11.

3 Plutarch, Περὶ τοῦ Εἰ τοῦ ἐν Δελφοῖς,

vol. ii. § 385; ἐπεὶ δὲ τοῦ φιλοσοφεῖν, ἔφη, τὸ ζητεῖν, τὸ θαυμάζειν, καὶ ἀπορεῖν. — ED.

4 Vol. viii. p. 8, (Montagu's ed.)

est semen sapientiæ," and copious illustrations of its truth, — illustrations which I shall not quote, but they deserve your private study.

No one, however, has so fully illustrated the play and effect of this motive as a distinguished philosopher of this country, Adam Smith; although he has attributed too little to the principal, too much to the subsidiary, momenta. He seems not to have been aware of what had been, previously to him, observed in regard to this principle by others. You will find the discussion among his posthumous essays, in that entitled *The Principles which lead and direct Philosophical Inquiries, illustrated by the History of Astronomy ;* — to this I must simply refer you.

We have already remarked, that the principle of wonder affords

Affords an explation of the order in which objects studied.

an explanation of the order in which the different objects of philosophy engaged the attention of mankind. The aim of all philosophy is the discovery of principles, that is, of higher causes; but, in the procedure to this end, men first endeavored to explain those phænomena which attracted their attention by arousing their wonder. The child is wholly absorbed in the observation of the world without; the world within first engages the contemplation of the man. As it is with the individual, so was it with the species. Philosophy, before attempting the problem of intelligence, endeavored to resolve the problem of nature. The spectacle of the external universe was too imposing not first to solicit curiosity, and to direct upon itself the prelusive efforts of philosophy. Thales and Pythagoras, in whom philosophy finds its earliest representatives, endeavored to explain the organization of the universe, and to substitute a scientific for a religious cosmogony. For a season their successors toiled in the same course ; and it was only after philosophy had tried, and tired, its forces on external nature, that the human mind recoiled upon itself, and sought in the study of its own nature the object and end of philosophy. The mind now became to itself its point of departure, and its principal object ; and its progress, if less ambitious, was more secure. Socrates was he who first decided this new destination of philosophy. From his epoch man sought in himself the solution of the great problem of existence, and the history of philosophy was henceforward only a development, more or less successful, more or less complete, of the inscription on the Delphic temple — Γνῶθι σεαυτόν — Know thyself. [1]

---

1 Plato, *Protagoras*, p. 343. — ED. [See Géruzez, *Nouveau Cours de Philosophie*, p. 1.]

LECTURE V.

THE DISPOSITIONS WITH WHICH PHILOSOPHY OUGHT TO BE STUDIED.

HAVING, in the previous Lectures, informed you, — 1°, What Philosophy is, and 2°, What are its Causes, I would now, in the third place, say a few words to you on the Dispositions with which Philosophy ought to be studied, for, without certain practical conditions a speculative knowledge of the most perfect Method of procedure, (our next following question,) remains barren and unapplied.

"To attain to a knowledge of ourselves," says Socrates, "we must banish prejudice, passion, and sloth;"[1] and no one who neglects this precept can hope to make any progress in the philosophy of the human mind, which is only another term for the knowledge of ourselves.

In the first place, then, all prejudices, — that is, all opinions formed on irrational grounds, — ought to be removed. A preliminary doubt is thus the fundamental condition of philosophy; and the necessity of such a doubt is no less apparent than is its difficulty. We do not approach the study of philosophy ignorant, but perverted. "There is no one who has not grown up under a load of beliefs — beliefs which he owes to the accidents of country and family, to the books he has read, to the society he has frequented, to the education he has received, and, in general, to the circumstances which have concurred in the formation of his intellectual and moral habits. These beliefs may be true, or they may be false, or, what is more probable, they may be a medley of truths and errors. It is, however, under their influence that he studies, and through them, as through a prism, that he views and judges the objects of knowledge. Everything is therefore seen by him in false colors, and in distorted relations. And this is the rea-

First condition of the study of Philosophy,— renunciation of prejudice.

[See Gatien-Arnoult, *Doctrine Philosophique*, p. 89.]

8

son why philosophy, as the science of truth, requires a renunciation of prejudices, (præ-judicia, opiniones præ-judicatæ), — that is, conclusions formed without a previous examination of their grounds."[1] In this, if I may without irreverence compare things human with

In this Christianity and Philosophy at one.

things divine, Christianity and Philosophy coincide, — for truth is equally the end of both. What is the primary condition which our Saviour requires of his disciples? That they throw off their old prejudices, and come with hearts willing to receive knowledge and understandings open to conviction. "Unless," He says, "ye become as little children, ye shall not enter the kingdom of heaven." Such is true religion; such also is true philosophy. Philosophy requires an emancipation from the yoke of foreign authority, a renunciation of all blind adhesion to the opinions of our age and country, and a purification of the intellect from all assumptive beliefs. Unless we can cast off the prejudices of the man, and become as children, docile and unperverted, we need never hope to enter the temple of philosophy. It is the neglect of this primary condition which has mainly occasioned men to wander from the unity of truth, and caused the endless variety of religious and philosophical sects. Men would not submit to approach the word of God in order to receive from that alone their doctrine and their faith; but they came in general with preconceived opinions, and, accordingly, each found in revelation only what he was predetermined to find. So, in like

Consciousness and the Bible.

manner, is it in philosophy. Consciousness is to the philosopher what the Bible is to the theologian. Both are revelations of the truth, — and both afford the truth to those who are content to receive it, as it ought to be received, with reverence and submission. But as it has, too frequently, fared with the one revelation, so has it with the other. Men turned, indeed, to consciousness, and professed to regard its authority as paramount, but they were not content humbly to accept the facts which consciousness revealed, and to establish these without retrenchment or distortion, as the only principles of their philosophy; on the contrary, they came with opinions already formed, with systems already constructed, and while they eagerly appealed to consciousness when its data supported their conclusions, they made no scruple to overlook, or to misinterpret, its facts when these were not in harmony with their speculations. Thus religion and philosophy, as they both terminate in the same end, so they both depart from the same fundamental condition. "Aditus ad reg-

---

[1] [Gatien-Arnoult, *Doct. Phil.*, pp. 39, 40.]

num hominis, quod fundatur in scientiis, quam ad regnum cœlorum, in quod, nisi sub persona infantis, intrare non datur." [1]

But the influence of early prejudice is the more dangerous, inasmuch as this influence is unobtrusive. Few of us are, perhaps, fully aware of how little we owe to ourselves, — how much to the influence of others. "Non licet," says Seneca, "ire recta via; trahunt in pravum parentes; trahunt servi; nemo errat uni sibi sed dementiam spargit in proximos accipitque invicem. Et ideo, in singulis vitia populorum sunt, quia illa populus dedit; dum facit quisque pejorem, factus est. Didicit deteriora, deinde docuit: effectaque est ingens illa nequitia, congesto in unum, quod cuique pessimum scitur. Sit ergo aliquis custos, et aurem subinde pervellat, abigatque rumores et reclamet populis laudantibus." [2]

Influence of early prejudice unobtrusive.

Man is by nature a social animal. "He is more political," says Aristotle, "than any bee or ant." [3] But the existence of society, from a family to a state, supposes a certain harmony of sentiment among its members; and nature has, accordingly, wisely implanted in us a tendency to assimilate in opinions and habits of thought to those with whom we live and act. There is thus, in every society great or small, a certain gravitation of opinions towards a common centre. As in our natural body, every part has a necessary sympathy with every other, and all together form, by their harmonious conspiration, a healthy whole; so, in the social body, there is always a strong predisposition, in each of its members, to act and think in unison with the rest. This universal sympathy, or fellow-feeling, of our social nature, is the principle of the different spirit dominant in different ages, countries, ranks, sexes, and periods of life. It is the cause why fashions, why political and religious enthusiasm, why moral example, either for good or evil, spread so rapidly, and exert so powerful an influence. As men are naturally prone to imitate others, they consequently regard, as important or insignificant, as honorable or disgraceful, as true or false, as good or bad, what those around them consider in the same light. They love and hate what they see others desire and eschew. This is not to be regretted; it is natural, and, consequently, it is right. Indeed, were it otherwise, society could not subsist, for nothing can be more apparent than that mankind in general, destined as they are to occupations incompatible with intellectual cultivation, are wholly incapable of forming opinions for themselves on many of the most impor-

Source of the power of custom. Man a social animal.

---

1 Bacon, *Nov. Org.* lib. i., aph. lxviii. 2 *Epist.* xciv. 3 *Polit.* i. 2. — ED.

tant objects of human consideration. If such, however, be the intentions of nature with respect to the unenlightened classes, it is manifest that a heavier obligation is thereby laid on those who enjoy the advantages of intellectual cultivation, to examine with diligence and impartiality the foundations of those opinions which have any connection with the welfare of mankind. If the multitude must be led, it is of consequence that it be led by enlightened conductors. That the great multitude of mankind are, by natural disposition, only what others are, is a fact at all times so obtrusive, that it could not escape observation from the moment a reflective eye was first turned upon man. "The whole conduct of Cambyses," says Herodotus,[1] the father of history, "towards the Egyptian gods, sanctuaries, and priests, convinces me that this king was in the highest degree insane, for otherwise he would not have insulted the worship and holy things of the Egyptians. If any one should accord to all men the permission to make free choice of the best among all customs, undoubtedly each would choose his own. That this would certainly happen can be shown by many examples, and, among others, by the following. The King Darius once asked the Greeks who were resident in his court, at what price they could be induced to devour their dead parents. The Greeks answered, that to this no price could bribe them. Thereupon the king asked some Indians who were in the habit of eating their dead parents, what they would take not to eat but to burn them; and the Indians answered even as the Greeks had done." Herodotus concludes this narrative with the observation, that "Pindar had justly entitled Custom — the Queen of the World."

Skeptical inference from the influence of custom.

The ancient skeptics, from the conformity of men in every country, their habits of thinking, feeling, and acting, and from the diversity of different nations in these habits, inferred that nothing was by nature beautiful or deformed, true or false, good or bad, but that these distinctions originated solely in custom. The modern skepticism of Montaigne terminates in the same assertion; and the sublime misanthropy of Pascal has almost carried him to a similar exaggeration. "In the just and the unjust," says he, "we find hardly anything which does not change its character in changing its climate. Three degrees of an elevation of the pole reverses the whole of jurisprudence. A meridian is decisive of truth, and a few years of possession. Fundamental laws change. Right has its epochs. A pleasant justice which a river or a mountain limits.

---

[1] Lib. iii. 37, 38.

Truth, on this side the Pyrenees, error on the other!"[1] This doctrine is exaggerated, but it has a foundation in truth; and the most zealous champions of the immutability of moral distinctions are unanimous in acknowledging the powerful influence which the opinions, tastes, manners, affections, and actions of the society in which we live, exert upon all and each of its members.[2]

Nor is this influence of man on man less unambiguous in times of social tranquillity, than in crises of social convulsion. In seasons of political and religious revolution, there arises a struggle between the resisting force of ancient habits and the contagious sympathy of new modes of feeling and thought.

This influence of man on man in times both of tranquility and convulsion.

In one portion of society, the inveterate influence of custom prevails over the contagion of example; in others, the contagion of example prevails over the conservative force of antiquity and habit. In either case, however, we think and act always in sympathy with others. "We remain," says an illustrious philosopher, "submissive so long as the world continues to set the example. As we follow the herd in forming our conceptions of what is respectable, so we are ready to follow the multitude also, when such conceptions come to be questioned or rejected; and are no less vehement reformers, when the current of opinion has turned against former establishments, than we were zealous abettors while that current continued to set in a different direction."[3]

Thus it is that no revolution in public opinion is the work of an individual, of a single cause, or of a day. When the crisis has arrived, the catastrophe must ensue; but the agents through whom it is apparently accomplished, though they may accelerate, cannot originate its occurrence.

Relation of the individual to social crises.

Who believes that but for Luther or Zwingli the Reformation would not have been? Their individual, their personal energy and zeal, perhaps, hastened by a year or two the event; but had the public mind not been already ripe for their revolt, the fate of Luther and Zwingli, in the sixteenth century, would have been that of Huss and Jerome of Prague in the fifteenth. Woe to the revolutionist who is not himself a creature of the revolution! If he anticipate, he is lost; for it requires, what no individual can supply, a long and powerful counter-sympathy in a nation to untwine the ties of custom which bind a people to the established and

1 *Pensées*, partie i. art. vi. § 8, (vol. ii. p. 126, ed. Faugère.)

2 See Meiners, *Untersuchungen über die Denk-* *kräfte und Willenskräfte des Menschen*, ii. 325, (ed. 1806.)

3 Ferguson's *Moral and Political Science*, vol. i. part. i. chap. ii. § 11, p. 135.

the old. This is finely expressed by Schiller, in a soliloquy from the mouth of the revolutionary Wallenstein : —

Schiller.　　" What is thy purpose? Hast thou fairly weighed it?
　　　　　　　　Thou seekest ev'n from its broad base to shake
　　　　　　　　The calm enthroned majesty of power,
　　　　　　　　By ages of possession consecrate —
　　　　　　　　Firm rooted in the rugged soil of custom —
　　　　　　　　And with the people's first and fondest faith,
　　　　　　　　As with a thousand stubborn tendrils twined.
　　　　　　　　That were no strife where strength contends with strength.
　　　　　　　　It is not strength I fear — I fear no foe
　　　　　　　　Whom with my bodily eye I see and scan;
　　　　　　　　Who, brave himself, inflames my courage too.
　　　　　　　　It is an unseen enemy I dread,
　　　　　　　　Who, in the hearts of mankind, fights against me —
　　　　　　　　Fearful to me but from his own weak fear.
　　　　　　　　Not that which proudly towers in life and strength
　　　　　　　　Is truly dreadful; but the mean and common,
　　　　　　　　The memory of the eternal *yesterday*,
　　　　　　　　Which, ever-warning, ever still returns,
　　　　　　　　And weighs to-morrow, for it weighed to-day;
　　　　　　　　Out of the common is man's nature framed,
　　　　　　　　And custom is the nurse to whom he cleaves.
　　　　　　　　Woe then to him whose daring hand profanes
　　　　　　　　The honored heir-looms of his ancestors!
　　　　　　　　There is a consecrating power in time;
　　　　　　　　And what is gray with years to man is godlike.
　　　　　　　　Be in possession, and thou art in right;
　　　　　　　　The crowd will lend thee aid to keep it sacred." [1]

This may enable you to understand how seductive is the influence of example; and I should have no end were I to quote to you all that philosophers have said of the prevalence and evil influence of prejudice and opinion.

We have seen that custom is called, by Pindar and Herodotus, the Queen of the World — and the same thing is expressed by the adage — "Mundus regitur opinionibus." "Opinion," says the great Pascal, "disposes of all things. It constitutes beauty, justice, happiness; and these are the all in all of the world. I would with all my heart see the Italian book of which I know only the

Testimonies of philosophers to the power of received opinion.

---

1 *Wallenstein.* (Translated by Mr. George Moir.) Act. i. scene 4, p. 15.

title, — a title, however, which is itself worth many books — *Della opinione regina del mondo.* I subscribe to it implicitly."[1] "Coutume," says Regnier,

> "Coutume, opinion, reines de notre sort,
> Vous réglez des mortels, et la vie, et la mort!"

"Almost every opinion we have," says the pious Charon, "we have but by authority; we believe, judge, act, live and die on trust, as common custom teaches us; and rightly, for we are too weak to decide and choose of ourselves. But the wise do not act thus."[2] "Every opinion," says Montaigne, "is strong enough to have had its martyrs;"[3] and Sir W. Raleigh — "It is opinion, not truth, that travelleth the world without passport."[4] "Opinion," says Heraclitus, "is a falling sickness;"[5] "and Luther — "O doxa! doxa! quam es communis noxa." In a word, as Hommel has it, "An ounce of custom outweighs a ton of reason."[6]

Such being the recognized universality and evil effect of prejudice, philosophers have, consequently, been unanimous in making doubt the first step towards philosophy. Aristotle has a fine chapter in his *Metaphysics*[7] on the utility of doubt, and on the things which we ought first to doubt of; and he concludes by establishing that the success of philosophy depends on the art of doubting well. This is even enjoined on us by the Apostle. For in saying "Prove" (which may be more correctly translated *test*) — "Test all things," he implicitly commands us to doubt all things.

"He," says Bacon, "who would become philosopher, must commence by repudiating belief;" and he concludes one of the most remarkable passages of his writings with the observation, that "were there a single man to be found with a firmness sufficient to efface from his mind the theories and notions vulgarly received, and to apply his intellect free and without prevention, the best hopes might be entertained of his success."[8] "To philosophize," says Descartes, "seriously, and to good effect, it is necessary for a man to renounce all prejudices; in other words, to apply the great-

Philosophers unanimous in making doubt the first step to philosophy.

Bacon.

Descartes.

1 *Pensées*, partie i. art. ¶ vi. 3. [Vol. ii. p. 52, ed. Faugère. M. Faugère has restored the original text of Pascal — "*La'imagination dispose de tout.*" The ordinary reading is *L'opinion.* — ED.]
2 *De la Sagesse*, liv. i. chap. xvi.
3 *Essais*, liv. i. chap. xl.
4 Preface to his *History of the World.*
5 Diog. Laert. lib. ix. ¶ 7.
6 [Alex. v. Joch (Hommel), *Über Belohnung und Strafe*, p. 111. See Krug. *Philosophisches Lexikon*, vol. v. p. 467, art. *Gewohnheit.*]
7 Lib. ii. c. 1. — ED.
8 "Nemo adhuc tanta mentis constantia in-

est care to doubt of all his previous opinions, so long as these have not been subjected to a new examination, and been recognized as true."[1] But it is needless to multiply authorities in support of so obvious a truth. The ancient philosophers refused to admit slaves to their instruction. Prejudice makes men slaves; it disqualifies them for the pursuit of truth; and their emancipation from prejudice is what philosophy first inculcates on, what it first requires of, its disciples.[2] Let us, however, beware that we act not the part of revolted slaves; that in asserting our liberty we do not run into license. Philosophical doubt is not an end but a mean. We doubt in order that we may believe; we begin that we may not end with doubt. We doubt once that we may believe always; we renounce authority that we may follow reason; we surrender opinion that we may obtain knowledge. We must be protestants, not infidels, in philosophy. "There is a great difference," says Malebranche, "between doubting and doubting.—We doubt through passion and brutality; through blindness and malice, and finally through fancy and from the very wish to doubt; but we doubt also from prudence and through distrust, from wisdom and through penetration of mind. The former doubt is a doubt of darkness, which never issues to the light, but leads us always further from it; the latter is a doubt which is born of the light, and which aids in a certain sort to produce light in its turn." Indeed, were the effect of philosophy the establishment of doubt, the remedy would be worse than the disease. Doubt, as a permanent state of mind, would be, in fact, little better than an intellectual death. The mind lives as it believes, — it lives in the affirmation of itself, of nature, and of God; a doubt upon any one of these would be a diminution of its life, — a doubt upon the three, were it possible, would be tantamount to a mental annihilation. It is well observed, by Mr. Stewart, "that it is not merely in order to free the mind from the influence of error, that it is useful to examine the foundation of established opinions. It is such

Philosophical doubt.

Malebranche.

Stewart.

ventus est, ut decreverit, et sibi imposuerit, theorias et notiones communes penitus abolere, et intellectum abrasum et æquum ad particularia, de integro, applicare. Itaque illa ratio humana quam habemus, ex multa fide, et multo etiam casu, nec non ex puerilibus, quas primo hausimus, notionibus, farrago quædam est, et congeries. Quod siquis ætate matura, et sensibus integris, et mente repurgata, se ad experientiam, et ad particularia de integro applicet, de eo melius sperandum est."—*Nov. Org.* i. aph. xcvii.; *Works,* vol. ix. p. 252, (Montagu's ed.) See also *omnino Nov. Org.* i. aph. lxviii.

1 *Prin. Phil.* pars i. § 75. [Cf. Clauberg, *De Dubitatione Cartesiana,* co. i. ii. *Opera,* p. 1131.—Ed.]

2 [Cf. Gatien-Arnoult, *Doct. Phil.,* p. 41.]

3 *Recherche de la Vérité,* liv. i chap. xx. § 3.

an examination alone, that, in an inquisitive age like the present, can secure a philosopher from the danger of unlimited skepticism. To this extreme, indeed, the complexion of the times is more likely to give him a tendency, than to implicit credulity. In the former ages of ignorance and superstition, the intimate association which had been formed, in the prevailing systems of education, between truth and error, had given to the latter an ascendant over the minds of men, which it could never have acquired if divested of such an alliance. The case has, of late years, been most remarkably reversed: the common sense of mankind, in consequence of the growth of a more liberal spirit of inquiry, has revolted against many of those absurdities which had so long held human reason in captivity; and it was, perhaps, more than could have been reasonably expected, that, in the first moments of their emancipation, philosophers should have stopped short at the precise boundary which cooler reflection and more moderate views would have prescribed. The fact is, that they have passed far beyond it; and that, in their zeal to destroy prejudices, they have attempted to tear up by the roots many of the best and happiest and most essential principles of our nature. That implicit credulity is a mark of a feeble mind, will not be disputed; but it may not, perhaps, be as generally acknowledged, that the case is the same with unlimited skepticism: on the contrary, we are sometimes apt to ascribe this disposition to a more than ordinary vigor of intellect. Such a prejudice was by no means unnatural, at that period in the history of modern Europe, when reason first began to throw off the yoke of authority, and when it unquestionably required a superiority of understanding, as well as of intrepidity, for an individual to resist the contagion of prevailing superstition. But, in the present age, in which the tendency of fashionable opinions is directly opposite to those of the vulgar, the philosophical creed, or the philosophical skepticism, of by far the greater number of those who value themselves on an emancipation from popular errors, arises from the very same weakness with the credulity of the multitude; nor is it going too far to say, with Rousseau, that 'he who, in the end of the eighteenth century, has brought himself to abandon all his early principles without discrimination, would probably have been a bigot in the days of the League.' In the midst of these contrary impulses of fashionable and vulgar prejudices, he alone evinces the superiority and the strength of his mind, who is able to disentangle truth from error; and to oppose the clear conclusions of his own unbiassed faculties to the united clamors of superstition and of false philosophy. Such are the men whom nature marks out to be the lights of the world; to fix the wavering opinions of the multitude, and to impress their own characters on that of their age."[1]

In a word, philosophy is, as Aristotle has justly expressed it, not the art of doubting, but the art of doubting well.[2]

Aristotle.

In the second place, in obedience to the precept of Socrates, the passions, under which we shall include sloth, ought to be subjugated.

Second practical condition, — subjugation of the passions.

These ruffle the tranquillity of the mind, and consequently deprive it of the power of carefully considering all that the solution of a question requires should be examined. A man under the agitation of any lively emotion, is hardly aware of aught but what has immediate relation to the passion which agitates and engrosses him. Among the affections which influence the will, and induce it to adhere to skepticism or error, there is none more dangerous than sloth. The greater proportion of mankind are inclined to spare themselves the trouble of a long and laborious inquiry; or they fancy that a superficial examination is enough; and the slightest agreement between a few objects, in a few petty points, they at once assume as evincing the correspondence of the whole throughout. Others apply themselves exclusively to the matters which it is absolutely necessary for them to know, and take no account of any opinion but that which they have stumbled on, — for no other reason than that they have embraced it, and are unwilling to recommence the labor of learning. They receive their opinion on the authority of those who have had suggested to them their own; and they are always facile scholars, for the slightest probability is, for them, all the evidence that they require.

Sloth.

Pride is a powerful impediment to a progress in knowledge. Under the influence of this passion, men seek honor, but not truth. They do not cultivate what is most valuable in reality, but what is most valuable in opinion. They disdain, perhaps, what can be easily accomplished, and apply themselves to the obscure and recondite; but as the vulgar and easy is the foundation on which the rare and arduous is built, they fail even in attaining the object of their ambition, and remain with only a farrago of confused and ill-assorted notions. In all its

Pride.

1 Coll. Works, vol. ii.; Elements, vol. i. book ii. § 1, p. 68, et seq.

2 Metaph. ii. 1. Ἔστι δὲ τοῖς εὐπορῆσαι βουλομένοις προὔργου τὸ διαπορῆσαι καλῶς· ἡ γὰρ ὕστερον εὐπορία λύσις τῶν πρότερον ἀπορουμένων ἐστί, λύειν δ' οὐκ ἔστιν ἀγνοοῦντας τὸν δεσμόν. — Ed.

phases, self-love is an enemy to philosophical progress; and the history of philosophy is filled with the illusions of which it has been the source. On the one side, it has led men to close their eyes against the most evident truths which were not in harmony with their adopted opinions. It is said that there was not a physician in Europe, above the age of forty, who would admit Harvey's discovery of the circulation of the blood. On the other hand, it is finely observed by Bacon, that "the eye of human intellect is not dry, but receives a suffusion from the will and from the affections, so that it may almost be said to engender any sciences it pleases. For what a man wishes to be true, that he prefers believing."[1] And, in another place, "if the human intellect hath once taken a liking to any doctrine, either because received and credited, or because otherwise pleasing, — it draws everything else into harmony with that doctrine, and to its support; and albeit there may be found a more powerful array of contradictory instances, these, however, it either does not observe, or it contemns, or by distinction extenuates and rejects."[2]

1 *Nov. Org.* lib. i. aph. xlix. 2 *Ibid.* xlvi.

LECTURE VI.

THE METHOD OF PHILOSOPHY.

THE next question we proceed to consider is, — What is the true Method or Methods of Philosophy?

There is only one possible method in philosophy; and what have been called the different methods of different philosophers, vary from each other only as more or less perfect applications of this one Method to the objects of knowledge.

All method[1] is a rational progress, — a progress towards an end;

Method a progress towards an end.

and the method of philosophy is the procedure conducive to the end which philosophy proposes. The ends, — the final causes of philosophy, — as we have seen, — are two; — first, the discovery of efficient causes; secondly, the generalization of our knowledge into unity; — two ends, however, which fall together into one, inasmuch as the higher we proceed in the discovery of causes, we necessarily approximate more and more to unity. The detection of the one in the many might, therefore, be laid down as the end

Philosophy has but one possible method.

to which philosophy, though it can never reach it, tends continually to approximate. But, considering philosophy in relation to both these ends, I shall endeavor to show you that it has only one possible method.

Considering philosophy, in the first place, in relation to its first end, — the discovery of causes, — we have seen

This shown in relation to the first end of Philosophy.

that causes, (taking that term as synonymous for all without which the effect would not be,) are only the coëfficients of the effect; an effect being nothing more than the sum or complement of all the partial causes, the concurrence of which constitute its existence. This being the case, — and as it is only by experience that we discover

---

[1] [On the difference between Order and Method, see Facciolati, *Rudimenta Logicæ*, parsiv. c. i. note: "Methodus differt ab Ordine; quia ordo facit ut rem unam discamus post aliam; Methodus ut unam per aliam." Cf. Zabarella, *Op. Log.*, pp. 139, 149, 223, 225; Molinæus, *Log.*, p. 234 *et seq.* p. 244 *et seq.*, ed. 1613.]

what particular causes must conspire to produce such or such an effect,— it follows, that nothing can become known to us as a cause except in and through its effect; in other words, that we can only attain to the knowledge of a cause by extracting it out of its effect. To take the example, we formerly employed, of a neutral salt. This, as I observed, was made up by the conjunction of three proximate causes, —viz. an acid, — an alkali, — and the force which brought the alkali and the acid into the requisite approximation. This last, as a transitory condition, and not always the same, we shall throw out of account. Now, though we might know the acid and the alkali in themselves as distinct phænomena, we could never know them as the concurrent causes of the salt, unless we had known the salt as their effect. And though, in this example, it happens that we are able to compose the effect by the union of its causes, and to decompose it by their separation, — this is only an accidental circumstance; for the far greater number of the objects presented to our observation, can only be decomposed, but not actually recomposed, and in those which can be recomposed, this possibility is itself only the result of a knowledge of the causes previously obtained by an original decomposition of the effect.

In so far, therefore, as philosophy is the research of causes, the one necessary condition of its possibility is the decomposition of effects into their constituted

Analysis.

causes. This is the fundamental procedure of philosophy, and is called by a Greek term *Analysis.* But though analysis be the fundamental procedure, it is still only a mean towards an end. We analyze only that we may comprehend; and we comprehend only inasmuch as we are able to reconstruct in thought the complex effects which we have analyzed into their elements. This mental reconstruction is, therefore, the final, the consummative procedure of philosophy, and it is familiarly known by the Greek term *Synthesis.* Analysis and synthesis, though

Synthesis.

commonly treated as two different methods, are, if properly understood, only the two necessary parts of the same method. Each is the relative and the correlative of the other. Analysis, without a subsequent synthesis, is incomplete; it is a mean cut off from its end. Synthesis, without a previous analysis, is baseless; for synthesis receives from analysis the elements which it recomposes. And, as synthesis supposes analysis as the prerequisite of its possibility, — so it is also dependent on analysis for the qualities of its existence. The value of every synthesis depends upon the value of the foregoing analysis. If the precedent analysis afford false elements, the subsequent synthesis of these elements will necessarily afford a false result. If the elements furnished by analysis are assumed, and not really discovered, — in other words, if they be hypothetical, the synthesis of these hypothetical elements will constitute only a conjectural theory. The legitimacy of every synthesis is thus necessarily dependent on the legitimacy of the analysis which it pre-supposes, and on which it founds.

These two relative procedures are thus equally necessary to each other. On the one hand, analysis without synthesis affords only a commenced, only an incomplete, knowledge. On the other, synthesis without analysis is a false knowledge, — that is, no knowledge at all. Both, therefore, are absolutely necessary to philosophy, and both are, in philosophy, as much parts of the same method as, in the animal body, inspiration and expiration are of the same vital function. But though these operations are each requisite to the other, yet were we to distinguish and compare what ought only to be considered as conjoined, it is to analysis that the preference must be accorded. An analysis is always valuable; for though now without a synthesis, this synthesis may at any time be added; whereas a synthesis without a previous analysis is radically and *ab initio* null.

Constitute a single method.

So far, therefore, as regards the first end of philosophy, or the discovery of causes, it appears that there is only one possible method, — that method of which analysis is the foundation, synthesis the completion. In the second place, considering philosophy in relation to its second end, the carrying up our knowledge into unity, — the same is equally apparent.

Everything presented to our observation, whether external or internal, whether through sense or self-consciousness, is presented in complexity. Through sense, the objects crowd upon the mind in multitudes, and each separate individual of these multitudes is itself a congeries of many various qualities. The same is the case with the phænomena of self-consciousness. Every modification of mind is a complex state; and the different elements of each state, manifest themselves only in and through each other. Thus, nothing but multiplicity is ever presented to our observation; and yet our faculties are so limited that they are able to comprehend at once only the very simplest conjunctions. There seems, therefore, a singular disproportion between our powers of knowledge and the objects to be known.

Only one possible method shown in relation to the second end of Philosophy.

How is the equilibrium to be restored? This is the great problem proposed by nature, and which analysis and synthesis, in combination, enable us to solve. For example, I perceive a tree, among other objects of an extensive landscape, and I wish to obtain a full and distinct conception of that tree. What ought I to do? *Divide et impera:* I must attend to it by itself, that is, to the exclusion of the other constituents of the scene before me. I thus analyze that scene; I separate a petty portion of it from the rest, in order to consider that portion apart. But this is not enough, the tree itself is not a unity, but, on the contrary, a complex assemblage of elements, far beyond what my powers can master at once. I must carry my analysis still farther. Accordingly, I consider successively its height, its breadth, its shape; I then proceed to its trunk, rise from that to its branches, and follow out its different ramifications; I now fix my attention on the leaves, and severally examine their form, color, etc. It is only after having thus, by analysis, detached all these parts, in order to deal with them one by one, that I am able, by reversing the process, fully to comprehend them again in a series of synthetic acts. By synthesis, rising from the ultimate analysis step by step, I view the parts in relation to each other, and, finally, to the whole of which they are the constituents; I reconstruct them; and it is only through these two counter-processes of analysis and synthesis that I am able to convert the confused perception of the tree, which I obtained at first sight, into a clear, and distinct, and comprehensive knowledge.[1]

But if analysis and synthesis be required to afford us a perfect knowledge even of one individual object of sense, still more are they required to enable the mind to reduce an indefinite multitude of objects, — the infinitude, we may say, of nature, — to the limits of its own finite comprehension. To accomplish this, it is requisite to extract the one out of the many, and thus to recall multitude to unity, — confusion to order. And how is this performed? The one in the many being that in which a plurality of objects agree, — or that in which they may be considered as the same; and the agreement of objects in any common quality being discoverable only by an observation and comparison of the objects themselves, it follows that a knowledge of the one can only be evolved out of a foregoing knowledge of the many. But this evolution can only be accomplished by an analysis and a synthesis. By analysis, from the infinity of objects presented to our observation, we select some. These we consider apart, and, further, only in certain points of

---

1 [On the subject of analysis and synthesis, compare Condillac, *Logique*, cc. i. ii.]

view, — and we compare these objects with others also considered in the same points of view. So far the procedure is analytic. Having discovered, however, by this observation and comparison, that certain objects agree in certain respects, we generalize the qualities in which they coincide, — that is, from a certain number of individual instances we infer a general law; we perform what

Induction.

is called an act of Induction. This induction is erroneously viewed as analytic; it is purely a synthetic process.[1] For example, from our experience, — and all experience, be it that of the individual or of mankind, is only finite, — from our limited experience, I say, that bodies, as observed by us, attract each other, we infer by induction the unlimited conclusion that all bodies gravitate towards each other. Now, here the consequent contains much more than was contained in the antecedent. Experience, the antecedent, only says, and only can say, this, that, and the other body gravitate, (that is, *some* bodies gravitate); the consequent educed from that antecedent, says, — *all* bodies gravitate. The antecedent is limited, — the consequent unlimited. Something, therefore, has been added to the antecedent in order to legitimate the inference, if we are not to hold the consequent itself as absurd; for, as you will hereafter learn, no conclusion must contain more than was contained in the premises from which it is drawn. What then is the *something?* If we consider the inductive process, this will be at once apparent.

The affirmation, this, that, and the other, body gravitate, is connected with the affirmation, all bodies gravitate, only by inserting between the two a third affirmation, by which the two other affirmations are connected into reason and consequent, — that is, into a logical cause and effect. What that is I shall explain. All scientific induction is founded on the presumption that nature is uniform in her operations. Of the ground and origin of this presumption, I am not now to speak. I shall only say, that, as it is a principle which we suppose in all our inductions, it cannot be itself a product of induction. It is, therefore, interpolated in the inductive reasoning by the mind itself. In our example the reasoning will, accordingly, run as follows:

This, that, and the other body, (some bodies,) are observed to gravitate;

---

[1] It may be considered as the one or the other, according as the whole and its parts are viewed in the relations of comprehension or of extension. The latter, however, is the simpler and more convenient point of view: and in this respect Induction is properly synthetic. See the Author's *Discussions*, p. 173. — ED.

But, (as nature is uniform in her operations,) this, that, and the other body, (some bodies,) represent all bodies, —

Therefore all bodies gravitate.

Now, in this and other examples of induction, it is the mind which binds up the separate substances observed and collected into a whole, and converts what is only the observation of many particulars into a universal law. This procedure is manifestly synthetic.

Now, you will remark that analysis and synthesis are here absolutely dependent on each other. The previous observation and comparison, — the analytic foundation, — are only instituted for the sake of the subsequent induction, — the synthetic consummation. What boots it to observe and to compare, if the uniformities we discover among objects are never generalized into laws? We have obtained an historical, but not a philosophical knowledge. Here, therefore, analysis without synthesis is incomplete. On the other hand, an induction which does not proceed upon a competent enumeration of particulars, is either doubtful, improbable, or null; for all synthesis is dependent on a foregone analysis for whatever degree of certainty it may pretend to. Thus, considering philosophy in relation to its second end, unity or system, it is manifest that the method by which it accomplishes that end, is a method involving both an analytic and a synthetic process.

Now, as philosophy has only one possible method, so the History of philosophy only manifests the conditions of this one method, more or less accurately fulfilled. There are aberrations in the method, — no aberrations from it.

The history of philosophy manifests the more or less accurate fulfilment of the conditions of the one Method.

Earliest problem of philosophy.

" Philosophy commenced with the first act of reflection on the objects of sense or self-consciousness, for the purpose of explaining them. And with that first act of reflection, the method of philosophy began, in its application of an analysis, and in its application of a synthesis, to its object. The first philosophers naturally endeavored to explain the enigma of external nature. The magnificent spectacle of the material universe, and the marvellous demonstrations of power and wisdom which it everywhere exhibited, were the objects which called forth the earliest efforts of speculation. Philosophy was thus, at its commencement, physical, not psychological; it was not the problem of the soul, but the problem of the world, which it first attempted to solve.

" And what was the procedure of philosophy in its solution of this problem? Did it first decompose the whole into its parts, in

10

order again to reconstruct them into a system? This it could not accomplish; but still it attempted this, and nothing else. A complete analysis was not to be expected from the first efforts of intelligence; its decompositions were necessarily partial and imperfect; a partial and imperfect analysis afforded only hypothetical elements; and the synthesis of these elements issued, consequently, only in a one-sided or erroneous theory.

"Thales, the founder of the Ionian philosophy, devoted an especial study to the phænomena of the material universe; and, struck with the appearances of power which water manifested in the formation of bodies, he analyzed all existences into this element, which he viewed as the universal principle, — the universal agent of creation. He proceeded by an incomplete analysis, and generalized by hypothesis the law which he drew by induction from the observation of a small series of phænomena.

Thales and the Ionic School.

"The Ionic school continued in the same path. They limited themselves to the study of external nature, and sought in matter the principle of existence. Anaximander of Miletus, the countryman and disciple of Thales, deemed that he had traced the primary cause of creation to an ethereal principle, which occupied space, and whose different combinations constituted the universe of matter. Anaximenes found the original element in air, from which, by rarefaction and condensation, he educed existences. Anaxagoras carried his analysis farther, and made a more discreet use of hypothesis; he rose to the conception of an intelligent first cause, distinct from the phænomena of nature; and his notion of the Deity was so far above the gross conceptions of his contemporaries, that he was accused of atheism.

"Pythagoras, the founder of the Italic school, analyzed the properties of number; and the relations which this analysis revealed, he elevated into principles of the mental and material universe. Mathematics were his only objects; his analysis was partial, and his synthesis was consequently hypothetical. The Italic school developed the notions of Pythagoras, and, exclusively preöccupied with the relations and harmonies of existence, its disciples did not extend their speculation to the consideration either of substance or of cause.

Pythagoras and the Italic School.

"Thus, these earlier schools, taking external nature for their point of departure, proceeded by an imperfect analysis, and a presumptuous synthesis, to the construction of exclusive systems, — in which Idealism, or Materialism, preponderated, according to the kind of data on which they founded.

"The Eleatic school, which is distinguished into two branches, the one of Physical, the other of Metaphysical, speculation, exhibits the same character, the same point of departure, the same tendency, and the same errors.

Eleatic School.

"These errors led to the skepticism of the Sophists, which was assailed by Socrates,—the sage who determined a new epoch in philosophy by directing observation on man himself, and henceforward the study of mind becomes the prime and central science of philosophy.

The Sophists. Socrates.

"The point of departure was changed, but not the method. The observation or analysis of the human mind, though often profound, remained always incomplete. Fortunately, the first disciples of Socrates, imitating the prudence of their master, and warned by the downfall of the systems of the Ionic, Italic, and Eleatic schools, made a sparing use of synthesis, and hardly a pretension to system.

"Plato and Aristotle directed their observation on the phæ-nomena of intelligence, and we cannot too highly admire the profundity of their analysis, and even the sobriety of their synthesis. Plato devoted himself more particularly to the higher faculties of intelligence; and his disciples were led by the love of generalization, to regard as the intellectual whole, those portions of intelligence which their master had analyzed; and this exclusive spirit gave birth to systems false, not in themselves, but as resting upon a too narrow basis. Aristotle, on the other hand, whose genius was of a more positive character, analyzed with admirable acuteness those operations of mind which stand in more immediate relation to the senses; and this tendency, which among his followers became often exclusive and exaggerated, naturally engendered systems which more or less tended to materialism."[1]

Plato and Aristotle.

The school of Alexandria, in which the systems resulting from those opposite tendencies were combined, endeavored to reconcile and to fuse them into a still more comprehensive system. Eclecticism, — conciliation, — union, were, in all things, the grand aim of the Alexandrian school. Geographically situated between Greece and Asia, it endeavored to ally Greek with Asiatic genius, religion with philosophy. Hence the Neoplatonic system, of which the last great representative is Proclus. This system is the result of the long labor of the Socratic schools. It is an edifice reared by synthesis out of the materials

School of Alexandria.

Proclus.

1 Géruzez, *Nouveau Cours de Philosophie*, p. 4-8. **Paris, 1834, (2d ed.)**

which analysis had collected, proved, and accumulated, from Socrates down to Plotinus.

But a synthesis is of no greater value than its relative analysis; and as the analysis of the earlier Greek philosophy was not complete, the synthesis of the Alexandrian school was necessarily imperfect.

In the scholastic philosophy, analysis and observation were too often neglected in some departments of philosophy, and too often carried rashly to excess in others.

The Scholastic Philosophy.

After the revival of letters, during the fifteenth and sixteenth centuries, the labors of philosophy were principally occupied in restoring and illustrating the Greek systems; and it was not until the seventeenth century, that a new epoch was determined by the genius of Bacon and Descartes. In Bacon and Descartes our modern philosophy may be said to originate, inasmuch as they were the first who made the doctrine of method a principal object of consideration. They both proclaimed, that, for the attainment of scientific knowledge, it is necessary to observe with care, — that is, to analyze; to reject every element as hypothetical, which this analysis does not spontaneously afford; to call in experiment in aid of observation; and to attempt no synthesis or generalization, until the relative analysis has been completely accomplished. They showed that previous philosophers had erred, not by rejecting either analysis or synthesis, but by hurrying on to synthetic induction from a limited or specious analytic observation. They propounded no new method of philosophy, they only expounded the conditions of the old. They showed that these conditions had rarely been fulfilled by philosophers in time past; and exhorted them to their fulfilment in time to come. They thus explained the petty progress of the past philosophy; — and justly anticipated a gigantic advancement for the future. Such was their precept, but such unfortunately was not their example. There are no philosophers who merit so much in the one respect, none, perhaps, who deserve less in the other.

Philosophy from the revival of letters.

Bacon and Descartes.

Of philosophy since Bacon and Descartes, we at present say nothing. Of that we shall hereafter have frequent occasion to speak. But to sum up what this historical sketch was intended to illustrate.

Result of this historical sketch of philosophy.

There is but one possible method of philosophy, — a combination of analysis and synthesis; and the purity and equilibrium of these two elements constitute its perfection. The aberrations of philosophy have been all so many violations of the laws of this one method. Philosophy has erred, because it built its systems upon incomplete or erroneous analysis, and it can only proceed in safety, if from accurate and unexclusive observation, it rise, by successive generalization, to a comprehensive system.

LECTURE VII.

THE DIVISIONS OF PHILOSOPHY.

I HAVE already endeavored to afford you a general notion of what Philosophy comprehends: I now proceed to say something in regard to the Parts into which it has been divided. Here, however, I must limit myself to the most famous distributions, and to those which, as founded on fundamental principles, it more immediately concerns you to know. For, were I to attempt an enumeration of the various Divisions of Philosophy which have been proposed, I should only confuse you with a multitude of contradictory opinions, with the reasons of which you could not, at present, possibly be made acquainted.

Seneca, in a letter to his young friend Lucilius, expresses the wish that the whole of philosophy might, like the spectacle of the universe, be at once submitted to our view. "Utinam quemadmodum universi mundi facies in conspectum venit, ita philosophia tota nobis posset occurrere, simillimum mundo spectaculum."[1] But as we cannot survey the universe at a glance, neither can we contemplate the whole of philosophy in one act of consciousness. We can only master it gradually and piecemeal; and this is in fact the reason why philosophers have always distributed their science, (constituting, though it does, one organic whole,) into a plurality of sciences. The expediency, and even necessity, of a division of philosophy, in order that the mind may be enabled to embrace in one general view its various parts, in their relation to each other, and to the whole which they constitute, is admitted by every philosopher. "Res utilis," continues Seneca, "et ad sapientiam properanti utique necessaria, dividi philosophiam, et ingens corpus ejus in membra disponi. Facilius enim per partes in cognitionem totius adducimur."[2]

Expediency of a division of Philosophy.

But, although philosophers agree in regard to the utility of such a distribution, they are almost as little at one in regard to the parts, as they are in respect to the definition, of their science; and, indeed, their differences in reference to the former, mainly arise from their

1 *Epist.* lxxxix.   2 *Epist.* lxxxix.

discrepancies in reference to the latter. For they who vary in their comprehension of the whole, cannot agree in their division of the parts.

The most ancient and universally recognized distinction of philosophy, is into Theoretical and Practical. These are discriminated by the different nature of their ends. Theoretical, called likewise speculative, and contemplative, philosophy, has for its highest end mere truth or knowledge. Practical philosophy, on the other hand, has truth or knowledge only as its proximate end,— this end being subordinate to the ulterior end of some practical action. In theoretical philosophy, we know for the sake of knowing, *scimus ut sciamus:* in practical philosophy, we know for the sake of acting, *scimus ut operemur.*[1] I may here notice the poverty of the English language, in the want of a word to express that practical activity which is contradistinguished from mere intellectual or speculative energy,— what the Greeks express by πράσσειν, the Germans by *handeln.* The want of such a word occasions frequent ambiguity; for, to express the species which has no appropriate word, we are compelled to employ the generic term *active.* Thus our philosophers divide the powers of the mind into Intellectual and Active. They do not, however, thereby mean to insinuate that the powers called intellectual are a whit less energetic than those specially denominated active. But, from the want of a better word, they are compelled to employ a term which denotes at once much more and much less than they are desirous of expressing. I ought to observe that the term *practical* has also obtained with us certain collateral significations, which render it in some respects unfit to supply the want.[2] But to return.

This distinction of Theoretical and Practical philosophy, was first explicitly enounced by Aristotle;[3] and the attempts of the later Platonists to carry it up to Plato and even to Pythagoras, are not worthy of statement, far less of refutation. Once promulgated, the division was, however, soon generally recognized. The Stoics borrowed it, as may be seen from Seneca:[4]— "Philosophia et contemplativa est et activa; spectat, simulque agit." It

The most ancient division into Theoretical and Practical.

The term Active.

History of the distinction of Theoretical and Practical.

---

1 Θεωρητικῆς μὲν ἐπιστήμης τέλος ἀλήθεια, πρακτικῆς δ' ἔργον. Arist. *Metaph.* A minor, c. 1; " or as Averroes has it, *Per speculativam scimus ut sciamus, per practicam scimus ut operemur.*"— *Discussions,* p. 134.— ED.

2 Cf. *Reid's Works,* p. 511, n. †.— ED.

3 *Metaph.* v. 1: Πᾶσα διάνοια ἢ πρακτικὴ ἢ ποιητικὴ ἢ θεωρητική. Cf. *Metaph.* x. 7; *Top.* vi. 6, viii. 8. But the division had been at least intimated by Plato: *Politicus,* p. 258: Ταύτῃ τοίνυν, συμπάσας ἐπιστήμας διαίρει, τὴν μὲν πρακτικὴν προσειπών, τὴν δὲ μόνον γνωστικήν.— ED.

4 *Ep.* xcv. 10.

was also adopted by the Epicureans; and, in general, by those Greek and Roman philosophers who viewed their science as versant either in the contemplation of nature (φυσική), or in the regulation of human action (ἠθική);[1] for by *nature* they did not denote the material universe alone, but their Physics included Metaphysics, and their Ethics embraced Politics and Economics. There was thus only a difference of nomenclature; for Physical and Theoretical, — Ethical and Practical Philosophy, — were with them terms absolutely equivalent.

I regard the division of philosophy into Theoretical and Practical as unsound, and this for two reasons.

The division of Philosophy into Theoretical and Practical unsound. The first is, that philosophy, as philosophy, is only cognitive, — only theoretical; whatever lies beyond the sphere of speculation or knowledge, transcends the sphere of philosophy; consequently, to divide philosophy by any quality ulterior to speculation, is to divide it by a difference which does not belong to it. Now, the distinction of practical philosophy from theoretical, commits this error. For, while it is admitted that all philosophy, as cognitive, is theoretical, some philosophy is again taken out of this category on the ground, that, beyond the mere theory, — the mere cognition, — it has an ulterior end in its application to practice.

But, in the second place, this difference, even were it admissible, would not divide philosophy; for, in point of fact, all philosophy must be regarded as practical, inasmuch as mere knowledge, — that is, the mere possession of truth, — is not the highest end of any philosophy, but, on the contrary, all truth or knowledge is valuable only inasmuch as it determines the mind to its contemplation, — that is, to practical energy. Speculation, therefore, inasmuch as it is not a negation of thought, but, on the contrary, the highest energy of intellect, is, in point of fact, preëminently practical. The practice of one branch of philosophy is, indeed, different from that of another; but all are still practical; for in none is mere knowledge the ultimate, — the highest end.

Among the ancients, the principal difference of opinion regarded the relation of Logic to Philosophy and its branches. But as this controversy is of very subordinate importance, and hinges upon distinctions, to explain which would require considerable detail, I

1 Sext. Emp. *Adv. Math.* vii. 14: Τῶν δὲ διμερῆ τὴν φιλοσοφίαν ὑποστησαμένων Ξενοφάνης μὲν ὁ Κολοφώνιος, τὸ φυσικὸν ἅμα καὶ λογικόν, ὥς φασί τινες, μετήρχετο, Ἀρχέλαος δὲ ὁ Ἀθηναῖος τὸ φυσικὸν καὶ ἠθικόν· μεθ' οὗ τινὲς καὶ τὸν Ἐπίκουρον τάττουσιν ὡς καὶ τὴν λογικὴν θεωρίαν ἐκβάλλοντα. Seneca, *Ep.* lxxxix.: "Epicurei quas partes philosophiæ putaverunt esse, Naturalem, atque Moralem: Rationalem remoderunt." — ED.

shall content myself with saying, — that, by the Platonists, Logic was regarded both as a part, and as the instru-

Controversy among ancients regarding the relation of Logic to Philosophy.

ment, of philosophy; — by the Aristotelians, (Aristotle himself is silent), as an instrument, but not as a part, of philosophy; — by the Stoics, as forming one of the three parts of philosophy, — Physics, or theoretical, Ethics, or practical philosophy, being the other two.[1] But as Logic, whether considered as a part of philosophy proper or not, was by all included under the philosophical sciences, the division of these sciences which latterly prevailed among the Academic, the Peripatetic, and the Stoical sects, was into Logic as the subsidiary or instrumental doctrine, and into the two principal branches of Theoretical and Practical Philosophy.[2]

It is manifest that in our sense of the term *practical*, Logic, as an instrumental science, would be comprehended under the head of practical philosophy.

I shall take this opportunity of explaining an anomaly which you

Application of the terms Art and Science.

will find explained in no work with which I am acquainted. Certain branches of philosophical knowledge are called Arts, — or Arts and Sciences indifferently; others are exclusively denominated Sciences. Were this distinction coincident with the distinction of sciences speculative and sciences practical, — taking the term practical in its ordinary acceptation, — there would be no difficulty; for, as every practical science necessarily involves a theory, nothing could be more natural than to call the same branch of knowledge an art, when viewed as relative to its practical application, and a science, when viewed in relation to the theory which that application supposes. But this is not the case. The speculative sciences, indeed, are never denominated arts; we may, therefore, throw them aside. The difficulty is exclusively confined to the practical. Of these some never receive the name of arts; others are called arts and sciences indifferently. Thus the sciences of Ethics, Economics, Politics, Theology, etc., though all practical, are never denominated arts; whereas this appellation is very usually applied to the practical sciences of Logic, Rhetoric, Grammar, etc.

1 Alexander Aphrodisiensis, *In Anal. Prior.* p. 2, (ed. 1520). Ammonius, *In Categ.* c. 4; Philoponus, *In Anal. Prior.* f. 4; Cramer's *Anecdota*, vol. iv. p. 417. Compare the Author's *Discussions*, p. 132. The division of Philosophy into Logic, Physics, and Ethics, probably originated with the Stoics. See Laertius, vii. 39; Pseudo-Plutarch, *De Plat. Phil.* Prœm. It is sometimes, but apparently without much reason, attributed to Plato. See Cicero, *Acad. Quæst.* i. 5; Eusebius, *Præf. Evan.* xi. 1; Augustin, *De Civ. Dei.* viii. 4. — ED.

2 Sext. Empir. *adv. Math.* vii. 16. — ED.

That the term art is with us not coëxtensive with practical science, is thus manifest; and yet these are frequently confounded. Thus, for example, Dr. Whately, in his definition of Logic, thinks that Logic is a science, in so far as it institutes an analysis of the process of the mind in reasoning, and an art, in so far as it affords practical rules to secure the mind from error in its deductions; and he defines an art the application of knowledge to practice.[1] Now, if this view were correct, art and practical science would be convertible terms. But that they are not employed as synonymous expressions is, as we have seen, shown by the incongruity we feel in talking of the art of Ethics, the art of Religion, etc., though these are eminently practical sciences.

The question, therefore, still remains, Is this restriction of the term art to certain of the practical sciences the result of some accidental and forgotten usage, or is it founded on any rational principle which we are able to trace? The former alternative seems to be the common belief; for no one, in so far as I know, has endeavored to account for the apparently vague and capricious manner in which the terms art and science are applied. The latter alternative, however, is the true; and I shall endeavor to explain to you the reason of the application of the term art to certain practical sciences, and not to others.

You are aware that the Aristotelic philosophy was, for many centuries, not only the prevalent, but, during the *Its historical origin.* middle ages, the one exclusive philosophy in Europe. This philosophy of the middle ages, or, as it is commonly called, the Scholastic Philosophy, has exerted the most extensive influence on the languages of modern Europe; and from this common source has been principally derived that community of expression which these languages exhibit. Now, the peculiar application of the term art was introduced into the vulgar tongues from the scholastic philosophy; and was borrowed by that philosophy from Aristotle. This is only one of a thousand instances which might be alleged of the unfelt influence of a single powerful mind, on the associations and habits of thought of generations to the end of time; and of Aristotle is preëminently true, what has been so beautifully said of the ancients in general :—

> " The great of old!
> The dead but sceptred sovrans who still rule
> Our spirits from their urns." [2]

Now, then, the application of the term art in the modern lan-

---

1 See *Discussions*, p. 131. — Ed.   2 Byron's *Manfred*, Act. iii. Scene iv.

guages being mediately governed by certain distinctions which the capacities of the Greek tongue allowed Aristotle to establish, these distinctions must be explained.

In the Aristotelic philosophy, the terms πρᾶξις and πρακτικός,—

Πρᾶξις.

that is, *practice* and *practical*, were employed both in a generic or looser, and in a special or stricter signification. In its generic meaning πρᾶξις, *practice*, was opposed to theory or speculation, and it comprehended under it, practice in its special meaning, and another coördinate term to which practice, in this its stricter signification, was opposed. This

Ποίησις.

term was ποίησις, which we may inadequately translate by *production*. The distinction of πρακτικός and ποιητικός consisted in this: the former denoted that action which terminated in action,—the latter, that action which resulted in some permanent product. For example, dancing and music are practical, as leaving no work after their performance; whereas, painting and statuary are productive, as leaving some product over and above their energy.[1]

Now Aristotle, in formally defining art, defines it as a habit pro-

Why Ethics, Politics, etc., designated Sciences; Logic, Rhetoric, etc., Arts.

ductive, and not as a habit practical, ἕξις ποιητικὴ μετὰ λόγου;—and, though he has not always himself adhered strictly to this limitation, his definition was adopted by his followers, and the term in its application to the practical sciences, (the term practical being here used in its generic meaning), came to be exclusively confined to those whose end did not result in mere action or energy. Accordingly as Ethics, Politics, etc., proposed happiness as their end,—and as happiness was an energy, or at least the concomitant of energy, these sciences terminated in action, and were consequently *practical*, not *productive*. On the other hand, Logic, Rhetoric, etc., did not terminate in a mere,—an evanescent action, but in a permanent,—an enduring product. For the end of Logic was the production of a reasoning, the end of Rhetoric the production of an oration, and so forth.[2] This distinction is not perhaps beyond the reach of criticism, and I am not here to vindicate its correctness. My only aim is to make you

1 See *Eth. Nic.* i. 1. Διαφορὰ δέ τις φαίνεται τῶν τέλων· τὰ μὲν γάρ εἰσιν ἐνέργειαι τὰ δὲ παρ' αὐτὰς ἔργα τινά. *Ibid.* vi. 4; *Magna Moralia*, i. 35. Cf. Quintilian, *Institut.* lib. ii. c. 18.—ED.

2 Cf. Burgersdyck, *Institut. Log.* lib. i. § 6. Logica dicitur ποιεῖν, id est, *facere* sive *efficere* syllogismos, definitiones, etc. Neque enim verum est, quod quidam aiunt, ποιεῖν semper significare ejusmodi actionem, qua ex palpabili materia opus aliquod efficitur quod etiam post actionem permanet. Nam Poetica dicta est ἀπὸ τοῦ ποιεῖν quæ tamen palpabilem materiam non tractat, neque opus facit ipsa Poetæ fictione durabilius. Quod enim poemata supersint, id non est ab ea actione qua efficiuntur sed a scriptione. Atque hæc de genere. See also Scheibler, *Opera*, Tract. Procem. § iii. p. 6.—ED.

aware of the grounds of the distinction, in order that you may comprehend the principle which originally determined the application of the term *art* to some of the practical sciences and not to others, and without a knowledge of which principle the various employment of the term must appear to you capricious and unintelligible. It is needless, perhaps, to notice that the rule applies only to the philosophical sciences, — to those which received their form and denominations from the learned. The mechanical dexterities were beneath their notice; and these were accordingly left to receive their appellations from those who knew nothing of the Aristotelic proprieties. Accordingly, the term art is in them applied, without distinction, to productive and unproductive operations. We speak of the art of rope-dancing, equally as of the art of rope-making. But to return.

The division of philosophy into Theoretical and Practical is the most important that has been made; and it is that which has entered into nearly all the distributions attempted by modern philosophers. Bacon was the first, after the revival of letters, who essayed a distribution of the sciences and of philosophy. He divided all human knowledge into History, Poetry, and Philosophy. Philosophy he distinguished into branches conversant about the Deity, about Nature, and about Man; and each of these had their subordinate divisions, which, however, it is not necessary to particularize.[1]

Universality of the division of Philosophy into Theoretical and Practical.

Bacon.

Descartes[2] distributed philosophy into theoretical and practical, with various subdivisions; but his followers adopted the division of Logic, Metaphysics, Physics, and Ethics.[3] Gassendi recognized, like the ancients, three parts of philosophy, Logic, Physics, and Ethics,[4] and this, along with many other of Gassendi's doctrines, was adopted by Locke.[5] Kant distinguished philosophy into theoretical and practical, with various subdivisions;[6] and the distribution into theoretical and practical was also established by Fichte.[7]

Descartes and his followers.

Gassendi; Locke; Kant; Fichte.

1 *Advancement of Learning, Works*, vol. ii. pp. 100, 124, (ed. Montagu.) *De Augmentis Scientiarum*, lib. ii. c. 1, lib. iii. c. 1; *Works*, vol. viii. pp. 87, 152. — ED.

2 See the Prefatory Epistle to the *Principia.* — ED.

3 See Sylvain Regis, *Cours entier de Philosophie*, contenant la Logique, la Metaphysique, la Physique, et la Morale. Cf. Clauberg: — "Physica .... Philosophia Naturalis dicitur; distincta a Supernaturali seu Metaphys-ica, et a Rationali seu Logica, necnon a Morali seu Practica. *Disput. Phys.* i., *Opera*, p. 54. — ED.

4 *Syntagma Philosophium*, Lib. Procem. c. 9. (*Opera.* Lugduni, 1658, vol. i. p. 29.) — ED.

5 *Essay*, book iv. ch. 21. — ED.

6 *Kritik der reinen Vernunft*, Methodenlehre, c. 3. — ED.

7 *Grundlage der gesammten Wissenchaftslehre*, § 4. (*Werke*, vol. i. p. 126.) — ED.

I have now concluded the Lectures generally introductory to the proper business of the Course. In these lectures, from the general nature of the subjects, I was compelled to anticipate conclusions, and to depend on your being able to supply a good deal of what it was impossible for me articulately to explain. I now enter upon the consideration of the matters which are hereafter to occupy our attention, with comparatively little apprehension, — for, in these, we shall be able to dwell more upon details, while, at the same time, the subject will open upon us by degrees, so that, every step that we proceed, we shall find the progress easier. But I have to warn you, that you will probably find the very commencement the most arduous, and this not only because you will come less inured to difficulty, but because it will there be necessary to deal with principles, and these of a general and abstract nature ; whereas, having once mastered these, every subsequent step will be comparatively easy.

Conclusion of Introductory Lectures.

Without entering upon details, I may now summarily state to you the order which I propose to follow in the ensuing Course. This requires a preliminary exposition of the different departments of Philosophy, in order that you may obtain a comprehensive view of the proper objects of our consideration, and of the relations in which they stand to others.

Order of the Course.

Science and philosophy are conversant either about Mind or about Matter. The former of these is Philosophy properly so called. With the latter we have nothing to do, except in so far as it may enable us to throw light upon the former, for Metaphysics, in whatever latitude the term be taken, is a science, or complement of sciences, exclusively occupied with mind. Now the Philosophy of Mind, — Psychology or Metaphysics, in the widest signification of the terms, — is *threefold;* for the object it immediately proposes for consideration may be either, 1°, PHÆNOMENA in general; or, 2°, LAWS; or, 3°, INFERENCES, — RESULTS. This I will endeavor to explain.

Distribution of the Philosophical Sciences.

The whole of philosophy is the answer to these three questions : 1°, What are the Facts or Phænomena to be observed ? 2°, What are the Laws which regulate these facts, or under which these phænomena appear ? 3°, What are the real Results, not immediately manifested, which these facts or phænomena warrant us in drawing ?

The three grand questions of Philosophy.

If we consider the mind merely with the view of observing and

generalizing the various phænomena it reveals, — that is, of analyzing them into capacities or faculties, — we have
I. Phænomenology of Mind.
one mental science, or one department of mental science; and this we may call the PHÆNOME-
NOLOGY OF MIND. It is commonly called PSYCHOLOGY — EMPIR-
ICAL PSYCHOLOGY, or the INDUCTIVE PHILOSOPHY of MIND; we
might call it PHÆNOMENAL PSYCHOLOGY. It is evident that the
divisions of this science will be determined by the classes into
which the phænomena of mind are distributed.

If, again, we analyze the mental phænomena with the view of
discovering and considering, not contingent ap-
II. Nomology of Mind.
pearances, but the *necessary* and *universal* facts,
— *i. e.* the Laws, by which our faculties are governed, to the end that we may obtain a criterion by which to judge
or to explain their procedures and manifestations, — we have a
science which we may call the NOMOLOGY OF MIND, — NOMOLOGICAL
PSYCHOLOGY. Now, there will be as many distinct classes of Nomological Psychology, as there are distinct classes
Its subdivisions.
of mental phænomena under the Phænomeno-
logical division. I shall, hereafter, show you that there are Three
great classes of these phænomena, — viz. 1°, The phænomena of
our Cognitive faculties, or faculties of Knowledge; 2°, The phænomena of our Feelings, or the phænomena of Pleasure and Pain;
and, 3°, The phænomena of our Conative powers, — in other words,
the phænomena of Will and Desire. (These you must, for the
present, take upon trust).[1] Each of these classes of phænomena
has accordingly a science which is conversant about its Laws. For
as each proposes a different end, and, in the accomplishment of that
end, is regulated by peculiar laws, each must, consequently, have a
different science conversant about these laws, — that is, a different
Nomology.

There is no one, no Nomological, science of the Cognitive faculties in general, though we have some older
1. Nomology of the Cognitive faculties.
treatises which, though partial in their subject,
afford a name not unsuitable for a nomology of
the cognitions, — viz. Gnoseologia or Gnostologia. There is no
independent science of the laws of Perception; if there were, it
might be called Æsthetic, which, however, as we shall see, would
be ambiguous. Mnemonic, or the science of the laws of Memory,
has been elaborated at least in numerous treatises; but the name
Anamnestic, the art of Recollection or Reminiscence, might be
equally well applied to it. The laws of the Representative faculty,

---

[1] See *infra.* Lect. XI. p. 183, *et seq.* — ED.

— that is, the laws of Association, have not yet been elevated into a separate nomological science. Neither have the conditions of the Regulative or Legislative faculty, the faculty itself of Laws, been fully analyzed, far less reduced to system; though we have several deservedly forgotten treatises, of an older date, under the inviting name of *Noologies.* The only one of the cognitive faculties, whose

Logic.

laws constitute the object-matter of a separate science, is the Elaborative, — the Understanding Special, the faculty of Relations, the faculty of Thought Proper. This nomology has obtained the name of LOGIC among other appellations, but not from Aristotle. The best name would have been DIANOETIC. Logic is the science of the laws of thought, in relation to the end which our cognitive faculties propose, — *i. e.* the TRUE. To this head might be referred Grammar, — Universal Grammar, — Philosophical Grammar, or the science conversant with the laws of Language, as the instrument of thought.

The Nomology of our Feelings, or the science of the laws which

2. Nomology of the feelings.

govern our capacities of enjoyment, in relation to the end which they propose, — *i. e.* the PLEASURABLE, — has obtained no precise name in our language. It has been called the Philosophy of Taste, and, on the Continent especially, it has been denominated Æsthetic. Neither name is unobjectionable. The first is vague, metaphorical, and even delusive. In regard to the second, you are aware that αἴσθησις in Greek means feeling in general, as well as sense in particular, as our term *feeling* means either the sense of touch in particular, or sentiment, — and the capacity of the pleasurable and painful in general. Both terms are, therefore, to a certain extent, ambiguous; but this objection can rarely be avoided, and Æsthetic, if not the best expression to be found, has already been long and generally employed. It is now nearly a century since Baumgarten, a celebrated philosopher of the Leibnitzio-Wolfian school, first applied the term Æsthetic to the doctrine which we vaguely and periphrastically denominate the Philosophy of Taste, the theory of the Fine Arts, the science of the Beautiful and Sublime,[1] etc., — and this term is now in general acceptance, not only in Germany, but throughout the other countries of Europe. The term Apolaustic would have been a more appropriate designation.

Finally, the Nomology of our Conative powers

3. Nomology of the Conative Powers.

is Practical Philosophy, properly so called; for practical philosophy is simply the science of the laws regulative of our Will and Desires, in relation to the end

---

1 Baumgarten's work on this subject, entitled *Æsthetica* (two vols.), was published in 1750-58. — ED.

which our conative powers propose, — *i. e.* the GOOD. This, as it

Ethics; Politics. considers these laws in relation to man as an individual, or in relation to man as a member of society, will be divided into two branches, — Ethics and Politics; and these again admit of various subdivisions.

So much for those parts of the Philosophy of Mind, which are conversant about Phænomena, and about Laws. The Third great branch of this philosophy is that which is engaged in the deduction of Inferences, or Results.

In the First branch, — the Phænomenology of mind, — philosophy is properly limited to the facts afforded in

III. Ontology, or
Metaphysics Proper. consciousness, considered exclusively in themselves. But these facts may be such as not only to be objects of knowledge in themselves, but likewise to furnish us with grounds of inference to something out of themselves. As effects, and effects of a certain character, they may enable us to infer the analogous character of their unknown causes; as phænomena, and phænomena of peculiar qualities, they may warrant us in drawing many conclusions regarding the distinctive character of that unknown principle, of that unknown substance, of which they are the manifestations. Although, therefore, existence be only revealed to us in phænomena, and though we can, therefore, have only a relative knowledge either of mind or of matter; still, by inference and analogy, we may legitimately attempt to rise above the mere appearances which experience and observation afford. Thus, for example, the existence of God and the Immortality of the Soul are not given us as phænomena, as objects of immediate knowledge; yet, if the phænomena actually given do necessarily require, for their rational explanation, the hypotheses of immortality and of God, we are assuredly entitled, from the existence of the former, to infer the reality of the latter. Now, the science conversant about all such inferences of unknown being from its known manifestations, is called ONTOLOGY, or METAPHYSICS PROPER. We might call it INFERENTIAL PSYCHOLOGY.

The following is a tabular view of the distribution of Philosophy as here proposed : —

Mind or Consciousness affords	Facts, — Phænomenology, Empirical Psychology.	Cognitions.
		Feelings.
		Conative Powers (Will and Desire).
	Laws, — Nomology, Rational Psychology.	Cognitions, — Logic.
		Feelings, — Æsthetic.
		Conative Powers. { Moral Philosophy. Political Philosophy.
	Results, — Ontology, Inferential Psychology.	Being of God.
		Immortality of the Soul, etc.

In this distribution of the philosophical sciences, you will observe that I take little account of the celebrated division of philosophy

Meaning of the term. into Speculative and Practical, which I have already explained to you,[1] for I call only one minor division of philosophy practical, — viz. the Nomology of the Conative powers, not because that science is not equally theoretical with any other, but simply because these powers are properly called practical, as tending to practice or overt action.

Such is the distribution of Philosophy, which I venture to propose as the simplest and most exhaustive, and I shall now proceed, in reference to it, to specify the particular branches which form the objects of our consideration in the present course.

The subjects assigned to the various chairs of the Philosophical

Distribution of subjects in Faculty of Philosophy in the Universities of Europe. Faculty, in the different Universities of Europe, were not calculated upon any comprehensive view of the parts of philosophy, and of their natural connection. Our universities were founded when the Aristotelic philosophy was the dominant, or rather the exclusive, system, and the parts distributed to the different classes, in the faculty of Arts or Philosophy, were regulated by the contents of certain of the Aristotelic books, and by the order in which they were studied. Of these, there were always Four great divisions. There was first Logic, in relation to the Organon of Aristotle; secondly, Metaphysics, relative to his books under that title; thirdly, Moral Philosophy, relative to his Ethics, Politics, and Economics; and, fourthly, Physics, relative to his Physics, and the collection of treatises styled in the schools the *Parva Naturalia*. But every university had not a full complement of classes, that is, did not devote a separate year to each of the four subjects of study; and, accordingly, in those seats of learning where three years formed the curriculum of philosophy, two of these branches were combined. In this university, Logic and Metaphysics were taught in the same year; in others, Metaphysics and Moral Philosophy were conjoined; and, when the old practice was abandoned of the several Regents or Professors carrying on their students through every department, the two branches which had been taught in the same year were assigned to the same chair. What is most curious in the matter is this, — Aristotle's treatise *On the Soul* being, (along with his lesser treatises on *Memory and Reminiscence*, on *Sense and its Objects*, etc.,) included in the *Parva Naturalia*, and, he having declared that the consideration of the soul was part of the philosophy of nature,[2] the science of Mind

---

1 See *ante*, p. 80. — ED.

2 *De Anima*, i. 1. Φυσικοῦ τὸ θεωρῆσαι περὶ ψυχῆς, ἢ πάσης ἢ τῆς τοιαύτης. Cf. *Metaph.* v. 1. Δῆλον πῶς δεῖ ἐν τοῖς φυσικοῖς

was always treated along with Physics. The professors of Natural Philosophy have, however, long abandoned the philosophy of mind, and this branch has been, as more appropriate to their departments, taught both by the Professors of Moral Philosophy and by the Professors of Logic and Metaphysics, — for you are not to suppose that metaphysics and psychology are, though vulgarly used as synonymous expressions, by any means the same. So much for the historical accidents which have affected the subjects of the different chairs.

I now return to the distribution of philosophy, which I have given you, and, first, by exclusion, I shall tell you what does not concern us. In this class, we have nothing to do with Practical Philosophy, — that is, Ethics, Politics, Economics. But, with this exception, there is no other branch of philosophy which is not either specially allotted to our consideration, or which does not fall naturally within our sphere. Of the former description, are Logic, and Ontology or Metaphysics Proper. Of the latter, are Psychology, or the Philosophy of Mind in its stricter signification, and Æsthetic.

Subjects appropriate to this Chair.

These subjects are, however, collectively too extensive to be overtaken in a single Course, and, at the same time, some of them are too abstract to afford the proper materials for the instruction of those only commencing the study of philosophy. In fact, the department allotted to this chair comprehends the two extremes of philosophy, — Logic, forming its appropriate introduction, — Metaphysics, its necessary consummation. I propose, therefore, in order fairly to exhaust the business of the chair, to divide its subjects between two Courses, — the one on Phænomenology, Psychology, or Mental Philosophy in general; the other, on Nomology, Logic, or the laws of the Cognitive Faculties in particular.[1]

Comprehension and order of the Course.

τὸ τί ἐστι ζητεῖν καὶ ὁρίζεσθαι, καὶ διότι καὶ περὶ ψυχῆς ἐνίας θεωρῆσαι τοῦ φυσικοῦ, ὅση μὴ ἄνευ τῆς ὕλης ἐστίν. — ED.

[1] From the following sentences, which appear in the manuscript lecture as superseded by the paragraph given in the text, it is obvious that the Author had originally designed to discuss specifically, and with greater detail, the three grand departments of Philosophy indicated in the distribution proposed by him: — "The plan which I propose to adopt in the distribution of the Course, or rather Courses, is the following:

"I shall commence with Mental Philosophy, strictly so called, with the science which is conversant with the Manifestations of Mind, — Phænomenology, or Psychology. I shall then proceed to Logic, the science which considers the Laws of Thought; and finally, to Ontology, or Metaphysics proper, the philosophy of Results. Æsthetic, or the theory of the Pleasurable, I should consider subsequently to Logic, and previously to Ontology." — On the propriety of according to Psychology the first place in the order of the philosophical sciences, see Cousin, *Cours de l' Histoire de la Philosophie*, Deuxième Série, tom. ii. p. 71-73 (ed. 1847). — ED.

LECTURE VIII.

PSYCHOLOGY, ITS DEFINITION. EXPLICATION OF TERMS.

I now pass to the First Division of my subject, which will occupy the present Course, and commence with a definition of Psychology, — The Phænomenology of Mind.

Psychology, or the Philosophy of the Human Mind, strictly so denominated, is the science conversant about the *phœnomena*, or *modifications*, or *states* of the *Mind*, or *Conscious-Subject*, or *Soul*, or *Spirit*, or *Self*, or *Ego*.

Definition of Psychology.

In this definition, you will observe that I have purposely accumulated a variety of expressions, in order that I might have the earliest opportunity of making you accurately acquainted with their meaning; for they are terms of vital importance and frequent use in philosophy. — Before, therefore, proceeding further, I shall pause a moment in explanation of the terms in which this definition is expressed. Without restricting myself to the following order, I shall consider the word *Psychology ;* the correlative terms *subject* and *substance, phœnomenon, modification, state*, etc., and, at the same time, take occasion to explain another correlative, the expression *object*, and, finally, the words *mind, soul, spirit, self*, and *ego*.

Explication of terms.

Indeed, after considering these terms, it may not be improper to take up, in one series, the philosophical expressions of principal importance and most ordinary occurrence, in order to render less frequent the necessity of interrupting the course of our procedure, to afford the requisite verbal explanations.

The term *Psychology*, is of Greek compound, its elements ψυχή, signifying *soul* or *mind*, and λόγος, signifying *discourse* or *doctrine*. Psychology, therefore, is the *discourse* or *doctrine treating of the human mind*. But, though composed of Greek elements, it is, like the greater number of the compounds of λόγος, of modern combination. I may be asked, — why use an exotic, a technical name? Why not be contented with the more popular terms, Philosophy of Mind, or Mental Philosophy, — Science of Mind or Mental

The term Psychology; its use vindicated.

Science? — expressions by which this department of knowledge has been usually designated by those who, in this country, have cultivated it with the most distinguished success. To this there are several answers. In the first place, philosophy itself, and all, or almost all, its branches, have, in our language, received Greek technical denominations; — why not also the most important of all, the science of mind? In the second place, the term psychology is now, and has long been, the ordinary expression for the doctrine of mind in the philosophical language of every other European nation. Nay, in point of fact, it is now naturalized in English, *psychology* and *psychological* having of late years come into common use; and their employment is warranted by the authority of the best English writers. It was familiarly employed by one of our best writers, and most acute metaphysicians, Principal Campbell of Aberdeen;[1] and Dr. Beattie, likewise, has entitled the first part of his *Elements of Moral Science*, — that which treats of the mental faculties, — Psychology. To say nothing of Coleridge, the late Sir James Mackintosh was also an advocate for its employment, and justly censured Dr. Brown for not using it, in place of his very reprehensible expression, — *Physiology of Mind*, the title of his unfinished text-book.[2] But these are reasons in themselves of comparatively little moment: they tend merely to show that, if otherwise expedient, the nomenclature is permissible; and that it is expedient, the following reasons will prove. For, in the third place, it is always of consequence for the sake of precision to be able to use one word instead of a plurality of words, — especially, where the frequent occurrence of a descriptive appellation might occasion tedium, distraction, and disgust; and this must necessarily occur in the treatment of any science, if the science be able to possess no single name vicarious of its definition. In this respect, therefore, *Psychology* is preferable to *Philosophy of Mind*. But, in the fourth place, even if the employment of the description for the name could, in this instance, be tolerated when used substantively, what are we to do when we require, (which we do unceasingly,) to use the denomination of the science adjectively? For example, I have occasion to say a psychological fact, a psychological law, a psychological curiosity, etc. How can we express these by the descriptive appellation? A psychological fact may indeed be styled a fact considered relatively to the philosophy of the human mind, — a psychological law may be called a law by which the

1 *Philosophy of Rhetoric*, vol. i. p. 143, (1st ed.); p. 123, (ed. 1816.) — ED.

2 *Dissertation on the progress of Ethical Phi-* losophy, in the Encyclopædia Britannica, vol. i. p. 399., (7th ed.) — ED.

mental phænomena are governed, — a psychological curiosity may be rendered — by what, I really do not know.   But how miserably weak, awkward, tedious, and affected, is the commutation when it can be made; not only do the vivacity and precision of the original evaporate, the meaning itself is not even adequately conveyed. But this defect is still more manifestly shown when we wish to place in contrast the matters proper to this science, with the matters proper to others.   Thus, for example, to say, — this is a psychological, not a physiological, doctrine — this is a psychological observation, not a logical inference.   How is the contradistinction to be expressed by a periphrasis?   It is impossible, — for the intensity of the contrast consists, first, in the two opposite terms being single words, and second, in their being both even technical and precise Greek.   This necessity has, accordingly, compelled the adoption of the terms psychology and psychological into the philosophical nomenclature of every nation, even where the same necessity did not vindicate the employment of a non-vernacular expression.   Thus in Germany, though the native language affords a facility of composition only inferior to the Greek, and though it possesses a word (*Seelenlehre*) exactly correspondent to ψυχολογία, yet because this substantive did not easily allow of an adjective flexion, the Greek terms, substantive and adjective, were both adopted, and have been long in as familiar use in the Empire, as the terms geography and geographical, — physiology and physiological, are with us.

What I have now said may suffice to show that, to supply necessity, we must introduce these words into our philosophical vocabulary.   But the propriety of this is still further shown by the inauspicious attempts that have been recently made on the name of the science.   As I have mentioned before, Dr. Brown, in the very title of the abridgment of his lectures on mental philosophy, has styled this philosophy, " *The Physiology of the Human Mind;*" and I have also seen two English publications of modern date, — one entitled the "*Physics of the Soul,*" the other "*Intellectual Physics.*"[1]   Now the term *nature*, (φύσις, *natura,*) though in common language of a more extensive meaning, has, in general, by philosophers, been applied appropriately to denote the laws which govern the appearances of the material universe.   And the words Physiology and Physics have been specially limited to denote sciences conversant about

The terms Physiology and Physics, as applied to the philosophy of mind, inappropriate.

---

1 *Intellectual Physics, an Essay concerning the Nature of Being and the Progression of existence.* London, 1795.   *Intellectual Physics, an Essay concerning the Nature of Being.* 1803.   By Governor Pownall. — ED.

these laws as regulating the phænomena of organic and inorganic bodies. The empire of nature is the empire of a mechanical necessity; the necessity of nature, in philosophy, stands opposed to the liberty of intelligence. Those, accordingly, who do not allow that mind is matter,—who hold that there is in man a principle of action superior to the determinations of a physical necessity, a brute or blind fate—must regard the application of the terms Physiology and Physics to the doctrine of the mind as either singularly inappropriate, or as significant of a false hypothesis in regard to the character of the thinking principle.

Mr. Stewart objects[1] to the term *Spirit*, as seeming to imply an hypothesis concerning the nature and essence of the sentient or thinking principle, altogether unconnected with our conclusions in regard to its phænomena, and their general laws; and, for the same reason, he is disposed to object to the words Pneumatology and Psychology; the former of which was introduced by the schoolmen. In regard to *Spirit* and *Pneumatology*, Mr. Stewart's criticism is perfectly just. They are unnecessary; and, besides the etymological metaphor, they are associated with a certain theological limitation, which spoils them as expressions of philosophical generality.[2] But this is not the case with *Psychology*. For though, in its etymology, it is like almost all metaphysical terms, originally of physical application, still this had been long forgotten even by the Greeks; and, if we were to reject philosophical expressions on this account, we should be left without any terms for the mental phænomena at all. The term *soul*, (and what I say of the term soul is true of the term *spirit*,) though in this country less employed than the term *mind*, may be regarded as another synonym for the unknown basis of the mental phænomena. Like nearly all the words significant of the internal world, there is here a metaphor borrowed from the external; and this is the case not merely in one, but, as far as we can trace the analogy, in all languages. You are aware that ψυχή, the Greek term for soul, comes from ψύχω, *I breathe* or *blow*,—as πνεῦμα in Greek, and *spiritus* in Latin, from verbs of the same signification. In like

Spirit, Soul.

Corresponding terms in other languages.

1 *Philosophical Essays*, Prelim. Dissert. ch. 1; *Works*, vol. v. p. 20.

2 [The terms *Psychology* and *Pneumatology*, or *Pneumatic*, are not equivalents. The latter word was used for the doctrine of spirit in general, which was subdivided into three branches, as it treated of the three orders of spiritual substances,— God, —Angels, and Devils,—and Man. Thus—

Pneumatologia or Pneumatica,
{
1. Theologia (Naturalis),
2. Angelographia, Dæmonologia.
3. Psychologia.
}

—See Theoph. Gale, Gale *Logica*, p. 455. (1681).]

manner, *anima* and *animus* are words which, though in Latin they have lost their primary signification, and are only known in their secondary or metaphorical, yet, in their original physical meaning, are preserved in the Greek ἄνεμος, *wind* or *air*. The English *soul*, and the German *Seele*, come from a Gothic root *saivala*,[1] which signifies to *storm*. *Ghost*, the old English word for spirit in general, and so used in our English version of the Scriptures, is the same as the German *Geist*,[2] and is derived from *Gas*, or *Gescht*, which signifies *air*. In like manner the two words in Hebrew for soul or spirit, *nephesh* and *ruach*, are derivatives of a root which means *to breathe;* and in Sanscrit the word *atmā* (analogous to the Greek ἀτμός, *vapor* or *air*) signifies both *mind* and *wind* or *air*.[3] *Sapientia*, in Latin, originally meant only the power of tasting; as *sagacitas* only the faculty of scenting. In French, *penser* comes from the Latin *pendere*, through *pensare* to weigh, and the terms, *attentio, intentio, (entendement,) comprehensio, apprehensio, penetratio, understanding*, etc., are just so many bodily actions transferred to the expression of mental energies.[4]

There is, therefore, on this ground, no reason to reject such useful terms as *psychology* and *psychological;* terms, too, now in such general acceptation in the philosophy of Europe. I may, however, add an historical notice of their introduction. Aristotle's principal treatise on the philosophy of mind is entitled Περὶ Ψυχῆς; but the first author who gave a treatise on the subject under the title *Psychologia*, (which I have observed to you is a modern compound), is Otto Casmann, who, in the year 1594, published at Hanau his very curious work, " *Psychologia Anthropologica, sive Animæ Humanæ Doctrina*." This was followed, in two years, by his "*Anthropologiæ Pars II., hoc est, de fabrica Humani Corporis*." This author had the merit of first giving the name *Anthropologia* to the science of man in general, which he divided into two parts, — the first, *Psychologia*, the doctrine of the Human Mind; the second, *Somatologia*, the doctrine of the Human Body; and these thus introduced and applied, still continue to be the usual appellations of these branches of knowledge in Germany. I would not say, however, that Casmann was the true author of the term

By whom the appellation Psychology first employed.

---

1 See Grimm, *Deutsche Grammatik*, vol. ii. p. 99. In Anglo-Saxon, *Sawel, Sawal, Sawl, Saul.* — ED.

2 Scotch, *Ghaist, Gastly.*

3 [See H. Schmid, *Versuch einer Metaphysik der inneren Natur*, p. 69, note. Scheidler's *Psychologie*, pp. 299-301, 320, *et seq.* Cf. Theop.

Gale, *Philosophia Generalis*, pp. 321, 322. Prichard, *Review of the Doctrine of a Vital Principle*, p. 5, 6.]

4 [On this point see Leibnitz, *Nouv. Ess.* lib. iii. c. i. § 5; Stewart, *Phil. Essays — Works*, vol. v. Essay v.; Brown, *Human Understanding*, p. 388, *et seq.*]

psychology, for his master, the celebrated Rudolphus Goclenius of Marburg, published, also in 1594, a work entitled, " Ψυχολογία, *hoc est, de Hominis Perfectione, Anima, etc*," being a collection of dissertations on the subject; in 1596 another, entitled "*De præcipuis Materiis Psychologicis;*" and in 1597 a third, entitled " *Authores Varii de Psychologia*," — so that I am inclined to attribute the origin of the name to Goclenius.[1] Subsequently, the term became the usual title of the science, and this chiefly through the authority of Wolf, whose two principal works on the subject are entitled " *Psychologia Empirica*," and " *Psychologia Rationalis*." Charles Bonnet, in his " *Essai de Psychologie*,"[2] familiarized the name in France; where, as well as in Italy, — indeed, in all the Continental countries, — it is now the common appellation.

In the second place, I said that Psychology is conversant about the *phænomena* of the thinking *subject*, etc., and I now proceed to expound the import of the correlative terms *phænomenon, subject,* etc.

But the meaning of these terms will be best illustrated by now stating and explaining the great axiom, that all human knowledge, consequently that all human philosophy, is only of the relative or phænomenal. In this proposition, the term *relative* is opposed to the term *absolute ;* and, therefore, in saying that we know only the

The correlative terms Phænomenon, Subject, illustrated by reference to the relativity of human knowledge.

relative, I virtually assert that we know nothing absolute, — nothing existing absolutely ; that is, in and for itself, and without relation to us and our faculties. I shall illustrate this by its application. Our knowledge is either of matter or of mind. Now, what is matter? What do we know of matter? Matter, or body, is to us the name either of something known, or of something unknown. In so far as matter is a name for something known, it means that which appears to us under the forms of extension, solidity, divisibility, figure, motion, roughness, smoothness, color, heat, cold, etc.; in short, it is a common name for a certain series, or aggregate, or complement, of appearances or phænomena manifested in coëxistence.

But as the phænomena appear only in conjunction, we are compelled by the constitution of our nature to think them conjoined in and by something; and as they are phænomena, we cannot think them the phænomena of nothing, but must regard them as the properties or qualities of something that is extended, solid, figured, etc. But this something, absolutely and in itself, — *i. e.* considered apart

---

1 [The term *psychology* is, however, used by Joannes Thomas Freigius in the *Catalogus Lo-* *corum Communium*, prefixed to his *Ciceronianus*, 1575. See also Gale, *Logica*, p. 455.]

2 Published in 1755. — ED.

from its phænomena,—is to us as zero. It is only in its qualities, only in its effects, in its relative or phænomenal existence, that it is cognizable or conceivable; and it is only by a law of thought, which compels us to think something, absolute and unknown, as the basis or condition of the relative and known, that this something obtains a kind of incomprehensible reality to us. Now, that which manifests its qualities,—in other words, that in which the appearing causes inhere, that to which they belong, is called their *subject*, or *substance*, or *substratum*. To this subject of the phænomena of extension, solidity, etc., the term *matter* or *material substance* is commonly given; and, therefore, as contradistinguished from these qualities, it is the name of something unknown and inconceivable.

The same is true in regard to the term *mind*. In so far as mind is the common name for the states of knowing, willing, feeling, desiring, etc., of which I am conscious, it is only the name for a certain series of connected phænomena or qualities, and, consequently, expresses only what is known. But in so far as it denotes that subject or substance in which the phænomena of knowing, willing, etc., inhere,—something behind or under these phænomena,—it expresses what, in itself or in its absolute existence, is unknown.

Thus, mind and matter, as known or knowable, are only two different series of phænomena or qualities; mind and matter, as unknown and unknowable, are the two substances in which these two different series of phænomena or qualities, are supposed to inhere. The existence of an unknown substance is only an inference we are compelled to make, from the existence of known phænomena; and the distinction of two substances is only inferred from the seeming incompatibility of the two series of phænomena to coinhere in one.

Our whole knowledge of mind and matter is thus, as we have said, only relative; of existence, absolutely and in itself, we know nothing; and we may say of man what Virgil says of Æneas, contemplating in the prophetic sculpture of his shield the future glories of Rome —

" Rerumque ignarus, imagine gaudet." [1]

This is, indeed, a truth, in the admission of which philosophers, in general, have been singularly harmonious; and the praise that has been lavished on Dr. Reid for this observation, is wholly unmerited. In fact, I am hardly aware of the philosopher who has not proceeded on the supposition, and there are few who have not explicitly enounced the observation. It is

General harmony of philosophers regarding the relativity of human knowledge.

1 *Æneid*, viii. 730. — ED.

only since Reid's death that certain speculators have arisen, who have obtained celebrity by their attempt to found philosophy on an immediate knowledge of the absolute or unconditioned. I shall quote to you a few examples of this general recognition, as they happen to occur to my recollection; and, in order to manifest the better its universality, I purposely overlook the testimonies of a more modern philosophy.

Aristotle, among many similar observations, remarks in regard to matter, that it is incognizable in itself;[1] while in regard to mind he says, "that the intellect does not know itself directly, but only indirectly, in knowing other things;"[2] and he defines the soul from its phænomena, "the principle by which we live, and move, and perceive, and understand."[3] St. Augustin, the most philosophical of the Christian fathers, admirably says of body, — "Materiam cognoscendo ignorari, et ignorando cognosci;"[4] and of mind, — "Mens se cognoscit cognoscendo se vivere, se meminisse, se intelligere, se velle, cogitare, scire, judicare."[5] "Non incurrunt," says Melanchthon, "ipsæ substantiæ in oculos, sed vestitæ et ornatæ accidentibus; hoc est, non possumus, in hac vita, acie oculorum perspicere ipsas substantias : sed utcunque, ex accidentibus quæ in sensus exteriores incurrunt, ratiocinamur, quomodo inter se differant substantiæ."[6]

Testimonies, — of Aristotle.

St. Augustin.

Melanchthon.

It is needless to multiply authorities, but I cannot refrain from adducing one other evidence of the general consent of philosophers to the relative character of our knowledge, as affording a graphic specimen of the manner of its ingenious author. "Substantiæ non a nobis cognoscuntur," says the elder Scaliger, "sed earum accidentia. Quis enim me doceat quid sit substantia, nisi miseris illis verbis, *res subsistens?* Scientiam ergo nostram constat esse umbram in sole. Et sicut vulpes, elusa a ciconia, lambendo vitreum vas pultem haud attingit : ita nos externa tantum accidentia percipiendo, formas internas non cognoscimus."[7]

The elder Scaliger.

---

1 *Metaph.* lib. vii. (vi.) c. 10: [ἡ ὕλη ἄγνωστος καθ' αὑτήν. —ED.]

2 *Metaph.* xii. (xi.) 7. Αὐτὸν δὲ νοεῖ ὁ νοῦς κατὰ μετάληψιν τοῦ νοητοῦ· νοητὸς γὰρ γίγνεται θιγγάνων καὶ νοῶν· Cf. *De Anima,* iii. 4. Καὶ αὐτὸς δὲ νοητός ἐστιν ὥσπερ τὰ νοητά. —ED.

3 *De Anima,* Lib. ii. c. 2. Ἡ ψυχὴ τούτοις ὥρισται, θρεπτικῷ, αἰσθητικῷ διανοητικῷ, κινήσει. —ED.

4 *Confess.* xii. 5. "Dum sibi hæc dicit humana cogitatio, conetur eam (materiam) vel nosse ignorando vel ignorare noscendo." —ED.

5 From the spurious treatise attributed to St. Austin, entitled *De Spiritu et Anima,* c. 32; but see *De Trinitate,* lib. x. § 16, tom. viii. p. 897, (ed. Ben.)

6 *Erotemata Dialectices,* lib. i., Pr. Substantia. [This is the text in the edition of Strigelius. It varies considerably in different editions. — ED.]

7 *De Subtilitate,* Ex. cccvii. § 21.

So far there is no difference of opinion among philosophers in general. We know mind and matter not in themselves, but in their accidents or phænomena.[1]

Thus our knowledge is of relative existence only, seeing that existence in itself, or absolute existence, is no object of knowledge.[2] But it does not follow that all relative existence is relative *to us ;* that all that can be known, even by a limited intelligence, is actually cognizable by us. We must, therefore, more precisely limit our sphere of knowledge, by adding, that all we know is known only under the special conditions of our faculties. This is a truth likewise generally acknowledged. "Man," says Protagoras, "is the measure of the universe," (πάντων χρημάτων μέτρον ἄνθρωπος), — a truth which Bacon has well expressed: "Omnes perceptiones tam sensus quam mentis, sunt ex analogia hominis, non ex analogia universi : estque intellectus humanus instar speculi inæqualis ad radios rerum, qui suam naturam naturæ rerum immiscet, eamque distorquet et inficit."[3] "Omne quod cognoscitur," says Boethius, "non secundum sui vim, sed secundum cognoscentium potius comprehenditur facultatem ;"[4] and this is expressed almost in the same terms by the two very opposite philosophers, Kant and Condillac, —"In perception" (to quote only the former) "everything is known according to the constitution of our faculty of sense."[5]

All relative existence not comprised in what is relative to us.

Now this principle, in which philosophers of the most opposite opinions equally concur, divides itself into two branches. In the first place, it would be unphilosophical to conclude that the properties of existence necessarily are, in number, only as the number of our faculties of apprehending them ; or, in the second, that the properties known, are known in their native purity, and without addition or modification from our organs of sense, or our capacities of intelligence. I shall illustrate these in their order.

This principle has two branches.

In regard to the first assertion, it is evident that nothing exists for us, except in so far as it is known to us, and that nothing is known to us, except certain properties or modes of existence, which are relative or analogous to our faculties. Beyond these modes we know, and can assert, the reality of no existence. But

---

1 For additional testimonies on this point, see the Author's *Discussions*, p. 644. — ED.

2 [Absolute in two senses: 1°, As opposed to partial ; 2°, As opposed to relative. Better if I had said that our knowledge not of absolute, and, therefore, only of the partial and relative.] — *Pencil Jotting on Blank Leaf of Lecture.*

3 *Novum Organum*, lib. i., Aph. xli. — ED.

4 *De Consol. Phil.* lib. v. Pr. 4. Quoted in *Discussions*, p. 645. — ED.

5 *Kritik der reinen Vernunft*, Vorrede zur zweiten Auflage. Quoted in *Discussions*, p. 646. Cf. *ibid.* Transc. Æsth. § 8. — ED.

if, on the one hand, we are not entitled to assert as actually existent except what we know; neither, on the other,

are we warranted in denying, as possibly existent, what we do not know. The universe may
be conceived as a polygon of a thousand, or a
hundred thousand, sides or facets,—and each of
these sides or facets may be conceived as representing one special mode of existence. Now,
of these thousand sides or modes all may be equally essential, but
three or four only may be turned towards us or be analogous to our
organs. One side or facet of the universe, as holding a relation to
the organ of sight, is the mode of luminous or visible existence;
another, as proportional to the organ of hearing, is the mode of
sonorous or audible existence; and so on. But if every eye to see,
if every ear to hear, were annihilated, the modes of existence to
which these organs now stand in relation, — that which could be
seen, that which could be heard, would still remain; and if the intelligences, reduced to the three senses of touch, smell, and taste,
were then to assert the impossibility of any modes of being except
those to which these three senses were analogous, the procedure
would not be more unwarranted, than if we now ventured to deny
the possible reality of other modes of material existence than those
to the perception of which our five senses are accommodated. I
will illustrate this by an hypothetical parallel. Let us suppose a
block of marble,[1] on which there are four different inscriptions, —
in Greek, in Latin, in Persic, and in Hebrew, and that four trav-
ellers approach, each able to read only the inscription in his native
tongue. The Greek is delighted with the information the marble
affords him of the siege of Troy. The Roman finds interesting
matter regarding the expulsion of the kings. The Persian deciphers
an oracle of Zoroaster. And the Jew is surprised by a commemoration of the Exodus. Here, as each inscription exists or is significant only to him who possesses the corresponding language; so the
several modes of existence are manifested only to those intelligences who possess the corresponding organs. And as each of the
four readers would be rash if he maintained that the marble could
be significant only as significant to him, so should we be rash, were
we to hold that the universe had no other phases of being than the
few that are turned towards our faculties, and which our five senses
enable us to perceive.

---

1 This illustration is taken from F. Hemsterhuis, *Sophyle ou de la Philosophie — Œuvres Philosophiques*, vol. i. p. 281, (ed. 1792.) — ED.

Voltaire, (*aliud agendo*), has ingeniously expressed this truth in one of his philosophical romances. " Tell me,"
says Micromegas, an inhabitant of one of the planets of the Dog-Star, to the secretary of the Academy of Sciences in the planet Saturn, at which he had recently arrived, in a journey through the heavens, — " Tell me, how many senses have the men on your globe ? " — " We have seventy-two senses," answered the academician, " and we are, every day, complaining of the smallness of the number. Our imagination goes far beyond our .wants. What are seventy-two senses! and how pitiful a boundary, even for beings with such limited perceptions, to be cooped up within our ring and our five moons. In spite of our curiosity, and in spite of as many passions as can result from six dozen of senses, we find our hours hang very heavily on our hands, and can always find time enough for yawning." — " I can very well believe it," says Micromegas, " for, in our globe, we have very near one thousand senses; and yet, with all these, we feel continually a sort of listless inquietude and vague desire, which are forever telling us that we are nothing, and that there are beings infinitely nearer perfection. I have travelled a good deal in the universe. I have seen many classes of mortals far beneath us, and many as much superior; but I have never had the good fortune to meet with any who had not always more desires than real necessities to occupy their life. And pray, how long may.you Saturnians live, with your few senses ? " continued the Sirian. " Ah! but a very short time indeed ! " said the little man of Saturn, with a sigh. " It is the same with us," said the traveller; " we are forever complaining of the shortness of life. It must be an universal law of nature." — " Alas! " said the Saturnian, " we live only five hundred great revolutions of the sun, (which is pretty much about fifteen thousand years of our counting). You see well, that this is to die almost the moment one is born. Our existence is a point, — our duration an instant, — our globe an atom. Scarcely have we begun to pick up a little knowledge, when death rushes in upon us, before we can have acquired anything like experience. As for me, I cannot venture even to think of any project. I feel myself but like a drop of water in the ocean; and, especially now, when I look to you and to myself, I really feel quite ashamed of the ridiculous appearance which I cut in the universe."

" If I did not know you to be a philosopher," replied Micromegas, " I should be afraid of distressing you, when I tell you, that our life is seven hundred times longer than yours. But what is even that ? and, when we come to the last moment, to have lived a single day, and to have lived a whole eternity, amount to the same thing. I have been in countries where they live a thousand times longer than with us; and I have always found them murmuring, just as we do ourselves. But you have seventy-two senses, and they must have told you something about your globe. How many properties has matter with you?"—"If you mean essential properties," said the Saturnian, "without which our globe could not subsist, we count three hundred,— extension, impenetrability, mobility, gravity, divisibility, and so forth."—"That small number," replied the gigantic traveller, "may be sufficient for the views which the Creator must have had with respect to your narrow habitation. Your globe is little; its inhabitants are so too. You have few senses; your matter has few qualities. In all this, Providence has suited you most happily to each other."

"The academician was more and more astonished with everything which the traveller told him. At length, after communicating to each other a little of what they knew, and a great deal of what they knew not, and reasoning as well and as ill as philosophers usually do, they resolved to set out together on a little tour of the universe."[1]

Before leaving this subject, it is perhaps proper to observe, that had we faculties equal in number to all the possible modes of existence, whether of mind or matter, still would our knowledge of mind or matter be only relative. If material existence could exhibit ten thousand phænomena, and if we possessed ten thousand senses to apprehend these ten thousand phænomena of material existence,— of existence absolutely and in itself, we should be then as ignorant as we are at present.

But the consideration that our actual faculties of knowledge are probably wholly inadequate in number to the possible modes of being, is of comparatively less importance than the other consideration to which we now proceed,—that whatever we know is not known as it is, but only as it seems to us to be; for it is of less importance that our knowledge should be limited than that our knowledge should be pure. It is, therefore, of the highest moment that we should be aware that what we know is not a simple relation apprehended between the object known and the subject knowing,— but that every knowledge is a sum made up of several elements, and that the great business of philosophy is to analyze and discriminate these elements, and to determine from whence these contributions have been derived. I shall explain what I

2. The properties of existence, not known in their native purity.

mean, by an example. In the perception of an external object, the mind does not know it in immediate relation to itself, but mediately in relation to the material organs of sense. If, therefore, we were to throw these organs out of consideration, and did not take into account what they contribute to, and how they modify, our knowledge of that object, it is evident, that our conclusion in regard to the nature of external perception would be erroneous. Again, an object of perception may not even stand in immediate relation to the organ of sense, but may make its impression on that organ through an intervening medium. Now, if this medium be thrown out of account, and if it be not considered that the real external object is the sum of all that externally contributes to affect the sense, we shall, in like manner, run into error. For example, I see a book, — I see that book through an external medium, (what that medium is, we do not now inquire,) — and I see it through my organ of sight, the eye. Now, as the full object presented to the mind (observe that I say the mind), in perception, is an object compounded of the external object emitting or reflecting light, i. e. modifying the external medium, — of this external medium, — and of the living organ of sense, in their mutual relation, — let us suppose, in the example I have taken, that the full or adequate object perceived is equal to twelve, and that this amount is made up of three several parts, — of four, contributed by the book, — of four, contributed by all that intervenes between the book and the organ, and of four, contributed by the living organ itself.[1]

I use this illustration to show, that the phænomenon of the external object is not presented immediately to the mind, but is known by it only as modified through certain intermediate agencies; and to show that sense itself may be a source of error, if we do not analyze and distinguish what elements, in an act of perception, belong to the outward reality, what to the outward medium, and what to the action of sense itself. But this source of error is not limited to our perceptions; and we are liable to be deceived, not merely by not distinguishing in an act of knowledge what is contributed by sense, but by not distinguishing what is contributed by the mind itself. This is the most difficult and important function of philosophy; and the greater number of its higher problems arise in the attempt to determine the shares to which the knowing subject, and the object known, may pretend in the total act of cognition. For according as we attribute a larger or a smaller proportion to

Illustrated by the act of perception.

---

1 This illustration is borrowed in an improved form from F. Hemsterhuis. See his *Sophyle ou de la Philosophie — Œuvres Philosophiques*, i. 279. — ED.

each, we either run into the extremes of Idealism and Materialism, or maintain an equilibrium between the two. But, on this subject, it would be out of place to say anything further at present.

From what has been said, you will be able, I hope, to understand what is meant by the proposition, that all our knowledge is only relative. It is relative, 1°, Because existence is not cognizable, absolutely and in itself, but only in special modes; 2°, Because these modes can be known only if they stand in a certain relation to our faculties; and, 3°, Because the modes, thus relative to our faculties, are presented to, and known by, the mind only under modifications determined by these faculties themselves. This general doctrine being premised, it will be proper now to take some special notice of the several terms significant of the relative nature of our knowledge. And here there are two opposite series of expressions, — 1°, Those which denote the relative and the known; 2°, Those which denote the absolute and the unknown. Of the former class, are the words *phænomenon, mode, modification, state,* — words which are employed in the definition of Psychology; and to these may be added the analogous terms, — *quality, property, attribute, accident.* Of the latter class, — that is, the absolute and the unknown, — is the word *subject*, which we have to explain as an element of the definition, and its analogous expressions, *substance* and *substratum.* These opposite classes cannot be explained apart; for, as each is correlative of the other, each can be comprehended only in and through its correlative.

In what senses human knowledge is relative.

Two opposite series of terms as applied to human knowledge.

The term *subject* (*subjectum,* ὑπόστασις, ὑποκείμενον) is used to denote the unknown basis which lies under the various phænomena or properties of which we become aware, whether in our internal or external experience. In the more recent philosophy, especially in that of Germany, it has, however, been principally employed to denote the basis of the various mental phænomena; but of this special signification we are hereafter more particularly to speak.[1] The word *substance* (*substantia*) may be employed in two, but two kindred, meanings. It may be used either to denote that which exists absolutely and of itself; in this sense it may be viewed as derived from *subsistendo,* and as meaning *ens per se subsistens;* or it may be viewed as the basis of attributes, in which sense it may be regarded as derived from *substando,* and as meaning *id quod*

The term Subject.

Substance.

---

[1] For the history and various meanings of the terms *Subject* and *Object,* see the Author's note, *Reid's Works,* p. 806. See also Trendelenburg. *Elementa Logices Aristotelicæ,* § 1.—ED.

substat accidentibus, like the Greek ὑπόστασις, ὑποκείμενον. In either case it will, however, signify the same thing, viewed in a different aspect. In the former meaning, it is considered in contrast to, and independent of, its attributes; in the latter, as conjoined with these, and as affording them the condition of existence. In different relations, a thing may be at once considered as a *substance*, and as an *attribute, quality*, or *mode*. This paper is a substance in relation to the attribute of white; but it is itself a mode in relation to the substance, matter. Substance is thus a term for the substratum we are obliged to think to all that we variously denominate a *mode*, a *state*, a *quality*, an *attribute*, a *property*, an *accident*, a *phænomenon*, an *appearance*, etc. These, though expressions generically the same, are, however, used with specific distinctions. The terms *mode, state, quality, attribute, property, accident*, are employed in reference to a substance, as existing; the terms *phænomenon, appearance*, etc. in reference to it, as known. But each of these expressions has also its

Mode.

peculiar signification. A *mode* is the manner of the existence of a thing. Take, for example, a piece of wax. The wax may be round, or square, or of any other definite figure; it may also be solid, or fluid. Its existence in any of these modes is not essential; it may change from one to the other without any substantial alteration. As the mode cannot exist without a substance, we can accord to it only a secondary or precarious existence in relation to the substance, to which we accord the privilege of existing by itself, *per se existere;* but though the substance be not astricted to any particular mode of existence, we must not suppose that it can exist, or, at least, be conceived by us to exist in none. All modes are, therefore, variable states; and though some mode is necessary for the existence of a thing, any

Modification.

individual mode is accidental. The word *modification* is properly the bringing a thing into a certain mode of existence, but it is very commonly employed for

State.

the mode of existence itself. *State* is a term nearly synonymous with mode, but of a meaning more extensive, as not exclusively limited to the mutable and contingent.

Quality is, likewise, a word of a wider signification, for there are essential and accidental qualities.[1] The essential qualities of a thing are those aptitudes, those manners of existence and action, which it cannot lose without ceasing to be. For example, in man the faculties of sense and intelligence; in body, the dimensions of

---

1 The term *quality* should, in strictness, be confined to accidental attributes. See the Author's note, *Reid's Works* p 836. — ED.

length, breadth, and thickness; in God, the attributes of eternity, omniscience, omnipotence, etc. By accidental qualities, are meant those aptitudes and manners of existence and action, which substances have at one time and not at another; or which they have always, but may lose without ceasing to be. For example, of the transitory class are the whiteness of a wall, the health which we enjoy, the fineness of the weather, etc. Of the permanent class are the gravity of bodies, the periodical movement of the planets, etc.

Quality, Essential and accidental.

The term *attribute* is a word properly convertible with *quality*, for every quality is an attribute, and every attribute is a quality; but, in our language, custom has introduced a certain distinction in their application. Attribute is considered as a word of loftier significance, and is, therefore, conventionally limited to qualities of a higher application. Thus, for example, it would be felt as indecorous to speak of the qualities of God, and as ridiculous to talk of the attributes of matter.

Attribute.

Property is correctly a synonym for peculiar quality;[1] but it is frequently used as coëxtensive with quality in general. *Accident*, on the contrary, is an abbreviated expression for accidental or contingent quality.

Property. Accident.

Phænomenon is the Greek word for *that which appears*, and may therefore be translated by *appearance*. There is, however, a distinction to be noticed. In the first place, the employment of the Greek term shows that it is used in a strict and philosophical application. In the second place, the English name is associated with a certain secondary or implied meaning, which, in some degree, renders it inappropriate as a precise and definite expression. For the term *appearance* is used to denote not only that which reveals itself to our observation, as existent, but also to signify that which only seems to be, in contrast to that which truly is. There is thus not merely a certain vagueness in the word, but it even involves a kind of contradiction to the sense in which it is used when employed for *phænomenon*. In consequence of this, the term phænomenon has been naturalized in our language, as a philosophical substitute for the term appearance.

Phænomenon.

---

1 In the older and Aristotelian sense of the term. See *Topics.* i. 5: Ἴδιον δ' ἐστὶν ὃ μὴ δηλοῖ μὲν τὸ τί ἦν εἶναι, μόνῳ δ' ὑπάρχει καὶ ἀντικατηγορεῖται τοῦ πράγματος. By the later Logicians, the term *property* was less correctly used to denote a necessary quality, whether peculiar or not. — ED.

LECTURE IX.

EXPLICATION OF TERMS — RELATIVITY OF HUMAN KNOWLEDGE.

Recapitulation. AFTER giving a definition of Psychology, or the Philosophy of Mind, in which I endeavored to comprise a variety of expressions, the explanation of which might smooth the way in our subsequent progress, I was engaged, during my last Lecture, in illustrating the principle, that all our knowledge of mind and matter is merely relative. We know, and can know, nothing absolutely and in itself: all that we know is existence in certain special forms or modes, and these, likewise, only in so far as they may be analogous to our faculties. We may suppose existence to have a thousand modes; — but these thousand modes are all to us as zero, unless we possess faculties accommodated to their apprehension. But were the number of our faculties coëxtensive with the modes of being, — had we, for each of these thousand modes, a separate organ competent to make it known to us, — still would our whole knowledge be, as it is at present, only of the relative. Of existence, absolutely and in itself, we should then be as ignorant as we are now. We should still apprehend existence only in certain special modes, — only in certain relations to our faculties of knowledge.

These relative modes, whether belonging to the world without or to the world within, are, under different points of view and different limitations, known under various names, as *qualities, properties, essence, accidents, phænomena, manifestations, appearances,* and so forth; — whereas the unknown something of which they are the modes, — the unknown ground, which affords them support, is usually termed their *substance* or *subject*. Of the signification and differences of these expressions, I stated only what was necessary in order to afford a general notion of their philosophical application. *Substance, (substantia,)* I noticed, is considered either in contrast to its accidents, as *res per se subsistens,* or in connection with them, as *id quod substat accidentibus.* It, therefore, comprehends both the Greek terms οὐσία and ὑποκείμενον,— οὐσία being equivalent to *substantia* in the meaning of *ens per se subsistens;*— ὑποκείμενον to it, as *id quod substat accidentibus.*[1] The term *subject* is used only for substance in its second meaning, and thus corresponds to ὑποκείμενον; its literal signification is, as its etymology expresses, that which lies, or is placed, *under* the phænomena. So much for the terms *substance* and *subject*, significant of unknown or absolute existence.

I then said a few words on the differences of the various terms expressive of known or relative existence, *mode, modification, state, quality, attribute, property, phænomenon, appearance;* but what I stated I do not think it necessary to recapitulate.

I at present avoid entering into the metaphysics of substance and phænomenon. I shall only observe in general, that philosophers have frequently fallen into one or other of three different errors. Some have denied the reality of any unknown ground of the known phænomena; and have maintained that mind and matter have no substantial existence, but are merely the two complements of two series of associated qualities. This doctrine is, however, altogether futile. It belies the veracity of our primary beliefs; it leaves unsatisfied the strongest necessities of our intellectual nature; it admits as a fact that the phænomena are connected, but allows no cause explanatory of the fact of their connection. Others, again, have fallen into an opposite error. They have attempted to speculate concerning the ·nature of the unknown grounds of the phænomena of mind and matter, apart from the phænomena, and have, accordingly, transcended the legitimate sphere of philosophy. A third party have taken some one, or more, of the phænomena themselves as the basis or substratum of the others. Thus Descartes, at least as understood and followed by Mallebranche and others of his disciples, made thought or consciousness convertible with the substance of mind;[2] and Bishops Brown and Law, with Dr. Watts, constituted solidity and extension

Philosophers have fallen into three different errors regarding Substance.

---

[1] Ὑπόστασις, here noted, by way of *interpolation*, as of theological application. [On this point see Melanchthon, *Erot. Dial.* (Strigelii) p. 145, *et seq.* "In philosophia, generaliter nomine *Essentiæ* utimur *pro re per sese considerata*, sive sit in prædicamento substantiæ, sive sit accidens. At ὑπόστασις significat *rem subsistentem*, quæ opponitur accidentibus. Ecclesia vero cum quodam discrimine his vocabulis utitur. Nam vocabulum *Essentiæ* sig- nificat *id quod revera est*, etiamsi est communicatum. Ὑπόστασις autem seu *Persona* est subsistens, vivum, individuum, intelligens, incommunicabile, non sustentatum in alio." Compare the relative annotation by Strigelius, and Höcker, *Clavis Phil. Arist.* p. 301. — ED.]

[2] *Principia*, pars 1. § 98, 51–53. On this point see Stewart, *Works*, vol. ii. p. 473, note A. — ED.

into the substance of body. This theory is, however, liable to all the objections which may be alleged against the first.[1]

I defined Psychology, the science conversant about the *phœnomena* of the *mind*, or *conscious-subject*, or *self*, or *ego*. The former parts of the definition have been explained; the terms *mind*, *conscious-subject*, *self*, and *ego*, come now to be considered. These are all only expressions for the unknown basis of the mental phænomena, viewed, however, in different relations.

Explanation of terms — (continued.)

Of these the word *mind* is the first. In regard to the etymology of this term,[2] it is obscure and doubtful; perhaps, indeed, none of the attempts to trace it to its origin are successful. It seems to hold an analogy with the Latin *mens*, and both are probably derived from the same common root. This root, which is lost in the European languages of Scytho-Indian origin, is probably preserved in the Sanscrit *mena, to know* or *understand*. The Greek νοῦς, *intelligence*, is, in like manner, derived from a verb of precisely the same meaning (νοέω). The word mind is of a more limited signification than the term *soul*. In the Greek philosophy, the term ψυχὴ, *soul*, comprehends, besides the sensitive and rational principle in man, the principle of organic life, both in the animal and vegetable kingdoms; and, in Christian theology, it is likewise used, in contrast to πνεῦμα or *spirit*, in a vaguer and more extensive signification.

Mind.

Since Descartes limited psychology to the domain of consciousness, the term mind has been rigidly employed for the self-knowing principle alone. Mind, therefore, is to be understood as the subject of the various internal phænomena of which we are conscious, or that subject of which consciousness is the general phænomenon. Consciousness is, in fact, to the mind what extension is to matter or body. Though both are phænomena, yet both are essential qualities; for we can neither conceive mind without consciousness, nor body without extension. Mind can be defined only *a posteriori*, — that is, only from its manifestations. What it is in itself, that is, apart from its manifestations, — we, philosophically, know nothing, and, accordingly, what we mean by mind is simply *that which perceives, thinks, feels, wills, desires*, etc. Mind, with us, is thus nearly coextensive with the Rational and Animal souls of Aristotle; for the faculty of voluntary motion, which is a function of

Mind can be defined only a posteriori.

1 *Encyclopædia Britannica*, art. *Metaphysics*, pp. 615, 646, (7th ed.) [Cf. Descartes, *Principia* pars i. § 53, pars ii. § 4. — ED.]

2 On etymology of *mind*, etc. — see Scheidler's *Psychologie*, p. 325.

the animal soul in the Peripatetic doctrine, ought not, as is generally done, to be excluded from the phænomena of consciouness and mind.

The definition of mind from its qualities is given by Aristotle; it forms the second definition in his *Treatise on the Soul*,[1] and after him, it is the one generally adopted by philosophers, and, among others, by Dr. Reid.[2] That Reid, therefore, should have been praised for having thus defined the mind, shows only the ignorance of his encomiasts. He has no peculiar merit in this respect at all.

The next term to be considered is *conscious subject*. And first, what is it to be conscious? Without anticipating the discussion relative to consciousness, as the fundamental function of intelligence, I may, at present, simply indicate to you what an act of consciousness denotes. This act is of the most elementary character; it is the condition of all knowledge; I cannot, therefore, define it to you; but, as you are all familiar with the thing, it is easy to enable you to connect the thing with the word. I know, — I desire, — I feel. What is it that is common to all these? *Knowing* and *desiring* and *feeling* are not the same, and may be distinguished. But they all agree in one fundamental condition. Can I know, without *knowing* that I know? Can I desire, without *knowing* that I desire? Can I feel, without *knowing* that I feel? This is impossible. Now this knowing that I know or desire or feel, — this common condition of self-knowledge, is precisely what is denominated Consciousness.[3]

So much at present for the adjective of *conscious* — now for the substantive, *subject,* — *conscious-subject.* Though consciousness be the condition of all internal phænomena, still it is itself only a phænomenon; and, therefore, supposes a subject in which it inheres; — that is, supposes something that is conscious, — something that manifests itself as conscious. And, since consciousness comprises within its sphere the whole phænomena of mind, the expression *conscious-subject* is a brief, but comprehensive, definition of mind itself.

I have already informed you of the general meaning of the word *subject* in its philosophical application, — viz. the unknown basis

Conscious-Subject.

---

1 *De Anima*, ii. 2. Ἡ ψυχὴ δὲ τοῦτο ᾧ ζῶμεν καὶ αἰσθανόμεθα καὶ διανοούμεθα πρώτως. Cf. Themistius. Εἰ δὲ χρὴ λέγειν τί ἕκαστον τούτων, οἷον τί τὸ νοητικὸν, ἢ τί τὸ αἰσθητικὸν, πρότερον ἐπισκεπτέον, τί τὸ νοεῖν, καὶ τί τὸ αἰσθάνεσθαι· πρότεραι γὰρ καὶ σαφέστεραι πρὸς ἡμᾶς τῶν δυνάμεών εἰσι αἱ ἐνέργειαι· προεντυγχάνομεν γὰρ αὐ-ταῖς, καὶ τὰς δυνάμεις ἀπὸ τούτων ἐπινοοῦμεν. In lib. ii. *De Anima*, p. 76, (Ald. Fol.) — ED.

2 *Intellectual Powers*, Essay i. c. 2; *Works*, p. 229. "By the mind of a man, we understand *that* in him which thinks, remembers, reasons, wills." — ED.

3 Compare *Discussions*, p. 47. — ED.

of phænomenal or manifested existence. It is thus, in its application, common equally to the external and to the internal worlds. But the philosophers of mind have, in a manner, usurped and appropriated this expression to themselves. Accordingly, in their hands, the phrases *conscious or thinking subject*, and *subject* simply, mean precisely the same thing; and custom has prevailed so far, that, in psychological discussions, *the subject* is a term now currently employed, throughout Europe, for the *mind* or *thinking principle*.[1]

The question here occurs, what is the reason of this employment?

Use of the term Subject vindicated.

If mind and subject are only convertible terms, why multiply synonyms? Why exchange a precise and proximate expression for a vague and abstract generality? The question is pertinent, and merits a reply; for unless it can be shown that the word is necessary, its introduction cannot possibly be vindicated. Now, the utility of this expression is founded on two circumstances. The first, that it affords an adjective; the second, that the terms *subject* and *subjective* have opposing relatives in the terms *object* and *objective*, so that the two pairs of words together, enable us to designate the primary and most important analysis and antithesis of philosophy, in a more precise and emphatic manner than can be done by any other technical expressions. This will require some illustration.

Terms Subjective and Objective; their origin and meaning.

Subject, we have seen, is a term for that in which the phænomena revealed to our observation, inhere; — what the schoolmen have designated the *materia in qua*. Limited to the mental phænomena, *subject* therefore, denotes the mind itself; and *subjective*, that which belongs to, or proceeds from, the thinking subject. *Object*, on the other hand, is a term for that about which the knowing subject is conversant, what the schoolmen have styled the *materia circa quam;* while *objective* means that which belongs to, or proceeds from, the object known, and not from the subject knowing; and thus denotes what is real in opposition to what is ideal, — what exists in nature, in contrast to what exists merely in the thought of the individual.

Now, the great problem of philosophy is to analyze the contents of our acts of knowledge, or cognitions, — to distinguish what elements are contributed by the knowing subject, what elements by the object known. There must, therefore, be terms adequate to designate these correlative opposites, and to discriminate the

---

1 See the Author's note, *Reid's Works*, p. 806. — ED.

share which each has in the total act of cognition. But, if we reject the terms *subject* and *subjective,* — *object* and *objective,* there
are no others competent to the purpose.

At this stage of your progress, Gentlemen, it is not easy to
make you aware of the paramount necessity of
such a distinction, and of such terms, — or to
show you how, from the want of words expressive of this primary antithesis, the mental

Errors arising from
want of the terms Sub-
ject and Object.

philosophy of this country has been checked in its development,
and involved in the utmost perplexity and misconception. It is
sufficient to remark at present, that to this defect in the language
of his psychological analysis, is, in a great measure, to be attributed
the confusion, not to say the errors of Reid, in the very cardinal
point of his philosophy, — a confusion so great that the whole
tendency of his doctrine was misconceived by Brown, who, in
adopting a modification of the hypothesis of a representative perception, seems not even to have suspected, that he, and Reid, and
modern philosophers in general, were not in this at one.[1] The
terms *subjective* and *objective* denote the primary distinction in
consciousness of *self* and *not-self,* and this distinction involves the
whole science of mind; for this science is nothing more than a
determination of the subjective and objective, in themselves and
in their mutual relations. The distinction is of paramount importance, and of infinite application, not only in Philosophy proper,
but in Grammar, Rhetoric, Criticism, Ethics, Politics, Jurisprudence,
Theology. I will give you an example, — a philological example.
Suppose a lexicographer had to distinguish the two meanings of
the word *certainty*. Certainty expresses either the firm conviction
which we have of the truth of a thing; or the character of the
proof on which its reality rests. The former is the *subjective* meaning; the latter the *objective*. By what other terms can they be
distinguished and described?

The distinction of subject and object, as marking out the fundamental and most thorough-going antithesis in
philosophy, we owe, among many other important benefits, to the schoolmen, and from the

History of the terms
Subject and Object.

schoolmen the terms passed, both in their substantive and adjective
forms, into the scientific language of modern philosophers. Deprived of these terms, the Critical Philosophy, indeed the whole philosophy of Germany and France, would be a blank. In this country,
though familiarly employed in scientific language, even subsequently

---

[1] See on this question the Author's *Discus-
sions*, p. 45, *et seq.*, and his *Supplementary Dis-* *sertations* to *Reid's Works*, notes B and C.—
ED.

to the time of Locke, the adjective forms seem at length to have dropt out of the English tongue. That these words waxed obsolete, was, perhaps, caused by the ambiguity which had gradually crept into the signification of the substantives. *Object*, besides its proper signification, came to be abusively applied to denote *motive, end, final cause*, (a meaning, by the way, not recognized by Johnson.) This innovation was probably borrowed from the French, in whose language the word had been similarly corrupted, after the commencement of the last century. Subject in English, as *sujet* in French, had not been rightly distinguished from object, taken in its proper meaning, and had thus returned to the original ambiguity of the corresponding term (ὑποκείμενον) in Greek. It is probable that the logical application of the word, (subject of predication), facilitated, or occasioned this confusion. In using the terms, therefore, we think that an explanation, but no apology, is required. The distinction is expressed by no other terms; and if these did not already enjoy a prescriptive right as denizens of the language, it cannot be denied, that, as strictly analogical, they are well entitled to sue out their naturalization. We shall have frequent occasion to recur to this distinction, — and it is eminently worthy of your attention.

The last parallel expressions are the terms *self* and *ego*. These we shall take together, as they are absolutely convertible. As the best preparative for a proper understanding of these terms, I shall translate to you a passage from the *First Alcibiades* of Plato.[1] The interlocutors are Socrates and Alcibiades.

Self, Ego — illustrated from Plato.

" *Socr.* Hold, now, with whom do you at present converse? Is it not with me? — *Alcib.* Yes.

Socr. And I also with you? — *Alcib.* Yes.

Socr. It is Socrates then who speaks? — *Alcib.* Assuredly.

Socr. And Alcibiades who listens? — *Alcib.* Yes.

Socr. Is it not with language that Socrates speaks? — *Alcib.* What now? of course.

Socr. To converse, and to use language, are not these then the same? — *Alcib.* The very same.

Socr. But he who uses a thing, and the thing used, — are these not different? — *Alcib.* What do you mean?

Socr. A currier, — does he not use a cutting knife, and other instruments? — *Alcib.* Yes.

---

[1] P. 129. The genuineness, however, of this Dialogue is questionable. See Ritter, *Hist. of Ancient Philosophy*, vol. ii. p. 164, (English translation); Schleiermacher's *Introduction*, translated by Dobson, p. 328; Brandis, *Gesch. der Gr. Rom. Philosophie*, vol. ii. p. 180. — ED.

Socr. And the man who uses the cutting knife, is he different from the instrument he uses? — *Alcib.* Most certainly.

Socr. In like manner, the lyrist, is he not different from the lyre he plays on? — *Alcib.* Undoubtedly.

Socr. This, then, was what I asked you just now, — does not he who uses a thing seem to you always different from the thing used? — *Alcib.* Very different.

Socr. But the currier, does he cut with his instruments alone, or also with his hands? — *Alcib.* Also with his hands.

Socr. He then uses his hands? — *Alcib.* Yes.

Socr. And in his work he uses also his eyes? — *Alcib.* Yes.

Socr. We are agreed, then, that he who uses a thing, and the thing used, are different? — *Alcib.* We are.

Socr. The currier and lyrist are, therefore, different from the hands and the eyes, with which they work? — *Alcib.* So it seems.

Socr. Now, then, does not a man use his whole body? — *Alcib.* Unquestionably.

Socr. But we are agreed that he who uses, and that which is used, are different? — *Alcib.* Yes.

Socr. A man is, therefore, different from his body? — *Alcib.* So I think.

Socr. What then is the man? — *Alcib.* I cannot say.

Socr. You can at least say that the man is that which uses the body? — *Alcib.* True.

Socr. Now, does anything use the body but the mind? — *Alcib.* Nothing.

Socr. The mind is, therefore, the man? — *Alcib.* The mind alone."

To the same effect, Aristotle asserts that the mind contains the man, not the man the mind.[1] "Thou art the soul," says Hierocles, "but the body is thine."[2] So Cicero — " Mens cujusque is est quisque, non ea figura quæ digito demonstrari potest;"[3] and Macrobius —"Ergo qui videtur, non ipse verus homo est, sed verus ille est, a quo regitur quod videtur."[4]

Arbuthnot.   No one has, however, more beautifully expressed this truth than Arbuthnot.[5]

"What am I, whence produced, and for what end?
Whence drew I being, to what period tend?

[1] That the mind is *the man*, is maintained by Aristotle in several places. Cf. *Eth. Nic.* ix. 8; x. 7; but these do not contain the exact words of the text. — ED.

[2] *In Aurea Pythagoreorum Carmina*, 26: Σὺ γὰρ εἶ ἡ ψυχή· τὸ δὲ σῶμα σόν. — ED.

[3] *Somnium Scipionis*, § 8. — ED.

[4] Macrobius, *In Somnium Scipionis*, lib. ii. c. 12. — ED.

[5] *Know thyself.* See Dodsley's *Collection*, vol. i p. 180. — ED.

Am I th' abandon'd orphan of blind chance,
Dropp'd by wild atoms in disordered dance?
Or, from an endless chain of causes wrought,
And of unthinking substance, born with thought.
Am I but what I seem, mere flesh and blood,
A branching channel with a mazy flood?
The purple stream that through my vessels glides,
Dull and unconscious flows, like common tides,
The pipes, through which the circling juices stray,
Are not that thinking I, no more than they:
This frame, compacted with transcendent skill,
Of moving joints, obedient to my will;
Nursed from the fruitful glebe, like yonder tree,
Waxes and wastes, — I call it mine, not me.
New matter still the mould'ring mass sustains;
The mansion chang'd, the tenant still remains;
And, from the fleeting stream, repair'd by food,
Distinct, as is the swimmer from the flood."

But let us come to a closer determination of the point; let us appeal to our experience. "I turn my attention on my being, and find that I have organs, and that I have thoughts. My body is the complement of my organs; am I then my body, or any part of my body? This I cannot be. The matter of my body, in all its points, is in a perpetual flux, in a perpetual process of renewal. I, — *I* do not pass away, I am not renewed. None probably of the molecules which constituted my organs some years ago, form any part of the material system which I now call mine. It has been made up anew; but I am still what I was of old. These organs may be mutilated; one, two, or any number of them may be removed; but not the less do I continue to be what I was, one and entire. It is even not impossible to conceive me existing, deprived of every organ, — I therefore, who have these organs, or this body, *I* am neither an organ nor a body.

The Self or Ego in relation to bodily organs, and thoughts.

"Neither am I identical with my thoughts, for they are manifold and various. I, on the contrary, am one and the same. Each moment they change and succeed each other; this change and succession takes place in me, but I neither change nor succeed myself in myself. Each moment, I am aware or am conscious of the existence and change of my thoughts: this change is sometimes determined by me, sometimes by something different from me; but I always can distinguish myself from them: I am a permanent being, an enduring subject, of whose existence these thoughts are only so many modes, appearances, or phænomena; — I who possess organs and thoughts am, therefore, neither these organs nor these thoughts.

"I can conceive myself to exist apart from every organ. But if I try to conceive myself existent without a thought, — without some form of consciousness, — I am unable. This or that thought may not be perhaps necessary; but of some thought it is necessary that I should be conscious, otherwise I can no longer conceive myself to be. A suspension of thought is thus a suspension of my intellectual existence; I am, therefore, essentially a thinking, — a conscious being; and my true character is that of an intelligence, — an intelligence served by organs."[1]

But this thought, this consciousness, is possible only in, and through, the consciousness of Self. The Self, the I, is recognized in every act of intelligence, as the subject to which that act belongs. It is I that perceive, I that imagine, I that remember, I that attend, I that compare, I that feel, I that desire, I that will, I that am conscious. The I, indeed, is only manifested in one or other of these special modes; but it is manifested in them all; they are all only the phænomena of the I, and, therefore, the science conversant about the phænomena of mind is, most simply and unambiguously, said to be conversant about the phænomena of the *I* or *Ego*.

This expression, as that which, in many relations, best marks and discriminates the conscious mind, has now become familiar in every country, with the exception of our own. Why it has not been naturalized with us is not unapparent. The French have two words for the Ego or I — *Je* and *Moi*. The former of these is less appropriate as an abstract term, being in sound ambiguous; but *le moi* admirably expresses what the Germans denote, but less felicitously, by their *Das Ich*. In English, *the I* could not be tolerated; because, in sound, it would not be distinguished from the word significant of the organ of sight. We must, therefore, either renounce the term, or resort to the Latin *Ego;* and this is perhaps no disadvantage, for, as the word is only employed in a strictly philosophical relation, it is better that this should be distinctly marked, by its being used in that relation alone. The term *Self* is more allowable; yet still the expressions *Ego* and *Non-Ego* are felt to be less awkward than those of *Self* and *Not-Self*.

So much in explanation of the terms involved in the definition which I gave you of Psychology.

1 Gatien-Arnoult, [*Doct. Phil.*, p. 34-36. — ED.]

LECTURE X.

EXPLICATION OF TERMS.

I NOW proceed, as I proposed, to the consideration of a few other words of frequent occurrence in philosophy, and which it is expedient to explain at once, before entering upon discussions in which they will continually recur. I take them up without order, except in so far as they may be grouped together by their meaning; and the first I shall consider, are the terms *hypothesis* and *theory*.

When a phænomenon is presented to us which can be explained by no cause within the sphere of our experi-

Hypothesis.

ence, we feel dissatisfied and uneasy. A desire arises to escape from this unpleasing state; and the consequence of this desire is an effort of the mind to recall the outstanding phænomenon to unity, by assigning it, *ad interim*, to some cause or class, to which we imagine that it may possibly belong, until we shall be able to refer it, permanently, to that cause, or class, to which we shall have proved it actually to appertain. The judgment by which the phænomenon is thus provisorily referred, is called an *hypothesis,* — a *supposition*.

Hypotheses have thus no other end than to satisfy the desire of the mind to reduce the objects of its knowledge to unity and system; and they do this in recalling them, *ad interim*, to some principle, through which the mind is enabled to comprehend them. From this view of their nature it is manifest how far they are permissible, and how far they are even useful and expedient, — throwing altogether out of account the possibility that what is at first assumed as hypothetical, may subsequently be proved true.

An hypothesis is allowable only under certain conditions. Of

Two conditions of legitimate hypothesis. The first.

these the first is, — that the phænomenon to be explained, should be ascertained actually to exist. It would, for example, be absurd to propose an hypothesis to account for the possibility of apparitions, until it be proved that ghosts do actually appear. This precept, to establish your fact before you attempt to conjecture its cause, may, perhaps, seem to you too elementary to be worth the statement. But a longer experience will convince you of the contrary. That the enunciation of the rule is not only not superfluous, but even highly requisite as an admonition, is shown by great and numerous examples of its violation in the history of science; and, as Cullen has truly observed, there are more false facts current in the world than false hypotheses to explain them. There is, in truth, nothing which men seem to admit so lightly as an asserted fact. Of this I might adduce to you a host of memorable examples. I shall content myself with one small but significant illustration.

Charles II., soon after the incorporation of the Royal Society, which was established under his patronage, sent to request of that learned body an explanation of the following phænomenon. When a live fish is thrown into a basin of water, the basin, water, and fish do not weigh more than the basin and water before the fish is thrown in; whereas, when a dead fish is employed, the weight of the whole is exactly equal to the added weights of the basin, the water, and the fish. Much learned discussion ensued regarding this curious fact, and several elaborate papers, propounding various hypotheses in explanation, were read on the occasion. At length a member, who was better versed in Aristotle than his associates, recollected that the philosopher had laid it down, as a general rule of philosophizing, to consider the *an sit* of a fact, before proceeding to investigate the *cur sit;* and he ventured to insinuate to his colleagues, that, though the authority of the Stagirite was with them, — the disciples of Bacon, — of small account, it might possibly not be altogether inexpedient to follow his advice on the present occasion; seeing that it did not, in fact, seem at variance with common sense, and that none of the hypotheses proposed were admitted to be altogether satisfactory. After much angry discussion, some members asserting the fact to be in itself notorious, and others declaring that to doubt of its reality was an insult to his majesty, and tantamount to a constructive act of treason, the experiment was made, — when lo! to the confusion of the wise men of Gotham, — the name by which the Society was then popularly known, — it was found that the weight was identical, whether a dead or a living fish were used.

This is only a past and petty illustration. It would be easy to adduce extensive hypotheses, very generally accredited, even at the present hour, which are, however, nothing better than assumptions founded on, or explanatory of, phænomena which do not really exist in nature.

The second condition of a permissible hypothesis is, — that the

The second. phænomenon cannot be explained otherwise than by an hypothesis. It would, for example, have been absurd, even before the discoveries of Franklin, to account for the phænomenon of lightning by the hypothesis of supernatural agency. These two conditions, of the reality of the phænomenon, and the necessity of an hypothesis for its explanation, being fulfilled, an hypothesis is allowable.[1]

But the necessity of some hypothesis being conceded, how are

Criteria of the excellence of an hypothesis. we to discriminate between a good and a bad, — a probable and an improbable hypothesis? The comparative excellence of an hypothesis requires, in the first place, that it involve nothing contradictory, either internally or externally, — that is, either between the parts of which it is composed, or between these and any established truths. Thus, the Ptolemaic hypothesis of the heavenly revolutions became worthless, from the moment that it was contradicted by the ascertained phænomena of the planets Venus and Mercury. Thus the Wernerian hypothesis in geology is improbable, inasmuch as it is obliged to maintain that water was originally able to hold in solution substances which it is now incapable of dissolving. The Huttonian hypothesis, on the contrary, is so far preferable, that it assumes no effect to have been produced by any agent, which that agent is not known to be capable of producing. In the second place, an hypothesis is probable in proportion as the phænomenon in question can be by it more completely explained. Thus, the Copernican hypothesis is more probable than the Tychonic and semi-Tychonic, inasmuch as it enables us to explain a greater number of phænomena. In the third place, an hypothesis is probable, in proportion as it is independent of all subsidiary hypotheses. In this respect, again, the Copernican hypothesis is more probable than the Tychonic. For, though both save all the phænomena, the Copernican does this by one principal assumption; whereas the Tychonic is obliged to call in the aid of several subordinate suppositions, to render the principal assumption available. So much for *hypothesis*.

I have dwelt longer on hypothesis than perhaps was necessary; for you must recollect that these terms are, at present, considered only in order to enable you to understand their signification when casually employed. We shall probably, in a subsequent part of the Course, have occasion to treat of them expressly, and with

1 [On the conditions of legitimate hypothesis compare John Christopher Sturm, *Phys-* *ica Electiva*, Diss. Prælim. art. 3, tom. i. p. 28.]

the requisite details. I shall, therefore, be more concise in treating of the cognate expression, — *theory*. This word is employed by English writers, in a very loose and improper sense. It is with them usually convertible with hypothesis, and hypothesis is commonly used as another term for conjecture. Dr. Reid, indeed, expressly does this; he identifies the two words, and explains them as philosophical conjectures, as you may see in his First Essay on the *Intellectual Powers*, (Chapter III.)[1] This is, however, wrong; wrong, in relation to the original employment of the terms by the ancient philosophers; and wrong, in relation to their employment by the philosophers of the modern nations.

The terms *theory* and *theoretical* are properly used in opposition

Theory; Practice.

to the terms *practice* and *practical;* in this sense they were exclusively employed by the ancients; and in this sense they are almost exclusively employed by the continental philosophers. Practice is the exercise of an art, or the application of a science, in life, which application is itself an art, for it is not every one who is able to apply all he knows; there being required, over and above knowledge, a certain dexterity and skill. Theory, on the contrary, is mere knowledge or science. There is a distinction, but no opposition, between theory and practice; each to a certain extent supposes the other. On the one hand, theory is dependent on practice; practice must have preceded theory; for theory being only a generalization of the principles on which practice proceeds, these must originally have been taken out of, or abstracted from, practice. On the other hand, this is true only to a certain extent; for there is no practice without a theory. The man of practice must have always known something, however little, of what he did, of what he intended to do, and of the means by which his intention was to be carried into effect. He was, therefore, not wholly ignorant of the principles of his procedure; he was a limited, he was, in some degree, an unconscious, theorist. As he proceeded, however, in his practice, and reflected on his performance, his theory acquired greater clearness and extension, so that he became at last distinctly conscious of what he did, and could give, to himself and others, an account of his procedure.

> "Per varios usus artem experientia fecit,
> Exemplo monstrante viam." [2]

In this view, theory is, therefore, simply a knowledge of the principles by which practice accomplishes its end.

1 *Works*, p. 235; see also p. 97. — ED.   2 [*Manilius*, i. 62.]

The opposition of Theoretical and Practical philosophy, is some-

Theoretical and Practical Philosophy.

what different; for these do not stand simply related to each other as theory and practice. Practical philosophy involves likewise a theory, —a theory, however, subordinated to the practical application of its principles; while theoretical philosophy has nothing to do with practice, but terminates in mere speculative or contemplative knowledge.[1]

The next group of associated words to which I would call your attention is composed of the terms, —*power, faculty, capacity, disposition, habit, act, operation, energy, function*, etc.

Of these the first is *power*, and the explanation of this, in a manner, involves that of all the others.

Power. Reid's criticism of Locke.

I have, in the first place, to correct an error of Dr. Reid, in relation to this term, in his criticism of Locke's statement of its import. — You will observe that I do not, at present, enter on the question, How do we acquire the notion of power? and I defend the following passage of Locke, only in regard to the meaning and comprehension of the term. "The mind," says Locke, "being every day informed, by the senses, of the alteration of those simple ideas it observes in things without, and taking notice how one comes to an end, and ceases to be, and another begins to exist which was not before; reflecting also on what passes within itself, and observing a constant change of its ideas, sometimes by the impression of outward objects on the senses, and sometimes by the determination of its own choice; and concluding from what it has so constantly observed to have been, that the like changes will, for the future, be made in the same things, by like agents, and by the like ways; considers, in one thing, the possibility of having any of its simple ideas changed, and, in another, the possibility of making that change; and so comes by that idea which we call power. Thus we say, fire has a power to melt gold, — that is, to destroy the consistency of its insensible parts and consequently its hardness, and make it fluid, and gold has a power to be melted: that the sun has a power to blanch wax, and wax a power to be blanched by the sun, whereby the yellowness is destroyed, and whiteness made to exist in its room. In which, and the like cases, the power, we consider, is in reference to the change of perceivable ideas; for we cannot observe any alteration to be made in, or operation upon, anything, but by the observable change of its sensible ideas; nor conceive

---

1 See *ante*, p. 80. — ED.

any alteration to be made, but by conceiving a change of some of its ideas. Power, thus considered, is twofold — viz. as able to make, or able to receive, any change: the one may be called *active*, and the other *passive* power."[1]

I have here only to call your attention to the distinction of power into two kinds, *active* and *passive* — the former meaning, *id quod potest facere*, that which *can effect* or *can do*, — the latter *id quod potest fieri* that which *can be effected* or *can be done*. In both cases the general notion of power is expressed by the verb *potest* or *can*. Now, on this, Dr. Reid makes the following strictures.[2] "On this account by Locke," he says, "of the origin of our idea of power, I would beg leave to make two remarks, with the respect that is most justly due to so great a philosopher and so good a man." We are at present concerned only with the first of these remarks by Dr. Reid, which is as follows, — "Whereas Locke distinguishes power into *active* and *passive*, I conceive passive power is no power at all. He means by it, the possibility of being changed. To call this *power*, seems to be a misapplication of the word. I do not remember to have met with the phrase *passive power* in any other good author. Mr. Locke seems to have been unlucky in inventing it; and it deserves not to be retained in our language. Perhaps he was unwarily led into it, as an opposite to *active power*. But I conceive we call certain powers *active*, to distinguish them from other powers that are called *speculative*. As all mankind distinguish action from speculation, it is very proper to distinguish the powers by which those different operations are performed, into active and speculative. Mr. Locke, indeed, acknowledges that active power is more properly called power: but I see no propriety at all in passive power; it is a powerless power, and a contradiction in terms."

These observations of Dr. Reid are, I am sorry to say, erroneous from first to last. The latter part, in which he attempts to find a reason for Locke being unwarily betrayed into making this distinction, is, supposing the distinction untenable, and Locke its author, wholly inadequate to account for his hallucination: for, surely, the powers by which we speculate are, in their operations, not more passive than those that have sometimes been styled *active*, but which are properly denominated *practical*. But in the censure itself on Locke, Reid is altogether mistaken. In the first place, so far was Locke from being unlucky in inventing the dis-

Active and Passive Power.

---

1 *Essay*, Book ii. ch. 21. § 1. — ED.   2 *Active Powers*, Essay i. ch. 3; *Works*, p. 519. — ED.

tinction, it was invented some two thousand years before. In the second place, to call the *possibility of being changed* a *power*, is no misapplication of the word. In the third place, so far is the phrase *passive power* from not being employed by any good author, — there is hardly a metaphysician previous to Locke, by whom it was not familiarly used. In fact, this was one of the most celebrated distinctions in philosophy. It was first formally enounced by Aristotle,[1] and from him was universally adopted. Active and passive power are in Greek styled δύναμις ποιητική, and δύναμις παθητική; in Latin, *potentia activa*, and *potentia passiva*.[2]

Power, therefore, is a word which we may use both in an active, and in a passive, signification, and, in psychology, we may apply it both to the active faculties, and to the passive capacities, of mind.

This leads to the meaning of the terms *faculties*, and *capacities*.

Faculty.

Faculty (*facultas*) is derived from the obsolete Latin *facul*, the more ancient form of *facilis*, from which again *facilitas* is formed. It is properly limited to active power, and, therefore, is abusively applied to the mere passive affections of mind.

Capacity.

Capacity (*capacitas*) on the other hand, is more properly limited to these. Its primary signification, which is literally *room for*, as well as its employment, favors this; although it cannot be denied, that there are examples of its usage in an active sense. Leibnitz, as far as I know, was the first who limited its psychological application to the passivities of mind. In his famous *Nouveaux Essais sur l' Entendement Humain*, a work written in refutation of Locke's *Essay* on the same subject, he observes: " We may say that power (*puissance*), in general, is the possibility of change. Now the change, or the act of this possibility, being action in one subject and passion in another, there will be two powers (*deux puissances*,) the one *passive*, the other *active*. The active may be called *faculty*, and perhaps the passive might be called *capacity*, or receptivity. It is true that the active power is sometimes taken in a higher sense, when, over and above the simple faculty, there is also a tendency, a *nisus*; and it is thus that I have used it in my dynamical considerations. We

---

1 See *Metaph.* iv. (v.) 12; viii. (ix.) 1. — ED.

2 This distinction is, indeed, established in the Greek language itself. That tongue has, among its other marvellous perfections, two sets of potential adjectives, the one for *active*, the other for *passive* power. Those for active power are denoted by terminations in τικός, those for passive power by terminations in τός. Thus ποιητικόν, that which can make; ποιητόν, that which can be made; κινητικόν, that which can move; κινητόν, that which can be moved; and so πρακτικός and πρακτός, αἰσθητικός and αἰσθητός, νοητικός and νοητός, οἰκοδομητικός and οἰκοδομητός, etc.

might give to it in this meaning the special name of *force*."[1] I may notice that Reid seems to have attributed no other meaning to the term power than that of force.

Power, then, is active and passive; faculty is active power,— capacity is passive power.

The two terms next in order, are *disposition*, in Greek, διάθεσις;

Disposition, Habit.

and *habit*, in Greek, ἕξις. I take these together as they are similar, yet not the same. Both are tendencies to action; but they differ in this, that disposition properly denotes a natural tendency, habit an acquired tendency. Aristotle distinguishes them by another difference. "Habit (ἕξις) is discriminated from disposition (διάθεσις) in this, that the latter is easily movable, the former of longer duration, and more difficult to be moved."[2] I may notice that habit is formed by the frequent repetition of the same action or passion, and that this repetition is called *consuetude*, or *custom*. The latter terms, which properly signify the cause, are not unfrequently abusively employed for habit, their effect.

I may likewise observe that the terms *power, faculty, capacity*, are more appropriately applied to natural, than to acquired, capabilities, and are thus inapplicable to mere habits. I say *mere* habits, for where habit is superinduced upon a natural capability, both terms may be used. Thus we can say both the faculty of abstraction, and the habit of abstraction,—the capacity of suffering, and the habit of suffering; but still the meanings are not identical.

The last series of cognate terms are *act, operation, energy*. They

Act, Operation, Energy.

are all mutually convertible, as all denoting the present exertion or exercise of a power, a faculty, or a habit. I must here explain to you the famous distinction of actual and potential existence; for, by this

Potential and Actual Existence.

distinction, act, operation, energy, are contra-discriminated from power, faculty, capacity, disposition, and habit. This distinction, when divested of certain subordinate subtleties of no great consequence, is manifest and simple. Potential existence means merely that the thing *may be* at some time; actual existence, that it now *is*.[1] Thus, the mathematician, when asleep or playing at cards, does not exercise his skill; his geometrical knowledge is all latent, but he is still a mathematician,— potentially.

---

1 *Nouveaux Essais*, liv. ii. ch. 21. § 1. — ED.
2 *Categ.* ch. 8. — ED.
3 This distinction is well illustrated in the

learned note of Trendelenburg on *Arist. de Anima*, ii. 1. — ED.

> 'Ut quamvis tacit Hermogenes, cantor tamen atque
> Optimus est modulator; — ut Alfenus vafer, omni
> Abjecto instrumento artis, clausaque taberna,
> Sutor erat." [1]

Hermogenes, says Horace, was a singer, even when silent; how? — a singer, not *in actu* but *in posse*. So Alfenus was a cobbler, even when not at work; that is, he was a cobbler *potential*; whereas, when busy in his booth, he was a cobbler *actual*.

In like manner, my sense of sight potentially exists, though my eyelids are closed; but when I open them, it exists actually. Now, *power, faculty, capacity, disposition, habit*, are all different expressions for potential or possible existence; *act, operation, energy*, for actual or present existence. Thus the *power* of imagination expresses the unexerted capability of imagining; the *act* of imagination denotes that power elicited into immediate, — into present existence. The different synonyms for potential existence, are existence ἐν δυνάμει, *in potentia, in posse, in power*; for actual existence, existence ἐν ἐνεργείᾳ, or ἐν ἐντελεχείᾳ, *in actu, in esse, in act, in operation, in energy*. The term *energy* is precisely the Greek term for act of operation; but it has vulgarly obtained the meaning of forcible activity. [2]

The word *functio*, in Latin, simply expresses performance or operation; *functio muneris* is the exertion of an energy of some determinate kind. But with us

Function.

the word *function* has come to be employed in the sense of *munus* alone, and means not the exercise, but the specific character, of a power. Thus the function of a clergyman does not mean with us the performance of his duties, but the peculiarity of those duties themselves. The function of nutrition does not mean the operation of that animal power, but its discriminate character.

So much by way of preliminary explanation of the psychological terms in most general and frequent use. Others, likewise, I shall, in the sequel, have occasion to elucidate; but these may, I think, more appropriately be dealt with as they happen to occur.

---

1 Horace, *Sat.* i. 3, 129. — ED.

2 But there is another relation of potentiality and actuality which I may notice, — Hermogenes, Alfenus, before, and after, acquiring the habits of singer, and cobbler. There is thus a double kind of potentiality and actuality, — for when Hermogenes has obtained the habit and power of singing, though not actually exercising, he is a singer *in actu*, in relation to himself, before he had acquired the accomplishment. This affords the distinction taken by Aristotle of first and second energy, — the first being the habit acquired, the second the immediate exercise of that habit. [Cf. *De Anima*, lib. ii. c. — ED.]

LECTURE XI.

I NOW proceed to the consideration of the important subject,—
the Distribution of the Mental Phænomena into
their primary or most general classes. In regard
to the distribution of the mental phænomena, I
shall not at present attempt to give any history or criticism of the
various classifications which have been proposed by different philosophers. These classifications are so numerous, and so contradictory, that, in the present stage of your knowledge, such a history
would only fatigue the memory, without informing the understanding; for you cannot be expected to be as yet able to comprehend,
at least many of the reasons which may be alleged for, or against,
the different distributions of the human faculties. I shall, therefore,
at once proceed to state the classification of these, which I have
adopted as the best.

Distribution of the mental phænomena.

In taking a comprehensive survey of the mental phænomena,
these are all seen to comprise one essential element, or to be possible only under one necessary
condition. This element or condition is Consciousness, or the knowledge that I,—that the
Ego exists, in some determinate state. In this
knowledge they appear, or are realized as phænomena, and with this
knowledge they likewise disappear, or have no longer a phænomenal
existence; so that consciousness may be compared to an internal
light, by means of which, and which alone, what passes in the mind
is rendered visible. Consciousness is simple,—is not composed of
parts, either similar or dissimilar. It always resembles itself, differing only in the degrees of its intensity; thus, there are not various
kinds of consciousness, although there are various kinds of mental
modes, or states, of which we are conscious. Whatever division,
therefore, of the mental phænomena may be adopted, all its members must be within consciousness itself, which must be viewed as

Consciousness,—the one essential element of the mental phæno-mena.

comprehensive of the whole phænomena to be divided; far less should we reduce it, as a special phænomenon, to a particular class. Let consciousness, therefore, remain one and indivisible, comprehending all the modifications, — all the phænomena, of the thinking subject.

But taking, again, a survey of the mental modifications, or phænomena, of which we are conscious, — these are seen to divide themselves into THREE great classes. In the first place, there are the phænomena of Knowledge; in the second place, there are the phænomena of Feeling, or the phænomena of Pleasure and Pain; and, in the third place, there are the phænomena of Will and Desire.[1]

Three grand classes of mental phænomena.

Let me illustrate this by an example. I see a picture. Now, first of all, — I am conscious of perceiving a certain complement of colors and figures, — I recognize what the object is. This is the phænomenon of Cognition or Knowledge. But this is not the only phænomenon of which I may be here conscious. I may experience certain affections in the contemplation of this object. If the picture be a masterpiece, the gratification will be unalloyed; but if it be an unequal production, I shall be conscious, perhaps, of enjoyment, but of enjoyment alloyed with dissatisfaction. This is the phænomenon of Feeling, — or of Pleasure and Pain. But these two phænomena do not yet exhaust all of which I may be conscious on the occasion. I may desire to see the picture long, — to see it often, — to make it my own, and, perhaps, I may will, resolve, or determine so to do. This is the complex phænomenon of Will and Desire.

The English language, unfortunately, does not afford us terms competent to express and discriminate, with even tolerable clearness and precision, these classes of phænomena. In regard to the first, indeed, we have comparatively little reason to complain, — the synonymous terms, *knowledge* and *cognition*, suffice to distinguish the phænomena of this class from those of the other two. In the second class, the defect of the language becomes more apparent. The word *feeling* is the only term under which we can possibly collect the phænomena of pleasure and pain, and yet this word is ambiguous. For it is not only employed to denote what we are conscious of as agreeable or disagreeable in our mental states, but it is likewise used as a

Their nomenclature.

---

1 Compare Stewart's *Works*, vol. i., Advertisement by Editor. — ED.

synonym for the sense of touch.[1] It is, however, principally in relation to the third class that the deficiency is manifested. In English, unfortunately, we have no term capable of adequately expressing what is common both to will and desire; that is, the *nisus* or *conatus*, — the tendency towards the realization of their end. By will is meant a free and deliberate, by desire a blind and fatal, tendency to act.[2] Now, to express, I say, the tendency to overt action, — the quality in which desire and will are equally contained, — we possess no English term to which an exception of more or less cogency may not be taken. Were we to say the phænomena of *tendency*, the phrase would be vague; and the same is true of the phænomena of *doing*. Again, the term phænomena of *appetency* is objectionable, because, (to say nothing of the unfamiliarity of the expression,) *appetency*, though perhaps etymologically unexceptionable, has both in Latin and English a meaning almost synonymous with desire. Like the Latin *appetentia*, the Greek ὄρεξις is equally ill-balanced, for, though used by philosophers to comprehend both will and desire, it more familiarly suggests the latter, and we need not, therefore, be solicitous, with Mr. Harris and Lord Monboddo, to naturalize in English the term *orectic*.[3] Again, the phrase phænomena of *activity* would be even worse; every possible objection can be made to the term *active powers*, by which the philosophers of this country have designated the *orectic faculties* of the Aristotelians. For you will observe, that all faculties are equally active; and it is not the overt performance, but the tendency towards it, for which we are in quest of an expression. The German is the only language I am acquainted with which is able to supply the term of which philosophy is in want. The expression *Bestrebungs Vermögen*, which is most nearly, though awkwardly and inadequately, translated by *striving faculties*, — faculties of effort or endeavor, — is now generally employed, in the philosophy of Germany, as the genus comprehending desire and will. Perhaps the phrase, phænomena of *exertion*, is, upon the whole, the best expression to denote the manifestations, and *exertive* faculties, the best expression to denote the faculties of will and desire. *Exero*, in Latin, means literally *to put forth*, — and, with us, *exertion* and *exertive* are the only endurable words that I can find which approximate, though distantly, to the strength and precision of the German

1 [Brown uses feeling for consciousness. — *Oral Interp.*]; *e. g. Philosophy of the Human Mind*, Lecture xi. "The mind is susceptible of a variety of feelings, every new feeling being a change of its state." Second edition, vol. i. p. 222. — ED.

2 Cf. Aristotle, *Rhet.* i. 10: Βούλησις, μετὰ λόγου ὄρεξις ἀγαθοῦ, ἄλογοι δ' ὀρέξεις, ὀργὴ καὶ ἐπιθυμία. — ED.

3 See Lord Monboddo's *Ancient Metaphysics*, book ii. chaps. vii. ix. — ED.

expression. I shall, however, occasionally employ likewise the term *appetency*, in the rigorous signification I have mentioned, — as a genus comprehending under it both desires and volitions.[1]

This division of the phænomena of mind into the three great classes of the Cognitive faculties, — the Feelings, or capacities of Pleasure and Pain, — and the Exertive or Conative Powers, — I do not propose as original. It was first promulgated by Kant;[2] and the felicity of the distribution was so apparent, that it has now been long all but universally adopted in Germany by the philosophers of every school; and, what is curious, the only philosopher of any eminence by whom it has been assailed, — indeed, the only philosopher of any reputation by whom it has been, in that country, rejected, is not an opponent of the Kantian philosophy, but one of its most zealous 'champions.[3] To the psychologists of this country, it is apparently wholly unknown. They still adhere to the old scholastic division into powers of the Understanding and powers of the Will; or, as it is otherwise expressed, into Intellectual and Active powers.[4]

By whom this three-fold distribution first made.

By its author, the Kantian classification has received no illustration; and by other German philosophers, it has apparently been viewed as too manifest to require any. Nor do I think it needs much; though a few words in explanation may not be inexpedient. An objection to the arrangement may, perhaps, be taken on the ground that the three classes are not coördinate. It is evident that every mental phænomenon is either an act of knowledge, or only possible through an act of knowledge, for consciousness is a knowledge, — a phænomenon of cognition; and, on this principle, many philosophers, — as Descartes, Leibnitz, Spinoza, Wolf, Platner, and others, — have been led to regard the knowing, or representative faculty, as they called it, — the faculty of cognition, as the fundamental power of mind, from which all others are derivative. To this the

Objection to the classification obviated.

---

1 1848. The term *Conative* (from *Conari*) is employed by Cudworth in his *Treatise on Free Will*, published some years ago from his MSS. in the British Museum. [*A Treatise on Free Will*, by Ralph Cudworth, D. D., edited by John Allen, M. A. London, 1838, p. 31. "Notwithstanding which, the hegemonic of the soul may, by conatives and endeavors, acquire more and more power over them." The terms *Conation* and *Conative* are those finally adopted by the Author, as the most appropriate expressions for the class of phænomena in question. — ED.

2 *Kritik der Urtheilskraft*, Einleitung. The same division is also adopted as the basis of his *Anthropologie*. — ED.

3 This philosopher is Krug, who attacked the Kantian division in his *Grundlage zu einer neuen Theorie der Gefühle und des sogenannten Gefühlsvermögens*, Konigsberg, 1823. See also his *Handwörterbuch der Philosophischen Wissenschaften*, art. *Gefühl* and *Seelenkräfte*. A fuller account of this controversy is given by Sir W. Hamilton in a subsequent Lecture. See Lectures on the Feelings. — ED.

4 See below, Lect. XX. — ED.

answer is easy. These philosophers did not observe that, although pleasure and pain — although desire and volition, are only as they are known to be; yet, in these modifications, a quality, a phænomenon of mind, absolutely new, has been superadded, which was never involved in, and could, therefore, never have been evolved out of, the mere faculty of knowledge. The faculty of knowledge is certainly the first in order, inasmuch as it is the *conditio sine qua non* of the others; and we are able to conceive a being possessed of the power of recognizing existence, and yet wholly void of all feeling of pain and pleasure, and of all powers of desire and volition. On the other hand, we are wholly unable to conceive a being possessed of feeling and desire, and, at the same time, without a knowledge of any object upon which his affections may be employed, and without a consciousness of these affections themselves.

We can farther conceive a being possessed of knowledge and feeling alone — a being endowed with a power of recognizing objects, of enjoying the exercise, and of grieving at the restraint, of his activity, — and yet devoid of that faculty of voluntary agency — of that conation, which is possessed by man. To such a being would belong feelings of pain and pleasure, but neither desire nor will, properly so called. On the other hand, however, we cannot possibly conceive the existence of a voluntary activity independently of all feeling; for voluntary conation is a faculty which can only be determined to energy through a pain or pleasure, — through an estimate of the relative worth of objects.

In distinguishing the cognitions, feelings, and conations, it is not, therefore, to be supposed that these phænomena are possible independently of each other. In our philosophical systems, they may stand separated from each other in books and chapters; — in nature, they are ever interwoven. In every, the simplest, modification of mind, knowledge, feeling, and desire or will, go to constitute the mental state; and it is only by a scientific abstraction that we are able to analyze the state into elements, which are never really existent but in mutual combination. These elements are found, indeed, in very various proportions in different states, — sometimes one preponderates, sometimes another; but there is no state in which they are not all coëxistent.

Let the mental phænomena, therefore, be distributed under the three heads of phænomena of Cognition, or the faculties of Knowledge; phænomena of Feeling, or the capacities of Pleasure and Pain; and phænomena of Desiring or Willing, or the powers of Conation.

The order of these is determined by their relative consecution.

Feeling and appetency suppose knowledge. The cognitive facul-

Order of the mental phænomena. ties, therefore, stand first. But as will, and desire, and aversion, suppose a knowledge of the pleasurable and painful, the feelings will stand second as intermediate between the other two.

Such is the highest or most general classification of the mental phænomena, or of the phænomena of which we

Consciousness, the first object of consideration. are conscious. But as these primary classes are, as we have shown, all included under one universal phænomenon, — the phænomenon of consciousness, — it follows that Consciousness must form the first object of our consideration.

I shall not attempt to give you any preliminary detail of the opinions of philosophers in relation to consciousness. The only effect of this would be to confuse you. It is necessary, in the first place, to obtain correct and definite notions on the subject, and having obtained these, it will be easy for you to understand in what respects the opinions that have been hazarded on the cardinal point of all philosophy, are inadequate or erroneous. I may notice that

No special account of consciousness by Reid or Stewart. Dr. Reid and Mr. Stewart have favored us with no special or articulate account of consciousness. The former, indeed, intended and promised this. In the seventh chapter of the first Essay *On the Intellectual Powers*, which is entitled *Division of the Powers of the Mind*, the concluding paragraph is as follows : —

" I shall not, therefore, attempt a complete enumeration of the powers of the human understanding. I shall only mention those which I propose to explain, and they are the following:

" 1st, The powers we have by means of our External Senses; 2dly, Memory; 3dly, Conception; 4thly, The powers of Resolving and Analyzing complex objects, and compounding those that are more simple; 5thly, Judging; 6thly, Reasoning; 7thly, Taste; 8thly, Moral Perception; and, last of all, Consciousness."[1]

The work, however, contains no essay upon Consciousness; but, in reference to this deficiency, the author, in the last paragraph of the book, states, — " As to Consciousness, what I think necessary to be said upon it has been already said; Essay vi., chap. v,"[2] — the chapter, to wit, entitled *On the First Principles of Contingent Truths*. To that chapter you may, however, add what is spoken of consciousness in the first chapter of the first Essay, entitled, *Explication of Words*, § 7.[3] We are, therefore, left to glean the opinion of both Reid and Stewart on the subject of consciousness, from

1 *Works*, p. 244. — ED.   2 *Ib.* p. 508. — ED.   3 *Ib.* p. 222. — ED.

incidental notices in their writings; but these are fortunately sufficient to supply us with the necessary information in regard to their opinions on this subject.

Nothing has contributed more to spread obscurity over a very transparent matter, than the attempts of philosophers to define consciousness. Consciousness cannot be defined; we may be ourselves fully aware what consciousness is, but we cannot, without confusion, convey to others a definition of what we ourselves clearly apprehend. The reason is plain. Consciousness lies at the root of all knowledge. Consciousness is itself the one highest source of all comprehensibility and illustration, — how, then, can we find aught else by which consciousness may be illustrated or comprehended? To accomplish this, it would be necessary to have a second consciousness, through which we might be conscious of the mode in which the first consciousness was possible. Many philosophers, — and among others Dr. Brown, — have defined consciousness a *feeling.*[1] But how do they define a feeling? They define, and must define it, as something of which we are conscious; for a feeling of which we are not conscious, is no feeling at all. Here, therefore, they are guilty of a logical see-saw, or circle. They define consciousness by feeling, and feeling by consciousness, — that is, they explain the same by the same, and thus leave us in the end no wiser than we were in the beginning. Other philosophers say that consciousness is a knowledge, — and others, again, that it is a belief or conviction of a knowledge. Here, again, we have the same violation of logical law. Is there any knowledge of which we are not conscious? Is there any belief of which we are not conscious? There is not, — there cannot be; therefore, consciousness is not contained under either knowledge or belief, but, on the contrary, knowledge and belief are both contained under consciousness. In short, the notion of consciousness is so elementary, that it cannot possibly be resolved into others more simple. It cannot, therefore, be brought under any genus, — any more general conception; and, consequently, it cannot be defined.

Consciousness cannot be defined.

But though consciousness cannot be logically defined, it may, however, be philosophically analyzed. This analysis is effected by observing and holding fast the phænomena or facts of consciousness, comparing these, and, from this comparison, evolving the universal conditions under which alone an act of consciousness is possible.

Consciousness admits of philosophical analysis.

---

[1] *Philosophy of the Human Mind.* Lecture xi.; vol. i. p. 227-237. Second edition. — Ed.

It is only in following this method that we can attain to precise and accurate knowledge of the contents of consciousness; and it need not afflict us if the result of our investigation be very different from the conclusions that have been previously held. -

But, before proceeding to show you in detail what the act of consciousness comprises, it may be proper, in the first place, to recall to you, in general, what kind of act the word is employed to denote. I know, I feel, I desire, etc. What is it that is necessarily involved in all these? It requires only to be stated to be admitted, that when I know, I must know that I know, — when I feel, I must know that I feel, — when I desire, I must know that I desire. The knowledge, the feeling, the desire, are possible only under the condition of being known, and being known by me. For if I did not know that I knew, I would not know, — if I did not know that I felt, I would not feel, — if I did not know that I desired, I would not desire. Now, this knowledge, which I, the subject, have of these modifications of my being, and through which knowledge alone these modifications are possible, is what we call *consciousness*. The expressions, *I know that I know, — I know that I feel, — I know that I desire,* — are thus translated by, *I am conscious that I know, — I am conscious that I feel, — I am conscious that I desire.* Consciousness is thus, on the one hand, the recognition by the mind or ego of its acts and affections; — in other words, the self-affirmation, that certain modifications are known by me, and that these modifications are mine. But, on the other hand, consciousness is not to be viewed as anything different from these modifications themselves, but is, in fact, the general condition of their existence, or of their existence within the sphere of intelligence. Though the simplest act of mind, consciousness thus expresses a relation subsisting between two terms. These terms are, on the one hand, an I or Self, as the subject of a certain modification, — and, on the other, some modification, state, quality, affection, or operation belonging to the subject. Consciousness, thus, in its simplicity, necessarily involves three things, — 1°, A recognizing or knowing subject; 2°, A recognized or known modification; and, 3°, A recognition or knowledge by the subject of the modification.

From this it is apparent, that consciousness and knowledge each involve the other. An act of knowledge may be expressed by the formula, *I know;* an act of consciousness by the formula, *I know that I know:* but as it is impossible for us to know without at the same time knowing that we know; so it is impossible to know that we know without our actually knowing. The one merely explicitly expresses what the other implicitly contains. Consciousness and knowledge are thus not opposed as really different. Why, then, it may be asked, employ two terms to express notions, which, as they severally infer each other, are really identical? To this the answer is easy. Realities may be in themselves insepara-

Nature of scientific analysis.

ble, while, as objects of our knowledge, it may be necessary to consider them apart. Notions, likewise, may severally imply each other, and be inseparable even in thought; yet, for the purposes of science, it may be requisite to distinguish them by different terms, and to consider them in their relations or correlations to each other. Take a geo-

Illustrated by a geometrical example.

metrical example, — a triangle. This is a whole composed of certain parts. Here the whole cannot be conceived as separate from its parts, and the parts cannot be conceived as separate from their whole. Yet it is scientifically necessary to have different names for each, and it is necessary now to consider the whole in relation to the parts, and now the parts in correlation to the whole. Again, the constituent parts of a triangle are sides and angles. Here the sides suppose the angles, — the angles suppose the sides, — and, in fact, the sides and angles are in themselves — in reality, one and indivisible. But they are not the same to us, — to our knowledge. For though we cannot abstract in thought, the sides from the angle, the angle from the sides, we may make one or other the principal object of attention. We may either consider the angles in relation to each other, and to the sides; or the sides in relation to each other, and to the angles. And to express all this, it is necessary to distinguish, in thought and in expression, what, in nature, is 'one and indivisible.

As it is in geometry, so it is in the philosophy of mind. We

By the distinction of consciousness and knowledge.

require different words, not only to express objects and relations different in themselves, but to express the same objects and relations under the different points of view in which they are placed by the mind, when scientifically considering them. Thus, in the present instance, consciousness and knowledge are not distinguished by different words as different things, but only as the same thing considered in different aspects. The verbal distinction is taken for the sake of brevity and precision, and its convenience warrants its establishment. Knowledge is a relation, and every relation supposes two terms. Thus, in the relation in question, there is, on the one hand, a subject of knowledge, — that is, the knowing mind, — and on the other, there is an object of knowledge, — that is, the thing known; and the knowledge itself is the relation between these two terms. Now, though each term of a relation necessarily supposes the other, nevertheless one of these terms may be to us the more interesting, and we may consider that term as the principal, and view the other only as subordinate and correlative. Now, this is the case in the present instance. In an act of knowledge, my attention may be principally attracted either to the object known, or to myself as the subject knowing; and, in the latter case, although no new element be added to the act, the condition involved in it, — *I know that I know,* — becomes the primary and prominent matter of consideration. And when, as in the philosophy of mind, the act of knowledge comes to be specially considered in relation to the knowing subject, it is, at last, in the progress of the science, found convenient, if not absolutely necessary, to possess a scientific word in which this point of view should be permanently and distinctively embodied. But, as the want of a technical and appropriate expression could be experienced only after psychological abstraction had acquired a certain stability and importance, it is evident that the appropriation of such an expression could not, in any language, be of very early date. And this is shown by the history of the synonymous terms for *consciousness* in the different languages, — a history which, though curious, you will find noticed in no publication whatever. The employment of the word *conscientia,* of which our term consciousness is a translation, is, in its psychological signification, not older than the philosophy of Descartes. Previously to him, this word was used almost exclusively in the ethical sense, expressed by our term *conscience,* and in the striking and apparently appropriate dictum of St. Augustin, —

History of the term consciousness.

"certissima scientia et clamante conscientia"[1] — which you may find so frequently paraded by the continental philosophers, when illustrating the certainty of consciousness; in that quotation, the term is, by its author, applied only in its moral or religious signification. Besides the moral application, the words *conscire* and *conscientia* were frequently employed to denote participation in a common knowledge. Thus the members of a conspiracy were said *conscire,* — and *conscius* is even used for conspirator; and, metaphorically, this com-

Its use by St. Augustin.

1 *De Trinitate,* xiii. 1. — ED.

munity of knowledge is attributed to inanimate objects, — as, wailing to the rocks, a lover says of himself, —

"Et conscia saxa fatigo." [1]

I would not, however, be supposed to deny that these words were sometimes used, in ancient Latinity, in the modern sense of consciousness, or being conscious. An unexceptionable example is afforded by Quintilian in his *Institutiones*, lib. xii., cap. xi.; [2] and more than one similar instance may be drawn from Tertullian, [3] and other of the Latin Fathers.

Until Descartes, therefore, the Latin terms *conscire* and *conscientia* were very rarely usurped in their present psychological meaning, — a meaning which, it is needless to add, was not expressed by any term in the vulgar languages; for, besides Tertullian, I am aware of only one or two obscure instances in which, as translations of the Greek terms συναισθάνομαι and συναίσθησις, of which we are about to speak, the terms *conscio* and *conscientia*, were, as the nearest equivalents, contorted from their established signification to the sense in which they were afterwards employed by Descartes. Thus, in the philosophy of the West, we may safely affirm that, prior to Descartes, there was no psychological term in recognized use for what, since his time, is expressed in philosophical Latinity by *conscientia*, in French by *conscience*, in English by *consciousness*, in Italian by *conscienza*, and in German by *Bewusstseyn*. It will be observed that in Latin, French, and Italian (and I might add the Spanish and other Romanic languages), the terms are analogous; the moral and psychological meaning being denoted by the same word.

First used by Descartes in present psychological meaning.

In Greek there was no term for consciousness until the decline of philosophy, and in the later ages of the language. Plato and Aristotle, to say nothing of other philosophers, had no special term to express the knowledge which the mind affords of the operations of its faculties, though this, of

No term for consciousness in Greek until the decline of philosophy.

---

[1] Compare Virgil, *Æneid*, ix. 429: "Cœlum hoc et conscia sidera testor."

[2] "Conscius sum mihi, quantum mediocritate valui, quæque antea scierim quæque operis hujusce gratia potuerim inquirere, candide me atque simpliciter in notitiam eorum, si qui forte cognoscere voluissent, protulisse." This sense, however, is not unusual. Cf. *Cic.*

Tusc. ii. 4: "Mihi sum conscius, nunquam me nimis cupidum fuisse vitæ." — ED.

[3 *De Testimonio Animæ*, c. 5: "Sed qui ejusmodi eruptiones animæ non putavit doctrinam esse naturæ et congenitæ et ingenitæ conscientiæ tacita commssa." *De Carne Christi*, c. 8 "Sed satis erat illi, inquis, conscientia sua." Cf. Augustin, *De Trinitate*, x. c. 7: "Et quia sibi bene conscia est principatus sui quo corpus regit."]

course, was necessarily a frequent matter of their consideration. Intellect was supposed by them to be cognizant of its own operations; it was only doubted whether by a direct or by a reflex act. In regard to sense, the matter was more perplexed; and, on this point, both philosophers seem to vacillate in their opinions. In his *Theœtetus*,[1] Plato accords to sense the power of perceiving that it perceives; whereas, in his *Charmides*,[2] this power he denies to sense, and attributes to intelligence, (νοῦς.) In like manner, an apparently different doctrine may be found in different works of Aristotle. In his *Treatise on the Soul* he thus cogently argues: "When we perceive that we see, hear, etc., it is necessary that by sight itself we perceive that we see, or by another sense. If by another sense, then this also must be a sense of sight, conversant equally about the object of sight, color. Consequently there must either be two senses of the same object, or every sense must be percipient of itself. Moreover, if the sense percipient of sight be different from sight itself, it follows either that there is a regress to infinity, or we must admit at last some sense percipient of itself; but if so, it is more reasonable to admit this in the original sense at once."[3] Here a consciousness is apparently attributed to each several sense. This, however, is expressly denied in his work "*On Sleep and Waking*,"[4] to say nothing of his *Problems*, which, I am inclined, however, to think, are not genuine. It is there stated that sight does not see that it sees, neither can sight or taste judge that sweet is a quality different from white; but that this is the function of some common faculty, in which they both converge. The apparent repugnance may, however, easily be reconciled. But, what concerns us at present, in all these discussions by the two philosophers, there is no single term employed to denote that special aspect of the phænomenon of knowledge, which is thus by them made a matter of consideration. · It is only under the later Platonists and Aristotelians that peculiar terms, tantamount to our consciousness, were adopted into the language of philosophy. In the text of Diogenes Laertius, indeed, (vii. 85,) I find

---

1 " Accedit testimonium Platonis in Theæteto, ubi ait sensum sentire quod sentit et quod non sentit." — *Conimbricenses in Arist. de Anim.* ii. 2. The passage referred to is probably *Theæt.*, p. 192: Ἀδύνατον . . . ὃ αἰσθάνεταί γε, ἕτερόν τι ὧν αἰσθάνεται, οἰηθῆναι εἶναι, καὶ ὃ αἰσθάνεται, ὧν τι μὴ αἰσθάνεται. This passage, however, is not exactly in point. — ED.

2 P. 167, *et seq.* Cf. Conimbricenses, l. c.

Plato, however, merely denies that there can be a sense which perceives the act of sensation without perceiving its object. — ED.

3 *De Anima*, iii. 2. — ED.

4 *De Somno*, c. 2. § 4. The passage in the *Problems*, which may perhaps have the same meaning, though it admits of a different interpretation, is sect. xi. § 33: Χωρισθεῖσα δὲ αἴσθησις διανοίας καθάπερ ἀναίσθητον πόνον ἔχει. See further, *Discussions*, p. 51. — ED.

συνείδησις manifestly employed in the sense of *consciousness*. This, however, is a corrupt reading; and the authority of the best man-

Terms tantamount to
consciousness adopted
by the later Platonists
and Aristotelians.

uscripts and of the best critics shows that σύνδε-σις is the true lection.[1] The Greek Platonists and Aristotelians, in general, did not allow that the recognition that we know, that we feel, that we desire, etc., was the act of any special faculty, but the general attribute of intellect; and the power of reflecting, of turning back upon itself, was justly viewed as the distinctive quality of intelligence. It was, however, necessary to possess some single term expressive of this intellectual retortion, — of this ἐπιστροφὴ πρὸς ἑαυτόν, and the term συναίσθησις was adopted. This I find employed particularly by Proclus, Plotinus and Simplicius.[2] The term συνείδησις, the one equivalent to the *conscientia* of the Latins, remained like *conscientia* itself, long exclusively applied to denote conscience or the moral faculty; and it is only in Greek writers who, as Eugenius of Bulgaria, have flourished since the time of Descartes and Leibnitz, that συνείδησις has, like the *conscientia* of the Latins, been employed in the psychological meaning of consciousness.[3] I may notice that the word συνεπίγνωσις, in the sense of consciousness, is also to be occasionally met with in the later authors on philosophy in the Greek tongue. The expression συναίσθησις, which properly denotes the self-recognition of sense and feeling, was, however, extended to mark consciousness in general. Some of the Aristotelians, how-

Certain of the Aris-
totelians attributed
the recognition of
sense and feeling to a
special faculty.

ever, like certain philosophers in this country, attributed this recognition to a special faculty. Of these I have been able to discover only three: Philoponus, in his commentary on Aristotle's treatise *Of the Soul;*[4] Michael Ephesius, in his commentary on Aristotle's treatise of *Memory and Remin-*

---

1 The correction σύνδεσις is made by Menage on the authority of Suidas, *v.* ὁρμή. Kuster, on the other hand, proposes, on the authority of Laertius, to read συνείδησις for σύνδεσις in Suidas. — ED.

2 [Plotinus, *Enn.* v. lib. iii. c. 2. Proclus, *Inst. Theol.* c. 39. Simplicius, *In Epict. Enchir.* p. 28, Heins. — (p. 49, Schweigh.)] In the two first of these passages, συναίσθησις appears to be used merely in its etymological sense of perception of an object in conjunction with other objects. In the last, however, it seems to be fully equivalent to the modern *consciousness;* as also in Hierocles, *In Aurea*

Pyth. Carm. 41, p. 213, ed. 1654. Sextus Empiricus, *Adv. Math.* ix. 68 (p. 407, Bekker). Michael Ephesius, *In Arist. de Memoria*, p. 134. Plutarch, *De Profectibus in Virtute*, c. 1, 3. Plotinus, *Enn.* iii. lib. 4, b. 4. Simplicius, *In Arist. Categ.* p. 83, *b.* ed. 1551. — ED.

3 See the *Logic* of Eugenius, p. 113. He also uses συνεπίγνωσις in the same sense. The title of his work is, Ἡ λογικὴ ἐκ παλαιῶντε καὶ νεωτέρων συνερανισθεῖσα· ὑπὸ Εὐγενίου διακόνου τοῦ Βουλγαρέως· ἐν Λε-ψίᾳ τῆς Σαξονίας. Ἔτει αψξς. (1766.) — ED.

4 On lib. iii. c. 2. He mentions this as the opinion of the more recent interpreters. — ED.

iscence;[1] and Michael Psellus, in his work on *Various Knowledge.*[2] It is doubted, however, whether the two last be not the same person; and their remarkable coincidence in the point under consideration, is even a strong argument for their identity. They assign this recognition to a faculty which they call τὸ προσεκτικόν, — that is τὸ προσεκτικὸν μέρος, the attentive part or function of mind. This is the first indication in the history of philosophy of that false analysis which has raised attention into a separate faculty. I beg you, however, to observe, that Philoponus and his follower, Michael Ephesius, do not distinguish attention from consciousness. This is a point we are hereafter specially to consider, when perhaps it may be found that, though wrong in making consciousness or attention a peculiar faculty, they were right, at least, in not dividing consciousness and attention into different faculties.

But to return from our historical digression. We may lay it down as the most general characteristic of consciousness, that it is the recognition by the thinking subject of its own acts or affections.

The most general characteristic of consciousness.

The special conditions of consciousness.

So far there is no difficulty and no dispute. In this all philosophers are agreed. The more arduous task remains of determining the special conditions of consciousness. Of these, likewise, some are almost too palpable to admit of controversy. Before proceeding to those in regard to which there is any doubt or difficulty, it will be proper, in the first place, to state and dispose of such determinations as are too palpable to be called in question. Of these admitted limitations, the first is, that consciousness is an actual and not a potential knowledge.[3] Thus a man is said to know, — *i. e.* is able to know, that 7 + 9 are = 16, though that equation be not, at the moment, the object of his thought; but we cannot say that he is conscious of this truth unless while actually present to his mind.

1. Those generally admitted.

Consciousness implies, 1, actual knowledge.

The second limitation is, that consciousness is an immediate, not a mediate knowledge. We are said, for example, to know a past occurrence when we represent it to the mind in an act of memory. We know the mental representation, and this we do immediately and

2. Immediate knowledge.

1 Rather in the Commentary on the *Nicomachean Ethics,* usually attributed to Eustratius, p. 160, *b.* It is not mentioned in the Commentary on the *De Memoria.* — ED.

2 [Psellus, *De Omnifaria Doctrina,* § 46:]

Προσοχὴ δὲ ἐστὶ καθ᾽ ἣν προσέχομεν τοῖς ἔργοις οἷς πράττομεν καὶ τοῖς λόγοις οἷς λέγομεν. — ED.

3 Compare Reid's *Coll. Works,* p. 810. — ED.

in itself, and are also said to know the past occurrence, as mediately knowing it through the mental modification which represents it. Now, we are conscious of the representation as immediately known, but we cannot be said to be conscious of the thing represented, which, if known, is only known through its representation. If, therefore, mediate knowledge be in propriety a knowledge, consciousness is not coëxtensive with knowledge. This is, however, a problem we are hereafter specially to consider. I may here also observe, that, while all philosophers agree in making consciousness an immediate knowledge, some, as Reid and Stewart, do not admit that all immediate knowledge is consciousness. They hold that we have an immediate knowledge of external objects, but they hold that these objects are beyond the sphere of consciousness.[1] This is an opinion we are, likewise, soon to canvass.

The third condition of consciousness, which may be held as universally admitted, is, that it supposes a contrast,

3. Contrast. Discrimination of one object from another.

—a discrimination; for we can be conscious only inasmuch as we are conscious of something; and we are conscious of something only inasmuch as we are conscious of what that something is, — that is, distinguish it from what it is not. This discrimination is of different kinds and degrees.

In the first place, there is the contrast between the two grand opposites, self and not-self, — ego and non-ego,

This discrimination of various kinds and degrees.

— mind and matter; (the contrast of subject and object is more general.) We are conscious of self only in and by its contradistinction from not-self; and are conscious of not-self only in and by its contradistinction from self. In the second place, there is the discrimination of the states or modifications of the internal subject or self from each other. We are conscious of one mental state only as we contradistinguish it from another; where two, three, or more such states are confounded, we are conscious of them as one; and were we to note no difference in our mental modifications, we might be said to be absolutely unconscious. Hobbes has truly said, "Idem semper sentire, et non sentire, ad idem recidunt."[2] In the third place, there is the distinction between the parts and qualities of the outer world. We are conscious of an external object only as we are conscious of it as distinct from others, — where several

1 See Reid, *Intellectual Powers*, Essay vi. ch. 5, § 1, 5. *Works*, pp. 442, 445. Stewart, *Outlines of Moral Philosophy*, part i. § 1, 2; *Collected Works*, vol. ii. p. 12. — ED.

2 *Elementa Philosophiæ*, part iv. c. 25, § 5. *Opera*, ed. Molesworth, vol. i. p. 321. *English Works*, vol. i. p. 394. — ED.

distinguishable objects are confounded, we are conscious of them as one; where no object is discriminated, we are not conscious of any. Before leaving this condition, I may parenthetically state, that, while all philosophers admit that consciousness involves a discrimination, many do not allow it any cognizance of aught beyond the sphere of self. The great majority of philosophers do this because they absolutely deny the possibility of an immediate knowledge of external things, and, consequently, hold that consciousness in distinguishing the non-ego from the ego, only distinguishes self from self; for they maintain, that what we are conscious of as something different from the perceiving mind, is only, in reality, a modification of that mind, which we are condemned to mistake for the material reality. Some philosophers, however, (as Reid and Stewart,) who hold, with mankind at large, that we do possess an immediate knowledge of something different from the knowing self, still limit consciousness to a cognizance of self; and, consequently, not only deprive it of the power of distinguishing external objects from each other, but even of the power of discriminating the ego and non-ego. These opinions we are afterwards to consider. With this qualification, all philosophers may be viewed as admitting that discrimination is an essential condition of consciousness.

The fourth condition of consciousness, which may be assumed as very generally acknowledged, is, that it involves judgment. A judgment is the mental act by which one thing is affirmed or denied of another. This fourth condition is in truth only a necessary consequence of the third, — for it is impossible to discriminate without judging, — discrimination, or contradistinction, being in fact only the denying one thing of another. It may to some seem strange that consciousness, the simple and primary act of intelligence, should be a judgment, — which philosophers, in general, have viewed as a compound and derivative operation. This is, however, altogether a mistake. A judgment is, as I shall hereafter show you, a simple act of mind, for every act of mind implies a judgment. Do we perceive or imagine without affirming, in the act, the external or internal existence of the object?[1] Now these fundamental affirmations are the affirmations, — in other words, the judgments, of consciousness.

4. Judgment.

The fifth undeniable condition of consciousness is memory. This condition also is a corollary of the third. For without memory our mental states could not be held fast, compared, distinguished from each other, and referred to

5. Memory.

—————
1 See Reid's *Works*, pp. 243, 414, with the Editor's Notes. — ED.

self. Without memory, each indivisible, each infinitesimal, moment in the mental succession, would stand isolated from every other, — would constitute, in fact, a separate existence. The notion of the ego or self, arises from the recognized permanence and identity of the thinking subject in contrast to the recognized succession and variety of its modifications. But this recognition is possible only through memory. The notion of self is, therefore, the result of memory. But the notion of self is involved in consciousness, so consequently is memory.

LECTURE XII.

CONSCIOUSNESS,—ITS SPECIAL CONDITIONS: RELATION TO COGNITIVE FACULTIES IN GENERAL.

So far as we have proceeded, our determination of the contents of consciousness may be viewed as that universally admitted; for

Recapitulation.

though I could quote to you certain counter-doctrines, these are not of such importance as to warrant me in perplexing the discussion by their refutation, which would indeed be nothing more than the exposition of very palpable mistakes. Let us, therefore, sum up the points we have established. We have shown, in general, that consciousness is the self-recognition that we know, or feel, or desire, etc. We have shown, in particular, 1°, That consciousness is an actual or living, and not a potential or dormant, knowledge;—2°, That it is an immediate and not a mediate knowledge;—3°, That it supposes a discrimination;—4°, That it involves a judgment;—and, 5°, That it is possible only through memory.

We are now about to enter on a more disputed territory; and the first thesis I shall attempt to establish, in-

II. Special conditions of consciousness not generally admitted.

volves several subordinate questions.

I state, then, as the first contested position which I am to maintain, that our consciousness is coëxtensive with our knowledge. But this assertion, that we have no knowledge of which we are not conscious, is tantamount to the other that consciousness is coëxtensive with our cognitive faculties,—and this

1. Our consciousness coëxtensive with our knowledge.

again is convertible with the assertion, that consciousness is not a special faculty, but that our special faculties of knowledge are only modifications of consciousness. The question, therefore, may be thus stated,—Is consciousness the genus under which our several faculties of knowledge are contained as species,—or, is consciousness itself a special faculty coördinate with, and not comprehending, these?

Before proceeding to canvass the reasonings of those who have

Error of Dr. Brown.
reduced consciousness from the general condition, to a particular variety, of knowledge, I may notice the error of Dr. Brown, in asserting that, "in the systems of philosophy which have been most generally prevalent, especially in this part of the island, consciousness has always been classed as one of the intellectual powers of the mind, differing from its other powers, as these mutually differ from each other."[1] This statement, in so far as it regards the opinion of philosophers in general, is not only not true, but the very reverse of truth. For, in place of consciousness being, "in the systems most generally prevalent," classed as a special faculty, it has, in all the greater schools of philosophy, been viewed as the universal attribute of the intellectual acts. Was consciousness degraded to a special faculty in the Platonic, in the Aristotelian, in the Cartesian, in the Lockian, in the Leibnitzian, in the Kantian philosophies? These are the systems which have obtained a more general authority than any others, and yet in none of these is the supremacy of consciousness denied; in all of them it is either expressly or implicitly recognized. Dr. Brown's assertion is so far true in relation to this country, that by Hutcheson, Reid, and Stewart, — to say nothing of inferior names, — consciousness has been considered as nothing higher than a special faculty. As I regard this opinion to be erroneous, and as the error is one affecting the very cardinal point of philosophy, — as it stands opposed to the peculiar and most important principles of the philosophy of Reid and Stewart themselves, and has even contributed to throw around their doctrine of perception an obscurity that has caused Dr. Brown absolutely to mistake it for its converse, and as I have never met with any competent refutation of the grounds on which it rests, — I shall endeavor to show you that, notwithstanding the high authority of its supporters, this opinion is altogether untenable.

As I previously stated to you, neither Dr. Reid nor Mr. Stewart

Reid and Stewart on consciousness.
has given us any regular account of consciousness; their doctrine on this subject is to be found scattered in different parts of their works. The two following brief passages of Reid contain the principal positions of that doctrine. The first is from the first chapter of the first Essay *On the Intellectual Powers :*[2] " Consciousness is a word used by philosophers to signify that immediate knowledge which we have of our present thoughts and purposes, and, in general, of all

the present operations of our minds. Whence we may observe that consciousness is only of things present. To apply consciousness to things past, which sometimes is done in popular discourse, is to confound consciousness with memory; and all such confusion of words ought to be avoided in philosophical discourse. It is likewise to be observed, that consciousness is only of things in the mind, and not of external things. It is improper to say, I am conscious of the table which is before me. I perceive it, I see it; but do not say I am conscious of it. As that consciousness by which we have a knowledge of the operations of our own minds, is a different power from that by which we perceive external objects, and as these different powers have different names in our language, and, I believe, in all languages, a philosopher ought carefully to preserve this distinction, and never to confound things so different in their nature." The second is from the fifth chapter of the sixth Essay *On the Intellectual Powers.*[1] "Consciousness is an operation of the understanding of its own kind, and cannot be logically defined. The objects of it are our present pains, our pleasures, our hopes, our fears, our desires, our doubts, our thoughts of every kind; in a word, all the passions and all the actions and operations of our own minds, while they are present. We may remember them when they are past; but we are conscious of them only while they are present." Besides what is thus said in general of consciousness, in his treatment of the different special faculties, Reid contrasts consciousness with each. Thus in his essays on Perception, on Conception or Imagination, and on Memory, he specially contradistinguishes consciousness from each of these operations;[2] and it is also incidentally by Reid,[3] but more articulately by Stewart,[4] discriminated from Attention and Reflection.

According to the doctrine of these philosophers, consciousness is thus a special faculty, coördinate with the other intellectual powers, having like them a particular operation and a peculiar object. And what is the peculiar object which is proposed to consciousness?[5] The peculiar objects of consciousness, says Dr. Reid, are all the present passions and operations of our minds. Consciousness thus has for its objects, among the other modifica-

Consciousness a special faculty, according to Reid and Stewart.

---

1 *Works*, p. 442.

2 See *Intellectual Powers*, Essay ii. *Works*, p. 297, and Essay i. *Works*, p. 222; Essay iii. *Works*, pp. 340, 351; Essay iv. *Works*, p. 368. — ED.

3 See *Works*, p 239. Compare pp. 240, 258, 347, 419-20, 443. — ED.

4 *Coll. Works*, vol. ii. p. 134, and pp. 122, 123. — ED.

5 See the same argument in the Author's *Discussions*, p. 47. — ED.

tions of the mind, the acts of our cognitive faculties. Now here a doubt arises. If consciousness has for its object the cognitive operations, it must know these operations, and, as it knows these operations, it must know their objects: consequently, consciousness is either not a special faculty, but a faculty comprehending every cognitive act; or it must be held that there is a double knowledge of every object, — first, the knowledge of that object by its particular faculty, and second, a knowledge of it by consciousness as taking cognizance of every mental operation. But the former of these alternatives is a surrender of consciousness as a coördinate and special faculty, and the latter is a supposition not only unphilosophical but absurd. Now, you will attend to the mode in which Reid escapes, or endeavors to escape, from this dilemma. This he does by assigning to consciousness, as its object, the various intellectual operations to the exclusion of their several objects. "I am conscious," he says, "of perception, but not of the object I perceive; I am conscious of memory, but not of the object I remember." By this limitation, if tenable, he certainly escapes the dilemma, for he would thus disprove the truth of the principle on which it proceeds — viz., that to be conscious of the operation of a faculty, is, in fact, to be conscious of the object of that operation.

Reid's limitation of the sphere of consciousness untenable.

The whole question, therefore, turns upon the proof or disproof of this principle, — for if it can be shown that the knowledge of an operation necessarily involves the knowledge of its object, it follows that it is impossible to make consciousness conversant about the intellectual operations to the exclusion of their objects. And that this principle must be admitted, is what, I hope, it will require but little argument to demonstrate.

No consciousness of a cognitive act, without a consciousness of its object.

Some things can be conceived by the mind each separate and alone; others only in connection with something else. The former are said to be things absolute; the latter, to be things relative. Socrates, and Xanthippe, may be given as examples of the former; husband and wife, of the latter. Socrates, and Xanthippe, can each be represented to the mind without the other; and if they are associated in thought, it is only by an accidental connection. Husband and wife, on the contrary, cannot be conceived apart. As relative and correlative, the conception of husband involves the conception of wife, and the conception of wife involves the conception of husband. Each is thought only in and through the other, and it is impossible to think of Socrates as the husband of Xanthippe, without thinking of Xanthippe as the wife of Socrates. We cannot, therefore, know what a husband is without also knowing what is a wife, as, on the other hand, we cannot know what a wife is without also knowing what is a husband. You will, therefore, understand from this example the meaning of the logical axiom, that the knowledge of relatives is one, — or that the knowledge of relatives is the same.

This being premised, it is evident that if our intellectual operations exist only in relation, it must be impossible that consciousness can take cognizance of one term of this relation without also taking cognizance of the other. Knowledge, in general, is a relation between a subject knowing and an object known, and each operation of our cognitive faculties only exists by relation to a particular object, — this object at once calling it into existence, and specifying the quality of its existence. It is, therefore, palpably impossible that we can be conscious of an act without being conscious of the object to which that act is relative. This, however, is what Dr. Reid and Mr. Stewart maintain. They maintain that I can know that I know, without knowing what I know, — or that I can know the knowledge without knowing what the knowledge is about; for example, that I am conscious of perceiving a book without being conscious of the book perceived, — that I am conscious of remembering its contents without being conscious of these contents remembered, — and so forth. The unsoundness of this opinion must, however, be articulately

Shown in detail with respect to the different cognitive faculties.

shown by taking the different faculties in detail, which they have contradistinguished from consciousness, and by showing, in regard to each, that it is altogether impossible to propose the operation of that faculty to the consideration of consciousness, and to withhold from consciousness its object.

I shall commence with the faculty of Imagination, to which Dr. Reid and Mr. Stewart have chosen, under various limitations, to give the name of Conception.[1] This faculty is peculiarly suited to evince the error of holding that consciousness is cognizant of acts, but not of the objects of these acts.

Imagination.

"Conceiving, Imagining, and Apprehending," says Dr. Reid, "are commonly used as synonymous in our language, and signify the same thing which the logicians call Simple Apprehension. This is an operation of the mind different from all those we have men-

---

1 Reid, *Intellectual Powers*, Essay iv. ch. 1 ; *Works*, p. 360, Stewart, *Elements*, vol. i. ch. 3; *Works*, vol. ii. p. 145. — ED.

tioned [Perception, Memory, etc.] Whatever we perceive, whatever we remember, whatever we are conscious of, we have a full persuasion or conviction of its existence. What never had an existence cannot be remembered; what has no existence at present cannot be the object of perception or of consciousness; but what never had, nor has any existence, may be conceived. Every man knows that it is as easy to conceive a winged horse or a centaur, as it is to conceive a horse or a man. Let it be observed, therefore, that to conceive, to imagine, to apprehend, when taken in the proper sense, signify an act of the mind which implies no belief or judgment at all. It is an act of the mind by which nothing is affirmed or denied, and which therefore can neither be true nor false." [1] And again : "Consciousness is employed solely about objects that do exist, or have existed. But conception is often employed about objects that neither do, nor did, nor will, exist. This is the very nature of this faculty, that its object, though distinctly conceived, may have no existence. Such an object we call a creature of imagination, but this creature never was created.

"That we may not impose upon ourselves in this matter, we must distinguish between that act or operation of the mind, which we call conceiving an object, and the object which we conceive. When we conceive anything, there is a real act or operation of the mind; of this we are conscious, and can have no doubt of its existence. But every such act must have an object; for he that conceives must conceive something. Suppose he conceives a centaur, he may have a distinct conception of this object, though no centaur ever existed." [2] And again : "I conceive a centaur. This conception is an operation of the mind of which I am conscious, and to which I can attend. The sole object of it is a centaur, an animal which, I believe, never existed." [3]

Now, here it is admitted by Reid, that imagination has an object, and, in the example adduced, that this object has no existence out of the mind. The object of imagination is, therefore, in the mind, — is a modification of the mind. Now, can it be maintained that there can be a modification of mind, — a modification of which we are aware, but of which we are not conscious? But let us regard the matter in another aspect. We are conscious, says Dr. Reid, of the imagination of a centaur, but not of the centaur imagined. Now, nothing can be more evident than that the object and the act of imagination, are identical. Thus, in the example alleged, the centaur imagined and the act of imagining it,

1 *Works*, p. 223.　　2 *Works*, p. 386.　　3 *Works*, p. 373.

are one and indivisible. What is the act of imagining a centaur but the centaur imaged, or the image of the centaur; what is the image of the centaur but the act of imagining it? The centaur is both the object and the act of imagination: it is the same thing viewed in different relations. It is called the object of imagination, when considered as representing a possible existence, — for everything that can be construed to the mind, everything that does not violate the laws of thought, in other words, everything that does not involve a contradiction, may be conceived by the mind as possible. I say, therefore, that the centaur is called the object of imagination, when considered as representing a possible existence; whereas the centaur is called the act of imagination, when considered as the creation, work, or operation, of the mind itself. The centaur imagined and the imagination of the centaur, are thus as much the same indivisible modification of mind as a square is the same figure, whether we consider it as composed of four sides, or as composed of four angles, — or as paternity is the same relation whether we look from the son to the father, or from the father to the son. We cannot, therefore, be conscious of imagining an object without being conscious of the object imagined, and as regards imagination, Reid's limitation of consciousness is, therefore, futile.

I proceed next to Memory: — "It is by Memory," says Dr. Reid,

Memory.

"that we have an immediate knowledge of things past. The senses give us information of things only as they exist in the present moment; and this information, if it were not preserved by memory, would vanish instantly, and leave us as ignorant at if it had never been. Memory must have an object. Every man who remembers must remember something, and that which he remembers is called the object of his remembrance. In this, memory agrees with perception, but differs from sensation, which has no object but the feeling itself. Every man can distinguish the thing remembered from the remembrance of it. We may remember anything which we have seen, or heard, or known, or done, or suffered; but the remembrance of it is a particular act of the mind which now exists, and of which we are conscious. To confound these two is an absurdity which a thinking man could not be led into, but by some false hypothesis which hinders him from reflecting upon the thing which he would explain by it."[1] "The object of memory, or thing remembered, must be something that is past; as the object of perception and of consciousness, must be something which is present. What now is, cannot be an object of memory; neither can that which is past and gone

---

[1] *Works*, p. 339.

be an object of perception, or of consciousness."[1] To these passages, which are taken from the first chapter of the third Essay *On the Intellectual Powers*, I must add another from the sixth chapter of the same Essay,—the chapter in which he criticises Locke's doctrine in regard to our Personal Identity. "Leaving," he says, "the consequences of this doctrine to those who have leisure to trace them, we may observe, with regard to the doctrine itself, first, that Mr. Locke attributes to consciousness the conviction we have of our past actions, as if a man may now be conscious of what he did twenty years ago. It is impossible to understand the meaning of this, unless by consciousness be meant memory, the only faculty by which we have an immediate knowledge of our past actions. Sometimes, in popular discourse, a man says he is conscious that he did such a thing, meaning that he distinctly remembers that he did it. It is unnecessary, in common discourse, to fix accurately the limits between consciousness and memory. This was formerly shown to be the case with regard to sense and memory. And, therefore, distinct remembrance is sometimes called sense, sometimes consciousness, without any inconvenience. But this ought to be avoided in philosophy, otherwise we confound the different powers of the mind, and ascribe to one what really belongs to another. If a man be conscious of what he did twenty years or twenty minutes ago, there is no use for memory, nor ought we to allow that there is any such faculty. The faculties of consciousness and memory are chiefly distinguished by this, that the first is an immediate knowledge of the present, the second an immediate knowledge of the past."[2]

From these quotations it appears that Reid distinguishes memory from consciousness in this,—that memory is an immediate knowledge of the past, consciousness an immediate knowledge of the present. We may, therefore, be conscious of the act of memory as present, but of the object of memory as past, consciousness is impossible. Now, if memory and consciousness be, as Reid asserts, the one an immediate knowledge of the past, the other an immediate knowledge of the present, it is evident that memory is a faculty whose object lies beyond the sphere of consciousness; and, consequently, that consciousness cannot be regarded as the general condition of every intellectual act. We have only, therefore, to examine whether this attribution of repugnant qualities to consciousness and memory be correct,—whether there be not assigned to one or other a function which does not really belong to it.

Now, in regard to what Dr. Reid says of consciousness, I admit

---

[1] *Works*, p. 340.　　　　　[2] *Works*, p. 351.

that no exception can be taken. Consciousness is an immediate knowledge of the present. We have, indeed, already shown that consciousness is an immediate knowledge, and, therefore, only of the actual or now-existent. This being admitted, and professing, as we do, to prove that consciousness is the one generic faculty of knowledge, we, consequently, must maintain that all knowledge is immediate, and only of the actual or present, — in other words, that what is called mediate knowledge, knowledge of the past, knowledge of the absent, knowledge of the non-actual or possible, is either no knowledge at all, or only a knowledge contained in, and evolved out of, an immediate knowledge of what is now existent and actually present to the mind. This, at first sight, may appear like paradox; I trust you will soon admit that the counter doctrine is self-repugnant.

I proceed, therefore, to show that Dr. Reid's assertion of memory being an immediate knowledge of the past, is not only false, but that it involves a contradiction in terms.[1]

Memory not an immediate knowledge of the past.

Let us first determine what immediate knowledge is, and then see whether the knowledge we have of the past, through memory, can come under the conditions of immediate knowledge. Now nothing can be more evident than the following positions: 1°, An object to be known immediately must be known in itself, — that is, in those modifications, qualities, or phænomena, through which it manifests its existence, and not in those of something different from itself; for, if we suppose it known not in itself, but in some other thing, then this other thing is what is immediately known, and the object known through it is only an object mediately known.

Conditions of immediate knowledge.

But 2°, If a thing can be immediately known only if known in itself, it is manifest that it can only be known in itself, if it be itself actually in existence, and actually in immediate relation to our faculties of knowledge.

Such are the necessary conditions of immediate knowledge; and they disprove at once Dr. Reid's assertion, that memory is an immediate knowledge of the past. An immediate knowledge is only conceivable of the now existent, as the now existent alone can be known in itself. But the past is only past, inasmuch as it is not now existent; and as it is not now existent, it cannot be known in itself. The immediate knowledge of the past is, therefore, impossible.

We have, hitherto, been considering the conditions of immediate

1 Compare *Discussions*, p. 50. — ED.

knowledge in relation to the object; let us now consider them in relation to the cognitive act. Every act, and consequently every act of knowledge, exists only as it now exists; and as it exists only in the *now*, it can be cognizant only of a now-existent object. Memory is an act, — an act of knowledge; it can, therefore, be cognizant only of a now-existent object. But the object known in memory is,

Application of these conditions to the knowledge we have in Memory.

ex hypothesi, past; consequently, we are reduced to the dilemma, either of refusing a past object to be known in memory at all, or of admitting it to be only mediately known, in and through a present object. That the latter alternative is the true, it will require a very few explanatory words to convince you. What are the contents of an act of memory? An act of memory is merely a present state of mind, which we are conscious of, not as absolute, but as relative to, and representing, another state of mind, and accompanied with the belief that the state of mind, as now represented, has actually been. I remember an event I saw, — the landing of George IV. at Leith. This remembrance is only a consciousness of certain imaginations, involving the conviction that these imaginations now represent ideally what I formerly really experienced. All that is immediately known in the act of memory, is the present mental modification; that is, the representation and concomitant belief. Beyond this mental modification, we know nothing; and this mental modification is not only known to consciousness, but only exists in and by consciousness. Of any past object, real or ideal, the mind knows and can know nothing, for *ex hypothesi*, no such object now exists; or if it be said to know such an object, it can only be said to know it mediately, as represented in the present mental modification. Properly speaking, however, we know only the actual and present, and all real knowledge is an immediate knowledge. What is said to be mediately known, is, in truth, not known to be, but only believed to be; for its existence is only an inference resting on the belief, that the mental modification truly represents what is in itself beyond the sphere of knowledge. What is immediately known must be; for what is immediately known is supposed to be known as existing. The denial of the existence, and of the existence within the sphere of consciousness, involves, therefore, a denial of the immediate knowledge of an object. We may, accordingly, doubt the reality of any object of mediate knowledge, without denying the reality of the immediate knowledge on which the mediate knowledge rests. In memory, for instance, we cannot deny the existence of the present representation and belief, for their existence is the consciousness of their existence itself.

To doubt their existence, therefore, is for us to doubt the existence of our consciousness. But as this doubt itself exists only through consciousness, it would, consequently, annihilate itself. But, though in memory we must admit the reality of the representation and belief, as facts of consciousness, we may doubt, we may deny, that the representation and belief are true. We may assert that they represent what never was, and that all beyond their present mental existence is a delusion. This, however, could not be the case if our knowledge of the past were immediate. So far, therefore, is memory from being an immediate knowledge of the past, that it is at best only a mediate knowledge of the past; while, in philosophical propriety, it is not a knowledge of the past at all, but a knowedge of the present and a belief of the past. But in whatever terms we may choose to designate the contents of memory, it is manifest that these contents are all within the sphere of consciousness.[1]

1 What I have said in regard to Dr. Reid's doctrine of memory as an immediate knowledge of the past, applies equally to his doctrine of conception or imagination, as an immediate knowledge of the distant,—a case which I deferred noticing, when I considered his contradistinction of that faculty from consciousness. "I can conceive," he says, "an individual object that really exists, such as St. Paul's Church in London. I have an idea of it; that is, I conceive it. The immediate object of this conception is four hundred miles distant; and I have no reason to think that it acts upon me, or that I act upon it; but I can think of it notwithstanding." This requires no comment. I shall, subsequently, have occasion to show how Reid confused himself about the term object,—this being part and parcel of his grand error in confounding representative or mediate, and intuitive or immediate knowledge.

LECTURE XIII.

CONSCIOUSNESS, — ITS SPECIAL CONDITIONS: RELATION TO COGNITIVE FACULTIES IN GENERAL.

WE now proceed to consider the third faculty which Dr. Reid specially contradistinguishes from Consciousness, — I mean Perception, or that faculty through which we obtain a knowledge of the external world. Now, you will observe that Reid maintains against the immense majority of all, and the entire multitude of modern philosophers, that we have a direct and immediate knowledge of the external world. He thus vindicates to mind not only an immediate knowledge of its own modifications, but also an immediate knowledge of what is essentially different from mind or self, — the modifications of matter. He did not, however, allow that these were known by any common faculty, but held that the qualities of mind were exclusively made known to us by Consciousness, the qualities of matter exclusively made known to us by Perception. Consciousness was, thus, the faculty of immediate knowledge, purely subjective; perception, the faculty of immediate knowledge, purely objective. The Ego was known by one faculty, the Non-Ego by another. "Consciousness," says Dr. Reid, "is only of things in the mind, and not of external things. It is improper to say, I am conscious of the table which is before me. I perceive it, I see it, but do not say I am conscious of it. As that consciousness by which we have a knowledge of the operations of our own minds, is a different power from that by which we perceive external objects, and as these different powers have different names in our language, and, I believe, in all languages, a philosopher ought carefully to preserve this distinction, and never to confound things so different in their nature."[1] And in another place he observes: — "Consciousness always goes along with perception; but they are different operations of the mind, and they have their different objects.

Our consciousness coëxtensive with our knowledge.
Reid contradistinguishes consciousness from perception.

---

[1] *Intellectual Powers*, Essay i., chap. i.   *Coll. Works*, p. 223.   •

Consciousness is not perception, nor is the object of consciousness the object of perception."[1]

Dr. Reid has many merits as a speculator, but the only merit which he arrogates to himself, — the principal merit accorded to him by others, — is, that he was the first philosopher, in more recent times, who dared, in his doctrine of immediate perception, to vindicate, against the unanimous authority of philosophers, the universal conviction of mankind. But this doctrine he has at best imperfectly developed, and, at the same time, has unfortunately obscured it, by errors of so singular a character, that some acute philosophers — for Dr. Brown does not stand alone — have never even suspected what his doctrine of perception actually is. One of these errors is the contradistinction of perception from consciousness.

Principal merit accorded to Reid as a philosopher.

I may here notice, by anticipation, that philosophers, at least modern philosophers, before Reid, allowed to the mind no immediate knowledge of the external reality. They conceded to it only a representative or mediate knowledge of external things. Of these some, however, held that the representative object — the object immediately known — was different from the mind knowing, as it was also different from the reality it represented; while others, on a simpler hypothesis, maintained that there was no intermediate entity, no *tertium quid*, between the reality and the mind, but that the immediate or representative object was itself a mental modification.[2] The latter thus granting to mind no immediate knowledge of aught beyond its own modification, could, consequently, only recognize a consciousness of self. The former, on the contrary, could, as they actually did, accord to consciousness a cognizance of not-self. Now, Reid, after asserting against the philosophers the immediacy of our knowledge of external things, would almost appear to have been startled by his own boldness, and, instead of carrying his principle fairly to its issue, by according to consciousness on his doctrine that knowledge of the external world as existing, which, in the doctrine of the philosophers, it obtained of the external world as represented, he inconsistently stopped short, split immediate knowledge into two parts,

Modern philosophers before Reid held a doctrine of representative perception, in one or other of two forms.

Reid exempts the object of perception from the sphere of consciousness.

---

1 *Ibid.*, Essay ii., chap. iii. *Coll. Works*, p. 297.

2 For a full discussion of the various theo-ries of knowledge and perception, see the Author's supplementary dissertations to Reid's Works, Notes B and C. — ED.

and bestowed the knowledge of material qualities on perception alone, allowing that of mental modifications to remain exclusively with consciousness. Be this, however, as it may, the exemption of the objects of perception from the sphere of consciousness, can be easily shown to be self-contradictory.

What! say the partisans of Dr. Reid, are we not to distinguish, as the product of different faculties, the knowledge we obtain of objects in themselves the most opposite? Mind and matter are mutually separated by the whole diameter of being. Mind and matter are, in fact, nothing but words to express two series of phænomena known less in themselves, than in contradistinction from each other. The difference of the phænomena to be known, surely legitimates a difference of faculty to know them. In answer to this, we admit at once, that — were the question merely whether we should not distinguish, under consciousness, two special faculties, — whether we should not study apart, and bestow distinctive appellations on consciousness considered as more particularly cognizant of the external world, and on consciousness considered as more particularly cognizant of the internal — this would be highly proper and expedient. But this is not the question. Dr. Reid distinguishes consciousness as a special faculty from perception as a special faculty, and he allows to the former the cognizance of the latter in its operation, to the exclusion of its object. He maintains that we are conscious of our perception of a rose, but not of the rose perceived. That we know the ego by one act of knowledge, the non-ego by another. This doctrine I hold to be erroneous, and it is this doctrine I now proceed to refute.

In the first place, it is not only a logical axiom, but a self-evident truth, that the knowledge of opposites is one. Thus, we cannot know what is tall without knowing what is short, — we know what is virtue only as we know what is vice, — the science of health is but another name for the science of disease. Nor do we know the opposites, the I and Thou, the ego and non-ego, the subject and object, mind and matter, by a different law. The act which affirms that this particular phænomenon is a modification of Me, virtually affirms that the phænomenon is not a modification of anything different from Me, and, consequently, implies a common cognizance of self and notself; the act which affirms that this other phænomenon is a modification of something different from Me, virtually affirms that the phænomenon is not a modification of Me, and, consequently, implies a common cognizance of not-self and self. But unless we are

That in this Reid is wrong shown, 1°, From the principle, that the knowledge of opposites is one.

prepared to maintain that the faculty cognizant of self and not-self is different from the faculty cognizant of not-self and self, we must allow that the ego and non-ego are known and discriminated in the same indivisible act of knowledge. What, then, is the faculty of which this act of knowledge is the energy? It cannot be Reid's consciousness, for that is cognizant only of the ego or mind, — it cannot be Reid's perception, for that is cognizant only of the non-ego or matter. But as the act cannot be denied, so the faculty must be admitted. It is not, however, to be found in Reid's catalogue. But though not recognized by Reid in his system, its necessity may, even on his hypothesis, be proved. For if with him we allow only a special faculty immediately cognizant of the ego, and a special faculty immediately cognizant of the non-ego, we are at once met with the question, By what faculty are the ego and non-ego discriminated? We cannot say by consciousness, for that knows nothing but mind, — we cannot say by perception, for that knows nothing but matter. But as mind and matter are never known apart and by themselves, but always in mutual correlation and contrast, this knowledge of them in connection must be the function of some faculty, not like Reid's consciousness and perception, severally limited to mind and to matter as exclusive objects, but cognizant of them as the ego and non-ego, — as the two terms of a relation. It is thus shown that an act and a faculty must, perforce, on Reid's own hypothesis, be admitted, in which these two terms shall be comprehended together in the unity of knowledge, — in short, a higher consciousness, embracing Reid's consciousness and perception, and in which the two acts, severally cognitive of mind and of matter, shall be comprehended, and reduced to unity and correlation. But what is this but to admit at last, in an unphilosophical complexity, the common consciousness of subject and object, of mind and matter, which we set out with denying in its philosophical simplicity?

But, in the second place, the attempt of Reid to make consciousness conversant about the various cognitive faculties to the exclusion of their objects, is equally impossible in regard to Perception, as we have shown it to be in relation to Imagination and Memory; nay, the attempt, in the case of perception, would, if allowed, be even suicidal of his great doctrine of our immediate knowledge of the external world.

2°, Reid's limitation of consciousness is suicidal of his doctrine of an immediate knowledge of the external world.

Reid's assertion, that we are conscious of the act of perception, but not of the object perceived, involves, first of all, a general absurdity. For it virtually asserts that we can know what we are not conscious of knowing. An act of percep-

It first of all involves a general absurdity.

tion is an act of knowledge; that we perceive, that we know. Now, if in perception there be an external reality known, but of which external reality we are, on Reid's hypothesis, not conscious, then is there an object known, of which we are not conscious. But as we know only inasmuch as we know that we know, — in other words, inasmuch as we are conscious that we know, — we cannot know an object without being conscious of that object as known; consequently, we cannot perceive an object without being conscious of that object as perceived.

But, again, how is it possible that we can be conscious of an operation of perception, unless consciousness be

And secondly, it destroys the distinction of consciousness itself.

coëxtensive with that act; and how can it be coëxtensive with the act, and not also conversant with its object? An act of knowledge is only possible in relation to an object, — and it is an act of one kind or another only by special relation to a particular object. Thus the object at once determines the existence, and specifies the character of the existence, of the intellectual energy. An act of knowledge existing and being what it is only by relation to its object, it is manifest that the act can be known only through the object to which it is correlative; and Reid's supposition that an operation can be known in consciousness to the exclusion of its object, is impossible. For example, I see the inkstand. How can I be conscious that my present modification exists, — that it is a perception, and not another mental state, — that it is a perception of sight to the exclusion of every other sense, — and, finally, that it is a perception of the inkstand and of the inkstand only, — unless my consciousness comprehend within its sphere the object, which at once determines the existence of the act, qualifies its kind, and distinguishes its individuality? Annihilate the inkstand, you annihilate the perception; annihilate the consciousness of the object, you annihilate the consciousness of the operation.

It undoubtedly sounds strange to say, I am conscious of the inkstand, instead of saying, I am conscious of

Whence the apparent incongruity of the expression, "Consciousness of the object in perception."

the perception of the inkstand. This I admit, but the admission can avail nothing to Dr. Reid, for the apparent incongruity of the expression arises only from the prevalence of that doctrine of perception in the schools of philosophy, which it is his principal merit to have so vigorously assailed. So long as it was universally assumed by the learned, that the mind is cognizant of nothing beyond, either, on one theory, its own representative modifications, or, on another, the species, ideas, or representative entities, different from itself, which it contains, and that all it knows of a material world is only an internal representation which, by the necessity of its nature, it mistakes for an external reality, — the supposition of an immediate knowledge of material phænomena was regarded only as a vulgar, an unphilosophical illusion, and the term consciousness, which was exclusively a learned or technical expression for all immediate knowledge, was, consequently, never employed to express an immediate knowledge of aught beyond the mind itself; and thus, when at length, by Reid's own refutation of the prevailing doctrine, it becomes necessary to extend the term to the immediate knowledge of external objects, this extension, so discordant with philosophic usage, is, by the force of association and custom, felt at first as strange and even contradictory. A slight consideration, however, is sufficient to reconcile us to the expression, in showing, if we hold the doctrine of immediate perception, the necessity of not limiting consciousness to our subjective states. In fact, if we look beneath the surface, consciousness was not, in general, restricted, even in philosophical usage, to the modifications of the conscious self. That great majority of philosophers who held that, in perception, we know nothing of the external reality as existing, but that we are immediately cognizant only of a representative something, different both from the object represented, and from the percipient mind, — these philosophers, one and all, admitted that we are conscious of this *tertium quid* present to, but not a modification of, mind, — for, except Reid and his school, I am aware of no philosophers who denied that consciousness was coëxtensive or identical with immediate knowledge.

But, in the third place, we have previously reserved a supposition on which we may possibly avoid some of the self-contradictions which emerge from Reid's proposing as the object of consciousness the act, but excluding from its cognizance the object, of perception; that is, the object of its own object. The supposition is, that Dr. Reid committed the same error in regard to perception, which he did in regard to memory and imagination, and that in maintaining our immediate knowledge in perception, he meant nothing more than to maintain, that the mind is not, in that act, cognizant of any representative object different from its own modification, of any *tertium quid* ministering between itself and the external reality; but that,

3°, A supposition on which some of the self-contradictions of Reid's doctrine may be avoided.

in perception, the mind is determined itself to represent the unknown external reality, and that, on this self-representation, he abusively bestowed the name of immediate knowledge, in contrast to that more complex theory of perception, which holds that there intervenes between the percipient mind and the external existence an intermediate something, different from both, by which the former knows, and by which the latter is represented. On the supposition of this mistake, we may believe him guiltless of the others; and we can certainly, on this ground, more easily conceive how he could accord to consciousness a knowledge only of the percipient act, — meaning by that act the representation of the external reality; and how he could deny to consciousness a knowledge of the object of perception, — meaning by that object the unknown reality itself. This is the only opinion which Dr. Brown and others ever suspect him of maintaining; and a strong case might certainly be made out to prove that this view of his doctrine is correct. But if such were, in truth, Reid's opinion, then has he accomplished nothing, — his whole philosophy is one mighty blunder. For, as I shall hereafter show, idealism finds in this simpler hypothesis of representation even a more secure foundation than on the other; and, in point of fact, on this hypothesis, the most philosophical scheme of idealism that exists, — the Egoistic or Fichtean, is established.

Taking, however, the general analogy of Reid's system, and a great number of unambiguous passages into account, I am satisfied that this view of his doctrine is erroneous; and I shall endeavor, when we come to treat of mediate and immediate knowledge, to explain how, from his never having formed to himself an adequate conception of these under all their possible forms, and from his historical ignorance of them as actually held by philosophers, — he often appears to speak in contradiction of the vital doctrine which, in equity, he must be held to have steadily maintained.

This supposition untenable.

Besides the operations we have already considered, — Imagination or Conception, Memory, and Perception, which Dr. Reid and Mr. Stewart have endeavored to discriminate from Consciousness, there are further to be considered Attention and Reflection, which, in like manner, they have maintained to be an act or acts, not subordinate to, or contained in, Consciousness. But, before proceeding to show that their doctrine on this point is almost equally untenable as on the preceding, it is necessary to clear up some confusion, and to notice certain collateral errors.

Reid and Stewart maintain, that Attention and Reflection are acts not subordinate to, or contained in, consciousness.

In the first place, on this head, these philosophers are not at one; for Mr. Stewart seems inadvertently to have

Certain collateral errors noticed. Stewart misrepresents Reid's doctrine of the meaning and difference of Attention and Reflection.

misrepresented the opinion of Dr. Reid in regard to the meaning and difference of Attention and Reflection. Reid either employs these terms as synonymous expressions, or he distinguishes them only by making attention relative to the consciousness and perception of the present; reflection to the memory of the past. In the fifth chapter of the second Essay on the *Intellectual Powers*,[1] he says, "In order, however, to our having a distinct notion of any of the operations of our own minds, it is not enough that we be conscious of them, for all men have this consciousness: it is farther necessary that we attend to them while they are exerted, and reflect upon them with care while they are recent and fresh in our memory. It is necessary that, by employing ourselves frequently in this way, we get the habit of this attention and reflection," etc. And in the first chapter of the sixth Essay, "Mr. Locke," he says, "has restricted the word *reflection* to that which is employed about the operations of our minds, without any authority, as I think, from custom, the arbiter of language: for surely I may reflect upon what I have seen or heard, as well as upon what I have thought. The word, in its proper and common meaning, is equally applicable to objects of sense, and to objects of consciousness. He has likewise confounded reflection with consciousness, and seems not to have been aware that they are different powers, and appear at very different periods of life."[2] In the first of these quotations, Reid might use *attention* in relation to the consciousness of the present, *reflection*, to the memory of the past; but in the second, in saying that reflection "is equally applicable to objects of sense and to objects of consciousness," he distinctly indicates that the two terms are used by

him as convertible. Reid (I may notice by the

Reid wrong in his censure of Locke's usage of the term Reflection.

way) is wholly wrong in his strictures on Locke for his restricted usage of the term *reflection;* for it was not until after his time that the term came, by Wolf, to be philosophically employed in a more extended signification than that in which Locke correctly applies it.[3] Reid is likewise wrong, if we literally understand his

1 *Coll. Works*, p. 258.
2 *Ibid.*, p. 420.
3 [Wolf, *Psychologia Empirica*, § 257: "Attentionis successiva directio ad ea quæ in re percepta insunt dicitur *Reflexio*. Unde simul liquet quid sit facultas reflectendi, scilicet quod sit facultas attentionem suam successive ad ea quæ in re percepta insunt, pro arbitrio dirigendi."] Reid is further criticized in the Author's edition of his works, pp. 347, 420. — ED.

words, in saying that reflection is employed in common language
in relation to objects of sense. It is never em-

And in saying that Reflection is employed in relation to objects of sense.

ployed except upon the mind and its contents.
We cannot be said to reflect upon any external
object, except in so far as that object has been
previously perceived, and its image become
part and parcel of our intellectual furniture. We may be said to
reflect upon it in memory, but not in perception. But to return.

Reid, therefore, you will observe, identifies attention and reflection. Now Mr. Stewart, in the chapter on Attention in the first
volume of his *Elements*,[1] says, "Some important observations on
the subject of attention occur in different parts of Dr. Reid's writings; particularly in his *Essays on the Intellectual Powers of Man*,
p. 62, and his *Essays on the Active Powers of Man*, p. 78 *et seq.*
To this ingenious author we are indebted for the remark, that attention to things external is properly called *observation;* and attention
to the subjects of our consciousness, *reflection*."[2]

I may, however, notice a more important inadvertence of Mr.

Locke not the first to use the term Reflection in its psychological application.

Stewart, and this it is the more requisite to do,
as his authority is worthy of high respect, not
only on account of philosophical talent, but of
historical accuracy. In various passages of his
writings, Mr. Stewart states that Locke seems
to have considered the employment of the term reflection, in its
psychological acceptation, as original to himself; and he notices
it as a curious circumstance that Sir John Davies, Attorney-General
to Queen Elizabeth, should, in his poem on the *Immortality of the
Soul*, have employed this term in the same signification. How Mr.
Stewart could have fallen into this error, is wholly inconceivable.
The word, as employed by Locke, was in common use in every
school of philosophy for fifteen hundred years previous to the publication of the *Essay on the Human Understanding*. It was a
term in the philosophy both of Descartes,[3] and of Gassendi;[4] and
it was borrowed by them from the schoolmen, with whom it was

---

1 *Works*, vol. ii. pp. 122, 123.

2 This distinction has been attempted by
others. [See Keckermann, *Opera*, tom. i. p.
1612, where he distinguishes *reflection*,—*intellectio reflexa, interna*, per quam homo intelligit
suum intellectum,—from the *intellectio externa*,
qua intellectus alias res extra se positas percipit. See also Mazure. *Cours de Philosophie*,
tom. i. p. 381.—ED.]

3 [Descartes, *Epist.*, P. ii., Ep. iv. (See Gru-
yer, *Essais Philosophiques*, tom. iv. p. 118.) De
la Forge, *De Mente Humana*, Præf., p. 9.]

4 [Gassendi, *Physica*, § iii. Memb. Post., lib.
ix. c. 3. (*Opera*, Leyden, 1658; vol. ii. p. 451.)
" Ad secundam vero operationem præsertim
spectat ipsa intellectus ad suam operationem
attentio, reflexione illa supra actionem propriam, qua se intelligere intelligit, cogitatve
se agitare."]

a household word.[1] From the schoolmen, indeed, Locke seems to have adopted the fundamental principle of his philosophy, the derivation of our knowledge through the double medium of sense and reflection, — at least, some of them had in terms articulately enounced this principle five centuries previous to the English philosopher, and enounced it also in a manner far more correct than was done by him;[2] for they did not, like Locke, regard reflection itself as a source of knowledge, — thus reducing all our knowledge to experience and its generalization, but viewed in reflection only the channel through which, along with the contingent phænomena of our internal experience, we discover the necessary judgments which are original or native to the mind.

There is, likewise, another oversight of Mr. Stewart which I may notice. "Although," he says, "the connection between attention and memory has been frequently remarked in general terms, I do not recollect that the power of attention has been mentioned by any of the writers on pneumatology in their enumeration of faculties of the mind; nor has it been considered by any one, so far as I know, as of sufficient importance to deserve a particular examination."[3] So far is this from being the case that there are many previous authors who have considered attention as a separate faculty, and treated of it even at greater length than Mr. Stewart himself. This is true not only of the celebrated Wolf,[4] but of the whole Wolfian school; and to these I may add Condillac,[5] Contzen,[6] Tiedemann,[7] Irwing,[8] Malebranche[9] and many others. But this by the way.

Taking, however, Attention and Reflection for acts of the same faculty, and supposing, with Mr. Stewart, that reflection is properly attention directed to the phænomena of mind; observation, atten-

1 [We have the scholastic brocard pointing to the difficulties of the study of self: "Reflexiva cogitatio facile fit deflexiva." See Keckermann, *Opera*, tom. i. p. 466.]

2 [See Scotus, *Super Universalibus Porphyrii*, Qu. iii.: "Ad tertium dico quod illa propositio Aristotelis, nihil est in intellectu quin prius fuerit in sensu, vera est de eo quod est primum intelligibile, quod est scilicet quod quid est rei materialis, non autem de omnibus per se intelligibilibus; quia multa per se intelliguntur, non quia speciem faciunt in sensu, sed per reflexionem intellectus." (By the Scotists the act of intellect was regarded as threefold: *Rectus*, — *Collativus*, — *Reflexus*. See Constantius (a Sarnano), *Tract. de Secundis Intentionibus*; Scoti *Opera*, p. 452.) See also Philip Mocenicus, *Contemplationes* (1581), passim. Goclenius, *Lexicon Philosophicum*, v. *Reflexus*. Keckermann, *Opera*, tom. i. pp. 1600, 1612. Conimbricenses in *Arist. de Anima*, pp. 370, 373.]

3 *Elements*, i. c. 2. *Collected Works*, vol. ii. p. 122. — ED.

4 *Psychologia Empirica*, § 234, *et seq.* — ED.

5 *Origine des Connoisances Humaines*, part. i. § ii. ch. 2. — ED.

6 *Prelectiones Logicæ et Metaphysicæ* auctore Adamo Contzen; Mechlin, 1830; vol. iii. p. 31. (Originally published in 1775-1780.) — ED.

7 *Handbuch der Pyschologie*, p. 121. — ED.

8 *Erfahrungen und Untersuchungen über den Menschen* von karl Franz von Irwing, Berlin, 1777, b. i. p. 411; b. ii. p. 209. — ED.

9 *De la Recherche de la Vérité*, lib. iii. ch. 4; lib. vi. ch. 2. *Traité de la Morale*, ch. 5. — ED.

tion directed to the phænomena of matter; the main question comes to be considered, Is attention a faculty different from consciousness, as Reid and Stewart maintain? As the latter of these philosophers has not argued the point himself, but merely refers to the arguments of the former in confirmation of their common doctrine, it will be sufficient to adduce the following passage from Reid, in which his doctrine on this head is contained. "I return," he says, "to what I mentioned as the main source of information on this subject, — attentive reflection upon the operations of our own minds.

Is Attention a faculty different from consciousness?

Reid quoted in reference to this question.

"All the notions we have of mind and its operations, are, by Mr. Locke, called *ideas of reflection*. A man may have as distinct notions of remembrance, of judgment, of will, of desire, as he has of any object whatever. Such notions, as Mr. Locke justly observes, are got by the power of reflection. But what is this power of reflection? 'It is,' says the same author, 'that power by which the mind turns its view inward, and observes its own actions and operations.' He observes elsewhere, 'That the understanding, like the eye, whilst it makes us see and perceive all other things, takes no notice of itself; and that it requires art and pains to set it at a distance, and make it its own object.'

"This power of the understanding to make its own operations its object: to attend to them, and examine them on all sides, is the power of reflection, by which alone we can have any distinct notion of the powers of our own or of other minds.

"This reflection ought to be distinguished from consciousness, with which it is too often confounded, even by Mr. Locke. All men are conscious of the operations of their own minds, at all times while they are awake; but there are few who reflect upon them, or make them objects of thought."[1]

Dr. Reid has rightly said that attention is a voluntary act. This remark might have led him to the observation, that attention is not a separate faculty, or a faculty of intelligence at all, but merely an act of will or desire, subordinate to a certain law of intelligence. This law is, that the greater the number of objects to which our consciousness is simultaneously extended, the smaller is the intensity with which it is able to consider each, and consequently the less vivid and distinct

What Attention is.

---

[1] *Intellectual Powers*, Essay i., chap. v. *Coll. Works*, p. 239.

will be the information it obtains of the several objects.[1] This law is expressed in the old adage,

"Pluribus intentus minor est ad singula sensus."

Such being the law, it follows that, when our interest in any particular object is excited, and when we wish to obtain all the knowledge concerning it in our power, it behooves us to limit our consideration to that object, to the exclusion of others. This is done by an act of volition or desire, which is called *attention*. But to view attention as a special act of intelligence, and to distinguish it from consciousness, is utterly inept. Consciousness may be compared to a telescope, attention to the pulling out or in of the tubes in accommodating the focus to the object; and we might, with equal justice, distinguish in the eye, the adjustment of the pupil from the general organ of vision, as, in the mind, distinguish attention from consciousness as separate faculties. Not, however, that they are to be accounted the same. Attention is consciousness, and something more. It is consciousness voluntarily applied, under its law of limitations, to some determinate object; it is consciousness concentrated. In this respect, attention is an interesting subject of consideration; and having now finished what I proposed in proof of the position, that consciousness is not a special faculty of knowledge, but coëxtensive with all our cognitions,

Attention as a general phænomenon of consciousness.

I shall proceed to consider it in its various aspects and relations; and having just stated the law of limitation, I shall go on to what I have to say in regard to attention as a general phænomenon of consciousness.

And, here, I have first to consider a question in which I am again sorry to find myself opposed to many distinguished philosophers, and in particular, to one whose opinion on this, as on every other point of psychological observation, is justly

Can we attend to more than a single object at once?

entitled to the highest consideration. The philosopher I allude to is Mr. Stewart. The question is, Can we attend to more than a single object at once? For if attention be nothing but the concentration of consciousness on a smaller number of objects than constitute its widest compass of simultaneous knowledge, it is evident that, unless this widest compass of consciousness be limited to only two objects, we do attend when we converge consciousness on any smaller number than that total complement of objects which it can embrace at once. For example, if we suppose that

1 [Cf. Steeb. *Über den Menschen*, ii. 673; and Fries, *Anthropologie*, i. 83.]

the number of objects which consciousness can simultaneously apprehend be six, the limitation of consciousness to five, or four, or three, or two, or one, will all be acts of attention, different in degree, but absolutely identical in kind.

Mr. Stewart's doctrine is as follows:—"Before," he says, "we leave the subject of Attention, it is proper to take notice of a question which has been stated with respect to it; whether we have the power of attending to more than one thing at one and the same instant; or, in other words, whether we can attend, at one and the same instant, to objects which we can attend to separately? This question has, if I am not mistaken, been already decided by several philosophers in the negative; and I acknowledge, for my own part, that although their opinion has not only been called in question by others, but even treated with some degree of contempt as altogether hypothetical, it appears to me to be the most reasonable and philosophical that we can form on the subject.

Stewart quoted in reference to this question.

"There is, indeed, a great variety of cases in which the mind apparently exerts different acts of attention at once; but from the instances which have already been mentioned, of the astonishing rapidity of thought, it is obvious that all this may be explained without supposing those acts to be coëxistent; and I may even venture to add, it may all be explained in the most satisfactory manner, without ascribing to our intellectual operations a greater degree of rapidity than that with which we know, from the fact, that they are sometimes carried on. The effect of practice in increasing this capacity of apparently attending to different things at once, renders this explanation of the phænomenon in question more probable than any other.

"The case of the equilibrist and rope-dancer already mentioned, is particularly favorable to this explanation, as it affords direct evidence of the possibility of the mind's exerting different successive acts in an interval of time so short, as to produce the same sensible effect as if they had been exerted at one and the same moment. In this case, indeed, the rapidity of thought is so remarkable, that if the different acts of the mind were not all necessarily accompanied with different movements of the eye, there can be no reason for doubting that the philosophers whose doctrine I am now controverting, would have asserted that they are all mathematically coëxistent.

"Upon a question, however, of this sort, which does not admit of a perfectly direct appeal to the fact, I would by no means be understood to decide with confidence; and, therefore, I should wish the conclusions I am now to state, to be received as only conditionally established. They are necessary and obvious consequences of the general principle, ' that the mind can only attend to one thing at once ;' but must stand or fall with the truth of that supposition.

"It is commonly understood, I believe, that in a concert of music, a good ear can attend to the different parts of the music separately, or can attend to them all at once, and feel the full effect of the harmony. If the doctrine, however, which I have endeavored to establish be admitted, it will follow that in the latter case the mind is constantly varying its attention from the one part of the music to the other, and that its operations are so rapid as to give us no perception of an interval of time.

"The same doctrine leads to some curious conclusions with respect to vision. Suppose the eye to be fixed in a particular position, and the picture of an object to be painted on the retina. Does the mind perceive the complete figure of the object at once, or is this perception the result of the various perceptions we have of the different points in the outline? With respect to this question, the principles already stated lead me to conclude that the mind does at one and the same time perceive every point in the outline of the object, (provided the whole of it be painted on the retina at the same instant,) for perception, like consciousness, is an involuntary operation. As no two points, however, of the outline are in the same direction, every point by itself constitutes just as distinct an object of attention to the mind, as if it were separated by an interval of empty space from all the rest. If the doctrine, therefore, formerly stated be just, it is impossible for the mind to attend to more than one of these points at once ; and as the perception of the figure of the object implies a knowledge of the relative situation of the different points with respect to each other, we must conclude that the perception of figure by the eye is the result of a number of different acts of attention. These acts of attention, however, are performed with such rapidity, that the effect, with respect to us, is the same as if the perception were instantaneous.

"In farther confirmation of this reasoning, it may be remarked, that if the perception of visible figure were an immediate consequence of the picture on the retina, we should have, at the first glance, as distinct an idea of a figure of a thousand sides as of a triangle or a square. The truth is, that when the figure is very simple, the process of the mind is so rapid that the perception seems to be instantaneous; but when the sides are multiplied beyond a certain number, the interval of time necessary for these different acts of attention becomes perceptible.

"It may, perhaps, be asked what I mean by a *point* in the outline of a figure, and what it is that constitutes this point *one* object of attention. The answer, I apprehend, is that this point is the *minimum visibile*. If the point be less, we cannot perceive it; if it be greater, it is not all seen in one direction.

"If these observations be admitted, it will follow that, without the faculty of memory, we could have had no perception of visible figure."[1]

On this point, Dr. Brown not only coincides with Mr. Stewart

Brown coincides with Stewart.

in regard to the special fact of attention, but asserts in general that the mind cannot exist at the same moment in two different states, that is, in two states in either of which it can exist separately. "If the mind of man," he says, "and all the changes which take place in it, from the first feeling with which life commenced to the last with which it closes, could be made visible to any other thinking being, a certain series of feelings alone, — that is to say, a certain number of successive states of mind, would be distinguishable in it, forming indeed a variety of sensations, and thoughts, and passions, as momentary states of the mind, but all of them existing individually, and successively to each other. To suppose the mind to exist in two different states, in the same moment, is a manifest absurdity."[2]

I shall consider these statements in detail. Mr. Stewart's first

Criticism of Stewart's doctrine. His first illustration from the phænomena of sound.

illustration of his doctrine is drawn from a concert of music, in which, he says, "a good ear can attend to the different parts of the music separately, or can attend to them all at once, and feel the full effect of the harmony." This example, however, appears to me to amount to a reduction of his opinion to the impossible. What are the facts in this example? In a musical concert, we have a multitude of different instruments and voices emitting at once an infinity of different sounds. These all reach the ear at the same indivisible moment in which they perish, and, consequently, if heard at all, much more if their mutual relation or harmony be perceived, they must be all heard simultaneously. This is evident. For if the mind can attend to each minimum of sound only successively, it, consequently, requires a minimum of time in which it is exclusively occupied with each minimum of sound. Now, in this minimum of

1 *Elements*, vol. i. chap. 2. *Works*, vol. ii. p. 140—143.

2 *Lectures on the Philosophy of the Human Mind*, Lect. xi. p. 67, (ed. 1830). — ED.

time, there coëxist with it, and with it perish, many minima of sound which, *ex hypothesi*, are not perceived, are not heard, as not attended to. In a concert, therefore, on this doctrine, a small number of sounds only could be perceived, and above this petty maximum, all sounds would be to the ear as zero. But what is the fact? No concert, however numerous its instruments, has yet been found to have reached, far less to have surpassed, the capacity of mind and its organ.

But it is even more impossible, on this hypothesis, to understand how we can perceive the relation of different sounds, that is, have any feeling of the harmony of a concert. In this respect, it is, indeed, *felo de se*. It is maintained that we cannot attend at once to two sounds, we cannot perceive them as coëxistent, — consequently, the feeling of harmony of which we are conscious, must proceed from the feeling of the relation of these sounds as successively perceived in different points of time. We must, therefore, compare the past sound, as retained in memory, with the present, as actually perceived. But this is impossible on the hypothesis itself. For we must, in this case, attend to the past sound in memory, and to the present sound in sense at once, or they will not be perceived in mutual relation as harmonic. But one sound in memory and another sound in sense, are as much two different objects as two different sounds in sense. Therefore, one of two conclusions is inevitable, — either we can attend to two different objects at once, and the hypothesis is disproved, or we cannot, and all knowledge of relation and harmony is impossible, which is absurd.

Impossible, on Stewart's doctrine, to understand how we can perceive the relation of different sounds.

The consequences of this doctrine are equally startling, as taken from Mr. Stewart's second illustration from the phænomena of vision. He holds that the perception of figure by the eye is the result of a number of separate acts of attention, and that each act of attention has for its object a point the least that can be seen, the *minimum visibile*. On this hypothesis, we must suppose that, at every instantaneous opening of the eyelids, the moment sufficient for us to take in the figure of the objects comprehended in the sphere of vision, is subdivided into almost infinitesimal parts, in each of which a separate act of attention is performed. This is, of itself, sufficiently inconceivable. But this being admitted, no difficulty is removed. The separate acts must be laid up in memory, in imagination. But how are they there to form a single whole,

His second illustration from the phænomena of vision.

unless we can, in imagination, attend to all the *minima visibilia* together, which in perception we could only attend to severally? On this subject I shall, however, have a more appropriate occasion of speaking, when I consider Mr. Stewart's doctrine of the relation of color to extension.

LECTURE XIV.

CONSCIOUSNESS,—ATTENTION IN GENERAL.

In the former part of our last Lecture, I concluded the argument against Reid's analysis of Consciousness
Recapitulation. into a special faculty, and showed you that,
even in relation to Perception, (the faculty by which we obtain a
knowledge of the material universe,) Consciousness is still the
common ground in which every cognitive operation has its root.
I then proceeded to prove the same in regard to Attention. After
some observations touching the confusion among philosophers, more
or less extensive, in the meaning of the term *reflection*, as a subordinate modification of attention, I endeavored to explain to you
what attention properly is, and in what relation it stands to consciousness. I stated that attention is consciousness applied to an
act of will or desire under a particular law. In so far as attention
is an act of the conative faculty, it is not an act of knowledge at
all, for the mere will or desire of knowing is not an act of cognition. But the act of the conative faculty is exerted by relation to
a certain law of consciousness, or knowledge, or intelligence. This
law, which we call the Law of Limitation, is, that the intension of
our knowledge is in the inverse ratio of its extension,—in other
words, that the fewer objects we consider at once, the clearer and
more distinct will be our knowledge of them. Hence the more
vividly we will or desire that a certain object should be clearly and
distinctly known, the more do we concentrate consciousness through
some special faculty upon it. I omitted, I find, to state that I think
Reid and Stewart incorrect in asserting that attention is only a
voluntary act, meaning by the expression *voluntary*, an act of free-
will. I am far from maintaining, as Brown and others do, that all
will is desire; but still I am persuaded that we
Attention possible are frequently determined to an act of atten-
without an act of free- tion, as to many other acts, independently of
will. our free and deliberate volition. Nor is it, I
conceive, possible to hold that, though immediately determined to

an act of attention by desire, it is only by the permission of our will that this is done; consequently, that every act of attention is still under the control of our volition. This I cannot maintain. Let us take an example: — When occupied with other matters, a person may speak to us, or the clock may strike, without our having any consciousness of the sound;[1] but it is wholly impossible for us to remain in this state of unconsciousness intentionally and with will. We cannot determinately refuse to hear by voluntarily withholding our attention; and we can no more open our eyes, and, by an act of will, avert our mind from all perception of sight, than we can, by an act of will, cease to live. We may close our ears or shut our eyes, as we may commit suicide; but we cannot, with our organs unobstructed, wholly refuse our attention at will. It, therefore, appears to me the more correct doctrine to hold that there is no consciousness without attention, — without concentration, but that attention is of three degrees or kinds. The first, a

Attention of three degrees or kinds. mere vital and irresistible act; the second, an act determined by desire, which, though involuntary, may be resisted by our will; the third, an act determined by a deliberate volition. An act of attention, — that is, an act of concentration, — seems thus necessary to every exertion of consciousness, as a certain contraction of the pupil is requisite to every exercise of vision. We have formerly noticed, that discrimination is a condition of consciousness; and a discrimination is only possible by a concentrative act, or act of attention. This, however, which corresponds to the lowest degree, — to the mere vital or automatic act of attention, has been refused the name; and *attention*, in contradistinction to this mere automatic contraction, given to the two other degrees, of which, however, Reid only recognizes the third.

Attention, then, is to consciousness, what the contraction of the

Nature and importance of attention. pupil is to sight; or to the eye of the mind, what the microscope or telescope is to the bodily eye. The faculty of attention is not, therefore, a special faculty, but merely consciousness acting under the law of limitation to which it is subjected. But whatever be its relations to the special faculties, attention doubles all their efficiency, and affords them a power of which they would otherwise be destitute. It is, in fact, as we are at present constituted, the primary condition of their activity.

Having thus concluded the discussion of the question regarding the relation of consciousness to the other cognitive faculties, I

---

1 See Reid, *Active Powers*, Essay ii. ch. 3. *Works*, p. 587. — ED.

proceeded to consider various questions, which, as not peculiar to any of the special faculties, fall to be discussed under the head of consciousness, and I commenced with the curious problem, Whether we can attend to more than a single object at once.

Can we attend to more than a single object at once?

Mr. Stewart maintains, though not without hesitation, the negative. I endeavored to show you that his arguments are not conclusive, and that they even involve suppositions which are so monstrous as to reduce the thesis he supports *ad impossibile*. I have now only to say a word in answer to Dr. Brown's assertion of the same proposition, though in different terms. In the passage I adduced in our last Lecture, he commences by the assertion, that the mind cannot exist, at the same moment, in two different states,—that is, in two states in either of which it can exist separately, and concludes with the averment that the contrary supposition is a manifest absurdity.

Brown's doctrine, that the mind cannot exist at the same moment in two different states.

I find the same doctrine maintained by Locke in that valuable, but neglected, treatise entitled *An Examination of Père Malebranche's Opinion of Seeing all Things in God*. In the thirty-ninth section he says: "Different sentiments are different modifications of the mind. The mind or the soul that perceives, is one immaterial, indivisible substance. Now, I see the white and black on this paper, I hear one singing in the next room, I feel the warmth of the fire I sit by, and I taste an apple I am eating, and all this at the same time. Now, I ask, take modification for what you please, can the same unextended, indivisible substance have different, nay, inconsistent and opposite, (as these of white and black must be,) modifications at the same time? Or must we suppose distinct parts in an indivisible substance, one for black, another for white, and another for red ideas, and so of the rest of those infinite sensations which we have in sorts and degrees; all which we can distinctly perceive, and so are distinct ideas, some whereof are opposite as heat and cold, which yet a man may feel at the same time?" Leibnitz has not only given a refutation of Locke's *Essay*, but likewise of his *Examination of Malebranche*. In reference to the passage I have just quoted Leibnitz says: "Mr. Locke asks, 'Can the same unextended, indivisible substance, have different, nay, inconsistent and opposite modifications, at the same time?' I reply, it can. What is inconsistent in the same object, is not inconsistent in the representation of different objects which we conceive at the same moment. For

This doctrine maintained by Locke.

Opposed by Leibnitz.

this there is no necessity that there should be different parts in the soul, as it is not necessary that there should be different parts in the point on which, however, different angles rest."[1]   The same thing had, however, been even better said by Aristotle, whose doctrine I prefer translating to you, as more perspicuous, in the following passage from Joannes Grammaticus, (better known by the surname Philoponus,) — a Greek philosopher, who flourished towards the middle of the sixth century.   It is taken from the Prologue to his valuable commentary on the *De Anima* of Aristotle; and, what is curious, the very supposition which on Locke's doctrine would infer the corporeal nature of mind, is alleged, by the Aristotelians and Condillac, in proof of its immateriality.   "Nothing bodily," says Aristotle, "can, at the same time, in the same part, receive contraries. The finger cannot at once be wholly participant of white and of black, nor can it, at once and in the same place, be both hot and cold.   But the sense at the same moment apprehends contraries. Wherefore, it knows that this is first, and that second, and that it discriminates the black from the white.   In what manner, therefore, does sight simultaneously perceive contraries?   Does it do so by the same? or does it by one part apprehend black, by another white?   If it does so by the same, it must apprehend these without parts, and it is incorporeal.   But if by one part it apprehends this quality, and by another that, — this, he says, is the same as if I perceived this, and you that.   But it is necessary that that which judges should be one and the same, and that it should even apprehend by the same the objects which are judged.   Body cannot, at the same moment and by the same part, apply itself to contraries or things absolutely different.   But sense at once applies itself to black and to white; it, therefore, applies itself indivisibly. It is thus shown to be incorporeal.   For if by one part it apprehended white, by another part apprehended black, it could not discern the one color from the other; for no one can distinguish that which is perceived by himself as different from that which is perceived by another."[2]   So far, Philoponus.

Aristotle opposed to foregoing doctrine.

His view, as paraphrased by Philoponus.

---

1 *Remarques sur le Sentiment du Père Malebranche; Opera Philosophica*, edit. Erdmann, p. 451. — ED.

2 The text of Aristotle here partially paraphrased, (Procem, f. 3*b* ed. 1535), and more fully in Commentary on texts, 144. 149, is as follows; —Ἦ καὶ δῆλον ὅτι ἡ σὰρξ οὐκ ἔστι τὸ ἔσχατον αἰσθητήριον· ἀνάγκη γὰρ ἦν ἁπτόμενον αὐτοῦ κρίνειν τὸ κρῖνον. Οὔτε δὴ κεχωρισμένοις ἐνδέχεται κρίνειν ὅτι ἕτερον τὸ γλυκὺ τοῦ λευκοῦ, ἀλλὰ δεῖ ἑνί τινι ἄμφω δῆλα εἶναι. Οὕτω μὲν γὰρ κἂν εἰ τοῦ μὲν ἐγὼ τοῦ δὲ σὺ αἴσθοιο, δῆλον ἂν εἴη ὅτι ἕτερα ἀλλήλων· Δεῖ δὲ τὸ ἓν λέγειν ὅτι ἕτερον· ἕτερον γὰρ τὸ γλυκὺ τοῦ λευκοῦ. Λέγει ἄρα τὸ αὐτό· Ὥστε ὡς λέγει, οὕτω καὶ νοεῖ καὶ αἰσθάνεται. Ὅτι μὲν οὖν οὐχ οἷόν τε κεχωρισμένοις κρίνειν τὰ κεχωρισμένα, δῆλον

Dr. Brown calls the sensation of sweet one mental state, the sensation of cold another; and as the one of these states may exist without the other, they are consequently different states. But will it be maintained that we cannot, at one and the same moment, feel the sensations of sweet and cold, or that sensations forming apart different states, do, when coëxistent in the same subject, form only a single state?

Criticism of Brown's doctrine.

The doctrine that the mind can attend to, or be conscious of, only a single object at a time, would, in fact, involve the conclusion that all comparison and discrimination are impossible; but comparison and discrimination being possible, this possibility disproves the truth of the counter proposition. An act of comparison or discrimination supposes that we are able to comprehend, in one indivisible consciousness, the different objects to be compared or discriminated. Were I only conscious of one object at one time, I could never possibly bring them into relation; each could be apprehended only separately, and for itself. For in the moment in which I am conscious of the object A, I am, *ex hypothesi*, unconscious of the object B; and in the moment I am conscious of the object B, I am unconscious of the object A. So far, in fact, from consciousness not being competent to the cognizance of two things at once, it is only possible under that cognizance as its condition. For without discrimination there could be no consciousness; and discrimination necessarily supposes two terms to be discriminated.

On this view comparison impossible.

No judgment could be possible were not the subject and predicate of a proposition thought together by the mind, although expressed in language one after the other. Nay, as Aristotle has observed, a syllogism forms in thought one simultaneous act;[1] and it is only the necessity of retailing it piecemeal and by succession, in order to accommodate thought to the imperfection of its vehicle, language, that affords the appearance of a consecutive existence. Some languages, as the Sanscrit, the Latin, and the Greek, express the syntactical relations by flexion, and not by mere juxtaposition.

ὅτι δ' οὐδ' ἐν κεχωρισμένῳ χρόνῳ, ἐντευθεν. Ὥπσερ γὰρ τὸ αὐτὸ λέγει ὅτι ἕτερον, τὸ ἀγαθὸν καὶ τὸ κακόν, οὕτω καὶ ὅτε θάτερον λέγει ὅτι ἕτερον καὶ θάτερον, οὐ κατὰ συμβεβηκὸς τὸ ὅτε· λέγω δ', οἷον νῦν λέγω ὅτι ἕτερον, οὐ μέντοι ὅτι νῦν ἕτερον. Ἀλλ' οὕτω λέγει, καὶ νῦν, καὶ ὅτι νῦν· ἅμα ἄρα. Ὥστε ἀχώριστον καὶ ἐν ἀχωρίστῳ χρόνῳ. *De Anima,* lib. iii. c. 2, ¶ 11. Cf. ¶¶ 9, 10, 12, 13, 14, with

the relative commentary by Philoponus. — ED.

[1] This is said by Aristotle of the act of judgment; but the remark applies to that of reasoning also. See *De Anima,* iii. 6: Ἐν οἷς τὸ ψεῦδος καὶ τὸ ἀληθές, σύνθεσίς τις ἤδη νοημάτων ὥσπερ ἓν ὄντων. . . . . Τὸ δὲ ἓν ποιοῦν, τοῦτο ὁ νοῦς ἕκαστον. —ED.

Their sentences are thus bound up in one organic whole, the preceding parts remaining suspended in the mind, till the meaning, like an electric spark, is flashed from the conclusion to the commencement. This is the reason of the greater rhetorical effect of terminating the Latin period by the verb. And to take a more elementary example, — "How could the mind comprehend these words of Horace,

'Bacchum in remotis carmina rupibus
Vidi docentem,'

unless it could seize at once those images in which the adjectives are separated from their substantives ? "[1]

The modern philosophers who have agitated this question, are not aware that it was once canvassed likewise in the schools of the middle ages. It was there expressed by the proposition, *Possitne intellectus noster plura simul intelligere.*[2] Maintaining the negative, we find St. Thomas, Cajetanus, Ferrariensis, Capriolus, Hervæus, Alexander Alensis, Albertus Magnus, and Durandus; while the affirmative was asserted by Scotus, Occam, Gregorius Ariminensis, Lichetus, Marsilius, Biel, and others.

This question canvassed in the schools of the middle ages.

Supposing that the mind is not limited to the simultaneous consideration of a single object, a question arises, How many objects can it embrace at once? You will recollect that I formerly stated that the greater the number of objects among which the attention of the mind is distributed, the feebler and less distinct will be its cognizance of each.

How many objects can the mind embrace at once?

" Pluribus intentus, minor est ad singula sensus."

Consciousness will thus be at its maximum of intensity when attention is concentrated on a single object; and the question comes to be, how many several objects can the mind simultaneously survey, not with vivacity, but without absolute confusion ? I find this problem stated and differently answered, by different philosophers, and apparently without a knowledge of each other. By Charles Bonnet[3] the mind is allowed to have a distinct notion of

---

[1] [Bonstetten, *Etudes de l'Homme*, tom. ii. p. 377, note.]

[2] [See Aquinas, *Summa*, pars i., Q. 85, art. 4. Cf. Alex. Aphrodisiensis, *De Anima*, lib. i. c. 22, p. 134, fol. *a* (ed. Ald.) Nemesius, *De Natura Hominis*, c. vii. p. 184—ed. Matthæi.]

[3] [*Essai de Psychologie*, c. xxxviii. p. 132. Compare his *Essai Analytique sur l'Ame*, tom. i. c. xiii. p. 163 *et seq.*]

six objects at once; by Abraham Tucker[1] the number is limited to four; while Destutt-Tracy[2] again amplifies it to six. The opinion of the first and last of these philosophers, appears to me correct. You can easily make the experiment for yourselves, but you must beware of grouping the objects into classes. If you throw a handful of marbles on the floor, you will find it difficult to view at once more than six, or seven at most, without confusion; but if you group them into twos, or threes, or fives, you can comprehend as many groups as you can units; because the mind considers these groups only as units, — it views them as wholes, and throws their parts out of consideration. You may perform the experiment also by an act of imagination.

Before leaving this subject, I shall make some observations on the value of attention, considered in its highest degree as an act of will, and on the importance of forming betimes the habit of deliberate concentration.

Value of attention considered in its highest degree as an act of will. The greater capacity of continuous thinking that a man possesses, the longer and more steadily can he follow out the same train of thought,—the stronger is his power of attention; and in proportion to his power of attention will be the success with which his labor is rewarded. All commencement is difficult; and this is more especially true of intellectual effort. When we turn for the first time our view on any given object, a hundred other things still retain possession of our thoughts. Even when we are able, by an arduous exertion, to break loose from the matters which have previously engrossed us, or which every moment force themselves on our consideration, — even when a resolute determination, or the attraction of the new object, has smoothed the way on which we are to travel; still the mind is continually perplexed by the glimmer of intrusive and distracting thoughts, which prevent it from placing that which should exclusively occupy its view, in the full clearness of an undivided light. How great soever may be the interest which we take in the new object, it will, however, only be fully established as a favorite when it has been fused into an integral part of the system of our previous knowledge, and of our established associations of thoughts, feelings, and desires. But this can only be accomplished by time and custom. Our imagination and our memory, to which we must

---

1 [*Light of Nature*, c. xiv. § 5.]

2 [*Idéologie*, tom. i. p. 453. Compare Degerando, *Des Signes*, i. 167, who allows us to embrace, at one view, five unities. D'Alembert, *Mélanges*, vol. iv. pp. 40, 151. Ancillon, *Nouveaux Mélanges*, tom. ii. p. 135. Malebranche, *Recherche*, liv. iii. c. 2, tom. i. p. 191.]

resort for materials with which to illustrate and enliven our new study, accord us their aid unwillingly, — indeed, only by compulsion. But if we are vigorous enough to pursue our course in spite of obstacles, every step, as we advance, will be found easier; the mind becomes more animated and energetic; the distractions gradually diminish; the attention is more exclusively concentrated upon its object; the kindred ideas flow with greater freedom and abundance, and afford an easier selection of what is suitable for illustration. At length, our system of thought harmonizes with our pursuit. The whole man becomes, as it may be, philosopher, or historian, or poet; he lives only in the trains of thought relating to this character. He now energizes freely, and, consequently, with pleasure; for pleasure is the reflex of unforced and unimpeded energy. All that is produced in this state of mind, bears the stamp of excellence and perfection. Helvetius justly observes, that the very feeblest intellect is capable of comprehending the inference of one mathematical position from another, and even of making such an inference itself.[1] Now, the most difficult and complicate demonstrations in the works of a Newton or a Laplace, are all made up of such immediate inferences. They are like houses composed of single bricks. No greater exertion of intellect is required to make a thousand such inferences than is requisite to make one; as the effort of laying a single brick is the maximum of any individual effort in the construction of such a house. Thus, the difference between an ordinary mind and the mind of a Newton, consists principally in this, that the one is capable of the application of a more continuous attention than the other, — that a Newton is able without fatigue to connect inference with inference in one long series towards a determinate end; while the man of inferior capacity is soon obliged to break or let fall the thread which he had begun

Sir Isaac Newton.

to spin. This is, in fact, what Sir Isaac, with equal modesty and shrewdness, himself admitted. To one who complimented him on his genius, he replied that if he had made any discoveries, it was owing more to patient attention than to any other talent.[2] There is but little analogy between mathematics and play-acting; but I heard the great Mrs. Siddons, in nearly the same language, attribute the whole superiority of her unrivalled talent to the more intense study which she bestowed upon her parts. If what Alcibiades, in the *Symposium*[3] of Plato,

Socrates.

narrates of Socrates were true, the father of Greek philosophy must have possessed this faculty of meditation or continuous attention in the highest degree.

1 *De l' Esprit* — Discours iii. c. iv. — ED.   2 See Reid's *Works*, p. 537.   3 P. 220. — ED.

The story, indeed, has some appearance of exaggeration; but it shows what Alcibiades, or rather Plato through him, deemed the requisite of a great thinker. According to this report, in a military expedition which Socrates made along with Alcibiades, the philosopher was seen by the Athenian army to stand for a whole day and a night, until the breaking of the second morning, motionless, with a fixed gaze, — thus showing that he was uninterruptedly engrossed with the consideration of a single subject: "And thus," says Alcibiades, "Socrates is ever wont to do when his mind is occupied with inquiries in which there are difficulties to be overcome. He then never interrupts his meditation, and forgets to eat, and drink, and sleep, — everything, in short, until his inquiry has reached its termination, or, at least, until he has seen some light in it." In this history there may be, as I have said, exaggeration; but still the truth of the principle is undeniable.

Descartes.

Like Newton, Descartes arrogated nothing to the force of his intellect. What he had accomplished more than other men, that he attributed to the superiority of his method;[1]

Bacon.

and Bacon, in like manner, eulogizes his method, — in that it places all men with equal attention upon a level, and leaves little or nothing to the prerogatives of genius.[2] Nay, genius itself has been analyzed by the shrewdest observers into a higher capacity of attention.

Helvetius.

"Genius," says Helvetius, whom we have already quoted, "is nothing but a continued attention," (une attention suivie).[3] "Genius," says Buffon,[4] "is only

Buffon.
Cuvier.

a protracted patience," (une longue patience). "In the exact sciences, at least," says Cuvier,[5] "it is the patience of a sound intellect, when invincible, which truly constitutes genius." And Chesterfield has also

Chesterfield.

observed, that "the power of applying an attention, steady and undissipated, to a single object, is the sure mark of a superior genius."[6]

These examples and authorities concur in establishing the important truth, that he who would, with success, attempt discovery, either by inquiry into the works of nature, or by meditation on the phænomena of mind, must acquire the faculty of abstracting himself, for a season, from the invasion of surrounding objects; must be

1 *Discours de la Méthode*, p. 1. — ED.

2 *Nov. Org.*, lib. i. aph. 61. — ED.

3 *De l' Esprit*, Discours iii. chap. iv. — ED.

4 [Quoted by Ponelle, *Manuel*, p. 371.]

5 *Eloge Historique de M. Haüy*, quoted by Toussaint, *De la Pensées*, p. 219.]

6 *Letters to his Son*. Letter lxxxix. [Compare Bonnet, *Essai Analytique*, tom. i., préface, p. 8.]

able even, in a certain degree, to emancipate himself from the dominion of the body, and live, as it were, a pure intelligence, within the

Instances of the pow-
er of Abstraction.

circle of his thoughts. This faculty has been
manifested, more or less, by all whose names are
associated with the progress of the intellectual
sciences. In some, indeed, the power of abstraction almost degen-
erated into a habit akin to disease, and the examples which now
occur to me, would almost induce me to retract what I have said
about the exaggeration of Plato's history of Socrates.

Archimedes,[1] it is well known, was so absorbed in a geometrical

Archimedes.

meditation, that he was first aware of the storm-
ing of Syracuse by his own death-wound, and
his exclamation on the entrance of Roman soldiers was, — *Noli
turbare circulos meos.* In like manner, Joseph Scaliger, the most

Joseph Scaliger.

learned of men, when a Protestant student in
Paris, was so engrossed in the study of Homer,
that he became aware of the massacre of St. Bartholomew, and of
his own escape, only on the day subsequent to the catastrophe. The

Carneades.

philosopher Carneades[2] was habitually liable to
fits of meditation, so profound, that, to prevent
him from sinking from inanition, his maid found it necessary to feed

Newton.

him like a child. And it is reported of Newton, that, while engaged in his mathematical
researches, he sometimes forgot to dine. Cardan,[3] one of the most

Cardan.

illustrious of philosophers and mathematicians,
was once, upon a journey, so lost in thought, that
he forgot both his way and the object of his journey. To the questions of his driver whither he should proceed, he made no answer;
and when he came to himself at nightfall, he was surprised to find
the carriage at a stand-still, and directly under a gallows. The

Vieta.

mathematician Vieta was sometimes so buried
in meditation, that for hours he bore more
resemblance to a dead person than to a living, and was then wholly
unconscious of everything going on around him. On the day of

Budæus.

his marriage, the great Budæus forgot everything in philological speculations, and he was
only awakened to the affairs of the external world by a tardy
embassy from the marriage-party, who found him absorbed in the
composition of his *Commentarii.*

It is beautifully observed by Malebranche, "that the discovery of

1 See Valerius Maximus, lib. viii. c. 7. — ED.   3 *Ibid.*, lib. viii. c. 7. — ED.
2 [Steeb, *Über den Menschen*, ii. 671]

truth can only be made by the labor of attention; because it is only the labor of attention which has light for its reward;"[1] and in another place:[2] "The attention of the intellect is a natural prayer by which we obtain the enlightenment of reason.

Malebranche quoted on place and importance of attention.

But since the fall, the intellect frequently experiences appalling droughts; it cannot pray; the labor of attention fatigues and afflicts it. In fact, this labor is at first great, and the recompense scanty; while, at the same time, we are unceasingly solicited, pressed, agitated by the imagination and the passions, whose inspiration and impulses it is always agreeable to obey. Nevertheless, it is a matter of necessity; we must invoke reason to be enlightened; there is no other way of obtaining light and intelligence but by the labor of attention. Faith is a gift of God which we earn not by our merits; but intelligence is a gift usually only conceded to desert. Faith is a pure grace in every sense; but the understanding of a truth is a grace of such a character that it must be merited by labor, or by the coöperation of grace. Those, then, who are capable of this labor, and who are always attentive to the truth which ought to guide them, have a disposition which would undoubtedly deserve a name more magnificent than those bestowed on the most splendid virtues. But although this habit or this virtue be inseparable from the love of order, it is so little known among us that I do not know if we have done it the honor of a particular name. May I, therefore, be pardoned in calling it by the equivocal name of *force of intellect*. To acquire this true force by which the intellect supports the labor of attention, it is necessary to begin betimes to labor; for, in the course of nature, we can only acquire habits by acts, and can only strengthen them by exercise. But perhaps the only difficulty is to begin. We recollect that we began, and that we were obliged to leave off. Hence we get discouraged; we think ourselves unfit for meditation; we renounce reason. If this be the case, whatever we may allege to justify our sloth and negligence, we renounce virtue, at least in part. For without the labor of attention, we shall never comprehend the grandeur of religion, the sanctity of morals, the littleness of all that is not God, the absurdity of the passions, and of all our internal miseries. Without this labor, the soul will live in blindness and in disorder; because there is naturally no other way to obtain the light that should conduct us; we shall be eternally under disquietude and in strange embarrassment; for we fear everything when we walk in darkness and surrounded by precipices. It is true that faith guides and supports; but it does so only as it

---

1 *Traité de Morale*, partie i. chap. vi. § 1.   2 *Ibid.*, partie i. chap. v, § 4. — ED.

produces some light by the attention which it excites in us; for light alone is what can assure minds, like ours, which have so many enemies to fear."

I have translated a longer extract than I intended when I began;
but the truth and importance of the observations are so great, and they are so admirably expressed in Malebranche's own inimitable style, that it was not easy to leave off. They are only a fragment of a very valuable chapter on the subject, to which I would earnestly refer you, — indeed, I may take this opportunity of saying, that there is no philosophical author who can be more profitably studied than Malebranche. As a thinker, he is perhaps the most profound that France has ever produced, and as a writer on philosophical subjects, there is not another European author who can be placed before him. His style is a model at once of dignity and of natural ease; and no metaphysician has been able to express himself so clearly and precisely without resorting to technical and scholastic terms. That he was the author of a celebrated, but exploded hypothesis, is, perhaps, the reason why he is far less studied than he otherwise deserves. His works are of principal value for the admirable observations on human nature which they embody; and were everything to be expunged from them connected with the *Vision of all things in the Deity*, and even with the Cartesian hypotheses in general, they would still remain an inestimable treasury of the acutest analyses, expressed in the most appropriate, and, therefore, the most admirable eloquence. In the last respect, he is only approached, certainly not surpassed, by Hume and Mendelssohn.

Study of the writings of Malebranche recommended.

I have dwelt at greater length upon the practical bearings of Attention, not only because this principle constitutes the better half of all intellectual power, but because it is of consequence that you should be fully aware of the incalculable importance of acquiring, by early and continued exercise, the habit of attention. There are, however, many points of great moment on which I have not touched, and the dependence of Memory upon Attention might alone form an interesting matter of discussion. You will find some excellent observations on this subject in the first and third volumes of Mr. Stewart's *Elements*.[1]

---

1 See *Works*, ii.; *Elements*, i. p. 122 *et seq.*, and p. 352. — Ed.

LECTURE XV.

CONSCIOUSNESS,—ITS EVIDENCE AND AUTHORITY.

HAVING now concluded the discussion in regard to what Consciousness is, and shown you that it constitutes the fundamental form of every act of knowledge;—I now proceed to consider it as the source from whence we must derive every fact in the Philosophy of Mind. And, in prosecution of this purpose, I shall, in the first place, endeavor to show you that it really is the principal, if not the only source, from which all knowledge of the mental phænomena must be obtained;[1] in the second place, I shall consider the character of its evidence, and what, under different relations, are the different degrees of its authority; and, in the last place, I shall state what, and of what nature, are the more general phænomena which it reveals. Having terminated these, I shall then descend to the consideration of the special faculties of knowledge, that is, to the particular modifications of which consciousness is susceptible.

Consciousness the source of Philosophy.

We proceed to consider, in the first place, the authority,—the certainty of this instrument. Now, it is at once evident, that philosophy, as it affirms its own possibility, must affirm the veracity of consciousness; for, as philosophy is only a scientific development of the facts which consciousness reveals, it follows, that philosophy, in denying or doubting the testimony of consciousness, would deny or doubt its own existence. If, therefore, philosophy be not *felo de se,* it must not invalidate the

The possibility of Philosophy implies the veracity of consciousness.

---

[1] Under the head here specified, the Author occasionally delivered from the Chair three lectures, which contained " a summary view of the nervous system in the higher animals, more especially in man; and a statement of some of the results obtained [by him] from an extensive and accurate induction on the size of the Encephalus and its principal parts, both in man and the lower animals,—serving to prove that no assistance is afforded to Mental Philosophy by the examination of the Nervous System, and that the doctrine, or doctrines, which found upon the supposed parallelism of brain and mind, are, as far as observation extends, wholly groundless." These lectures, as foreign in their details from the general subject of the Course, are omitted in the present publication. A general summary of the principal conclusions to which the researches of the Author on this subject conducted him, will be found in Appendix II.—ED.

integrity of that which is, as it were, the heart, the *punctum saliens*, of its being; and as it would actively maintain its own credit, it must be able positively to vindicate the truth of consciousness: for, as Lucretius[1] well observes,

" . . . Ut in Fabrica, si prava est Regula prima,
　Normaque si fallax rectis regionibus exit,
　Omnia mendose fieri, atque obstipa necessum est;
　Sic igitur Ratio tibi rerum prava necesse est,
　Falsaque sit, falsis quæcunque ab Sensibus orta est."

And Leibnitz[2] truly says,— "If our immediate internal experience could possibly deceive us, there could no longer be for us any truth of fact (*vérité de fait*), nay, nor any truth of reason (*vérité de raison*)."

So far there is, and can be, no dispute; if philosophy is possible, the evidence of consciousness is authentic. No philosopher denies its authority, and even the Skeptic can only attempt to show, on the hypothesis of the Dogmatist, that consciousness, as at variance with itself, is, therefore, on that hypothesis, mendacious.

But if the testimony of consciousness be in itself confessedly above all suspicion, it follows, that we inquire into the conditions or laws which regulate the legitimacy of its applications. The conscious mind being at once the source from which we must derive our knowledge of its phænomena, and the mean through which that knowledge is obtained, Psychology is only an evolution, by consciousness, of the facts which consciousness itself reveals. As every system of Mental Philosophy is thus only an exposition of these facts, every such system, consequently, is true and complete, as it fairly and fully exhibits what, and what only, consciousness exhibits.

But, it may be objected, — if consciousness be the only revelation we possess of our intellectual nature, and

Consciousness, as the criterion of philosophy, naturally clear and unerring.

if consciousness be also the sole criterion by which we can interpret the meaning of what this revelation contains, this revelation must be very obscure, — this criterion must be very uncertain, seeing that the various systems of philosophy all equally appeal to this revelation and to this criterion, in support of the most contradictory opinions. As to the fact of the variety and contradiction of philosophical systems, — this cannot be denied, and it is also true that all these systems either openly profess allegiance to

---

[1] *De Rerum Natura*, lib. v. 516.　　[2] *Nouveaux Essais*, lib. ii. c. 27, § 13. —ED.

consciousness, or silently confess its authority. But admitting all this, I am still bold enough to maintain, that consciousness affords not merely the only revelation, and only criterion of philosophy, but that this revelation is naturally clear, — this criterion, in itself, unerring. The history of philosophy, like the history of theology, is only, it is too true, the history of variations, and we must admit of the book of consciousness what a great Calvinist divine [1] bitterly confessed of the book of Scripture, —

> " Hic liber est in quo quærit sua dogmata quisque;
> Invenit et pariter dogmata quisque sua."

In regard, however, to either revelation, it can be shown that the source of this diversity is not in the book, but in the reader. If men will go to the Bible, not to ask of it what they shall believe, but to find in it what they believe already, the standard of unity and truth becomes in human hands only a Lesbian rule.[2] And if philosophers, in place of evolving their doctrines out of consciousness, resort to consciousness only when they are able to quote its authority in confirmation of their preconceived opinions, philosophical systems, like the sandals of Theramenes,[3] may fit any feet, but can never pretend to represent the immutability of nature. And that philosophers have been, for the most part, guilty of this, it is not extremely difficult to show. They have seldom or never taken the facts of consciousness, the whole facts of consciousness, and nothing but the facts of consciousness. They have either overlooked, or rejected, or interpolated.

Cause of variation in philosophy.

Before we are entitled to accuse consciousness of being a false, or vacillating, or ill-informed witness, — we are bound, first of all, to see whether there be any rules by which, in employing the testimony of consciousness, we must be governed; and whether philosophers have evolved their systems out of consciousness in obedience to these rules. For if there be rules under which alone the evidence of consciousness can be fairly and fully given, and, consequently, under which alone consciousness can serve as

We are bound to inquire whether there be any rules by which in employing the testimony of consciousness, we must be governed.

1 S. Werenfels, *Dissertationes.* Amstel. 1716, vol. ii. p. 391. — ED.

2 Aristotle, *Eth. Nic.*, v. 10: Τοῦ γὰρ ἀορίστου ἀόριστος καὶ ὁ κανών ἐστιν, ὥσπερ καὶ τῆς Λεσβίας οἰκοδομῆς ὁ μολίβδινος κανών· πρὸς γὰρ τὸ σχῆμα τοῦ λίθου μετακινεῖται καὶ οὐ μένει ὁ κανών. — ED.

3 Θηραμένης διὰ τὸ μὴ μόνιμον ἀλλὰ καὶ ἐπαμφοτερίζον ἀεὶ τῇ προαιρέσει τῆς πολιτείας, ἐπεκλήθη Κόθορνος. Plutarch, *Nicias*, vol. i. p. 525 (ed. 1599). — ED.

an infallible standard of certainty and truth, and if philosophers have despised or neglected these,—then, must we remove the reproach from the instrument, and affix it to those blundering workmen who have not known how to handle and apply it. In attempting to vindicate the veracity and perspicuity of this, the natural, revelation of our mental being, I shall, therefore, first, endeavor to enumerate and explain the general rules by which we must be governed in applying consciousness as a mean of internal observation, and thereafter show how the variations and contradictions of philosophy have all arisen from the violation of one or more of these laws. If I accomplish this at present but imperfectly, I may at least plead in excuse, that the task I undertake is one that has not been previously attempted. I, therefore, request that you will view what I am to state to you on this subject rather as the outline of a course of reasoning, than as anything pretending to finished argument.

In attempting a scientific deduction of the philosophy of mind from the data of consciousness, there are, in all, if I generalize correctly, three laws which afford the exclusive conditions of psychological legitimacy. These laws, or regulative conditions, are self-evident, and yet they seem never to have been clearly proposed to themselves by philosophers,—in philosophical speculation, they have certainly never been adequately obeyed.

Three grand Laws, under which consciousness can be legitimately applied to the consideration of its own phænomena.

The First of these rules is,—That no fact be assumed as a fact of consciousness but what is ultimate and simple. This I would call the law of Parcimony.

1. The law of Parcimony.

The Second,—that which I would style the law of Integrity, is—That the whole facts of consciousness be taken without reserve or hesitation, whether given as constituent, or as regulative data.

2. The law of Integrity.

The Third is,—That nothing but the facts of consciousness be taken, or, if inferences of reasoning be admitted, that these at least be recognized as legitimate only as deduced from, and in subordination to, the immediate data of consciousness, and every position rejected as illegitimate, which is contradictory of these. This I would call the law of Harmony.

3. The law of Harmony.

I shall consider these in their order.

I. The first law, that of Parcimony, is,—That no fact be assumed as a fact of consciousness but what is ultimate and simple. What

I. The law of Parcimony.

Fact of consciousness — what?

is a fact of consciousness? This question of all others requires a precise and articulate answer, but I have not found it adequately answered in any psychological author.

In the first place, — every mental phænomenon may be called a fact of consciousness. But as we distinguish

1. Primary and universal.

consciousness from the special faculties, though these are all only modifications of consciousness, — only branches of which consciousness is the trunk, so we distinguish the special and derivative phænomena of mind from those that are primary and universal, and give to the latter the name of *facts of consciousness*, as more eminently worthy of that appellation. In an act of perception, for example, I distinguish the pen I hold in my hand, and my hand itself, from my mind perceiving them. This distinction is a particular fact, — the fact of a particular faculty, perception. But there is a general fact, a general distinction, of which this is only a special case. This general fact is the distinction of the Ego and non-Ego, and it belongs to consciousness as the general faculty. Whenever, therefore, in our analysis of the intellectual phænomena, we arrive at an element which we cannot reduce to a generalization from experience, but which lies at the root of all experience, and which we cannot, therefore, resolve into any higher principle, — this we properly call a fact of consciousness. Looking to such a fact of consciousness as the last result of an analysis, we call it an *ultimate* principle; looking from it as the first constituent of all intellectual combination, we call it a *primary* principle. A fact of consciousness is, thus, a simple, and, as we regard it, either an ultimate, or a primary, datum of intelligence. It obtains also various denominations; sometimes it is called an *a priori principle*, sometimes a *fundamental law* of mind, sometimes a *transcendental condition* of thought,[1] etc., etc.

But, in the second place, this, its character of ultimate priority,

2. Necessary.

supposes its character of necessity. It must be impossible not to think it. In fact, by its necessity alone can we recognize it as an original datum of intelligence, and distinguish it from any mere result of generalization and custom.

In the third place, this fact, as ultimate, is also given to us with a mere belief of its reality; in other words, consciousness reveals that it is, but not why or how it is. This is evident. Were this

---

1 See *Reid's Works*, p. 755 *et seq.* — ED.

fact given us, not only with a belief, but with a knowledge of how
or why it is, in that case it would be a derivative
and not a primary datum. For that whereby we
were thus enabled to comprehend its how and
why, — in other words, the reason of its existence, — this would be
relatively prior, and to it or to its antecedent must we ascend, until
we arrive at that primary fact, in which we must at last believe, —
which we must take upon trust, but which we could not comprehend, that is, think under a higher notion.

3. Given with a mere
belief of its reality.

A fact of consciousness is thus, — that whose existence is
given and guaranteed by an original and necessary belief. But
there is an important distinction to be here made, which has not
only been overlooked by all philosophers, but has led some of the
most distinguished into no inconsiderable errors.

The facts of consciousness are to be considered in two points of
view; either as evidencing their own ideal or
phænomenal existence, or as evidencing the
objective existence of something else beyond
them.[1] A belief in the former is not identical
with a belief in the latter. The one cannot, the
other may possibly be refused. In the case of a
common witness, we cannot doubt the fact of
his personal reality, nor the fact of his testimony as emitted, — but we can always doubt the truth of that
which his testimony avers. So it is with consciousness. We cannot possibly refuse the fact
of its evidence as given, but we may hesitate to
admit that beyond itself of which it assures us.
I shall explain by taking an example. In the
act of External Perception, consciousness gives
as a conjunct fact, the existence of Me or Self as perceiving, and the
existence of something different from Me or Self as perceived. Now
the reality of this, as a subjective datum, — as an ideal phænomenon,
it is absolutely impossible to doubt without doubting the existence
of consciousness, for consciousness is itself this fact; and to doubt
the existence of consciousness is absolutely impossible; for as such
a doubt could not exist, except in and through consciousness, it
would, consequently, annihilate itself. We should doubt that we
doubted. As contained, — as given, in an act of consciousness, the
contrast of mind knowing and matter known cannot be denied.

But the whole phænomenon as given in consciousness may be

The facts of con-
sciousness to be con-
sidered in two points
of view; either as
evidencing their own
ideal existence, or
the objective existence
of something beyond
them.

How far doubt is
possible in regard to
a fact of Conscious-
ness. Illustrated in
the case of Percep-
tion.

---

1 See *Reid's Works.* Note A, p. 743, *et seq.* — ED.

admitted, and yet its inference disputed.   It may be said, consciousness gives the mental subject as perceiving an external object, contradistinguished from it as perceived; all this we do not, and cannot, deny.   But consciousness is only a phænomenon; the contrast between the subject and object may be only apparent, not real; the object given as an external reality, may only be a mental representation, which the mind is, by an unknown law, determined unconsciously to produce, and to mistake for something different from itself.   All this may be said and believed, without self-contradiction, — nay, all this has, by the immense majority of modern philosophers, been actually said and believed.

In like manner, in an act of Memory consciousness connects a present existence with a past.   I cannot deny

In the case of Memory.

the actual phænomenon, because my denial would be suicidal, but I can, without self-contradiction, assert that consciousness may be a false witness in regard to any former existence; and I may maintain, if I please, that the memory of the past, in consciousness, is nothing but a phænomenon, which has no reality beyond the present.   There are many other facts of consciousness which we cannot but admit as ideal phænomena, but may discredit as guaranteeing aught beyond their phænomenal existence itself.   The legality of this doubt I do not at present consider, but only its possibility; all that I have now in view being to show that we must not confound, as has been done, the double import of the facts, and the two degrees of evidence for their reality.   This mistake has, among others, been made by Mr. Stewart.[1]   "The belief," he says, "which accompanies consciousness, as to the present existence of its appro-

Stewart confounds these two degrees of evidence.

priate phænomena, has been commonly considered as much less obnoxious to cavil, than any of the principles which philosophers are accustomed to assume as self-evident, in the formation of their metaphysical systems.   No doubts on this head have yet been suggested by any philosopher, how skeptical soever; even by those who have called in question the existence both of mind and of matter.   And yet the fact is, that it rests on no foundation more solid than our belief of the existence of external objects; or our belief, that other men possess intellectual powers and faculties similar to those of which we are conscious in ourselves.   In all these cases, the only account that can be given of our belief is, that it forms a necessary part of our constitution; against which metaphysicians may easily

1 *Phil. Essays*   *Works*, vol. v. p. 57.

argue, so as to perplex the judgment, but of which it is impossible for us to divest ourselves for a moment, when we are called on to employ our reason, either in the business of life, or in the pursuits of science. While we are under the influence of our appetites, passions, or affections, or even of a strong speculative curiosity, all those difficulties which bewildered us in the solitude of the closet, vanish before the essential principles of the human frame."

With all the respect to which the opinion of so distinguished a philosopher as Mr. Stewart is justly entitled, I must be permitted to say, that I cannot but regard his assertion, — that the present exist-

Criticism of Stewart's view.

ence of the phænomena of consciousness, and the reality of that to which these phænomena bear witness, rest on a foundation equally solid, — as wholly untenable. The second fact, the fact testified to, may be worthy of all credit, — as I agree with Mr. Stewart in thinking that it is; but still it does not rest on a foundation equally solid as the fact of the testimony itself. Mr. Stewart confesses that of the former no doubt had ever been suggested by the boldest skeptic; and the latter, in so far as it assures us of our having an immediate knowledge of the external world, —which is the case alleged by Mr. Stewart, — has been doubted, nay denied, not merely by skeptics, but by modern philosophers almost to a man. This historical circumstance, therefore, of itself, would create a strong presumption, that the two facts must stand on very different foundations; and this presumption is confirmed when we investigate what these foundations themselves are.

The one fact, — the fact of the testimony, is an act of consciousness itself; it cannot, therefore, be invalidated without self-contradiction. For, as we have frequently observed, to doubt the reality of that of which we are conscious is impossible; for as we can only doubt through consciousness, to doubt of consciousness is to doubt of consciousness by consciousness. If, on the one hand, we affirm the reality of the doubt, we thereby explicitly affirm the reality of consciousness, and contradict our doubt; if, on the other hand, we deny the reality of consciousness, we implicitly deny the reality of our denial itself. Thus, in the act of perception, consciousness gives as a conjunct fact, an ego or mind, and a non-ego or matter, known together, and contradistinguished from each other. Now, as a present phænomenon, this double fact cannot possibly be denied. I cannot, therefore, refuse the fact, that, in perception, I am conscious of a phænomenon, which I am compelled to regard as the attribute of something different from my mind or self. This I must perforce admit, or run into self-contradiction. But admitting this, may I not still, without self-contradiction, maintain that what I am compelled to view as the phænomenon of something different from me is nevertheless (unknown to me), only a modification of my mind? In this I admit the fact of the testimony of consciousness as given, but deny the truth of its report. Whether this denial of the truth of consciousness as a witness, is or is not legitimate, we are not, at this moment, to consider: all I have in view at present is, as I said, to show that we must distinguish in consciousness two kinds of facts, — the fact of consciousness testifying, and the fact of which consciousness testifies; and that we must not, as Mr. Stewart has done, hold that we can as little doubt of the fact of the existence of an external world, as of the fact that consciousness gives, in mutual contrast, the phænomenon of self, in contrast to the phænomenon of not-self.[1]

Under this first law, let it, therefore, be laid down, in the first

Results of the Law of Parcimony.

place, that by a fact of consciousness properly so called, is meant a primary and universal fact of our intellectual being; and, in the second, that such facts are of two kinds, — 1°, The facts given in the act of consciousness itself; and, 2°, The facts which consciousness does not at once give, but to the reality of which it only bears evidence. And as simplification is always a matter of importance, we may throw out of account altogether the former class of these facts; for of such no doubt can be, or has been, entertained. It is only the authority of these facts as evidence of something beyond themselves, — that is, only the second class of facts, — which become matter of discussion; it is not the reality of consciousness that we have to prove, but its veracity.[2]

The second rule is, That the whole facts of consciousness be

II. The Law of Integrity.

taken without reserve or hesitation, whether given as constituent, or as regulative, data. This rule is too manifest to require much elucidation. As philosophy is only a development of the phænomena and laws of consciousness, it is evident that philosophy can only be complete, as it comprehends, in one harmonious system, all the constituent, and all the regulative, facts of consciousness. If any phænomenon or constituent fact of consciousness be omitted, the system is not complete; if any law or regulative fact is excluded, the system is not legitimate.

---

1 The only philosopher whom I have met with, touching on the question, is Father Buffier, and he seems to strike the nail upon the head. He says, as I recollect, — "He who gainsays the evidence of consciousness of an external world is not self-contradictory; by no means, — he is only mad." — *Traité des Premieres Vérités*, c. xi. § 98. [See *Reid's Works*, p. 787. — ED.]

2 See *Reid's Works*, pp. 743-754, *et seq.* — ED.

The violation of this second rule is, in general, connected with a

III. The Law of
Harmony.

violation of the third, and we shall accordingly illustrate them together. The third is, — That nothing but the facts of consciousness be taken, or if inferences of reasoning be admitted, that these at least be recognized as legitimate only as deduced from, and only in subordination to, the immediate data of consciousness, and that every position be rejected as illegitimate which is contradictory to these.

The truth and necessity of this rule are not less evident than the

These illustrated in
conjunction.

truth and necessity of the preceding. Philosophy is only a systematic evolution of the contents of consciousness, by the instrumentality of consciousness; it, therefore, necessarily supposes, in both respects, the veracity of consciousness.

But, though this be too evident to admit of doubt, and though

How Skepticism ari-
ses out of partial dog-
matic systems.

no philosopher has ever openly thrown off allegiance to the authority of consciousness, we find, nevertheless, that its testimony has been silently overlooked, and systems established upon principles in direct hostility to the primary data of intelligence. It is only such a violation of the integrity of consciousness, by the dogmatist, that affords, to the skeptic, the foundation on which he can establish his proof of the nullity of philosophy. The skeptic cannot assail the truth of the facts of consciousness in themselves. In attempting this he would run at once into self-contradiction. In the first place, he would enact the part of a dogmatist, — that is, he would positively, dogmatically, establish his doubt. In the second, waiving this, how can he accomplish what he thus proposes? For why? He must attack consciousness either from a higher ground, or from consciousness itself. Higher ground than consciousness there is none; he must, therefore, invalidate the facts of consciousness from the ground of consciousness itself. On this ground, he cannot, as we have seen, deny the facts of consciousness as given; he can only attempt to invalidate their testimony. But this again can be done only by showing that consciousness tells different tales, — that its evidence is contradictory, — that its data are repugnant. But this no skeptic has ever yet been able to do. Neither does the skeptic or negative philosopher himself assume his principles; he only accepts those on which the dogmatist or positive philosopher attempts to establish his doctrine; and this doctrine he reduces to zero, by showing that its principles are either mutually repugnant, or repugnant to facts of consciousness, on which, though it may not expressly found, still, as facts of consciousness, it cannot refuse to recognize without denying the possibility of philosophy in general.

I shall illustrate the violation of this rule by examples taken from the writings of the late ingenious Dr. Thomas

Violations of the Second and Third laws in the writings of Dr. Thomas Brown.

Brown. — I must, however, premise that this philosopher, so far from being singular in his easy way of appealing to, or overlooking, the facts of consciousness, as he finds them convenient or inconvenient for his purpose, supplies only a specimen of the too ordinary style of philosophizing. Now,

Brown's doctrine of External Perception involves an inconsistency.

you must know, that Dr. Brown maintains the common doctrine of the philosophers, that we have no immediate knowledge of anything beyond the states or modifications of our own minds, — that we are only conscious of the ego, — the non-ego, as known, being only a modification of self, which mankind at large are illusively determined to view as external and different from self. This doctrine is contradictory of the fact to which consciousness testifies, — that the object of which we are conscious in perception, is the external reality as existing, and not merely its representation in the percipient mind. That this is the fact testified to by consciousness, and believed by the common sense of mankind, is admitted even by those philosophers who reject the truth of the testimony and the belief. It is of no consequence to us at present what are the grounds on which the principle is founded, that the mind can have no knowledge of aught besides itself; it is sufficient to observe that, this principle being contradictory of the testimony of consciousness, Dr. Brown, by adopting it, virtually accuses consciousness of falsehood. But if consciousness be false in its testimony to one fact, we can have no confidence in its testimony to any other; and Brown, having himself belied the veracity of consciousness, cannot, therefore, again appeal to this veracity as to a credible authority. But he is not thus consistent. Although he does not allow that we have any knowledge of the existence of an outer world, the existence of that world he still maintains. And on what grounds? He admits the reasoning of the idealist, that is, of the philosopher who denies the reality of the material universe, — he admits this to be invincible. How, then, is this conclusion avoided? Simply by appealing to the universal belief of mankind in favor of the existence of external things,[1] — that is, to the authority of a fact of consciousness. But to him this appeal is incompetent.

---

[1] *Philosophy of the Human Mind,* lecture xxviii., p. 50, 2d edition. See this argument further pursued in the Author's *Discussions,* p. 92. — ED.

For, in the first place, having already virtually given up, or rather positively rejected, the testimony of consciousness, when consciousness deposed to our immediate knowledge of external things, — how can he even found upon the veracity of that mendacious principle, when bearing evidence to the unknown existence of external things? I cannot but believe that the material reality exists; therefore, it does exist, for consciousness does not deceive us, — this reasoning Dr. Brown employs when defending his assertion of an outer world. I cannot but believe that the material reality is the object immediately known in perception; therefore, it is immediately known, for consciousness does not deceive us, — this reasoning Dr. Brown rejects when establishing the foundation of his system. In the one case, he maintains, — this belief, because irresistible, is true; in the other case he maintains, — this belief, though irresistible, is false. Consciousness is veracious in the former belief, mendacious in the latter. I approbate the one, I reprobate the other. The inconsistency of this is apparent. It becomes more palpable when we consider, in the second place, that the belief which Dr. Brown assumes as true rests on — is, in fact, only the reflex of — the belief which he repudiates as false. Why do mankind believe in the existence of an outer world? They do not believe in it as in something unknown; but, on the contrary, they believe it to exist, only because they believe that they immediately know it to exist. The former belief is only as it is founded on the latter. Of all absurdities, therefore, the greatest is to assert, — on the one hand, that consciousness deceives us in the belief that we know any material object to exist, and, on the other, that the material object exists, because, though on false grounds, we believe it to exist.

I may give you another instance, from the same author, of the

The same is true of Brown's proof of our Personal Identity.

wild work that the application of this rule makes, among philosophical systems not legitimately established. Dr. Brown, with other philosophers, rests the proof of our Personal Identity, and of our Mental Individuality, on the ground of beliefs, which, as "intuitive, universal, immediate, and irresistible," he, not unjustly, regards as the "internal and never-ceasing voice of our Creator, — revelations from on high, omnipotent [and veracious] as their Author.[1] To him this argument is, however, incompetent, as contradictory.

What we know of self or person, we know only as a fact of con-

---

1 *Philosophy of the Human Mind*, lecture xiii., p. 269, 2d edition, also Sir W. Hamilton's Discussions, p. 96. — ED.

sciousness. In our perceptive consciousness, there is revealed, in contrast to each, a self and a not-self. This contrast is either true or false. If true, then am I conscious of an object different from me,— that is, I have an immediate perception of the external reality. If false, then am I not conscious of anything different from me, but what I am constrained to regard as not-me is only a modification of me, which, by an illusion of my nature, I mistake, and must mistake, for something different from me.

Now, will it be credited that Dr. Brown — and be it remembered that I adduce him only as the representative of a great majority of philosophers — affirms or denies, just as he finds it convenient or inconvenient, this fact, — this distinction of consciousness? In his doctrine of perception, he explicitly denies its truth, in denying that mind is conscious of aught beyond itself. But, in other parts of his philosophy, this false fact, this illusive distinction, and the deceitful belief founded thereupon, are appealed to, (I quote his expressions,) as "revelations from on high, — as the never-ceasing voice of our Creator," etc.

Thus, on the veracity of this mendacious belief, Dr. Brown establishes his proof of our personal identity. Touching the object of perception, when its evidence is inconvenient, this belief is quietly passed over, as incompetent to distinguish not-self from self; in the question regarding our personal identity, where its testimony is convenient, it is clamorously cited as an inspired witness, exclusively competent to distinguish self from not-self. Yet why, if, in the one case, it mistook self for not-self, it may not, in the other, mistake not-self for self, would appear a problem not of the easiest solution.

The same belief, with the same inconsistency, is called in to prove the Individuality of mind.[1] But if we are falla-

And of our Individuality.

ciously determined, in our perceptive consciousness, to regard mind both as mind and as matter, — for, on Brown's hypothesis, in perception, the object perceived is only a mode of the percipient subject, — if, I say, in this act, I must view what is supposed one and indivisible, as plural, and different, and opposed, — how is it possible to appeal to the authority of a testimony so treacherous as consciousness for an evidence of the real simplicity of the thinking principle? How, says the materialist to Brown, — how can you appeal against me to the testimony of consciousness, which you yourself reject when against your own opinions, and how can you, on the authority of that testimony,

---

1 Lecture xii. vol. i. p. 241, 2d edition. — ED.

maintain the unity of self to be more than an illusive appearance, when self and not-self, as known to consciousness, are, on your own hypothesis, confessedly only modifications of the same percipient subject? If, on your doctrine, consciousness can split what you hold to be one and indivisible into two, not only different but opposed, existences, — what absurdity is there, on mine, that consciousness should exhibit as phænomenally one, what we both hold to be really manifold? If you give the lie to consciousness in favor of your hypothesis, you can have no reasonable objection that I should give it the lie in favor of mine. If you can maintain that not-self is only an illusive phænomenon, — being, in fact, only self in disguise; I may also maintain, *a contra*, that self itself is only an illusive phænomenon, — and that the apparent unity of the ego is only the result of an organic harmony of action between the particles of matter.

From these examples, the truth of the position I maintain is manifest, — that a fact of consciousness can only be rejected on the supposition of falsity, and that, the falsity of one fact of consciousness being admitted, the truth of no other fact of consciousness can be maintained. The legal brocard, *Falsus in uno, falsus in omnibus*, is a rule not more applicable to other witnesses than to consciousness. Thus, every system of philosophy which implies the negation of any fact of consciousness, is not only necessarily unable, without self-contradiction, to establish its own truth by any appeal to consciousness; it is also unable, without self-contradiction, to appeal to consciousness against the falsehood of any other system. If the absolute and universal veracity of consciousness be once surrendered, every system is equally true, or rather all are equally false; philosophy is impossible, for it has now no instrument by which truth can be discovered, — no standard by which it can be tried; the root of our nature is a lie. But though it is thus manifestly the common interest of every scheme of philosophy to preserve intact the integrity of consciousness, almost every scheme of philosophy is only another mode in which this integrity has been violated. If, therefore, I am able to prove the fact of this various violation, and to show that the facts of consciousness have never, or hardly ever, been fairly evolved, it will follow, as I said, that no reproach can be justly addressed to consciousness as an ill-informed, or vacillating, or perfidious witness, but to those only who were too proud, or too negligent, to accept its testimony, to employ its materials, and to obey its laws. And on this suppo-

> The absolute and universal veracity of consciousness must be maintained.

sition, so far should we be from despairing of the future advance of philosophy from the experience of its past wanderings, that we ought, on the contrary, to anticipate for it a steady progress, the moment that philosophers can be persuaded to look to consciousness, and to consciousness alone, for their materials and their rules.

LECTURE XVI.

CONSCIOUSNESS, — VIOLATIONS OF ITS AUTHORITY.

ON the principle, which no one has yet been found bold enough formally to deny, and which, indeed, requires only to be understood to be acknowledged, — namely, that as all philosophy is evolved from consciousness, so, on the truth of consciousness, the possibility of all philosophy is dependent, — it is manifest, at once and without further reasoning, that no philosophical theory can pretend to truth except that single theory which comprehends and develops the fact of consciousness on which it founds, without retrenchment, distortion, or addition. Were a philosophical system to pretend that it culls out all that is correct in a fact of consciousness, and rejects only what is erroneous, — what would be the inevitable result? In the first place, this system admits, and must admit, that it is wholly dependent on consciousness for its constituent elements, and for the rules by which these are selected and arranged, — in short, that it is wholly dependent on consciousness for its knowledge of true and false. But, in the second place, it pretends to select a part, and to reject a part, of a fact given and guaranteed by consciousness. Now, by what criterion, by what standard, can it discriminate the true from the false in this fact? This criterion must be either consciousness itself, or an instrument different from consciousness. If it be an instrument different from consciousness, what is it? No such instrument has ever yet been named — has ever yet been heard of. If it exist, and if it enable us to criticize the data of consciousness, it must be a higher source of knowledge than consciousness, and thus it will replace consciousness as the first and generative principle of philosophy. But of any principle of this character, different from consciousness, philosophy is yet in ignorance. It remains unenounced and unknown. It may therefore, be safely assumed not to be. The standard, therefore, by which any philosophical theory can profess

> Consciousness, the first and generative principle of Philosophy.

to regulate its choice among the elements of any fact of consciousness, must be consciousness itself. Now, mark the dilemma. The theory makes consciousness the discriminator between what is true and what is false in its own testimony. But if consciousness be assumed to be a mendacious witness in certain parts of its evidence, how can it be presumed a veracious witness in others? This it cannot be. It must be held as false in all, if false in any; and the philosophical theory which starts from this hypothesis, starts from a negation of itself in the negation of philosophy in general. Again, on the hypothesis that part of the deliverance of consciousness is true, part false, how can consciousness enable us to distinguish these? This has never yet been shown; it is, in fact, inconceivable. But, further, how is it discovered that any part of a datum of consciousness is false, another true? This can only be done if the datum involve a contradiction. But if the facts of consciousness be contradictory, then is consciousness a principle of falsehood; and the greatest of conceivable follies would be an attempt to employ such a principle in the discovery of truth. And such an act of folly is every philosophical theory which, departing from an admission that the data of consciousness are false, would still pretend to build out of them a system of truth. But, on the other hand, if the data of consciousness are not contradictory, and consciousness, therefore, not a self-convicted deceiver, how is the unapparent falsehood of its evidence to be evinced? This is manifestly impossible; for such falsehood is not to be presumed; and, we have previously seen, there is no higher principle by which the testimony of consciousness can be canvassed and redargued. Consciousness, therefore, is to be presumed veracious; a philosophical theory which accepts one part of the harmonious data of consciousness and rejects another, is manifestly a mere caprice, a chimera not worthy of consideration, far less of articulate disproof. It is *ab initio* null.

I have been anxious thus again to inculcate upon you this view in regard to the relation of Philosophy to Consciousness, because it contains a preliminary refutation of all those proud and wayward systems which, though they can only pretend to represent the truth inasmuch as they fully and fairly develop the revelations vouchsafed to us through consciousness, still do, one and all of them, depart from a false or partial acceptance of these revelations themselves; and because it affords a clear and simple criterion of certainty in our own attempts at philosophical construction. If it be correct, it sweeps away at once a world of metaphysical speculation; and if it curtail the dominions of human reason, it firmly establishes our authority over what remains.

In order still further to evince to you the importance of the precept (namely, that we must look to conscious-
ness and to consciousness alone for the materials and rules of philosophy), and to show articulately how all the variations of philosophy
have been determined by its neglect, I will take those facts of consciousness which lie at the very root of philosophy, and with which,
consequently, all philosophical systems are necessarily and primarily
conversant; and point out how, besides the one true doctrine which
accepts and simply states the fact as given, there are always as
many various actual theories as there are various possible modes of
distorting or mutilating this fact.   I shall commence with that
great fact to which I have already alluded, — that
we are immediately conscious in perception of
an ego and a non-ego, known together, and
known in contrast to each other. This is the fact of the Duality
of Consciousness. It is clear and manifest. When I concentrate
my attention in the simplest act of perception, I return from my
observation with the most irresistible conviction of two facts, or
rather two branches of the same fact; — that I am, — and that
something different from me exists. In this act, I am conscious of
myself as the perceiving subject, and of an external reality as the
object perceived; and I am conscious of both existences in the same
indivisible moment of intuition.   The knowledge of the subject
does not precede, nor follow, the knowledge of the object, — neither
determines, neither is determined by, the other.

*Violations of the au-
thority of conscious-
ness illustrated.*

*The Duality of Con-
sciousness.*

Such is the fact of perception revealed in consciousness, and as it
determines mankind in general in their almost
equal assurance of the reality of an external
world, as of the existence of their own minds.
Consciousness declares our knowledge of material qualities to be intuitive or immediate, — not
representative or mediate. Nor is the fact, as
given, denied even by those who disallow its truth. So clear is
the deliverance, that even the philosophers who reject an intuitive
perception, find it impossible not to admit, that their doctrine
stands decidedly opposed to the voice of consciousness, — to the
natural convictions of mankind. I may give you some examples of
the admission of this fact, which it is of the utmost importance to
place beyond the possibility of doubt. I quote, of course, only from
those philosophers whose systems are in contradiction of the testimony of consciousness, which they are forced to admit. I might
quote to you confessions to this effect from Descartes, *De Passion-*

*The fact of the testi-
mony of conscious-
ness in Perception al-
lowed by those who
deny its truth.*

ibus, article 23, and from Malebranche, *Recherche,* liv. iii. c. 1. To these I only refer you.

The following is from Berkeley, towards the conclusion of the third and last Dialogue, in which his system of Idealism is established: — " When Hylas is at last entirely converted, he observes to Philonous, — 'After all, the controversy about matter, in the strict acceptation of it, lies altogether between you and the philosophers, whose principles, I acknowledge, are not near so natural, or so agreeable to the common sense of mankind, and Holy Scripture, as yours.' Philonous observes in the end, — ' That he does not pretend to be a setter-up' of new notions; his endeavors tend only to unite, and to place in a clearer light, that truth which was before shared between the vulgar and the philosophers; the former being of opinion, that those things they immediately perceive are the real things; and the latter, that the things immediately perceived are ideas which exist only in the mind; which two things put together do, in effect, constitute the substance of what he advances.' And he concludes by observing,— ' That those principles which at first view lead to skepticism, pursued to a certain point, bring men back to common sense.' " [1]

Berkeley.

Here you will notice that Berkeley admits that the common belief of mankind is, that the things immediately perceived are not representative objects in the mind, but the external realities themselves. Hume, in like manner, makes the same confession; and the confession of that skeptical idealist, or skeptical nihilist, is of the utmost weight.

" It seems evident that men are carried by a natural instinct or prepossession to repose faith in their senses; and that, without any reasoning, or even almost before the use of reason, we always suppose an external universe, which depends not on our perception, but would exist though we and every sensible creature were absent or annihilated. Even the animal creation are governed by a like opinion, and preserve this belief of external objects in all their thoughts, designs, and actions.

Hume.

" It seems also evident that, when men follow this blind and powerful instinct of nature, they always suppose the very images presented by the senses to be the external objects, and never entertain any suspicion that the one are nothing but representations of the other. This very table, which we see white, and which we feel hard, is believed to exist, independent of our perception, and to be something external to our mind, which perceives it. Our presence bestows not being on it, — our absence does not annihilate it. It

---

1 See *Reid's Works,* p. 284. — ED.

preserves its existence uniform and entire, independent of the situation of intelligent beings, who perceive or contemplate it.

"But this universal and primary opinion of all men is soon destroyed by the slightest philosophy, which teaches us that nothing can ever be present to the mind but an image or perception, and that the senses are only the inlets through which these images are conveyed, without being able to produce any immediate intercourse between the mind and the object. The table, which we see, seems to diminish as we remove farther from it; but the real table, which exists independent of us, suffers no alteration; it was, therefore, nothing but its image which was present to the mind. These are the obvious dictates of reason; and no man who reflects, ever doubted that the existences which we consider, when we say, *this house* and *that tree*, are nothing but perceptions in the mind, and fleeting copies or representations of other existences, which remain uniform and independent. . . . . .

"Do you follow the instincts and propensities of nature, may they say, in assenting to the veracity of sense? But these lead you to believe that the very perception or sensible image is the external object. Do you disclaim this principle, in order to embrace a more rational opinion, that the perceptions are only representations of something external? You here depart from your natural propensities and more obvious sentiments; and yet are not able to satisfy your reason, which can never find any convincing argument from experience to prove that the perceptions are connected with any external objects."[1]

The fact that consciousness does testify to an immediate knowledge by mind of an object different from any modification of its own, is thus admitted even by those philosophers who still do not hesitate to deny the truth of the testimony; for to say that all men do naturally believe in such a knowledge, is only, in other words, to say that they believe it upon the authority of consciousness. A fact of consciousness, and a fact of the common sense of mankind, are only various expressions of the same import. We may, therefore, lay it down as an undisputed truth, that consciousness gives, as an ultimate fact, a primitive duality; — a knowledge of the ego in relation and contrast to the non-ego; and a knowledge of the non-ego in relation and contrast to the ego. The ego and non-ego are, thus, given in an original synthesis, as conjoined in the unity of knowl-

---

[1] *Essays*, vol. ii. pp. 154, 155, 156, 157 (edit. 1788). Similar confessions are made by Hume in his *Treatise of Human Nature*, vol. i. pp. 330, 338, 353, 358, 361, 369, (original edit); — in a word, you may read from 330 to 370; and the same thing is acknowledged by Kant, by Fichte, by Schelling, by Tennemann, by Jacobi. Several of these testimonies you will find extracted and translated in a note of my *Discussions on Philosophy*, p. 92.

edge, and, in an original antithesis, as opposed in the contrariety of existence. In other words, we are conscious of them in an indivisible act of knowledge together and at once, — but we are conscious of them as, in themselves, different and exclusive of each other.

Again, consciousness not only gives us a duality, but it gives its elements in equal counterpoise and independence. The ego and non-ego — mind and matter — are not only given together, but in absolute coëquality. The one does not precede, the other does not follow; and, in their mutual relations, each is equally dependent, equally independent. Such is the fact as given in and by consciousness.

The Ego and Non-Ego given by consciousness in equal counterpoise and independence.

Philosophers have not, however, been content to accept the fact in its integrity, but have been pleased to accept it only under such qualifications as it suited their systems to devise. In truth, there are just as many different philosophical systems originating in this fact, as it admits of various possible modifications. An enumeration of these modifications, accordingly, affords an enumeration of philosophical theories.

As many different philosophical systems originate in this fact, as it admits of various possible modifications.

In the first place, there is the grand division of philosophers into those who do, and those who do not, accept the fact in its integrity.[1] Of modern philosophers, almost all are comprehended under the latter category, while of the former, if we do not remount to the schoolmen and the ancients, — I am only aware of a single philosopher[2] before Reid, who did not reject, at least in part, the fact as consciousness affords it. As it is always expedient to possess a precise name for a precise distinction, I would be inclined to denominate those who implicitly acquiesce in the primitive duality as given in consciousness, the Natural Realists or Natural Dualists, and their doctrine, Natural Realism or Natural Dualism.

I. Those who do, and those who do not, accept in its integrity the fact of the Duality of Consciousness.

The former called Naturalists or Natural Dualists.

In the second place, the philosophers who do not accept the fact, and the whole fact, may be divided and subdivided into various classes by various principles of distribution.

The latter, variously subdivided.

The first subdivision will be taken from the total, or partial,

---

1 See the Author's Suppl. Disser. to *Reid's Works*, Note C. — ED.

2 This philosopher is doubtless Peter Poiret.

John Sergeant is subsequently referred to by Sir W. Hamilton, as holding a similar doctrine in a paradoxical form. See pp. 331, 353. — ED.

rejections of the import of the fact. I have previously shown you that to deny any fact of consciousness as an actual phænomenon is utterly impossible. But, though necessarily admitted as a present phænomenon, the import of this phænomenon, — all beyond our actual consciousness of its existence, may be denied. We are able, without self-contradiction, to suppose, and, consequently, to assert, that all to which the phænomenon of which we are conscious refers, is a deception, — that, for example, the past to which an act of memory refers, is only an illusion involved in our consciousness of the present, — that the unknown subject to which every phænomenon of which we are conscious involves a reference, has no reality beyond this reference itself, — in short, that all our knowledge of

Into Realists and Nihilists.

mind or matter, is only a consciousness of various bundles of baseless appearances. This doctrine, as refusing a substantial reality to the phænomenal existence of which we are conscious, is called Nihilism; and, consequently, philosophers, as they affirm or deny the authority of consciousness in guaranteeing a substratum or substance to the manifestations of the ego and non-ego, are divided into Realists or Substantialists, and into Nihilists or Non-Substantialists. Of positive or dogmatic Nihilism there is no example in modern philosophy, for Oken's deduction of the universe from the original nothing,[1] — the nothing being equivalent to the Absolute or God, is only the paradoxical foundation of a system of realism; and, in ancient philosophy, we know too little of the book of Gorgias the Sophist, entitled Περὶ τοῦ μὴ ὄντος, ἢ περὶ φύσεως,[2] — *Concerning Nature or the Non-Existent*, — to be able to affirm whether it were maintained by him as a dogmatic and *bona fide* doctrine. But as a skeptical conclusion from the premises of previous philosophers we have an illustrious example of Nihilism in Hume; and the celebrated Fichte admits that the speculative principles of his own idealism would, unless corrected by his practical, terminate in this result.[3]

The Realists or Substantialists are again divided into Dualists,

Realists divided into Hypothetical Dualists and Monists.

and into Unitarians or Monists, according as they are, or are not, contented with the testimony of consciousness to the ultimate duplicity of subject and object in perception. The Dualists, of whom we are now first speaking, are distinguished from the Natural Dualists of whom we formerly spoke, in this, — that the

---

1 See *Oken's Physiophilosophy*, translated for the Ray Society by Tulk, § 31-43. — ED.

2 See Sextus Empiricus, *Adv. Math.* vii. 65. — ED.

3 See a remarkable passage in the *Bestimmung des Menschen*, p. 174, (*Werke*, vol. ii. p. 245), translated by Sir W. Hamilton. *Reid's Works*, p. 129. — ED.

latter establish the existence of the two worlds of mind and matter on the immediate knowledge we possess of both series of phænomena,—a knowledge of which consciousness assures us; whereas the former, surrendering the veracity of consciousness to our immediate knowledge of material phænomena, and, consequently, our immediate knowledge of the existence of matter, still endeavor, by various hypotheses and reasonings, to maintain the existence of an unknown external world. As we denominate those who maintain a dualism as involved in the fact of consciousness, Natural Dualists; so we may style those dualists who deny the evidence of consciousness to our immediate knowledge of aught beyond the sphere of mind, Hypothetical Dualists or Cosmothetic Idealists.

To the class of Cosmothetic Idealists, the great majority of modern philosophers are to be referred. Deny-

The majority of modern philosophers belong to the former of these classes, and are subdivided according to their view of the representation in perception.

ing an immediate or intuitive knowledge of the external reality, whose existence they maintain, they, of course, hold a doctrine of mediate or representative perception; and, according to the various modifications of that doctrine, they are again subdivided into those who view, in the immediate object of perception, a representative entity present to the mind, but not a mere mental modification, and into those who hold that the immediate object is only a representative modification of the mind itself. It is not always easy to determine to which of these classes some philosophers belong. To the former, or class holding the cruder hypothesis of representation, certainly belong the followers of Democritus and Epicurus, those Aristotelians who held the vulgar doctrine of species, (Aristotle himself was probably a natural dualist,)[1] and in recent times, among many others, Malebranche, Berkeley, Clarke, Newton, Abraham Tucker, etc. To these is also, but problematically, to be referred Locke. To the second, or class holding the finer hypothesis of representation, belong, without any doubt, many of the Platonists, Leibnitz, Arnauld, Crousaz, Condillac, Kant, etc., and to this class is also probably to be referred Descartes.[2]

The philosophical Unitarians or Monists, reject the testimony of consciousness to the ultimate duality of the sub-

Monists, subdivided,

ject and object in perception, but they arrive at the unity of these in different ways. Some admit the testimony of

1 Aristotle's opinion is doubtful. In the *De Anima*, i. 5, he combats the theory of Empedocles, that like is known by like, and appears as a natural realist. But in the *Nicomachean Ethics*, vi. 1, he adopts the principle of similarity as the basis of all knowledge. See the Author's Notes, *Reid's Works*, pp. 300, 886; and M. St. Hilaire's preface to his translation of the *De Anima*, p. 22. — ED.

2 See the Author's *Discussions*, p. 57 *seq.* — ED.

consciousness to the equipoise of the mental and material phænomena, and do not attempt to reduce either mind to matter, or
matter to mind. They reject, however, the evidence of consciousness to their antithesis in existence, and maintain that mind and
matter are only phænomenal modifications of the same common
substance. This is the doctrine of Absolute
Identity,—a doctrine of which the most illustrious representatives among recent philosophers
are Schelling, Hegel, and Cousin. Others again
deny the evidence of consciousness to the equipoise of the subject
and object as coördinate and coöriginal elements; and as the balance is inclined in favor of the one relative or the other, two opposite schemes of psychology are determined. If the subject be
taken as the original and genetic, and the object
evolved from it as its product, the theory of
Idealism is established. On the other hand, if the object be assumed as the original and genetic, and the sub-
ject evolved from it as its product, the theory
of Materialism is established.

Into, 1. Those who hold the doctrine of Absolute Identity;

2. Idealists;

3. Materialists.

In regard to these two opposite schemes of a one-sided philosophy, I would at present make an observation to
which it may be afterwards necessary to recur
—viz., that a philosophical system is often prevented from falling into absolute idealism or
absolute materialism, and held in a kind of
vacillating equilibrium, not in consequence of
being based on the fact of consciousness, but
from the circumstance, that its materialistic tendency in one opinion
happens to be counteracted by its idealistic tendency in another;—
two opposite errors, in short, coöperating to the same result as one
truth. On this ground is to be explained, why the philosophy of
Locke and Condillac did not more easily slide into materialism.
Deriving our whole knowledge, mediately or immediately, from
the senses, this philosophy seemed destined to be fairly analyzed
into a scheme of materialism; but from this it was for a long time
preserved, in consequence of involving a doctrine, which, on the
other hand, if not counteracted, would have naturally carried it
over into idealism. This was the doctrine of a representative perception. The legitimate issue of such a doctrine is now admitted,
on all hands, to be absolute idealism; and the only ground on which
it has been latterly thought possible to avoid this conclusion,—an
appeal to the natural belief of mankind in the existence of an
external world,—is, as I showed you, incompetent to the hypo-

How a philosophical system is often prevented from falling into absolute idealism or absolute material-ism.

thetical dualist or cosmothetic idealist. In his hands such an appeal is self-contradictory. For if this universal belief be fairly applied, it only proves the existence of an outer world by disproving the hypothesis of a representative perception.

To recapitulate what I have now said : — The philosophical systems concerning the relation of mind and matter, are coëxtensive with the various possible modes in which the fact of the Duality of Consciousness may be accepted or refused. It may be accepted either wholly and without reserve, or it may not. The former alternative affords the class of Natural Realists or Natural Dualists.

Those, again, who do not accept the fact in its absolute integrity, are subdivided in various manners. They are, first of all, distinguished into Realists or Substantialists, and into Nihilists, as they do, or do not, admit a subject, or subjects, to the two opposite series of phænomena which consciousness reveals. The former class is again distributed into Hypothetical Dualists or Cosmothetic Idealists, and into Unitarians or Monists.

The Hypothetical Dualists or Cosmothetic Idealists, are divided, according to their different theories of the representation in perception, into those who view in the object immediately perceived, a *tertium quid* different both from the external reality and from the conscious mind, and into those who identify this object with a modification of the mind itself.

The Unitarians or Monists fall into two classes as they do, or do not, preserve the equilibrium of subject and object. If, admitting the equilibrium of these, they deny the reality of their opposition, the system of Absolute Identity emerges, which carries thought and extension, mind and matter, up into modes of the same common substance.

It would be turning aside from my present purpose, were I to attempt any articulate refutation of these various systems. What I have now in view is to exhibit to you how, the moment that the fact of consciousness in its absolute integrity is surrendered, philosophy at once falls from unity and truth into variety and error. In reality, by the very act of refusing any one datum of consciousness, philosophy invalidates the whole credibility of consciousness, and consciousness ruined as an instrument, philosophy is extinct. Thus, the refusal of philosophers to accept the fact of the duality of consciousness, is virtually an act of philosophical suicide. Their various systems are now only so many empty spectres, — so many enchanted corpses, which the first exorcism of the skeptic reduces to their natural nothingness. The mutual polemic of these sys-

Recapitulation of foregoing.

tems is like the warfare of shadows; as the heroes in Valhalla, they hew each other into pieces, only in a twinkling to be reünited, and again to amuse themselves in other bloodless and indecisive contests.[1]

Having now given you a general view of the various systems of philosophy, in their mutual relations, as founded

Hypotheses proposed in regard to the mode of intercourse between Mind and Body.

on the great fact of the Duality of Consciousness, I proceed, in subordination to this fact, to give you a brief account of certain famous hypotheses which it is necessary for you to know, — hypotheses proposed in solution of the problem of how intercourse of substances so opposite as mind and body could be accomplished. These hypotheses, of course, belong exclusively to the doctrine of Dualism, for in the Unitarian system the difficulty is resolved by the annihilation of the opposition, and the reduction of the two substances to one. The hypotheses I allude

Four in number.

to, are known under the names, 1°, Of the system of Assistance or of Occasional Causes; 2°, Of the Preëstablished Harmony; 3°, Of the Plastic Medium; and, 4°, Of Physical Influence. The first belongs to Descartes, De la Forge, Malebranche, and the Cartesians in general; the second to Leibnitz and Wolf, though not universally adopted by their school; the third was an ancient opinion revived in modern times by Cudworth and Leclerc;[2] the fourth is the common doctrine of the Schoolmen, and, though not explicitly enounced, that generally prevalent at present; — among modern philosophers, it has been expounded with great perspicuity by Euler.[3] We shall take these in their order.

The hypothesis of Divine Assistance or of Occasional Causes,

1. Occasional Causes.

sets out from the apparent impossibility involved in Dualism of any actual communication between a spiritual and a material substance, — that is, between extended and non-extended existences; and it terminates in the assertion, that the Deity, on occasion of the affections of matter — of the motions in the bodily organism, excites in the mind correspondent thoughts and representations; and on occasion of thoughts or representations arising in the mind, that He, in like manner, produces the correspondent movements in the body. But more explicitly: — "God, according to the advocates of this scheme, governs the

[1] This simile is taken from Kant, *Kritik der reinen Vernunft*, p. 784 (edit. 1799) — ED.

[2] Cudworth, *Intellectual System of the Universe*, b. i. c. iii. § 87. Leclerc, *Bibliothèque*

Choisée, vol. ii. p. 107, *et seq.* See also Leibnitz, *Considérations sur la Principe de Vie.* *Opera*, edit. Erdmann, p. 429. — ED.

[3] *Lettres d une Princesse d' Allemagne*, part ii. let. 14, ed. Cournot. — ED.]

universe, and its constituent existences, by the laws according to which He has created them; and as the world was originally called into being by a mere fiat of the divine will, so it owes the continuance of its existence from moment to moment only to the unremitted perseverance of the same volition. Let the sustaining energy of the divine will cease, but for an instant, and the universe lapses into nothingness. The existence of created things is thus exclusively maintained by a creation, as it were, incessantly renewed. God is, thus, the necessary cause of every modification of body, and of every modification of mind; and his efficiency is sufficient to afford an explanation of the union and intercourse of extended and unextended substances.

"External objects determine certain movements in our bodily organs of sense, and these movements are, by the nerves and animal spirits, propagated to the brain. The brain does not act immediately and really upon the soul; the soul has no direct cognizance of any modification of the brain; this is impossible. It is God himself who, by a law which he has established, when movements are determined in the brain, produces analogous modifications in the conscious mind. In like manner, suppose the mind has a volition to move the arm; this volition is, of itself, inefficacious, but God, in virtue of the same law, causes the answering motion in our limb. The body is not, therefore, the real cause of the mental modifications; nor the mind the real cause of the bodily movements. Nevertheless, as the soul would not be modified without the antecedent changes in the body, nor the body moved without the antecedent determination of the soul, — these changes and determinations are in a certain sort necessary. But this necessity is not absolute; it is only hypothetical or conditional. The organic changes, and the mental determinations, are nothing but simple conditions, and not real causes; in short, they are occasions or occasional causes."[1] This doctrine of occasional causes is called, likewise, the Hypothesis of Assistance, as supposing the immediate coöperation or intervention of the Deity. It is involved in the Cartesian theory, and, therefore, belongs to Descartes; but it was fully evolved by De la Forge, Malebranche, and other followers of Descartes.[2] It may, however, be traced far higher. I find it first explicitly, and in all its extent, maintained in the commencement of the twelfth

---

1 [Laromiguière *Leçons de Philosophie*, tom. ii. p. 255–6.]

2 See Descartes *Principia*, part ii. § 36. De

la Forge, *Traité de l' Esprit de l' Homme*, c. xvi. Malebranche, *Recherche de la Vérité*, lib. vi. part ii. c. 3, *Entretiens sur la Métaphysique*, Ent. vii. — ED.

century by Algazel,[1] or Elgazali, of Bagdad, surnamed the Imaum of the world; — from him it passed to the schools of the West, and many of the most illustrious philosophers of the middle ages maintained that God is the only real agent in the universe.[2] To this doctrine Dr. Reid inclines,[3] and it is expressly maintained by Mr. Stewart.[4]

This hypothesis did not satisfy Leibnitz. "He reproaches the Cartesians with converting the universe into a perpetual miracle, and of explaining the natural, by a supernatural, order. This would annihilate philosophy; for philosophy consists in the investigation and discovery of the second causes which produce the various phænomena of the universe.[5] You degrade the Divinity, he subjoined; — you make him act like a watchmaker, who, having constructed a timepiece, would still be obliged himself to turn the hands, to make it mark the hours. A skilful mechanist would so frame his clock that it would go for a certain period without assistance or interposition. So when God created man, he disposed his organs and faculties in such a manner that they are able of themselves to execute their functions and maintain their activity from birth to death."[6]

2. Preëstablished Harmony.

Leibnitz thought he had devised a more philosophical scheme, in the hypothesis of the preëstablished or predetermined Harmony, (*Systema Harmoniæ Præstabilitæ vel Prædeterminatæ.*) This hypothesis denies all real connection, not only between spiritual and material substances, but between substances in general; and explains their apparent communion from a previously decreed coärrangement of the Supreme Being, in the following manner: — "God, before creating souls and bodies, knew all these souls and bodies; he knew also all possible souls and bodies.[7] Now, in this infinite variety of possible souls and bodies, it was necessary that there should be souls whose series of per-

---

1 In his *Destructio Philosophorum*, now only known through the refutation of it by Averroes, called *Destructio Destructionis*, preserved in a barbarous Latin translation, in the ninth volume of Aristotle's Works, Venice, 1550. A full account of this treatise is given in Tennemann's *Geschichte der Philosophie*, vol. viii. p. 387 *et seq.* See also Degerando, *Histoire Comparée*, vol. iv. p. 226. — ED.

2 Averroes, l. c. p. 56: "Agens combustionis creavit nigredinem in stuppa et combustionem in partibus ejus, et posuit eam combustam et cinerem, et est Deus gloriosus mediantibus angelis, aut immediate." See Tennemann, l. c. p. 405. — ED.

3 See *Works*, pp. 257, 527. — ED.

4 See *Works*, vol. ii. pp. 97, 476—479; vol. ii. pp. 230, 248, 389—391. — ED.

5 *Système Nouveau de la Nature*, § 18. *Opera*, ed. Erdmann, p. 127. Cf. *Théodicée*, § 61. *Ibid.*, p. 520. — ED.

6 [Laromiguière, *Leçons*, ii. 256–7] *Troisième Eclaircissement. Opera*, ed. Erdmann, p. 134. — ED.

7 *Système Nouveau de la Nature*, § 14. *Théodicée*, § 62. These passages contain the substance of the remarks in the text, but not the words. — ED.

ceptions and determinations would correspond to the series of movements which some of these possible bodies would execute; for in an infinite number of souls, and in an infinite number of bodies, there would be found all possible combinations. Now, suppose that, out of a soul whose series of modifications corresponded exactly to the series of modifications which a certain body was destined to perform, and of this body whose successive movements were correspondent to the successive modifications of this soul, God should make a man,— it is evident, that between the two substances which constitute this man, there would subsist the most perfect harmony. It is, thus, no longer necessary to devise theories to account for the reciprocal intercourse of the material and the spiritual substances. These have no communication, no mutual influence. The soul passes from one state, from one perception, to another by virtue of its own nature. The body executes the series of its movements without any participation or interference of the soul in these. The soul and body are like two clocks accurately regulated, which point to the same hour and minute, although the spring which gives motion to the one is not the spring which gives motion to the other.[1] Thus the harmony which appears to combine the soul and body is, however, independent of any reciprocal action. This harmony was established before the creation of man; and hence it is called the preëstablished or predetermined harmony."[2]

It is needless to attempt a refutation of this hypothesis, which its author himself probably regarded more as a specimen of ingenuity than as a serious doctrine.

The third hypothesis is that of the Plastic Medium between the soul and body. "This medium participates of the two natures; it is partly material, partly spiritual. As material, it can be acted on by the body; and as spiritual, it can act upon the mind. It is the middle term of a continuous proportion. It is a bridge thrown over the abyss which separates matter from spirit. This hypothesis is too absurd for refutation; it annihilates itself. Between an extended and unextended substance, there can be no middle existence; [these being not simply different in degree, but contradictory.] If the medium be neither body nor soul, it is a chimera; if it is at once body and soul, it is contradictory; or if, to avoid the contradiction, it is said to be, like us, the union of soul and body, it is itself in want of a medium."[3]

8. Plastic Medium.

---

1 *Troisième Eclaircissement. Opera*, edit. Erd- 2 [Laromiguière *Leçons*, tom. ii. p. 257-8.]
mann, p. 135. — ED. 3 [Laromiguière, *Leçons*, tom. ii. p. 253-4.]

The fourth hypothesis is that of Physical Influence, (*Influxus Physicus.*) "On this doctrine, external objects

4. Physical Influence.

affect our senses, and the organic motion they determine is communicated to the brain. The brain acts upon the soul, and the soul has an idea, — a perception. The mind thus possessed of a perception or idea, is affected for good or ill. If it suffers, it seeks to be relieved of pain. It acts in its turn upon the brain, in which it causes a movement in the nervous system; the nervous system causes a muscular motion in the limbs, — a motion directed to remove or avoid the object which occasions the sensation of pain.

" The brain is the seat of the soul, and, on this hypothesis, the soul has been compared to a spider seated in the centre of its web. The moment the least agitation is caused at the extremity of this web, the insect is advertised and put upon the watch. In like manner, the mind situated in the brain has a point on which all the nervous filaments converge; it is informèd of what passes at the different parts of the body; and forthwith it takes its measures accordingly. The body thus acts with a real efficiency on the mind, and the mind acts with a real efficiency upon the body. This action or influence being real, — physical, in the course of nature, — the body exerts a physical influence upon the soul, the soul a physical influence upon the body.

" This system is simple, but it affords us no help in explaining the mysterious union of an extended and an unextended substance.

'Tangere enim et tangi nisi corpus nulla potest res.' [1]

Nothing can touch and be touched but what is extended; and if the soul be unextended, it can have no connection by touch with the body, and the physical influence is inconceivable or contradictory." [2]

If we consider these hypotheses in relation to their historical manifestation, — the doctrine of Physical In-

Historical order of these hypotheses. Physical influence, first.

fluence would stand first; for this doctrine, which was only formally developed into system by the later Peripatetics, was that prevalent in the earlier schools of Greece. The Aristotelians, — who held that the soul was the substantial form, the vital principle, of the body, that the soul was all in the whole and all in every part of the body, — naturally allowed a reciprocal influence of these. By influence, (in Latin *influxus*,)

1 Lucretius, i. 305.— Ed.　　　2 [Laromiguière, *Leçons*, tom. ii. p. 251—3.]

you are to understand the relation of a cause to its effect, and the term, now adopted into every vulgar language of Europe, was brought into use principally by the authority of Suarez, a Spanish Jesuit, who flourished at the close of the sixteenth and beginning of the seventeenth centuries, and one of the most illustrious metaphysicians of modern times. By him a cause is defined, *Principium per se influens esse in aliud.*[1] This definition, however, and the use of the metaphysical term *influence,* (for it is nothing more,) are not, as is supposed, original with him. They are to be found in the pseudo-Aristotelic treatise *De Causis.* This is a translation from the Arabic, but a translation made many centuries before Suarez.[2] But this by the way.

The second hypothesis in chronological order, is that of the Plastic Medium. It is to be traced to Plato. That philosopher, in illustrating the relation of the two constituents of man, says that the soul is in the body like a sailor in a ship; that the soul employs the body as its instrument; but that the energy, or life and sense of the body, is the manifestation of a different substance, — of a substance which holds a kind of intermediate existence between mind and matter. This conjecture, which Plato only obscurely hinted at, was elaborated with peculiar partiality by his followers of the Alexandrian school, and, in their psychology, the ὄχος, or vehicle of the soul, the medium through which it is united to the body, is a prominent element and distinctive principle.[3] To this opinion St. Austin,[4] among other

Plastic Medium, second.

---

1 *Disputationes Metaphysicæ*, Disp. xii., § ii. 4. — ED.

2 The *Libellus de Causis* is printed in a Latin version made from a Hebrew one, in the seventh volume of the Latin edition of Aristotle's Works, Venice, 1550, f. 144. It has been attributed to Aristotle, to Avempace, to Alfarabi, and to Proclus. The above definition does not occur in it verbatim, though it may be gathered in substance from Prop. I. — ED.

3 The passage referred to in Plato is probably *Timæus*, p. 69: Οἱ δὲ μιμούμενοι παραλαβόντες ἀρχὴν ψυχῆς ἀθάνατον, τὸ μετὰ τοῦτο θνητὸν σῶμα αὐτῇ περιετόρνευσαν ὄχημά τε πᾶν τὸ σῶμα ἔδοσαν κ.τ.λ. This passage, as well as the simile of the chariot in the *Phædrus*, p. 246, were interpreted in this sense by the later Platonists. See Ficinus, *Theologia Platonica*, lib. xviii. c. 4: "Ex quo sequitur rationales animas tanquam medias

tales esse debere, ut virtute quidem semper separabiles sint, ... actu autem sint semper conjunctæ, quia familiare corpus nanciscuntur ex æthere, quod servant per immortalitatem propriam immortale, quod Plato currum tum deorum tum animarum vocat in Phædro, vehiculum in Timæo." The *ship* is more definitely expressed by Maximus Tyrius, *Diss.* xl. ε (referred to by Stallbaum, on the *Timæus*, l. c.): Οὐχ ὁρᾶς καὶ τὸν ἐν τῇ θαλάττῃ πλοῦν, ἔνθα ὁ μὲν κυβερνήτης ἄρχει, ὡς ψυχὴ σώματος, ἡ δὲ νοῦς ἄρχεται, ὡς ὑπὸ ψυχῆς σῶμα. Cf. also Proclus, *Inst. Theol.* c. 206 *et seq.*; Cudworth, *Intellectual System*, b. i. c. v. § 3. Platner, *Phil. Aphorismen*, i. p. 627. — ED.

4 St. Augustin seems to have adopted the ancient and Platonic dogma that *matter* (ὕλη) is incorporeal (ἀσώματος.) He regarded *matter* as "quiddam inter formatum et nihil, nec formatum nec nihil, informe prope nihil." *Confessions*, lib. xii. c. vi. — ED.

Christian fathers, was inclined, and, in modern times, it has been revived and modified by Gassendi,[1] Cudworth,[2] and Le Clerc.[3]

Descartes agrees with the Platonists in opposition to the Aristotelians, that the soul is not the substantial form of the body, but is connected with it only at a single point in the brain — viz., the pineal gland. The pineal gland, he supposes, is the central point at which the organic movements of the body terminate, when conveying to the mind the determinations to voluntary motion.[4] But Descartes did not allow, like the Platonists, any intermediate or connecting substance. The nature of the connection he himself does not very explicitly state; — but his disciples have evolved the hypothesis, already explained, of Occasional Causes, in which God is the connecting principle, — an hypothesis at least implicitly contained in his philosophy.[5]

Occasional Causes, third.

Finally, Leibnitz and Wolf agree with the Cartesians, that there is no real, but only an apparent intercourse between mind and body. To explain this apparent intercourse, they do not, however, resort to the continual assistance or interposition of the Deity, but have recourse to the supposition of a harmony between mind and body, established before the creation of either.[6]

Preëstablished Harmony, fourth.

All these theories are unphilosophical, because they all attempt to establish something beyond the sphere of observation, and, consequently, beyond the sphere of genuine philosophy; and because they are either, like the Cartesian and Leibnitzian theories, contradictions of the fact of consciousness; or, like the two other hypotheses, at variance with the fact which they suppose. What St. Austin so admirably says of the substance, either of mind or of body, — "Materiam spiritumque cognoscendo ignorari et ignorando cognosci,"[7] — I would exhort you to adopt as your opinion in regard to the union of these two existences. In short, in the words of Pascal,[8] "Man is to himself the mightiest prodigy of nature; for he is unable to conceive what is body, still less what is mind, but least of all is he able to conceive how a body can be united to a mind; yet this is his proper

These hypotheses unphilosophical.

---

1 Gassendi, in his *Physica*, divides the human soul into two parts, the one rational and incorporeal, the other corporeal, including the nutritive and sensitive faculties. The latter he regards as the medium of connection between the rational soul and the body. See *Opera*, vol. ii. p. 256, 1658. — ED.

2 See above, p. 208, note 1. — ED.

3 See above p. 208, note 1. — ED.

4 *De Passionibus Animæ*, art. 31, 32. *De Homine*, art. 63. — ED.

5 See above, p. 209, note 1. — ED.

6 [On these hypotheses in general, see Zedler's *Lexicon*, v. *Seele*, p. 98 *et seq.*]

7 *Confessions*, xii. 5. See *ante*, p. 98. — ED.

8 *Pensées*, partie i. art. vi.. 26. Vol. ii. p. 74, edit. Faugère. — ED.

being." A contented ignorance is, indeed, wiser than a presumptuous knowledge; but this is a lesson which seems the last that philosophers are willing to learn. In the words of one of the acutest of modern thinkers[1] — " Magna immo maxima pars sapientiæ est, quædam æquo animo nescire velle."

1 Julius Cæsar Scaliger. The passage is quoted more correctly in the Author's *Discussions*, p. 640. — Ed.

LECTURE XVII.

CONSCIOUSNESS,—GENERAL PHÆNOMENA,—ARE WE ALWAYS CONSCIOUSLY ACTIVE?

THE second General Fact of Consciousness which we shall consider, and out of which several questions of great interest arise, is the fact, or correlative facts, of the Activity and Passivity of Mind.

Activity and Passivity of Mind.

There is no pure activity, no pure passivity in creation. All things in the universe of nature are reciprocally in a state of continual action and counter-action; they are always active and passive at once. God alone must be thought of as a being active without any mixture of passivity, as his activity is subjected to no limitation. But precisely because it is unlimited, is it for us wholly incomprehensible.

No pure activity or passivity in creation.

Activity and passivity are not, therefore, in the manifestations of mind, distinct and independent phænomena. This is a great, though a common error. They are always conjoined. There is no operation of mind which is purely active; no affection which is purely passive. In every mental modification action and passion are the two necessary elements or factors of which it is composed. But though both are always present, each is not, however, always present in equal quantity. Sometimes the one constituent preponderates, sometimes the other; and it is from the preponderance of the active element in some modifications, of the passive element in others, that we distinguish these modifications by different names, and consider them as activities or passivities according as they approximate to one or other of the two factors. Thus *faculty, operation, energy,* are words that we employ to designate the manifestations in which activity is predominant. *Faculty* denotes an active power; *action, operation, energy,* denote its present exertion. On the other hand, *capacity* expresses a passive power; *affection, passion,* express a present suffering. The terms *mode, modification, state,* may be used indifferently to signify

Activity and Passivity always conjoined in the manifestations of mind.

both phænomena; but it must be acknowledged that these, especially the word *state*, are now closely associated with the passivity of mind, which they, therefore, tend rather to suggest. The passivity of mind is expressed by another term, *receptivity;* for passivity is only the condition, the necessary antecedent of activity, only the property possessed by the mind of standing in relation to certain foreign causes, — of receiving from them impressions, determinations to act.

It is to be observed, that we are never directly conscious of passivity. Consciousness only commences with, is only cognizant of, the reäction consequent upon the foreign determination to act, and this reäction is not itself passive. In so far, therefore, as we are conscious, we are active; whether there may be a mental activity of which we are not conscious, is another question.[1]

We are never directly conscious of passivity.

There are certain arduous problems connected with the activity of mind, which will be more appropriately considered in a subsequent part of the course, when we come to speak of the Inferences from the Phænomenology of Mind, or of Metaphysics Proper. At present, I shall only treat of those questions which are conversant about the immediate phænomena of activity. Of these, the first that I shall consider is one of considerable interest, and which, though variously determined by different philosophers, does not seem to lie beyond the sphere of observation. I allude to the question, Whether we are always consciously active?

The question, Are we always consciously active? raised.

It is evident that this question is not convertible with the question, Have we always a memory of our consciousness? — for the latter problem must be at once answered in the negative. It is also evident, that we must exclude the consideration of those states in which the mind is apparently without consciousness, but in regard to which, in reality, we can obtain no information from experiment. Concerning these we must be contented to remain in ignorance; at least only to extend to them the analogical conclusions which our observations on those within the sphere of experiment warrant us inferring. Our question, as one of possible solution, must, therefore, be limited to the states of sleep and somnambulism, to the exclusion of those states of insensibility which we cannot terminate suddenly at will. It is hardly necessary to observe, that with the nature of sleep and somnambulism as psychological phænomena, we have at present nothing to do; our consideration is now strictly limited to the inquiry,

Distinguished from other questions.

1 See below, Lect. xviii. p. 235. — ED.

Whether the mind, in as far as we can make it matter of observation, is always in a state of conscious activity.

Treatment of the question by philosophers.

The general problem in regard to the ceaseless activity of the mind has been one agitated from very ancient times, but it has also been one on which philosophers have pronounced less on grounds of experience than of theory. Plato and the Platonists were

Plato and Platonists.

unanimous in maintaining the continual energy of intellect. The opinion of Aristotle appears doubtful, and passages may be quoted from his works in favor of

Aristotle and the Aristotelians.

either alternative. The Aristotelians, in general, were opposed, but a considerable number were favorable, to the Platonic doctrine. This doctrine was adopted by

Cicero and St. Augustin.

Cicero and St. Augustin. "Nunquam animus," says the former, "cogitatione et motu vacuus esse potest."[1] "Ad quid menti," says the latter, "præceptum est, ut se ipsam cognoscat, nisi ut semper vivat, et semper sit in actu."[2] The question, however, obtained its principal importance in the philosophy of Descartes. That

Descartes.

philosopher made the essence, the very existence, of the soul to consist in actual thought,[3] under which he included even the desires and feelings; and *thought* he defined all of which we are conscious.[4] The assertion, therefore, of Descartes, that the mind always thinks, is, in his employment of language, tantamount to the assertion that the mind is always conscious.

That the mind is always conscious, though a fundamental position of the Cartesian doctrine, was rather assumed than proved by an appeal to fact and experience. All is theoretical in Descartes; all is theoretical in his disciples. Even Malebranche assumes our con-

Malebranche.

sciousness in sleep, and explains our oblivion only by a mechanical hypothesis.[5] It was, therefore, easy for Locke to deny the truth of the Cartesian opinion, and

Locke.

to give a strong semblance of probability to his own doctrine by its apparent conformity with the phænomena. Omitting a good deal of what is either irrelevant

1 *De Divinatione*, ii. 62: "Naturam eam dico, qua nunquam animus insistens *agitatione*, et motu esse vacuus potest."— ED.

2 Eugenios, Ψυχολογία, p. 29.—[Book iii. of his Στοιχεῖα τῆς Μεταφυσικῆς, (edit. 1805). The reference in Eugenios is to *De Trinitate*, l. x. c. v., where a passage occurs, resembling in words the one quoted in the text, but hardly supporting the doctrine in question. It is as follows: "Ut quid ergo ei præceptum est, ut se ipsam cognoscat? Credo

ut se ipsam cogitet, et secundum naturam suam vivat." But in the *De Anima et ejus Origine*, lib. iv. c. vi. § 7, t. x. p. 391, (edit. Ben.) occurs the following explicit statement: "Sicut motus non cessat in corde, unde se pulsus diffundit usquequaque venarum, ita non quiescimus aliquid cogitando versare."— ED.]

3 *Principia*, part i. § 53.— ED.

4 *Principia*, part i. § 9.— ED.

5 *Recherche de la Vérité*, lib. iii. c. 2.— ED.

to the general question, or what is now admitted to be false, as founded on his erroneous doctrine of personal identity, the following is the sum of Locke's argument upon the point. "It is an opinion," he says,[1] "that the soul always thinks, and that it has the actual perception of ideas in itself constantly, as long as it exists; and that actual thinking is as inseparable from the soul, as actual extension is from the body; which if true, to inquire after the beginning of a man's ideas, is the same as to inquire after the beginning of his soul. For by this account, soul and its ideas, as body and its extension, will begin to exist both at the same time.

Locke's argument for the negative.

"But whether the soul be supposed to exist antecedent to, or coëval with, or some time after, the first rudiments, or organization, or the beginnings of life in the body, I leave to be disputed by those who have better thought of that matter. I confess myself to have one of those dull souls that doth not perceive itself always to contemplate ideas; nor can conceive it any more necessary for the soul always to think than for the body always to move: the perception of ideas being (as I conceive) to the soul, what motion is to the body; not its essence, but one of its operations. And, therefore, though thinking be supposed ever so much the proper action of the soul, yet it is not necessary to suppose that it should be always thinking, always in action. That perhaps is the privilege of the infinite Author and Preserver of things, who never slumbers nor sleeps; but is not competent to any finite being, at least not to the soul of man. We know certainly by experience that we sometimes think, and thence draw this infallible consequence, that there is something in us that has a power to think: but whether that substance perpetually thinks or no, we can be no further assured than experience informs us. For to say that actual thinking is essential to the soul, and inseparable from it, is to beg what is in question, and not to prove it by reason; which is necessary to be done if it be not a self-evident proposition. But whether this, 'that the soul always thinks,' be a self-evident proposition, that everybody assents to at first hearing, I appeal to mankind. It is doubted whether I thought all last night or no; the question being about a matter of fact, it is begging it to bring as a proof for it an hypothesis which is the very thing in dispute; by which way one may prove anything; and it is but supposing that all watches, whilst the balance beats, think; and it is sufficiently proved, and past doubt, that my watch thought all last night. But he that would not deceive himself, ought to

---

[1] *Essay*, book ii. chap. i., §§ 9, 10, 14 *et seq.*

build his hypothesis on matter of fact, and make it out by sensible experience, and not presume on matter of fact, because of his hypothesis; that is, because he supposes it to be so; which way of proving amounts to this, that I must necessarily think all last night because another supposes I always think, though I myself cannot perceive that I always do so." . . . . "It will perhaps be said that 'the soul thinks even in the soundest sleep, but the memory retains it not.' That the soul in a sleeping man should be this moment busy a-thinking, and the next moment in a waking man not remember nor be able to recollect one jot of all those thoughts, is very hard to be conceived, and would need some better proof than bare assertion to make it be believed. For who can, without any more ado but being barely told so, imagine that the greatest part of men do, during all their lives for several hours every day, think of something which, if they were asked even in the middle of these thoughts, they could remember nothing at all of? Most men, I think, pass a great part of their sleep without dreaming. I once knew a man that was bred a scholar and had no bad memory, who told me he had never dreamed in his life till he had that fever he was then newly recovered of, which was about the five or six and twentieth year of his age. I suppose the world affords more such instances; at least every one's acquaintance will furnish him with examples enough of such as pass most of their nights without dreaming." . . . . And again, "If they say that a man is always conscious to himself of thinking; I ask how they know it? 'Consciousness is the perception of what passes in a man's own mind. Can another man perceive that I am conscious of anything, when I perceive it not myself?' No man's knowledge here can go beyond his experience. Wake a man out of a sound sleep, and ask him what he was that moment thinking on. If he himself be conscious of nothing he then thought on, he must be a notable diviner of thoughts that can assure him that he was thinking: may he not with more reason assure him he was not asleep? This is something beyond philosophy; and it cannot be less than revelation that discovers to another thoughts in my mind when I can find none there myself; and they must needs have a penetrating sight who can certainly see what I think when I cannot perceive it myself, and when I declare that I do not. This some may think to be a step beyond the Rosicrucians, it being easier to make one's self invisible to others, than to make another's thoughts visible to one which are not visible to himself. But it is but defining the soul to be 'a substance that always thinks,' and the business is done. If such definition be of any authority, I know not what it can serve for, but to make many men suspect that they have no souls at all, since they find a good part of their lives pass away without thinking. For no definitions that I know, no suppositions of any sect, are of force enough to destroy constant experience; and perhaps it is the affectation of knowing beyond what we perceive that makes so much useless dispute and noise in the world."

This decision of Locke was rejected by Leibnitz in the *New Essays on the Human Understanding*,[1] the great work in which he canvassed from beginning to end the Essay, under the same title, of the English philosopher. He observes, in reply to the supposition that continual consciousness is an attribute of Him " who neither slumbereth nor sleepeth," 'that this affords no inference that in sleep we are wholly without perception.' To the remark, " that it is difficult to conceive, that a being can think and not be conscious of thought," he replies, 'that in this lies the whole knot and difficulty of the matter. But this is not insoluble.' " We must observe," he says, " that we think of a multitude of things at once, but take heed only of those thoughts that are the more prominent. Nor could it be otherwise. For were we to take heed of everything, it would be necessary to attend to an infinity of matters at the same moment, all of which make an effectual impression on the senses. Nay, I assert that there remains always something of all our past thoughts, — that none is ever entirely effaced. Now, when we sleep without dreaming, and when stunned by a blow or other accident, there are formed in us an affinity of small confused perceptions." And again he remarks: " That even when we sleep without dreaming, there is always some feeble perception. The act of awakening, indeed, shows this: and the more easily we are roused, the clearer is the perception we have of what passes without, although this perception is not always strong enough to cause us to awake."

Now, in all this it will be observed, that Leibnitz does not precisely answer the question we have mooted. He maintains that the mind is never without perceptions, but, as he holds that perceptions exist without consciousness, he cannot, though he opposes Locke, be considered as affirming that the mind is never without consciousness during sleep, — in short, does always dream. The doctrine of Wolf on this point is the same with that of his master,[2] though the *Nouveaux Essais* of Leibnitz were not published till long after the death of Wolf.

But if Leibnitz cannot be adduced as categorically asserting that

Marginal notes:

Locke's view opposed by Leibnitz.

Wolf.

---

there is no sleep without its dream, this cannot be said of Kant.

Kant.

That great thinker distinctly maintains that we always dream when asleep; that to cease to dream would be to cease to live; and that those who fancy that they have not dreamt have only forgotten their dream.[1] This is all that the manual of *Anthropology*, published by himself, contains upon the question; but in a manuscript in my possession, which bears to be a work of Kant, but is probably only a compilation from notes taken at his lectures on Anthropology, it is further stated that we can dream more in a minute than we can act during a day, and that the great rapidity of the train of thought in sleep, is one of the principal causes why we do not always recollect what we dream.[2] He elsewhere also observes that the cessation of a force to act, is tantamount to its cessation to be.

Though the determination of this question is one that seems not

The question dealt with by philosophers rather by hypothesis than by experiment.

extremely difficult, we find it dealt with by philosophers, on the one side and the other, rather by hypothesis than by experiment; at least, we have, with one partial exception, which I am soon to quote to you, no observations sufficiently accurate and detailed to warrant us in establishing more than a very doubtful conclusion. I have myself at different times turned my

Conclusion from experiments made by the Author.

attention to the point, and, as far as my observations go, they certainly tend to prove that, during sleep, the mind is never either inactive or wholly unconscious of its activity. As to the objection of Locke and others, that, as we have often no recollection of dreaming, we have, therefore, never

Locke's assumption, that consciousness and the recollection of consciousness are convertible, disproved by the phænomena of somnambulism.

dreamt, it is sufficient to say that the assumption in this argument — that consciousness, and the recollection of consciousness, are convertible — is disproved in the most emphatic manner by experience. You have all heard of the phænomenon of somnambulism. In this remarkable state, the various mental faculties are usually in a higher degree of power than in the natural. The patient has recollections of what he has wholly forgotten. He speaks languages of which, when awake, he remembers not a word. If he use a vulgar dialect when out of this state, in it he employs only a correct and elegant phraseology. The imagination, the sense of propriety, and the fac-

---

1 *Anthropologie*, §§ 30, 36. — ED.
2 The substance of this passage is published in the *Menschenkunde oder Philosophische An-* thropologie, edited by Starke in 1831, from Kant's Lectures. See p. 164. — ED.

ulty of reasoning, are all in general exalted.[1] The bodily powers are in high activity, and under the complete control of the will; and, it is well known, persons in this state have frequently performed feats, of which, when out of it, they would not even have imagined the possibility. And what is even more remarkable, the difference of the faculties in the two states, seems not confined merely to a difference in degree. For it happens, for example, that a person who has no ear for music when awake, shall, in his somnambulic crisis, sing with the utmost correctness and with full enjoyment of his performance. Under this affection persons sometimes live half their lifetime, alternating between the normal and abnormal states, and performing the ordinary functions of life indifferently in both, with this distinction, that if the patient be dull and doltish when he is said to be awake, he is comparatively alert and intelligent when nominally asleep. I am in possession of three works, written during the crisis by three different somnambulists.[2] Now it is evident that consciousness, and an exalted consciousness, must be allowed in somnambulism. This cannot possibly be denied, — but mark what follows. It is the peculiarity of somnambulism —

Consciousness without memory, the characteristic of somnambulism.

it is the differential quality by which that state is contradistinguished from the state of dreaming — that we have no recollection, when we awake, of what has occurred during its continuance. Consciousness is thus cut in two; memory does not connect the train of consciousness in the one state with the train of consciousness in the other. When the patient again relapses into the state of somnambulism, he again remembers all that had occurred during every former alternative of that state; but he not only remembers this, he recalls also the events of his normal existence; so that, whereas the patient in his somnambulic crisis, has a memory of his whole life, in his waking intervals he has a memory only of half his life.

At the time of Locke, the phænomena of somnambulism had been very little studied; nay, so great is the

Dreaming possible without memory.

ignorance that prevails in this country in regard to its nature even now, that you will find this, its distinctive character, wholly unnoticed in the best works upon the subject.[3] But this distinction, you observe, is incompetent always to discriminate the states of dreaming and somnambulism.

---

1 For some interesting illustrations of this state, see Abercrombie *On the Intel. Powers*, pt. ii. § iv. 92. — ED.

2 Of these works we have failed to discover any trace. — ED.

3 This deficiency has been ably supplied by Dr. Carpenter. See his *Principles of Human Physiology*, § 827.— ED.

It may be true that if we recollect our visions during sleep, this recollection excludes somnambulism, but the want of memory by no means proves that the visions we are known by others to have had, were not common dreams. The phænomena, indeed, do not always enable us to discriminate the two states. Somnambulism may exist in many different degrees; the sleep-walking from which it takes its name is only one of its higher phænomena, and one comparatively rare. In general, the subject of this affection does not leave his bed, and it is then frequently impossible to say whether the manifestations exhibited, are the phænomena of somnambulism or of dreaming. Talking during sleep, for example, may be a symptom of either, and it is often only from our general knowledge of the habits and predispositions of the sleeper, that we are warranted in referring this effect to the one and not to the other class of phænomena. We have, however, abundant evidence to prove that forgetfulness is not a decisive criterion of somnambulism. Persons whom there is no reason to suspect of this affection, often manifest during sleep the strongest indications of dreaming, and yet, when they awaken in the morning, retain no memory of what they may have done or said during the night. Locke's argument, that because we do not always remember our consciousness during sleep, we have not, therefore, been always conscious, is thus, on the ground of fact and analogy, disproved.

But this is not all. We can not only show that the fact of the mind remaining conscious during sleep is possible, is even probable, we can also show, by an articulate experience, that this actually occurs. The following observations are the result of my personal experience, and similar experiments every one of you is competent to institute for himself.

That the mind remains conscious during sleep established by experience.

In the first place, when we compose ourselves to rest, we do not always fall at once asleep, but remain for a time in a state of incipient slumber, — in a state intermediate between sleep and waking. Now, if we are gently roused from this transition-state, we find ourselves conscious of being in the commencement of a dream; we find ourselves occupied with a train of thought, and this train we are still able to follow out to a point when it connects itself with certain actual perceptions. We can still trace imagination to sense, and show how, departing from the last sensible impressions of real objects, the fancy proceeds in its work of distorting, falsifying, and perplexing these, in order to construct out of their ruins its own grotesque edifices.

Results of the Author's personal experience.

In the second place, I have always observed, that when suddenly awakened during sleep (and to ascertain the fact I have caused myself to be roused at different seasons of the night), I have always been able to observe that I was in the middle of a dream. The recollection of this dream was not always equally vivid. On some occasions, I was able to trace it back until the train was gradually lost at a remote distance; on others, I was hardly aware of more than one or two of the latter links of the chain; and, sometimes, was scarcely certain of more than the fact, that I was not awakened from an unconscious state. Why we should not always be able to recollect our dreams, it is not difficult to explain. In our waking and our sleeping states, we are placed in two worlds of thought, not only different but contrasted, and contrasted both in the character and in the intensity of their representations. When snatched suddenly from the twilight of our sleeping imaginations, and placed in the meridian lustre of our waking perceptions, the necessary effect of the transition is at once to eclipse or obliterate the traces of our dreams. The act itself also of rousing us from sleep, by abruptly interrupting the current of our thoughts, throws us into confusion, disqualifies us for a time from recollection, and before we have recovered from our consternation, what we could at first have easily discerned is fled or flying.

A sudden and violent is, however, in one respect, more favorable than a gradual and spontaneous wakening to the observation of the phænomena of sleep. For in the former case, the images presented are fresh and prominent; while in the latter, before our attention is applied, the objects of observation have withdrawn darkling into the background of the soul. We may, therefore, I think, assert, in general, that whether we recollect our dreams or not, we always dream. Something similar, indeed, to the rapid oblivion of our sleeping consciousness, happens to us occasionally even when awake. When our mind is not intently occupied with any subject, or more frequently when fatigued, a thought suggests itself. We turn it lazily over and fix our eyes in vacancy; interrupted by the question what we are thinking of, we attempt to answer, but the thought is gone; we cannot recall it, and say that we are thinking of nothing.

The observations I have hitherto made tend only to establish the fact, that the mind is never wholly inactive, and that we are never wholly unconscious of its activity. Of the degree and character of that activity, I at present say nothing; this may form the subject of our future consideration. But in confirmation of the opinion I have

General conclusions from foregoing.

now hazarded, and in proof of something more even than I have
ventured to maintain, I have great pleasure in quoting to you the
substance of a remarkable essay on sleep by one of the most dis-

Jouffroy quoted in confirmation of the Author's view, and in proof of sundry other conclusions.

tinguished of the philosophers of France, — living when the extract was made, but now unfortunately lost to the science of mind, which he
cultivated with most distinguished success; —
I refer to M. Jouffroy, who, along with M.
Royer Collard, was at the head of the pure school of Scottish
Philosophy in France.[1]

"I have never well understood those who admit that in sleep the
mind is dormant. When we dream, we are

The mind frequent-ly awake when the senses asleep.

assuredly asleep, and assuredly also our mind is
not asleep, because it thinks; it is, therefore,
manifest, that the mind frequently wakes when
the senses are in slumber. But this does not prove that it never
sleeps along with them. To sleep is for the mind not to dream;
and it is impossible to establish the fact, that there are in sleep
moments in which the mind does not dream. To have no recollection of our dreams, does not prove that we have not dreamt; for it
can be often proved that we have dreamt, although the dream has
left no trace on our memory.

"The fact, then, that the mind sometimes wakes while the senses
are asleep, is thus established; whereas the fact,

Probable that the mind is always awake.

that it sometimes sleeps along with them is
not; the probability, therefore, is, that it wakes
always. It would require contradictory facts to destroy the force
of this induction, which, on the contrary, every fact seems to confirm.
I shall proceed to analyze some of these which appear to me curious
and striking. They manifestly imply this conclusion, that the
mind, during sleep, is not in a peculiar state, but that its activity
is carried on precisely as when awake.

"When an inhabitant of the province comes to Paris, his sleep
is at first disturbed, and continually broken, by

Induction of facts in support of this con-clusion.

the noise of the carriages passing under his
window. He soon, however, becomes accustomed to the turmoil, and ends by sleeping at
Paris as he slept in his village.

"The noise, however, remains the same, and makes an equal
impression on his senses; how comes it that this noise at first
hinders, and then, at length, does not hinder him from sleeping?

"The state of waking presents analogous facts. Every one

---

[1] *Mélanges*, p. 318, [p. 290, second edition. — ED.]

knows that it is difficult to fix our attention on a book, when sur-rounded by persons engaged in conversation; at length, however, we acquire this faculty. A man unaccustomed to the tumult of the streets of Paris is unable to think consecutively while walking through them; a Parisian finds no difficulty. He meditates as tran-quilly in the midst of the crowd and bustle of men and carriages, as he could in the centre of the forest. The analogy between these facts taken from the state of waking, and the fact which I men-tioned at the commencement, taken from the state of sleep, is so close, that the explanation of the former should throw some light upon the latter. We shall attempt this explanation.

"Attention is the voluntary application of the mind to an object.

Analysis and expla-nation of these phæ-nomena. Attention and Distraction.

It is established, by experience, that we cannot give our attention to two different objects at the same time. Distraction (*être distrait*) is the removal of our attention from a matter with which we are engaged, and our bestowal of it on another which crosses us. In distraction, attention is only diverted because it is attracted by a new perception or idea, solicit-ing it more strongly than that with which it is occupied; and this diversion diminishes exactly in proportion as the solicitation is weaker on the part of the intrusive idea. All experience proves this. The more strongly attention is applied to a subject, the less susceptible is it of distraction; thus it is, that a book which awakens a lively curiosity, retains the attention captive; a person occupied with a matter affecting his life, his reputation, or his fortune, is not easily distracted; he sees nothing, he understands nothing, of what passes around him; we say that he is deeply preöccupied. In like manner, the greater our curiosity, or the more curious the things that are spoken of around us, the less able are we to rivet our attention on the book we read. In like manner, also, if we are waiting in expectation of any one, the slightest noises occasion distraction, as these noises may be the signal of the approach we anticipate. All these facts tend to prove that distraction results only when the intrusive idea solicits us more strongly than that with which we are occupied.

"Hence it is that the stranger in Paris cannot think in the bustle of the streets. The impressions which assail his eyes and ears on every side being for him the signs of things new or little known, when they reach his mind, interest him more strongly than the matter even to which he would apply his thoughts. Each of these impressions announces a cause which may be beautiful, rare, curi-ous, or terrific; the intellect cannot refrain from turning out to verify the fact. It turns out, however, no longer when experience has made it familiar with all that can strike the senses on the streets of Paris; it remains within, and no longer allows itself to be deranged.

"The other admits of a similar explanation. To read without distraction in the midst of an unknown company, would be impossible. Curiosity would be too strong. This would also be the case if the subject of conversation were very interesting. But in a familiar circle, whose ordinary topics of conversation are well known, the ideas of the book make an easy conquest of our thoughts.

"The will, likewise, is of some avail in resisting distraction. Not that it is able to retain the attention when disquieted and curious; but it can recall, and not indulge it in protracted absences, and, by constantly remitting it to the object of its volition, the interest of this object becomes at last predominant. Rational considerations, and the necessity of remaining attentive, likewise exert an influence; they come in aid of the idea, and lend it, so to speak, a helping hand in concentrating on it the attention.

"But, howsoever it may be with all these petty influences, it remains evident that distraction and non-distraction are neither of them matters of sense, but both matters of intelligence. It is not the senses which become accustomed to hear the noises of the street and the sounds of conversation, and which end in being less affected by them; if we are at first vehemently affected by the noises of the street or drawing-room, and then little or not at all, it is because at first attention occupies itself with these impressions, and afterwards neglects them; when it neglects them it is not diverted from its object, and distraction does not take place; when, on the contrary, it accords them notice, it abandons its object, and is then distracted.

Distraction and Non-distraction matters of intelligence.

"We may observe, in support of this conclusion, that the habit of hearing the same sounds renders us sometimes highly sensible to these, as occurs in savages and in the blind; sometimes, again, almost insensible to them, as exemplified in the apathy of the Parisian for the noise of carriages. If the effect were physical, — if it depended on the body and not on the mind, there would be a contradiction, for the habit of hearing the same sounds either blunts the organ or sharpens it; it could not at once have two, and two contrary effects, — it could have only one. The fact is, it neither blunts nor sharpens; the organ remains the same; the same sensations are determined; but when these sensations interest the mind, it applies itself to them, and becomes accustomed to their discrimination; when they do not interest it, it becomes accustomed to neglect, and does not discriminate them. This is the whole mystery; the phænomenon is psychological, not physiological.

"Let us now turn our attention to the state of sleep, and consider whether analogy does not demand a similar explanation of the fact which we stated at the commencement. What takes place when a noise hinders us from sleeping? The body fatigued begins to slumber; then, of a sudden, the senses are struck, and we awake; then fatigue regains the ascendant, we relapse into drowsiness, which is soon again interrupted; and so on for a certain continuance. When, on the contrary, we are accustomed to noise, the impressions it makes no longer disturb our first sleep; the drowsiness is prolonged, and we fall asleep. That the senses are more torpid in sleep than in our waking state, is not a matter of doubt. But when I am once asleep, they are then equally torpid on the first night of my arrival in Paris as on the hundredth. The noise being the same, they receive the same impressions, which they transmit in equal vivacity to the mind. Whence comes it, then, that on the first night I am awakened, and not on the hundredth? The physical facts are identical; the difference can originate only in the mind, as in the case of distraction and of non-distraction in the waking state. Let us suppose that the soul has fallen asleep along with the body; on this hypothesis, the slumber would be equally deep, in both cases, for the mind and for the senses, and we should be unable to see why, in the one case, it was aroused more than in the other. It remains, therefore, certain that it does not sleep like the body; and that, in the one case, disquieted by unusual impressions, it awakens the senses to inquire what is the matter; whilst in the other, knowing by experience of what external fact these impressions are the sign, it remains tranquil, and does not disturb the senses to obtain a useless explanation.

"For let us remark, that the mind has need of the senses to obtain a knowledge of external things. In sleep, the senses are some of them closed, as the eyes; the others half torpid, as touch and hearing. If the soul be disquieted by the impressions which reach it, it requires the senses to ascertain the cause, and to relieve its inquietude. This is the cause why we find ourselves in a disquieted state, when aroused by an extraordinary noise; and this could not have occurred had we not been occupied with this noise before we awoke.

Application of the foregoing analysis to the phænomena of sleep.

"This is, also, the cause why we sometimes feel, during sleep, the efforts we make to awaken our senses, when an unusual noise or any painful sensation disturbs our rest. If we are in a profound sleep, we are for a long time agitated before we have it in our power to awake, — we say to ourselves, we must awake in order to get out of pain; but the sleep of the senses resists, and it is only by little and little that we are able to rouse them from torpidity. Sometimes, when the noise ceases before the issue of the struggle, the awakening does not take place, and, in the morning, we have a confused recollection of having been disturbed during our sleep, — a recollection which becomes distinct only when we learn from others that such and such an occurrence has taken place while we were asleep.

"I had given orders some time ago, that a parlor adjoining to my bedroom should be swept before I was called in the morning. For the first two days the noise awoke me; but, thereafter, I was not aware of it. Whence arose the difference? The noises are the same and at the same hour, I am in the same degree of slumber; the same sensations, consequently, take place. Whence comes it that I awoke, and do no longer awake? For this, it appears to me, there is but one explanation, — viz., that my mind which wakes, and which is now aware of the cause of these sensations, is no longer disquieted, and no longer rouses my senses. It is true that I do not retain the recollection of this reasoning; but this oblivion is not more extraordinary than that of so many others which cross our mind both when awake and when asleep.

Illustrated by the personal experience of the writer.

"I add a single observation. The noise of the brush on the carpet of my parlor is as nothing compared with that of the heavy wagons which pass under my windows at the same hour, and which do not trouble my repose in the least. I was, therefore, awakened by a sensation much feebler than a crowd of others, which I received at the same time. Can that hypothesis afford the reason, which supposes that the awakening is a necessary event; that the sensations rouse the senses, and that the senses rouse the mind? It is evident that my mind alone, and its activity, can explain why the fainter sensation awoke me; as these alone can explain why, when I am reading in my study, the small noise of a mouse playing in a corner can distract my attention, while the thundering noise of a passing wagon does not affect me at all.

"The explanation fully accounts for what occurs with those who sleep in attendance on the sick. All noises foreign to the patient have no effect on them; but let the patient turn him on the bed, let

him utter a groan or sigh, or let his breathing become painful or
interrupted, forthwith the attendant awakes,
however little inured to the vocation, or interested in the welfare of the patient. Whence
comes this discrimination between the noises which deserve the attention of the attendant, and those which do not, if, whilst the senses
are asleep, the mind does not remain observant, — does not act the
sentinel, does not consider the sensations which the senses convey,
and does not awaken the senses as it finds these sensations disquiet-
ing or not? It is by being strongly impressed, previous to going
to sleep, with the duty of attending to the respiration, motions,
complaints of the sufferer, that we come to awaken at all such
noises, and at no others. The habitual repetition of such an impression gives this faculty to professional sick-nurses; a lively interest in
the health of the patient gives it equally to the members of his family.

Experience of those attendant on the sick.

" It is in precisely the same manner that we waken at the appointed
hour, when before going to sleep we have made
a firm resolution of so doing. I have this power
in perfection, but I notice that I lose it if I
depend on any one calling me. In this latter case, my mind does
not take the trouble of measuring the time or of listening to the clock.
But in the former, it is necessary that it do so, otherwise the phænomenon is inexplicable. Every one has made, or can make, this
experiment; when it fails it will be found, if I mistake not, either
that we have not been sufficiently preöccupied with the intention, or
were over-fatigued; for when the senses are strongly benumbed, they
convey to the mind, on the one hand, more obtuse sensations of the
monitory sounds, and, on the other, they resist for a longer time the
efforts the mind makes to awaken them, when these sounds have
reached it.

Awaking at an appointed hour.

" After a night passed in this effort, we have, in general, the recollection, in the morning, of having been constantly occupied during
sleep with this thought. The mind, therefore, watched, and, full of
its resolution, awaited the moment. It is thus that when we go to
bed much interested with any subject, we remember, on wakening,
that during sleep we have been continually haunted by it. On these
occasions, the slumber is light, for, the mind being untranquil, its
agitation is continually disturbing the torpor of the senses. When
the mind is calm, it does not sleep more, but it is less restless.

" It would be curious to ascertain, whether persons of a feeble
memory, and of a volatile disposition, are not less capable than
others of awakening at an appointed hour; for these two circumstances ought to produce this effect, if the notion I have formed of

the phænomenon be correct. A volatile disposition is unable strongly to preöccupy itself with the thought, and to form a determined resolution; and, on the other hand, it is the memory which preserves a recollection of the resolution taken before falling asleep. I have not had an opportunity of making the experiment.

General conclusions. "It appears to me, that from the previous observations it inevitably follows:

1°, That in sleep the senses are torpid, but that the mind wakes.

2°, That certain of our senses continue to transmit to the mind the imperfect sensations they receive.

3°, That the mind judges these sensations, and that it is in virtue of its judgments that it awakens, or does not awaken, the senses.

4°, That the reason why the mind awakens the senses is, that sometimes the sensation disquiets it, being unusual or painful, that sometimes the sensation warns it to rouse the senses, as being an indication of the moment when it ought to do so.

5°, That the mind possesses the power of awakening the senses, but that it only accomplishes this by its own activity overcoming their torpor; that this torpor is an obstacle, — an obstacle greater or less as it is more or less profound.

"If these inferences are just, it follows that we can waken ourselves at will and at appointed signals; that the instrument called an alarum (*réveil-matin*) does not act so much by the noise it makes as by the association we have established in going to bed between the noise and the thought of wakening; that, therefore, an instrument much less noisy, and emitting only a feeble sound, would probably produce the same effect. It follows, moreover, that we can inure ourselves to sleep profoundly in the midst of the loudest noises; that to accomplish this it is perhaps sufficient, on the first night, to impress it on our minds that these sounds do not deserve attention, and ought not to awaken us; and that by this mean, any one may probably sleep as well in the mill as the miller himself. It follows, in fine, that the sleep of the strong and courageous ought to be less easily disturbed, all things equal, than the sleep of the weak and timid. Some historical facts may he quoted in proof of this last conclusion."

I shall not quote to you the observations of M. Jouffroy on Reverie,[1] which form a sequel, and a confirmation, of those he has made upon sleep. Before terminating this subject, I may, however, notice a rather curious case which occurs to my recollection, and which tends to corroborate the theory of the French psychologist. I give it on the authority of Junker, a cele-

Jouffroy's theory corroborated by the case of the postman of Halle.

[1] See *Mélanges*, p. 304 *et seq.* — Ed.

brated physician and professor of Halle, who flourished during the first half of last century, and he says that he took every pains to verify the facts by frequent personal observation. I regret that I am unable at the moment to find the book in which the case is recorded, but of all its relevant circumstances I have a vivid remembrance. The object of observation was the postman between Halle and a town, I forget which, some eight miles distant. This distance the postman was in the habit of traversing daily. A considerable part of his way lay across a district of unenclosed champaign meadow-land, and in walking over this smooth surface the postman was generally asleep. But at the termination of this part of his road, there was a narrow foot-bridge over a stream, and to reach this bridge it was necessary to ascend some broken steps. Now, it was ascertained as completely as any fact of the kind could be, — the observers were shrewd, and the object of observation was a man of undoubted probity, — I say, it was completely ascertained : — 1°, That the postman was asleep in passing over this level course ; 2°, That he held on his way in this state without deflection towards the bridge ; and, 3°, That before arriving at the bridge, he awoke. But this case is not only deserving of all credit from the positive testimony by which it is vouched ; it is also credible as only one of a class of analogous cases which it may be adduced as representing. This case, besides showing that the mind must be active though the body is asleep, shows also that certain bodily functions may be dormant, while others are alert. The locomotive faculty was here in exercise, while the senses were in slumber. This suggests to me another example of the same phænomenon. It is found in a story told by Erasmus [1] in one of his letters, concern

Case of Oporinus.

ing his learned friend Oporinus, the celebrated professor and printer of Basle. Oporinus was on a journey with a bookseller ; and, on their road, they had fallen in with a manuscript. Tired with their day's travelling, — travelling was then almost exclusively performed on horseback, — they came at nightfall to their inn. They were, however, curious to ascertain the contents of their manuscript, and Oporinus undertook the task of reading it aloud. This he continued for some time, when the bookseller found it necessary to put a question concerning a word which he had not rightly understood. It was now discovered that Oporinus was asleep, and being awakened by his companion, he found that he had no recollection of what for a considerable time he had been reading.

---

1 This story is told by Felix Platerus (Observationes, lib. i. p. 11). The person to whom Oporinus read, was the father of the narrator, Thomas Platerus. See Bohn, Noctambulatio; (Haller, Disputationes ad Morborum Hist. et Curat., t. vii. p. 443.) — ED.

Most of you, I daresay, have known or heard of similar occurrences, and I do not quote the anecdote as anything remarkable. But, still, it is a case concurring with a thousand others to prove, 1°, That one bodily sense or function may be asleep while another is awake; and, 2°, That the mind may be in a certain state of activity during sleep, and no memory of that activity remain after the sleep has ceased. The first is evident; for Oporinus, while reading, must have had his eyes and the muscles of his tongue and fauces awake, though his ears and other senses were asleep; and the second is no less so, for the act of reading supposed a very complex series of mental energies. I may notice, by the way, that physiologists have observed, that our bodily senses and powers do not fall asleep simultaneously, but in a certain succession. We all know that the first symptom of slumber is the relaxation of the eyelids; whereas, hearing continues alert for a season after the power of vision has been dormant. In the case last alluded to, this order was, however, violated; and the sight was forcibly kept awake while the hearing had lapsed into torpidity.

In the case of sleep, therefore, so far is it from being proved that the mind is at any moment unconscious, that the result of observation would incline us to the opposite conclusion.

LECTURE XVIII.

CONSCIOUSNESS,—GENERAL PHÆNOMENA,—IS THE MIND EVER UNCONSCIOUSLY MODIFIED?

I PASS now to a question in some respects of still more proximate interest to the psychologist than that discussed in the preceding Lecture; for it is one which, according as it is decided, will determine the character of our explanation of many of the most important phænomena in the philosophy of mind, and, in particular, the great phænomena of Memory and Association. The question I refer to is, Whether the mind exerts energies, and is the subject of modifications, of neither of which it is conscious. This is the most general expression of a problem which has hardly been mentioned, far less mooted, in this country; and when it has attracted a passing notice, the supposition of an unconscious action or passion of the mind, has been treated as something either unintelligible, or absurd. In Germany, on the contrary, it has not only been canvassed, but the alternative which the philosophers of this country have lightly considered as ridiculous, has been gravely established as a conclusion which the phænomena not only warrant, but enforce. The French philosophers, for a long time, viewed the question in the same light as the British. Condillac, indeed, set the latter the example;[1] but of late a revolution is apparent, and two recent French psychologists[2] have marvellously propounded the doctrine, long and generally established in Germany, as something new and unheard of before their own assertion of the paradox.

This question is one not only of importance, but of difficulty; I shall endeavor to make you understand its purport by arguing it upon broader grounds than has hitherto been done, and shall prepare you, by some preliminary information, for its discussion. I shall first of all adduce some proof of the fact, that the mind may, and does, contain far more latent furniture than consciousness informs us it possesses. To simplify the discussion, I shall distinguish three degrees of this mental latency.

Is the mind ever unconsciously modified?

Three degrees of mental latency.

---

[1] *Essai sur l' Origine des Connoissances Humaines.* Sect. ii. ch. 1. § 4—13. — ED.

[2] Cardaillac and Damiron. See below, p. 252. — ED.

In the first place, it is to be remembered that the riches, the

The first.

possessions of our mind, are not to be measured
by its present momentary activities, but by the
amount of its acquired habits. I know a science, or language, not
merely while I make a temporary use of it, but inasmuch as I can
apply it when and how I will. Thus the infinitely greater part of
our spiritual treasures, lies always beyond the sphere of consciousness, hid in the obscure recesses of the mind. This is the first
degree of latency. In regard to this, there is no difficulty, or dispute; and I only take it into account in order to obviate misconception, and because it affords a transition towards the other two
degrees which it conduces to illustrate.

The second degree of latency exists when the mind contains cer-

The second.

tain systems of knowledge, or certain habits of
action, which it is wholly unconscious of pos-
sessing in its ordinary state, but which are revealed to consciousness in certain extraordinary exaltations of its powers. The evidence on this point shows that the mind frequently contains whole
systems of knowledge, which, though in our normal state they have
faded into absolute oblivion, may, in certain abnormal states, as
madness, febrile delirium, somnambulism, catalepsy, etc., flash out
into luminous consciousness, and even throw into the shade of unconsciousness those other systems by which they had, for a long
period, been eclipsed, and even extinguished. For example, there
are cases in which the extinct memory of whole languages was suddenly restored, and, what is even still more remarkable, in which
the faculty was exhibited of accurately repeating, in known or unknown tongues, passages which were never within the grasp of
conscious memory in the normal state. This degree, this phænomenon of latency, is one of the most marvellous in the whole
compass of philosophy, and the proof of its reality will prepare us
for an enlightened consideration of the third, of which the evidence, though not less certain, is not equally obtrusive. But, however remarkable and important, this phænomenon has been almost
wholly neglected by psychologists,[1] and the cases which I adduce in
illustration of its reality have never been previously collected and
applied. That in madness, in fever, in somnambulism, and other
abnormal states, the mind should betray capacities and extensive
systems of knowledge, of which it was at other times wholly unconscious, is a fact so remarkable that it may well demand the highest
evidence to establish its truth. But of such a character is the

---

1 These remarks were probably written before the publication of Abercrombie on the
Intellectual Powers. He collects some very curious instances; see p. 314, 10th edition. — ED.

evidence which I am now to give you. It consists of cases reported by the most intelligent and trustworthy observers, — by observers wholly ignorant of each other's testimony; and the phænomena observed were of so palpable and unambiguous a nature that they could not possibly have been mistaken or misinterpreted.

Evidence from cases of madness.

The first, and least interesting, evidence I shall adduce, is derived from cases of madness; it is given by a celebrated American physician, Dr. Rush.

"The records of the wit and cunning of madmen," says the Doctor, "are numerous in every country. Talents for eloquence, poetry, music, and painting, and uncommon ingenuity in several of the mechanical arts, are often evolved in this state of madness. A gentleman, whom I attended in an hospital in the year 1810, often delighted as well as astonished the patients and officers of our hospital by his displays of oratory, in preaching from a table in the hospital yard every Sunday. A female patient of mine who became insane, after parturition, in the year 1807, sang hymns and songs of her own composition during the latter stage of her illness, with a tone of voice so soft and pleasant that I hung upon it with delight every time I visited her. She had never discovered a talent for poetry or music, in any previous part of her life. Two instances of a talent for drawing, evolved by madness, have occurred within my knowledge. And where is the hospital for mad people, in which elegant and completely rigged ships, and curious pieces of machinery, have not been exhibited by persons who never discovered the least turn for a mechanical art, previously to their derangement? Sometimes we observe in mad people an unexpected resuscitation of knowledge; hence we hear them describe past events, and speak in ancient or modern languages, or repeat long and interesting passages from books, none of which, we are sure, they were capable of recollecting in the natural and healthy state of their mind."[1]

From cases of fever.

The second class of cases are those of fever; and the first I shall adduce is given on the authority of the patient himself. This is Mr. Flint, a very intelligent American clergyman. I take it from his *Recollections of the Valley of the Mississippi.* He was travelling in the State of Illinois, and suffered the common lot of visitants from other climates, in being taken down with a bilious fever. "I am aware," he remarks, "that every sufferer in this way is apt to think his own case extraordinary. My physicians agreed with all who saw me that my case

1 Beasley, *On the Mind*, p. 474.

was so. As very few live to record the issue of a sickness like mine, and as you have requested me, and as I have promised, to be particular, I will relate some of the circumstances of this disease. And it is in my view desirable, in the bitter agony of such diseases, that more of the symptoms, sensations and sufferings, should have been recorded than have been; and that others in similar predicaments may know that some before them have had sufferings like theirs, and have survived them. I had had a fever before, and had risen, and been dressed every day. But in this, with the first day I was prostrated to infantine weakness, and felt, with its first attack, that it was a thing very different from what I had yet experienced. Paroxysms of derangement occurred the third day, and this was to me a new state of mind. That state of disease in which partial derangement is mixed with a consciousness generally sound, and a sensibility preternaturally excited, I should suppose the most distressing of all its forms. At the same time that I was unable to recognize my friends, I was informed that my memory was more than ordinarily exact and retentive, and that I repeated whole passages in the different languages which I knew, with entire accuracy. I recited, without losing or misplacing a word, a passage of poetry which I could not so repeat after I recovered my health."

The following more curious case, is given by Lord Monboddo in his *Antient Metaphysics*.[1]

Case of the Comtesse de Laval.

"It was communicated in a letter from the late Mr. Hans Stanley, a gentleman well known both to the learned and political world, who did me the honor to correspond with me upon the subject of my first volume of metaphysics. I will give it in the words of that gentleman. He introduces it, by saying, that it is an extraordinary fact in the history of mind, which he believes stands single, and for which he does not pretend to account; then he goes on to narrate it: 'About six-and-twenty years ago, when I was in France, I had an intimacy in the family of the late Maréchal de Montmorenci de Laval. His son, the Comte de Laval, was married to Mademoiselle de Maupeaux, the daughter of a Lieutenant-General of that name, and the niece of the late Chancellor. This gentleman was killed at the battle of Hastenbeck; his widow survived him some years, but is since dead.

"'The following fact comes from her own mouth. She has told it me repeatedly. She was a woman of perfect veracity, and very good sense. She appealed to her servants and family for the truth.

Nor did she, indeed, seem to be sensible that the matter was so extraordinary as it appeared to me. I wrote it down at the time; and I have the memorandum among some of my papers.

"'The Comtesse de Laval had been observed, by servants who sate up with her on account of some indisposition, to talk in her sleep a language that none of them understood; nor were they sure, or, indeed, herself able to guess, upon the sounds being repeated to her, whether it was or was not gibberish.

"'Upon her lying in of one of her children, she was attended by a nurse, who was of the province of Brittany, and who imme. diately knew the meaning of what she said, it being in the idiom of the natives of that country; but she herself, when awake, did not understand a single syllable of what she had uttered in her sleep, upon its being retold her.

"'She was born in that province, and had been nursed in a family where nothing but that language was spoken; so that, in her first infancy, she had known it, and no other; but, when she returned to her parents, she had no opportunity of keeping up the use of it; and, as I have before said, she did not understand a word of *Breton* when awake, though she spoke it in her sleep.

"'I need not say that the Comtesse de Laval never said or imagined that she used any words of the Breton idiom, more than were necessary to express those ideas that are within the compass of a child's knowledge of objects,'" etc.

A highly interesting case is given by Mr. Coleridge in his *Biographia Literaria.*[1]

Case given by Coleridge.

"It occurred," says Mr. Coleridge, "in a Roman Catholic town in Germany, a year or two before my arrival at Göttingen, and had not then ceased to be a frequent subject of conversation. A young woman of four or five and twenty, who could neither read nor write, was seized with a nervous fever; during which, according to the asseverations of all the priests and monks of the neighborhood, she became possessed, and, as it appeared, by a very learned devil. She continued incessantly talking Latin, Greek, and Hebrew, in very pompous tones, and with most distinct enunciation. This possession was rendered more probable by the known fact that she was or had been a heretic. Voltaire humorously advises the devil to decline all acquaintance with medical men; and it would have been more to his reputation, if he had taken this advice in the present instance. The case had attracted the particular attention of a young physician, and by his statement many eminent physiologists and psychologists

---

1 Vol. i. p. 117, (edit. 1847).

visited the town, and cross-examined the case on the spot. Sheets full of her ravings were taken down from her own mouth, and were found to consist of sentences, coherent and intelligible each for itself, but with little or no connection with each other. Of the Hebrew, a small portion only could be traced to the Bible, the remainder seemed to be in the Rabbinical dialect. All trick or conspiracy was out of the question. Not only had the young woman ever been a harmless, simple creature; but she was evidently laboring under a nervous fever. In the town, in which she had been resident for many years as a servant in different families, no solution presented itself. The young physician, however, determined to trace her past life step by step; for the patient herself was incapable of returning a rational answer. He at length succeeded in discovering the place where her parents had lived: travelled thither, found them dead, but an uncle surviving; and from him learned that the patient had been charitably taken by an old Protestant pastor at nine years old, and had remained with him some years, even till the old man's death. Of this pastor the uncle knew nothing, but that he was a very good man. With great difficulty, and after much search, our young medical philosopher discovered a niece of the pastor's who had lived with him as his housekeeper, and had inherited his effects. She remembered the girl; related that her venerable uncle had been too. indulgent, and could not bear to hear the girl scolded; that she was willing to have kept her, but that, after her patron's death, the girl herself refused to stay. Anxious inquiries were then, of course, made concerning the pastor's habits; and the solution of the phænomenon was soon obtained. For it appeared that it had been the old man's custom, for years, to walk up and down a passage of his house into which the kitchen-door opened, and to read to himself, with a loud voice, out of his favorite books. A considerable number of these were still in the niece's possession. She added, that he was a very learned man, and a great Hebraist. Among the books were found a collection of Rabbinical writings, together with several of the Greek and Latin fathers; and the physician succeeded in identifying so many passages with those taken down at the young woman's bedside, that no doubt could remain in any rational mind concerning the true origin of the impressions made on her nervous system."

What general fact
these cases establish.

These cases thus evince the general fact, that a mental modification is not proved not to be, merely because consciousness affords us no evidence of its existence. This general fact being established, I now proceed to consider the question in relation to the third class

The third degree of latency.

or degree of latent modifications,— a class in relation to, and on the ground of which alone, it has ever hitherto been argued by philosophers.

The problem, then, in regard to this class is, — Are there, in ordinary, mental modifications,— *i. e.* mental

The problem in regard to this degree stated.

activities and passivities, of which we are unconscious, but which manifest their existence by effects of which we are conscious?

I have thus stated the question, because this appears to me the most unambiguous form in which it can be ex-

To be considered in itself, and in its history.

pressed; and in treating of it, I shall, in the first place, consider it in itself, and, in the second place, in its history. I adopt this order, because the principal difficulties which affect the problem arise from the equivocal and indeterminate language of philosophers. These it is obviously necessary to avoid in the first instance; but, having obtained an insight into the question itself, it will be easy, in a subsequent historical narrative, to show how it has been perplexed and darkened by the mode in which it has been handled by philosophers. I request your attention to this matter, as in the solution of this general problem is contained the solution of several important questions, which will arise under our consideration of the special faculties. It is impossible, however, at the present stage of our progress, to exhibit all, or even the strongest part of, the evidence for the alternative which I adopt; and you must bear in mind that there is much more to be said in favor of this opinion than what I am able at present to adduce to you.

In the question proposed, I am not only strongly inclined to the affirmative,— nay, I do not hesitate to maintain,

The affirmative of this question maintained.

that what we are conscious of is constructed out of what we are not conscious of,— that our whole knowledge, in fact, is made up of the unknown and the incognizable.

This at first sight may appear not only paradoxical, but contradictory. It may be objected, 1°, How can we

To the affirmative two objections.

know that to exist which lies beyond the one condition of all knowledge,— consciousness? And 2°, How can knowledge arise out of ignorance, — consciousness out of unconsciousness, — the cognizable out of the incognizable, — that is, how can one opposite proceed out of the other?

In answer to the first objection,— how can we know that of

which we are conscious, seeing that consciousness is the condi-

tion of knowledge, — it is enough to allege, that there are many things which we neither know nor can know in themselves, — that is, in their direct and immediate relation to our faculties of knowledge, but which manifest their existence indirectly through the medium of their effects. This is the case with the mental

modifications in question; they are not in themselves revealed to consciousness, but as certain facts of consciousness necessarily suppose them to exist, and to exert an influence in the mental processes, we are thus constrained to admit, as modifications of mind, what are not in themselves phænomena of

consciousness. The truth of this will be apparent, if, before descending to any special illustration, we consider that consciousness cannot exist independently of some peculiar modification of mind; we are only conscious as we are conscious of a determinate state. To be conscious, we must be conscious of some particular perception, or remembrance, or imagination, or feeling, etc.; we have no general consciousness. But as consciousness supposes a special mental modification as its object, it must be remembered, that this modification or state supposes a change, — a transition from some other state or modification. But as the modification must be present, before we have a consciousness of the modification, it is evident, that we can have no consciousness of its rise or awakening; for its rise or awakening is also the rise or awakening of consciousness.

But the illustration of this is contained in an answer to the

second objection which asks, — How can knowledge come out of ignorance, — consciousness out of unconsciousness, — the known out of the unknown, — how can one opposite be made up of the other?

In the removal of this objection, the proof of the thesis which I

support is involved. And without dealing in any general speculation, I shall at once descend to the special evidence which appears to me not merely to warrant, but to necessitate the conclusion, that the sphere of our conscious modifications is only a small circle in the centre of a far wider sphere of action and passion, of which we are only conscious through its effects.

Let us take our first example from Perception, — the perception
of external objects, and in that faculty, let us
commence with the sense of sight. Now, you
either already know, or can be at once informed,
what it is that has obtained the name of *Minimum Visibile*. You are of course aware, in
general, that vision is the result of the rays of light, reflected from
the surface of objects to the eye ; a greater number of rays is reflected from a larger surface ; if the superficial extent of an object,
and, consequently, the number of the rays which it reflects, be diminished beyond a certain limit, the object becomes invisible; and
the *minimum visibile* is the smallest expanse which can be seen, —
which can consciously affect us, — which we can be conscious of
seeing. This being understood, it is plain that if we divide this
minimum visibile into two parts, neither half can, by itself, be an
object of vision, or visual consciousness. They are, severally and
apart, to consciousness as zero. But it is evident, that each half
must, by itself, have produced in us a certain modification, real
though unperceived ; for as the perceived whole is nothing but the
union of the unperceived halves, so the perception — the perceived
affection itself of which we are conscious — is only the sum of two
modifications, each of which severally eludes our consciousness.
When we look at a distant forest, we perceive a certain expanse of
green. Of this, as an affection of our organism, we are clearly and
distinctly conscious. Now, the expanse of which we are conscious
is evidently made up of parts of which we are not conscious. No
leaf, perhaps no tree, may be separately visible. But the greenness
of the forest is made up of the greenness of the leaves; that is, the
total impression of which we are conscious, is made up of an infinitude of small impressions of which we are not conscious.

Take another example, from the sense of hearing. In this sense,
there is, in like manner, a *Minimum Audibile*,
that is, a sound the least which can come into
perception and consciousness. But this *mini-
mum audibile* is made up of parts which severally affect the sense,
but of which affections, separately, we are not conscious, though of
their joint result we are. We must, therefore, here likewise admit
the reality of modifications beyond the sphere of consciousness.
To take a special example. When we hear the distant murmur of
the sea, — what are the constituents of the total perception of
which we are conscious ? This murmur is a sum made up of parts,
and the sum would be as zero if the parts did not count as some-

I. External Percep-
tion.

1. The sense of
Sight.
Minimum Visibile.

2. Sense of Hearing.
Minimum Audibile.

thing. The noise of the sea is the complement of the noise of its several waves; —

$$\pi o \nu \tau \iota \omega \nu \ \tau \epsilon \ \kappa \upsilon \mu \acute{\alpha} \tau \omega \nu$$
$$\text{'}A \nu \acute{\eta} \rho \iota \vartheta \mu o \nu \ \gamma \acute{\epsilon} \lambda \alpha \sigma \mu \alpha \cdot \ [1]$$

and if the noise of each wave made no impression on our sense, the noise of the sea, as the result of these impressions, could not be realized. But the noise of each several wave, at the distance we suppose, is inaudible; we must, however, admit that they produce a certain modification, beyond consciousness, on the percipient subject; for this is necessarily involved in the reality of their result. The same is equally the case in the other senses; the taste or smell
3. The other senses. of a dish, be it agreeable or disagreeable, is composed of a multitude of severally imperceptible effects, which the stimulating particles of the viand cause on different points of the nervous expansion of the gustatory and olfactory organs; and the pleasant or painful feeling of softness or roughness is the result of an infinity of unfelt modifications, which the body handled determines on the countless papillæ of the nerves of touch. [2]

Let us now take an example from another mental process. We
II. Association of Ideas. have not yet spoken of what is called the Association of Ideas; and it is enough for our present purpose that you should be aware, that one thought suggests another in conformity to certain determinate laws, — laws to which the succession of our whole mental states are subjected. Now it sometimes happens, that we find one thought rising immediately after another in consciousness, but whose consecution we can reduce to no law of association. Now in these cases we can generally discover, by an attentive observation, that these two thoughts, though not themselves associated, are each associated with certain other thoughts; so that the whole consecution would have been regular, had these intermediate thoughts come into consciousness, between the two which are not immediately associated. Suppose, for instance, that A, B, C, are three thoughts, — that A and C cannot immediately suggest each other, but that each is associated with B, so that A will naturally suggest B, and B naturally suggest C. Now it may happen, that we are conscious of A, and immediately thereafter of C. How is the anomaly to be explained? It can only be explained on the principle of latent modifications. A suggests C, not immediately, but through B; but as B, like the

[1] Æschylus, *Prometheus*, l. 89. — ED.
[2] See Leibnitz, *Nouveaux Essais*, Avant-Propos, p. 8, 9, (ed. Raspe); and lib. ii. c. i. § 9 et seq. — ED.

half of the *minimum visibile* or *minimum audibile*, does not rise into consciousness, we are apt to consider it as non-existent. You are probably aware of the following fact in mechanics. If a number of billiard balls be placed in a straight row and touching each other, and if a ball be made to strike, in the line of the row, the ball at one end of the series, what will happen? The motion of the impinging ball is not divided among the whole row; this, which we might *a priori* have expected, does not happen, but the impetus is transmitted through the intermediate balls which remain each in its place, to the ball at the opposite end of the series, and this ball alone is impelled on. Something like this seems often to occur in the train of thought. One idea mediately suggests another into consciousness, — the suggestion passing through one or more ideas which do not themselves rise into consciousness. The awakening and awakened ideas here correspond to the ball striking and the ball struck off; while the intermediate ideas of which we are unconscious, but which carry on the suggestion, resemble the intermediate balls which remain moveless, but communicate the impulse. An instance of this occurs to me with which I was recently struck. Thinking of Ben Lomond, this thought was immediately followed by the thought of the Prussian system of education. Now, conceivable connection between these two ideas in themselves, there was none. A little reflection, however, explained the anomaly. On my last visit to the mountain, I had met upon its summit a German gentleman, and though I had no consciousness of the intermediate and unawakened links between Ben Lomond and the Prussian schools, they were undoubtedly these, — the German, — Germany, — Prussia, — and, these media being admitted, the connection between the extremes was manifest.

I should perhaps reserve for a future occasion, noticing Mr. Stewart's explanation of this phænomenon. He admits that a perception or idea may pass through the mind without leaving any trace in the memory, and yet serve to introduce other ideas connected with it by the laws of association.[1] Mr. Stewart can hardly be said to have contemplated the possibility of the existence and agency of mental modifications of which we are unconscious. He grants the necessity of interpolating certain intermediate ideas, in order to account for the connection of thought, which could otherwise be explained by no theory of association; and he admits that these intermediate ideas are not

Stewart's explanation of the phænomenon of Association here adduced.

---

[1] *Elements*, part ii. chap. ii.; *Works*, vol. ii. pp. 121, 122.

known by memory to have actually intervened. So far, there is no difference in the two doctrines. But now comes the separation. Mr. Stewart supposes that the intermediate ideas are, for an instant, awakened into consciousness, but, in the same moment, utterly forgot; whereas the opinion I would prefer, holds that they are efficient without rising into consciousness. Mr.

Difficulties of Stewart's doctrine.

Stewart's doctrine on this point is exposed to all the difficulties, and has none of the proofs in its favor which concur in establishing the other.

In the first place, to assume the existence of acts of consciousness

1. Assumes acts of consciousness of which there is no memory.

2. Violates the analogy of consciousness.

of which there is no memory beyond the moment of existence, is at least as inconceivable an hypothesis as the other. But, in the second place, it violates the whole analogy of consciousness, which the other does not. Consciousness supposes memory; and we are only conscious as we are able to connect and contrast one instance of our intellectual existence with another. Whereas, to suppose the existence and efficiency of modifications beyond consciousness, is not at variance with its conditions; for consciousness, though it assures us of the reality of what is within its sphere, says nothing against the reality of what is without. In the third place,

3. Presumption in favor of latent acts in association.

it is demonstrated, that, in perception, there are modifications, efficient, though severally imperceptible; why, therefore, in the other faculties, should there not likewise be modifications, efficient, though unapparent? In the fourth place, there must be some

4. Stewart's hypothesis must take refuge in the counter doctrine.

reason for the assumed fact, that there are perceptions or ideas of which we are conscious, but of which there is no memory. Now, the only reason that can possibly be assigned is that the consciousness was too faint to afford the condition of memory. But of consciousness, however faint, there must be some memory, however short. But this is at variance with the phænomenon, for the ideas A and C may precede and follow each other without any perceptible interval, and without any the feeblest memory of B. If there be no memory, there could have been no consciousness; and, therefore, Mr. Stewart's hypothesis, if strictly interrogated, must, even at last, take refuge in our doctrine; for it can easily be shown, that the degree of memory is directly in proportion to the degree of consciousness, and, consequently, that an absolute negation of memory is an absolute negation of consciousness.

Let us now turn to another class of phænomena, which in like manner are capable of an adequate explanation only on the theory I have advanced; — I mean the operations resulting from our Acquired Dexterities and Habits.

III. Our Acquired Dexterities and Habits.

To explain these, three theories have been advanced. The first regards them as merely mechanical or automatic, and thus denying to the mind all active or voluntary intervention, consequently removes them beyond the sphere of consciousness. The second, again, allows to each several motion a separate act of conscious volition; while the third, which I would maintain, holds a medium between these, constitutes the mind the agent, accords to it a conscious volition over the series, but denies to it a consciousness and deliberate volition in regard to each separate movement in the series which it determines.

To explain these, three theories advanced.
The first.
The second.
The third.

The first of these has been maintained, among others, by two philosophers who in other points are not frequently at one, — by Reid and Hartley. "Habit," says Reid, "differs from instinct, not in its nature, but in its origin; the last being natural, the first acquired. Both operate without will or intention, without thought, and therefore may be called mechanical principles."[1] In another passage, he expresses himself thus: "I conceive it to be a part of our constitution, that what we have been accustomed to do, we acquire not only a facility but a proneness to do on like occasions; so that it requires a particular will or effort to forbear it, but to do it requires very often no will at all."[2]

The first or mechanical theory, maintained by Reid and Hartley.

The same doctrine is laid down still more explicitly by Dr. Hartley. "Suppose," says he, "a person, who has a perfectly voluntary command over his fingers, to begin to learn to play on the harpsichord. The first step is to move his fingers, from key to key, with a slow motion, looking at the notes, and exerting an express act of volition in every motion. By degrees the motions cling to one another, and to the impressions of the notes, in the way of *association*, so often mentioned; the acts of volition growing less and less express all the time, till, at last, they become evanescent and imperceptible. For an expert performer will play from notes, or ideas laid up in the memory, and at the same time carry on a quite different train of thoughts in his mind; or even hold a conversation with another. Whence we conclude, that there is no intervention of the

---

1 *Active Powers*, Essay iii., part i. chap. 3; *Coll. Works*, p. 550.   2 *Ibid.*

idea, or state of mind called will." Cases of this sort Hartley calls "transitions of voluntary actions into automatic ones." [1]

The second theory is maintained against the first by Mr. Stewart; and I think his refutation valid, though not his confirmation. "I cannot help thinking it," he says, "more philosophical to suppose that those actions which are originally voluntary always continue so, although in the case of operations, which are become habitual in consequence of long practice, we may not be able to recollect every different volition. Thus, in the case of a performer on the harpsichord, I apprehend that there is an act of the will preceding every motion of every finger, although he may not be able to recollect these volitions afterwards, and although he may, during the time of his performance, be employed in carrying on a separate train of thought. For it must be remarked, that the most rapid performer can, when he pleases, play so slowly as to be able to attend to, and to recollect, every separate act of his will in the various movements of his fingers; and he can gradually accelerate the rate of his execution till he is unable to recollect these acts. Now, in this instance, one of two suppositions must be made. The one is, that the operations in the two cases are carried on precisely in the same manner, and differ only in the degree of rapidity; and that when this rapidity exceeds a certain rate, the acts of the will are too momentary to leave any impression on the memory. The other is, that when the rapidity exceeds a certain rate, the operation is taken entirely out of our hands, and is carried on by some unknown power, of the nature of which we are as ignorant as of the cause of the circulation of the blood, or of the motion of the intestines. The last supposition seems to me to be somewhat similar to that of a man who should maintain, that although a body projected with a moderate velocity is seen to pass through all the intermediate spaces in moving from one place to another, yet we are not entitled to conclude that this happens when the body moves so quickly as to become invisible to the eye. The former supposition is supported by the analogy of many other facts in our constitution. Of some of these I have already taken notice, and it would be easy to add to the number. An expert accountant, for example, can sum up, almost with a single glance of his eye, a long column of figures. He can tell the sum, with unerring certainty, while, at the same time, he is unable to recollect any one of the figures of which that sum is composed; and yet nobody doubts that each of these figures has passed

The second theory maintained, validly as against the first, by Stewart.

---

[1] Vol. i. pp. 108, 109. [*Observations on Man*, prop. xxi. — ED.]

through his mind, or supposes that when the rapidity of the process becomes so great that he is unable to recollect the various steps of it, he obtains the result by a sort of inspiration. This last supposition would be perfectly analogous to Dr. Hartley's doctrine concerning the nature of our habitual exertions.

"The only plausible objection which, I think, can be offered to the principles I have endeavored to establish on this subject, is founded on the astonishing and almost incredible rapidity they necessarily suppose in our intellectual operations. When a person, for example, reads aloud, there must, according to this doctrine, be a separate volition preceding the articulation of every letter; and it has been found by actual trial, that it is possible to pronounce about two thousand letters in a minute. Is it reasonable to suppose that the mind is capable of so many different acts, in an interval of time so very inconsiderable?

"With respect to this objection, it may be observed, in the first place, that all arguments against the foregoing doctrine with respect to our habitual exertions, in so far as they are founded on the inconceivable rapidity which they suppose in our intellectual operations, apply equally to the common doctrine concerning our perception of distance by the eye. But this is not all. To what does the supposition amount which is considered as so incredible? Only to this, that the mind is so formed as to be able to carry on certain intellectual processes in intervals of time too short to be estimated by our faculties; a supposition which, so far from being extravagant, is supported by the analogy of many of our most certain conclusions in natural philosophy. The discoveries made by the microscope have laid open to our senses a world of wonders, the existence of which hardly any man would have admitted upon inferior evidence; and have gradually prepared the way for those physical speculations which explain some of the most extraordinary phænomena of nature by means of modifications of matter far too subtile for the examination of our organs. Why, then, should it be considered as unphilosophical, after having demonstrated the existence of various intellectual processes which escape our attention in consequence of their rapidity, to carry the supposition a little farther, in order to bring under the known laws of the human constitution a class of mental operations which must otherwise remain perfectly inexplicable? Surely our ideas of time are merely relative, as well as our ideas of extension; nor is there any good reason for doubting that, if our powers of attention and memory were more perfect than they are, so as to give us the same advantage in examining rapid events, which the microscope gives for examining minute portions of extension, they would enlarge our views with respect to the intellectual world, no less than that instrument has with respect to the material."[1]

This doctrine of Mr. Stewart, — that our acts of knowledge are made up of an infinite number of acts of atten-

The principle of Stewart's theory already shown to involve contradictions.

tion, that is, of various acts of concentrated consciousness, there being required a separate act of attention for every minimum possible of knowledge, — I have already shown you, by various examples, to involve contradictions. In the present instance, its admission would constrain our assent to the

But here specially refuted.

most monstrous conclusions. Take the case of a person reading. Now, all of you must have experienced, if ever under the necessity of reading aloud, that, if the matter be uninteresting, your thoughts, while you are going on in the performance of your task, are wholly abstracted from the book and its subject, and you are perhaps deeply occupied in a train of serious meditation. Here the process of reading is performed without interruption, and with the most punctual accuracy; and, at the same time, the process of meditation is carried on without distraction or fatigue. Now this, on Mr. Stewart's doctrine, would seem impossible; for what does his theory suppose? It supposes that separate acts of concentrated consciousness or attention, are bestowed on each least movement in either process. But be the velocity of the mental operations what it may, it is impossible to conceive how transitions between such contrary operations could be kept up for a continuance without fatigue and distraction, even if we throw out of account the fact that the acts of attention to be effectual must be simultaneous, which on Mr. Stewart's theory is not allowed.

We could easily give examples of far more complex operations; but this, with what has been previously said, I deem sufficient to show, that we must either resort to the first theory, which, as nothing but the assumption of an occult and incomprehensible principle, in fact explains nothing, or adopt the theory that there are acts of mind so rapid and minute as to elude the ken of consciousness.

I shall now say something of the history of this opinion. It is a

History of the doctrine of unconscious mental modifications.

curious fact that Locke, in the passage I read to you a few days ago, attributes this opinion to the Cartesians, and he thinks it was employed by them to support their doctrine of the ceaseless activity of mind.[2] In this, as in many other points of the Car-

<hr>

[1] *Elements*, vol. i. chap. ii.; *Works*, vol. ii. p. 127—131.

[2] *Essay on Human Understanding*, book ii.

c. 1, § 18, 19. The Cartesians are intended though not expressly mentioned. — Ed.

tesian philosophy, he is, however, wholly wrong. On the contrary, the Cartesians made consciousness the essence of thought;[1] and their assertion that the mind always thinks is, in their language, precisely tantamount to the assertion that the mind is always conscious.

But what was not maintained by the Cartesians, and even in opposition to their doctrine, was advanced by Leibnitz.[2] To this great philosopher belongs the honor of having originated this opinion, and of having supplied some of the strongest arguments in its support. He was, however, unfortunate in the terms which he employed to propound his doctrine. The latent modifications, — the unconscious activities of mind, he denominated *obscure ideas, obscure representations, perceptions without apperception or consciousness, insensible perceptions*, etc. In this he violated the universal usage of language.

Leibnitz the first to proclaim this doctrine.

Unfortunate in the terms he employed to designate it.

For perception, and idea, and representation, all properly involve the notion of consciousness, — it being, in fact, contradictory to speak of a representation not really represented — a perception not really perceived — an actual idea of whose presence we are not aware.

The close affinity of mental modifications with perceptions, ideas, representations, and the consequent commutation of these terms, have been undoubtedly the reasons why the Leibnitzian doctrine was not more generally adopted, and why, in France and in Britain, succeeding philosophers have almost admitted as a self-evident truth that there can be no modification of mind, devoid of consciousness. As to any refutation of the Leibnitzian doctrine, I know of none. Condillac is, indeed, the only psychologist who can be said to have formally proposed the question. He, like Mr. Stewart, attempts to explain why it can be supposed that the mind has modifications of which we are not conscious, by asserting that we are in truth conscious of the modification, but that it is immediately forgotten.[3] In Germany, the doctrne of Leibnitz was almost universally adopted. I am not aware of a philosopher of the least note by whom it has been rejected. In France, it has, I see, lately been broached by M. de Cardaillac,[4] as a theory of his own, and this, his

Fate of the doctrine in France and Britain.

Condillac.

The doctrine of Leibnitz adopted in Germany.

---

1 Descartes, *Principia*, pt. 1. § 9. — ED.
2 *Nouveaux Essais*, ii. 7. *Monadologie*, § 41. *Principes de la Natur et de la Grace*, § 4. — ED.

3 *Origine des Connoissances Humaines*, sect. ii. c. 1, § 4—13. — ED.
4 *Etudes Elémentaires de Philosophie*, t. ii. pp. 138, 139.

originality, is marvellously admitted by authors like M. Damiron,[1]

De Cardaillac.　　　whom we might reasonably expect to have been better informed. It is hardly worth adding that as the doctrine is not new, so nothing new has been contrib-

Damiron.　　　uted to its illustration. To British psychologists, the opinion would hardly seem to have been known. By none, certainly, is it seriously considered.[2]

---

[1] In the *second* edition of Damiron's *Psychologie,* vol. i. p. 188, Leibnitz is expressly cited. In the *first* edition, however, though the doctrine of latency is stated, (t. i. p. 190), there is no reference to Leibnitz. — ED.

[2] Qualified exception; Kames's *Essays on the principles of Morality and Natural Religion,* (3d edit.), p. 289, to end, Ess. iv., on Matter and Spirit. [With Kames compare Carus, *Psychologie,* ii. p. 185, (edit. 1808). Tucker, *Light of Nature,* c. 10, § 4. Tralles, *De Immortalitate Animæ,* p. 39, *et seq.* On the general subject of acts of mind beyond the sphere of consciousness, compare Kant, *Anthropologie,* § 5. Reinhold, *Theorie des Menschlichen Erkenntnissvermögens und Metaphysik,* i. p. 279, *et seq.* Fries, *Anthropologie,* i. p. 77, (edit. 1820). Schulze, *Philosophische Wissenschaften,* i. p. 16, 17. H. Schmid, *Versuch einer Metaphysik der inneren Natur,* pp. 23, 232 *et seq.* Damiron, *Cours de Philosophie,* i. p. 190, (edit. 1834), Maass, *Einbildungskraft,* § 24, p. 65 *et seq.,* (edit. 1797). Sulzer, *Vermischte Schriften,* i. pp. 99, 109, (edit. 1808), Denzinger, *Institutiones Logicæ,* § 260, i. p. 226, (edit. 1824). Beneke, *Lehrbuch der Psychologie,* § 96 *et seq.,* p. 72, (edit. 1833). Platner, *Philosophische Aphorismen,* i. p. 70.]

LECTURE XIX.

CONSCIOUSNESS, — GENERAL PHÆNOMENA. — DIFFICULTIES AND FACILITIES OF PSYCHOLOGICAL STUDY.

IN our last Lecture we were occupied with the last and principal part of the question, Are there mental agencies beyond the sphere of Consciousness? — in other words, Are there modifications of mind unknown in themselves, but the existence of which we must admit, as the necessary causes of known effects? In dealing with this question, I showed, first of all, that there is indisputable evidence for the general fact, that even extensive systems of knowledge may, in our ordinary state, lie latent in the mind, beyond the sphere of consciousness and will; but which, in certain extraordinary states of organism, may again come forward into light, and even engross the mind to the exclusion of its everyday possessions. The establishment of the fact, that there are in the mind latent capacities, latent riches, which may occasionally exert a powerful and obtrusive agency, prepared us for the question, Are there, in ordinary, latent modifications of mind — agencies unknown themselves as phæ-nomena, but secretly concurring to the production of manifest effects? This problem, I endeavored to show you, must be answered in the affirmative. I took for the medium of proof various operations of mind, analyzed these, and found as a residuum a certain constituent beyond the sphere of consciousness, and the reality of which cannot be disallowed, as necessary for the realization of the allowed effect. My first examples were taken from the faculty of External Perception. I showed you, in relation to all the senses, that there is an ultimate perceptible minimum; that is, that there is no conscious-ness, no perception of the modification determined by its object in any sense, unless that object determines in the sense a certain

Recapitulation.

Are there, in ordinary, latent modifica-tions of mind, concur-ring to the production of manifest effects?

Proof from the fac-ulty of External Per-ception.

quantum of excitement. Now, this quantum, though the minimum that can be consciously perceived, is still a whole composed even of an infinity of lesser parts. Conceiving it, however, only divided into two, each of these halves is unperceived — neither is an object of consciousness; the whole is a percept made up of the unperceived halves. The halves must, however, have each produced its effect towards the perception of the whole; and, therefore, the smallest modification of which consciousness can take account, necessarily supposes, as its constituents, smaller modifications, real, but eluding the ken of consciousness. Could we magnify the discerning power of consciousness, as we can magnify the power of vision by the microscope, we might enable consciousness to extend its cognizance to modifications twice, ten times, ten thousand times less, than it is now competent to apprehend; but still there must be some limit. And as every mental modification is a quantity, and as no quantity can be conceived not divisible *ad infinitum*, we must, even on this hypothesis, allow (unless we assert that the ken of consciousness is also infinite) that there are modifications of mind unknown in themselves, but the necessary coëfficients of known results. On the ground of perception, it is thus demonstratively proved that latent agencies — modifications of which we are unconscious — must be admitted as a groundwork of the Phænomenology of Mind.

The fact of the existence of such latent agencies being proved in reference to one faculty, the presumption is established that they exert an influence in all. And this presumption holds, even if, in regard to some others, we should be unable to demonstrate, in so direct and exclusive a manner, the absolute necessity of their admission. This is shown in regard to the Association of Ideas. In order to explain this, I stated to you that the laws, which govern the train or consecution of thought, are sometimes apparently violated; and that philosophers are perforce obliged, in order to explain the seeming anomaly, to interpolate, hypothetically, between the ostensibly suggesting and the ostensibly suggested thought, certain connecting links of which we have no knowledge. Now, the necessity of such interpolation being admitted, as admitted it must be, the question arises, How have these connecting thoughts, the reality of which is supposed, escaped our cognizance? In explanation of this, there can possibly be only two theories. It may be said, in the first place, that these intermediate ideas did rise into conscious-

The fact of the existence of latent agencies in one faculty, a presumption that they exert an influence in all.

Association of Ideas.
The laws of Association sometimes apparently violated.

ness, operated their suggestion, and were then instantaneously forgotten. It may be said, in the second place, that these intermediate ideas never did rise into consciousness, but, remaining latent themselves, still served to awaken into consciousness the thought, and thus explain its suggestion.

The former of these theories, which is the only one whose possibility is contemplated in this country, I endeavored to show you ought not to be admitted, being obnoxious to the most insurmountable objections. It violates the whole analogy of consciousness; and must at last found upon a reason which would identify it with the second theory. At the same time it violates the law of philosophizing, called the law of Parcimony, which prescribes that a greater number of causes are not to be assumed than are necessary to explain the phænomena. Now, in the present case,

The anomaly solved by the doctrine of latent agencies.

if the existence of unconscious modifications,— of latent agencies, be demonstratively proved by the phænomena of perception, which they alone are competent to explain, why postulate a second unknown cause to account for the phænomena of association, when these can be better explained by the one cause, which the phænomena of perception compel us to admit?

The fact of latent agencies being once established, and shown to be applicable, as a principle of psychological solution, I showed you, by other examples, that it enables us to account, in an easy and satisfactory manner, for some of the most perplexing phæ-

The same principle explains the operations of our Acquired Dexterities and Habits.

nomena of mind. In particular, I did this by reference to our Acquired Dexterities and Habits. In these the consecution of the various operations is extremely rapid; but it is allowed on all hands, that, though we are conscious of the series of operations,— that is, of the mental state which they conjunctly constitute,— of the several operations themselves as acts of volition we are wholly incognizant. Now, this incognizance may be explained, as I stated to you, on three possible hypotheses. In the first place, we may say that the whole process is effected without either volition, or even any action of the thinking principle, it being merely automatic or mechanical. The incognizance to be explained is thus involved in this hypothesis. In the second place, it may be said that each individual act of which the process is made up, is not only an act of mental agency, but a conscious act of volition; but that, there being no memory of these acts, they, consequently, are unknown to us when past. In the third place, it may be said that each individual act

of the process is an act of mental agency, but not of consciousness
and separate volition. The reason of incog-
nizance is thus apparent. The first opinion is
unphilosophical, because, in the first place, it
assumes an occult, an incomprehensible principle, to enable us to
comprehend the effect. In the second place, admitting the agency
of the mind in accomplishing the series of movements before the
habit or dexterity is formed, it afterwards takes it out of the hands
of the mind, in order to bestow it upon another agent. This
hypothesis thus violates the two great laws of philosophizing, —
to assume no occult principle without necessity, — to assume no
second principle without necessity. This doctrine was held by
Reid, Hartley, and others.

The mechanical theory.

The second hypothesis which Mr. Stewart adopts, is at once
complex and contradictory. It supposes a consciousness and no memory. In the first place,
in this it is altogether hypothetical, — it cannot
advance a shadow of proof in support of the
fact which it assumes, that an act of consciousness does or can take
place without any, the least, continuance in memory. In the
second place, this assumption is disproved by the whole analogy
of our intellectual nature. It is a law of mind,
that the intensity of the present consciousness
determines the vivacity of the future memory.
Memory and consciousness are thus in the direct
ratio of each other. On the one hand, looking from cause to effect,
— vivid consciousness, long memory; faint consciousness, short
memory; no consciousness, no memory: and, on the other, looking
from effect to cause, — long memory, vivid consciousness; short
memory, faint consciousness; no memory, no consciousness. Thus,
the hypothesis which postulates consciousness without memory,
violates the fundamental laws of our intellectual being. But, in
the third place, this hypothesis is not only a psychological sole-
cism, — it is, likewise, a psychological pleonasm; it is at once illegitimate and superfluous. As we must admit, from the analogy of
perception, that efficient modifications may exist without any consciousness of their existence, and as this admission affords a solution of the present problem, the hypothesis in question here again
violates the law of parcimony, by assuming without necessity a
plurality of principles to account for what one more easily suffices.

The theory of Consciousness without Memory.

Consciousness and Memory in the direct ratio of each other.

The third hypothesis, then, — that which employs the single principle of latent agencies to account for so numerous a class of
mental phænomena, — how does it explain the phænomenon under

consideration? Nothing can be more simple and analogical than
its solution. As, to take an example from vis-
*The theory of laten-
cy shown to explain
the phænomena in ac-
cordance with anal-
ogy.*
ion, — in the external perception of a station-
ary object, a certain space, an expanse of surface, is necessary to the *minimum visibile;* in
other words, an object of sight cannot come into
consciousness unless it be of a certain size; in
like manner, in the internal perception of a series of mental operations, a certain time, a certain duration, is necessary for the smallest
section of continuous energy to which consciousness is competent.
Some minimum of time must be admitted as the condition of consciousness; and as time is divisible *ad infinitum,* whatever minimum be taken, there must be admitted to be, beyond the cognizance
of consciousness, intervals of time, in which, if mental agencies be
performed, these will be latent to consciousness. If we suppose
that the minimum of time to which consciousness can descend, be
an interval called six, and that six different movements be performed in this interval, these, it is evident, will appear to consciousness as a simple indivisible point of modified time; precisely as
the *minimum visibile* appears as an indivisible point of modified
space. And, as in the extended parts of the *minimum visibile,*
each must determine a certain modification on the percipient subject, seeing that the effect of the whole is only the conjoined effect
of its parts, in like manner, the protended parts of each conscious
instant, — of each distinguishable minimum of time, — though themselves beyond the ken of consciousness, must contribute to give the
character to the whole mental state which that instant, that minimum, comprises. This being understood, it is easy to see how we
lose the consciousness of the several acts, in the rapid succession
of many of our habits and dexterities. At first, and before the
habit is acquired, every act is slow, and we are conscious of the
effort of deliberation, choice, and volition; by degrees the mind
proceeds with less vacillation and uncertainty; at length the acts
become secure and precise: in proportion as this takes place, the
velocity of the procedure is increased, and as this acceleration rises,
the individual acts drop one by one from consciousness, as we lose
the leaves in retiring further and further from the tree; and, at last,
we are only aware of the general state which results from these
unconscious operations, as we can at last only perceive the greenness which results from the unperceived leaves.

I have thus endeavored to recapitulate and vary the illustration
of this important principle. At present, I can only attempt to
offer you such evidence of the fact as lies close to the surface.

When we come to the discussion of the special faculties, you will find that this principle affords an explanation of many interesting phænomena, and from them receives confirmation in return.

Before terminating the consideration of the general phænomena of consciousness, there are Three Principal Facts which it would be improper altogether to pass over without notice, but the full discussion of which I reserve for that part of the course which is conversant with Metaphysics Proper, and when we come to establish upon their foundation our conclusions in regard to the Immateriality and Immortality of Mind;—I mean the fact of our Mental Existence or Substantiality, the fact of our Mental Unity or Individuality, and the fact of our Mental Identity or Personality. In regard to these three facts, I shall, at present, only attempt to give you a very summary view of what place they naturally occupy in our psychological system.

The first of these—the fact of our own Existence—I have already incidentally touched on, in giving you a view of the various possible modes in which the fact of the Duality of Consciousness may be conditionally accepted.

The various modifications of which the thinking subject, Ego, is conscious, are accompanied with the feeling, or intuition, or belief,—or by whatever name the conviction may be called,—that I, the thinking subject, exist. This feeling has been called by philosophers the apperception or consciousness of our own existence; but, as it is a simple and ultimate fact of consciousness, though it be clearly given, it cannot be defined or described. And for the same reason that it cannot be defined, it cannot be deduced or demonstrated; and the apparent enthymeme of Descartes,—*Cogito ergo sum*,—if really intended for an inference,—if really intended to be more than a simple enunciation of the proposition, that the fact of our existence is given in the fact of our consciousness, is either tautological, or false. Tautological, because nothing is contained in the conclusion which was not explicitly given in the premise,—the premise, *Cogito, I think*, being only a grammatical equation of *Ego sum cogitans, I am* or *exist, thinking*. False, inasmuch as there would, in the first place, be postulated the reality of thought as a quality or modification, and then, from the fact of this modification, inferred the fact of existence, and of the existence of a subject;

Three Principal Facts to be noticed in connection with the general phænomena of consciousness.

1. Self-Existence.

Descartes' Cogito ergo sum.

whereas it is self-evident, that in the very possibility of a quality or modification, is supposed the reality of existence, and of an existing subject. Philosophers, in general, among whom may be particularly mentioned Locke and Leibnitz, have accordingly found the evidence in a clear and immediate belief in the simple datum of consciousness; and that this was likewise the opinion of Descartes himself, it would not be difficult to show.[1]

2. Mental Unity.

The second fact — our Mental Unity or Individuality — is given with equal evidence as the first. As clearly as I am conscious of existing, so clearly am I conscious at every moment of my existence, (and never more so than when the most heterogeneous mental modifications are in a state of rapid succession,) that the conscious Ego is not itself a mere modification, nor a series of modifications of any other subject, but that it is itself something different from all its modifications, and a self-subsistent entity. This feeling, belief, datum, or fact of

The truth of the testimony of consciousness to our mental unity, doubted.

our mental individuality or unity, is not more capable of explanation than the feeling or fact of our existence, which it indeed always involves. The fact of the deliverance of consciousness to our mental unity has, of course, never been doubted; but philosophers have been found to doubt its truth. According to Hume,[2] our thinking

Hume.

Ego is nothing but a bundle of individual impressions and ideas, out of whose union in the imagination, the notion of a whole, as of a subject of that which is felt and thought, is formed. According to Kant,[3] it cannot be

Kant.

properly determined whether we exist as substance or as accident, because the datum of individuality is a condition of the possibility of our having thoughts and feelings; in other words, of the possibility of consciousness; and, therefore, although consciousness gives — cannot but give — the phænomenon of individuality, it does not follow that this phænomenon may not be only a necessary illusion. An articulate refutation of these opinions I cannot attempt at present, but their refutation is, in fact, involved in their statement. In regard to Hume, his skeptical conclusion is only an inference from the premises of the dogmatical philosophers, who founded their systems on a violation or distortion

1 That Descartes did not intend to prove the fact of existence from that of thought, but to state that personal existence consists in consciousness, is shown in M. Cousin's Dissertation, *Sur le vrai sens du cogito ergo sum;* printed in the earlier editions of the *Frag-*

ments Philosophiques, and in vol. i. p. 27 of the collected edition of his works. — ED.

2 *Treatise of Human Nature*, part iv. sect. v., vi. — ED.

3 *Kritik der reinen Vernunft*, Trans. Dial. b. ii. c. 1. — ED.

of the facts of consciousness. His conclusion is, therefore, refuted in the refutation of their premises, which is accomplished in the simple exposition that they at once found on, and deny, the veracity of consciousness. And by this objection the doctrine of Kant is overset. For if he attempts to philosophize, he must assert the possibility of philosophy. But the possibility of philosophy supposes the veracity of consciousness as to the contents of its testimony; therefore, in disputing the testimony of consciousness to our mental unity and substantiality, Kant disputes the possibility of philosophy, and, consequently, reduces his own attempts at philosophizing to absurdity.

The third datum under consideration is the Identity of Mind or Person. This consists in the assurance we have,

8. Mental Identity.

from consciousness, that our thinking Ego, notwithstanding the ceaseless changes of state or modification, of which it is the subject, is essentially the same thing, — the same person, at every period of its existence. On this subject, laying out of account certain subordinate differences on the mode of stating the fact, philosophers, in general, are agreed. Locke,[1] in the *Essay on the Human Understanding;* Leibnitz,[2] in the *Nouveaux Essais;* Butler,[3] and Reid,[4] are particularly worthy of attention. In regard to this deliverance of consciousness, the truth of which is of vital importance, affording, as it does, the basis of moral responsibility and hope of immortality, — it is, like the last, denied by Kant to afford a valid ground of scientific certainty. He maintains that there is no cogent proof of the substantial permanence of our thinking self, because the feeling of identity is only the condition under which thought is possible. Kant's doubt in regard to the present fact is refuted in the same manner as his doubt in regard to the preceding, and there are also a number of special grounds on which it can be shown to be untenable. But of these at another time.

We have now terminated the consideration of Consciousness as the general faculty of thought, and as the only

The peculiar diffi-
culties and facilities
of psychological in-
vestigation.

instrument and only source of Philosophy. But before proceeding to treat of the Special Faculties, it may be proper here to premise some observations in relation to the peculiar Difficulties and peculiar Facilities which we may expect in the applica-

---

1 Book ii. c. 27, especially § 9 *et seq.* — Ed.

2 Liv. ii. c. 27. — Ed.

3 *Analogy,* Diss. i. Of Personal Identity. · Ed.

4 *Int. Powers,* Essay iii. cc. iv. vi. — Ed.

tion of consciousness to the study of its own phænomena. I shall first speak of the difficulties.

The first difficulty in psychological observation arises from this,

I. Difficulties.

that the conscious mind is at once the observing subject and the object observed. What are the consequences of this? In the first place, the mental energy, instead of being concentrated, is divided, and divided in two divergent directions. The state of mind ob-

1. The conscious mind at once the observing subject and the object observed.

served, and the act of mind observing, are mutually in an inverse ratio; each tends to annihilate the other. Is the state to be observed intense, all reflex observation is rendered impossible; the mind cannot view as a spectator; it is wholly occupied as an agent or patient. On the other hand, exactly in proportion as the mind concentrates its force in the act of reflective observation, in the same proportion must the direct phænomenon lose in vivacity, and, consequently, in the precision and individuality of its character. This difficulty is manifestly insuperable in those states of mind, which, of their very nature, as suppressing consciousness, exclude all contemporaneous and voluntary observation, as in sleep and fainting. In states like dreaming, which allow at least of a mediate, but, therefore, only of an imperfect observation, through recollection, it is not altogether exclusive. In all states of strong mental emotion, the passion is itself, to a certain extent, a negation of the tranquillity requisite for observation, so that we are thus impaled on the awkward dilemma, — either we possess the necessary tranquillity for observation, with little or nothing to observe, or there is something to observe, but we have not the necessary tranquillity for observation. All this is completely opposite in our observation of the external world. There the objects lie always ready for our inspection; and we have only to open our eyes and guard ourselves from the use of hypotheses and green spectacles, to carry our observations to an easy and successful termination.[1]

In the second place, in the study of external nature, several

2. Want of mutual coöperation.

observers may associate themselves in the pursuit; and it is well known how coöperation and mutual sympathy preclude tedium and languor, and brace up the faculties to their highest vigor. Hence the old proverb, *unus homo, nullus homo.* "As iron," says Solomon, "sharpeneth iron, so a man sharpeneth the understanding of his

---

1 [Cf. Biunde, *Versuch einer systematischen Behandlung der empirischen Psychologie,* i. p. 55.]

friend."[1] "In my opinion," says Plato,[2] "it is well expressed by Homer,

> 'By mutual confidence and mutual aid,
>   Great deeds are done, and great discoveries made;

for if we labor in company, we are always more prompt and capable for the investigation of any hidden matter. But if a man works out anything by solitary meditation, he forthwith goes about to find some one with whom he may commune, nor does he think his discovery assured until confirmed by the acquiescence of others." Aristotle,[3] in like manner, referring to the same passage of Homer, gives the same solution. "Social operation," he says, "renders us more energetic both in thought and action;" a sentiment which is beautifully illustrated by Ovid,[4]

> "Scilicet ingeniis aliqua est concordia junctis,
>   Et servat studii fœdera quisque sui.
> Utque meis numeris tua dat facundia nervos,
>   Sic venit a nobis in tua verba nitor."

Of this advantage the student of Mind is in a great measure deprived. He who would study the internal world must isolate himself in the solitude of his own thought; and for man, who, as Aristotle observes,[5] is more social by nature than any bee or ant, this isolation is not only painful in itself, but, in place of strengthening his powers, tends to rob them of what maintains their vigor, and stimulates their exertion.

In the third place, "In the study of the material universe, it is not necessary that each observer should himself make every observation. The phænomena are here so palpable and so easily described, that the experience of one observer suffices to make the facts which he has witnessed intelligible and credible to all. In point of fact, our knowledge of the external world is taken chiefly upon trust. The phænomena of the internal world, on the contrary, are not thus capable of being described; all that the first observer can do is to lead others to repeat his experience: in the science of mind, we can believe nothing upon authority, take nothing upon trust. In the physical sciences, a fact viewed in different aspects and in different circumstances, by one or more observers of acknowl-

3. No fact of consciousness can be accepted at second-hand.

---

1 *Proverbs*, xxvii. 17. The authorized version is *countenance.* — ED.

2 *Protagoras*, p. 848. — ED.

3 *Eth. Nic.*, viii. 1. Cf. *ibid.*, ix. 9. — ED

4 *Epist ex Ponto*, ii. 5, 59, 69. — ED.

5 *Polit.* i. 2. — ED.

edged sagacity and good faith, is not only comprehended as clearly by those who have not seen it for themselves, but is also admitted without hesitation, independently of all personal verification. Instruction thus suffices to make it understood, and the authority of the testimony carries with it a certainty which almost precludes the possibility of doubt.

"But this is not the case in the philosophy of mind. On the contrary, we can here neither understand nor believe at second hand. Testimony can impose nothing on its own authority; and instruction is only instruction when it enables us to teach ourselves. A fact of consciousness, however well observed, however clearly expressed, and however great may be our confidence in its observer, is for us as nothing, until, by an experience of our own, we have observed and recognized it ourselves. Till this be done we cannot comprehend what it means, far less admit it to be true. Hence it follows that, in philosophy proper, instruction is limited to an indication of the position in which the pupil ought to place himself, in order by his own observation to verify for himself the facts which his instructor pronounces true."[1]

In the fourth place, the phænomena of consciousness are not arrested during observation, — they are in a ceaseless and rapid flow; each state of mind is indivisible, but for a moment, and there are not two states or two moments of whose precise identity we can be assured. Thus, before we can observe a modification, it is already altered; nay, the very intention of observing it, suffices for the change. It hence results that the phænomena can only be studied through its reminiscence; but memory reproduces it often very imperfectly, and always in lower vivacity and precision. The objects of the external world, on the other hand, remain either unaltered during our observation, or can be renewed without change; and we can leave off at will and recommence our investigation without detriment to its result.[2]

4. Phænomena of consciousness not arrested during observation, but only to be studied through memory.

In the fifth place, "The phænomena of the mental world are not, like those of the material, placed by the side of each other in space. They want that form by which external objects attract and fetter our attention; they appear only in rows on the thread of time, occupying their fleeting moment, and then vanishing into oblivion; whereas, external objects stand before us steadfast, and distinct, and simultaneous, in all the life and emphasis of extension, figure, and color."[3]

5. Presented only in succession.

1 Cardaillac, *Etudes de Philosophie*, i. p. 6.
2 [Ancillon, *Nouv. Mélanges*, ii. 102. Cardaillac, *Etudes de Philos.*, i. 3, 4.]
Psychologie, vol. i. p. 56.]
3 Biunde,

In the sixth place, the perceptions of the different qualities of external objects are decisively discriminated by

6. Naturally blend with each other, and are presented in complexity.

different corporeal organs, so that color, sound, solidity, odor, flavor, are, in the sensations themselves, contrasted, without the possibility of confusion. In an individual sense, on the contrary, it is not always easy to draw the line of separation between its perceptions, as these are continually running into each other. Thus red and yellow are, in their extreme points, easily distinguished, but the transition point from one to the other is not precisely determined. Now, in our internal observation, the mental phænomena cannot be discriminated like the perceptions of one sense from the perceptions of another, but only like the perceptions of the same. Thus the phænomenon of feeling, — of pleasure or pain, and the phænomenon of desire, are, when considered in their remoter divergent aspects, manifestly marked out and contradistinguished as different original modifications; whereas, when viewed on their approximating side, they are seen to slide so insensibly into each other, that it becomes impossible to draw between them any accurate line of demarcation. Thus the various qualities of our internal life can be alone discriminated by a mental process called Abstraction; and abstraction is exposed to many liabilities of error. Nay, the various mental operations do not present themselves distinct and separate; they are all bound up in the same unity of action, and as they are only possible through each other, they cannot, even in thought, be dealt with as isolated and apart. In the perception of an external object, the qualities are, indeed, likewise presented by the different senses in connection, as, for example, vinegar is at once seen as yellow, felt as liquid, tasted as sour, and so on; nevertheless, the qualities easily allow themselves in abstraction to be viewed as really separable, because they are all the properties of an extended and divisible body; whereas in the mind, thoughts, feelings, desires, do not stand separate, though in juxtaposition, but every mental act contains at once all these qualities, as the constituents of its indivisible simplicity.

In the seventh place, the act of reflection on our internal modifications is not accompanied with that frequent and varied sentiment of pleasure, which we experience from the impression of external things. Self-observation costs us a greater effort, and has less excitement than the contemplation of the material world; and the higher and more refined gratification which it supplies when its habit has been once formed, cannot be conceived by those who have not as yet been trained to its enjoyment.[1] "The first part of our life is fled before we possess the capacity of reflective observation; while the impressions which, from earliest infancy, we receive from material objects, the wants of our animal nature, and the prior development of our external senses, all contribute to concentrate, even from the first breath of life, our attention on the world with-out. The second passes without our caring to observe ourselves. The outer life is too agreeable to allow the soul to tear itself from its gratifications, and return frequently upon itself. And at the period when the material world has at length palled upon the senses, when the taste and the desire of reflection gradually become predominant, we then find ourselves, in a certain sort, already made up, and it is impossible for us to resume our life from its commencement, and to discover how we have become what we now are."[2] "Hitherto external objects have exclusively riveted our attention; our organs have acquired the flexibility requisite for this peculiar kind of observation; we have learned the method, acquired the habit, and feel the pleasure which results from perform-ing what we perform with ease. But let us recoil upon ourselves; the scene changes; the charm is gone; difficulties accumulate; all that is done is done irksomely and with effort; in a word, every-thing within repels, everything without attracts; we reach the age of manhood without being taught another lesson than reading what takes place without and around us, whilst we possess neither the habit nor the method of studying the volume of our own thoughts."[3] "For a long time, we are too absorbed in life to be able to detach ourselves from it in thought; and when the desires and the feelings are at length weakened or tranquillized, — when we are at length restored to ourselves, we can no longer judge of the preceding state, because we can no longer reproduce or replace it. Thus it is that our life, in a philosophical sense, runs like water through our fingers. We are carried along lost, whelmed in our life; we live, but rarely see ourselves to live.

"The reflective Ego, which distinguishes self from its transitory modifications, and which separates the spectator from the spectacle of life, which it is continually representing to itself, is never devel-oped in the majority of mankind at all, and even in the thoughtful

Marginal note: 7. The act of reflec-tion not accompanied with the frequent and varied sentiment of pleasure, which we experience from the impression of external things.

1 [Biunde, *Psychologie*, vol. i. p. 56.]   3 [Ancillon, *Nouv. Mélanges*, t. ii. p. 103.]
2 [Cardaillac, *Etudes de Philosophie*, t. i. p. 3.]

and reflective few, it is formed only at a mature period, and is even then only in activity by starts and at intervals." [1]

But Philosophy has not only peculiar difficulties, it has also peculiar facilities. There is indeed only one external condition on which it is dependent, and that is language; and when, in the progress of civilization, a language is once formed of a copiousness and pliability capable of embodying its abstractions without figurative ambiguity, then a genuine philosophy may commence. With this one condition all is given; the Philosopher requires for his discoveries no preliminary preparations, — no apparatus of instruments and materials. He has no new events to seek, as the Historian; no new combinations to form, as the Mathematician. The Botanist, the Zoölogist, the Mineralogist, can accumulate only by care, and trouble, and expense, an inadequate assortment of the objects necessary for their labors and observations. But that most important and interesting of all studies of which man himself is the object, has no need of anything external; it is only necessary that the observer enter into his inner self in order to find there all he stands in need of, or rather it is only by doing this that he can hope to find anything at all. If he only effectively pursue the method of observation and analysis, he may even dispense with the study of philosophical systems. This is at best only useful as a mean towards a deeper and more varied study of himself, and is often only a tribute paid by philosophy to erudition. [2]

II. The facilities of philosophical study.

---

1 [Ancillon, *Nouv. Mélanges*, t. ii. pp. 103, 104, 105.]

2 [Cf. Fries, *Logik*, § 126, p. 587 (edit. 1819).

Thurot, *Introduction à l' Etude de la Philosophie*, t. i., Disc. Prél. p. 85.]

LECTURE XX.

DISTRIBUTION OF THE SPECIAL COGNITIVE FÀCULTIES.

GENTLEMEN:—We have now concluded the consideration of Consciousness, viewed in its more general relations, and shall proceed to analyze its more particular modifications, that is, to consider the various Special Faculties of Knowledge.

The Special Faculties of Knowledge.

It is here proper to recall to your attention the division I gave you of the Mental Phænomena into three great classes,—viz., the phænomena of Knowledge, the phænomena of Feeling, and the phænomena of Conation. But as these various phænomena all suppose Consciousness as their condition,—those of the first class, the phænomena of knowledge, being, indeed, nothing but consciousness in various relations,—it was necessary, before descending to the consideration of the subordinate, first to exhaust the principal; and in doing this the discussion has been protracted to a greater length than I anticipated.

Three great classes of mental phænomena.

I now proceed to the particular investigation of the first class of the mental phænomena,—those of Knowledge or Cognition,—and shall commence by delineating to you the distribution of the cognitive faculties which I shall adopt;—a distribution different from any other with which I am acquainted. But I would first premise an observation in regard to psychological powers, and to psychological divisions.

The first class,—Phænomena of Knowledge.

As to mental powers,—under which term are included mental faculties and capacities,—you are not to suppose entities really distinguishable from the thinking principle, or really different from each other. Mental powers are not like bodily organs. It is the same simple substance which exerts every energy of every faculty, however various, and which is affected in every mode of every capacity, however opposite. This has frequently been wilfully or ignorantly misunderstood; and,

Mental powers.

among others, Dr. Brown has made it a matter of reproach to philosophers in general, that they regarded the fac-

Brown wrong as to
the common philo-
sophical opinion re-
garding these.

ulties into which they analyzed the mind as so
many distinct and independent existences.[1] No
reproach, however, can be more unjust, no mistake more flagrant; and it can easily be shown
that this is perhaps the charge, of all others, to which the very smallest number of psychologists need plead guilty. On this point Dr.
Brown does not, however, stand alone as an accuser; and, both before and since his time, the same charge has been once and again preferred, and this, in particular, with singular infelicity, against Reid
and Stewart. To speak only of the latter, — he sufficiently declares
his opinion on the subject in a foot-note of the *Dissertation :* — "I
quote," he says, " the following passage from Addison, *not* as a specimen of his metaphysical acumen, but as a proof of his good sense in
divining and obviating a difficulty, which, I believe, most persons
will acknowledge occurred to themselves when they first entered on
metaphysical studies : — 'Although we divide the soul into several
powers and faculties, there is no such division in the soul itself, since
it is the *whole soul* that remembers, understands, wills, or imagines.
Our manner of considering the memory, understanding, will, imagination, and the like faculties, is for the better enabling us to express
ourselves in such abstracted subjects of speculation, not that there
is any such division in the soul itself.' In another part of the same
paper, Addison observes, 'that what we call the faculties of the soul
are only the different ways or modes in which the soul can exert
herself.' — *Spectator*, No. 600." [2]

I shall first state to you what is intended by the terms *mental power*,

What meant by men-
tal power; and the rel-
ative opinion of phi-
losophers.

faculty, or *capacity ;* and then show you that
no other opinion has been generally held by
philosophers.

It is a fact too notorious to be denied, that the
mind is capable of different modifications, that
is, can exert different actions, and can be affected by different passions. This is admitted. But these actions and passions are not all
dissimilar; every action and passion is not different from every
other. On the contrary, they are like, and they are unlike. Those,
therefore, that are like, we group or assort together in thought, and
bestow on them a common name; nor are these groups or assortments manifold, — they are in fact few and simple. Again, every
action is an effect; every action and passion a modification. But

---

1 *Philosophy of the Human Mind*, Lecture xvi. vol. i. p. 338, (second edition.) — ED.
2 *Collected Works*, vol. i. p. 334.

every effect supposes a cause; every modification supposes a subject. When we say that the mind exerts an energy, we virtually say that the mind is the cause of the energy; when we say that the mind acts or suffers, we say in other words, that the mind is the subject of a modification. But the modifications, that is, the actions and passions, of the mind, as we stated, all fall into a few resembling groups, which we designate by a peculiar name; and as the mind is the common cause and subject of all these, we are surely entitled to say in general that the mind has the faculty of exerting such and such a class of energies, or has the capacity of being modified by such and such an order of affections. We here excogitate no new, no occult principle. We only generalize certain effects, and then infer that common effects must have a common cause; we only classify certain modes, and conclude that similar modes indicate the same capacity of being modified. There is nothing in all this contrary to the most rigid rules of philosophizing; nay, it is the purest specimen of the inductive philosophy.

On this doctrine, a *faculty* is nothing more than a general term for the causality the mind has of originating a certain class of energies; a *capacity* only a general term for the susceptibility the mind has of being affected by a particular class of emotions.[1] All mental powers are thus, in short, nothing more than names determined by various orders of mental phænomena. But as these phænomena differ from, and resemble, each other in various respects, various modes of classification may, therefore, be adopted, and consequently, various faculties and capacities, in different views, may be the result.

Faculty and Capacity distinguished.

And this is what we actually see to be the case in the different systems of philosophy; for each system of philosophy is a different view of the phænomena of mind. Now, here I would observe that we might fall into one or other of two errors, either by attributing too great or too small importance to a systematic arrangement of the mental phænomena. It must be conceded to those who affect to undervalue psychological system, that system is neither the end first in the order of time, nor that paramount in the scale of importance. To attempt a definitive system or synthesis, before we have fully analyzed and accumulated the facts to be arranged, would be preposterous, and necessarily futile; and system is only valuable when it is not arbitrarily devised, but arises naturally out of an observation of the facts, and of the whole facts, themselves; τῆς πολλῆς πείρας τελευταῖον ἐπιγέννημα.

Philosophical System, — its true place and importance.

1 See above, p. 123, *et seq.* — ED.

On the other hand, to despise system is to despise philosophy; for the end of philosophy is the detection of unity. Even in the progress of a science, and long prior to its consummation, it is indeed better to assort the materials we have accumulated, even though the arrangement be only temporary, only provisional, than to leave them in confusion. For without such arrangement, we are unable to overlook our possessions; and as experiment results from the experiment it supersedes, so system is destined to generate system in a progress never attaining, but ever approximating to, perfection.

Having stated what a psychological power in propriety is, I may add that this, and not the other, opinion, has been the one prevalent in the various schools and ages of philosophy. I could adduce to you passages in which the doctrine that the faculties and capacities are more than mere possible modes, in which the simple indivisible principle of thought may act and exist, is explicitly denied by Galen,[1] Lactantius,[2] Tertullian,[3] St. Austin,[4] Isidorus,[5] Irenæus,[6] Synesius,[7] and Gregory of Nyssa,[8] among the fathers of

The opinion generally prevalent regarding mental powers.

[1] Galen, however, adopting Plato's threefold division of the faculties (*Ratio, Iracundia, Cupiditas*), expressly teaches that these have separate local seats, and that the mind is a whole composed of parts different both in kind and in nature (*genere et natura*). See his *De Hippocratis et Platonis Decretis*, lib. vi. *Opera*, pp. 1003, 1004, *et seq.* (edit. Basle, 1549). Cf. lib. v. c. viii. — ED.

[2] [*De Opificio Dei*, c. 18.] [*Opera*, ii. 125 (edit. 1784); where, however, Lactantius merely pronounces the question in regard to the identity or difference of the *anima* and *animus*, insoluble, and gives the arguments on both sides. — ED.]

[3] [*De Anima*, c. 18.] [*Opera*, ii. 304, (edit. 1630): " Quid sensus, nisi ejus rei quæ sentitur, intellectus? Quid intellectus nisi ejus rei quæ intelligitur sensus? Unde ista tormenta cruciandæ simplicitatis, et suspendendæ veritatis? Quis mihi exhibebit sensum non intelligentem quod sentit? aut intellectum non sentientem quod intelligit? . . . Si corporalia quidem sentiuntur, incorporalia vero intelliguntur: verum genera diversa sunt non domicilia sensus et intellectus, id est, non anima et animus." — ED.]

[4] See *De Trinitate*, lib. x. c. 8, § 18. *Opera*, viii. p. 898 (edit. Bened.): " Hæc tria, memoria, intelligentia, voluntas, quoniam non sunt tres vitæ, sed una vita, nec tres mentes, sed una mens; consequenter utique, nec tres substantiæ sunt, sed una substantia. . . . . . Quocirca tria hæc eo sunt unum, quo una vita, una mens, una essentia." Cf. *ibid.*,

lib. xi. c. 3. §§ 5, 6, *Opera*, viii. p. 903, (edit. Bened.) L. ix. c iv. § 3, and c. v. § 8. The doctrine of St. Augustin on this point, however, divided the schoolmen. Henry of Ghent, and Gregory of Rimini, maintained that his opinion was Nominalistic, while others held that it might be identified with that of Aquinas. See Fromondus, *Philosophia Christiana de Anima*, lib. i. c. vi. art. iii. p. 160 *et seq.* (ed. 1649). — ED.

[5] [*Originum*, lib. xi. c. 1.] [*Opera*, p. 94, (edit. 1617) : " Hæc omnia adjuncta sunt animæ, ut una res sit. Pro efficientiis enim causarum diversa nomina sortita est anima. Nam et *memoria* mens est: dum ergo vivificat corpus, *anima* est; dum scit, *mens* est; dum vult, *animus* est; dum recolit, *memoria* est," — ED.]

[6] [*Contra Hæreses*, lib. ii. c. 29.] [*Opera*, t. i. p. 392, (edit. Leipsic, 1848): " Sensus hominis, mens, et cogitatio, et intentio mentis, et ea quæ sunt hujusmodi, non aliud quid præter animam sunt ; sed ipsius animæ motus et operationes, nullam sine anima habentes substantiam." — ED.]

[7] [*De Insomniis*,] [*Opera*, p. 103, (edit. 1553): Ὅλῳ ἀκούει τῷ πνεύματι, καὶ ὅλῳ βλέπει, καὶ τὰ λοιπὰ πάντα δύναται. Δυνάμεις μία μὲν πᾶσαι κατὰ τὴν κοινὴν ῥίζαν· πολλαὶ δὲ κατὰ περίοδον. — ED.

[8] [*De Hominis Opificio*, c. vi.] [*Opera*, i. p. 55.] [Οὐδὲ γὰρ ἡμῖν πολλαί τινες εἰσὶν αἱ ἀντιληπτικαὶ τῶν πραγμάτων δυνάμεις, εἰ καὶ πολυτρόπως διὰ τῶν αἰσθήσεων τῶν κατὰ

the Church; by Iamblichus,[1] Plotinus,[2] Proclus,[3] Olympiodorus,[4] and the pseudo Hermes Trismegistus,[5] among the Platonists; by the Aphrodisian,[6] Ammonius Hermiæ,[7] and Philoponus[8] among the Aristotelians. Since the restoration of letters the same doctrine is explicitly avowed by the elder Scaliger,[9] Patricius,[10] and Campanella;[11] by Descartes,[12] Malebranche,[13] Leibnitz,[14] and Wolf;[15] by Condillac,[16] Kant,[17] and the whole host of recent philosophers.

ζωὴν ἐφαπτώμεθα. Μία γάρ τις ἐστὶ δύναμις, αὐτος ὁ ἐγκείμενος νοῦς, ὁ δι᾽ ἑκάστου τῶν αἰσθητηρίων διεξιὼν, καὶ τῶν ὄντων ἐπιδρασσόμενος. — ED.]

1 " Anima quamvis videatur omnes rationes et totas in se species exhibere, tamen determinata semper est secundum aliquid unum, id est, unam speciem." *De Mysteriis*, as paraphrased by Marsilius Ficinus. *Opera*, p. 1879. — ED.

2 *Ennead*, iv. lib. iii. § iii. p. 374, (ed. 1615): Τοῦτο δὲ οὐκέτ᾽ ἂν τὴν μὲν [ψυχὴν] ὅλην, τὴν δὲ μέρος ἂν εἶναι παράσχοιτο· καὶ μάλιστα, οἷς τὸ αὐτὸ δυνάμεως πάρεστιν· ἐπεὶ καὶ οἷς ἄλλο ἔργον, τῷ δὲ ἄλλο οἷον ὀφθαλμοῖς καὶ ὠσὶν· οὐ μόριον ἄλλο ψυχῆς ὁράσει, ἄλλο δὲ ὠσὶ λεκτέον παρεῖναι, (ἄλλων δὲ, τὸ μερίζειν οὕτως), ἀλλὰ τὸ αὐτὸ, κἂν ἄλλη δύναμις ἐν ἑκατέροις ἐνεργῇ. *Ibid.*, lib. ii. p. 363: Ψυχὴ μεριστὴ μὲν, ὅτι ἐν πᾶσι μέρεσι τοῦ ἐν ᾧ ἐστιν· ἀμέριστος δὲ ὅτι ὅλη ἐν πᾶσι, καὶ ἐν ὁτωοῦν αὐτοῦ ὅλη. Cf. lib. i. p. 361. — ED.

3 *In Platonis Theologiam*, lib. iv. c. xvi. p. p. 210, (edit. 1618): Διὰ γὰρ τὴν ἄκραν μετουσίαν τῆς συνοχῆς, ἀμέριστος ὁ νοῦς. Διὰ δὲ τὸ δεύτερα μέτρα τῆς μεθέξεως, ἡ ψυχὴ μεριστὴ, καὶ ἀμέριστος ἐστι, κατὰ μίαν σύγκρασιν. *Ibid.*, lib. i. c. xi. p. 25: Τὴν δὲ ψυχὴν ἓν καὶ πολλὰ; — thus rendered in the Latin version of Portus: " Animam unam et multa, [propter varias unius animæ facultates, et variarum rerum cognitionem, quam una anima habet."] — ED.

4 Olympiodorus adopts Plato's division of the soul into three principles. As regards the unity of the rational soul alone, something may perhaps be inferred from the Commentary on the *First Alcibiades*, where the rational soul is identified with the personal self. See especially pp. 203, 226, edit. Creuzer. Compare also a passage from his Commentary on the *Phædo*, cited by Cousin, *Fragments Philosophiques*, tom. i. p. 421, (ed. 1847). Neither passage, however, bears decisively on this question. — ED.

5 *De Intellectione et Sensu*, lib. xv. f. 42.] [Patricii, *Nova de Universis Philosophia*, (edit. 1593): Ἐν γὰρ τοῖς ἄλλοις ζώοις ἡ αἴσθησις τῇ

φύσει ἥνωται, ἐν δ᾽ ἀνθρώποις ἡ νόησις. Νοήσεως δὲ ὁ νοῦς διαφέρεται τοσοῦτον, ὅσον ὁ Θεὸς θειότητος. Ἡ μὲν γὰρ θειότης ὑπὸ τοῦ θεοῦ γίνεται, ἡ δὲ νόησις ὑπὸ τοῦ νοῦ, ἀδελφὴ οὖσα τοῦ λόγου, καὶ ὄργανα ἀλλήλων. — ED.]

6 Πᾶσαι γὰρ αὗται (sc. ψυχὴ θρεπτικὴ, αἰσθητικὴ, φανταστικὴ, ὁρμητικὴ, ὀρεκτικὴ) μία οὖσαι κατὰ τὸ ὑποκείμενον, ταῖς διαφοραῖς τῶν δυνάμεων αὐταῖς διήρηνται. *In De Anima*, lib. i. f. 140a, (edit. Ven. 1534.) — ED.

7 Τῆς ἡμετέρας ψυχῆς διτταὶ αἱ ἐνέργειαι, αἱ μὲν γνωστικαὶ, οἷον νοῦς, δόξα, αἴσθησις, φαντασία, διάνοια, αἱ δὲ ζωτικαὶ καὶ ὀρεκτικαὶ, οἷον βούλησις, προαίρεσις, θυμὸς, καὶ ἐπιθυμία. *In Quinque Voces Porphyrii*, f. 7a. (edit. Aldine, 1546). — ED.

8 *In De Anima*, Prœm, f. 4a.: Οὐ γὰρ οἶδεν ἑαυτὴν ἡ ὄψις, ἤ ἡ ἀκοή, ἤ ἁπλῶς ἡ αἴσθησις· οὐδὲ ζητεῖ ποίας ἐστὶ φύσεως· ἡ μέντοι ψυχὴ ἡ λογικὴ, αὐτὴ ἑαυτὴν γινώσκει· αὕτη γοῦν ἐστιν ἡ ζητοῦσα· αὕτη ἡ ζητουμένη· αὕτη ἡ εὑρίσκουσα, αὕτη ἡ εὑρισκομένη· ἡ γινώσκουσα, καὶ γινωσκομένη. Cf. In lib. i. c. v., text 89, to end. — ED.

9 *Exercitationes*, [ccxcvii. § 1; cccvii. § 87.] [Cf. cccvii. § 15.] — ED.

10 *Mystica Ægyptiorum*, lib. ii. c. iii. f. 4, col. 2: " Anima unica est et simplex; sed multiplicantur virtutes ejus, ultra substantiam, et si videtur operari plurima simul, ejus opera sunt multa ratione patientum. Si quidem corpora non recipiunt operationes animæ equaliter, sed pro conditione sua; ergo pluralitas operationum inest rebus, non animæ." — ED.

11 " Eandem animam sentientem et memorativam esse imaginativam et discursivam." See *De Sensu Rerum*, lib. ii. c. xxi. p. 77, (edit. 1637). Cf. cc. xix. xx. — ED.

12 [*De Passionibus*, pars. ii. art. 68.]

13 *Recherche de la Vérité*, lib. iii. c. i. § 1. — ED.

14 [*Nouveaux Essais*, lib. ii. c. xxi. § 6. p. 132 — edit. Raspe.]

15 [*Psychologia Rationalis*, § 81.]

16 [*De l' Art de penser*, c. viii. *Cours*, t. iii. p. 304.]

17 *Kritik der reinen Vernunft* — Transac. Dial., B. ii. H. 1. (p. 407, edit. 1799). Kant, how-

During the middle ages, the question was indeed one which divided the schools. St. Thomas,[1] at the head of one party, held that the faculties were distinguished not only from each other, but from the essence of the mind; and this, as they phrased it, really and not formally. Henry of Ghent,[2] at the head of another party, maintained a modified opinion,—that the faculties were really distinguished from each other, but not from the essence of the soul. Scotus,[3] again, followed by Occam[4] and the whole sect of Nominalists, denied all real difference either between the several faculties, or between the faculties and the mind; allowing between them only a formal or logical distinction. This last is the doctrine that has subsequently prevailed in the latter ages of philosophy; and it is a proof of its universality, that few modern psychologists have ever thought it necessary to make an explicit profession of their faith in what they silently assumed. No accusation can, therefore, be more ungrounded than that which has been directed against philosophers,—that they have generally harbored the opinion that faculties are, like organs in the body, distinct constituents of mind. The Aristotelic

The Aristotelic doctrine regarding the relation of the soul to the body.

principle, that in relation to the body "the soul is all in the whole and all in every part,"—that it is the same indivisible mind that operates in sense, in imagination, in memory, in reasoning, etc., differently indeed, but differently only because operating in different relations,[5]—this opinion is the one

---

ever, while he admits this unity of the subject, as a conception involved in the fact of consciousness, denies that the conception can be legitimately transferred to the soul as a real substance.— Ed.

[1] *Summa*, pars i. Q. 77, art. i. *et seq. Ibid.*, Q. 54. art. iii. Cf. *In Sent.*, lib. i. dist. iii. Q. 4, art. ii. St. Thomas is followed by Capreolus, Cajetan, Ferrariensis, and Marsilius Ficinus. See Cottunius, *De Trip. Stat. Animæ Rationalis*, p. 281. — Ed.

[2] Henry of Ghent is, by Fromondus, classed with Gregory of Rimini and the Nominalists. See *De Anima*, lib. ii. c. vi. But see Genovesi, *Element. Metapha.* pars ii. p. 120. — Ed.

[3] See Zabarella, *De Rebus Naturalibus. Lib. De Facultatibus Animæ*, p. 685. Tennemann, *Gesch. der Philosophie*, viii. 2. p. 751.] ["Dico igitur," says Scotus, "quod potest sustineri, quod essentia animæ indistincta re et ratione, est principium plurium actionum sine diversitate reali potentiarum, ita quod sint vel partes animæ vel accidentia, vel respectus. . . . . Dices, quod erit ibi saltem differentia rationis. Concedo, sed hac nihil faciet ad principium operationis realis. *In Sent.*, lib. ii. dist. 16.

Q. 2, (quoted by Tennemann.) The Conimbricenses distinguish between the doctrine of Scotus, and that held in common by Gregory (Ariminensis), Occam, Gabriel Biel, Marsilius, and almost the whole sect of the Nominalists, —who, they say, concur in affirming, — "potentias [animæ] nec re ipsa, nec formaliter, et natura rei, ab animæ essentia distingui, licet anima ex varietate actionum diversa nomina sortiatur;" whereas Scotus, according to them, is of opinion that, while the faculties cannot in reality (re ipsa) be distinguished from the mind, these may, however, be distinguished "formaliter, et ex natura rei." *In De Anima*, lib. ii. c. iii. Q 4, p. 150. Cottunius attributes the latter opinion to the Scotists universally. See his *De Triplici Statu Animæ Rationalis*, p. 280, (ed. 1628.) Cf. Toletus, *In De Anima*, lib. ii. c. iv. f. 69. — Ed.]

[4] *In Sent.*, lib. ii. dist. 16, qq. 24, 26. See Conimbricenses, *In De Anima*, p. 150. Cottunius, *De Trip. Stat. An Rat.*, p. 280. — Ed.

[5] *De Anima*, i. v. 31: 'Αλλ' οὐδὲν ἧττον ἐν ἑκατέρῳ τῶν μορίων ἅπαντ' ἐνυπάρχει τὰ μόρια τῆς ψυχῆς, κ. τ. λ. Cf. Plotinus, above, p. 271, note 2.—Ed.

dominant among psychologists, and the one which, though not always formally proclaimed, must, if not positively disclaimed, be in justice presumptively attributed to every philosopher of mind. Those who employed the old and familiar language of philosophy, meant, in truth, exactly the same as those who would establish a new doctrine on a newfangled nomenclature.

From what I have now said, you will be better prepared for what I am about to state in regard to the classifica-

Psychological Division, what.

tion of the first great order of mental phæno- mena, and the distribution of the faculties of Knowledge founded thereon. I formerly told you that the mental qualities—the mental phænomena — are never presented to us sep- arately; they are always in conjunction, and it is only by an ideal analysis and abstraction that, for the purposes of science, they can be discriminated and considered apart.[1] The problem proposed in such an analysis, is to find the primary threads which, in their com- position, form the complex tissue of thought. In what ought to be accomplished by such an analysis, all philosophers are agreed, how- ever different may have been the result of their attempts. I shall not state and criticize the various classifications propounded of the cognitive faculties, as I did not state and criticize the classifications propounded of the mental phænomena in general. The reasons are the same. You would be confused, not edified. I shall only delin- eate the distribution of the faculties of knowledge, which I have adopted, and endeavor to afford you some general insight into its principles. At present I limit my consideration to the phænomena of Knowledge; with the two other classes — the phænomena of Feeling and the phænomena of Conation — we have at present no concern.

I again repeat that consciousness constitutes, or is coëxtensive with, all our faculties of knowledge, — these

The special faculties of knowledge, evolved out of Consciousness.

faculties being only special modifications under which consciousness is manifested. It being, therefore, understood that consciousness is not a special faculty of knowledge, but the general faculty out of which the special faculties of knowledge are evolved, I proceed to this evolution.

In the first place, as we are endowed with a faculty of Cognition, or Consciousness in general, and since it cannot

I. The Presentative Faculty.

be maintained that we have always possessed the knowledge which we now possess, it will be admitted, that we must have a faculty of acquiring knowledge.

1 See above, p. 130.— ED.

But this acquisition of knowledge can only be accomplished by the immediate presentation of a new object to consciousness, in other words, by the reception of a new object within the sphere of our cognition. We have thus a faculty which may be called the Acquisitive, or the Presentative, or the Receptive.

Now, new or adventitious knowledge may be either of things external, or of things internal; in other words, either of the phænomena of the non-ego, or of the phænomena of the ego; and this distinction of object will determine a subdivision of this, the Acquisitive Faculty. If the object of knowledge be external, the faculty receptive or presentative of the qualities of such object, will be a consciousness of the non-ego. This has obtained the name of External Perception, or of Perception simply. If, on the other hand, the object be internal, the faculty receptive or presentative of the qualities of such subject-object, will be a consciousness of the ego. This faculty obtains the name of Internal or Reflex Perception, or of Self-Consciousness. By the foreign psychologists this faculty is termed also the Internal Sense.

Subdivided, as External and Internal, into Perception and Self-Consciousness.

Under the general faculty of cognition is thus, in the first place, distinguished an Acquisitive, or Presentative, or Receptive Faculty; and this acquisitive faculty is subdivided into the consciousness of the non-ego, or External Perception, or Perception simply, and into the consciousness of the ego, or Self-Consciousness, or Internal Perception.

This acquisitive faculty is the faculty of Experience. External perception is the faculty of external, self-consciousness is the faculty of internal, experience. If we limit the term Reflection in conformity to its original employment and proper signification, — an attention to the internal phænomena, — *reflection* will be an expression for self-consciousness concentrated.

In the second place, inasmuch as we are capable of knowledge, we must be endowed not only with a faculty of acquiring, but with a faculty of retaining or conserving it when acquired. By this faculty, I mean merely, and in the most limited sense, the power of mental retention. We have thus, as a second necessary faculty, one that may be called the Conservative or Retentive. This is Memory, strictly so denominated, — that is, the power of retaining knowledge in the mind, but out of consciousness; I say retaining knowledge in the mind, but out of consciousness, for to bring the *retentum* out of memory into consciousness, is the function of a totally different faculty, of which we are immediately to speak.

II. The Conservative Faculty, — Memory Proper.

Under the general faculty of cognition is thus, in the second place, distinguished the Conservative or Retentive Faculty, or Memory Proper. Whether there be subdivisions of this faculty, we shall not here inquire.

But, in the third place, if we are capable of knowledge, it is not

III. The Reproductive Faculty.

enough that we possess a faculty of acquiring, and a faculty of retaining it in the mind, but out of consciousness; we must further be endowed with a faculty of recalling it out of unconsciousness into consciousness, in short, a reproductive power. This Reproductive Faculty is governed by the laws which regulate the succession of our thoughts, — the laws, as they are called, of Mental Association.

Subdivided as without, or with Will, into Suggestion and Reminiscence.

If these laws are allowed to operate without the intervention of the will, this faculty may be called Suggestion, or Spontaneous Suggestion; whereas, if applied under the influence of the will, it will properly obtain the name of Reminiscence or Recollection. By *reproduction*, it should be observed, that I strictly mean the process of recovering the absent thought from unconsciousness, and not its representation in consciousness. This reproductive faculty is commonly confounded with the conservative, under the name of Memory; but most erroneously. These qualities of mind are totally unlike, and are possessed by different individuals in the most different degrees. Some have a strong faculty of conservation, and a feeble faculty of reproduction; others, again, a prompt and active reminiscence, but an evanescent retention. Under the general faculty of cognition, there is thus discriminated, in the third place, the Reproductive Faculty.

In the fourth place, as capable of knowledge, we must not only

IV. The Representative Faculty, — Imagination.

be endowed with a presentative, a conservative, and a reproductive faculty; there is required for their consummation — for the keystone of the arch — a faculty of representing in consciousness, and of keeping before the mind the knowledge presented, retained, and reproduced. We have thus a Representative Faculty; and this obtains the name of Imagination or Phantasy.

The element of imagination is not to be confounded with the element of reproduction, though this is frequently, nay commonly, done; and this either by comprehending these two qualities under imagination, or by conjoining them with the quality of retention under memory. The distinction I make is valid. For the two faculties are possessed by different individuals in very different degrees. It is not, indeed, easy to see how, without a representative act, an object can be reproduced. But the fact is certain, that the two powers have no necessary proportion to each other. The representative faculty has, by philosophers, been distinguished into the Productive or Creative, and into the Reproductive, Imagination. I shall hereafter show you that this distinction is untenable.

Thus, under the general cognitive faculty, we have a fourth special faculty discriminated, — the Representative Faculty, — Phantasy, or Imagination.

In the fifth place, all the faculties we have considered are only subsidiary. They acquire, preserve, call out, and hold up, the materials, for the use of a higher faculty which operates upon these materials, and which we may call the Elaborative or Discursive Faculty. This faculty has only one operation, it only compares, — it is Comparison, — the faculty of Relations. It may startle you to hear that the highest function of mind is nothing higher than comparison, but, in the end, I am confident of convincing you of the paradox. Under comparison, I include the conditions, and the result, of comparison. In order to compare, the mind must divide or separate, and conjoin or compose. Analysis and synthesis are, therefore, the conditions of comparison. Again, the result of comparison is either the affirmation of one thing of another, or the negation of one thing of another. If the mind affirm one thing of another, it conjoins them, and is thus again synthesis. If it deny one thing of another, it disjoins them, and is thus again analysis. Generalization, which is the result of synthesis and analysis, is thus an act of comparison, and is properly denominated Conception. Judgment is only the comparison of two terms or notions directly together; Reasoning, only the comparison of two terms or notions with each other through a third. Conception or Generalization, Judgment and Reasoning, are thus only various applications of comparison, and not even entitled to the distinction of separate faculties.

V. The Elaborative Faculty, — Comparison.

Analysis and Synthesis.

Conception or Generalization.

Judgment. Reasoning.

Under the general cognitive faculty, there is thus discriminated a fifth special faculty in the Elaborative Faculty, or Comparison. This is Thought, strictly so called; it corresponds to the Διάνοια of the Greek, to the *Discursus* of the Latin, to the *Verstand* of the German philosophy; and its laws are the object of Logic.

But, in the sixth and last place, the mind is not altogether indebted to experience for the whole apparatus of its knowledge, — its knowledge is not all adventitious. What we know by experience, without experience we should not have known; and as all our experience is contingent, all the knowledge derived from experience is contingent also. But there are cognitions in the mind which are not contingent, — which are necessary, — which we cannot but think, — which thought supposes as its fundamental condition. These cognitions, therefore, are not mere generalizations from experience. But if not derived from experience, they must be native to the mind; unless, on an alternative that we need not at present contemplate, we suppose with Plato, St. Austin, Cousin, and other philosophers, that Reason, or more properly Intellect, is impersonal, and that we are conscious of these necessary cognitions in the divine mind. These native, these necessary cognitions, are the laws by which the mind is governed in its operations, and which afford the conditions of its capacity of knowledge. These necessary laws, or primary conditions, of intelligence, are phænomena of a similar character; and we must, therefore, generalize or collect them into a class; and on the power possessed by the mind of manifesting these phænomena, we may bestow the name of the Regulative Faculty. This faculty corresponds in some measure to what, in the Aristotelic philosophy, was called Noûs, — νοῦς (*intellectus, mens*), when strictly employed, being a term, in that philosophy, for the place of principles, — the *locus principiorum*. It is analogous, likewise, to the term *Reason*, as occasionally used by some of the older English philosophers, and to the *Vernunft* (*reason*) in the philosophy of Kant, Jacobi, and others of the recent German metaphysicians, and from them adopted into France and England. It is also nearly convertible with what I conceive to be Reid's, and certainly Stewart's, notion of Common Sense. This, the last general faculty which I would distinguish under the Cognitive Faculty, is thus what I would call the Regulative or Legislative, — its synonyms being Noûs, Intellect, or Common Sense.

VI. The Regulative Faculty, — Reason or Common Sense.

You will observe that the term *faculty* can be applied to the class of phænomena here collected under one name, only in a very different signification from what it bears when applied to the preceding powers. For νοῦς, intelligence or common sense, meaning merely the complement of the fundamental principles or laws of thought, is not properly a faculty, that is, it is not an active power at all. As it is, however, not a capacity, it is not easy to see by what other word it can be denoted.

The term Faculty not properly applicable to Reason or Common Sense.

Such are the six special Faculties of Cognition; — 1°, The Acquisitive or Presentative or Receptive Faculty divided into Perception and Self-Consciousness; 2°, The Conservative or Retentive Fac-

These constitute the
whole fundamental
faculties of cognition.

ulty, Memory; 3°, The Reproductive or Revo-
cative Faculty, subdivided into Suggestion and
Reminiscence; 4°, The Representative Faculty
or Imagination; 5°, The Elaborative Faculty
or Comparison, Faculty of Relations; and, 6°, The Regulative
or Legislative Faculty, Intellect or Intelligence Proper, Common
Sense. Besides these faculties, there are, I conceive, no others;
and, in the sequel, I shall endeavor to show you, that while these
are attributes of mind not to be confounded,—not to be analyzed into
each other, — the other faculties which have been devised by philosophers are either factitious and imaginary, or easily reducible to
these.

The following is a tabular view of the distribution of the Special
Faculties of Knowledge:

Cognitive Faculties.	I. Presentative	External = Perception. Internal = Self-consciousness.
	II. Conservative	= Memory.
	III. Reproductive	Without will = Suggestion. With will = Reminiscence.
	IV. Representative	= Imagination.
	V. Elaborative	= Comparison, — Faculty of Relations.
	VI. Regulative	= Reason, — Common Sense.

LECTURE XXI.

THE PRESENTATIVE FACULTY.

I. PERCEPTION. — REID'S HISTORICAL VIEW OF THE THEORIES OF PERCEPTION.

HAVING concluded the consideration of Consciousness as the

Recapitulation. common condition of the mental phænomena, and of those more general phænomena which pertain to consciousness as regarded in this universal relation, I proceeded, in our last Lecture, to the discussion of consciousness viewed in its more particular modifications, — that is, to the discussion of the Special powers, — the Special Faculties and Capacities of Mind. And, having called to your recollection the primary distribution of the mental phænomena into three great classes, — the phænomena included under our general faculty of Knowledge, or Thought, the phænomena included under our general capacity of Feeling, or of Pleasure and Pain, and the phænomena included under our general power of Conation, that is, of Will and Desire, — I passed on to the consideration of the first of these classes, — that is, the phænomena of Knowledge. This class of phænomena are, in strictest propriety, mere modifications of consciousness, being consciousness only in different relations; and consciousness may, therefore, be regarded as the general faculty of knowledge : whereas the phænomena of the other classes, though they suppose consciousness as the condition of their manifestation, inasmuch as we cannot feel, nor will, nor desire, without knowing or being aware that we so do or suffer, — these phænomena are, however, something more than mere modifications of consciousness, seeing a new quality is superadded to that of cognition.

I may notice, parenthetically, the reason why I frequently employ

Employment of the term Cognition vindicated. *cognition* as a synonym of knowledge. This is not done merely for the sake of varying the expression. In the first place, it is necessary to have a word of this signification, which we can use in the plural. Now the term *knowledges* has waxed obsolete, though I think it ought to be revived. It is frequently employed by Bacon.[1] We must, therefore, have recourse to the term *cognition*, of which the plural is in common usage. But, in the second place, we must likewise have a term for knowledge, which we can employ adjectively. The word *knowledge* itself has no adjective, for the participle *knowing* is too vague and unemphatic to be employed, at least alone. But the substantive *cognition* has the adjective *cognitive*. Thus, in consequence of having a plural and an adjective, *cognition* is a word we cannot possibly dispense with in psychological discussion. It would also be convenient, in the third place, for psychological precision and emphasis, to use the word *to cognize* in connection with its noun *cognition*, as we use the decompound *to recognize* in connection with its noun *recognition*. But in

Condition under which the employment of new terms in philosophy is allowable.

this instance the necessity is not strong enough to warrant our doing what custom has not done. You will notice, such an innovation is always a question of circumstances; and though I would not subject Philosophy to Rhetoric more than Gregory the Great would Theology to Grammar, still, without an adequate necessity, I should always recommend you, in your English compositions, to prefer a word of Saxon to a word of Greek or Latin derivation. It would be absurd to sacrifice meaning to its mode of utterance,—to make thought subordinate to its expression; but still where no higher authority, no imperious necessity, dispenses with philological precepts, these, as themselves the dictates of reason and philosophy, ought to be punctiliously obeyed. "It is not in language," says Leibnitz, "that we ought to play the puritan;"[2] but it is not either for the philosopher or the theologian to throw off all deference to the laws of language,—to proclaim of their doctrines,

> "Mysteria tanta
> Turpe est grammaticis submittere colla capistris."[3]

The general right must certainly be asserted to the philosopher of usurping a peculiar language, if requisite to express his peculiar analyses; but he ought to remember that the exercise of this right, as odious and suspected, is *strictissimi juris*, and that, to avoid the pains and penalties of grammatical recusancy, he must always be able to plead a manifest reason of philosophical necessity.[4] But to return from this digression.

---

1 See above, p. 40.—ED.

2 *Unvorgreiffliche Gedancken betreffend die Ausübung und Verbesserung der Teutschen Sprache. Opera*, (edit. Dutens), vol. vi. pars ii. p. 13.—ED.

3 Buchanan, *Franciscanus*, l. 632.—ED.

4 Οὐχ ἡμεῖς οἱ ἐν τῷ τοιῷδε χορεύοντες, τῶν λόγων ὑπηρέται, ἀλλ' οἱ λόγοι οἱ ἡμέτεροι ὥσπερ οἰκέται.—Plato.] [Theætetus, p. 178.—ED.] ["Hac enim necessario extor-

Having, I say, recalled to your observation the primary distribution of the mental phænomena into these three classes, — a distribution which, you will remember, I stated to you, was first promulgated by Kant, — I proceeded to the subdivision of the first class of the general faculty of knowledge into its various special faculties, — a subdivision, I noticed, for the defects of which I am individually accountable. But, before displaying to you a general view of my scheme of distribution, I first informed you what is meant by a power of mind, active or passive; in other words, what is meant by a mental faculty or a mental capacity; and this both in order to afford you a clear conception of the matter, and, likewise, to obviate some frivolous objections which have been made to such an analysis, or rather to such terms.

The phænomena of mind are never presented to us undecomposed and simple, that is, we are never conscious of any modification of mind which is not made up of many elementary modes; but these simple modes we are able to distinguish, by abstraction, as separate forms or qualities of our internal life, since, in different states of mind, they are given in different proportions and combinations. We are thus able to distinguish as simple, by an ideal abstraction and analysis, what is never actually given except in composition; precisely as we distinguish color from extension, though color is never presented to us apart, nay, cannot even be conceived as actually separable, from extension. The aim of the psychologist is thus to analyze, by abstraction, the mental phænomena into those ultimate or primary qualities, which, in their combination, constitute the concrete complexities of actual thought. If the simple constituent phænomenon be a mental activity, we give to the active power thus possessed by the mind of eliciting such elementary energy the name of *faculty;* whereas, if the simple or constituent phænomenon be a mental passivity, we give to the passive power thus possessed by the mind of receiving such an elementary affection, the name of *capacity.* Thus it is that there are just as many simple faculties as there are ultimate activities of mind; as many simple capacities as there are ultimate passivities of mind; and it is consequently manifest that a system of the mental powers can never be final and complete, until we have accomplished a full and accurate analysis of the various fundamental phænomena of our internal life. And what does such an

Phænomena of mind presented in composition.

---

quenda sunt a sapiente, quasi monstra monstris, absurda absurdis, inepta ineptis, ut inscitiæ minutissimas latebras vestigatas ex- pugnemus." Scaliger, *In Arist. De Plant.*, lib. ii.] [f. 135*b*, ed. 1556. — ED.]

analysis suppose? Manifestly three conditions: 1°, That no phænomenon be assumed as elementary which can be resolved into simpler principles; 2°, That no elementary phænomenon be overlooked; and, 3°, That no imaginary element be interpolated.

Three rules of psychological analysis.

These are the rules which ought evidently to govern our psychological analyses. I could show, however, that these have been more or less violated in every attempt that has been made at a determination of the constituent elements of thought; for philosophers have either stopped short of the primary phænomenon, or they have neglected it, or they have substituted another in its room. I decline, however, at present, an articulate criticism of the various systems of the human powers proposed by philosophers, as this would, in your present stage of advancement, tend rather to confuse than to inform you, and, moreover, would occupy a longer time than we are in a condition to afford: I therefore pass on to a summary recapitulation of the distribution of the cognitive faculties given in last Lecture. It is evident that such a distribution, as the result of an analysis, cannot be appreciated until the analysis itself be understood; and this can only be understood after the discussion of the several faculties and elementary phænomena has been carried through. You are, therefore, at present to look upon this scheme as little more than a table of contents to the various chapters, under which the phænomena of knowledge will be considered. I now only make a statement of what I shall subsequently attempt to prove. The principle of the distribution is, however, of such a nature that I flatter myself it can, in some measure, be comprehended even on its first enunciation: for the various elementary phænomena and the relative faculties which it assumes, are of so notorious and necessary a character, that they cannot possibly be refused; and, at the same time, they are discriminated from each other, both by obvious contrast, and by the fact that they are manifested in different individuals, each in very various proportions to each other.

These have not been observed by psychologists.

If a man has a faculty of knowledge in general, and if the contents of his knowledge be not all innate, it is evident that he must have a special faculty of acquiring it, — an acquisitive faculty. But to acquire knowledge is to receive an object within the sphere of our consciousness; in other words, to present it, as existing, to the knowing mind.

Evolution of Special Faculties of Knowledge from Consciousness.

I. The Acquisitive Faculty.

This Acquisitive Faculty may, therefore, be also called a Receptive or Presentative Faculty. The latter term, *Presentative Faculty*, I use, as you will see, in contrast and correlation to a *Representative Faculty*, of which I am immediately to speak. That the acquisition of knowledge is an ultimate phænomenon of mind, and an acquisitive faculty a necessary condition of the possession of knowledge, will not be denied. This faculty is the faculty of experience, and affords us exclusively all the knowledge we possess *a posteriori*, that is, our whole contingent knowledge,— our whole knowledge of fact. It is subdivided into two, according as its object is external or internal. In the former case it is called External Perception, or simply Perception; in the latter, Internal Perception, Reflex Perception, Internal Sense, or more properly, Self-Consciousness. Reflection, if limited to its original and correct signification, will be an expression for self-consciousness attentively applied to its objects, — that is, for self-consciousness concentrated on the mental phænomena.

In the second place, the faculty of acquisition enables us to know, — to cognize an object, when actually

II. The Conservative Faculty.

presented within the sphere of external or of internal consciousness. But if our knowledge of that object terminated when it ceased to exist, or to exist within the sphere of consciousness, our knowledge would hardly deserve the name; for what we actually perceive by the faculties of external and of internal perception, is but an infinitesimal part of the knowledge which we actually possess. It is, therefore, necessary that we have not only a faculty to acquire, but a faculty to keep possession of knowledge; in short, a Conservative or Retentive Faculty. This is Memory strictly so denominated; that is, the simple power of retaining the knowledge we have once acquired. This conservation, it is evident, must be performed without an act of consciousness, — the immense proportion of our acquired and possessed riches must lie beyond the sphere of actual cognition. What at any moment we really know, or are really conscious of, forms an almost infinitesimal fraction of what at any moment we are capable of knowing.

Now, this being the case, we must, in the third place, possess a faculty of calling out of unconsciousness into living

III. The Reproductive Faculty.

consciousness the materials laid up by the conservative faculty, or memory. This act of calling out of memory into consciousness, is not identical with the act of conservation. They are not even similar or proportional; and yet, strange to say, they have always, or almost always, in the analyses of philosophers, been considered as inseparable. The faculty of which this act of revocation is the energy, I call the Reproductive. It is governed by the laws of Mental Association, or rather these laws are the conditions of this faculty itself. If it act spontaneously and without volition or deliberate intention, Suggestion is its most appropriate name; if, on the contrary, it act in subordination to the will, it should be called Reminiscence. The term Recollection, if not used as a synonym for reminiscence, may be employed indifferently for both.

In the fourth place, the general capability of knowledge neces-

IV. The Representative Faculty.

sarily requires that, besides the power of evoking out of unconsciousness one portion of our retained knowledge in preference to another, we possess the faculty of representing in consciousness what is thus evoked. I will, hereafter, show you that the act of representation in the light of consciousness, is not to be confounded with the antecedent act of reproduction or revocation, though they severally, to a certain extent, infer each other. This Representative Faculty is Imagination or Phantasy. The word Fancy is an abbreviation of the latter; but with its change of form, its meaning has been somewhat modified. *Phantasy*, which latterly has been little used, was employed in the language of the older English philosophers as, like its Greek original, strictly synonymous with *Imagination*.

In the fifth place, these four acts of acquisition, conservation,

V. The Elaborative Faculty.

reproduction, and representation, form a class of faculties which we may call the Subsidiary, as furnishing the materials to a higher faculty, the function of which is to elaborate these materials. This elaborative or discursive faculty is Comparison; for under comparison may be comprised all the acts of Synthesis and Analysis, Generalization and Abstraction, Judgment and Reasoning. Comparison, or the Elaborative or Discursive Faculty, corresponds to the Διάνοια of the Greeks, to the *Verstand* of the Germans. This faculty is Thought Proper; and Logic, as we shall see, is the science conversant about its laws.

In the sixth place, the previous faculties are all conversant about

VI. The Regulative Faculty.

facts of experience, — acquired knowledge, — knowledge *a posteriori*. All such knowledge is contingent. But the mind not only possesses contingently a great apparatus of *a posteriori*, adventitious, knowledge; it possesses necessarily a small complement of *a priori*, native, cognitions. These *a priori* cognitions are the laws or conditions of thought in general; consequently, the laws and conditions under which our knowledge *a posteriori* is possible.

By the way, you will please to recollect these two relative expressions. As used in a psychological sense, a knowledge *a posteriori* is a synonym for knowledge empirical, or from experience; and, consequently, is adventitious to the mind, as subsequent to, and in consequence of, the exercise of its faculties of observation. Knowledge *a priori*, on the contrary, called likewise native, pure, or transcendental knowledge, embraces those principles which, as the conditions of the exercise of its faculties of observation and thought, are, consequently, not the result of that exercise. True it is that, chronologically considered, our *a priori* is not antecedent to our *a posteriori* knowledge; for the internal conditions of experience can only operate when an object of experience has been presented. In the order of time our knowledge, therefore, may be said to commence with experience, but to have its principle antecedently in the mind. Much as has been written on this matter by the greatest philosophers, this all-important doctrine has never been so well stated as in an unknown sentence of an old and now forgotten thinker: "Cognitio omnis a mente primam originem, a sensibus exordium habet primum."[1] These few words are worth many a modern volume of philosophy. You will observe the felicity of the expression. The whole sentence has not a superfluous word, and yet is absolute and complete. *Mens*, the Latin term for νοῦς, is the best possible word to express the intellectual source of our *a priori* principles, and is well opposed to *sensus*. But the happiest contrast is in the terms *origo* and *exordium;* the former denoting priority in the order of existence, the latter priority in the order of time.

Knowledge a priori and a posteriori, explained.

Relation of our knowledge to experience,—how best expressed.

But to return whence I have diverged. These *a priori* principles form one of the most remarkable and peculiar of the mental phænomena; and we must class them under the head of a common power or principle of the mind. This power,—what I would call the Regulative Faculty,—corresponding to the Greek νοῦς when used as the *locus principiorum*, may be denominated Reason, using that word in the sense in which, as opposed to Reasoning, it was applied by some of the older English writers, and by Kant, Jacobi, and others of the more modern German philosophers. It may also be considered as equivalent to the term Common Sense, in the more correct acceptation of this expression.

----

1 [Patricius, *Nova de Universis Philosophia*, p. 1.]

The general faculty of knowledge is thus, according to this distribution, divided into six special faculties: first, the Acquisitive, Presentative, or Receptive; second, the Conservative; third the Reproductive; fourth, the Representative; fifth, the Elaborative; and sixth, the Regulative. The first of these, the Acquisitive, is again subdivided into two faculties, — Perception and Self-Consciousness; the third into Suggestion and Reminiscence; and the fifth may likewise admit of subdivisions, into Conception, Judgment, and Reasoning, which, however, as merely applications of the same act in different degrees, hardly warrant a distinction into separate faculties.

Having thus varied, amplified, and abridged the outline which I gave you in my last Lecture of the several constituents of the class of Cognitive Faculties, I now proceed to consider these faculties in detail.

The special faculties of Knowledge, considered in detail.

Perception, or the consciousness of external objects, is the first power in order. And, in treating of this faculty, — the faculty on which turns the whole question of Idealism and Realism, — it is perhaps proper, in the first place, to take an historical survey of the hypotheses of philosophers in regard to Perception. In doing this, I shall particularly consider the views which Reid has given of these hypotheses: his authority on this the most important part of his philosophy is entitled to high respect; and it is requisite to point out to you, both in what respects he has misrepresented others, and in what been misrepresented himself.

I. The Presentative Faculty — Perception. Historical survey of hypotheses in regard to Perception, proposed.

Before commencing this survey, it is proper to state, in a few words, the one, the principal, point in regard to which opinions vary. The grand distinction of philosophers is determined by the alternative they adopt on the question, — Is our perception, or our consciousness of external objects, mediate or immediate?

The principal point in regard to Perception, on which opinions vary.

As we have seen, those who maintain our knowledge of external objects to be immediate, accept implicitly the datum of consciousness which gives as an ultimate fact, in this act, an ego immediately known, and a non-ego immediately known. Those again who deny that an external object can be immediately known, do not accept one-half of the fact of consciousness, but substitute some hypothesis in its place, — not, however, always the same. Consciousness declares that we have an immediate knowledge of a non-ego, and of an external non-ego. Now, of the philosophers who reject this fact, some admit our immediate knowledge of a non-ego, but not of an external non-ego. They do not limit the consciousness or immediate knowledge of the mind to its own modes, but conceiving it impossible for the external reality to be brought within the sphere of consciousness, they hold that it is represented by a vicarious image, numerically different from mind, but situated somewhere, either in the brain or mind, within the sphere of consciousness. Others, again, deny to the mind not only any consciousness of an external non-ego, but of a non-ego at all, and hold that what the mind immediately perceives, and mistakes for an external object, is only the ego itself peculiarly modified. These two are the only generic varieties possible of the representative hypothesis. And they have each their respective advantages and disadvantages. They both equally afford a basis for idealism. On the former, Berkeley established his Theological, on the latter, Fichte his Anthropological Idealism. Both violate the testimony of consciousness, the one the more complex and the clumsier, in denying that we are conscious of an external non-ego, though admitting that we are conscious of a non-ego within the sphere of consciousness, either in the mind or brain. The other, the simpler and more philosophical, outrages, however, still more flagrantly, the veracity of consciousness, in denying not only that we are conscious of an external non-ego, but that we are conscious of a non-ego at all.

Two grand hypotheses of Mediate Perception.

Each of these hypotheses of a representative perception admits of various subordinate hypotheses. Thus the former, which holds that the representative or immediate object is a *tertium quid*, different both from the mind and from the external reality, is subdivided, according as the immediate object is viewed as material, as immaterial, or as neither, or as both, as something physical or as something hyperphysical, as propagated from the external object, as generated in the medium, or as fabricated in the soul itself; and this latter either in the intelligent mind or in the animal life, as infused by God or by angels, or as identical with the divine substance, and so forth. In the latter, the representative modification has been regarded either as factitious, that is, a mere product of mind; or as innate, that is, as independent of any mental energy.[1]

Each of these admits of various subordinate hypotheses.

1 See *Reid's Works*, Note C, p. 816—819. — Ed.

I must return on this subject more articulately, when I have finished the historical survey.   At present I only beg to call

Historical survey of opinions in regard to Perception.

your attention to two facts which it is necessary to bear in mind : the first regards a mistake of Reid, the second a mistake of Brown ; and the proper understanding of these will enable you easily to apprehend how they have both wandered so widely from the truth.

Reid,[1] who, as I shall hereafter endeavor to show you, probably holds the doctrine of an Intuitive or Immediate Perception, never generalized, never articulately understood, the distinction of the two forms of the Representative Hypothesis.   This was the cause of the most important errors on his part. In the first place, it prevented him from drawing the obtrusive and vital distinction between Perception, to him a faculty immediately cognitive, or presentative of external objects and the faculties of Imagination and Memory, in which external objects can only be known to the mind mediately or in a representation.

Reid did not distinguish the two forms of the representative hypothesis.

In the second place, this, as we shall see, causes him the greatest perplexity, and sometimes leads him into errors in his history of the opinions of previous philosophers, in regard to which he has, independently of this, been guilty of various mistakes.   As to Brown, again, he holds the simple doctrine of a representative perception, — a doctrine which Reid does not seem to have understood; and this opinion he not only holds himself, but attributes, with one or two exceptions, to all modern philosophers, nay, even to Reid himself, whose philosophy he thus maintains to be one great blunder, both in regard to the new truths it professes to establish, and to the old errors it professes to refute.   It turns out, however, that Brown in relation to Reid is curiously wrong from first to last, — not one of Reid's numerous mistakes, historical and philosophical, does he touch, far less redargue ; whereas in every point on which he assails Reid, he himself is historically or philosophically in error.

Brown's general error in regard to Reid.

I meant to have first shown you Reid's misrepresentations of the opinions of other philosophers, and then to have shown you Brown's misrepresentations of Reid.   I find it better to effect both purposes together, which, having now prepared you by a statement of Brown's general error, it will not, I hope, be difficult to do.

---

1 See the Author's *Discussions*, p. 89, *et seq.*, and his Supplementary Dissertations to Reid, Notes B and C. — ED.

This being premised, I now proceed to follow Reid through his historical view and scientific criticism of the various theories of Perception; and I accordingly commence with the Platonic. In this, however, he is unfortunate, for the simile of the cave which is applied by Plato in the seventh book of the Republic, was not intended by him as an illustration of the mode of our sensible perception at all. "Plato," says Reid,[1] "illustrates our manner of perceiving the objects of sense, in this manner. He supposes a dark subterraneous cave, in which men lie bound in such a manner that they can direct their eyes only to one part of the cave: far behind, there is a light, some rays of which come over a wall to that part of the cave which is before the eyes of our prisoners. A number of persons, variously employed, pass between them and the light, whose shadows are seen by the prisoners, but not the persons themselves.

Reid's historical view of the theories of Perception. The Platonic.

"In this manner, that philosopher conceived that, by our senses, we perceive the shadows of things only, and not things themselves. He seems to have borrowed his notions on this subject from the Pythagoreans, and they very probably from Pythagoras himself. If we make allowance for Plato's allegorical genius, his sentiments on this subject correspond very well with those of his scholar Aristotle, and of the Peripatetics. The shadows of Plato may very well represent the species and phantasms of the Peripatetic school, and the ideas and impressions of modern philosophers."

Reid's account of the Platonic theory of perception is utterly wrong.[2] Plato's simile of the cave he completely misapprehends. By his cave, images, and shadows, this philosopher intended only to illustrate the great principle of his philosophy, that the sensible or ectypal world, — the world phænomenal, transitory, ever becoming but never being (ἀεὶ γιγνόμενον, μηδέποτε ὄν), stands to the noetic or archetypal world, — the world substantial, permanent (ὄντως ὄν), in the same relation of comparative unreality, in which the shadows of the images of sensible existences themselves, stand to the objects of which they are the dim and distant adumbrations. The Platonic theory of these two worlds and their relations, is accurately stated in some splendid verses of Fracastorius, — a poet hardly inferior to Virgil, and a philosopher far superior to his age.

Reid wrong in regard to the Platonic theory of perception, and misapprehends Plato's simile of the cave.

Fracastorius quoted.

" An nescis, quæcunque heic sunt, quæ hac nocte teguntur,
    Omnia res prorsus veras non esse, sed umbras,
    Aut specula, unde ad nos aliena elucet imago?
    Terra quidem, et maria alta, atque his circumfluus aer,
    Et quæ consistunt ex iis, hæc omnia tenueis
    Sunt umbræ, humanos quæ tanquam somnia quædam
    Pertingunt animos, fallaci et imagine ludunt,
    Nunquam eadem, fluxu semper variata perenni.
    Sol autem, Lunæque globus, fulgentiaque astra
    Cætera, sint quamvis meliori prædita vita,
    Et donata ævo immortali, hæc ipsa tamen sunt
    Æterni specula, in quæ animus, qui est inde profectus,
    Inspiciens, patriæ quodam quasi tactus amore,
    Ardescit.   Verum quoniam heic non perstet et ultra
    Nescio quid sequitur secum, tacitusque requirit,
    Nosse licet circum hæc ipsum consistere verum
    Non finem : sed enim esse aliud quid, cujus imago
    Splendet in iis, quod per se ipsum est, et principium esse
    Omnibus æternum, ante omnem numerumque diemque;
    In quo alium Solem atque aliam splendescere Lunam
    Adspicias, aliosque orbes, alia astra manere,
    Terramque, fluviosque alios, atque aera, et ignem,
    Et nemora, atque aliis errare animalia silvis." 1

Now, as well might it be said of these verses, that they are intended to illustrate a theory of perception, as of Plato's cave. But
not only is Reid wrong in regard to the meaning of the cave, he is
curiously wrong in regard to Plato's doctrine, at least of vision.
For so far was Plato from holding that we only perceive in consequence of the representations of objects being thrown upon the percipient mind,— he, on the contrary, maintained, in the *Timæus*,[2] that,
in vision, a percipient power of the sensible soul sallies out towards
the object, the images of which it carries back into the eye, — an
opinion, by the way, held likewise by Empedocles,[3] Alexander of

---

1 These lines are given in the Author's note,
Reid's Works, p. 262, and occur in the *Carmen
ad M. Antonium Flaminium et Galeatium Flori-
montium* — *Opera*, Venet., 1584, f. 206. — ED.

2 P. 45. — ED.

3 " Visionem fieri per *extramissionem* " (as
opposed to the *intromissionem* of Democritus,
Leucippus, and Epicurus), " ait Empedocles,
cui et Hipparchus astipulatus est, ita, ut radii
exeuntes quasi manu comprehendant imagines rerum quæ visionis sint effectrices."
Gabriel Buratellus, *An Visio Fiat Extramitten-*

do, lib. v. Cf. *Empedoclis Fragmenta*, ed. Sturz,
p. 416. Stallbaum, *In Plat. Timæum.* p. 45.
Burateleus thus states Plato's doctrine of vision : " Visionem Plato fieri sentit ut oculi ex
se naturam quandam lucidam habeant, ex
qua visivi radii effluentes in extremam æris
lucem objectæ rei imaginem adducant, et in
animo repræsentent, ex qua repræsentatione
fit visus." — *Ibid.* Cf. Leo Hebræus, *De Amore*,
Dial. iii. Chalcidius, *In Timæum Platonis*, p.
388. See Bernardus, *Seminarium Philosophiæ
Platonicæ*, p. 922. — ED.

Aphrodisias,[1] Seneca,[2] Chalcidius,[3] Euclid,[4] Ptolemy,[5] Alchindus,[6] Galen,[7] Lactantius,[8] and Lord Monboddo.[9]

The account which Reid gives of the Aristotelic doctrine is, likewise, very erroneous. "Aristotle seems to have thought that the soul consists of two parts, or rather that we have two souls, — the animal and the rational; or, as he calls them, the soul and the intellect. To the *first* belong the senses, memory and imagination; to the *last*, judgment, opinion, belief, and reasoning. The first we have in common with brute animals; the last is peculiar to man. The animal soul he held to be a certain form of the body, which is inseparable from it, and perishes at death. To this soul the senses belong; and he defines a sense to be that which is capable of receiving the sensible forms or species of objects, without any of the matter of them; as wax receives the form of the seal without any of the matter of it. The forms of sound, of color, of taste, and of other sensible qualities, are, in a manner, received by the senses. It seems to be a necessary consequence of Aristotle's doctrine, that bodies are constantly sending forth, in all directions, as many different kinds of forms without matter as they have different sensible qualities; for the forms of color must enter by the eye, the forms of sound by the ear, — and so of the other senses. This, accordingly, was maintained by the followers of Aristotle, though not, as far as I know, expressly mentioned by himself. They disputed concerning the nature of those forms of species, whether they were real beings or nonentities; and some held them to be of an intermediate nature between the two. The whole doctrine of the Peripatetics and schoolmen concerning forms, substantial and accidental, and concerning the transmission of sensible species from objects of sense to the mind, if it be at all intelligible, is so far above my comprehension that I should perhaps do it injustice by entering into it more minutely."[10]

In regard to the statement of the Peripatetic doctrine of species,

1 *In Arist. De Sensu*, f. 95, 96, edit. Ald. The Conimbricenses refer to the (probably spurious) *Problemata*, (lib. i. § 57, Lat. tr. 59, ed. Ald.) — ED.

2 *Naturalium Quæstionum*, lib. i. c. 5-7. — ED.

3 *In Timæum Platonis*, p. 338. Cf. p. 329 *et seq.*, (edit. Leyden, 1617). — ED.

4 See Conimbricenses, *In De Anima*, lib. ii. c. vii. q. 5, art. i. p. 231, (edit. 1629). — ED.

5 See Conimbricenses, *ibid.* — ED.

6 See Conimbricenses, *ibid.* — ED.

7 *De Plac. Hippocratis et Platonis*, lib. vii. c. 5 (vol. v. p. 215, edit. Chartier). — ED.

8 *De Opificio Dei*, c. viii. *Opera*, ii. (edit. 1784), where Lactantius, moreover, denies the necessity of visual species. See Conimbricenses, as above, and compare Stallbaum's note on the *Timæus*, p. 45, B. — ED.

9 *Antient Metaphysics*, vol. i. book ii. chap. ii. p. 151. Cf. *Origin and Progress of Language*, vol. i. p. 26, (2d edit.) — ED.

10 *Coll. Works*, p. 267. — ED.

I must observe that it is ' correct only as applied to the doctrine
taught as the Aristotelic in the schools of the
middle ages; and even in these schools there was

Only partially correct.

a large party who not only themselves disavowed
the whole doctrine of species, but maintained that it received no
countenance from the authority of Aristotle.[1] This opinion is correct; and I could easily prove to you, had we time, that there is
nothing in the metaphorical expressions of εἶδος and τύπος, which,
on one or two occasions, he cursorily uses,[2] to warrant the attribution to him of the doctrine of his disciples. This is even expressly

1 [See Durandus, In Sent., lib. ii. dist. iii.
Q. 6, § 9: "Species originaliter introductæ
videntur esse propter sensum visus, et sensibilia illius sensus. .... Sed quia quidam
credunt quod species coloris in oculo representat visui colorem, cujus est species, ideo po-
nunt in intellectu quasdam species adrepre-
sentandum res ut cognoscantur.

§ 10: "Hoc autem non reputo verum nec
in sensu nec in intellectu. Et quod non sit
ponere speciem in sensu, patet sic:—Omne
illud per quod tanquam per representativum
potentia cognitiva fertur in alterum est primo
cognitum; sed species coloris in oculo non
est primo cognita seu visa ab eo, immo nullo
modo est visa ab eo; ergo, per ipsam tanquam
per representativum, visus, non fertur in aliquid aliud.

§ 11: "Quamvis enim color imprimat in
medio et in oculo suam speciem propter simi-
lem dispositionem diaphaneitatis quæ est in
eis, illa tamen nihil fecit ad visionem, neque
visui representat colorem ut videatur.

§ 21: "Sensibilia secundum præsentia sen-
sui cognoscuntur per sensum, puta omnia
colorata, et omnia lucentia, quæ secundum
se præsentialiter objiciuntur visui, statim videntur, quia unum est visivum et aliud visibile,
propter quod, eis approximatis, statim sequitur vitio, a quocunque sit (fit?) effective. Et
similiter est de aliis Sensibus." Durandus
thus reduces species to the physical impression
of the external object, which is unknown to
the mind, and not like the object.] [See
Conimbricenses, In De Anima, lib. ii. c. vi. Q.
2, p. 188. The Conimbricenses refer besides
to Occam, Gregory (Ariminensis), and Biel,
among the schoolmen, as concurring with
Durandus on this point. The doctrine of
species was also rejected by the Nominalists.
See Toletus, In De Anima, lib. ii. c. xii. f. 109,
(edit. 1594.) Cf. Plotinus, Ennead, iv. lib. iii.
c. xxvi. p. 891, (edit. Basle, 1516): Τί οὖν; εἰ
αὐτὴ μὲν μνημονεύει, τῷ δὲ ἐν σώματι εἶναι,
τῷ μὴ καθαρᾷ εἶναι· ἀλλ' ὥσπερ ποιωθεῖσα

ἀναμάττεσθαι δύναται τοὺς τῶν αἰσθητῶν
τύπους, καὶ τὸ οἷον ἕδραν ἐν τῷ σώματι πρὸς
τὸ παραδέχεσθαι, καὶ μὴ ὥσπερ παπαρρεῖν.
'Αλλὰ πρῶτον μὲν οἱ τύποι, οὐ μεγέθη· οὐδ'
ὥσπερ αἱ ἐνσφραγίσεις, οὐδ' ἀντερείσεις, ἢ
τυπώσεις, ὅτι μηδ' ὠθισμός· μηδ' ὥσπερ ἐν
κηρῷ, ἀλλ' ὁ τρόπος οἷον νόησις, καὶ ἐπὶ τῶν
αἰσθητῶν. See also Galen, De Placitis Hippocratis et Platonis, lib. vii. c. ix. It should be
observed, however, that the great majority of
the schoolmen attributed species both to the
external and internal senses, and held that
this was the doctrine of Aristotle. To this
class belong Anselm, John of Damascus, Augustin, Aquinas, Alensis, Albertus Magnus,
Bonaventura, Scotus, Argentinas, Richardus,
Capreolus, Marsilius, Hervæus, and Ægidius.
See Conimbricenses, In De Anima, p. 192, and
Toletus, In De Anima, f. 109. — ED.]

2 See De Anima, lib. ii. c. xii. § 1, (edit.
Trend.): Καθόλου δὲ περὶ πάσης αἰσθήσεως
δεῖ λαβεῖν ὅτι ἡ μὲν αἴσθησίς ἐστι τὸ δεκτικὸν τῶν αἰσθητῶν εἰδῶν ἄνευ τῆς ὕλης, οἷον
ὁ κηρὸς τοῦ δακτυλίου ἄνευ τοῦ σιδήρου καὶ
τοῦ χρυσοῦ δέχεται τὸ σημεῖον, λαμβάνει τε
τὸ χρυσοῦν ἢ τὸ χαλκοῦν σημεῖον, ἀλλ' οὐχ
ᾗ χρυσὸς ἢ χαλκός. κ. τ. λ. Ibid.. iii. c. ii.
§ 3, 4: Τὸ γὰρ αἰσθητήριον δεκτικὸν τοῦ αἰσθητοῦ ἄνευ τῆς ὕλης ἕκαστον· διὸ καὶ ἀπελ-
θόντων τῶν αἰσθητῶν ἔνεισιν αἱ αἰσθήσεις
καὶ φαντασίαι ἐν τοῖς αἰσθητηρίοις. 'Η δὲ
τοῦ αἰσθητοῦ ἐνέργεια καὶ τῆς αἰσθήσεως ἡ
αὐτὴ μέν ἐστι καὶ μία, τὸ δ' εἶναι οὐ ταὐτὸν
αὐταῖς. Cf. De Memoria et Reminiscentia, c.
i., and De. An., lib. ii. c. iv.; lib. iii. c. viii—
ED. [On Aristotle's doctrine in these passages; see Gassendi, Syntag. Philos. Physica, s.
iii., Mem Post. lib. vi. c. ii., Opera, t. ii. p. 389,
(edit. 1658). Cf. Ibid., p. 337, and t. i. p. 443;
t. iii. p. 467; Piccolomini, In Phys., p. 1308;
Zabarella, De Rebus Naturalibus, p. 989, Liber,
De Speciebus Intelligibilibus; Devillemandy,
Scepticismus Debellatus, c. xxiv. p. 165.] [Cf.
Reid's Works, p. 827, note. — ED.]

maintained by several of his Greek commentators, — as the Aphrodisian,[1] Michael Ephesius,[2] and Philoponus.[3] In fact, Aristotle appears to have held the same doctrine in regard to perception as Reid himself. He was a natural realist.[4]

Reid gives no account of the famous doctrine of perception held

Theory of Democritus and Epicurus, omitted by Reid.

by Epicurus, and which that philosopher had borrowed from Democritus, — namely, that the εἴδωλα, ἀπόῤῥοιαι, *imagines, simulacra rerum*, etc., are like pellicles continually flying off from objects; and that these material likenesses, diffusing themselves everywhere in the air, are propagated to the perceptive organs. In the words of Lucretius, —

> "Quæ, quasi Membranæ, summo de cortice rerum
> Dereptæ volitant ultro citroque per auras."[5]

Reid's statement of the Cartesian doctrine of perception is not

1 [*In De Anima*, lib. i. f. 136a, (edit. Ald. 1534): Χρὴ δὲ τοῦ τύπου κοινότερον ἐπὶ τῆς φαντασίας ἀκούειν· κυρίως μὲν γὰρ τύπος, τὸ κατ' εἰσοχήν τε καὶ ἐξοχήν. *Ἢ τὸ τοῦ τυποῦντος ἐν τῷ τυπουμένῳ σχῆμα γινόμενον, ὡς ὁρῶμεν τὰ ἐπὶ τῶν σφραγίδων ἔχοντα. Οὐχ οὕτω δὲ τὰ ἀπὸ τῶν αἰσθητῶν ἐγκαταλείμματα γίνεται ἐν ἡμῖν. Οὐδὲ γὰρ τὴν ἀρχὴν κατὰ σχῆμά τι ἡ τῶν αἰσθητῶν ἀντίληψις. Ποῖον γὰρ σχῆμα τὸ λευκὸν, ἢ ὅλως τὸ χρῶμα· ἢ ποῖον σχῆμα, ἢ ὀσμή. Ἀλλὰ δι' ἀπορίαν κυρίου τινὸς ὀνόματος, τὸ ἴχνος καὶ ἐγκατάλημμα τὸ ὑπομένον ἀπὸ τῶν αἰσθητῶν ἐν ἡμῖν τύπον καλούμενον· μεταφέροντες τοὔνομα.] [Cf. *Ibid.*, lib. i. f. 135b: Ἀπὸ τῶν ἐνεργειῶν τῶν περὶ τὰ αἰσθητά, οἷον τύπον τινὰ καὶ ἀναζωγράφημα ἐν τῷ πρώτῳ αἰσθητηρίῳ . . . . μήποτε δὲ οὐχ ὁ τύπος αὐτὸς ἡ φαντασία, ἀλλὰ ἡ περὶ τὸν τύπον οὖτον τῆς φανταστικῆς δυνάμεως ἐνέργεια. The Aphrodisian is literally followed by Themistius *In De Memoria et Reminiscentia*, c. i. f. 96b; cf. also the same, *In De Anima*, lib. ii. c. vi. ff. 78a, 83a, 93a, 96b, (edit. Ald. 1534); and by Simon Simonius, *In De Memoria et Reminiscentia*, c. i. §§ 12, 14, p. 290-91, (edit. 1566). — ED.

2 [*In De Memoria et Reminiscentia*, Procem,] [fol. 127b, (edit. 1527). — ED.]

3 *In De Anima*, lib. ii. c. v. text 62: Δύναμίς δέ ἐστι τὸ αἰσθητικὸν οἷον τὸ αἰσθητὸν κατὰ τὴν δευτέραν δύναμιν· οὐ γὰρ παθόντα· οὐδὲ ὑπ' ἐναντίας ἕξεως μεταβάλλον ὁμοιοῦται αὐτῷ. Ἀλλὰ τὸ εἶδος αὐτοῦ δεξάμενον· οὐχ ὡς ὕλη αὐτοῦ γινόμενον, οὐδὲ γὰρ λευκὴ

γίνεται ἡ αἴσθησις δεξαμένη τὸ εἶδος τοῦ αἰσθητοῦ. Διὸ οὐδὲ πάσχειν οὐδὲ ἀλλοιοῦσθαι κυρίως λέγεται, ἀλλὰ τὸν λόγον τοῦ εἴδους γνωστικῶς ἐν ἑαυτῇ δεχομένη. Ὥσπερ γὰρ τὸν κηρὸν φαμὲν δυνάμει εἶναι ὅπερ τὸν δακτύλιον. Διότι παθὼν ὑπ' αὐτοῦ γίνεται ὅπέρ ἐστιν ἐκεῖνος ἐνεργείᾳ· οὐ τὴν ὕλην αὐτοῦ δεξάμενος, ἀλλὰ μόνον τό εἶδος. Οὕτω καὶ ἡ αἴσθησις παθοῦσα ὑπὸ τῶν αἰσθητῶν τὰ εἴδη αὐτῶν ἀσωμάτως ἀναμάττεται. Διαφέρει δὲ, ὅτι ὁ μὲν κηρὸς αὐτὸς ὕλη γίνεται τοῦ εἴδους τοῦ ἐν τῷ δακτυλίῳ· ἡ δ' αἴσθησις, οὐχ ὕλη γίνεται τοῦ αἰσθητοῦ· ἀλλὰ γνωστικῶς τὴν ἰδέαν αὐτοῦ ἐκμάττεται. Ἔχει δέ τι πλέον ἡ αἴσθησις παρὰ τὸν κηρόν· ὁ μὲν κηρὸς γὰρ εἰ καὶ ὕλη γίνεται τοῦ εἴδους τοῦ ἐν τῷ δακτυλίῳ, ἀλλὰ οὐ δι' ὅλον αὐτοῦ δέχεται τὸ εἶδος, ἀλλ' ἐπιπολῆς· ἡ μέν τοι αἰσθητικὴ δύναμις ὅλη δι' ὅλης ζωτικῆς τὰς τῶν αἰσθητῶν ἀπομάττεται ἰδέας. Cf. *Ibid.*, c. xii. t. 121. In this passage Philoponus closely approximates to the doctrine of the Platonists, as expounded by Priscianus Lydus, according to which, perception takes place on condition of an assimilation between the living organ and the object, by means of forms and immaterial reasons (κατὰ τὰ εἴδη καὶ τοὺς λόγους ἄνευ τῆς ὕλης.) See Μετάφρασις τοῦ Θεοφράστου Περὶ Αἰσθήσεως, c. i. (Version of Ficinus, s. i. *et seq.*), and *Reid's Works*, p. 262, note. — ED.

4 See above, p. 205, note. — ED.

5 Lib. iv. 35. So quoted in the Author's *Discussions*, p. 71, but the usual reading is *corpore*, not *cortice.* — ED.

exempt from serious error. After giving a long, and not very accurate, account of the philosophy of Descartes in general, he proceeds: — "To return to Des Cartes's notions of the manner of our perceiving external objects, from which a concern to do justice to the merit of that great reformer in philosophy has led me to digress, he took it for granted, as the old philosophers had done, that what we immediately perceive must be either in the mind itself, or in the brain, to which the mind is immediately present. The impressions made upon our organs, nerves, and brain, could be nothing, according to his philosophy, but various modifications of extension, figure, and motion. There could be nothing in the brain like sound or color, taste or smell, heat or cold; these are sensations in the mind, which, by the laws of the union of soul and body, are raised on occasion of certain traces in the brain; and although he gives the name of ideas to these traces in the brain, he does not think it necessary that they should be perfectly like to the things which they represent, any more than that words or signs should resemble the things they signify. But, says he, that we may follow the received opinion as far as is possible, we may allow a slight resemblance. Thus we know that a print in a book may represent houses, temples, and groves; and so far is it from being necessary that the print should be perfectly like the thing it represents, that its perfection often requires the contrary; for a circle must often be represented by an ellipse, a square by a rhombus, and so of other things. . . . .

"The writings of Des Cartes have, in general, a remarkable degree of perspicuity; and he undoubtedly intended that, in this particular, his philosophy should be a perfect contrast to that of Aristotle; yet, in what he has said, in different parts of his writings, of our perceptions of external objects, there seems to be some obscurity, and even inconsistency; whether owing to his having had different opinions on the subject at different times, or to the difficulty he found in it, I will not pretend to say.

"There are two points, in particular, wherein I cannot reconcile him to himself: the *first*, regarding the place of the ideas or images of external objects, which are the immediate objects of perception; the *second*, with regard to the veracity of our external senses.

"As to the *first*, he sometimes places the ideas of material objects in the brain, not only when they are perceived, but when they are remembered or imagined; and this has always been held to be the Cartesian doctrine; yet he sometimes says, that we are not to conceive the images or traces in the brain to be perceived, as if there

Reid's statement of the Cartesian doctrine of Perception.

were eyes in the brain; these traces are only occasions on which, by the laws of the union of soul and body, ideas are excited in the mind; and, therefore, it is not necessary that there should be an exact resemblance between the traces and the things represented by them, any more than that words or signs should be exactly like the things signified by them.

"These two opinions, I think, cannot be reconciled. For, if the images or traces in the brain are perceived, they must be the objects of perception, and not the occasions of it only. On the other hand, if they are only the occasions of our perceiving, they are not perceived at all. Descartes seems to have hesitated between the two opinions, or to have passed from the one to the other."[1]

I have quoted to you this passage in order that I may clearly exhibit to you, in the first place, Reid's misrepresentations of Descartes; and, in the second, Brown's misrepresentation of Reid.

In regard to the former, Reid's principal error consists in charging Descartes with vacillation and inconsistency,

Cardinal principle of the Cartesian philosophy.

and in possibly attributing to him the opinion that the representative object of which the mind is conscious in perception, is something material, — something in the brain. This arose from his ignorance of the fundamental principle of the Cartesian doctrine.[2] By those not possessed of the key to the Cartesian theory, there are many passages in the writings of its author which, taken by themselves, might naturally be construed to import, that Descartes supposed the mind to be conscious of certain motions in the brain, to which, as well as to the modifications of the intellect itself, he applies the terms *image* and *idea*. Reid, who did not understand the Cartesian philosophy as a system, was puzzled by these superficial ambiguities. Not aware that the cardinal point of that system is, that mind and body, as essentially opposed, are naturally to each other as zero; and that their mutual intercourse can, therefore, only be supernaturally maintained by the concourse of the Deity, Reid was led into the error of attributing, by possibility, to Descartes, the opinion that the soul was immediately cognizant of material images in the brain. But in the Cartesian theory, mind is only conscious of itself; the affections of body may, by the law of union, be proximately the occasions, but can never constitute the imme-

---

1 *Intellectual Powers*, Essay ii. chap. viii. *Coll. Works*, p. 272.

2 The following remarks have been printed in the Author's article on Reid and Brown. See *Discussions*, p. 72. — ED.

diate objects, of knowledge. Reid, however, supposing that nothing could obtain the name of *image*, which
did not represent a prototype, or the name of
idea, which was not an object of thought, wholly
misinterpreted Descartes, who applies, abusively
indeed, these terms to the occasion of perception, that is, the
motion in the sensorium, unknown in itself, and representing nothing; as well as to the object of thought, that is, the representation of which we are conscious in the mind itself. In the Leibnitzio-Wolfian system, two elements, both also denominated *ideas*,
are in like manner accurately to be contradistinguished in the
process of perception. The idea in the brain, and the idea in the
mind, are, to Descartes, precisely what the "*material idea*" and
the "*sensual idea*" are to the Wolfians. In both philosophies, the
two ideas are harmonic modifications, correlative and coëxistent;
but in neither is the organic affection or sensorial idea an object of
consciousness. It is merely the unknown and arbitrary condition
of the mental representation; and in the hypothesis, both of
Assistance and of Preëstablished Harmony, the presence of the
one idea implies the concomitance of the other, only by virtue of
the hyperphysical determination.

Twofold use of the term idea by Descartes.

LECTURE XXII.

THE PRESENTATIVE FACULTY.

I. PERCEPTION. — REID'S HISTORICAL VIEW OF THE THEORIES OF PERCEPTION.

IN our last Lecture, after recapitulating, with varied illustrations,
the Distribution of the Cognitive Faculties,
which I had detailed to you in the Lecture
before, I entered upon the particular consideration of the Special
Faculties themselves, and commenced with that which stands first
in order, and which I had denominated the Acquisitive, or Receptive, or Presentative. And as this faculty is again subdivided into
two, according as it is conversant either about the phænomena of
matter, or about the phænomena of mind, the non-ego, or the ego,
I gave precedence to the former of these, — the faculty known
under the name of External Perception. Perception, as matter of psychological consideration, is of the very highest importance in philosophy; as the doctrine in regard to the object
and operation of this faculty affords the immediate data for determining the great question touching the existence or non-existence of an external world; and there is hardly a problem of any
moment in the whole compass of philosophy, of which it does not
mediately affect the solution. The doctrine of perception may
thus be viewed as a cardinal point of philosophy. It is also exclusively in relation to this
faculty, that Reid must claim his great, his distinguishing glory, as a philosopher; and of this no one was more
conscious than himself. "The merit," he says, in a letter to Dr.
James Gregory, "of what you are pleased to call my philosophy,
lies, I think, chiefly in having called in question the common theory
of ideas or images of things in the mind being the only objects of
thought — a theory founded on natural prejudices, and so universally received as to be interwoven with the structure of language."
"I think," he adds, "there is hardly anything that can be called
science in the philosophy of the mind, which does not follow with

Recapitulation.

The doctrine of Perception a cardinal point in Philosophy.

Its place in the philosophy of Reid.

38

ease from the detection of this prejudice."[1] The attempts, therefore, among others, of Priestley, Gleig, Beasley,[2] and, though last not least, of Brown, to show that Reid in his refutation of the previous theory of perception, was only fighting with a shadow —was only combating philosophers who, on the point in question, really coincided with himself, would, if successful, prove not merely that the philosophical reputation of Reid is only based upon a blunder, but would, in fact, leave us no rational conclusion short, not of idealism only, but of absolute skepticism. For, as I have shown you, Brown's doctrine of perception, as founded on a refusal of the testimony of consciousness to our knowledge of an external world, virtually discredits consciousness as an evidence at all; and in place of his system being, as its author confidently boasts, the one "which allows the skeptic no place for his foot — no fulcrum for the instrument he uses," — it is, on the contrary, perhaps the system which, of all others, is the most contradictory and suicidal, and which, consequently, may most easily be developed into skepticism. The determination of this point, is, therefore, a matter affecting the vital interests of philosophy; for if Reid, as Brown and his coadjutors maintain, accomplished nothing, then is all philosophical reputation empty, and philosophy itself a dream.

In preparing you for the discussion that was to follow, I stated to you that it would not be in my power to maintain Reid's absolute immunity from error, either in his philosophical or in his historical views; on the contrary, I acknowledged that I found him frequently at fault in both. His mistakes, however, I hope to show you, are not of vital importance, and I am confident their exposure will only conduce to illustrate and confirm the truths which he has the merit, though amid cloud and confusion, to have established. But as to Brown's elaborate attack on Reid, — this, I have no hesitation in asserting, to be not only unsuccessful in its results, but that in all its details, without a single, even the most insignificant, exception, it has the fortune to be regularly and curiously wrong. Reid had errors enough to be exposed, but Brown has not been so lucky as to stumble even upon one. Brown, however, sung his pæan as if his victory were complete; and, what

Reid, philosophically and historically, not free from errors.

But Brown's criticism of Reid wholly wrong.

---

1 *Collected Works*, p. 88. — ED.

2 See Priestley, *Examination of Reid, Beattie, and Oswald*, sect. iii.; Bishop Gleig, art. *Metaphysics Encyc. Britan.*, vol. xiv. p. 604,

7th edit.; Beasley, *Search of Truth in the Science of the Human Mind*, book ii. c. iii. p. 123 *et seq.* Cf. cc. iv. v. vi. (Philadelphia, U. S., 1822.) — ED.

is singular, he found a general chorus to his song.   Even Sir James Mackintosh talks of Brown's triumphant exposure of Reid's marvellous mistakes.

To enable you provisionally to understand Reid's errors, I showed you how, holding himself the doctrine of an intuitive or immediate perception of external things, he did not see that the counter doctrine of a mediate or representative perception admitted of a subdivision into two forms, — a simpler and a more complex.   The simpler, that the immediate or representative object is a mere modification of the percipient mind, — the more complex, that this representative object is something different both from the reality and from the mind.   His ignorance of these two forms has caused him great confusion, and introduced much subordinate error into his system, as he has often confounded the simpler form of the representative hypothesis with the doctrine of an intuitive perception; but if he be allowed to have held the essential doctrine of an immediate perception, his errors in regard to the various forms of the representative hypothesis must be viewed as accidental, and comparatively unimportant.

General source of Reid's errors, — which however, are comparatively unimportant.

Brown's errors, on the contrary, are vital.   In the first place, he is fundamentally wrong in holding, in the teeth of consciousness, that the mind is incapable of an immediate knowledge of aught but its own modes.   He adopts the simpler form of a representative perception.   In the second place, he is wrong in reversing Reid's whole doctrine, by attributing to him the same opinion on this point which he himself maintains. In the third place, he is wrong in thinking that Reid only attacked the more complex, and not the more dangerous, form of the representative hypothesis, and did not attack the hypothesis of representation altogether.   In the fourth place, he is wrong in supposing that modern philosophers in general held the simpler form of the representative hypothesis, and that Reid was, therefore, mistaken in supposing them to maintain the more complex, — mistaken, in fact, in supposing them to maintain a doctrine different from his own.

Brown's errors vital.

Having thus prepared you for the subsequent discussion, I proceeded to consider Reid's historical account of the opinions on Perception held by previous philosophers.   This historical account is without order, and at once redundant and imperfect. The most important doctrines are altogether omitted; of others the statement is repeated over and over in different places, and yet never completely done at last; no chrono-

General character of Reid's historical account of philosophical opinions on Perception.

logical succession, no scientific arrangement, is followed, and with all this the survey is replete with serious mistakes. Without, therefore, following Reid's confusion, I took up the opinions on which he touched in the order of time. Of these the first was the doctrine of Plato; in regard to which I showed you, that Reid was singularly erroneous in mistaking what Plato meant by the simile of the cave. Then followed the doctrine of Aristotle and his school, in relation to whom he was hardly more correct. Did our time allow me to attempt a history of the doctrines on perception, I could show you that Aristotle must be presumed to have held the true opinion in regard to this faculty;[1] but in respect to a considerable number of the Aristotelic schoolmen, I could distinctly prove, not only that the whole hypothesis of species was by them rejected, but that their hitherto neglected theory of perception is, even at this hour, the most philosophical that exists.[2] I have no hesitation in saying that, on this point, they are incomparably superior to Reid: for while he excuses Brown's misinterpretation, and, indeed, all but annihilates his own doctrine of perception, by placing that power in a line with imagination and memory, as all faculties immediately cognizant of the reality; they, on the contrary, distinguish Perception as a faculty intuitive, Imagination and Memory as faculties representative of their objects.

Following Reid in his descent to modern philosophers, I showed you how, in consequence of his own want of a systematic knowledge of the Cartesian philosophy, he had erroneously charged Descartes with vacillation and contradiction, in sometimes placing the idea of a representative image in the mind, and sometimes placing it in the brain.

Such is the error of Reid in relation to Descartes, which I find it necessary to acknowledge. But, on the other hand, I must defend him on another point from Brown's charge of having not only ignorantly misunderstood, but of having exactly reversed, the notorious doctrine of Descartes; in supposing that this philosopher held the more complex hypothesis of a representative perception, which views in the representative image something different from the mind, instead of holding, with Reid himself and Brown, the simpler hypothesis, which views in this image only a mode of the percipient mind itself.

Reid right in supposing that Descartes held the more complex hypothesis of Representative Perception.

Now here you must observe that it would not be enough to convict Reid and to justify Brown, if it were made out that the former

---

1 See p. 205, and p. 202 *et seq.* — ED.

2 See above, p. 292 *et seq.*, and below, p. 316. — ED.

was wrong, the latter right, in their statement of Descartes' opinion; and I might even hold with Brown that Descartes had adopted the simpler theory of representation, and still vindicate Reid against his reproach of ignorant misrepresentation, — of reading the acknowledged doctrine of a philosopher, whose perspicuity he himself admits, in a sense "exactly the reverse" of truth. To determine with certainty what Descartes' theory of perception actually is, may be difficult, perhaps impossible. It here suffices to show that his opinion on the point in question is doubtful, — is even one mooted among his disciples; and that Brown, wholly unacquainted with the doubts and difficulties of the problem, dogmatizes on the basis of a single passage of Descartes, — nay, of a passage wholly irrelevant to the matter in dispute. The opinion attributed by Reid to Descartes is the one which was almost universally held in the Cartesian school as the doctrine of its founder; and Arnauld is the only Cartesian who adopted an opinion upon perception identical with Brown's, and who also assigned that opinion to Descartes. The doctrine of Arnauld was long regarded throughout Europe as a paradox, original and peculiar to himself.

Malebranche,[1] the most illustrious name in the school, after its founder, and who, not certainly with less ability,

Malebranche cited in regard to opinion of Descartes.

may be supposed to have studied the writings of his master with far greater attention than either Reid or Brown, ridicules, as "contrary to common sense and justice," the supposition that Descartes had rejected ideas in "the ordinary acceptation," and adopted the hypothesis of their being representations, not really distinct from their perception. And while he "was certain as he possibly can be in such matters," that Descartes had not dissented from the general doctrine, he taunts Arnauld with resting his paradoxical interpretation of that philosopher's doctrine, "not on any passages of his Metaphysics contrary to the 'common opinion,' but on his own arbitrary limitation of 'the ambiguous term perception.'"[2] That ideas are "found in the mind, not formed by it," and, consequently, that in the act of knowledge, the representation is really distinct from the cognition proper, is strenuously asserted as the doctrine of his master by the Cartesian Röell,[3] in the controversy he maintained with the anti-Cartesian De Vries. But it is idle to multiply proofs. Brown's charge of ignorance falls back upon himself; and Reid may lightly bear the reproach of "exactly

1 Given in *Discussions*, p. 74. — ED.

2 *Reponse au Livre des Idées*, passim. — AR-NAULD, *Œuvres*, xxxviii. pp. 838, 389.

3 Cf. Röell, *Dissertationes Philosophicæ*, i. § 43: iii. § 46. — ED.

reversing" the notorious doctrine of Descartes, when thus borne along with him by the profoundest of that philosopher's disciples.

Malebranche and Arnauld are the next philosophers, in chrono-

Reid's account of the opinion of Malebranche.

logical order, of whom Reid speaks. Concerning the former, his statements, though not complete, cannot be considered as erroneous; and Dr. Brown, admitting that Malebranche is one of the two, and only two modern philosophers (Berkeley is the other) who held the more complex doctrine of representation, of course does not attempt to accuse Reid of misrepresentation in reference to him. One error, however, though only an historical one, Reid does commit, in regard to this philosopher. He explains the polemic which Arnauld waged with Malebranche, on the ground of the antipathy between Jansenist and Jesuit. Now Malebranche was not a Jesuit, but a priest of the Oratory.

In treating of Arnauld's opinion, we see the confusion arising

Reid confused in his account of the view of Arnauld.

from Reid's not distinctly apprehending the two forms of the representative hypothesis. Arnauld held, and was the first of the philosophers noticed by Reid or Brown who clearly held the simpler of these forms. Now, in his statement of Arnauld's doctrine, Reid was perplexed, — was puzzled. As opposing the philosophers who maintained the more complex doctrine of representation, Arnauld seemed to Reid to coincide in opinion with himself; but yet, though he never rightly understood the simpler doctrine of representation, he still feels that Arnauld did not hold with him an intuitive perception. Dr. Brown is, therefore, wrong in asserting that Reid admits Arnauld's opinion on perception and his own, to be identical.[1] "To these authors," says Dr. Brown, "whose opinions on the subject of perception Dr. Reid has misconceived, I may add one whom even he himself allows to have shaken off the ideal system, and to have considered the idea and the perception as not distinct, but the same, — a modification of the mind, and nothing more. I allude to the celebrated Jansenist writer, Arnauld, who maintains this doctrine as expressly as Dr. Reid himself, and makes it the foundation of his argument in his controversy with Malebranche."[2] If this statement be true, then is Dr. Brown's interpretation of Reid himself correct. A representative perception under its third and simplest modification, is held by Arnauld as by Brown; and his exposition is so clear and articulate that all essential misconception of these doctrines is precluded. In these circumstances, if Reid avow the identity of

---

[1] See *Discussions*, p 76. — Ed. [2] Lect. xxvii. 178 (edit. 1830).

Arnauld's opinion and his own, this avowal is tantamount to a declaration that his peculiar doctrine of perception is a scheme of representation; whereas, on the contrary, if he signalize the contrast of their two opinions, he clearly evinces the radical antithesis, and his sense of the radical antithesis, of his doctrine of intuition, to every, even the simplest, form of the hypothesis of representation. And this last he does.

It cannot be maintained, that Reid admits a philosopher to hold an opinion convertible with his own, whom he states to "profess the doctrine, universally received, that we perceive not material things immediately, — that it is their ideas that are the immediate objects of our thoughts, — and that it is in the idea of everything that we perceive its properties."[1] This fundamental contrast being established, we may safely allow that the original misconception, which caused Reid to overlook the difference of our intuitive and representative faculties, caused him, likewise, to believe that Arnauld had attempted to unite two contradictory theories of perception. Not aware that it was possible to maintain a doctrine of perception in which the idea was not really distinguished from its cognition, and yet to hold that the mind had no immediate knowledge of external things: Reid supposes, in the first place, that Arnauld, in rejecting the hypothesis of ideas, as representative existences, really distinct from the contemplative act of perception, coincided with him in viewing the material reality, as the immediate object of that act; and, in the second, that Arnauld again deserted this opinion, when, with the philosophers, he maintained that the idea, or act of the mind representing the external reality, and not the external reality itself, was the immediate object of perception. Arnauld's theory is one and indivisible; and, as such, no part of it is identical with Reid's. Reid's confusion, here as elsewhere, is explained by the circumstance, that he had never speculatively conceived the possibility of the simplest modification of the representative hypothesis. He saw no medium between rejecting ideas as something different from thought, and his own doctrine of an immediate knowledge of the material object. Neither does Arnauld, as Reid[2] supposes, ever assert against Malebranche, "that we perceive external things immediately," that is, in themselves: maintaining that all our perceptions are modifications essentially representative, he everywhere avows, that he denies ideas, only as existences distinct from the act itself of perception.[3]

Reid not satisfied with Arnauld's opinion.

---

1 *Intellectual Powers,* Essay ii. ch. xiii. *Coll. Works,* p. 295.

2 *Ibid.,* p. 296.

3 *Œuvres,* tom. xxxviii. 187, 198, 199, 889. [See *Discussions,* p. 77. — ED.]

Reid was, therefore, wrong, and did Arnauld less than justice, in viewing his theory "as a weak attempt to reconcile two inconsistent doctrines:" he was wrong, and did Arnauld more than justice, in supposing that one of these doctrines was not incompatible with his own. The detection, however, of this error only tends to manifest more clearly, how just, even when under its influence, was Reid's appreciation of the contrast, subsisting between his own and Arnauld's opinion, considered as a whole; and exposes more glaringly Brown's general misconception of Reid's philosophy, and his present gross misrepresentation, in affirming that the doctrines of the two philosophers were identical, and by Reid admitted to be the same.

Locke is the philosopher next in order, and it is principally against

Reid on Locke.

Reid's statement of the Lockian doctrine of ideas, that the most vociferous clamour has been raised, by those who deny that the cruder form of the representative hypothesis was the one prevalent among philosophers, after the decline of the scholastic theory of species; and who do not see that, though Reid's refutation, from the cause I have already noticed, was ostensibly directed only against that cruder form, it was virtually and in effect levelled against the doctrine of a representative perception altogether. Even supposing that Reid was wrong in attributing this particular modification of the representative hypothesis to Locke, and the philosophers in general, — this would be a trivial error, provided it can be shown that he was opposed to every doctrine of perception, except that founded on the fact of the duality of consciousness. But let us consider whether Reid be really in error when he attributes to Locke the opinion in question. And let us first hear the charge of his opponents. Of these, I shall only particularly refer to the first and last, — to Priestley and to Brown, — though the same argument is confidently maintained by several other philosophers, in the interval between the publications of Priestley and of Brown.

Priestley asserts that Reid's whole polemic is directed against a

Priestley quoted on Reid's view of Locke's opinion.

phantom of his own creation, and that the doctrine of ideas which he combats was never seriously maintained by any philosopher, ancient or modern. "Before," says Priestley, "Dr. Reid had rested so much upon this argument, it behooved him, I think, to have examined the strength of it a little more carefully than he seems to have done; for he appears to me to have suffered himself to be misled in the very foundation of it, merely by philosophers happening to call ideas *images* of external things; *as if this was not known to be a figurative expression* denoting, *not* that the actual shapes of things were delineated in the brain, or upon the mind, but only that impressions of some kind or other were conveyed to the mind by means of the organs of sense and their corresponding nerves, and that between these impressions and the sensations existing in the mind, there is a real and necessary, though at present an unknown, connection."[1]

Brown does not go the length of Priestley; he admits that, in more ancient times, the obnoxious opinion was prevalent, and allows even two among modern philosophers, Malebranche and Berkeley, to have been guilty of its adoption. Both Priestley and Brown strenuously contend against Reid's interpretation of the doctrine of Locke, who states it as that philosopher's opinion, " that images of external objects were conveyed to the brain; but whether he thought with Descartes [*lege omnino* Dr. Clarke] and Newton, that the images in the brain are perceived by the mind, there present, or that they are imprinted on the mind itself, is not so evident."[2]

Brown coincides with Priestley in censuring Reid's view of Locke's opinion.

[3] This, Brown, Priestley, and others, pronounce a flagrant misrepresentation. Not only does Brown maintain that Locke never conceived the idea to be substantially different from the mind, as a material image in the brain; but, that he never supposed it to have an existence apart from the mental energy of which it is the object. Locke, he asserts, like Arnauld, considered the idea perceived and the percipient act, to constitute the same indivisible modification of the conscious mind. This we shall consider.

In his language, Locke is of all philosophers the most figurative, ambiguous, vacillating, various, and even contradictory; as has been noticed by Reid and Stewart, and Brown himself, — indeed, we believe, by every philosopher who has had occasion to animadvert on Locke. The opinions of such a writer are not, therefore, to be assumed from isolated and casual expressions, which themselves require to be interpreted on the general analogy of the system; and yet this is the only ground on which Dr. Brown attempts to establish his conclusions. Thus, on the matter under discussion, though really distinguishing, Locke verbally confounds, the objects of sense and of pure intellect, the operation and its object, the objects immediate and mediate, the object and its relations, the images of fancy and the notions of the understanding. Conscious-

General character of Locke's philosophical style.

1 *Remarks on Reid, Beattie, and Oswald,* § 3, (p. 30, 2d edition). On Priestley, see Stewart, *Phil. Essays,* Note H, *Works,* vol. v. p. 422.—ED.

2 *Intellectual Powers,* Essay ii. ch. iv. *Coll. Works,* p. 256.

3 See *Discussions,* p. 73. — ED.

ness is converted with Perception; Perception with Idea; Idea with the object of Perception, and with Notion, Conception, Phantasm, Representation, Sense, Meaning, etc. Now, his language identifying ideas and perceptions, appears conformable to a disciple of Arnauld; and now it proclaims him a follower of Democritus and Digby, — explaining ideas by mechanical impulse and the propagation of material particles from the external reality to the brain. In one passage, the idea would seem an organic affection, — the mere occasion of a spiritual representation; in another, a representative image, in the brain itself. In employing thus indifferently the language of every hypothesis, may we not suspect that he was anxious to be made responsible for none? One, however, he has formally rejected, and that is the very opinion attributed to him by Dr. Brown, — that the idea, or object of consciousness in perception, is only a modification of the mind itself.

I do not deny that Locke occasionally employs expressions, which, in a writer of more considerate language, would imply the identity of ideas with the act of knowledge; and, under the circumstances, I should have considered suspense more rational than a dogmatic confidence in any conclusion, did not the following passage, which has never, I believe, been noticed, afford a positive and explicit contradiction of Dr. Brown's interpretation. It is from Locke's *Examination of Malebranche's Opinion*, which, as subsequent to the publication of the *Essay*, must be held decisive in relation to the doctrines of that work. At the same time, the statement is articulate and precise, and possesses all the authority of one cautiously emitted in the course of a polemical discussion. Malebranche coincided with Arnauld, Reid, and recent philosophers in general, and consequently with Locke, as interpreted by Brown, to the extent of supposing that *sensation proper* is nothing but a state or modification of the mind itself; and Locke had thus the opportunity of expressing, in regard to this opinion, his agreement or dissent. An acquiescence in the doctrine, that the secondary qualities, of which we are conscious in sensation, are merely mental states, by no means involves an admission that the primary qualities, of which we are conscious in perception, are nothing more. Malebranche, for example, affirms the one and denies the other. But if Locke be found to ridicule, as he does, even the opinion which merely reduces the secondary qualities to mental states, *a fortiori*, and this on the principle of his own philosophy, he must be held to reject the doctrine, which would reduce not only the non-resembling sensations of the secondary, but

The interpretation adopted by Brown of Locke's opinion, explicitly contradicted by Locke himself.

even the resembling, and consequently extended, ideas of the primary qualities of matter, to modifications of the immaterial unextended mind. In these circumstances, the following passage is superfluously conclusive against Brown; and equally so, whether we coincide or not in all the principles it involves.

Locke quoted.

"But to examine their doctrine of *modification* a little farther. — Different sentiments (sensations) are different modifications of the mind. The mind, or soul, that perceives, is one immaterial indivisible substance. Now I see the white and black on this paper; I hear one singing in the next room; I feel the warmth of the fire I sit by; and I taste an apple I am eating, and all this at the same time. Now, I ask, take modification for what you please, can the same unextended indivisible substance have different, nay, inconsistent and opposite (as these of white and black must be) modifications at the same time? Or must we suppose distinct parts in an indivisible substance, one for black, another for white, and another for red ideas, and so of the rest of those infinite sensations, which we have in sorts and degrees; all which we can distinctly perceive, and so are distinct ideas, some whereof are opposite, as heat and cold, which yet a man may feel at the same time? I was ignorant before, how sensation was performed in us: this they call an explanation of it! Must I say now I understand it better? If this be to cure one's ignorance, it is a very slight disease, and the charm of two or three insignificant words will at any time remove it; *probatum est.*"[1] This passage is correspondent to the doctrine held, on this point, by Locke's personal friend and philosophical follower, Le Clerc.

But if it be thus evident that Locke held neither the third form of representation, that lent to him by Brown, nor even the second; it follows, that Reid did him anything but injustice, in supposing him to maintain that ideas are objects, either in the brain, or in the mind itself. Even the more material of these alternatives has been the one generally attributed to him by his critics,[2] and the one adopted from him by his disciples.[3] Nor is this to be deemed an opinion too monstrous to be entertained by so enlightened a philosopher. It was the common opinion of the age; the opinion, in particular, held by the most illustrious philosophers, his countrymen and contemporaries, — by Newton, Clarke, Willis, Hook, etc.[4]

Descartes, Arnauld, and Locke, are the only philosophers in regard

---

1 Section 39.

2 E. g. Sergeant and Cousin. See *Discussions*, p. 80, note*; and Stewart, *Phil. Essays*, note H, *Works*, v. 422. — ED.

3 Tucker's *Light of Nature*, i. pp. 15, 18, (2d edit.) See *Discussions*, p. 80, note. †. — ED.

4 See *Discussions*, p. 80. — ED.

to whom Brown attempts articulately to show, that Reid's account of their opinions touching the point at issue is erroneous. But there are others, such as Newton, Clarke, Hook, Norris, whom Reid charged with holding the obnoxious hypothesis, and whom Brown passes over without an attempt to vindicate, although Malebranche and Berkeley be the only two philosophers in regard to whom he explicitly avows that Reid is correct. But as an instance of Reid's error, Brown alleges Hobbes; and as an evidence of its universality, the authority of Le Clerc and Crousaz.

Brown passes over Reid's interpretation of the opinions of certain philosophers.

[1] To adduce Hobbes as an instance of Reid's misrepresentation of the "common doctrine of ideas," betrays, on the part of Brown, a total misapprehension of the conditions of the question; or he forgets that Hobbes was a materialist. The doctrine of representation, under all its modifications, is properly subordinate to the doctrine of a spiritual principle of thought; and on the supposition, all but universally admitted among philosophers, that the relation of knowledge implied the analogy of existence, it was mainly devised to explain the possibility of a knowledge by an immaterial subject, of an existence so disproportioned to its nature, as the qualities of a material object. Contending, that an immediate cognition of the accidents of matter, infers an essential identity of matter and mind, Brown himself admits, that the hypothesis of representation belongs exclusively to the doctrine of dualism;[2] whilst Reid, assailing the hypothesis of ideas only as subverting the reality of matter, could hardly regard it as parcel of that scheme, which acknowledges the reality of nothing else. But though Hobbes cannot be adduced as a competent witness against Reid, he is, however, valid evidence against Brown. Hobbes, though a materialist, admitted no knowledge of an external world. Like his friend Sorbiere, he was a kind of material idealist. According to him, we know nothing of the qualities or existence of any outward reality. All that we know is the "seeming," the "apparition," the "aspect," the "phænomenon," the "phantasm," within ourselves; and this subjective object, of which we are conscious, and which is consciousness itself, is nothing more than the "agitation" of our internal organism, determined by the unknown "motions," which are supposed, in like manner, to constitute the world without. Perception he reduces to Sensation. Memory and Imagination are faculties specifically identical with

But adduces Hobbes as an instance of Reid's error.

---

[1] See *Discussions*, p. 75. — ED.   [2] Lect. xxv. pp. 159, 160 (edit. 1830.)

Sense, differing from it simply in the degree of their vivacity; and this difference of intensity, with Hobbes as with Hume, is the only discrimination between our dreaming and our waking thoughts. — A doctrine of perception identical with Reid's!

[1] Dr. Brown at length proceeds to consummate his victory, by "that most decisive evidence, found not in treatises, read only by a few, but in the popular elementary works of science of the time, the general text-books of schools and colleges." He quotes however, only two, — the *Pneumatology* of Le Clerc, and the *Logic* of Crousaz.

Le Clerc and Crousaz, referred to by Brown.

"Le Clerc," says Dr. Brown, "in his chapter on the nature of ideas, gives the history of the opinions of philosophers on this subject, and states among them the very doctrine which is most forcibly and accurately opposed to the ideal system of perception. '*Alii putant ideas et perceptiones idearum easdem esse, licet relationibus differant.* Idea, uti censent, proprie ad objectum refertur, quod mens considerat; — perceptio, vere ad mentem ipsam quæ percepit: sed duplex illa relatio ad unam modificationem mentis pertinent. Itaque, secundum hosce philosophos, nullæ sunt, proprie loquendo, ideæ a mente nostra distinctæ.' What is it, I may ask, which Dr. Reid considers himself as having added to this very philosophical view of perception? and if he added nothing, it is surely too much to ascribe to him the merit of detecting errors, the counter-statement of which had long formed a part of the elementary works of the schools."[2]

Le Clerc.

In the first place, Dr. Reid certainly "added" nothing "to this very philosophical view of perception," but he exploded it altogether. In the second, it is false either that this doctrine of perception "had long formed part of the elementary works of the schools," or that Le Clerc affords any countenance to this assertion. On the contrary, it is virtually stated by him to be the novel paradox of a single philosopher; nay, it is already, as such a singular opinion, discussed and referred to its author by Reid himself. Had Dr. Brown proceeded from the tenth paragraph, which he quotes, to the fourteenth, which he could not have read, he would have found that the passage extracted, so far from containing the statement of an old and familiar dogma in the schools, was neither more nor less than a statement of the contemporary hypothesis of Antony Arnauld, and of Antony Arnauld alone. In the third place, from the mode in which he cites Le Clerc, his silence to the contrary, and the general tenor of his statement, Dr. Brown would lead us to

---

[1] See *Discussions*, p. 81. — ED.   [2] Lect. xxvii. p. 174 (edit. 1830.) — ED.

believe that Le Clerc himself coincides in "this very philosophical view of perception." So far, however, from coinciding with Arnauld, he pronounces his opinion to be false; controverts it upon very solid grounds; and in delivering his own doctrine touching ideas, though sufficiently cautious in telling us what they are, he has no hesitation in assuring us, among other things which they cannot be, that they are not modifications or essential states of mind. "*Non est* (idea *sc.*) *modificatio aut essentia mentis:* nam præterquam quod sentimus ingens esse discrimen inter ideæ *perceptionem* et *sensationem;* quid habet mens nostra simile monti, aut innumeris ejusmodi ideis?" Such is the judgment of that authority to which Dr. Brown appealed as the most decisive."[1]

In Crousaz, Dr. Brown has actually succeeded in finding one example (he might have found twenty) of a philosopher, before Reid, holding the same theory of ideas with Arnauld and himself.[2]

Crousaz.

[1] *Pneumatologia,* § 1. c. 5, § 10. — ED.
[2] See this subject further pursued in *Discussions,* p. 82 *et seq.* — ED.

LECTURE XXIII.

THE PRESENTATIVE FACULTY.

I.—PERCEPTION,—WAS REID A NATURAL REALIST?

IN our last Lecture, I concluded the review of Reid's Historical Account of the previous Opinions on Perception. In entering upon this review, I proposed the following ends. In the first place, to afford you, not certainly a complete, but a competent, insight into the various theories on this subject; and this was sufficiently accomplished by limiting myself to the opinions touched upon by Reid. My aim, in the second place, was to correct some errors of Reid arising from, and illustrative of, those fundamental misconceptions which have infected his whole doctrine of the cognitive faculties with confusion and error; and, in the third place, I had in view to vindicate Reid from the attack made on him by Brown. I, accordingly, showed you, that though not without mistakes, owing partly to his limited acquaintance with the works of previous philosophers, and partly to not having generalized to himself the various possible modifications of the hypothesis of representative perception,—I showed you, I say, that Reid, though certainly anything but exempt from error, was, however, absolutely guiltless of all and every one of that marvellous tissue of mistakes, with which he is so recklessly accused by Brown,—whereas Brown's own attack is, from first to last, itself that very series of misconceptions which he imputes to Reid. Nothing, indeed, can be more applicable to himself than the concluding observations which he makes in reference to Reid; and as these observations, addressed to his pupils, embody in reality an edifying and well-expressed advice, they will lose nothing of their relevancy or effect, if the one philosopher must be substituted for the other.[1] "That a mind so vigorous as that of Dr. Reid should have been capable of the series of misconceptions which we have traced, may seem wonderful, and truly is so; and equally, or rather

Margin note: Ends proposed in the review of Reid's account of opinions on Perception.

---

1 *Discussions*, p. 82. — ED.

still more wonderful, is the general admission of his merit in this respect. I trust it will impress you with one important lesson — to consult the opinions of authors in their own works, and not in the works of those who profess to give a faithful account of them. From my own experience I can most truly assure you, that there is scarcely an instance in which I have found the view which I had received of them to be faithful. There is usually something more, or something less, which modifies the general result; and by the various additions and subtractions thus made, so much of the spirit of the original doctrine is lost, that it may, in some cases, be considered as having made a fortunate escape, if it be not at last represented as directly opposite to what it is."[1]

The mistakes of Dr. Brown in relation to Reid, on which I have hitherto animadverted, are comparatively unimportant. Their refutation only evinces that Reid did not erroneously attribute to philosophers in general the cruder form of the representative hypothesis of perception; and that he was fully warranted in this attribution, is not only demonstrated by the disproval of all the instances which Brown has alleged against Reid, but might be shown by a whole crowd of examples, were it necessary to prove so undeniable a fact. In addition to what I have already articulately proved, it will be enough now simply to mention that the most learned and intelligent of the philosophers of last century might be quoted to the fact, that the opinion attributed by Reid to psychologists in general, was in reality the prevalent; and that the doctrine of Arnauld, which Brown supposes to have been the one universally received, was only adopted by the few. To this point Malebranche, Leibnitz, and Brucker, the younger Thomasius, 'S Gravesande, Genovesi, and Voltaire,[2] are conclusive evidence.

Reid right in attributing to philosophers in general the cruder doctrine of Representative Perception.

But a more important historical question remains, and one which even more affects the reputations of Reid and Brown. It is this:—Did Reid, as Brown supposes, hold, not the doctrine of Natural Realism, but the finer hypothesis of a Representative Perception?

Was Reid himself a Natural Realist?

If Reid did hold this doctrine, I admit at once that Brown is right.[3] Reid accomplished nothing; his philosophy is a blunder, and his whole polemic against the philosophers, too insignificant for refutation or comment. The one form of representation may

---

1 *Philosophy of the Human Mind,* Lect. xxvii. p. 175 (edit. 1830).

2 These testimonies are given in full, *Discussions,* p. 83. — ED.

3 See *Discussions,* p. 91. — ED.

be somewhat simpler and more philosophical than the other; but the substitution of the former for the latter is hardly deserving of notice; and of all conceivable hallucinations the very greatest would be that of Reid, in arrogating to himself the merit of thus subverting the foundation of Idealism and Skepticism, and of philosophers at large in acknowledging the pretension. The idealist and skeptic can establish their conclusions indifferently on either form of a representative perception; nay, the simpler form affords a securer, as the more philosophical, foundation. The idealism of Fichte is accordingly a system far more firmly founded than the idealism of Berkeley; and as the simpler involves a contradiction of consciousness more extensive and direct, so it furnishes to the skeptic a longer and more powerful lever.

Before, however, discussing this question, it may be proper here to consider more particularly a matter of which we have hitherto treated only by the way, — I mean the distinction of Immediate or Intuitive, in contrast to Mediate or Representative Knowledge. This is a distinction of the most important kind, and it is one which has, however, been almost wholly overlooked by philosophers. This oversight is less to be wondered at in those who allowed no immediate knowledge to the mind, except of its proper modes; in their systems the distinction, though it still subsisted, had little relevancy or effect, as it did not discriminate the faculty by which we are aware of the presence of external objects, from that by which, when absent, these are imaged to the mind. In neither case, on this doctrine, are we conscious or immediately cognizant of the external reality, but only of the mental mode through which it is represented. But it is more astonishing that those who maintain that the mind is immediately percipient of external things, should not have signalized this distinction; as on it is established the essential difference of Perception as a faculty of intuitive, Imagination as a faculty of representative, knowledge. But the marvel is still more enhanced when we find that Reid and Stewart — (if to them this opinion really belongs) so far from distinguishing Perception as an immediate and intuitive, from Imagination (and under Imagination, be it observed, I include both the Conception and the Memory of these philosophers), as a mediate or representative, faculty, — in language make them both equally immediate.

The distinction of Intuitive and Representative Knowledge, to be first considered.

Reid's view of this distinction obscure.

You will recollect the refutation I formerly gave you of Reid's self-contradictory assertion, that in Memory we are immediately cognizant of that which, as past, is not now existent, and cannot, therefore, be known in itself; and that, in Imagination, we are immediately cognizant of that which is distant, or of that which is not, and probably never was, in being.[1] Here the term *immediate* is either absurd, as contradictory; or it is applied only, in a certain special meaning, to designate the simpler form of representation, in which nothing is supposed to intervene between the mental cognition and the external reality; in contrast to the more complex, in which the representative or vicarious image is supposed to be something different from both. Thus, in consequence of this distinction not only not having been traced by Reid, as the discriminative principle of his doctrine, but having been even overlaid, obscured, and perplexed, his whole philosophy has been involved in haze and confusion; insomuch that a philosopher of Brown's acuteness could (as we have seen and shall see) actually so far misconceive, as even to reverse its import. The distinction is, therefore, one which, on every account, merits your most sedulous attention; but though of primary importance, it is fortunately not of any considerable difficulty.

His whole philosophy hence involved in confusion.

As every cognitive act which, in one relation, is a mediate or representative, is, in another, an immediate or intuitive, knowledge, let us take a particular instance of such an act; as hereby we shall at once obtain an example of the one kind of knowledge, and of the other, and these also in proximate contrast to each other. I call up an image of the *High Church.* Now, in this act, what do I know immediately or intuitively; what mediately or by representation? It is manifest that I am conscious or immediately cognizant of all that is known as an act or modification of my mind, and, consequently, of the modification or act which constitutes the mental image of the Cathedral. But as, in this operation, it is evident, that I am conscious or immediately cognizant of the Cathedral, as imaged in my mind; so it is equally manifest, that I am not conscious or immediately cognizant of the Cathedral as existing. But still I am said to know it; it is even called the object of my thought. I can, however, only know it mediately, — only through the mental image which represents it to consciousness; and it can only be styled the object of thought, inasmuch as a reference to it is necessarily involved in the act of representation. From this example is manifest, what in general

This distinction in general stated and illustrated.

---

1 See Lect. xii. p. 151 *et seq.* — ED.

is meant by immediate or intuitive,—what by mediate or representative knowledge. All philosophers are at one in regard to the immediate knowledge of our present mental modifications; and all are equally agreed, if we remove some verbal ambiguities, that we are only mediately cognizant of all past thoughts, objects, and events, and of every external reality not at the moment within the sphere of sense. There is but one point on which they are now at variance,— viz., whether the thinking subject is competent to an intuitive knowledge of aught but the modifications of the mental self; in other words, whether we can have any immediate perception of external things. Waiving, however, this question for the moment, let us articulately state what are the different conditions involved in the two kinds of knowledge.

The contrasts between Intuitive and Representative Cognition.

In the first place, considered as acts.—An act of immediate knowledge is simple; there is nothing beyond the mere consciousness, by that which knows, of that which is known. Here consciousness is simply contemplative. On the contrary, an act of mediate knowledge is complex; for the mind is not only conscious of the act as its own modification, but of this modification as an object representative of, or relative to, an object beyond the sphere of consciousness. In this act, consciousness is both representative and contemplative of the representation.

1. Considered as acts.

In the second place, in relation to their objects.—In an immediate cognition, the object is single, and the term unequivocal. Here the object in consciousness, and the object in existence, are the same; in the language of the schools, the *esse intentionale* or *representativum*, coincides with the *esse entitativum*. In a mediate cognition, on the other hand, the object is twofold, and the term equivocal; the object known and representing being different from the object unknown, except as represented. The immediate object, or object known in this act, should be called the *subjective object*, or *subject-object*, in contradistinction to the mediate or unknown object, which might be discriminated as the *object-object*. A slight acquaintance with philosophical writings will show you how necessary such a distinction is; the want of it has caused Reid to puzzle himself, and Kant to perplex his readers.

2. In relation to their objects.

In the third place, considered as judgments (for you will recollect that every act of Consciousness involves an affirmation).—In an intuitive act, the object known is known as actually existing; the cognition, therefore, is

3. As judgments.

assertory, inasmuch as the reality of that, its object, is given unconditionally as a fact. In a representative act, on the contrary, the represented object is unknown as actually existing; the cognition, therefore, is problematical, the reality of the object represented being only given as a possibility, on the hypothesis of the object representing.

In the fourth place, in relation to their sphere. — Representative

4. In relation to their sphere.

knowledge is exclusively subjective, for its immediate object is a mere mental modification, and its mediate object is unknown, except in so far as that modification represents it. Intuitive knowledge, on the other hand, if consciousness is to be credited, is either subjective or objective, for its single object may be either a phænomenon of the ego or of the non-ego, — either mental or material.

In the fifth place, considered in reference to their perfection. —

5. In reference to their perfection.

An intuitive cognition, as an act, is complete and absolute, as irrespective of aught beyond the dominion of consciousness; whereas, a representative cognition, as an act, is incomplete, being relative to, and vicarious of, an existence beyond the sphere of actual knowledge. The object likewise of the former is complete, being at once known and real; whereas, in the latter, the object known is ideal, the real object unknown. In their relations to each other, immediate knowledge is complete, as self-sufficient; mediate knowledge, on the contrary, is incomplete, as dependent on the other for its realization.[1]

Such are the two kinds of knowledge which it is necessary to distinguish, and such are the principal contrasts they present. I said a little ago that this distinction, so far from being signalized, had been almost abolished by philosophers. I ought, however, to

This distinction taken by certain of the schoolmen.

have excepted certain of the schoolmen,[2] by whom this discrimination was not only taken, but admirably applied; and, though I did not originally borrow it from them, I was happy to find that what I had thought out for myself, was confirmed by the

---

1 For a fuller statement of the points of distinction between Immediate and Mediate Knowledge, see *Reid's Works*, Suppl. Dissert. Note B, p. 804-815. — ED.

2 [See Durandus, *In Sent.*, Prologus, q. 3, § 6: " Cognitio *intuitiva*, illa quæ immediate tendit ad rem sibi præsentem objective, secundum ejus actualem existentiam: sicut cum video colorem existentem in pariete, vel rosam quam in manu teneo. *Abstractiva* dicitur om-

nis cognitio quæ habetur de re, non sic realiter præsente in ratione objecti immediate cogniti. § 9: Actus sensuum exteriorum sunt intuitivi, propter immediatum ordinem ad objecta sua." Cf. John Major, *In Sent.*, lib. i. dist. iii. q. 2, f. 33, and Tellez, *Summa Philosophiæ*, tom. ii. p. 952.] [Besides Durandus, the Conimbricenses refer to Scotus, Ferrariensis, Anselm, Hugo a Sancto Victore, the Master of Sentences, Aquinas, Gregory Ariminensis

authority of these subtle spirits. The names given in the schools
to the immediate and mediate cognitions were *intuitive* and *abstractive* (*cognitio intuitiva, cognitio abstractiva*), meaning by the
latter term not merely what we, with them, call abstract knowledge, but also the representations of concrete objects in the imagination or memory.

Now, possessed of this distinction, of which Reid knew nothing,
and asserting far more clearly and explicitly than he has ever done
the doctrine of an intuitive perception, I think the affirmation I
made in my last Lecture is not unwarranted, — that a considerable
section of the schoolmen were incomparably superior to Reid, or
any modern philosopher, in their exposition of the true theory of
that faculty. It is only wonderful that this, their doctrine, has not
hitherto attracted attention, and obtained the celebrity it merits.

Having now prepared you for the question concerning Reid, I
shall proceed to its consideration; and shall, in
the first place, state the arguments that may be
adduced in favor of the opinion, that Reid did
not assert a doctrine of Natural Realism, — did not accept the fact
of the duality of consciousness in its genuine integrity, but only
deluded himself with the belief that he was originating a new or
an important opinion, by the adoption of the simpler form of Representation; and, in the second place, state the arguments that
may be alleged in support of the opposite conclusion, that his
doctrine is in truth the simple doctrine of Natural Realism.

But before proceeding to state the grounds on which alone I
conceive any presumption can be founded, that
Reid is not a Natural Realist, but, like Brown,
a Cosmothetic Idealist, I shall state and refute
the only attempt made by Brown to support
this, his interpretation of Reid's fundamental
doctrine. Brown's interpretation of Reid seems,
in fact, not grounded on anything which he
found in Reid, but simply on his own assumption of what Reid's opinion must be. For,
marvellous as it may sound, Brown hardly seems to have contemplated the possibility of an immediate knowledge of anything
beyond the sphere of self; and I should say, without qualification,
that he had never at all imagined this possibility, were it not for

*Order of the dis-
cussion.*

*1. Grounds on
which Reid may be
supposed not a Nat-
ural Realist.
Brown's single ar-
gument in support of
the view that Reid
was a Cosmothetic
Idealist, refuted.*

Paludanus, Cajetan, as distinguishing between knowledge *intuitive* and *abstractive.*
See *In De Anima*, lib. ii. c. vi. q. 3, p. 198, and

Reid's Works, Suppl. Diss. B, p. 812. — See
above, L. xxi. p. 292, and L. xxii. p. 300. —
ED.]

the single attempt he makes at a proof of the impossibility of Reid holding such an opinion, when on one occasion Reid's language seems for a moment to have actually suggested to him the question: Might that philosopher not perhaps regard the external object as identical with the immediate object in perception? In the following passage, you will observe, by anticipation, that by Sensation, which ought to be called Sensation Proper, is meant the subjective feeling, — the pleasure or pain involved in an act of sensible perception; and by Perception, which ought to be called Perception Proper, is meant the objective knowledge which we have, or think we have, of the external object in that act. "'Sensation,' says Dr. Reid, 'can be nothing else than

Brown quoted.

it is felt to be. Its very essence consists in being felt; and when it is not felt, it is not. There is no difference between the sensation and the feeling of it; they are one and the same thing.' But this is surely equally true of what he terms perception, which, as a state of the mind, it must be remembered, is, according to his own account of it, as different from the object perceived as the sensation is. We may say of the mental state of perception, too, in his own language, as indeed we must say of all our states of mind, whatever they may be, that it can be nothing else than it is felt to be. Its very essence consists in being felt; and when it is not felt, it is not. There is no difference between the perception and the feeling of it; they are one and the same thing. The sensation, indeed, which is mental, is different from the object exciting it, which we term material; but so also is the state of mind which constitutes perception; for Dr. Reid was surely too zealous an opponent of the systems which ascribe everything to mind alone, or to matter alone, to consider the perception as itself the object perceived. That in sensation, as contradistinguished from perception, there is no reference made to an external object, is true; because, when the reference is made, we then use the new term of perception; but that in sensation there is no object distinct from that act of the mind by which it is felt, — no object independent of the mental feeling, is surely a very strange opinion of this philosopher; since what he terms perception is nothing but the reference of this very sensation to its external object. The sensation itself he certainly supposes to depend on the presence of an external object, which is all that can be understood in the case of perception, when we speak of its objects, or, in other words, of those external causes to which we refer our sensations; for the material object itself he surely could not consider as forming a part of the perception, which is a state of the mind alone. To be the object of perception, is nothing more than to be the foreign cause or occasion, on which this state of the mind directly or indirectly arises; and an object, in this only intelligible sense, as an occasion or cause of a certain subsequent effect, must, on his own principles, be equally allowed to sensation. Though he does not inform us what he means by the term *object*, as peculiarly applied to perception, — (and, indeed, if he had explained it, I cannot but think that a great part of his system, which is founded on the confusion of this single word, as something different from a mere external cause of an internal feeling, must have fallen to the ground), — he yet tells us very explicitly, that to be the object of perception, is something more than to be the external occasion on which that state of the mind arises which he terms perception; for, in arguing against the opinion of a philosopher who contends for the existence of certain images or traces in the brain, and yet says, 'that we are not to conceive the images or traces in the brain to be perceived, as if there were eyes in the brain; these traces are only occasions, on which, by the laws of the union of soul and body, ideas are excited in the mind; and, therefore, it is not necessary that there should be an exact resemblance between the traces and the things represented by them, any more than that words or signs should be exactly like the things signified by them,' he adds: 'These two opinions, I think, cannot be reconciled. For if the images or traces in the brain are perceived, they must be the objects of perception, and not the occasions of it only. On the other hand, if they are only the occasions of our perceiving, they are not perceived at all.' Did Dr. Reid, then, suppose that the feeling, whatever it may be, which constitutes perception as a state of the mind, or, in short, all of which we are conscious in perception, is not strictly and exclusively mental, as much as all of which we are conscious in remembrance, or in love, or hate; or did he wish us to believe that matter itself, in any of its forms, is, or can be, a part of the phænomena or states of the mind, — a part, therefore, of that mental state or feeling which we term a perception? Our sensations, like our remembrances or emotions, we refer to some cause or antecedent. The difference is, that in the one case we consider the feeling as having for its cause some previous feeling or state of the mind itself; in the other case we consider it as having for its cause something which is external to ourselves, and independent of our transient feelings, — something which, in consequence of former feelings suggested at the moment, it is impossible for us not to regard as extended and resisting. But still, what we thus regard as extended and resisting, is known to us only by the feelings which it occasions in our mind. What matter, in its relation to percipient mind, can be, but the cause or occasion, direct or indirect, of that class of feelings which I term sensations or perceptions, it is absolutely impossible for me to conceive.

"The percipient mind, in no one of its affections, can be said to be the mass of matter which it perceives, unless the separate existence, either of matter or of mind, be abandoned by us, the existence of either of which, Dr. Reid would have been the last of philosophers to yield. He acknowledges that our perceptions are consequent on the presence of external bodies, not from any necessary connection subsisting between them, but merely from the arrangement which the Deity, in his wisdom, has chosen to make of their mutual phænomena; which is surely to say, that the Deity has rendered the presence of the external object the occasion of that affection of the mind which is termed perception; or, if it be not to say this, it is to say nothing. Whatever state of mind perception may be; whether a primary result of a peculiar power, or a mere secondary reference of association that follows the particular sensation, of which the reference is made, it is itself, in either view of it, but a state of the mind; and to be the external occasion or antecedent of this state of mind, since it is to produce, directly or indirectly, all which constitutes perception, is surely, therefore, to be perceived, or there must be something in the mere word perceived, different from the physical reality which it expresses."[1]

[2] Now the sum and substance of this reasoning is, as far as I can comprehend it, to the following effect:—To assert an immediate perception of material qualities, is to assert an identity of matter and mind; for that which is immediately known must be the same in nature as that which immediately knows.

Brown's reasoning stated and refuted.

But Reid was not a materialist, was a sturdy spiritualist; therefore he could not really maintain an immediate perception of the qualities of matter.

The whole validity of this argument consists in the truth of the major proposition (for the minor proposition that Reid was not a materialist is certain),—To assert an immediate perception of material qualities, is to assert an identity of matter and mind; for that which is immediately known must be the same in essence as that which immediately knows.

Now in support of the proposition which constitutes the founda-

1 *Lectures on the Philosophy of the Human Mind.* Lect. xxv. p. 159, 160.
2 See *Discussions*, p. 60.—ED.

tion of his argument, Brown offers no proof. He assumes it as an axiom. But so far from his being entitled to do so, by its being too evident to fear denial, it is, on the contrary, not only not obtrusively true, but, when examined, precisely the reverse of truth.

His fundamental proposition assumed.

In the first place, if we appeal to the only possible arbiter in the case, — the authority of consciousness, — we find that consciousness gives as an ultimate fact, in the unity of knowledge, the duality of existence; that is, it assures us that, in the act of perception, the percipient subject is at once conscious of something which it distinguishes as a modification of self, and of something which it distinguishes as a modification of not-self. Reid, therefore, as a dualist, and a dualist founding not on the hypotheses of philosophers, but on the data of consciousness, might safely maintain the fact of our immediate perception of external objects, without fear of involving himself in an assertion of the identity of mind and matter.

In the first place, disproved by consciousness.

But, in the second place, if Reid did not maintain this immediacy of perception, and assert the veracity of consciousness, he would at once be forced to admit one or other of the unitarian conclusions of materialism or idealism. Our knowledge of mind and matter, as substances, is merely relative; they are known to us only in their qualities; and we can justify the postulation of two different substances, exclusively on the supposition of the incompatibility of the double series of phænomena to coinhere in one. Is this supposition disproved? — The presumption against dualism is again decisive. Entities are not to be multiplied without necessity; a plurality of principles is not to be assumed, where the phænomena can be explained by one. In Brown's theory of perception, he abolishes the incompatibility of the two series; and yet his argument, as a dualist, for an immaterial principle of thought, proceeds on the ground that this incompatibility subsists.[1] This philosopher denies us an immediate knowledge of aught beyond the accidents of mind. The accidents which we refer to body, as known to us, are only states or modifications of the percipient subject itself; in other words, the qualities we call *material*, are known by us to exist, only as they are known by us to inhere in the same substance as the qualities we denominate *mental*. There is an apparent antithesis, but a real identity. On this doctrine, the hypothesis of a double principle losing its necessity, becomes philo-

In the second place, would prove the converse of what Brown employs it to establish.

[1] *Philosophy of the Human Mind*, Lect. xxvi. pp. 646, 647.

sophically absurd; on the law of parcimony, a psychological unitarianism is established. To the argument, that the qualities of the object, are so repugnant to the qualities of the subject, of perception, that they cannot be supposed the accidents of the same substance, the unitarian — whether materialist, idealist, or absolutist, — has only to reply: — that so far from the attributes of the object being exclusive of the attributes of the subject, in this act, the hypothetical dualist himself establishes, as the fundamental axiom of his philosophy of mind, that the object known is universally identical with the subject knowing. The materialist may now derive the subject from the object, the idealist derive the object from the subject, the absolutist sublimate both into indifference, nay, the nihilist subvert the substantial reality of either; — the hypothetical realist, so far from being able to resist the conclusion of any, in fact accords their assumptive premises to all.

So far, therefore, is Brown's argument from inferring the conclusion, that Reid could not have maintained our immediate perception of external objects, that not only is its inference expressly denied by Reid, but if properly applied, it would prove the very converse of what Brown employs it to establish.

But there is a ground considerably stronger than that on which Brown has attempted to evince the identity of Reid's opinion on perception with his own. This ground is his equalizing Perception and Imagination. (Under Imagination, you will again observe, that I include Reid's Conception and Memory.) Other philosophers brought perception into unison with imagination, by making perception a faculty of mediate knowledge. Reid, on the contrary, has brought imagination into unison with perception, by calling imagination a faculty of immediate knowledge. Now as it is manifest that, in an act of imagination, the object-object is and can possibly be known only, mediately, through a representation, it follows that we must perforce adopt one of two alternatives, — we may either suppose that Reid means by immediate knowledge only that simpler form of representation from which the idea or *tertium quid*, intermediate between the external reality and the conscious mind, is thrown out, or that, in his extreme horror of the hypothesis of ideas, he has altogether overlooked the fundamental distinction of mediate and immediate cognition, by which the faculties of perception and imagination are discriminated; and that thus his very anxiety to separate more widely his own doctrine of

Reid's equalizing Perception and Imagination, a ground on which he may be supposed not a Natural Realist.

But may be explained consistently with his doctrine of Natural Realism.

intuition from the representative hypothesis of the philosophers, has, in fact, caused him almost inextricably to confound the two opinions.

That this latter alternative is greatly the more probable, I shall now proceed to show you; and in doing this, I beg you to keep in mind the necessary contrasts by which an immediate or intuitive is opposed to a mediate or representative cognition. The question to be solved is, — Does Reid hold that in perception we immediately know the external reality, in its own qualities, as existing; or only mediately know them, through a representative modification of the mind itself? In the following proof, I select only a few out of a great number of passages which might be adduced from the writings of Reid, in support of the same conclusions. I am, however, confident that they are sufficient; and quotations longer or more numerous would tend rather to obscure than to illustrate. [1]

Positive evidence that Reid held Natural Realism.

In the first place, knowledge and existence are then only convertible when the reality is known in itself; for then only can we say, that it is known because it exists, and exists since it is known. And this constitutes an immediate or intuitive cognition, rigorously so called. Nor did Reid contemplate any other. "It seems admitted," he says, "as a first principle, by the learned and the unlearned, that what is really perceived must exist, and that to perceive what does not exist, is impossible. So far the unlearned man and the philosopher agree."[2]

Application of the conditions of Immediate Knowledge to Reid's statements.

In the second place, philosophers agree, that the idea or representative object, in their theory, is, in the strictest sense, immediately perceived. And so Reid understands them. "I perceive not, says the Cartesian, the external object itself (so far he agrees with the Peripatetic, and differs from the unlearned man); but I perceive an image, or form, or idea, in my own mind, or in my brain. I am certain of the existence of the idea, because I immediately perceive it."[3]

In the third place, philosophers concur in acknowledging that mankind at large believe that the external reality itself constitutes the immediate and only object of perception. So also Reid: "On the same principle, the unlearned man says, I perceive the external object, and I perceive it to exist." — "The vulgar undoubtedly

1 See this question discussed in *Reid's Works*, Suppl. Dissert. Note C, § ii. p. 819 *et seq.* Compare *Discussions*, p. 58 *et seq.* — ED.

2 *Works*, p. 274. — ED.

3 *Ibid.* — ED.

believe that it is the external object which we immediately perceive, and not a representative image of it only. It is for this reason that they look upon it as perfect lunacy to call in question the existence of external objects."[1] — "The vulgar are firmly persuaded that the very identical objects which they perceive, continue to exist when they do not perceive them: and are no less firmly persuaded, that when ten men look at the sun or the moon they all see the same individual object."[2] Speaking of Berkeley,— "The vulgar opinion he reduces to this, that the very things which we perceive by our senses do really exist. This he grants."[3] — "It is, therefore, acknowledged by this philosopher to be a natural instinct or prepossession, an universal and primary opinion of all men, that the objects which we immediately perceive by our senses are not images in our minds, but external objects, and that their existence is independent of us and our perception."[4]

In the fourth place, all philosophers agree that consciousness has an immediate knowledge, and affords an absolute certainty of the reality, of its object. Reid, as we have seen, limits the name of consciousness to self-consciousness, that is, to the immediate knowledge we possess of the modifications of self; whereas, he makes perception the faculty by which we are immediately cognizant of the qualities of the not-self.

In these circumstances, if Reid either, 1°, Maintain, that his immediate perception of external things is convertible with their reality; or, 2°, Assert, that, in his doctrine of perception, the external reality stands to the percipient mind face to face, in the same immediacy of relation which the idea holds in the representative theory of the philosophers; or, 3°, Declare the identity of his own opinion with the vulgar belief, as thus expounded by himself and the philosophers; or, 4°, Declare, that his Perception affords us equal evidence of the existence of external phænomena, as his Consciousness affords us of the existence of internal; — in all and each of these suppositions, he would unambiguously declare himself a natural realist, and evince that his doctrine of perception is one not of a mediate or representative, but of an immediate or intuitive knowledge. And he does all four.

The first and second. — "We have before examined the reasons given by philosophers to prove that ideas, and not external objects, are the immediate objects of perception. We shall only here observe, that if external objects be perceived immediately" [and

<hr />

1 *Works*, p. 274. — ED.
2 *Ibid.*, p. 284. — ED.
3 *Works*, p. 284. — ED.
4 *Ibid.*, p. 299. — ED.

he had just before asserted for the hundredth time that they were so perceived], " we have the same reason to believe their existence as philosophers have to believe the existence of ideas, while they hold them to be the immediate objects of perception."[1]

The third. — Speaking of the perception of the external world, — " We have here a remarkable conflict between two contradictory opinions, wherein all mankind are engaged. On the one side, stand all the vulgar, who are unpractised in philosophical researches, and guided by the uncorrupted primary instincts of nature. On the other side, stand all the philosophers, ancient and modern; every man, without exception, who reflects. In this division, to my great humiliation, I find myself classed with the vulgar."[2]

The fourth. — "Philosophers sometimes say that we perceive ideas, — sometimes that we are conscious of them. I can have no doubt of the existence of anything which I either perceive, or of which I am conscious; but I cannot find that I either perceive ideas or am conscious of them."[3]

Various other proofs of the same conclusion could be adduced; these, for brevity, we omit.

On these grounds, therefore, I am confident that Reid's doctrine of Perception must be pronounced a doctrine of Intuition, and not of Representation; and though, as I have shown you, there are certainly some plausible arguments which might be alleged in support of the opposite conclusion; still, these are greatly overbalanced by stronger positive proofs, and by the general analogy of his philosophy. And here I would impress upon you an important lesson. That Reid, a distinguished philosopher, and even the founder of an illustrious school, could be so greatly misconceived, as that an eminent disciple of that school itself should actually reverse the fundamental principle of his doctrine, — this may excite your wonder, but it ought not to move you to disparage either the talent of the philosopher misconceived, or of the philosopher misconceiving. It ought, however, to prove to you the permanent importance, not only in speculation, but in practice, of precise thinking. You ought never to rest content, so long as there is aught vague or indefinite in your reasonings, — so long as you have not analyzed every notion into its elements, and excluded the possibility of all lurking ambiguity in your expressions. One great, perhaps the one greatest advantage, resulting

General conclusion, and caution.

---

1 *Works*, p. 446. Cf. pp. 263, 272. — ED.　　　2 *Works*, p. 302. — ED.
3 *Works*, p. 373. — ED.

from the cultivation of Philosophy, is the habit it induces of vigorous thought, that is, of allowing nothing to pass without a searching examination, either in your own speculations, or in those of others. We may never, perhaps, arrive at truth, but we can always avoid self-contradiction.

LECTURE XXIV.

THE PRESENTATIVE FACULTY.

I. — PERCEPTION. — THE DISTINCTION OF PERCEPTION PROPER FROM SENSATION PROPER.

IN my last Lecture, having concluded the review of Reid's

Recapitulation.

Historical Account of Opinions on Perception, and of Brown's attack upon that account, I proceeded to the question, — Is Reid's own doctrine of perception a scheme of Natural Realism, that is, did he accept in its integrity the datum of consciousness, — that we are immediately cognitive both of the phænomena of matter and of the phænomena of mind; or did he, like Brown, and the greater number of more recent philosophers, as Brown assumes, hold only the finer form of the representative hypothesis, which supposes that, in perception, the external reality is not the immediate object of consciousness, but that the ego is only determined in some unknown manner to represent the non-ego, which representation, though only a modification of mind or self, we are compelled, by an illusion of our nature, to mistake for a modification of matter, or not-self? I stated to you how, on the determination of this question, depended nearly the whole of Reid's philosophical reputation; his philosophy professes to subvert the foundations of idealism and skepticism, and it is as having accomplished what he thus attempted, that any principal or peculiar glory can be awarded to him. But if all he did was merely to explode the cruder hypothesis of representation, and to adopt in its place the finer, — why, in the first place, so far from depriving idealism and skepticism of all basis, he only placed them on one firmer and more secure; and, in the second, so far from originating a new opinion, he could only have added one to a class of philosophers, who, after the time of Arnauld, were continually on the increase, and who, among the contemporaries of Reid himself, certainly constituted the majority. His philosophy would thus be at once only a silly blunder; its pretence to originality only a proclamation of ignorance; and so far from being an honor to the nation from which it arose, and by whom it was respected, it would, in fact, be a scandal and a reproach to the philosophy of any country in which it met with any milder treatment than derision.

Previously, however, to the determination of this question, it was necessary to place before you, more distinctly than had hitherto been done, the distinction of Mediate or Representative from Immediate or Intuitive knowledge, — a distinction which, though overlooked, or even abolished, in the modern systems of philosophy, is, both in itself and in its consequences, of the highest importance in psychology. Throwing out of view, as a now exploded hypothesis, the cruder doctrine of representation, — that, namely, which supposes the immediate, or representative object to be something different from a mere modification of mind, — from the mere energy of cognitions, — I articulately displayed to you these two kinds of knowledge in their contrasts and correlations. They are thus defined. Intuitive or immediate knowledge is that in which there is only one object, and in which that object is known in itself, or as existing. Representative or mediate knowledge, on the contrary, is that in which there are two objects, — an immediate and a mediate object; — the immediate object or that known in itself, being a mere subjective or mental mode relative to and representing a reality beyond the sphere of consciousness; — the mediate object is that reality, thus supposed and represented. As an act of representative knowledge involves an intuitive cognition, I took a special example of such an act. I supposed that we called up to our minds the image of the *High Church*. Now, here the immediate object, — the object of consciousness, is the mental image of that edifice. This we know, and know not as an absolute object, but as a mental object relative to a material object which it represents; which material object, in itself, is, at present, beyond the reach of our faculties of immediate knowledge, and is, therefore, only mediately known in its representation. You must observe that the mental image, — the immediate object, is not really different from the cognitive act of imagination itself. In an act of mediate or representative knowledge, the cognition and the immediate object are really an identical modification, — the cognition and the object, — the imagination and the image, being nothing more than the mental representation, — the mental reference itself. The indivisible modification is distinguished by two names, because it involves a relation between two terms (the two terms being the mind knowing and the thing represented), and may, consequently, be viewed in more proximate reference to the one or to the other of these. Looking to the mind knowing, it is called a cognition, an act of knowledge, an imagination, etc.;—looking to the thing represented, it is called a representation, an object, an image, an idea, etc.

All philosophers admit that the knowledge of our present mental states is immediate: if we discount some verbal ambiguities, all would admit that our actual knowledge of all that is not now existent, or not now existent within the sphere of consciousness, must be mediate or representative. The only point on which any serious difference of opinion can obtain is,—Whether the ego or mind can be more than mediately cognizant of the phænomena of the non-ego or matter.

I then detailed to you the grounds on which it ought to be held

Summary of the reasons for holding Reid a Natural Realist.

that Reid's doctrine of Perception is one of Natural Realism, and not a form of Cosmothetic Idealism, as supposed by Brown. An immediate or intuitive knowledge is the knowledge of a thing as existing,—consequently, in this case, knowledge and existence infer each other. On the one hand, we know the object because it exists,—and, on the other, the object exists, since it is known. This is expressly maintained by Reid, and universally admitted by philosophers. In the first place, on this principle, the philosophers hold that ideas (whether on the one hypothesis of representation, or on the other) necessarily exist, because immediately known. Now, if Reid, fully aware of this, assert that, on his doctrine, the external reality holds, in the act of perception, the same immediate relation to the mind, in which the idea or representative image stands in the doctrine of philosophers; and that, consequently, on the one opinion, we have the same assurance of the existence of the material world, as, on the other, of the reality of the ideal world;—if, I say, he does this, he unambiguously proclaims himself a natural realist. And that this he actually does, I showed you by various quotations from his writings.

In the second place, upon the same principle, mankind at large believe in the existence of the external universe, because they believe that the external universe is by them immediately perceived. This fact, I showed you, is acknowledged both by the philosophers, who regard the common belief itself as an illusion, and by Reid. In these circumstances, if Reid declares that he coincides with the vulgar, in opposition to the learned, belief, he must again be held unambiguously to pronounce his doctrine of perception a scheme of natural realism. And that he emphatically makes this declaration, I also proved to you by sundry passages.

In the third place, Reid and all philosophers are at one in maintaining that self-consciousness, as immediately cognizant of our mental modifications, affords us an absolute assurance of their existence. If then Reid hold that perception is as immediately cognizant of the external modification, as self-consciousness is of the internal, and that the one cognition thus affords us an equal certainty of the reality of its object as does the other, — on this supposition, it is manifest that Reid, a third time, unambiguously declares his doctrine of perception a doctrine of natural realism. And that he does so, I proved by various quotations.

I might have noticed, in the fourth place, that Reid's assertion, that our belief in the existence of external things is immediate, and not the result of inference or reasoning, is wholly incompatible with the doctrine of a representative perception. I do not, however, lay much stress on this argument, because we may possibly suspect that he makes the same mistake in regard to the term *immediate*, as applied to this belief, which he does in its application to our representative cognitions. But, independently of this, the three former arguments are amply sufficient to establish our conclusion.

These are the grounds on which I would maintain that Brown has not only mistaken, but absolutely reversed the fundamental principle of Reid's philosophy; although it must be confessed, that the error and perplexity of Reid's exposition, arising from his non-distinction of the two possible forms of representation, and his confusion of representative and of intuitive knowledge, afford a not incompetent apology for those who might misapprehend his meaning. In this discussion, it may be matter of surprise, that I have not called in the evidence of Mr. Stewart. The truth is, — his writings afford no applicable testimony to the point at issue. His own statements of the doctrine of perception are brief and general, and he is content to refer the reader to Reid for the details.

Of the doctrine of an intuitive perception of external objects, — which, as a fact of consciousness, ought to be unconditionally admitted, — Reid has the merit, in these latter times, of being the first champion.

Reid the first champion of Natural Realism in these latter times.

I have already noticed that, among the scholastic philosophers, there were some who maintained the same doctrine, and with far greater clearness and comprehension than Reid.[1] These opinions are, however, even at this moment, I may say, wholly unknown; and it would be ridiculous to suppose that their speculations had exerted any influence, direct or indirect,

1 See above, pp 292, 300, 316, notes. — Ed.

upon a thinker so imperfectly acquainted with what had been done by previous philosophers, as Reid.   Since the revival of letters, I have met with only two, anterior to Reid, whose doctrine on the present question coincided with his.   One of these may, indeed, be discounted; for he has stated his opinions in so paradoxical a manner, that his authority is hardly worthy of notice.[1]   The other,[2] who flourished about a century before Reid, has, on the contrary, stated the doctrine of an intuitive, and refuted the counter hypothesis of a representative perception, with a brevity, perspicuity, and precision, far superior to the Scottish philosopher. Both of these authors, I may say, are at present wholly unknown.

Two modern philosophers, previously to Reid, held Intuitive Perception.

Having concluded the argument by which I endeavored to satisfy you that Reid's doctrine is Natural Realism, I should now proceed to show that Natural Realism is a more philosophical doctrine than Hypothetical Realism.   Before, however, taking up the subject, I think it better to dispose of certain subordinate matters, with which it is proper to have some preparatory acquaintance.

Of these the first is the distinction of Perception Proper from Sensation Proper.

---

1 The philosopher here meant is probably John Sergeant, who inculcated a doctrine of Realism against modern philosophers generally, and Locke in particular, — in his *Method to Science* (1696), and *Solid Philosophy asserted against the Fancies of the Ideists* (1697). See, of the latter work, Preface, especially §§ 7, 18, 19; pp. 23, 42, 44, 58 *et seq.*, 142, 338 *et seq.* See below, p. 353. — ED.

2 The latter of the two philosophers here referred to, is doubtless Peter Poiret. He is mentioned in the Author's Common-Place Book, as holding a more correct opinion than Reid on the point raised in the text. Poiret was born in 1646, and died in 1719. He states his doctrine as follows: "In nobis duplicis generis (saltem quantum ad cognitionem, voce hac late sumpta) facultates inesse; reales alteras, quæ res ipsas; alteras umbratiles, quæ rerum picturas, umbrasve sive *ideas* exhibeant: et utrasque quidem facultates illas iterum duplices existere; nempe, vel reales spiritales, pro rebus spiritalibus; vel reales corporeas, pro rebus materialibus. *Spiritales reales* sunt passivus intellectus sensusque spiritales et intimi, qui ab objectis ipsis realibus ac spiritalibus, eorumve effluviis veris afficiuntur. . . . *Corporeæ reales* facultates sunt (hoc in negotio) visus sensusque ceteri corporei qui ab objectis ipsis corporeis affecti, eorum exhibent nobis *cognitionem sensuale*. Umbratiles autem facultates (quæ sunt ipsa hominis, *Ratio*

sive intellectus activus) comparent maxime, quando objectis sive rebus quæ facultates reales affecerunt, eorumque affectione et effluviis absentibus, mens activitate sua eorumdem imagines sive ideas in se excitat et considerat. Et hoc quidem modo *idealiter* sive per *ideam* possunt quoque cognosci, *Deus, Mentes, Corpora.*" *Cogitationes Rationales,* lib. ii. c. iv. p. 176, (edit. 1715) — first published apparently in 1675.   Again he says: "Intellectus triplex. . . . . . Intellectus sive facultas percipiendi, cujus objectum ipsemet Deus est ejusque divinæ operationes ac emanationes, dicitur a me *intellectus divinus,* ac mere *passivus* sive receptivus; qui etiam *intelligentia* dici potest. Intellectus, sive facultas percipiendi, cujus objectum sunt res hujus mundi naturales earumque realia effluvia, dicitur a me intellectus animalis sive *sensualis,* qui quoque mere *passivus* est. Intellectus vero cujus objecta sunt picturæ et imagines ac ideæ rerum, quas ipsemet format et varie regit, sive imagines illæ ideæve sint de rebus spiritalibus sive de corporeis, dicitur a me Ratio *humana* vel intellectus *activus* et *picturarius* . . . intellectus *idealis. Defensio Methodi Inveniendi Verum,* §§ 2, 4, p. 113. Cf. §§ I, 5, *Opera Posthuma,* (edit. 1721). Cf. his *De Vera Methodo Inveniendi Verum,* pars i. §§ 20, 21, pp. 23, 24, (1st edit. 1692), — prefixed to his *De Eruditione.* See p. 203, note 2. — ED.

I have had occasion to mention, that the word *Perception* is, in the language of philosophers previous to Reid, used in a very extensive signification. By Descartes, Malebranche, Locke, Leibnitz, and others, it is employed in a sense almost as unexclusive as consciousness in its widest signification. By Reid, this word was limited to our faculty acquisitive of knowledge, and to that branch of this faculty whereby, through the senses, we obtain a knowledge of the external world. But his limitation did not stop here. In the act of external perception, he distinguished two elements, to which he gave the names of Perception and Sensation. He ought, perhaps, to have called these *perception proper* and *sensation proper*, when employed in his special meaning; for, in the language of other philosophers, *sensation* was a term which included his Perception, and *perception* a term comprehensive of what he called Sensation.

The distinction of Perception Proper from Sensation Proper.
Use of the term Perception previously to Reid.

There is a great want of precision in Reid's account of Perception and Sensation. Of Perception he says: "If, therefore, we attend to that act of our mind, which we call the perception of an external object of sense, we shall find in it these three things. *First,* Some conception or notion of the object perceived. *Secondly,* A strong and irresistible conviction and belief of its present existence; and, *Thirdly,* That this conviction and belief are immediate, and not the effect of reasoning.

Reid's account of Perception.

"*First,* it is impossible to perceive an object without having some notion or conception of what we perceive. We may indeed conceive an object which we do not perceive; but when we perceive the object, we must have some conception of it at the same time; and we have commonly a more clear and steady notion of the object while we perceive it, than we have from memory or imagination, when it is not perceived. Yet, even in perception, the notion which our senses give of the object may be more or less clear, more or less distinct in all possible degrees."[1]

Now here you will observe that the "having a notion or conception," by which he explains the act of perception, might at first lead us to conclude that he held, as Brown supposes, the doctrine of a representative perception; for notion and conception are generally used by philosophers for a representation or mediate knowledge of a thing.

Wanting in precision.

---

[1] *Intellectual Powers*, Essay ii. c. v. *Works*, p. 258.

But, though Reid cannot escape censure for ambiguity and vagueness, it appears, from the analogy of his writings, that by *notion* or *conception* he meant nothing more than knowledge or cognition.

Sensation he thus describes : "Almost all our perceptions have corresponding sensations, which constantly accompany them, and, on that account, are very

Sensation.

apt to be confounded with them. Neither ought we to expect that the sensation, and its corresponding perception, should be distinguished in common language, because the purposes of common life do not require it. Language is made to serve the purposes of ordinary conversation; and we have no reason to expect that it should make distinctions that are not of common use. Hence it happens that a quality perceived, and the sensation corresponding to that perception, often go under the same name.

"This makes the names of most of our sensations ambiguous, and this ambiguity hath very much perplexed the philosophers. It will be necessary to give some instances, to illustrate the distinction between our sensations and the objects of perception.

"When I smell a rose, there is in this operation both sensation and perception. The agreeable odor I feel, considered by itself, without relation to any external object, is merely a sensation. It affects the mind in a certain way; and this affection of the mind may be conceived, without a thought of the rose or any other object. This sensation can be nothing else than it is felt to be. Its very essence consists in being felt; and when it is not felt, it is not. There is no difference between the sensation and the feeling of it; they are one and the same thing. It is for this reason, that we before observed, that in sensation, there is no object distinct from that act of mind by which it is felt; and this holds true with regard to all sensations.

"Let us next attend to the perception which we have in smelling a rose. Perception has always an external object; and the object of my perception, in this case, is that quality in the rose which I discern by the sense of smell. Observing that the agreeable sensation is raised when the rose is near, and ceases when it is removed, I am led, by my nature, to conclude some quality to be in the rose which is the cause of this sensation. This quality in the rose is the object perceived; and that act of the mind, by which I have the conviction and belief of this quality, is what in this case I call perception."[1]

By *perception*, Reid, therefore, means the objective knowledge we

---

[1] *Intellectual Powers*, Essay ii. ch. 16.   *Coll. Works*, p. 310.

have of an external reality, through the senses; by *sensation*, the subjective feeling of pleasure or pain, with which the organic operation of sense is accom-

Reid anticipated in his distinction of Per-ception from Sensa-tion.

panied. This distinction of the objective from the subjective element in the act is important. Reid is not, however, the author of this distinc-tion. He himself notices of Malebranche that "he distinguished more accurately than any philosopher had done before, the objects which we perceive from the sensations in our own minds, which, by the laws of nature, always accompany the perception of the object. As in many things, so particularly in this, he has great merit; for this, I apprehend, is a key that opens the way to a right understanding both of our external senses, and of other powers of the mind."[1]　I

Malebranche.

may notice that Malebranche's distinction is into *Idée*, corresponding to Reid's Perception, and *Sentiment*, corresponding to his Sensation; and this distinction is as precisely marked in Malebranche[2] as in Reid. Subsequently to Malebranche, the distinction became even common; and there is

Crousaz, Hutcheson, Le Clerc, Sinsart, Buf-fier.

no reason for Mr. Stewart[3] being struck when he found it in Crousaz and Hutcheson. It is to be found in Le Clerc,[4] in Sinsart,[5] in Buffier,[6] in Genovesi,[7] and in many other philosophers. It is curious that Malebranche's distinction was apprehended neither by Locke nor by Leibnitz, in their counter examinations of the theory of that philosopher. Both totally mistake its import. Male-branche, however, was not the original author of the distinction.

Descartes.

He himself professedly evolves it out of Des-cartes.[8]　But long previously to Descartes, it had been clearly established. It formed a part of that admirable doctrine of perception maintained by the party of the Schoolmen to whom I have already alluded.[9] I find it, however, long prior to

Plotinus.

them. It is, in particular, stated with great precision by Plotinus,[10] and even some inferences drawn from it, which are supposed to be the discoveries of modern philosophy.

---

1 *Intellectual Powers*, Essay ii. ch. vii. *Coll. Works*, p. 265.

2 *Recherche de la Vérité*, lib. iii. part ii. ch. vi. and vii., with Eclaircissement on text. See *Reid's Works*, pp. 834, 887.—Ed.

3 *Philosophical Essays*, notes F and G. The passages from Hutcheson and Crousaz are given in Sir W. Hamilton's edition of the *Collected Works*, vol. v. p. 420.—Ed.

4 *Pneumatologia*, § i. chap. v. *Opera Phi-losophica*, tom. ii. p. 31 (edit. 1726).—Ed.

5 [*Recueil des Pensées sur l' Immortalité de l' Ame*, 119.]

6 *First Truths*, part i. ch. xiv. §§ 109—111, Cf. Remarks on Crousaz, art. viii. p. 427 (Eng. Trans).—Ed.

7 [*Elementa Metaphysicæ*, pars ii. p. 12.]

8 See *Reid's Works*, p. 831.—Ed.

9 See above, l. xxiii. p. 816, and *Reid's Works*, p. 887.—Ed.

10 *Enn.* iii. vi. 2. See *Reid's Works*, p. 887.—Ed.

Before proceeding to state to you the great law which regulates the mutual relation of these phænomena, — a law which has been wholly overlooked by our psychologists, — it is proper to say a few words, illustrative of the nature of the phænomena themselves; for what you will find in Reid, is by no means either complete or definite.

The nature of the phænomena, — Perception and Sensation, illustrated.

The opposition of Perception and Sensation is true, but it is not a statement adequate to the generality of the contrast. Perception is only a special kind of knowledge, and sensation only a special kind of feeling; and *Knowledge* and *Feeling*, you will recollect, are two out of the three great classes, into which we primarily divided the phænomena of mind. *Conation* was the third.

The contrast of Perception and Sensation, the special manifestation of a contrast which universally divides Knowledge and Feeling.

Now, as perception is only a special mode of knowledge, and sensation only a special mode of feeling, so the contrast of perception and sensation is only the special manifestation of a contrast, which universally divides the generic phænomena themselves. It ought, therefore, in the first place, to have been noticed, that the generic phænomena of knowledge and feeling are always found coëxistent, and yet always distinct; and the opposition of perception and sensation should have been stated as an obtrusive, but still only a particular example of the general law. But not only is the distinction of perception and sensation not generalized, — not referred to its category, by our psychologists; it is not concisely and precisely stated. A cognition is objective, that is, our consciousness is then relative to something different from the present state of the mind itself; a feeling, on the contrary, is subjective, that is, our consciousness is exclusively limited to the pleasure or pain experienced by the thinking subject. Cognition and feeling are always coëxistent. The purest act of knowledge is always colored by some feeling of pleasure or pain; for no energy is absolutely indifferent, and the grossest feeling exists only as it is known in consciousness. This being the case of cognition and feeling in general, the same is true of perception and sensation in particular. Perception proper is the consciousness, through the senses, of the qualities of an object known as different from self; Sensation proper is the consciousness of the subjective affection of pleasure or pain, which accompanies that act of knowledge. Perception is thus the objective element in the complex state, — the element of cognition; sensation is the subjective element, — the element of feeling.

Perception Proper and Sensation Proper, precisely distinguished.

The most remarkable defect, however, in the present doctrine
upon this point, is the ignorance of our psychologists in regard to the law by which the phænomena of cognition and feeling, — of perception
and sensation, are governed, in their reciprocal
relation. This law is simple and universal; and,
once enounced, its proof is found in every mental manifestation. It is this: Knowledge and
Feeling, — Perception and Sensation, though always coëxistent, are
always in the inverse ratio of each other.[1] That these two elements
are always found in coëxistence, as it is an old and a notorious
truth, it is not requisite for me to prove. But that these elements
are always found to coëxist in an inverse proportion, — in support
of this universal fact, it will be requisite to adduce proof and illustration.

The grand law by which the phænomena of Knowledge and Feeling, — Perception and Sensation, are governed in their reciprocal relation.

In doing this I shall, however, confine myself to the relation of
Perception and Sensation. These afford the
best examples of the generic relation of knowledge and feeling; and we must not now turn
aside from the special faculty with which we are engaged.

Established and illustrated.

The first proof I shall take from a comparison of the several
senses; and it will be found that, precisely as
a sense has more of the one element, it has less
of the other. Laying Touch aside for the moment, as this requires a special explanation, the
other four Senses divide themselves into two classes, according as
perception, the objective element, or sensation, the subjective element, predominates. The two in which the former element prevails,
are Sight and Hearing; the two in which the latter, are Taste and
Smell.[2]

1. From a comparison of the several senses.

Now, here, it will be at once admitted, that Sight, at the same
instant, presents to us a greater number and a
greater variety of objects and qualities, than
any other of the senses. In this sense, therefore, perception, — the
objective element, is at its maximum. But sensation, — the subjective element, is here at its minimum; for, in the eye, we experience less organic pleasure or pain from the impressions of its appropriate objects (colors), than we do in any other sense.

Sight.

Next to Sight, Hearing affords us, in the shortest interval, the

---

[1] This law is enunciated by Kant, *Anthropologie*, § 20. Kant's words are, "Je stärker
die Sinne, bei eben demselben Grade des auf
sie geschehenen Einflusses, sich *afficirt* fühlen,
desto weniger *lehren* sie. Umgekehrt; wenn
sie viel lehren sollen, müssen sie mässig affici-
ren." *Anthr.* § 20,(*Werke*, edit. Rosenkranz and
Schubert, vii. part 2, p. 51.) Sect. 20 of this
edition corresponds to § 19, edit. 1800. — Ed.

[2] Compare Kant, *Anthropologie*, § 15. — Ed.

greatest variety and multitude of cognitions; and as sight divides
space almost to infinity, through color, so hear-
ing does the same to time, through sound. Hear-

Hearing.

ing is, however, much less extensive in its sphere of knowledge or
perception than sight; but in the same proportion is its capacity of
feeling or sensation more intensive. We have greater pleasure and
greater pain from single sounds than from single colors; and, in like
manner, concords and discords, in the one sense, affect us more agreeably or disagreeably, than any modifications of light in the other.[1]

In Taste and Smell, the degree of sensation, that is, of pleasure
or pain, is great in proportion as the perception,

Taste and Smell.

that is, the information they afford, is small. In
all these senses, therefore, — Sight, Hearing, Taste, Smell, it will be
admitted that the principle holds good. ·

The sense of Touch, or Feeling strictly so called, I have reserved, as this requires a word of comment.

Touch.

Some philosophers include under this name all
our sensitive perceptions, not obtained through some of the four
special organs of sense, that is, sight, hearing, taste, smell; others,
again, divide the sense into several. To us at present this difference is of no interest: for it is sufficient for us to know, that in
those parts of the body where sensation predominates, perception
is feeble; and in those where perception is lively, sensation is obtuse.
In the finger points, tactile perception is at its height; but there
is hardly another part of the body in which sensation is not more
acute. Touch, or Feeling strictly so called, if viewed as a single
sense, belongs, therefore, to both classes, — the objective and subjective. But it is more correct, as we shall see, to regard it as a
plurality of senses, in which case Touch, prop-

Touch properly a plu-
rality of Senses.

erly so called, having a principal organ in the
finger points, will belong to the first class, — the
class of objective senses, — the perceptions, — that class in which
philosophy proper predominates.

The analogy, then, which we have thus seen to hold good in the
several senses in relation to each other, prevails

2. From the several
impressions of the
same sense.

likewise among the several impressions of the
same sense. Impressions in the same sense,
differ both in degree and in quality or kind. By
impression you will observe that I mean no explanation of the

1 [In regard to the subjective and objective
nature of the sensations of the several senses,
or rather the perceptions we have through
them, it may be observed, that what is more
objective is more easily remembered; whereas, what is more subjective affords a much
less distinct remembrance. Thus, what we
perceive by the eye, is better remembered
than what we hear.] — *Oral Interpolation.*

mode in which the external reality acts upon the sense (the metaphor you must disregard), but simply the fact of the agency itself.

Difference in degree. Taking, then, their difference in degree, and supposing that the degree of the impression determines the degree of the sensation, it cannot certainly be said, that the minimum of sensation infers the maximum of perception; for perception always supposes a certain quantum of sensation: but this is undeniable, that, above a certain limit, perception declines, in proportion as sensation rises. Thus, in the sense of sight, if the impression be strong we are dazzled, blinded, and consciousness is limited to the pain or pleasure of the sensation, in the intensity of which, perception has been lost.

Take now the difference, in kind, of impressions in the same sense.

Difference in kind. Sight; Color, and Figure, as sources of pleasure. Of the senses, take again that of Sight. Sight, as will hereafter be shown, is cognizant of color, and, through color, of figure. But though figure is known only through color, a very imperfect cognizance of color is necessary, as is shown in the case (and it is not a rare one) of those individuals who have not the faculty of discriminating colors. These persons, who probably perceive only a certain difference of light and shade, have as clear and distinct a cognizance of figure, as others who enjoy the sense of sight in absolute perfection. This being understood, you will observe, that, in the vision of color, there is more of sensation; in that of figure, more of perception. Color affords our faculties of knowledge a far smaller number of differences and relations than figure; but, at the same time, yields our capacity of feeling a far more sensual enjoyment. But if the pleasure we derive from color be more gross and vivid, that from figure is more refined and permanent. It is a law of our nature, that the more intense a pleasure, the shorter is its duration. The pleasures of sense are grosser and more intense than those of intellect; but, while the former alternate speedily with disgust, with the latter we are never satiated. The same analogy holds among the senses themselves. Those in which sensation predominates, in which pleasure is most intense, soon pall upon us; whereas those in which perception predominates, and which hold more immediately of intelligence, afford us a less exclusive but a more enduring gratification. How soon are we cloyed with the pleasures of the palate, compared with those of the eye; and, among the objects of the former, the meats that please the most are soonest objects of disgust. This is too notorious in regard to taste to stand in need of proof. But it is no less certain in the case of vision. In Painting, there is a pleasure derived from a vivid and harmonious coloring, and a pleasure from the drawing and grouping of the figures. The two pleasures are distinct, and even, to a certain extent, incompatible. For if we attempt to combine them, the grosser and more obtrusive gratification, which we find in the coloring, distracts us from the more refined and intellectual enjoyment we derived from the relation of figure; while, at the same time, the disgust we soon experience from the one tends to render us insensible to the other. This is finely expressed by a modern Latin poet of high genius:

Joannes Secundus quoted.

"Mensura rebus est sua dulcibus;
　Ut quodque mentes suavius afficit,
　　Fastidium sic triste secum .
　　　Limite proximiore ducit. [1]

"Est modus et dulci: nimis immoderata voluptas
　Tædia finitimo limite semper habet.
Cerne novas tabulas; rident florente colore,
　Picta velut primo Vere coruscat humus.
Cerne diu tamen has, hebetataque lumina flectes,
　Et tibi conspectus nausea mollis erit;
Subque tuos oculos aliquid revocare libebit,
　Prisca quod inculta secla tulere manu." [2]

His learned commentator, Bosscha, has nòt, however, noticed that these are only paraphrases of a remarkable passage of Cicero.[3] Cicero and Secundus have not, however, expressed the principle more explicitly than Shakspeare:

Paraphrases Cicero.

Shakspeare.

"These violent delights have violent ends,
　And in their triumph die. The sweetest honey
Is loathsome in its own deliciousness,
　And in the taste confounds the appetite.
Therefore, love moderately; long love doth so.
Too swift arrives as tardy as too slow." [4]

The result of what I have now stated, therefore, is, in the first place, that, as philosophers have observed, there is a distinction

---

[1] Joannes Secundus, *Basia*, ix. *Opera*, p. 85, (edit. 1631). — ED.

[2] Joannes Secundus, *Epigrammata*, liii. [*Opera*, p. 115. — ED.]

[3] *De Oratore*, iii. 25: "Difficile enim dictu est, quænam causa sit, cur ea, quæ maxime sensus, nostros impellunt voluptate, et specie prima acerrime commovent, ab iis celerrime fastidio quodam et satietate abalienemur," etc. — ED.

[4] *Romeo and Juliet*, act. ii. scene 6.

between Knowledge and Feeling, — Perception and Sensation, as

Result in sum of foregoing discussion.

between the objective and the subjective element; and, in the second, that this distinction is, moreover, governed by the law, — That the two elements, though each necessarily supposes the other, are still always in a certain inverse proportion to each other.[1] .

Before leaving this subject, I may notice that the distinction of perception proper and sensation proper, though

The distinction of Perception from Sensation, of importance only in the doctrine of Intuitive Perception.

recognized as phænomenal by philosophers who hold the doctrine of a representative perception, rises into reality and importance only in the doctrine of an intuitive perception. In the former doctrine, perception is supposed to be only apparently objective; being, in reality, no less subjective than sensation proper, — the subjective element itself. Both are nothing more than mere modes of the ego. The philosophers who hold the hypothesis of a representative perception, make the difference of the two to consist only in this; — that in perception proper, there is reference to an unknown object, different from me; in sensation, there is no reference to aught beyond myself. Brown, on the supposition that Reid held that doctrine in common with himself and philosophers at large, states sensation, as understood by Reid, to be "the simple feeling that immediately follows the action of an external body on any of our organs of sense, considered merely as a feeling of the mind; the corresponding perception being the reference of this feeling to the external body as its cause."[2] The distinction he allows to be a convenient one, if the nature of the complex process which it expresses be rightly understood. "The only question," he says, "that seems, philosophically, of importance, with respect to it, is whether the perception in this sense, — the reference of the sensation to its external corporeal cause, — implies, as Dr. Reid contends, a peculiar mental power, coëxtensive with sensation, to be distinguished by a peculiar name in the catalogue of our faculties; or be not merely one of the results of a more general power, which is afterwards to be considered by us, — the power of association, — by which one feeling suggests, or induces, other feelings that have formerly coëxisted with it."[3]

If Brown be correct in his interpretation of Reid's general doctrine of perception, his criticism is not only true but trite. In the hands of a cosmothetic idealist, the distinction is only superficial,

---

[1] For historical notices of approximations, to this Law, see *Reid's Works*, Note D*, p. 887. — Ed.

[2] Lecture xxvi. p. 1. second edition. — Ed.

[3] *Ibid.* — Ed.

and manifestly of no import; and the very fact, that Reid laid so great a stress on it, would tend to prove, independently of what we have already alleged, that Brown's interpretation of his doctrine is erroneous. You will remark, likewise, that Brown (and Brown only speaks the language of all philosophers who do not allow the mind a consciousness of aught beyond its own states) misstates the phænomenon, when he asserts that, in perception, there is a reference from the internal to the external, from the known to the unknown. That this is not the fact, an observation of his phænomenon will at once convince you. In an act of perception, I am conscious of something as self, and of something as not-self: — this is the simple fact. The philosophers, on the contrary, who will not accept this fact, misstate it. They say that we are there conscious of nothing but a certain modification of mind; but this modification involves a reference to, — in other words, a representation of, something external, as its object. Now this is untrue. We are conscious of no reference, — of no representation; we believe that the object of which we are conscious is the object which exists. Nor could there possibly be such reference or representation; for reference or representation supposes a knowledge already possessed of the object referred to or represented; but perception is the faculty by which our first knowledge is acquired, and, therefore, cannot suppose a previous knowledge as its condition. But this I notice only by the way; this matter will be regularly considered in the sequel.

That Reid laid stress on this distinction, serves to determine the nature of his doctrine of Perception.

No reference from the internal to the external in Perception, as Brown states.

I may here notice the false analysis, which has endeavored to take perception out of the list of our faculties, as being only a compound and derivative power. Perception, say Brown and others, supposes memory and comparison and judgment; therefore, it is not a primary faculty of mind. Nothing can be more erroneous than this reasoning. In the first place, I have formerly shown you that consciousness supposes memory, and discrimination, and judgment; and, as perception does not pretend to be simpler than consciousness, but in fact only a modification of consciousness, that, therefore, the objection does not apply. But, in the second place, the objection is founded on a misapprehension of what a faculty properly is. It may be very true that an act of perception cannot be realized simply and alone. I have often told you that the mental phænomena are never simple, and that as tissues

Perception taken out of the list of primary faculties, through a false analysis.

are woven out of many threads, so a mental phænomenon is made up of many acts and affections, which we can only consider separately by abstraction, but can never even conceive as separately existing. In mathematics, we consider a triangle or a square, the sides and the angles apart from each other, though we are unable to conceive them existing independently of each other. But because the angles and sides exist only through each other, would it be correct to deny their reality as distinct mathematical elements? As in geometry, so is it in psychology. We admit that no faculty can exist itself alone; and that it is only by viewing the actual manifestations of mind in their different relations, that we are able by abstraction to analyze them into elements, which we refer to different faculties. Thus, for example, every judgment, every comparison, supposes two terms to be compared, and, therefore, supposes an act of representative, or an act of acquisitive cognition. But go back to one or other of these acts, and you will find that each of them supposes a judgment and a memory. If I represent in imagination the terms of comparison, there is involved a judgment; for the fact of their representation supposes the affirmation or judgment that they are called up, that they now ideally exist; and this judgment is only possible, as the result of a comparison of the present consciousness of their existence with a past consciousness of their non-existence, which comparison, again, is only possible through an act of memory.

Connected with the preceding distinction of Perception and Sensation, is the distinction of the Primary and Secondary Qualities of matter. This distinction cannot be omitted; but I shall not attempt to follow out the various difficult and doubtful problems which it presents.[1]

The Primary and Secondary Qualities of matter.

It would only confuse you were I to attempt to determine, how far this distinction was known to the Atomic Physiologists, prior to Aristotle, and how far Aristotle himself was aware of the principle on which it proceeds. — It is enough to notice, as the most remarkable opinion of antiquity, that of Democritus, who, except the common qualities of body which are known by Touch, denied that the senses afforded us any information concerning the real properties of matter. Among modern philosophers, Descartes was the first who recalled attention to the distinction. According to him, the primary qualities differ from the secondary in this, —

Historical notices of this distinction.

Democritus.

Descartes.

---

[1] For a fuller and more accurate account of the history of this distinction, see *Reid's Works*, note D. — Ed.

that our knowledge of the former is more clear and distinct than of the latter. "Longe alio modo cognoscimus quid sit in corpore magnitudo vel figura quam quid sit, in eodem corpore, color, vel odor, vel sapor. — Longe evidentius cognoscimus quid sit in corpore esse figuratum quam quid sit esse coloratum."[1]

"The qualities of external objects," says Locke,[2] "are of two sorts; first, Original or Primary; such are solidity, extension, motion or rest, number and figure. These are inseparable from body, and such as it constantly keeps in all its changes and alterations. Thus, take a grain of wheat, divide it into two parts; each part has still solidity, extension, figure, mobility; divide it again, and it still retains the same qualities; and will do so still, though you divide it on till the parts become insensible.

Locke.

"Secondly, Secondary qualities, such as colors, smells, tastes, sounds, etc., which, whatever reality we by mistake may attribute to them, are, in truth, nothing in the objects themselves, but powers to produce various sensations in us; and depend on the qualities before mentioned.

"The ideas of primary qualities of bodies are resemblances of them; and their patterns really exist in bodies themselves: but the ideas produced in us by secondary qualities, have no resemblance of them at all: and what is sweet, blue, or warm in the idea, is but the certain bulk, figure, and motion of the insensible parts in the bodies themselves, which we call so."

Reid adopted the distinction of Descartes: he holds that our knowledge of the primary qualities is clear and distinct, whereas our knowledge of the secondary qualities is obscure.[3] "Every man," he says, "capable of reflection, may easily satisfy himself, that he has a perfectly clear and distinct notion of extension, divisibility, figure, and motion. The solidity of a body means no more, but that it excludes other bodies from occupying the same place at the same time. Hardness, softness, and fluidity, are different degrees of cohesion in the parts of a body. It is fluid, when it has no sensible cohesion; soft when the cohesion is weak; and hard when it is strong: of the cause of this cohesion we are ignorant, but the thing itself we understand perfectly, being immediately informed of it by the sense of touch. It is evident, therefore, that of the primary qualities we have a clear and distinct notion; we know what they are,

Reid.

---

1 *Principia*, i. § 69. — Ed.

2 *Essay* ii. 8, 9. The text is an abridgment of Locke, not an exact quotation. — Ed.

3 *Intellectual Powers*, Essay ii. ch. xvii. *Works*, p. 314. — Ed.

though we may be ignorant of the causes." But he did more, he endeavored to show that this difference arises from the circumstance, — that the perception, in the case of the primary qualities, is direct; in the case of the secondary, only relative. This he explains: "I observe, further, that the notion we have of primary qualities is direct and not relative only. A relative notion of a thing is, strictly speaking, no notion of the thing at all, but only of some relation which it bears to something else.

"Thus gravity sometimes signifies the tendency of bodies towards the earth; sometimes it signifies the cause of that tendency; when it means the first, I have a direct and distinct notion of gravity; I see it, and feel it, and know perfectly what it is; but this tendency must have a cause; we give the same name to the cause; and that cause has been an object of thought and of speculation. Now, what notion have we of this cause when we think and reason about it? It is evident we think of it as an unknown cause of a known effect. This is a relative notion, and it must be obscure, because it gives us no conception of what the thing is, but of what relation it bears to something else. Every relation which a thing unknown bears to something that is known, may give a relative notion of it; and there are many objects of thought, and of discourse, of which our faculties can give no better than a relative notion.

"Having premised these things to explain what is meant by a relative notion, it is evident, that our notion of Primary Qualities is not of this kind; we know what they are, and not barely what relation they bear to something else.

"It is otherwise with Secondary Qualities. If you ask me, what is that quality or modification in a rose which I call its smell, I am at a loss what to answer directly. Upon reflection I find, that I have a distinct notion of the sensation which it produces in my mind. But there can be nothing like to this sensation in the rose, because it is insentient. The quality in the rose is something which occasions the sensation in me; but what that something is, I know not. My senses give me no information upon this point. The only notion, therefore, my senses give is this, that smell in the rose is an unknown quality or modification which is the cause or occasion of a sensation which I know well. The relation which this unknown quality bears to the sensation with which nature hath connected it, is all I learn from the sense of smelling; but this is evidently a relative notion. The same reasoning will apply to every secondary quality.

"Thus I think it appears, that there is a real foundation for the distinction of primary from secondary qualities; and that they are distinguished by this, that of the primary we have by our senses a direct and distinct notion; but of the secondary only a relative notion, which must, because it is only relative, be obscure; they are conceived only as the unknown causes or occasions of certain sensations, with which we are well acquainted."

You will observe that the lists of the primary qualities given by Locke and Reid do not coincide. According to Locke, these are Solidity, Extension, Motion, Hardness, Softness, Roughness, Smoothness, and Fluidity.

The list of primary qualities given by Locke, and that of Reid, do not coincide. Stewart.

Mr. Stewart proposes another line of demarcation. "I distinguish," he says, "Extension and Figure by the title of the *Mathematical Affections* of matter; restricting the phrase, *Primary Qualities*, to Hardness and Softness, Roughness and Smoothness, and other properties of the same description. The line which I would draw between *Primary* and *Secondary Qualities* is this, that the former necessarily involve the notion of *Extension*, and consequently of *externality* or *outness;* whereas the latter are only conceived as the unknown causes of known sensations; and *when first apprehended by the mind*, do not imply the existence of anything locally distinct from the subjects of its own consciousness."[1]

All these Primary Qualities, including Mr. Stewart's Mathematical Affections of matter, may easily be reduced to two,—Extension and Solidity. Thus: Figure, is a mere limitation of extension; Hardness, Softness, Fluidity, are only Solidity variously modified, — only its different degrees; while Roughness and Smoothness denote only the sensations connected with certain perceptions of Solidity. On the other hand, in regard to Divisibility (which is proper to Reid), and to Motion, —these can hardly be mere data of sense. Divisibility supposes division, and a body divided supposes memory; for if we did not remember that it had been one, we should not know that it is now two; we could not compare its present with its former state; and it is by this comparison alone that we learn the fact of division. As to Motion, this supposes the exercise of memory, and the notion of time, and, therefore, we do not owe it exclusively to sense. Finally, as to Number, which is peculiar to Locke, it is evident that this, far from being a quality of matter, is only an abstract

The Primary Qualities reducible to two, —Extension and Solidity.

---

1 *Phil. Essays, Works,* vol. v. pp. 116, 117.

notion, — the fabrication of the intellect, and not a datum of sense.[1]

Thus, then, we have reduced all primary qualities to Extension and Solidity, and we are, moreover, it would seem, beginning to see light, inasmuch as the primary qualities are those in which perception is dominant, the secondary those in which sensation prevails. But here we are again thrown back: for extension is only another name for space, and our notion of space is not one which we derive exclusively from sense, — not one which is generalized only from experience; for it is one of our necessary notions, — in fact, a fundamental condition of thought itself. The analysis of Kant, independently of all that has been done by other philosophers, has placed this truth beyond the possibility of doubt, to all those who understand the meaning and conditions of the problem. For us, however, this is not the time to discuss the subject. But, taking it for granted that the notion of space is native or *a priori*, and not adventitious or *a posteriori*, are we not at once thrown back into idealism? For if extension itself be only a necessary mental mode, how can we make it a quality of external objects, known to us by sense; or how can we contrast the outer world, as the extended, with the inner, as the unextended world? To this difficulty, I see only one possible answer. It is this: — It cannot be denied that space, as a necessary notion, is native to the mind; but does it follow, that, because there is an *a priori* space, as a form of thought, we may not also have an empirical knowledge of extension, as an element of existence? The former, indeed, may be only the condition through which the latter is possible. It is true that, if we did not possess the general and necessary notion of space anterior to, or as the condition of, experience, from experience we should never obtain more than a generalized and contingent notion of space. But there seems to me no reason to deny, that because we have the one, we may not also have the other. If this be admitted, the whole difficulty is solved; and we may designate by the name of *extension* our empirical knowledge of space, and reserve the term *space* for space considered as a form or fundamental law of thought.[2] This matter

This reduction involves a difficulty.

What, and how solved.

Space known a priori; Extension a posteriori.

---

1 In this reduction of the primary qualities to Extension and Solidity, the author follows Royer-Collard, whose remarks will be found quoted in *Reid's Works*, p. 844. From the notes appended to that quotation, it will be seen that Sir W. Hamilton's final opinion differs in some respects from that expressed in the present text. — ED.

2 Here, on blank leaf of MS., are jotted the words, "So Causality." [Causality depends, first, on the *a priori* necessity in the mind to think some cause; and, second, on experience, as revealing to us the particular cause of any effect.] — *Oral Interpolation*, but not at this passage. — ED.

will, however, come appropriately to be considered, in treating of the Regulative Faculty.

The following is the result of what I think an accurate analysis would afford, though there are no doubt many difficulties to be explained. — That our knowledge of all the qualities of matter is merely relative. But though the qualities of matter are all known only in relation to our faculties, and the total or absolute cognition in perception is only matter in a certain relation to mind, and mind in a certain relation to matter; still, in different perceptions, one term of the relation may predominate, or the other. Where the objective element predominates, — where matter is known as principal in its relation to mind, and mind only known as subordinate in its correlation to matter, — we have Perception Proper, rising superior to sensation; this is seen in the Primary Qualities. Where, on the contrary, the subjective element predominates, — where mind is known as principal in its relation to matter, and matter is only known as subordinate in its relation to mind, — we have Sensation Proper rising superior to perception; and this is seen in the Secondary Qualities. The adequate illustration of this would, however, require both a longer, and a more abstruse, discussion than we can afford.[1]

General result. — In the Primary Qualities, Perception predominates; in the Secondary, Sensation.

1 Cf. *Reid's Works*, Notes D and D*. — ED.

LECTURE XXV.

THE PRESENTATIVE FACULTY.

I. — PERCEPTION. — OBJECTIONS TO THE DOCTRINE OF NATURAL REALISM.

FROM our previous discussions, you are now, in some measure, prepared for a consideration of the grounds on which philosophers have so generally asserted the scientific necessity of repressing the testimony of consciousness to the fact of our immediate perception of external objects, and of allowing us only a mediate knowledge of the material world: a procedure by which they either admit, or cannot rationally deny, that Consciousness is a mendacious witness; that Philosophy and the Common Sense of mankind are placed in contradiction; nay, that the only legitimate philosophy is an absolute and universal skepticism. That consciousness, in perception, affords us, as I have stated, an assurance of an intuitive cognition of the non-ego, is not only notorious to every one who will interrogate consciousness as to the fact, but is, as I have already shown you, acknowledged not only by cosmothetic idealists, but even by absolute idealists and skeptics. "It seems evident," says Hume, who in this concession must be allowed to express the common acknowledgment of philosophers, "that when men follow this blind and powerful instinct of nature, they always suppose the very images, presented by the senses, to be the external objects, and never entertain any suspicion, that the one are nothing but representations of the other. This very table, which we see white, and which we feel hard, is believed to exist, independent of our perception, and to be something external to our mind, which perceives it. Our presence bestows not being on it: our absence does not annihilate it. It preserves its existence, uniform and entire, independent of the situation of intelligent beings, who perceive or contemplate it. But this universal and primary opinion of all men is soon destroyed by the slightest philosophy, which teaches us that nothing can ever be present to the mind but an image or

Objections to the doctrine of Natural Realism.

The testimony of Consciousness in perception, notorious, and acknowledged by philosophers of all classes.

Hume quoted.

perception, and that the senses are only the inlets, through which these images are received, without being ever able to produce any immediate intercourse between the mind and the object."[1]

In considering this subject, it is manifest that, before rejecting the testimony of consciousness to our immediate knowledge of the non-ego, the philosophers were bound, in the first place, to evince the absolute necessity of their rejection; and, in the second place, in substituting an hypothesis in the room of the rejected fact, they were bound to substitute a legitimate hypothesis, — that is, one which does not violate the laws under which an hypothesis can be rationally proposed. I shall, therefore, divide the discussion into two sections. In the former, I shall state the reasons, as far as I have been able to discover them, on which philosophers have attempted to manifest the impossibility of acquiescing in the testimony of consciousness, and the general belief of mankind; and, at the same time, endeavor to refute these reasons, by showing that they do not establish the necessity required. In the latter, I shall attempt to prove that the hypothesis proposed by the philosophers, in place of the fact of consciousness, does not fulfil the conditions of a legitimate hypothesis, — in fact, violates them almost all.

The discussion divided into two parts.

In the first place, then, in regard to the reasons assigned by philosophers for their refusal of the fact of our immediate perception of external things, — of these I have been able to collect in all five. As they cannot be very briefly stated, I shall not first enumerate them together, and then consider each in detail; but shall consider them one after the other, without any general and preliminary statement.

I. Reasons for rejecting the testimony of Consciousness in perception, detailed and criticized.

The first, and highest, ground on which it may be held, that the object immediately known in perception is a modification of the mind itself, is the following: Perception is a cognition or act of knowledge; a cognition is an immanent act of mind; but to suppose the cognition of anything external to the mind, would be to suppose an act of the mind going out of itself, in other words, a transeunt act; but action supposes existence, and nothing can act where it is not; therefore, to act out of self is to exist out of self, which is absurd.[2]

The first ground of rejection.

1 *Enquiry concerning Human Understanding,* § xii., *Essays,* etc. [*Of the Academical or Skeptical Philosophy, Essays,* p. 367, edit. 1758. *Philosophical Works,* vol. iv. p. 177. — ED.]

2 See Biunde, *Versuch einer systematischen* *Behandlung der empirischen Psychologie,* vol. i. § 31, p. 139. [Biunde refers to Fichte as holding the principle of this argument. — ED.] Cf. Schulze, *Anthropologie,* § 53, p. 107, (edit. 1826.) [Cicero, *Acad. Quæst.,* iv. 24. — ED.]

This argument, though I have never met with it explicitly announced, is still implicitly supposed in the arguments of those philosophers who hold, that the mind cannot be conscious of aught beyond its own modifications. It will not stand examination. It is very true that we can neither prove, nor even conceive, how the ego can be conscious or immediately cognitive of the non-ego; but this, our ignorance, is no sufficient reason on which to deny the possibility of the fact. As a fact, and a primary fact, of consciousness, we must be ignorant of the why and how of its reality, for we have no higher notion through which to comprehend it, and, if it involve no contradiction, we are, philosophically, bound to accept it. But if we examine the argument a little closer, we shall find that it proves too much; for, on the same principle, we should establish the impossibility of any overt act of volition, — nay, even the impossibility of all agency and mutual causation. For if, on the ground that nothing can act out of itself, because nothing exists out of itself, we deny to mind the immediate knowledge of things external; on the same principle, we must deny to mind the power of determining any muscular movement of the body. And if the action of every existence were limited to the sphere of that existence itself, then, no one thing could act upon any other thing, and all action and reäction, in the universe, would be impossible. This is a general absurdity, which follows from the principle in question. But there is a peculiar and proximate absurdity into which this theory runs, in the attempt it makes to escape the inexplicable. It is this: — The cosmothetic idealists, who found their doctrine on the impossibility of mind acting out of itself, in relation to matter, are obliged to admit the still less conceivable possibility of matter acting out of itself, in relation to mind. They deny that mind is immediately conscious of matter; and, to save the phænomenon of perception, they assert that the non-ego, as given in that act, is only an illusive representation of the non-ego, in, and by, the ego. Well, admitting this, and allowing them to belie the testimony of consciousness to the reality of the non-ego as perceived, what do they gain by this? They surrender the simple datum of consciousness, — that the external object is immediately known; and, in lieu of that real object, they substitute a representative object. But still they hold (at least those who do not fly to some hyperphysical hypothesis) that the mind is determined to this

Refuted.

1. Our inability to conceive how the fact of consciousness is possible, no ground for denying its possibility.

2. The reason adduced involves a general absurdity.

3. Involves a special absurdity.

representation by the material reality, to which material reality they must, therefore, accord the very transeunt efficiency which they deny to the immaterial principle. This first and highest ground, therefore, on which it is attempted to establish the necessity of a representative perception, is not only insufficient, but self-contradictory.

The second ground on which it has been attempted to establish

The second ground of rejection.

the necessity of this hypothesis, is one which has been more generally and more openly founded on than the preceding. Mind and matter, it is said, are substances, not only of different, but of the most opposite, natures; separated, as some philosophers express it, by the whole diameter of being: but what immediately knows must be of a nature correspondent, analogous, to that which is known; mind cannot, therefore, be conscious or immediately cognizant of what is so disproportioned to its essence as matter.

This principle is one whose influence is seen pervading the whole

This principle has influenced the whole history of philosophy.

history of philosophy, and the tracing of this influence would form the subject of a curious treatise.[1] To it we principally owe the doctrine of a *representative perception*, in one or other of its forms; and in a higher or lower potence, according as the representative object was held to be, in relation to mind, of a nature either the same or similar. Derivative from the principle in its lower potence or degree (that is, the immediate object being supposed to be only something similar to the mind), we have, among other less celebrated and less definite theories, the *intentional species* of the schoolmen (at least as generally held), and the *ideas* of Malebranche and Berkeley. In its higher potence (that is, where the representative object is supposed to be of a nature not merely similar to, but identical with, mind, though it may be numerically different from individual minds), it affords us, among other modifications, the *gnostic reasons* (λόγοι γνωστικοί) of the Platonists, the *preëxisting species* of Avicenna and other Arabian Aristotelians, the *ideas* of Descartes, Arnauld, Leibnitz, Buffier, and Condillac, the *phœnomena* of Kant, and the *external states* of Dr. Brown. It is doubtful to which head we should refer Locke, and Newton, and Clarke, — nay, whether we should not refer them to the class of those who, like Democritus, Epicurus, and Digby, viewed the representative or immediate object, as a material efflux or propagation from the external reality to the brain.

This principle also indirectly determined many celebrated theo-

1 Cf. *Reid's Works*, p. 300, note, and *Discussions*, p. 61. — ED.

ries in philosophy, as the *hierarchical gradation of souls or sub-stantial faculties*, held by many followers of Aristotle, the ὄχοι or *vehicular media* of the Platonists, the *plastic medium* of Cudworth and Le Clerc, the doctrine of the *community, oneness*, or *identity of the human intellect* in all men, maintained by the Aphrodisian, Themistius, Averroes, Cajetanus, and Zabarella, the *vision of all things in the Deity* of Malebranche, and the Cartesian and Leibnitzian doctrine of *assistance* and *preëstablished harmony*. To the influence of the same principle, through the refusal of the testimony of consciousness to the duality of our knowledge, are also mediately to be traced the unitarian systems of *absolute identity, materialism,* and *idealism*.

But, if no principle was ever more universal in its effects, none was ever more arbitrarily assumed. It not only

But, 1. Is perfectly arbitrary.

can pretend to no necessity; it has absolutely no probability in its favor. Some philosophers, as Anaxagoras, Heraclitus, Alcmæon, have even held that the relation of knowledge supposes, not a similarity or sameness between subject and object, but, in fact, a contrariety or opposition; and Aristotle himself is sometimes in favor of this opinion, though, sometimes, it would appear, in favor of the other.[1] But, however

2. Is unphilosophical.

this may be, each assertion is just as likely, and just as unphilosophical, as its converse. We know, and can know, nothing *a priori* of what is possible or impossible to mind, and it is only by observation and by generalization *a posteriori*, that we can ever hope to attain any insight into the question. But the very first fact of our experience

3. Contradicted by the first fact of our experience.

contradicts the assertion, that mind, as of an opposite nature, can have no immediate cognizance of matter; for the primary datum of consciousness is, that, in perception, we have an intuitive knowledge of the ego and of the non-ego, equally and at once. This second ground, therefore, affords us no stronger necessity than the first, for denying the possibility of the fact of which consciousness assures us.

The third ground on which the representative hypothesis of perception is founded, and that apparently alone

The third ground of rejection.

contemplated by Reid and Stewart, is, that the mind can only know immediately that to which it is immediately present; but as external objects can neither themselves come into the mind, nor the mind go out to them, such presence is impossible; therefore, external objects can only be

---

[1] See above, p. 205, note. — ED.

mediately known, through some representative object, whether that object be a modification of mind, or something in immediate relation to the mind. It was this difficulty of bringing the subject and object into proximate relation, that, in part, determined all the various schemes of a representative perception; but it seems to have been the one which solely determined the peculiar form of that doctrine in the philosophy of Democritus, Epicurus, Digby, and others, under which it is held, that the immediate or internal object is a representative emanation, propagated from the external reality to the sensorium.

Now this objection to the immediate cognition of external objects, has, as far as I know, been redargued in three different ways. In the first place, it has been denied, that the external reality cannot itself come into the mind. In the second, it has been asserted, that a faculty of the mind itself does actually go out to the external reality; and, in the third place, it has been maintained that, though the mind neither goes out, nor the reality comes in, and though subject and object are, therefore, not present to each other, still that the mind, through the agency of God, has an immediate perception of the external object.

Has been redargued in three different ways.

The first mode of obviating the present objection to the possibility of an immediate perception, might be thought too absurd to have been ever attempted. But the observation of Varro,[1] that there is nothing so absurd which has not been asserted by some philosopher, is not destined to be negatived in the present instance. In opposition to Locke's thesis, " that the mind knows not things immediately, but only by the intervention of the ideas it has of them," and in opposition to the whole doctrine of representation, it is maintained, in terms, by Sergeant, that " I know the very thing; therefore, the very thing is in my act of knowledge; but my act of knowledge is in my understanding; therefore, the thing which is in my knowledge, is also in my understanding."[2] We may suspect that this is only a paradoxical way of stating his opinion; but though this author, the earliest and one of the most eloquent of Locke's antagonists, be destitute neither of learning nor of acuteness, I must

The first by Sergeant.

---

1 In a fragment of his satire *Eumenides*, preserved by Nonius Marcellus, *De Proprietate Sermonis*, c. i. n. 275, v. *Infans*: —

" Postremo nemo ægrotus quicquam somniat

Tam infandum quod non aliquis dicat philosophus."

But the words in the text occur more exactly in Cicero; *De Divinatione*, ii. 58: " Sed, nescio quomodo, nihil tam absurde dici potest, quod non dicatur ab aliquo philosophorum."— ED.

2 *Solid Philosophy*, p. 29. [See above, lect. xxiv. p. 331.— ED.]

confess, that Locke and Molyneux cannot be blamed in pronouncing his doctrine unintelligible.

The second mode of obviating the objection, — by allowing to the mind a power of sallying out to the external reality, has higher authority in its favor. That vision is effected by a perceptive emanation from the eye, was held by Empedocles, the Platonists, and Stoics, and was adopted also by Alexander the Aphrodisian, by Euclid, Ptolemy, Galen, and Alchindus.[1] This opinion, as held by these philosophers, was limited; and, though erroneous, is not to be viewed as irrational. But in the hands of Lord Monboddo, it is carried to an absurdity which leaves even Sergeant far behind. "The mind," says the learned author of *Antient Metaphysics*, "is not where the body is, when it perceives what is distant from the body, either in time or place, because nothing can act but when and where it is. Now the mind acts when it perceives. The mind, therefore, of every animal who has memory or imagination, acts, and, by consequence, exists, when and where the body is not; for it perceives objects distant from the body, both in time and place."[2]

The second by Empedocles, the Platonists, etc.

The third mode is apparently that adopted by Reid and Stewart, who hold, that the mind has an immediate knowledge of the external reality, though the subject and object may not be present to each other; and, though this be not explicitly or obtrusively stated, that the mind obtains this immediate knowledge through the agency of God. Dr. Reid's doctrine of perception is thus summed up by Mr. Stewart: "To what then, it may be asked, does this statement amount? Merely to this: that the mind is so formed that certain impressions produced on our organs of sense by external objects, are followed by correspondent sensations and that these sensations, (which have no more resemblance to the qualities of matter than the words of a language have to the things they denote), are followed by a perception of the existence and qualities of the bodies, by which the impressions are made; that all the steps of this process are equally incomprehensible; and that, for anything we can prove to the contrary, the connection between the sensation and the perception, as well as that between the impression and the sensation, may be both arbitrary; that it is therefore by no means impossible, that our sensations may be merely the occasions on which the correspondent perceptions are excited; and that, at any rate, the consideration of these sensations, which are attributes of mind, can throw

The third by Reid and Stewart.

---

[1] See above, lect. xxi. p. 290. — ED.

[2] See *Antient Metaphysics*, vol. ii. p. 306, and above, lect. xxi. p. 291. — ED.

no light on the manner in which we acquire our knowledge of the existence and qualities of body. From this view of the subject it follows, that it is the external objects themselves, and not any species or images of the objects, that the mind perceives; and that, although, by the constitution of our nature, certain sensations are rendered the constant antecedents of our perceptions, yet it is just as difficult to explain how our perceptions are obtained by their means, as it would be upon the supposition that the mind were all at once inspired with them, without any concomitant sensations whatever."[1]

This statement, when illustrated by the doctrine of these philoso-

Their opinion almost identical with the doctrine of Occasional Causes.

phers in regard to the distinctions of Efficient and Physical Causes, might be almost identified with the Cartesian doctrine of Occasional Causes. According to Reid and Stewart,[2] — and the opinion has been more explicitly asserted by the latter, — there is no really efficient cause in nature but one, viz., the Deity. What are called physical causes and effects being antecedents and consequents, but not in virtue of any mutual and necessary dependence; — the only efficient being God, who, on occasion of the antecedent, which is called the physical cause, produces the consequent, which is called the physical effect. So in the case of perception; the cognition of the external object is not, or may not be, a consequence of the immediate and natural relation of that object to the mind, but of the agency of God, who, as it were, reveals the outer existence to our perception. A similar doctrine is held by a great German philosopher, Frederick Henry Jacobi.[3]

To this opinion many objections occur. In the first place, so far is it from being, as Mr. Stewart affirms, a plain

And exposed to many objections.
1. Hypothetical.
2. Mystical.
3. Hyperphysical.

statement of the facts, apart from all hypothesis, it is manifestly hypothetical. In the second place, the hypothesis assumes an occult principle; — it is mystical. In the third place, the hypothesis is hyperphysical, — calling in the proximate assistance of the Deity, while the necessity of such intervention is not established. In the fourth place,

4. Goes to frustrate a doctrine of Intuitive Perception.

it goes even far to frustrate the whole doctrine of the two philosophers in regard to perception, as a doctrine of intuition. For if God has bestowed on me the faculty of immediately perceiving the external

---

1 *Stewart's Works*, vol. ii. pp. 111, 112.

2 Reid, *Intellectual Powers*, Essay ii. c. vi.; *Active Powers*, Essay i. c. v. vi.: Essay iv. c. ii. iii. Stewart, *Elements*, vol. i. c. i. § 2; vol. ii. c. iv. § 1.—ED.

3 *David Hume, über den Glauben*, Werke, ii. p. 165; *Über die Lehre des Spinoza*, Werke, iv. p. 211. Quoted by Sir W. Hamilton, *Reid's Works*, p. 793.—ED.

object, there is no need to suppose the necessity of an immediate intervention of the Deity to make that act effectual; and if, on the contrary, the perception I have of the reality is only excited by the agency of God, then I can hardly be held to know that reality, immediately and in itself, but only mediately, through the notion of it determined in my mind.

Let us try, then, whether it be impossible, not to explain (for that it would be ridiculous to dream of attempting),

The possibility of an immediate perception of external objects intelligible.

but to render intelligible the possibility of an immediate perception of external objects; without assuming any of the three preceding hypotheses, and without postulating aught that can fairly be refused.

Now in the first place, there is no good ground to suppose, that the mind is situate solely in the brain, or ex-

1. No ground to suppose that the mind is situated solely in any one part of the body.

clusively in any one part of the body. On the contrary, the supposition that it is really present wherever we are conscious that it acts, — in a word, the Peripatetic aphorism, the soul is all in the whole and all in every part,[1] — is more philosophical, and, consequently, more probable than any other opinion. It has not been always noticed, even by those who deem themselves the chosen

We materialize mind in attributing to it the relations of matter.

champions of the immateriality of mind, that we materialize mind when we attribute to it the relations of matter. Thus, we cannot attribute a local seat to the soul, without clothing it with the properties of extension and place, and those who suppose this seat to be but a point, only aggravate the difficulty. Admitting the spirituality of mind, all that we know of the relation of soul and body is, that the former is connected with the latter in a way of which we are wholly ignorant; and that it holds relations, different both in degree and kind, with different parts of the organism. We have no right, however, to say that it is limited to any one part of the organism; for even if we admit that the nervous system is the part to which it is proximately united, still the nervous system is itself universally ramified throughout the body; and we have no more right to deny that the mind feels at the finger-points, as consciousness assures us, than to assert that it thinks exclusively in the brain. The sum of our knowledge of the connection of mind and body is, therefore, this, — that the mental modifications are depen-

---

1 *Arist. de Anima* i. 5, 31; 'Εν ἑκατέρῳ τῶν μορίων ἅπαντ' ἐνυπάρχει τὰ μόρια τῆς ψυχῆς. Augustin, *De Trinitate,* vi. 6: " Ideo simplicior est corpore, quia non mole diffunditur per spatium loci, sed in unoquoque corpore et in toto tota est, et in qualibet ejus parte tota est." See above, lect. xx. p. 271, note 11. — ED.

dent on certain corporeal conditions; but of the nature of these
conditions we know nothing. For example, we
know, by experience, that the mind perceives
only through certain organs of sense, and that,
through these different organs, it perceives in a
different manner. But whether the senses be instruments, whether
they be media, or whether they be only partial outlets to the mind
incarcerated in the body, — on all this we can only theorize and conjecture. We have no reason whatever to believe, contrary to the
testimony of consciousness, that there is an action or affection of
the bodily sense previous to the mental perception; or that the
mind only perceives in the head, in consequence of the impression
on the organ. On the other hand, we have no reason whatever to
doubt the report of consciousness, that we actually perceive at the external point of sensation,
and that we perceive the material reality. But
what is meant by perceiving the material reality?

Sum of our knowledge of the connection of mind and body.

What is meant by perceiving the material reality?

In the first place, it does not mean that we perceive the material
reality absolutely and in itself, that is, out of
relation to our organs and faculties; on the
contrary, the total and real object of perception is the external object under relation to our
sense and faculty of cognition. But though thus relative to us,
the object is still no representation, — no modification of the ego.
It is the non-ego, — the non-ego modified, and relative, it may be,
but still the non-ego. I formerly illustrated this to you by a supposition. Suppose that the total object of consciousness in perception is = 12; and suppose that the external reality contributes 6,
the material sense 3, and the mind 3; — this may enable you to
form some rude conjecture of the nature of the object of perception.[1]

The total and real object of Perception, what.

But, in the second place, what is meant by the external object
perceived? Nothing can be conceived more
ridiculous than the opinion of philosophers in
regard to this. For example, it has been curiously held (and Reid is no exception), that in
looking at the sun, moon, or any other object of sight, we are, on
the one doctrine, actually conscious of these distant objects; or,
on the other, that these distant objects are those really represented
in the mind. Nothing can be more absurd: we perceive, through
no sense, aught external but what is in immediate relation and in
immediate contact with its organ; and that is true which Demo-

What is meant by the external object perceived?

1 See above, lect. viii. p. 103. — Ed.

critus of old asserted, that all our senses are only modifications of touch.[1] Through the eye we perceive nothing but the rays of light in relation to, and in contact with, the retina; what we add to this perception must not be taken into account. The same is true of the other senses. Now, what is there

Nothing especially inconceivable in the doctrine of an immediate perception.

monstrous or inconceivable in this doctrine of an immediate perception? The objects are neither carried into the mind, nor the mind made to sally out to them; nor do we require a miracle to justify its possibility. In fact, the consciousness of external objects, on this doctrine, is not more inconceivable than ·the consciousness of species or ideas on the doctrine of the school-men, Malebranche, or Berkeley. In either case, there is a consciousness of the non-ego, and, in either case, the ego and non-ego are in intimate relation. There is, in fact, on this hypothesis, no greater marvel, that the mind should be cognizant of the external reality, than that it should be connected with a body at all. The latter being the case, the former is not even improbable; all inexplicable as both equally remain. "We are unable," says Pascal, "to conceive what is mind; we are unable to conceive what is matter; still less are we able to conceive how these are united; — yet this is our proper nature."[2] So much in refutation of the third ground of difficulty to the doctrine of an immediate perception.

The fourth ground of rejection is that of Hume. It is alleged by him in the sequel of the paragraph of which

The fourth ground of rejection.
Hume quoted.

I have already quoted to you the commencement: "This universal and primary opinion of all men is soon destroyed by the slightest philosophy, which teaches us, that nothing can ever be present to the mind but an image or perception, and that the senses are only the inlets, through which these images are conveyed, without being ever able to produce any immediate intercourse between the mind and the object. The table which we see, seems to diminish, as we remove farther from it: but the real table which exists independent of us suffers no alteration: it was, therefore, nothing but its image, which was present to the mind. These are the obvious dictates of reason; and no man, who reflects, ever doubted that the existences, which we consider, when we say *this house*, and *that tree*, are nothing but perceptions in the mind, and fleeting copies or representations of other existences, which remain uniform and independent."[3]

---

1 See below, lect. xxvii. p. 374. — ED.

2 *Pensées* [partie i. art. vi. 26; vol ii p. 74, edit. Faugère. — ED.]

3 *Enquiry concerning Human Understanding,* sect. xii. [*Of the Academical or Skeptical Philosophy,* p. 367, 368, edit. 1758. — ED.]

This objection to the veracity of consciousness will not occasion us much trouble. Its refutation is, in fact, con-

Proceeds on a mistake of what the object in perception is.

tained in the very statement of the real external object of perception. The whole argument consists in a mistake of what that object is. That a thing, viewed close to the eye, should appear larger and differently figured, than when seen at a distance, and that, at too great a distance, it should even become for us invisible altogether;—this only shows that what changes the real object of sight,—the reflected rays in contact with the eye,—also changes, as it ought to change, our perception of such object. This ground of difficulty could be refuted through the whole senses; but its weight is not sufficient to entitle it to any further consideration.[1]

The fifth ground on which the necessity of substituting a representative for an intuitive perception has been

The fifth ground of rejection.

maintained, is that of Fichte.[2] It asserts that the nature of the ego, as an intelligence endowed with will, makes it absolutely necessary, that, of all external objects of perception, there should be representative modifications in the mind. For as the ego itself is that which wills; therefore, in so far as the will tends toward objects, these must lie within the ego. An external reality cannot lie within the ego; there must, therefore, be supposed, within the mind, a representation of this reality different from the reality itself.

This fifth argument involves sundry vices, and is not of greater value than the four preceding.

Involves sundry vices.

1. Asserts that the objects on which the will is directed must lie within the ego.

In the first place, it proceeds on the assertion, that the objects on which the will is directed, must lie within the willing ego itself. But how is this assertion proved? That the will can only tend toward those things of which the ego has itself a knowledge, is undoubtedly true. But from this it does not follow, that the object to which the knowledge is relative, must, at the same time, be present with it in the ego; but if there be a perceptive cognition, that is, a consciousness of some object external to the ego, this perception is competent to excite, and to direct, the will, notwithstanding that its object lies without the ego. That, therefore, no immediate knowledge of external objects is possible, and that consciousness

---

1 Vide Schulze, *Anthropologie*, ii. 49.

2 See especially his *Grundlage der gesammten Wissenschaftslehre*, §§ 4, 10. *Werke*, i. pp. 134,

313 *et seq.*; and his *Bestimmung des Menschen*. *Werke*, ii. p. 217 *et seq.* — Ed.

is exclusively limited to the ego, is not evinced, by this argument of Fichte, but simply assumed.

In the second place, this argument is faulty, in that it takes no account of the difference between those cogni-

2. Takes no account of the difference between cognitions.

tions which lie at the root of the energies of will, and the other kinds of knowledge. Thus, our will never tends to what is present, — to what we possess, and immediately cognize; but is always directed on the future, and is concerned either with the continuance of those states of the ego, which are already in existence, or with the production of wholly novel states. But the future cannot be intuitively, immediately, perceived, but only represented and mediately conceived. That a mediate·cognition is necessary, as the condition of an act of will, — this does not prove, that every cognition must be mediate.[1]

We have thus found by an examination of the various grounds on which it has been attempted to establish

These grounds of rejection are thus, one and all, incompetent.

the necessity of rejecting the testimony of consciousness to the intuitive perception of the external world, that these grounds are, one and all, incompetent. I shall proceed in my next Lecture to the second section of the discussion, — to consider the nature of the hypothesis of Representation or Cosmothetic Idealism, by which it is proposed to replace the fact of consciousness, and the doctrine of Natural Realism; and shall show you that this hypothesis, though, under various modifications, adopted in almost every system of philosophy, fulfils none of the conditions of a legitimate hypothesis.

---

1 Vide Schulze, *Anthropologie*, ii. p. 52. [Cf. § 53, third edit. — Ed.]

LECTURE XXVI.

THE PRESENTATIVE FACULTY.

I. — PERCEPTION. — THE REPRESENTATIVE HYPOTHESIS.

Recapitulation. No opinion has perhaps been so universally adopted in the various schools of philosophy, and more especially of modern philosophy, as the doctrine of a Representative Perception; and, in our last Lecture, I was engaged in considering the grounds on which this doctrine reposes. The order of the discussion was determined by the order of the subject. It is manifest, that, in rejecting the testimony of consciousness to our immediate knowledge of the non-ego, the philosophers were bound to evince the absolute necessity of their rejection; and, in the second place, in substituting an hypothesis in the room of the rejected fact, they were bound to substitute a legitimate hypothesis, that is, one which does not violate the laws under which an hypothesis can be rationally proposed. I stated, therefore, that I should divide the criticism of their doctrine into two sections: that, in the former, I should state the reasons which have persuaded philosophers of the impossibility of acquiescing in the evidence of consciousness, endeavoring at the same time to show that these reasons afford no warrant to the conclusion which they are supposed even to necessitate; and, in the latter, attempt to prove, that the hypothesis proposed by philosophers in lieu of the fact of consciousness, does not fulfil the conditions of a legitimate hypothesis, and is, therefore, not only unnecessary, but inadmissible. The first of these sections terminated the Lecture. I stated that there are in all five grounds, on which philosophers have deemed themselves compelled to reject the fact of our immediate consciousness of the non-ego in perception, and to place philosophy in contradiction to the common sense of mankind. The grounds I considered in detail, and gave you some of the more manifest reasons which went to prove their insufficiency. This discussion I shall not attempt to recapitulate; and now proceed

II. The nature of the hypothesis of a Representative Perception. It violates all the conditions of a legitimate hypothesis.

46

to the second section of the subject, — to consider the hypothesis of a Representative Perception, by which it is proposed to replace the fact of consciousness which testifies to our immediate perception of the external world. On the *hypothesis*, the doctrine of Cosmothetic Idealism is established: on the *fact*, the doctrine of Natural Dualism.

[1]In the first place, from the grounds on which the cosmothetic idealist would vindicate the necessity of his rejection of the datum of consciousness, the hypothesis itself is unnecessary. The examination of these grounds proves, that the fact of consciousness is not shown to be impossible.

Conditions of a legitimate hypothesis. — First, — That it be necessary. The hypothesis in question unnecessary.

So far, therefore, there is no necessity made out for its rejection. But it is said the fact of consciousness is inexplicable; we cannot understand how the immediate perception of an external object is possible: whereas the hypothesis of representation enables us to comprehend and explain the phænomenon, and is, therefore, if not absolutely necessary, at least entitled to favor and preference. But even on this lower, — this precarious ground, the hypothesis is absolutely unnecessary. That, on the incomprehensibility of the fact of consciousness, it is allowable to displace the fact by an hypothesis, is of all absurdities the greatest. As a fact, — an ultimate fact of consciousness, it must be incomprehensible; and were it comprehensible, that is, did we know it in its causes, — did we know it as contained in some higher notion, — it would not be a primary fact of consciousness, — it would not be an ultimate datum of intelligence. Every *how* (διότι) rests ultimately on a *that* (ὅτι), every demonstration is deduced from something given and indemonstrable; all that is comprehensible hangs from some revealed[2] fact, which we must believe as actual, but cannot construe to the reflective intellect in its possibility. In consciousness, in the original spontaneity of intelligence (νοῦς, *locus principiorum*), are revealed the primordial facts of our intelligent nature.

But the cosmothetic idealist has no right to ask the natural realist for an explanation of the fact of consciousness; supposing even that his own hypothesis were in itself both clear and probable, — supposing that the consciousness of self were intelligible, and the consciousness of the not-self the reverse. For, on this supposition, the intelligible consciousness of self could not be an ultimate fact, but

1 See *Discussions*, p. 63.

2 [This expression is not meant to imply anything hyperphysical. It is used to denote the ultimate and incomprehensible nature of the fact; of the fact which must be believed, though it connot be understood, cannot be explained.] *Discussions*, p. 63, note. — ED.

must be comprehended through a higher cognition, — a higher consciousness, which would again be itself either comprehensible or not. If comprehensible, this would of course require a still higher cognition, and so on till we arrive at some datum of intelligence, which, as highest, we could not understand through a higher; so that, at best, the hypothesis of representation, proposed in place of the fact of consciousness, only removes the difficulty by one or two steps. The end to be gained is thus of no value; and, for this end, as we have seen and shall see, there would be sacrificed the possibility of philosophy as a rational knowledge altogether; and, in the possibility of philosophy, of course, the possibility of the very hypothesis itself.

But is the hypothesis really in itself a whit more intelligible than the fact which it displaces? The reverse

The hypothesis not more intelligible than the fact which it displaces.

is true. What does the hypothesis suppose? It supposes that the mind can represent that of which it knows nothing, — that of which it is ignorant. Is this more comprehensible than the simple fact, that the mind immediately knows what is different from itself, and what is really an affection of the bodily organism? It seems, in truth, not only incomprehensible, but contradictory. The hypothesis of a representative perception thus violates the first condition of a legitimate hypothesis, — it is unnecessary; — nay, not only unnecessary, it cannot do what it professes, — it explains nothing, it renders nothing comprehensible.

The second condition of a legitimate hypothesis is, that it shall not subvert that which it is devised to explain;

Second, — That the hypothesis shall not subvert that which it is devised to explain.

— that it shall not explode the system of which it forms a part. But this, the hypothesis in question does; it annihilates itself in the destruction of the whole edifice of knowledge. Belying the testimony of consciousness to our immediate perception of an outer world, it belies the veracity of consciousness altogether; and the truth of consciousness is the condition of the possibility of all knowledge.

The third condition of a legitimate hypothesis, is, that the fact or facts, in explanation of which it is devised,

Third, — That the fact or facts in explanation of which it is devised, be not hypothetical.

be ascertained really to exist, and be not themselves hypothetical. But so far is the principal fact which the hypothesis of a representative perception is proposed to explain, from being certain, that its reality is even rendered problematical by the proposed explanation itself. The facts which this

hypothesis supposes to be ascertained and established are two —
first, the fact of an external world existing; sec-

ond, the fact of an internal world knowing.
These, the hypothesis take for granted. For it
is asked, How are these connected?—How can
the internal world know the external world
existing? And, in answer to this problem, the
hypothesis of representation is advanced as explaining the mode of
their correlation. This hypothesis denies the immediate connection of the two facts; it denies that the mind, the internal world,
can be immediately cognizant of matter, the external; and between
the two worlds it interpolates a representation which is at once the
object known by mind, and as known, an image vicarious or representative of matter, *ex hypothesi*, in itself unknown.

But mark the vice of the procedure. We can only, 1°, Assert
the existence of an external world, inasmuch

as we know it to exist; and we can only, 2°,
Assert that one thing is representative of another,
inasmuch as the thing represented is known, independently of the
representation. But how does the hypothesis of a representative
perception proceed? It actually converts the fact into an hypothesis; actually converts the hypothesis into a fact. On this theory,
we do not know the existence of an external world, except on the
supposition that that which we do know, truly represents it as
existing. The hypothetical realist cannot, therefore, establish the
fact of the external world, except upon the fact of its representation. This is manifest. We have, therefore, next to ask him, how
he knows the fact, that the external world is actually represented.
A representation supposes something represented, and the representation of the external world supposes the existence of that
world. Now, the hypothetical realist, when asked how he proves
the reality of the outer world, which, *ex hypothesi*, he does not
know, can only say that he infers its existence from the fact of its
representation. But the fact of the representation of an external
world supposes the existence of that world; therefore, he is again
at the point from which he started. He has been arguing in a
circle. There is thus a see-saw between the hypothesis and the
fact; the fact is assumed as an hypothesis; the hypothesis explained as a fact; each is established, each is expounded, by the
other. To account for the possibility of an unknown external
world, the hypothesis of representation is devised; and to account
for the possibility of representation, we imagine the hypothesis
of an external world.

The cosmothetic idealist thus begs the fact which he would explain. And, on the hypothesis of a representative* perception, it is admitted by the philosophers themselves who hold it, that the descent to absolute idealism is a logical precipice, from which they can alone attempt to save themselves by appealing to the natural beliefs, — to the common-sense of mankind, that is to the testimony of that very consciousness to which their own hypothesis gives the lie.

In the fourth place, a legitimate hypothesis must save the phænomena which it is invented to explain, that is, it must account for them adequately and without exclusion, distortion, or mutilation. But the hypothesis of a representative perception proposes to accomplish its end only by first destroying, and then attempting to recreate, the phænomena, for the fact of which it should, as a legitimate hypothesis, only afford a reason. The total, the entire phænomenon to be explained, is the phænomenon given in consciousness of the immediate knowledge by me, or mind, of an existence different from me, or mind.

Fourth, — That it save the phænomena which it is invented to explain.

This phænomenon, however, the hypothesis in question does not preserve entire. On the contrary, it hews it into two; — into the immediate knowledge by me, and into the existence of something different from me; — or more briefly, into the intuition and the existence. It separates, in its explanation, what is given it to explain as united. This procedure is, at best, monstrous; but this is not the worst. The entire phænomenon being cut in two, you will observe how the fragments are treated. The existence of the non-ego, — the one fragment, it admits; its intuition, its immediate cognition by the ego, — the other fragment, it disallows. Now mark what is the character of this proceeding. The former fragment of the phænomenon, — the fragment admitted, to us exists only through the other fragment which is rejected. The existence of an external world is only given us through its intuition, — we only believe it to exist because we believe that we immediately know it to exist, or are conscious of it as existing. The intuition is the *ratio cognoscendi*, and, therefore, to us the *ratio essendi*, of a material universe. Prove to me that I am wrong in regard to my intuition of an outer world, and I will grant at once, that I have no ground for supposing I am right in regard to the existence of that world. To annihilate the intuition is to annihilate what is prior and constitutive in the phænomenon; and to annihilate what is prior and consti-

The hypothesis in question sunders and subverts the phænomenon to be explained.

tutive in the phænomenon, is to annihilate the phænomenon altogether. The existence of a material world is no longer, therefore,
even a truncated, even a fractional, fact of consciousness; for the
fact of the existence of a material world, given in consciousness,
necessarily vanished with the fact of the intuition on which it
rested. The absurdity is about the same as if we should attempt
to explain the existence of color, on an hypothesis which denied
the existence of extension. A representative perception is thus
an hypothetical explanation of a supposititious fact; it creates the
nature it interprets.[1]

In the fifth place, the fact which a legitimate hypothesis explains,
must be within the sphere of experience; but
the fact of an external world, for which the
cosmothetic idealist would account, transcends,
ex hypothesi, all experience, being unknown in
itself, and a mere hyperphysical assumption.

Fifth, — That the fact
to be explained lie
within the sphere of
experience.

In the sixth place, an hypothesis is probable in proportion as it
works simply and naturally; that is, in propor-
tion as it is dependent on no subsidiary hypothesis, — as it involves nothing petitory, occult,
supernatural, as part and parcel of its explanation. In this respect,
the doctrine of a representative perception is not less vicious than
in others; to explain at all, it must not only postulate subsidiary
hypotheses, but subsidiary miracles. The doctrine in question
attempts to explain the knowledge of an unknown world, by the
ratio of a representative perception: but it is impossible by any
conceivable relation, to apply the ratio to the facts. The mental
modification, of which, on the doctrine of representation, we are
exclusively conscious in perception, either represents a real external
world, or it does not. The latter is a confession of absolute idealism; we have, therefore, only to consider the former.

Sixth, — The hypoth-
esis must be single.

The hypothesis of a representative perception supposes, that the
mind does not know the external world, which it represents; for

---

1 [With the hypothetical realist or cosmothetic idealist, it has been a puzzling problem
to resolve how, on their doctrine of a representative perception, the mind can attain the
notion of externality, or outness, far more
be impressed with the invincible belief of the
reality, and known reality, of an external
world. Their attempts at this solution, are
as unsatisfactory as they are operose. On
the doctrine of an intuitive perception, all
this is given in the fact of an immediate
knowledge of the non-ego. To us, therefore,
the problem does not exist; and Mr. Stewart
appears to me to have misunderstood the
conditions of his own doctrine, or rather not
to have formed a very clear conception of
an intuitive perception, when he endeavors
to explain, by inference and hypothesis, a
knowledge and belief in the outness of the
objects of sense, and when he denies the
reality of our sensations at the points where
we are conscious that they are] [See Stewart,
Phil. Essays, Works, v. 101 *et seq.* — Ed.]

this hypothesis is expressly devised only on the supposed impossibility of an immediate knowledge of aught different from, and external to, the mind. The percipient mind must, therefore, be, somehow or other, determined to represent the reality of which it is ignorant. Now, here one of two alternatives is necessary;—either the mind blindly determines itself to this representation, or it is determined to it by some intelligent and knowing cause, different from itself. The former alternative would be preferable, inasmuch as it is the more simple, and assumes nothing hyperphysical, were it not irrational, as wholly incompetent to account for the phænomenon. On this alternative, we should suppose, that the mind represented, and truly represented, that of whose existence and qualities it knew nothing. A great effect is here assumed, absolutely without a cause; for we could as easily conceive the external world springing into existence without a creator, as mind representing that external world to itself, without a knowledge of that which it represented. The manifest absurdity of this first alternative has accordingly constrained the profoundest cosmothetic idealists to call in supernatural aid by embracing the second. To say nothing of less illustrious schemes, the systems of Divine Assistance, of a Preëstablished Harmony, and of the Vision of all things in the Deity, are only so many subsidiary hypotheses;—so many attempts to bridge, by supernatural machinery, the chasm between the representation and the reality, which all human ingenuity had found, by natural means, to be insuperable. The hypothesis of a representative perception thus presupposes a miracle to let it work. Dr. Brown and others, indeed, reject, as unphilosophical, these hyperphysical subsidiaries; but they only saw less clearly the necessity for their admission. The rejection, indeed, is another inconsequence added to their doctrine. It is undoubtedly true that, without necessity, it is unphilosophical to assume a miracle, but it is doubly unphilosophical first to originate this necessity, and then not to submit to it. It is a contemptible philosophy that eschews the *Deus ex machina*, and yet ties the knot which can only be loosed by his interposition. Nor will it here do for the cosmothetic idealist to pretend that the difficulty is of nature's, not of his, creation. In fact, it only arises, because he has closed his eyes upon the light of nature, and refused the guidance of consciousness: but having swamped himself in following the *ignis fatuus* of a theory, he has no right to refer its private absurdities to the imbecility of human reason, or to excuse his

The hypothesis of Representation dependent on subsidiary hypotheses.

self-contracted ignorance by the narrow limits of our present knowledge.[1]

So much for the merits of the hypothesis of a Representative Perception, — an hypothesis which begins by denying the veracity of consciousness, and ends, when carried to its legitimate issue, in absolute idealism, in utter skepticism. This hypothesis has been, and is, one more universally prevalent among philosophers than any other; and I have given to its consideration a larger share of attention than I should otherwise have done, in consequence of its being one great source of the dissensions in philosophy, and of the opprobrium thrown on consciousness as the instrument of philosophical observation, and the standard of philosophical certainty and truth.

With this terminates the most important of the discussions to which the Faculty of Perception gives rise: the other questions are not, however, without interest, though their determination does not affect the vital interests of philosophy. Of these the first that I shall touch upon, is the problem; — Whether, in Perception, do we first obtain a general knowledge of the complex wholes presented to us by sense, and then, by analysis and limited attention, obtain a special knowledge of their several parts; or do we not first obtain a particular knowledge of the smallest parts to which sense is competent, and then, by synthesis, collect them into greater and greater wholes?

Other questions connected with the faculty of External Perception.

1. Whether we first obtain a knowledge of the whole, or of the parts, of the object in Perception.

The second alternative in this question is adopted by Mr. Stewart; it is, indeed, involved in his doctrine in regard to Attention, — in holding that we recollect nothing without attention, that we can attend only to a single object at once, which one object is the very smallest that is discernible through sense. "It is commonly," he says, "understood, I believe, that, in a concert of music, a good ear can attend to the different parts of the music separately, or can attend to them all at once, and feel the full effect of the harmony. If the doctrine, however, which I have endeavored to establish, be admitted, it will follow, that in the latter case the mind is constantly varying its attention from the one part of the music to the other, and that its operations are so rapid, as to give us no perception of an interval of time.

Second alternative adopted by Mr. Stewart.

Stewart quoted.

1 See *Discussions*, pp. 67, 68. — Ed.

"The same doctrine leads to some curious conclusions with respect to vision. Suppose the eye to be fixed in a particular position, and the picture of an object to be painted on the retina. Does the mind perceive the complete figure of the object at once, or is this perception the result of the various perceptions we have of the different points in the outline? With respect to this question, the principles already stated lead me to conclude, that the mind does at one and the same time perceive every point in the outline of the object (provided the whole of it be painted on the retina at the same instant) ; for perception, like consciousness, is an involuntary operation. As no two points, however, of the outline are in the same direction, every point by itself constitutes just as distinct an object of attention to the mind, as if it were separated by an interval of empty space from all the rest. If the doctrine, therefore, formerly stated be just, it is impossible for the mind to attend to more than one of these points at once ; and as the perception of the figure of the object implies a knowledge of the relative situation of the different points with respect to each other, we must conclude, that the perception of figure by the eye, is the result of a number of different acts of attention. These acts of attention, however, are performed with such rapidity, that the effect with respect to us, is the same as if the perception were instantaneous.

　　　*　　　*　　　*　　　*　　　*　　　*　　　*

"It may perhaps be asked, what I mean by a *point* in the outline of a figure, and what it is that constitutes this point *one* object of attention. The answer, I apprehend, is, that this point is the *minimum visibile*. If the point be less, we cannot perceive it ; if it be greater, it is not all seen in one direction.

"If these observations be admitted, it will follow, that, without the faculty of memory, we could have had no perception of visible figure."[1]

The same conclusion is attained, through a somewhat different process, by Mr. James Mill, in his ingenious *Analysis of the Phœnomena of the Human Mind*. This author, following Hartley and Priestley, has pushed the principle of Association to an extreme which refutes its own exaggeration, — analzying not only our belief in the relation of effect and cause into that principle, but even the primary logical laws. According to Mr. Mill, the necessity under which we lie of thinking that one contradictory excludes another, — that a thing cannot at once be and not be, is only the result of asso-

The same view maintained by James Mill.

Elements of the Philosophy of the Human Mind, vol, i. c. ii. *Works*, vol. ii. p. 141—143.

ciation and custom.[1] It is not, therefore, to be marvelled at, that he should account for our knowledge of complex wholes in perception, by the same universal principle; and this he accordingly does.[2]

Mill quoted.

"Where two or more ideas have been often repeated together, and the association has become very strong, they sometimes spring up in such close combination as not to be distinguishable. Some cases of sensation are analogous. For example; when a wheel, on the seven parts of which the seven prismatic colors are respectively painted, is made to revolve rapidly, it appears not of seven colors, but of one uniform color, white By the rapidity of the succession, the several sensations cease to be distinguishable; they run, as it were, together, and a new sensation, compounded of all the seven, but apparently a simple one, is the result. Ideas, also, which have been so often conjoined, that whenever one exists in the mind, the others immediately exist along with it, seem to run into one another, to coalesce, as it were, and out of many to form one idea; which idea, however in reality complex, appears to be no less simple than any one of those of which it is compounded."

＊   ＊   ＊   ＊   ＊   ＊   ＊

[3] "It is to this great law of association that we trace the formation of our ideas of what we call external objects; that is, the ideas of a certain number of sensations, received together so frequently that they coalesce as it were, and are spoken of under the idea of unity. Hence, what we call the idea of a tree, the idea of a stone, the idea of a horse, the idea of a man.

"In using the names, tree, horse, man, the names of what I call objects, I am referring, and can be referring, only to my own sensations; in fact, therefore, only naming a certain number of sensations, regarded as in a particular state of combination; that is, concomitance. Particular sensations of sight, of touch, of the muscles, are the sensations, to the ideas of which, color, extension, roughness, hardness, smoothness, taste, smell, so coalescing as to appear one idea, I give the name, idea of a tree.

＊   ＊   ＊   ＊   ＊   ＊   ＊

"Some ideas are by frequency and strength of association so closely combined, that they cannot be separated. If one exists, the other exists along with it, in spite of whatever effort we make to disjoin them.

"For example; it is not in our power to think of color, without thinking of extension; or of solidity, without figure. We have

---

[1] Chap. iii. p. 75. — ED.   [2] Chap. iii. p. 68. — ED.   [3] Chap. iii. p. 70. — ED.

seen color constantly in combination with extension, — spread, as it were, upon a surface. We have never seen it except in this connection. Color and extension have been invariably conjoined. The idea of color, therefore, uniformly comes into the mind, bringing that of extension along with it; and so close is the association, that it is not in our power to dissolve it. We cannot, if we will, think of color, but in combination with extension. The one idea calls up the other, and retains it, so long as the other is retained.

" This great law of our nature is illustrated in a manner equally striking, by the connection between the ideas of solidity and figure. We never have the sensations from which the idea of solidity is derived, but in conjunction with the sensations whence the idea of figure is derived. If we handle anything solid, it is always either round, square, or of some other form. The ideas correspond with the sensations. If the idea of solidity rises, that of figure rises along with it. The idea of figure which rises, is, of course, more obscure than that of extension; because figures being innumerable, the general idea is exceedingly complex, and hence, of necessity, obscure. But, such as it is, the idea of figure is always present when that of solidity is present; nor can we, by any effort, think of the one without thinking of the other at the same time."

Now, in opposition to this doctrine, nothing appears to me clearer than the first alternative, — and that, in place of ascending upwards from the minimum of perception to its maxima, we descend from masses to details. If the opposite doctrine were correct, what would it involve? It would involve as a primary inference, that, as we know the whole through the parts, we should know the parts better than the whole. Thus, for example, it is supposed that we know the face of a friend, through the multitude of perceptions which we have of the different points of which it is made up; in other words, that we should know the whole countenance less vividly than we know the forehead and eyes, the nose and mouth, etc., and that we should know each of these more feebly than we know the various ultimate points, in fact, unconscious minima, of perceptions, which go to constitute them. According to the doctrine in question, we perceive only one of these ultimate points at the same instant, the others by memory incessantly renewed. Now let us take the face out of perception into memory altogether. Let us close our eyes, and let us represent in imagination the countenance of our friend. This we can do with the utmost vivacity; or, if we see a picture of it, we can determine,

The counter alternative maintained against Stewart and Mill.

The doctrine of these philosophers implies, that we know the parts better than the whole.

with a consciousness of the most perfect accuracy, that the portrait is like or unlike. It cannot, therefore, be denied that we have the fullest knowledge of the face as a whole, — that we are familiar with its expression, with the general result of its parts. On the hypothesis, then, of Stewart and Mill, how accurate should be our knowledge of these parts themselves. But make the experiment.

This supposition shown to be erroneous. You will find that, unless you have analyzed, — unless you have descended from a conspectus of the whole face to a detailed examination of its parts, — with the most vivid impression of the constituted whole, you are almost totally ignorant of the constituent parts. You may probably be unable to say what is the color of the eyes, and if you attempt to delineate the mouth or nose, you will inevitably fail. Or look at the portrait. You may find it unlike, but unless, as I said, you have analyzed the countenance, unless you have looked at it with the analytic scrutiny of a painter's eye, you will assuredly be unable to say in what respect the artist has failed, — you will be unable to specify what constituent he has altered, though you are fully conscious of the fact and effect of the alteration. What we have shown from this example may equally be done from any other, — a house, a tree, a landscape, a concert of music, etc. But it is needless to multiply illustrations. In fact, on the doctrine of these philosophers, if the mind, as they maintain, were unable to comprehend more than one perceptible minimum at a time, the greatest of all inconceivable marvels would be, how it has contrived to realize the knowledge of wholes and masses which it has. Another refutation of this opinion might be drawn from the doctrine of latent modifications, — the obscure perceptions of Leibnitz, — of which we have recently treated. But this argument I think unnecessary.[1]

---

[1] Show this also, 1°, By the millions of acts of attention requisite in each of our perceptions. [Cf. Dr. T. Young's *Lectures on Natural Philosophy*, vol. ii. Ess. v. *The Mechanism of the Eye*, § iii. p. 574, edit. 1807. — ED.] 2°, By imperfection of Touch, which is a synthetic sense, as Sight is analytic. — *Marginal Jotting.*

LECTURE XXVII.

THE PRESENTATIVE FACULTY.

I. PERCEPTION. — GENERAL QUESTIONS IN RELATION TO THE SENSES.

In my last Lecture, I was principally occupied in showing that the hypothesis of a Representative Perception considered in itself, and apart from the grounds on which philosophers have deemed themselves authorized to reject the fact of consciousness, which testifies to our immediate perception of external things, violates, in many various ways, the laws of a legitimate hypothesis; and having, in the previous Lecture, shown you that the grounds on which the possibility of an intuitive cognition of external objects had been superseded, are hollow, I thus, if my reasoning be not erroneous, was warranted in establishing the conclusion that there is nothing against, but everything in favor of, the truth of consciousness, and the doctrine of immediate perception. At the conclusion of the Lecture, I endeavored to prove, in opposition to Mr. Stewart and Mr. Mill, that we are not percipient, at the same instant, only of certain *minima*, our cognitions of which are afterwards, by memory or association, accumulated into masses; but that we are at once and primarily percipient of masses, and only require analysis to obtain a minute and more accurate knowledge of their parts, — that, in short, we can, within certain limits, make a single object out of many. For example, we can extend our attentive perception to a house, and to it as only one object; or we can contemplate its parts, and consider each of these as separate objects.[1]

Resuming consideration of the more important psychological questions that have been agitated concerning the Senses, I proceed to take up those connected with the sense of Touch.

Recapitulation.

---

[1] Sir W. Hamilton here occasionally introduced an account of the mechanism of the organs of Sense; observing the following order, — Sight, Hearing, Taste, Smell, and Touch. This, he remarks, is the reverse of the order of nature, and is adopted by him because under Touch certain questions arise, the discussion of which requires some preliminary knowledge of the nature of the senses. As the Lecture devoted to this subject mainly consists of a series of extracts from Young and Bostock, and is purely physiological, it is here omitted. See Young's *Lectures on Natural Philosophy*, vol. i. pp. 387, 447 *et seq.*; vol. ii. p. 574, (4to edit.) Bostock's *Physiology*, pp. 692 *et seq.*, 723, 729—733. (3d edit.) — ED.

The problems which arise under this sense, may be reduced to two

Two problems under
sense of Touch.

opposite questions. The first asks, May not all the Senses be analyzed into Touch? The second asks, Is not Touch or Feeling, considered as one of the five senses, itself only a bundle of various sense?

In regard to the first of these questions,—it is an opinion as old

1. May all the Sen-
ses be analyzed into
Touch? Democritus.
Aristotle.

at least as Democritus, and one held by many of the ancient physiologists, that the four senses of Sight, Hearing, Taste, and Smell, are only modifications of Touch. This opinion Aristotle records in the fourth chapter of his book *On Sense and the Object of Sense* (*De Sensu et Sensili*), and contents himself with

In what sense the af-
firmative correct.

refuting it by the assertion that its impossibility is manifest. So far, however, from being manifestly impossible, and, therefore, manifestly absurd, it can now easily be shown to be correct, if by touch is understood the contact of the external object of perception with the organ of sense. The opinion of Democritus was revived, in modern

Telesius.

times, by Telesius,[1] an Italian philosopher of the sixteenth century, and who preceded Bacon and Descartes, as a reformer of philosophical methods. I say the opinion of Democritus can easily be shown to be correct; for it is only a con-

The proper object of
Perception.

fusion of ideas, or of words, or of both together, to talk of the perception of a distant object, that is, of an object not in relation to our senses. An external object is only perceived inasmuch as it is in relation to our sense, and it is only in relation to our sense inasmuch as it is present to it. To say, for example, that we perceive by sight the sun or moon, is a false or an elliptical expression. We perceive nothing but certain modifications of light in immediate relation to our organ of vision; and so far from Dr. Reid being philosophically correct, when he says that "when ten men look at the sun or moon, they all see the same individual object," the truth is that each of these persons sees a different object, because each person sees a different complement of rays, in relation to his individual organ.[2] In fact, if we look alternately with

---

1 [*De Rerum Natura*, lib. vii. c. viii.] From this reduction Telesius excepts Hearing. With regard to the senses of Taste, Smell, and Sight, he says:—"Non recte iidem . . . . gustum olfactumque et visum a tactu diversum posuere, qui non tactus modo sunt omnes, sed multo etiam quam qui tactus dicitur exquisitiores. Non scilicet ea modo, quæ universo in corpore percipiuntur, et quæ actilia (ut dictum est) dicuntur, propterea

percipiuntur, quod eorum actio et vis substantiaque spiritum contingit, sed magis quæ in lingua, et multo etiam magis quæ per nares, et quæ in oculis percipiuntur."—*Loc. cit.*—ED.

2 On this point, see Adam Smith, *Essays on Philosophical Subjects — Ancient Logics and Metaphysics*, p. 153. Cf. *Of the External Senses*, p. 289, (edit. 1800.)—ED.

each, we have a different object in our right, and a different object in our left, eye.   It is not by perception, but by a process of reasoning, that we connect the objects of sense with existences beyond the sphere of immediate knowledge.   It is enough that perception affords us the knowledge of the non-ego at the point of sense.   To arrogate to it the power of immediately informing us of external things, which are only the causes of the object we immediately perceive, is either positively erroneous, or a confusion of language, arising from an inadequate discrimination of the phænomena.   Such assumptions tend only to throw discredit on the doctrine of an intuitive perception ; and such assumptions you will find scattered over the works both of Reid and Stewart. I would, therefore, establish as a fundamental position of the doctrine of an immediate perception, the opinion of Democritus, that all our senses are only modifications of touch ; in other words, that the external object of perception is always in contact with the organ of sense.

This determination of the first problem does not interfere with the consideration of the second ; for, in the second, it is only asked, Whether, considering Touch or Feeling as a special sense, there are not comprehended under it varieties of perception and sensation so different, that these varieties ought to be viewed as constituting so many special senses.   This question, I think, ought to be answered in the affirmative ; for, though I hold that the other senses are not to be discriminated from Touch, in so far as Touch signifies merely the contact of the organ and the object of perception, yet, considering Touch as a special sense distinguished from the other four by other and peculiar characters, it may easily, I think, be shown, that if Sight and Hearing, if Smell and Taste, are to be divided from each other and from Touch Proper, under Touch there must, on the same analogy, be distinguished a plurality of special senses.   This problem, like the other, is of ancient date.   It is mooted by Aristotle in the eleventh chapter of the second book *De Anima*, but his opinion is left doubtful.   His followers were consequently left doubtful upon the point.[1]   Among his Greek interpreters, Themistius[2] adopts the opinion, that there is a plurality of senses under

2. Does Touch comprehend a plurality of senses?

Affirmative maintained.

Historical notices of this problem.
Aristotle.
Greek commentators.

1 See Conimbricenses, *In Arist. de Anima*, [lib. ii. c. xi. p. 326. — ED.
2 *In De Anima*, lib. ii. c. xi. fol. 82*a*, (edit. Ald., 1534.) Οὐκ ἔστι μία αἴσθησις ἡ ἁφή· σημεῖον ἄν τις νομίζοι, τὸ μὴ μιᾶς ἐναντιώσεως . . . . κριτικήν, ταύτην τὴν αἴσθησιν· ὥσπερ τὴν ὄψιν λευκοῦ καὶ μέλανος μόνον, καὶ τῶν μεταξύ· καὶ τὴν ἀκοὴν, ὀξέως καὶ βαρέως, καὶ τῶν μεταξύ· καὶ τὴν γεῦσιν πικροῦ καὶ γλυκέος· ἐν δὲ τοῖς, ἁπτοῖς, πολλαί εἰσιν ἐναντιώσεις καὶ πᾶσαι ἔμμεσοι, μεσότητος καθ' ἑκάστην οἰκείας θεωρουμένης· οἷον θερμὸν, ψυχρόν· ξηρὸν, ὑγρόν· σκληρὸν, μαλακόν· βαρὺ κοῦφον· λεῖον, ταχύ.   Cf. Aristotle, texts 106, 107. — ED.

touch. Alexander[1] favors, but not decidedly, the opposite opinion, which was espoused by Simplicius[2] and Philoponus.[3] The doctrine of Themistius was, however, under various modifications, adopted by

Arabian and Latin Schoolmen.

Averroes and Avicenna among the Arabian, and by Apollinaris, Albertus Magnus, Ægidius, Jandunus, Marcellus, and many others among the Latin, schoolmen.[4] These, however, and succeeding philosophers, were not at one in regard to the number of the senses, which they would distinguish. Themistius[5] and Avicenna[6]

Themistius and Avicenna.

allowed as many senses as there were different qualities of tactile feeling; but the number of these they did not specify. Avicenna, however, appears to have distinguished as one sense the feeling of pain from the lesion of a wound, and as another, the feeling of titillation.[7] Others, as Ægidius,[8] gave two senses, one for the hot and cold, an-

Ægidius.
Averroes.
Galen.
Cardan.

other for the dry and moist. Averroes[9] secerns a sense of titillation and a sense of hunger and thirst. Galen[10] also, I should observe, allowed a sense of heat and cold. Among modern philosophers, Cardan[11] distinguishes four senses of touch or feeling; one of the four primary tactile qualities of Aristotle (that is, of cold and hot, and wet and dry); a second, of the light and heavy; a third, of pleasure and pain; and a fourth, of titillation. His antagonist, the elder Scaliger,[12] distinguished as a sixth special sense the sexual appetite, in which he

Bacon, Buffon, Voltaire, Locke.

has been followed by Bacon[13] Voltaire[14] and others. From these historical notices you will see how marvellously incorrect is the statement[15] that Locke was the first philosopher who originated this question, in al-

---

1 *Problemata*, ii. 62 (probably spurious. — ED.

2 *In De Anima*, lib. ii. c. xi. text 106, fol. 44ab (edit. Ald. 1527). — ED.

3 *In De Anima*, lib. ii. c. xi. texts 106, 107. — ED.

4 See Conimbricenses, *In De Anima*, lib. ii. c. xi. p. 826. — ED.

5 See preceding page, note 2, and Conimbricenses, as above, p. 827. — ED.

6 See Conimbricenses, as above, p. 327. — ED.

7 See *ibid.* — ED.

8 See *ibid.* [Cf. De Raei, *Clavis Philosophiæ Naturalis, De Mentis Humanæ Facultatibus*, § 76, p. 366. D'Alembert, *Mélanges*, t. v. p. 115. Cf. Scaliger, *De Subtilitate*, Ex. cix., where he observes that, in paralysis, heat is felt, after the power of apprehending gravity is gone.]

9 See Conimbricenses, *In De Anima*, lib. ii. c. xi. p. 827. — ED.

10 [Leidenfrost, *De Mente Humana*, c. ii. § 4, p. 16.]

11 *De Subtilitate*, lib. xiii. See *Reid's Works*, p. 867. — ED.

12 *De Subtilitate*, Ex. cclxxxvi. § 3. — ED.

13 [*Sylva Sylvarum*, cent. vii. 698. *Works*, edit. Montagu, iv. 361.]

14 See *Reid's Works*, p. 124; and Poor, *Theoria Sensuum*, pars i. § 34, p. 38. Voltaire, *Dict. Philosophique*, art. *Sensation*, reduces this sense to that of Touch. Cf. *Traité de Metaphysique*, ch. iv. *Œuvres Complètes*, tom. vi. p. 651 (edit. 1817). — ED.

15 See *Lectures on Intellectual Philosophy*, by John Young, LL. D., p. 80.

lowing hunger and thirst to be the sensations of a sense different from
tactile feeling. Hutcheson, in his work on the *Passions*,[1] says, "the division of our external senses into five common classes is ridiculously imperfect. Some sensations, such as hunger and thirst, weariness and sickness, can be reduced to none of them; or if they are reduced to feelings, they are perceptions as different from the other ideas of touch, such as cold, heat, hardness, softness, as the ideas of taste or smell. Others have hinted at an external sense different from all of these." What that is, Hutcheson does not mention; and some of our Scotch philosophers have puzzled themselves to conceive the meaning of his allusion. There is no doubt that he referred to the sixth sense of Scaliger.

Adam Smith, in his posthumous *Essays*,[2] observes that hunger and thirst are objects of feeling, not of touch; and that heat and cold are felt not as pressing on the organ, but as in the organ. Kant[3] divides the whole bodily senses into two,—into a Vital Sense (*Sensus Vagus*), and an Organic Sense (*Sensus Fixus*). To the former class belong the sensations of heat and cold, shuddering, quaking, etc. The latter is divided into the five senses, of Touch Proper, Sight, Hearing, Taste, and Smell.

This division has now become general in Germany, the Vital Sense receiving from various authors various synonyms, as *cœnæsthesis, common feeling, vital feeling* and *sense of feeling, sensu latiori*, etc.; and the sensations attributed to it are heat and cold, shuddering, feeling of health, hunger and thirst, visceral sensations, etc. This division is, likewise, adopted by Dr. Brown. He divides our sensations into those which are less definite, and into those which are more definite; and these, his two classes, correspond precisely to the *sensus vagus* and *sensus fixus* of the German philosophers.[4]

The propriety of throwing out of the sense of Touch those sensations which afford us indications only of the subjective condition of the body, in other words, of dividing touch from sensible feeling, is apparent. In the first place, this is manifest on the analogy of the other special senses. These, as we have seen, are divided into two classes, according as perception proper or

Marginal notes:
Hutcheson.
Adam Smith.
Kant.
Kant's division general in Germany.
Brown.
Touch to be divided from sensible feeling.
1. From the analogy of the special senses.

---

1 Sect. i., third edition, p. 3, note.—ED.
2 *Of the External Senses*, p. 262 (ed. 1800).—ED.
3 *Anthropologie*, § 15.—ED. [Previously to Kant, whose *Anthropologie* was first published in 1798, Leidenfrost, in his *De Mente Humana*, (1793), c. ii. § 2, p. 14, distinguished the Vital Sense from the Organic Senses. See also Hübner's *Dissertation* (1794). Cf. Gruithuisen, *Anthropologie*, § 475, p. 364 (edit. 1810).]
4 Lectures xvii. xviii. — ED.

sensation proper predominates ; the sense of Sight and Hearing pertaining to the first, those of Smell and Taste to the second. Here each is decidedly either perceptive or sensitive. But in Touch, under the vulgar attribution of qualities, perception and sensation both find their maximum. At the finger-points, this sense would give us objective knowledge of the outer world, with the least possible alloy of subjective feeling; in hunger and thirst, etc., on the contrary it would afford us a subjective feeling of our own state, with the least possible addition of objective knowledge. On this ground, therefore, we ought to attribute to different senses perceptions and sensations so different in degree.

But, in the second place, it is not merely in the opposite degree of these two counter elements that this distinction is to be founded, but likewise on the different quality of the groups of the perceptions and sensations themselves. There is nothing similar between these different groups, except the negative circumstance that there is no special organ to which positively to refer them ; and, therefore, they are exclusively slumped together under that sense which is not obtrusively marked out and isolated by the mechanism of a peculiar instrument.

2. From the different quality of the perceptions and sensations themselves.

Limiting, therefore, the special sense of Touch to that of objective information, it is sufficient to say that this sense has its seat at the extremity of the nerves which terminate in the skin; its principal organs are the finger-points, the toes, the lips, and the tongue. Of these, the first is the most perfect. At the tips of the fingers, a tender skin covers the nervous papillæ, and here the nail serves not only as a protecting shield to the organ, but, likewise, by affording an opposition to the body which makes an impression on the finger-ends, it renders more distinct our perception of the nature of its surface. Through the great mobility of the fingers, of the wrist, and of the shoulder-joint, we are able with one, and still more effectually, with both hands, to manipulate an object on all sides, and thereby to attain a knowledge of its figure. We likewise owe to the sense of Touch a perception of those conformations of a body, according to which we call it rough or smooth, hard or soft, sharp or blunt. The repose or motion of a body is also perceived through the touch.

Special Sense of Touch,—its sphere and organic seat.

To obviate misunderstanding, I should, however, notice that the proper organ of Touch — the nervous papillæ — requires as the condition of its exercise, the movement of the voluntary muscles. This condition however, ought not to be viewed as a part of the organ itself. This being understood, the perception of the weight of a body will not fall under this sense, as the nerves lying under the epidermis or scurf skin have little or no share in this knowledge. We owe it almost exclusively to the consciousness we have of the exertion of the muscles, requisite to lift with the hand a heavy body from the ground, or when it is laid on the shoulders or head, to keep our own body erect, and to carry the burthen from one place to another.

Proper organ of Touch requires, as condition of its exercise, the movement of the voluntary muscles.

I next proceed to consider two counter-questions, which are still agitated by philosophers. The first is, — Does Sight afford us an original knowledge of extension, or do we not owe this exclusively to Touch? The second is, — Does Touch afford us an original knowledge of extension, or do we not owe this exclusively to Sight?

Two counter questions regarding sphere of Sight.

Both questions are still undetermined; and consequently, the vulgar belief is also unestablished, that we obtain a knowledge of extension originally both from sight and touch.

I commence, then, with the first, — Does Vision afford us a primary knowledge of extension, or do we not owe this knowledge exclusively to Touch? But, before entering on its discussion, it is proper to state to you, by preamble, what kind of extension it is that those would vindicate to sight, who answer this question in the affirmative. The whole primary objects of sight, then, are colors, and extensions, and forms or figures of extension. And here you will observe, it is not all kind of extension and form that is attributed to sight. It is not figured extension in all the three dimensions, but only extension as involved in plane figures; that is, only length and breadth.

1. Does Vision afford us a primary knowledge of extension? or do we not owe this exclusively to Touch?

It has generally been admitted by philosophers, after Aristotle, that color is the proper object of sight, and that extension and figure, common to sight and touch, are only accidentally its objects, because supposed in the perception of color.

Color the proper object of Sight. This generally admitted.

The first philosopher, with whom I am acquainted, who doubted or denied that vision is conversant with extension, was Berkeley; but the clear expression of his opinion is contained in his *Defence of the Theory of Vision*, an extremely rare tract, which has escaped the knowledge of all his editors and biographers, and is consequently not to be found in any of the editions of his collected works. It was almost certainly, therefore, wholly unknown to Condillac, who is the next philoso-

Berkeley the first to deny that extension object of Sight.

Condillac.

pher who maintained the same opinion. This, however, he did not do either very explicitly or without change; for the new doctrine which he hazards in his earlier work, in his later he again tacitly replaces by the old.[1] After its surrender by Condillac, the opinion was, however, supported, as I find, by Laboulinière.[2] Mr. Stewart maintains that extension is not an object of sight. "I formerly," he says, "had occasion to mention several instances of very intimate associations formed between two ideas which have no necessary connection with each other. One of the most remarkable is, that which exists in every person's mind between the notions of *color* and *extension*. The former of these words expresses (at least in the sense in which we commonly employ it) a sensation in the mind, the latter denotes a quality of an external object; so that there is, in fact, no more connection between the two notions than between those of pain and of solidity; and yet in consequence of our always perceiving extension at the same time at which the sensation of color is excited in the mind, we find it impossible to think of that sensation without conceiving extension along with it."[3] But before and after Stewart, a doctrine, virtually the same, is maintained by the Hartleian school; who assert, as a consequence of their universal principle of association, that the perception of color suggests the notion of extension.[4]

Laboulinière.
Stewart.

Hartleian School.

Then comes Dr. Brown, who, in his *Lectures*, after having repeatedly asserted, that it is, and always has been, the universal opinion of philosophers, that the superficial extension of length and breadth becomes known to us by sight originally, proceeds, as he says, for the first time, to controvert this opinion;[5] though it is wholly impossible that he could

Brown.

---

1 The order of Condillac's opinions is the reverse of that stated in the text. In his earliest work, the *Origine des Connoissances Humaines*, part i. sect. vi., he combats Berkeley's theory of vision, and maintains that extension exterior to the eye is discernible by sight. Subsequently, in the *Traité des Sensations*, part i. ch. xi., part ii. ch. iv. v., he asserts that the eye is incapable of perceiving extension beyond itself, and that this idea is originally due solely to the sense of touch. This opinion he again repeats in *l'Art de Penser*, part i. ch. xi. But neither Condillac nor Berkeley goes so far as to say that color, regarded as an affection of the visual organism, is apprehended as absolutely unextended, as a mathematical point. Nor is this the question in dispute. But granting, as Condillac in his later view expressly asserts, that color, as a visual sensation, necessarily occupies space, do we, by means of that sensation, acquire also the proper idea of extension, as composed of parts exterior to each other? In other words, does the sensation of different colors, which is necessary to the distinction of parts at all, necessarily suggest different and contiguous localities? This question is explicitly answered in the negative by Condillac, and in the affirmative by Sir W. Hamilton. Cf. *The Theory of Vision vindicated and explained.* London, 1733. See especially, §§ 41, 42, 44, 45, 46. — Ed.

2 See *Reid's Works*, p. 868. — Ed.

3 *Elements of the Philosophy of the Human Mind*, vol. i. chap. v. part ii. § 1. *Works*, vol. ii. p. 306. [Cf. *Ibid.*, note P. — Ed.]

4 See Priestley, *Hartley's Theory*, prop. 20. James Mill, *Analysis of Human Mind*, vol. i. p. 73. — Ed.

5 Lecture xxviii. — Ed.

have been ignorant that the same had been done, at least by Condillac and Stewart. Brown himself, however, was to be treated somewhat in the fashion in which he treats his predecessors. Some twenty years ago, there were published the *Lectures on Intellectual Philosophy*, by the late John Young, LL. D.,

John Young.

Professor of Philosophy in Belfast College; a work which certainly shows considerable shrewdness and ingenuity. This unfortunate speculator seems, however, to have been fated, in almost every instance, to be anticipated by Brown; and, as far as I have looked into these Lectures, I have been amused with the never-failing preamble, — of the astonishment, the satisfaction, and so forth, which the author expresses on finding, on the publication of Brown's *Lectures*, that the opinions which he himself, as he says, had always held and taught, were those also which had obtained the countenance of so distinguished a philosopher. The coincidence is, however, too systematic and precise to be the effect of accident; and the identity of opinion between the two doctors can only (plagiarism apart), be explained by borrowing from the hypothesis of a Preëstablished Harmony between their minds.[1] Of course, they are both at one on the problem under consideration.[2]

But to return to Brown, by whom the argument against the common doctrine is most fully stated. He

Brown quoted.

says:

"The universal opinion of philosophers is, that it is not color merely which it (the simple original sensation of vision) involves, but extension also, — that there is a visible figure, as well as a tangible figure, — and that the visible figure involves, in our instant original perception, superficial length and breadth, as the tangible figure, which we learn to see, involves length, breadth, and thickness.

"That it is impossible for us, at present, to separate, in the sensation of vision, the color from the extension, I admit; though not more completely impossible, than it is for us to look on the thousand feet of a meadow, and to perceive only the small inch of greenness on our retina; and the one impossibility, as much as the other, I conceive to arise only from intimate association, subsequent to the original sensations of sight. Nor do I deny, that a certain part of the retina — which, being limited, must therefore have figure — is affected by the rays of light that fall on it, as a certain breadth of nervous expanse is affected in all the other organs. I

---

1 I now find, and have elsewhere stated, that the similarity between these philosophers arises from their borrowing, I may say stealing, from the same source, — De Tracy. See *Dissertations on Reid*, note D, p. 868.

2 See Young, *Lectures on Intellectual Philosophy*, p. 116.

contend only, that the perception of this limited figure of the portion of the retina affected, does not enter into the sensation itself, more than, in our sensations of any other species, there is a perception of the nervous breadth affected.

"The immediate perception of visible figure has been assumed as indisputable, rather than attempted to be proved, — as before the time of Berkeley, the immediate visual perception of distance, and of the three dimensions of matter, was supposed, in like manner, to be without any need of proof; — and it is, therefore, impossible to refer to arguments on the subject. I presume, however, that the reasons which have led to this belief, of the immediate perception of a figure termed visible, as distinguished from that tangible figure, which we learn to see, are the following two, — the only reasons which I can even imagine, — that it is absolutely impossible, in our present sensations of sight, to separate color from extension, — and that there are, in fact, a certain length and breadth of the retina, on which the light falls."[1]

He then goes on to argue, at a far greater length than can be quoted, that the mere circumstance of a certain definite space, viz., the extended retina, being affected by certain sensations, does not necessarily involve the notion of extension. Indeed, in all those cases in which it is supposed, that a certain diffusion of sensations excites the notion of extension, it seems to be taken for granted that the being knows already, that he has an extended body, over which these sensations are thus diffused. Nothing but the sense of touch, however, and nothing but those kinds of touch which imply the idea of continued resistance, can give us any notion of body at all. All mental affections which are regarded merely as feelings of the mind, and which do not give us a conception of their external causes, can never be known to arise from anything which is extended or solid. So far, however, is the mere sensation of color from being able to produce this, that touch itself, as felt in many of its modifications, could give us no idea of it. That the sensation of color is quite unfit to give us any idea of extension, merely by its being diffused over a certain expanse of the retina, seems to be corroborated by what we experience in the other senses, even after we are perfectly acquainted with the notion of extension. In hearing, for instance, a certain quantity of the tympanum of the ear must be affected by the pulsations of the air; yet it gives us no idea of the dimensions of the part affected. The same may, in general, be said of taste and smell.

Summary of Brown's argument.

---

[1] Lect. xxix. p. 185 (edit. 1830). — ED.

Now, in all their elaborate argumentation on this subject, these philosophers seem never yet to have seen the

The perception of extension necessarily given in the perception of colors.

real difficulty of their doctrine. It can easily be shown that the perception of color involves the perception of extension. It is admitted that we have by sight a perception of colors, consequently, a perception of the difference of colors. But a perception of the distinction of colors necessarily involves the perception of a discriminating line; for if one color be laid beside or upon another, we only distinguish them as different by perceiving that they limit each other, which limitation necessarily affords a breadthless line, —a line of demarcation. One color laid upon another, in fact, gives a line returning upon itself, that is, a figure. But a line and a figure are modifications of extension. The perception of extension, therefore, is necessarily given in the perception of colors.

LECTURE XXVIII.

THE PRESENTATIVE FACULTY.

I. PERCEPTION. — RELATIONS OF SIGHT AND TOUCH TO EXTENSION.

Recapitulation. In my last Lecture, after showing you that the vulgar distribution of the Senses into five, stands in need of correction, and stating what that correction is, I proceeded to the consideration of some of the more important philosophical problems, which arise out of the relation of the senses to the elementary objects of Perception.

I then stated to you two counter-problems in relation to the genealogy of our empirical knowledge of extension; and as, on the one hand, some philosophers maintain that we do not perceive extension by the eye, but obtain this notion through touch, so, on the other, there are philosophers who hold that we do not perceive extension through the touch, but exclusively by the eye. The consideration of these counter-questions will, it is evident, involve a consideration of the common doctrine intermediate between these extreme opinions, — that we derive our knowledge of extension from both senses. I keep aloof from this discussion the opinion, that space, under which extension is included, is not an empirical or adventitious notion at all, but a native form of thought; for admitting this, still if space be also a necessary form of the external world, we shall also have an empirical perception of it by our senses, and the question, therefore, equally remains, — Through what sense, or senses, have we this perception?

In relation to the first problem, I stated that the position which denies to visual perception all cognizance of extension, was maintained by Condillac, by Laboulinière, by Stewart, by the followers of Hartley (Priestley, Belsham, Mill, etc.), and by Brown, — to say nothing of several recent authors in this country, and in America. I do not think it necessary to state to you the long process of reasoning on which, especially by Brown, this paradox has been grounded. It is sufficient to say, that there is no reason whatsoever adduced in its support, which carries with it the smallest weight. The whole argumentation in reply to the objections supposed by its defenders, is in reply to objections which no one, I conceive, who understood his case, would ever dream of advancing; while the only objection which it was incumbent on the advocates of the paradox to have answered, is passed over in total silence.

This objection is stated in three words. All parties are, of course, at one in regard to the fact that we see color. Those who hold that we see extension, admit that we see it only as colored; and those who deny us any vision of extension, make color the exclusive object of sight. In regard to this first position, all are, therefore, agreed. Nor are they less harmonious in reference to the second; — that the power of perceiving color involves the power of perceiving the differences of colors. By sight we, therefore, perceive color, and discriminate one color, that is, one colored body, — one sensation of color, from another. This is admitted. A third position will also be denied by none, that the colors discriminated in vision, are, or may be, placed side by side in immediate juxtaposition; or, one may limit another by being superinduced partially over it. A fourth position is equally indisputable, — that the contrasted colors, thus bounding each other, will form by their meeting a visible line, and that, if the superinduced color be surrounded by the other, this line will return upon itself, and thus constitute the outline of a visible figure.

Proof that Sight is cognizant of extension.

These four positions command a peremptory assent; they are all self-evident. But their admission at once explodes the paradox under discussion. And thus: A line is extension in one dimension, — length; a figure is extension in two, — length and breadth. Therefore, the vision of a line is a vision of extension in length; the vision of a figure, the vision of extension in length and breadth. This is an immediate demonstration of the impossibility of the opinion in question; and it is curious that the ingenuity which suggested to its supporters the petty and recondite objections, they have so operosely combated, should not have shown them this gigantic difficulty, which lay obtrusively before them.

So far, in fact, is the doctrine which divorces the perceptions of color and extension from being true, that we cannot even represent extension to the mind except as colored. When we come to the consideration of the Representative Faculty, — Imagination, — I shall endeavor to show you (what has not been observed by psychologists), that in the repre-

Extension cannot be represented to the mind except as colored.

sentation, — in the imagination, of sensible objects, we always

represent them in the organ of Sense through which we originally perceived them. Thus, we cannot imagine any particular odor but in the nose; nor any sound but in the ear; nor any taste but in the mouth; and if we would represent any pain we have ever·felt, this can only be done through the local nerves. In like manner, when we imagine any modification of light we do so in the eye; and it is a curious confirmation of this, as is well known to physiologists, that when not only the external apparatus of the eye, which is a mere mechanical instrument, but the real organ of sight, — the optic nerves and their thalami, have become diseased, the patient loses, in proportion to the extent of the morbid affection, either wholly or in part, the faculty of recalling visible phænomena to his mind. I

mention this at present in order to show, that Vision is not only a sense competent to the perception of extension, but the sense κατ’ ἐξοχήν, if not exclusively, so competent, — and this in the following manner: You either now know, or will hereafter learn, that no notion, whether native and general, or adventitious and generalized, can be represented in imagination, except in a concrete or singular example. For instance, you cannot imagine a triangle which is not either an equilateral, or an isosceles, or a scalene, — in short, some individual form of a triangle; nay, more, you cannot imagine it, except either large or small, on paper, or on a board, of wood or of iron, white or black or green; in short, except under all the special determinations which give it, in thought, as in existence, singularity or individuality. The same happens, too, with extension. Space I admit to be a native form of thought, — not an adventitious notion. We cannot but think it. Yet I cannot actually represent space in imagination, stript of all individualizing attributes. In this act, I can easily annihilate all corporeal existence, — I can imagine empty space. But there are two attributes of which I cannot divest it, that is, shape and color. This may sound almost ridiculous at first statement, but if you attend to the phænomenon, you will soon be satisfied of its truth. And first as to shape.

Your minds are not infinite, and cannot, therefore, positively conceive infinite space. Infinite space is only conceived negatively, — only by conceiving it inconceivable; in other words, it cannot be conceived at all. But if we do our utmost to realize this notion of infinite extension by a positive act of imagination, how do we proceed? Why, we think out from a centre, and endeavor to carry the circumference of the sphere to infinity. But by no one effort of imagination can we accomplish this; and as we cannot do it at once by one infinite act, it would require an eternity of successive finite efforts, — an endless series of imaginings beyond imaginings, to equalize the thought with its object. The very attempt is contradictory. But when we leave off, has the imagined space a shape? It has: for it is finite; and a finite, that is, a bounded, space, constitutes a figure. What, then, is this figure? It is spherical, — necessarily spherical; for as the effort of imagining space is an effort outwards from a centre, the space represented in imagination is necessarily circular. If there be no shape, there has been no positive imagination; and for any other shape than the orbicular, no reason can be assigned. Such is the figure of space in a free act of phantasy.

This, however, will be admitted without scruple; for if real space, as it is well described by St. Augustin, be a sphere whose centre is everywhere, and whose circumference is nowhere,[1] imagined space may be allowed to be a sphere whose circumference is represented at any distance from its centre. But will its color be as easily allowed? In explanation of this, you will observe

Nor without color.

that under color I of course include black as well as white; the transparent as well as the opaque, — in short, any modification of light or darkness. This being understood, I maintain that it is impossible to imagine figure, extension, space, except as colored in some determinate mode. You may represent it under any, but you must represent it under some, modification of light, — color. Make the experiment, and you will find I am correct.

But I anticipate an objection. The non-percep-

Objection obviated.

tion of color or the inability of discriminating colors, is a case of not unfrequent occurrence, though the subjects of this deficiency are, at the same time, not otherwise defective in

---

1 The editors have not been able to discover this passage in St. Augustin. As quoted in the text, with reference to space, it closely resembles the words of Pascal, *Pensées*, part i art. iv. (vol. ii. p. 64, edit. Faugère): "Tout ce monde visible n'est qu'un trait imperceptible dans l'ample sien de la nature. Nulle idée n'en approche. Nous avons beau enfler nos conceptions audelà des espaces imaginables nous n'enfantons que des atomes, au prix de la réalité des choses. C'est une sphère infinie, dont le centre est partout, la circonférence nulle part." But the expression is more usually cited as a definition of the Deity. In this relation it has been attributed to the mythical Hermes Trismegistus (see Alex. Ales., *Summa Theol.* part i. qu. vii. memb. 1), and to Empedocles (see Vincentius Bellovacensis, *Speculum Historiale*, lib. ii. c. 1; *Speculum Naturale*, lib. i. c. 4). It was a favorite expression with the mystics of the middle ages. See Müller, *Christian Doctrine of Sin*, vol. ii. p. 134 (Eng. transl.). Some interesting historical notices of this expression will be found in a learned note in M. Havet's edition of Pascal's *Pensées*, p. 3. — Eᴅ.

vision. In cases of this description, there is, however, necessarily a discrimination of light and shade, and the colors that to us appear in all "the sevenfold radiance of effulgent light," to them appear only as different gradations of clare-obscure. Were this not the case, there could be no vision. Such persons, therefore, have still two great contrasts of color, — black and white, and an indefinite number of intermediate gradations, in which to represent space to their imaginations. Nor is there any difficulty in the case of the blind, the absolutely blind, — the blind from birth. Blindness is the non-perception of color; the non-perception of color is simple darkness. The space, therefore, represented by the blind, if represented at all, will be represented black. Some modification of ideal light or darkness is thus the condition of the imagination of space. This of itself powerfully supports the doctrine, that vision is conversant with extension as its object. But if the opinion I have stated be correct, that an act of imagination is only realized through some organ of sense, the impossibility of representing space out of all relation to light and color at once establishes the eye as the appropriate sense of extension and figure.

In corroboration of the general view I have taken of the relation of Sight to extension, I may translate to you a passage by a distinguished mathematician and philosopher, who, in writing it, probably had in his eye the paradoxical speculation of Condillac. "It is certain," says D'Alembert,[1] "that sight alone, and independently of touch, affords us the idea of extension; for extension is the necessary object of vision, and we should see nothing if we did not see it extended. I even believe that sight must give us the notion of extension more readily than touch, because sight makes us remark more promptly and perfectly than touch, that contiguity, and, at the same time, that distinction of parts in which extension consists. Moreover, vision alone gives us the idea of the color of objects. Let us suppose now parts of space differently colored, and presented to our eyes; the difference of colors will necessarily cause us to observe the boundaries or limits which separate two neighboring colors, and, consequently, will give us an idea of figure; for we conceive a figure when we conceive a limitation or boundary on all sides."

D'Alembert quoted in support of the view now given of the relation of Sight to extension.

I am confident, therefore, that we may safely establish the conclusion, that Sight is a sense principally conversant with extension; whether it be the only sense thus conversant, remains to be considered.

---

1 *Mélanges*, t. v. p. 109. — ED.

I proceed, therefore, to the second of the counter-problems, — to inquire whether Sight be exclusively the sense

2. Does Touch afford us an original knowledge of extension, or do we owe this exclusively to Sight?

which affords us a knowledge of extension, or whether it does this only conjunctly with Touch. As some philosophers have denied to vision all perception of extension and figure, and given this solely to touch, so others have equally refused this perception to touch, and accorded it exclusively to vision.

This doctrine is maintained among others by Platner, — a man no less celebrated as an acute philosopher, than

The affirmative of the latter question maintained by Platner.

as a learned physician, and an elegant scholar. I shall endeavor to render his philosophical German into intelligible English, and translate some of the preliminary sentences with which he introduces a curious observation made by him on a blind subject.

Platner quoted.

"It is very true, as my acute antagonist observes, that the gloomy extension which imagination presents to us as an actual object, is by no means the pure a priori representation of space. It is very true, that this is only an empirical or adventitious image, which itself supposes the pure or a priori notion of space (or of extension), in other words, the necessity to think everything as extended. But I did not wish to explain the origin of this mental condition or form of thought objectively, through the sense of sight, but only to say this much: — that empirical space, empirical extension, is dependent on the sense of sight, — that, allowing space or extension, as a form of thought, to be in us, were there even nothing correspondent to it out of us, still the unknown external things must operate upon us, and, in fact, through the sense of sight, do operate upon us, if this unconscious form is to be brought into consciousness."

And after some other observations he goes on: "In regard to the visionless representation of space or extension, — the attentive observation of a person born blind, which I formerly instituted, in the year 1785, and, again, in relation to the point in question, have continued for three whole weeks, — this observation, I say, has convinced me, that the sense of touch, by itself, is altogether incompetent to afford us the representation of extension and space, and is not even cognizant of local exteriority (oertliches Auseinanderseyn), in a word, that a man deprived of sight has absolutely no perception of an outer world, beyond the existence of something effective, different from his own feeling of passivity, and in general only of the numerical diversity, — shall I say of impressions, or of things? In fact, to those born blind, time serves instead of space. Vicinity and distance means in their mouths nothing more than the shorter or longer time, the smaller or greater number of feelings, which they find necessary to attain from some one feeling to some other. That a person blind from birth employs the language of vision, — that may occasion considerable error, and did, indeed, at the commencement of my observations, lead me wrong; but, in point of fact, he knows nothing of things as existing out of each other; and (this in particular I have very clearly remarked), if objects, and the parts of his body touched by them, did not make different kinds of impression on his nerves of sensation, he would take everything external for one and the same. In his own body he absolutely did not discriminate head and foot at all by their distance, but merely by the difference of the feelings (and his perception of such difference was incredibly fine), which he experienced from the one and from the other; and, moreover, through time. In like manner, in external bodies, he distinguished their figure merely by the varieties of impressed feelings; inasmuch, for example, as the cube, by its angles, affected his feeling differently from the sphere. No one can conceive how deceptive is the use of language accommodated to vision. When my acute antagonist appeals to Cheselden's case, which proves directly the reverse of what it is adduced to refute, he does not consider that the first visual impressions which one born blind receives after couching, do not constitute vision. For the very reason, that space and extension are empirically only possible through a perception of sight, — for that very reason, must such a patient, after his eyes are freed from the cataract, first learn to live in space; if he could do this previously, then would not the distant seem to him near, — the separate would not appear to him as one. These are the grounds which make it impossible for me to believe empirical space in a blind person; and from these I infer, that this form of sensibility, as Mr. Kant calls it, and which, in a certain signification, may very properly be styled a pure representation, cannot come into consciousness otherwise than through the medium of our visual perception; without, however, denying that it is something merely subjective, or affirming that sight affords anything similar to this kind of representation. The example of blind geometers would likewise argue nothing against me, even if the geometers had been born blind; and this they were not, if, even in their early infancy, they had seen a single extended object."[1]

To what Platner has here stated I would add, from personal

---

[1] *Philosophische Aphorismen*, vol. i. § 765, p. 439 *et seq*, edit 1793. — ED.

experiment, and observation upon others, that if any one who is not
Phænomena that fa-
vor Platner's doctrine. blind will go into a room of an unusual shape, wholly unknown to him, and into which no ray of light is allowed to penetrate, he may grope about for hours, — he may touch and manipulate every side and corner of it; still, notwithstanding every endeavor, — notwithstanding all the previous subsidiary notions he brings to the task, he will be unable to form any correct idea of the room. In like manner, a blind-folded person will make the most curious mistakes in regard to the figure of objects presented to him, if these are of any considerable circumference. But if the sense of touch in such favorable circumstances can effect so little, how much less could it afford us any knowledge of forms, if the assistance which it here brings with it from our visual conceptions, were wholly wanting?

This view is, I think, strongly confirmed by the famous case of a
Supported also by
Cheselden's case of
couching. young gentleman, blind from birth, couched by Cheselden; — a case remarkable for being perhaps, of those cured, that in which the cataract was most perfect (it only allowed of a distinction of light and darkness); and, at the same time, in which the phænomena have been most distinctly described. In this latter respect, it is, however, very deficient; and it is saying but little in favor of the philosophical acumen of medical men, that the narrative of this case, with all its faults, is, to the present moment, the one most to be relied on.[1]

Now I contend (though I am aware I have high authority against me), that if a blind man had been able to form a conception of a square or globe by mere touch, he would, on first perceiving them by sight, be able to discriminate them from each other;[2] for this supposes only that he had acquired the primary notions of a straight and of a curved line. Again, if touch afforded us the notion of space or extension in general, the patient, on obtaining sight, would certainly be able to conceive the possibility of space or extension beyond the actual boundary of his vision. But of both of these Cheselden's patient was found incapable. As it is a celebrated case, I shall quote to you a few passages in illustration: you will find it at large in the *Philosophical Transactions* for the year 1728.

"Though we say of this gentleman, that he was blind," observes Mr. Cheselden, "as we do of all people who have ripe cataracts; yet

1 See Nunneley, *On the Organs of Vision*, p. 81 (1858), for a recent case of couching, with careful observations. — ED.

2 On this question, see Locke, *Essay on the Human Understanding*, ii. 9; and Sir. W. Hamilton's note, *Reid's Works*, p. 137.— ED.

they are never so blind from that cause but that they can discern

Cheselden quoted. day from night; and for the most part, in a strong light, distinguish black, white, and scarlet; but they cannot perceive the shape of anything; for the light by which these perceptions are made, being let in obliquely through the aqueous humor, or the anterior surface of the crystalline (by which the rays cannot be brought into a focus upon the retina), they can discern in no other manner than a sound eye can through a glass of broken jelly, where a great variety of surfaces so differently refract the light, that the several distinct pencils of rays cannot be collected by the eye into their proper foci; wherefore the shape of an object in such a case cannot be at all discerned, though the color may; and thus it was with this young gentleman, who, though he knew those colors asunder in a good light, yet when he saw them after he was couched, the faint ideas he had of them before were not sufficient for him to know them by afterwards; and therefore he did not think them the same which he had before known by those names."

* * * * * *

" When he first saw, he was so far from making any judgment about distances, that he thought all objects whatever touched his eyes (as he expressed it) as what he felt did his skin; and thought no objects so agreeable as those which were smooth and regular, though he could form no judgment of their shape, or guess what it was in any object that was pleasing to him. He knew not the shape of anything, nor any one thing from another, however different in shape or magnitude: but upon being told what things were, whose form he before knew from feeling, he would carefully observe, that he might know them again; but having too many objects to learn at once, he forgot many of them; and (as he said) at first learned to know, and again forgot a thousand things in a day. One particular only (though it may appear trifling) I will relate: Having often forgot which was the cat, and which the dog, he was ashamed to ask; but catching the cat (which he knew by feeling) he was observed to look at her steadfastly, and then setting her down, said, ' So, puss! I shall know you another time.' "

* * * * * *

" We thought he soon knew what pictures represented which were showed to him, but we found afterwards we were mistaken; for about two months after he was couched, he discovered at once they represented solid bodies, when, to that time, he considered them only as parti-colored plains, or surfaces diversified with variety of paints; but even then he was no less surprised, expecting the pictures would feel like the things they represented, and was amazed when he found those parts, which by their light and shadow appeared now round and uneven, felt only flat like the rest; and asked which was the lying sense, feeling or seeing." [1]

The whole of this matter is still enveloped in great uncertainty, and I should be sorry either to dogmatize myself, or to advise you to form any decided opinion. Without, however, going the length of Platner, in denying the possibility of a geometer blind from birth, we may allow this, and yet vindicate exclusively to sight the power of affording us our empirical notions of space. The explanation of this supposes, however, an acquaintance with the doctrine of pure or *a priori* space as a form of thought; it must, therefore, for the present be deferred.

The Author professes no decided opinion on the question.

The last question on which I shall touch, and with which I shall conclude the consideration of Perception in general, is, — How do we obtain our knowledge of Visual Distance? Is this original, or acquired?

How do we obtain our knowledge of Visual Distance?

Visual distance, before Berkeley, regarded as an original perception.

With regard to the method by which we judge of distance, it was formerly supposed to depend upon an original law of the constitution, and to be independent of any knowledge gained through the medium of the external senses. This opinion was attacked by Berkeley in his *New Theory of Vision*, one of the finest examples, as Dr. Smith justly observes, of philosophical analysis to be found in our own or in any other language; and in which it appears most clearly demonstrated, that our whole information on this subject is acquired by experience and association. This conclusion is supported by many circumstances of frequent occurrence, in which we fall into the greatest mistakes with respect to the distance of objects, when we form our judgment solely from the visible impression made upon the retina, without attending to the other circumstances which ordinarily direct us in forming our conclusions. It also obtains confirmation from the case of Cheselden, which I have already quoted. It clearly appears that, in the first instance the patient had no correct ideas of distance; and we are expressly told that he supposed all objects to touch the eye, until he learned to correct his visible, by means of his tangible, impressions, and thus gradually to acquire more correct notions of the situation of surrounding bodies with respect to his own person.

---

1 See Adam Smith's *Essays on Philosophical Subjects.* [Pp. 294, 295, 296, edit. 1800. Cf. Reid's *Works*, note, p. 137. — ED.]

On the hypothesis that our ideas of distance are acquired, it remains for us to investigate the circumstances which assist us in forming our judgment respecting them. We shall find that they may be arranged under two heads, some of them depending upon certain states of the eye itself, and others upon various accidents that occur in the appearance of the objects. With respect to distances that are so short as to require the adjustment of the eye in order to obtain distinct vision, it appears that a certain voluntary effort is necessary to produce the desired effect: this effort, whatever may be its nature, causes a corresponding sensation, the amount of which we learn by experience to appreciate; and thus, through the medium of association, we acquire the power of estimating the distance with sufficient accuracy.

Circumstances which assist us in forming our judgment respecting visual distance depend, 1. On certain states of the eye.

When objects are placed at only a moderate distance, but not such as to require the adjustment of the eye, in directing the two eyes to the object we incline them inwards; as is the case likewise with very short distances: so that what are termed the axes of the eyes, if produced, would make an angle at the object, the angle varying inversely as the distance. Here, as in the former case, we have certain perceptions excited by the muscular efforts necessary to produce a proper inclination of the axes, and these we learn to associate with certain distances. As a proof that this is the mode by which we judge of those distances where the optic axes form an appreciable angle, when the eyes are both directed to the same object, while the effort of adjustment is not perceptible, — it has been remarked, that persons who are deprived of the sight of one eye, are incapable of forming a correct judgment in this case.

When we are required to judge of still greater distances, where the object is so remote as that the axes of the two eyes are parallel, we are no longer able to form our opinion from any sensation in the eye itself. In this case, we have recourse to a variety of circumstances connected with the appearance of the object; for example, its apparent size, the distinctness with which it is seen, the vividness of its colors, the number of intervening objects, and other similar accidents, all of which obviously depend upon previous experience, and which we are in the habit of associating with different distances, without, in each particular case, investigating the cause on which our judgment is founded.

2. On certain conditions of the object.

The conclusions of science seem in this case to be decisive; and yet the whole question is thrown into doubt by the analogy of the lower animals. If in man the perception of distance be not original but acquired, the perception of distance must be also acquired by them. But as this is not the case in regard to animals, this confirms the reasoning of those who would explain the perception of distance in man, as an original, not as an acquired, knowledge. That the Berkeleian doctrine is opposed by the analogy of the lower animals, is admitted by one of its most intelligent supporters, — Dr. Adam Smith.[1]

Berkeley's proof thrown into doubt by the analogy of the lower animals.

"That, antecedent to all experience," says Smith, "the young of at least the greater part of animals possess some instinctive perception of this kind, seems abundantly evident. The hen never feeds her young by dropping the food into their bills, as the linnet and the thrush feed theirs. Almost as soon as her chickens are hatched, she does not feed them, but carries them to the field to feed, where they walk about at their ease, it would seem, and appear to have the most distinct perception of all the tangible objects which surround them. We may often see them, accordingly, by the straightest road, run to and pick up any little grains which she shows them, even at the distance of several yards; and they no sooner come into the light than they seem to understand this language of Vision as well as they ever do afterwards. The young of the partridge and the grouse seem to have, at the same early period, the most distinct perceptions of the same kind. The young partridge, almost as soon as it comes from the shell, runs about among long grass and corn, the young grouse among long heath; and would both most essentially hurt themselves if they had not the most acute as well as distinct perception of the tangible objects which not only surround them but press upon them on all sides. This is the case, too, with the young of the goose, of the duck, and, so far as I have been able to observe, with those of at least the greater part of the birds which make their nests upon the ground, with the greater part of those which are ranked by Linnæus in the orders of the hen and the goose, and of many of those long-shanked and wading birds which he places in the order that he distinguishes by the name of Grallæ.

Adam Smith quoted.

     *   *   *   *   *

"It seems difficult to suppose that man is the only animal of which the young are not endowed with some instinctive perception of this kind. The young of the human species, however, continue so long in a state of entire dependency, they must be so long carried about in the arms of their mothers or of their nurses, that such an instinc-

---

[1] See *Essays — Of the External Senses*, p. 299—304, edit. 1800. — ED.

tive perception may seem less necessary to them than to any other race of animals. Before it could be of any use to them, observation and experience may, by the known principle of the association of ideas, have sufficiently connected in their young minds each visible object with the corresponding tangible one which it is fitted to represent. Nature, it may be said, never bestows upon any animal any faculty which is not either necessary or useful, and an instinct of this kind would be altogether useless to an animal which must necessarily acquire the knowledge which the instinct is given to supply, long before that instinct could be of any use to it. Children, however, appear at so very early a period to know the distance, the shape, and magnitude of the different tangible objects which are presented to them, that I am disposed to believe that even they may have some instinctive perception of this kind; though possibly in a much weaker degree than the greater part of other animals. A child that is scarcely a month old, stretches out its hands to feel any little plaything that is presented to it. It distinguishes its nurse, and the other people who are much about it, from strangers. It clings to the former, and turns away from the latter. Hold a small looking-glass before a child of not more than two or three months old, and it will stretch out its little arms behind the glass, in order to feel the child which it sees, and which it imagines is at the back of the glass. It is deceived, no doubt; but even this sort of deception sufficiently demonstrates that it has a tolerably distinct apprehension of the ordinary perspective of Vision, which it cannot well have learnt from observation and experience."

LECTURE XXIX.

THE PRESENTATIVE FACULTY.

II. SELF-CONSCIOUSNESS.

HAVING, in our last Lecture, concluded the consideration of External Perception, I may now briefly recapitulate certain results of the discussion, and state in what principal respects the doctrine I would maintain, differs from that of Reid and Stewart, whom I suppose always to hold, in reality, the system of an Intuitive Perception.

Recapitulation.
Principal points of difference between the Author's doctrine of Perception, and that of Reid and Stewart.

In the first place, — in regard to the relation of the external object to the senses. The general doctrine on this subject is thus given by Reid: "A law of our nature regarding perception is, that we perceive no object, unless some impression is made upon the organ of sense, either by the immediate application of the object, or by some medium which passes between the object and the organ. In two of our senses, viz., Touch and Taste, there must be an immediate application of the object to the organ. In the other three, the object is perceived at a distance, but still by means of a medium, by which some impression is made upon the organ."[1]

1. In regard to the relation of the external object to the senses.

Now this, I showed you, is incorrect. The only object ever perceived is the object in immediate contact, — in immediate relation, with the organ. What Reid, and philosophers in general, call the distant object, is wholly unknown to Perception; by reasoning we may connect the object perceived with certain antecedents, — certain causes; but these, as the result of an inference, cannot be the objects of perception. The only objects of perception are in all the senses equally immediate. Thus the object of my vision at present is not the paper or letters at a foot from my eye, but the rays of light reflected from these upon the retina. The object of your hearing is

---

1 *Intellectual Powers*, Essay ii. c. ii. [*Works*, p. 247. — ED.]

not the vibrations of my larynx, nor the vibrations of the intervening air; but the vibrations determined thereby in the cavity of the internal ear, and in immediate contact with the auditory nerves. In both senses, the external object perceived is the last effect of a series of unperceived causes. But to call these unperceived causes the *object* of perception, and to call the perceived effect, — the real object, only the *medium* of perception, is either a gross error or an unwarrantable abuse of language. My conclusion is, therefore, that, in all the senses, the external object is in contact with the organ, and thus, in a certain signification, all the senses are only modifications of Touch. This is the simple fact, and any other statement of it is either the effect or the cause of misconception.

In all the senses, the external object in contact with the organ.

In the second place, — in relation to the number and consecution of the elementary phænomena, — it is, and must be, admitted, on all hands, that perception must be preceded by an impression of the external object on the sense; in other words, that the material reality and the organ must be brought into contact, previous to, and as the condition of, an act of this faculty. On this point there can be no dispute. But the case is different in regard to the two following. It is asserted by philosophers in general: — 1°. That the impression made on the organ must be propagated to the brain, before a cognition of the object takes place in the mind, — in other words, that an organic action must precede and determine the intellectual action; and, 2°. That Sensation Proper precedes Perception Proper. In regard to the former assertion, — if by this were only meant, that the mind does not perceive external objects out of relation to its bodily organs, and that the relation of the object to the organism, as the condition of perception, must, therefore, in the order of nature, be viewed as prior to the cognition of that relation, — no objection could be made to the statement. But if it be intended, as it seems to be, that the organic affection precedes in the order of time the intellectual cognition, — of this we have no proof whatever. The fact as stated would be inconsistent with the doctrine of an intuitive perception; for if the organic affection were chronologically prior to the act of knowledge, the immediate perception of an object different from our bodily senses would be impossible, and the external world would thus be represented only in the subjective affections of our own organism. It is, therefore, more correct to hold, that the corporeal move-

2. In regard to the number and consecution of the elementary phænomena.

Common doctrine of philosophers regarding the organic impression.

In what respect inaccurate.

ment and the mental perception are simultaneous; and in place of holding that the intellectual action commences after the bodily has terminated, — in place of holding that the mind is connected with the body only at the central extremity of the nervous system, it is more simple and philosophical to suppose that it is united with the nervous system in its whole extent. The mode of this union is of course inconceivable: but the latter hypothesis of union is not more inconceivable than the former; and, while it has the testimony of consciousness in its favor, it is otherwise not obnoxious to many serious objections to which the other is exposed.

In regard to the latter assertion, — viz., that a perception proper is always preceded by a sensation proper, — this, though maintained by Reid and Stewart, is even more manifestly erroneous than the former assertion, touching the precedence of an organic to a mental action. In summing up Reid's doctrine of Perception, Mr. Stewart says: "To what does the statement of Reid amount? Merely to this: that the mind is so formed, that certain impressions produced on our organs of sense by external objects, are followed by correspondent sensations; and that these sensations (which have no more resemblance to the qualities of matter, than the words of a language have to the things they denote) are followed by a perception of the existence and qualities of the bodies by which the impressions are made."[1] You will find in Reid's own works expressions which, if taken literally, would make us believe that he held perception to be a mere inference from sensation. Thus: " Observing that the agreeable sensation is raised when the rose is near, and ceases when it is removed, I am led, by my nature, to conclude some quality to be in the rose, which is the cause of this sensation. This quality in the rose is the object perceived; and that act of my mind, by which I have the conviction and belief of this quality, is what in this case I call perception."[2] I have, however, had frequent occasion to show you that we must not always interpret Reid's expressions very rigorously; and we are often obliged to save his philosophy from the consequences of his own loose and ambiguous language. In the present instance, if Reid were taken at his word, his perception would be only an instinctive belief, consequent on a sensation, that there is some unknown external quality the cause of the sensation. Be this, however, as it may, there is no more ground for holding that sensation precedes perception, than for holding that perception precedes sensation. In fact, both exist only as they coëxist. They do not indeed always coëxist in the same degree of intensity, but they

Relation of Sensation proper to Perception proper.

[1] *Elements*, vol. i. c. ii. § 3. *Works*, vol. ii. p. 111.   [2] *Intell. Powers*, Essay ii. c. xvi. *Works*. p. 310

are equally original; and it is only by an act, not of the easiest abstraction, that we are able to discriminate them scientifically from each other.[1]

So much for the first of the two faculties by which we acquire

The faculty of Self-Consciousness.

knowledge,—the faculty of External Perception. The second of these faculties is Self-consciousness, which has likewise received, among others, the name of Internal or Reflex Perception. This faculty will not occupy us long, as the principal questions regarding its nature and operation have been already considered, in treating of Consciousness in general.[2]

I formerly showed you that it is impossible to distinguish Percep-

Self-Consciousness a branch of the Presentative Faculty.

tion, or the other Special Faculties, from Consciousness,—in other words, to reduce Consciousness itself to a special faculty; and that the attempt to do so by the Scottish philosophers is self-contradictory.[3] I stated to you, however, that though it be incompetent to establish a faculty for the immediate knowledge of the external world, and a faculty for the immediate knowledge of the internal, as two ultimate powers, exclusive of each other, and not merely subordinate forms of a higher immediate knowledge, under which they are comprehended or carried up into one, — I stated, I say, that though the immediate knowledges of matter and of mind are still only modifications of consciousness, yet that their discrimination, as subaltern faculties, is both allowable and convenient. Accordingly, in the scheme which I gave you of the distribution of Consciousness into its special modes, — I distinguished a faculty of External, and a faculty of Internal, Apprehension, constituting together a more general modification of consciousness, which I called the Acquisitive or Presentative or Receptive Faculty.

In regard to Self-consciousness, — the faculty of Internal Experi-

Philosophers less divided in their opinions touching Self-consciousness than in regard to Perception.

ence, — philosophers have been far more harmonious than in regard to External Perception. In fact, their differences touching this faculty originate rather in the ambiguities of language, and the different meanings attached to the same form of expression, than in any fundamental opposition of opinion in regard to its reality and nature. It is admitted equally by all to exist and to exist as a source of knowledge; and the supposed differences of philosophers in this respect, are, as I shall show you, mere errors in the historical statement of their opinions.

---

[1] Compare *Reid's Works*, Note D*, p. 882 *et seq.* — ED.

[2] See above, lect. xi. *et seq.* — ED.

[3] See above, lect. xiii. p. 155, *et seq.* — ED.

The sphere and character of this faculty of acquisition, will be best illustrated by contrasting it with the other.

Self-consciousness contrasted with Perception. Their fundamental forms.

Perception is the power by which we are made aware of the phænomena of the external world; Self-consciousness the power by which we apprehend the phænomena of the internal. The objects of the former are all presented to us in Space and Time; space and time are thus the two conditions, — the two fundamental forms, of external perception. The objects of the latter are all apprehended by us in Time and in Self; time and self are thus the two conditions, — the two fundamental forms, of Internal Perception or Self-consciousness. Time is thus a form or condition common to both faculties; while space is a form peculiar to the one, self a form peculiar to the other. What I mean by the form or con-

What meant by the form of a faculty.

dition of a faculty, is that frame, — that setting (if I may so speak), out of which no object can be known. Thus we only know, through Self-consciousness, the phænomena of the internal world, as modifications of the indivisible ego or conscious unit; we only know, through Perception, the phænomena of the external world, under space, or as modifications of the extended and divisible non-ego or known plurality. That the forms are native, not adventitious, to the mind, is involved in their necessity. What I cannot but think, must be *a priori*, or original to thought; it cannot be engendered by experience upon custom. But this is not a subject the discussion of which concerns us at present.

It may be asked, if self or ego be the form of Self-consciousness,

Objection obviated.

why is the not-self, the non-ego, not in like manner called the form of Perception? To this I reply, that the not-self is only a negation, and, though it discriminates the objects of the external cognition from those of the internal, it does not afford to the former any positive bond of union among themselves. This, on the contrary, is supplied to them by the form of space, out of which they can neither be perceived, nor imagined by the mind; — space, therefore, as the positive condition under which the non-ego is necessarily known and imagined, and through which it receives its unity in consciousness, is properly said to afford the condition or form of External Perception.

But a more important question may be started. If space, — if extension, be a necessary form of thought, this, it may be argued, proves that the mind itself is extended. The reasoning here proceeds upon the assumption, that the qualities of the subject knowing must be similar to the qualities of the object known. This, as I have already stated,[1] is a mere philosophical crotchet, — an assumption without a shadow even of probability in its favor. That the mind has the power of perceiving extended objects, is no ground for holding that it is itself extended.

If space be a necessary form of thought, is the mind itself extended?

Still less can it be maintained, that because it has ideally a native or necessary conception of space, it must really occupy space. Nothing can be more absurd. On this doctrine, to exist as extended is supposed necessary in order to think extension. But if this analogy hold good, the sphere of ideal space which the mind can imagine, ought to be limited to the sphere of real space which the mind actually fills. This is not, however, the case; for though the mind be not absolutely unlimited in its power of conceiving space, still the compass of thought may be viewed as infinite in this respect, as contrasted with the petty point of extension, which the advocates of the doctrine in question allow it to occupy in its corporeal domicile.

The faculty of Self-consciousness affords us a knowledge of the phænomena of our minds. It is the source of internal experience. You will, therefore, observe, that, like External Perception, it only

The sphere of Self-consciousness.

furnishes us with facts; and that the use we make of these facts, — that is, what we find in them, what we deduce from them, — belongs to a different process of intelligence. Self-consciousness affords the materials equally to all systems of philosophy; all equally admit it, and all elaborate the materials which this faculty supplies, according to their fashion. And here I may merely notice, by the way, what, in treating of the Regulative Faculty,

Two modes of dealing with the phænomena given in Self-consciousness, — viz: either by Induction alone, or by Induction and analysis together.

will fall to be regularly discussed, that these facts, these materials, may be considered in two ways. We may employ either Induction alone, or also Analysis. If we merely consider the phænomena which Self-consciousness reveals, in relation to each other, — merely compare them together, and generalize the qualities which they display in common, and thus arrange them into classes or groups governed by the same laws, we perform the process of Induction. By this process we obtain what is general, but not what is necessary. For example, having observed that external objects presented in perception are extended, we generalize the notion of extension or space. We have thus explained the possibility of a conception of

---

[1] See above, lect. xxv. 351 *et seq.* — ED.

space, but only of space as a general and contingent notion; for if we hold that this notion exists in the mind only as the result of such a process, we must hold it to be *a posteriori* or adventitious, and, therefore, contingent. Such is the process of Induction, or of Simple Observation. The other process, that of Analysis or Criticism, does not rest satisfied with this comparison and generalization, which it, however, supposes. It proposes not merely to find what is general in the phænomena, but what is necessary and universal. It, accordingly, takes mental phænomena, and, by abstraction, throws aside all that it is able to detach, without annihilating the phænomena altogether, — in short, it analyzes thought into its essential or necessary, and its accidental or contingent, elements.

Thus, from Observation and Induction, we discover what experience affords as its general result; from Analysis and Criticism, we discover what experience supposes as its necessary condition. You will notice, that the critical analysis of which I now speak, is limited to the objects of our internal observation; for in the phænomena of mind alone can we be conscious of absolute necessity.

The sphere of Critical Analysis.

All necessity is, in fact, to us subjective; for a thing is conceived impossible only as we are unable to construe it in thought. Whatever does not violate the laws of thought, is, therefore, not to us impossible, however firmly we may believe that it will not occur. For example, we hold it absolutely impossible, that a thing can begin to be without a cause. Why? Simply because the mind cannot realize to itself the conception of absolute commencement. That a stone should ascend into the air, we firmly believe will never happen; but we find no difficulty in conceiving it possible. Why? Merely because gravitation is only a fact generalized by induction and observation; and its negation, therefore, violates no law of thought. When we talk, therefore, of the *necessity* of any external phænomenon, the expression is improper, if the necessity be only an inference of induction, and not involved in any canon of intelligence. For induction proves to us only what is, not what must be, — the actual, not the necessary.

All necessity to us subjective.

The two processes of Induction or Observation, and of Analysis or Criticism, have been variously employed by different philosophers. Locke, for instance, limited himself to the former, overlooking altogether the latter. He, accordingly, discovered nothing necessary, or *a priori*, in the phænomena of our internal experience. To him all axioms are only generalizations of experience. In this respect he

Historical notice of the employment of the Inductive and Critical Methods in philosophy.

Locke.

was greatly excelled by Descartes and Leibnitz. The latter, indeed,

Descartes.
Leibnitz,—the first to enounce necessity as the criterion of truth native to the mind.

was the philosopher who clearly enunciated the principle, that the phænomenon of necessity, in our cognitions, could not be explained on the ground of experience. "All the examples," he says, "which confirm a general truth, how numerous soever, would not suffice to establish the universal necessity of this same truth; for it does not follow, that what has hitherto occurred will always occur in future."[1] "If Locke," he adds, "had sufficiently considered the difference between truths which are necessary or demonstrative, and those which we infer from induction alone, he would have perceived that necessary truths could only be proved from principles which command our assent by their intuitive evidence; inasmuch as our senses can inform us only of what is, not of what must necessarily be." Leibnitz, however, was not himself fully aware of the import of the principle, — at least he failed in carrying it out to its most important applications; and though he triumphantly demonstrated,

Kant,—the first who fully applied this criterion.

in opposition to Locke, the *a priori* character of many of those cognitions which Locke had derived from experience, yet he left to Kant the honor of having been the first who fully applied the critical analysis in the philosophy of mind.

The faculty of Self-consciousness corresponds with the Reflection of Locke. Now, there is an interesting ques-

. Has the philosophy of Locke been misrepresented by Condillac, and other of his French disciples?

tion concerning this faculty, — whether the philosophy of Locke has been misapprehended and misrepresented by Condillac, and other of his French disciples, as Mr. Stewart maintains; or, whether Mr. Stewart has not himself attempted to vindicate the tendency of Locke's philosophy on grounds which will not bear out his conclusions. Mr. Stewart has canvassed this point at considerable length, both in his *Essays*[2] and in his *Dissertation on the Progress of Metaphysical, Ethical, and Political Philosophy.* In the latter, the point at issue is thus briefly stated:

Stewart quoted in vindication of Locke.

"The objections to which Locke's doctrine concerning the origin of our ideas, or, in other words, concerning the sources of our knowledge, are, in my judgment, liable, I have stated so fully in a former

[1] *Nouveaux Essais,* Avant-propos, p. 5 (edit. Raspe). — Ed. [Cf. lib. i. c. i. § 5, p. 36; lib. ii. c. xvii. § 1, p. 116. Letter to Burnet of Kemney (1706), *Opera,* t. vi. p. 274 (edit. Dutens). Letter to Bierling (1710), *Opera,* t. v. p.

858. *Theodicée* (1710), i. § 2, p. 480 (Erd.), or *Opera,* t. i. p. 65 (Dutens). *Monadologie* (1714), p. 707 (edit. Erdmann).]

[2] *Works,* vol. v. part i., Essay i., p. 55 *et seq.* — Ed.

work, that I shall not touch on them here. It is quite sufficient, on the present occasion, to remark, how very unjustly this doctrine (imperfect, on the most favorable construction, as it undoubtedly is) has been confounded with those of Gassendi, of Condillac, of Diderot, and of Horne Tooke. The substance of all that is common in the conclusions of these last writers, cannot be better expressed than in the words of their master, Gassendi. 'All our knowledge,' he observes in a letter to Descartes, 'appears plainly to derive its origin from the senses; and although you deny the maxim, 'Quicquid est intellectu præesse debere in sensu,' yet this maxim appears, nevertheless, to be true; since our knowledge is all ultimately obtained by an *influx* or *incursion* from things external; which knowledge afterwards undergoes various modifications by means of analogy, composition, division, amplification, extenuation, and other similar processes, which it is unnecessary to enumerate.' This doctrine of Gassendi's coincides exactly with that ascribed to Locke by Diderot and by Horne Tooke; and it differs only verbally from the more concise statement of Condillac, that 'our ideas are nothing more than transformed sensations.' 'Every idea,' says the first of these writers, 'must necessarily, when brought to its state of ultimate decomposition, resolve itself into a sensible representation or picture; and since everything in our understanding has been introduced there by the channel of sensation, whatever proceeds out of the understanding is either chimerical, or must be able, in returning by the same road, to reättach itself to its sensible archetype. Hence an important rule in philosophy, — that every expression which cannot find an external and a sensible object, to which it can thus establish its affinity, is destitute of signification.' Such is the exposition given by Diderot, of what is regarded in France as Locke's great and capital discovery; and precisely to the same purpose we are told by Condorcet, that 'Locke was the first who proved that all our ideas are compounded of sensations.' If this were to be admitted as a fair account of Locke's opinion, it would follow that he has not advanced a single step beyond Gassendi and Hobbes; both of whom have repeatedly expressed themselves in nearly the same words with Diderot and Condorcet. But although it must be granted, in favor of their interpretation of his language, that various detached passages may be quoted from his work, which seem, on a superficial view, to justify their comments; yet of what weight, it may be asked, are these passages, when compared with the stress laid by the author on *Reflection*, as an original source of our ideas, altogether different from *Sensation?* 'The other fountain,' says Locke, 'from which experience furnisheth the understanding with ideas, is the perception of the operations of our own minds within us, as it is employed about the ideas it has got; which operations, when the soul comes to reflect on and consider, do furnish the understanding with another set of ideas, which could not be had from things without; and such are Perception, Thinking, Doubting, Believing, Reasoning, Knowing, Willing, and all the different actings of our own minds, which, we being conscious of, and observing in ourselves, do from these receive into our understandings ideas as distinct as we do from bodies affecting our senses. This source of ideas every man has wholly in himself; and though it be not sense, as having nothing to do with external objects, yet it is very like it, and might properly enough be called *Internal Sense*. But as I call the other Sensation, so I call this Reflection; the ideas it affords being such only as the mind gets by reflecting on its own operations within itself.'[1] Again, 'The understanding seems to me not to have the least glimmering of any ideas which it does not receive from one of these two. External objects furnish the mind with the ideas of sensible qualities; and the mind furnishes the understanding with ideas of its own operations.' "[2]

On these observations I must remark, that they do not at all

Stewart's vindication unsatisfactory. satisfy me; and I cannot but regard Locke and Gassendi as exactly upon a par, and both as deriving all our knowledge from experience. The French philosophers, are therefore, in my opinion, fully justified in their interpretation of Locke's philosophy;

Condillac justified in his simplification of Locke's doctrine. and Condillac must, I think, be viewed as having simplified the doctrine of his master, without doing the smallest violence to its spirit. In the first place, I cannot concur with Mr. Stewart in allowing any weight to Locke's distinction of Reflection, or Self-consciousness, as a second source of our knowledge. Such a source of experience no sensualist ever denied, because no sensualist ever denied that

The Reflection of Locke, — compatible with Sensualism. sense was cognizant of itself. It makes no difference, that Locke distinguished Reflection from Sense, " as having nothing to do with external objects," admitting, however, that "they are very like," and that Reflection "might properly enough be called Internal Sense,"[3] while Condillac makes it only a modification of sense. It is a matter of no importance, that we do not call

---

[1] Locke, *Works*, vol. i. p. 78. [*Essay*, B. ii. c. i. § 4. — ED.]

[2] *Ibid.* p. 79. [*Ess.* B. ii. c. i. § 5. — Stewart,

Dissertation, p. ii. § i. *Works*, vol. i. p. 224 *et seq.* — ED.]

[3] *Essay*, B. ii. c. i. § 4. — ED.

Self-consciousness by the name of *Sense*, if we allow that it is only conversant about the contingent. Now, no interpretation of Locke can ever pretend to find in his Reflection a revelation to him of aught native or necessary to the mind, beyond the capability to act and suffer in certain manners, — a capability which no philosophy ever dreamt of denying. And if this be the case, it follows, that the formal reduction, by Condillac, of Reflection to Sensation, is only a consequent following out of the principles of the doctrine itself.

Of how little import is the distinction of Reflection from Sensation, in the philosophy of Locke, is equally shown in the philosophy of Gassendi; in regard to which I must correct a fundamental error of Mr. Stewart. I had formerly occasion to point out to you the unaccountable mistake of this very learned philosopher, in relation to Locke's use of the term Reflection, [1] which, both in his *Essays*, and his *Dissertation*, he states was a word first employed by Locke in its psychological signification. [2] Nothing, I stated, could be more incorrect. When adopted by Locke, it was a word of universal currency, in a similar sense, in every contemporary system of philosophy, and had been so employed for at least a thousand years previously. This being understood, Mr. Stewart's mistake in regard to Gassendi, is less surprising. " The word *Reflection*," says Mr. Stewart, " expresses the peculiar and characteristical doctrine, by which his system is distinguished from that of the Gassendists and Hobbists. All this, however, serves only to prove still more clearly, how widely remote his real opinion on this subject was from that commonly ascribed to him by the French and German commentators. For my own part, I do not think, notwithstanding some casual expressions which may seem to favor the contrary supposition, that Locke would have hesitated for a moment to admit, with Cudworth and Price, that the *Understanding* is itself a source of new ideas. That it is by *Reflection* (which, according to his own definition, means merely the exercise of the *Understanding* on the internal phenomena), that we get our ideas of Memory, Imagination, Reasoning, and of all other intellectual powers, Mr. Locke has again and again told us; and from this principle it is so obvious an inference, that all the simple ideas which are necessarily implied in our intellectual operations, are ultimately to be referred to the same source, that we can-

Fundamental error of Stewart in regard to the philosophy of Gassendi.

1 See above, lect. xiii. p. 162. — ED.
2 Lee on Locke, makes apparently the same mistake. [See *Anti-Skepticism: or, Notes upon* each *Chapter of Mr. Locke's Essay concerning Humane Understanding,* by Henry Lee, B.D., Preface, p. 7; London, 1702. — ED.]

not reasonably suppose a philosopher of Locke's sagacity to admit the former proposition, and to withhold his assent to the latter."[1]

The inference which, in the latter part of this quotation, Mr.

Gassendi, though a Sensationalist, admitted Reflection as a source of knowledge. Stewart speaks of, is not so obvious as he supposes, seeing that it was not till Leibnitz that the character of necessity was enounced, and clearly enounced, as the criterion by which to discriminate the native from the adventitious cognitions of the mind. This is, indeed, shown by the example of Gassendi himself, who is justly represented by Mr. Stewart as a Sensationalist of the purest water; but wholly misrepresented by him, as distinguished from Locke by his negation of any faculty corresponding to Locke's Reflection. So far is this from being correct, — Gassendi not only allowed a faculty of Self-consciousness analogous to the Reflection of Locke, he actually held such a faculty, and even attributed to it far higher functions than did the English philosopher; nay, what is more, held it under the very name of Reflection.[2] In fact, from the French philosopher, Locke borrowed this, as he did the principal part of his whole philosophy; and it is saying but little either for the patriotism or intelligence of their countrymen, that the works of Gassendi and Descartes should have been so long eclipsed in France by those of Locke, who was in truth only a follower of the one, and a mistaken refuter of the other. In respect to Gassendi, there are reasons that explain this neglect apart from any want of merit in himself; for he is a thinker fully equal to Locke in independence and vigor of intellect, and, with the exception of Leibnitz, he is, of all the great philosophers of modern times, the most varied and profound in learning.

Now, in regard to the point at issue, so far is Gassendi from

And did not assimilate Reflection to Sense. assimilating Reflection to Sense, as Locke virtually, if not expressly, does, and for which assimilation he has been principally lauded by those of his followers who analyzed every mental process into Sensation, — so far, I say, is Gassendi from doing this, that he places Sense and Reflection at the opposite mental poles, making the former a mental function wholly dependent upon the bodily organism; the latter, an energy of intellect wholly inorganic and abstract from matter. The cognitive phænom-

His division of the cognitive phænomena of mind. ena of mind Gassendi reduces to three general classes of faculties: — 1°. Sense, 2°. Phantasy (or Imagination), and 3°. Intellect. The two former are, however, virtually one, inasmuch as Phantasy, on his

1 *Dissertation*, p. ii. § 1. foot-note, *Works*, vol. i. p. 280. — ED.
2 See above, lect. xiii. p. 162. — ED.

doctrine, is only cognizant about the forms, which it receives from Sense, and is, equally with Sense, dependent on a corporeal organ. Intellect, on the contrary,

Intellect according to Gassendi, has three functions, — 1. Intellectual Apprehension.

he holds, is not so dependent, and that its functions are, therefore, of a kind superior to those of an organic faculty. These functions or faculties of Intellect he reduces to three. "The first," he says (and I literally translate his words in order that I may show you how flagrantly he has been misrepresented), "is Intellectual Apprehension, — that is, the apprehension of things which are beyond the reach of Sense, and which, consequently, leaving no trace in the brain, are also beyond the ken of Imagination. Such, especially, is spiritual or incorporeal nature, as, for example, the Deity. For although in speaking of God, we say that He is incorporeal, yet in attempting to realize Him to Phantasy, we only imagine something with the attributes of body. It must not, however, be supposed that this is all; for, besides and above the corporeal form which we thus imagine, there is, at the same time, another conception, which that form contributes, as it were, to veil and obscure. This conception is not confined to the narrow limits of Phantasy (præter Phantasiæ cancellos est); it is proper to Intellect; and, therefore, such an apprehension ought not to be called an *imagination*, but an *intelligence* or *intellection* (non *imaginatio*, sed *intelligentia* vel *intellectio*, dici oportet)."[1] In his doctrine of Intellect, Gassendi takes, indeed, far higher ground than Locke; and it is a total reversal of his doctrine, when it is stated, that he allowed to the mind no different, no higher, apprehensions than the derivative images of sense. He says, indeed, and he says truly, that if we attempt to figure out the Deity in imagination, we cannot depict Him in that faculty, except under sensible forms — as, for example, under the form of a venerable old man. But does he not condemn this attempt as derogatory; and does he not allow us an intellectual conception of the Divinity, superior to the grovelling conditions of Phantasy? The Cartesians, however, were too well disposed to overlook the limits under which Gassendi had advanced his doctrine, — that the senses are the source of all our knowledge; and Mr. Stewart has adopted, from the Port Royal *Logic*, a statement of Gassendi's opinion, which is, to say the least of it, partial and incomplete.

The second function which Gassendi assigns to Intellect, is Reflection, and the third is Reasoning. It is with the former of these

---

1 *Physica*, sect. iii., Memb. Post., lib. ix. c. 8. *Opera*, Lugd. 1658, vol. ii. p. 451. — ED

that we are at present concerned. Mr. Stewart, you have seen,
distinguishes the philosophy of Locke from that
of his predecessor in this,—that the former
introduced Reflection or Self-consciousness as
a source of knowledge, which was overlooked or disallowed by
the latter. Mr. Stewart is thus wrong in the fact of Gassendi's
rejection of any source of knowledge of the name and nature of
Locke's Reflection. So far is this from being the case, that Gassendi attributes far more to this faculty than Locke; for he not
only makes it an original source of knowledge, but founds upon the
nature of its action a proof of the immateriality of mind. "To
the second operation," he says, "belongs the Attention or Reflection
of the intellect upon its proper acts,—an operation by which it
understands that it understands, and thinks that it thinks (qua se
intelligere intelligit, cogitatve se cogitare). "We have formerly,"
he adds, "shown that it is above the power of Phantasy to imagine that it imagines, because, being of a corporeal nature, it
cannot act upon itself; in fact, it is as absurd to say that I imagine
myself to imagine, as that I see myself to see." He then goes on
to show, that the knowledge we obtain of all our mental operations
and affections, is by this reflection of Intellect; that it is necessarily of an inorganic or purely spiritual character; that it is peculiar
to man, and distinguishes him from the brutes; and that it aids us
in the recognition of disembodied substances, in the confession of a
God, and in according to Him the veneration which we owe Him.

From what I have now said, you will see, that the mere admission of a faculty of Self-consciousness, as a source
of knowledge, is of no import in determining
the rational,—the anti-sensual, character of a
philosophy; and that even those philosophers
who discriminated it the most strongly from
Sense, might still maintain that experience is
not only the occasion, but the source, of all our
knowledge. Such philosophers were Gassendi and Locke. On this
faculty I do not think it necessary to dwell longer; and, in our
next Lecture, I shall proceed to consider the Conservative Faculty,
—Memory, properly so called.

2. Reflection.
3 Reasoning.

The mere admission
of a faculty of Self-
consciousness, of no
import in determining
the anti-sensual char-
acter of a philosophy.

LECTURE XXX.

THE CONSERVATIVE FACULTY. — MEMORY PROPER.

I COMMENCED and concluded, in my last Lecture, the consideration of the second source of knowledge, — the
faculty of Self-Consciousness or Internal Perception. Through the powers of External and
Internal Perception we are enabled to acquire
information, — experience: but this acquisition
is not of itself independent and complete; it
supposes that we are also able to retain the knowledge acquired, for
we cannot be said to get what we are unable to keep. The faculty
of Acquisition is, therefore, only realized through another faculty, —
the faculty of Retention or Conservation. Here, we have another
example of what I have already frequently had
occasion to suggest to your observation, — we
have two faculties, two elementary phænomena,
evidently distinct, and yet each depending on
the other for its realization. Without a power
of acquisition, a power of conservation could
not be exerted; and without the latter, the former would be frustrated, for we should lose as fast as we acquired. But as the
faculty of Acquisition would be useless without the faculty of
Retention, so the faculty of Retention would be useless without the
faculties of Reproduction and Representation. That the mind
retained, beyond the sphere of consciousness, a treasury of knowledge, would be of no avail, did it not possess the power of bringing
out, and of displaying, in other words, of reproducing, and representing, this knowledge in consciousness. But because the faculty
of Conservation would be fruitless without the ulterior faculties of
Reproduction and Representation, we are not to confound these
faculties, or to view the act of mind which is their joint result, as a
simple and elementary phænomenon. Though mutually dependent
on each other, the faculties of Conservation, Reproduction, and

*Elementary phæ-
nomena may be dis-
tinct, while they de-
pend on each other
for their realization.*

*This general princi-
ple illustrated by the
phænomena of Acqui-
sition, Retention, Re-
production, and Rep-
resentation.*

Representation are governed by different laws, and, in different individuals, are found greatly varying in their comparative vigor.

Hence these three faculties not distinguished by philosophers; nor in ordinary language.

The intimate connection of these three faculties, or elementary activities, is the cause, however, why they have not been distinguished in the analysis of philosophers; and why their distinction is not precisely marked in ordinary language. In ordinary language we have indeed words which, without excluding the other faculties, denote one of these more emphatically. Thus in the term *Memory*, the Conservative Faculty, — the phænomenon of Retention is the central notion, with which, however, those of Reproduction and Representation are associated. In the term *Recollection*, again, the phænomenon of Reproduction is the principal notion, accompanied, however, by those of Retention and Representation, as its subordinates. This being the case, it is evident what must be our course in regard to the employment of common language. We must either abandon it altogether, or take the term that more proximately expresses our analysis, and, by definition, limit and specify its signification. Thus, in the Conservative Faculty, we may either content ourselves with the scientific terms of *Conservation* and *Retention* alone, or we may moreover use as a synonym the vulgar term *Memory*, determining its application, in our mouths, by a preliminary definition. And that the word *Memory* principally and properly denotes the power the mind possesses of retaining hold of the knowledge it has acquired, is generally admitted by philologers, and is not denied by philosophers. Of the latter, some have expressly avowed this. Of these I shall quote to you only two or three, which happen to occur the first to my recollection. Plato considers Memory simply as the faculty of Conservation (ἡ μνήμη σωτηρία αἰσθήσεως).[1] Aristotle distinguishes Memory (μνήμη) as the faculty of Conservation from Reminiscence (ἀνάμνησις), the faculty of Reproduction.[2] St. Augustin, who is not only the most illustrious of the Christian fathers, but one of the profoundest thinkers of antiquity, finely contrasts Memory with Recollection or Reminiscence, in one of the most eloquent and philosophical chapters of his

Ordinary use of the terms Memory and Recollection.

Memory properly denotes the power of Retention.

Acknowledged by Plato.

Aristotle.

St. Augustin.

---

[1] *Philebus,* [p. 34.—Ed.]
[2] *De Memoria et Reminiscentia* [c. 2, § 25

Cf. Conimbricenses, *In De Mem. et Rem. c.* vii. p. 10.—Ed.]

Confessions:[1] — "Hæc omnia recipit *recolenda,* cum opus est, et *retractanda* grandis memoriæ recessus. Et nescio qui secreti atque ineffabiles sinus ejus; quæ omnia suis quæque foribus intrant ad eam, et reponuntur in ea. Nec ipsa tamen intrant, sed rerum sensarum imagines illic præsto sunt, cogitationi *reminiscenti* eas." The

Julius Cæsar Scaliger.

same distinction is likewise precisely taken by one of the acutest of modern philosophers, the elder Scaliger.[2] "*Memoriam* voco hujusce cognitionis *conservationem. Reminiscentiam* dico, repetitionem disciplinæ, quæ e memoria delapsa fuerat." This is from his commentary on Aristotle's *History of Animals;* the following is from his *De Subtilitate:*[3] — "Quid *Memoria?* Vis animæ communis ad *retinendum* tam rerum imagines, *i. e.* phantasmata, quam notiones universales; easque, vel simplices, vel complexas. Quid *Recordatio?* Opera intellectus, species recolentis. Quid *Reminiscentia?* Disquisitio tectarum specierum; amotio importunarum, digestio obturbatarum." The father suggests the son, and the following occurs in the *Secunda Scaligerana,* which is one of the two collections

Joseph Scaliger.

we have of the table-talk of Joseph Scaliger. The one from which I quote was made by the brothers Vassan, whom the Dictator of Letters, from friendship to their learned uncles (the Messrs. Pithou), had received into his house, when pursuing their studies in the University of Leyden; and *Secunda Scaligerana* is made up of the notes they had taken of the conversations he had with them, and others in their presence. Scaliger, speaking of himself, is made to say: "I have not a good memory, but a good reminiscence; proper names do not easily recur to me, but when I think on them I find them out."[4] It is sufficient for our purpose that the distinction is here taken between the Retentive Power, — Memory, and the Reproductive Power, — Reminiscence. Scaliger's memory could hardly be called bad, though his reminiscence might be better; and these elements in conjunction go to constitute a good memory, in the comprehensive sense of the expression. I say the retentive faculty of that man is surely not to be despised, who was able to commit to memory Homer in twenty-one days, and the whole Greek poets in three months,[5] and who, taking him all in all, was the most learned man the world has ever seen. I might adduce many other authorities to

1 Lib. x. c. 8. — ED.

2 [*Aristotelis Historia de Animalibus, Julio Cæsare Scaligero Interprete.* Tolosæ 1619, p. 80.]

3 [Exercit. cccvii. 28]

4 Tom. ii. p. 552. — ED.

5 See Heinsius, *In Josephi Scaligeri Obitum; Funebris Oratio* (1609), p. 15. His words are: — "Uno et viginti diebus Homerum, reliquos intra quartum mensum poetas, cæteros autem intra biennium scriptores perdisceret." See below lect. xxxi. p. 413. — ED.

the same effect; but this, I think, is sufficient to warrant me in using the term *Memory* exclusively to denote the faculty possessed by the mind of preserving what has once been present to consciousness, so that it may again be recalled and represented in consciousness.[1] So much for the verbal consideration.

By Memory or Retention, you will see, is only meant the condi-

Memory,—what. tion of Reproduction; and it is, therefore, evident that it is only by an extension of the term that it can be called a faculty, that is, an active power. It is more a passive resistance than an energy, and ought, therefore, perhaps to receive rather the appellation of a capacity.[2] But the nature of this capacity or faculty we must now proceed to consider.

In the first place, then, I presume that the fact of retention is

The fact of retention admitted. admitted. We are conscious of certain cognitions as acquired, and we are conscious of these cognitions as resuscitated. That, in the interval, when out of consciousness, these cognitions do continue to subsist in the mind, is certainly an hypothesis, because whatever is out of consciousness can only be assumed; but it is an hypothesis which we are not only warranted, but necessitated, by the phænomena, to establish. I recollect, indeed, that one philosopher has proposed

The hypothesis of Avicenna regarding retention. another hypothesis. Avicenna, the celebrated Arabian philosopher and physician, denies to the human mind the conservation of its acquired knowledge; and he explains the process of recollection by an irradiation of divine light, through which the recovered cognition is infused into the intellect.[3] Assuming, however, that the knowledge we have acquired is retained in and by the human mind, we must, of course, attribute to the mind a power of thus retaining it. The fact of memory is thus established.

But if it cannot be denied, that the knowledge we have acquired

Retention admits of explanation. by Perception and Self-consciousness, does actually continue, though out of consciousness, to endure; can we, in the second place, find any ground on which to explain the possibility of this endurance? I think we can, and shall adduce such an explanation, founded on the general analogies of our mental nature. Before, however, com-

---

1 Suabedissen makes Memory equivalent to Retention; see his *Grundzüge der Lehre von dem Menschen*, p. 107. So Fries, Schmid. [Cf. Leibnitz, *Nouv. Ess.*, lib i. c. i. § 5; lib. ii. c. xix § 1. Conimbricenses, *In De Mem. et Rem.* c i. p 2] [Fracastorius, *De Intellectione*, 1. i., *Opera*, f. 126 (ed. 1584). — ED.]

2 See Suabedissen, as above.

3 See Conimbricenses, *In De Memoria et Reminiscentia*, [c. i. p. 2, edit. 1631. Cf. the same, *In De Anima*, lib. iii. c. v. q. ii. art. ii. p. 430. — ED.]

mencing this, I may notice some of the similitudes which have been suggested by philosophers, as illustrative of this faculty. It has been compared to a store-house, — Cicero calls it "*thesaurus omnium rerum*,"[1] — provided with cells or pigeon-holes, in which its furniture is laid up and arranged.[2]

Similitudes suggested in illustration of the faculty of Retention.
Cicero.

It has been likened to a tablet on which characters were written or impressed.[3] But of all these sensible resemblances, none is so ingenious as that of Gassendi[4] to the folds in a piece of paper or cloth; though I do not recollect to have seen it ever noticed. A sheet of paper, or cloth, is capable of receiving innumerable folds, and the folds in which it has been oftenest laid, it takes afterwards of itself. "Concipi charta valeat plicarum innumerabilium, inconfusarumque, et juxta suos ordines, suasque series repetendarum capax. Silicet ubi unam seriem subtilissimarum induxerimus, superinducere licet alias, quæ primam quidem refringant transversum, et in omnem obliquitatem; sed ita tamen, ut dum novæ, plicæ, plicarumque series superinducuntur priores omnes non modo remaneant, verum etiam possint facili negotio excitari, redire, apparere, quatenus una plica arrepta, cæteræ, quæ in eadem serie quadam quasi sponte sequuntur."

Gassendi.

All these resemblances, if intended as more than metaphors, are unphilosophical. We do not even obtain any insight into the nature of Memory from any of the physiological hypotheses which have been stated; indeed all of them are too contemptible even for serious criticism. "The mind affords us, however, in itself, the very explanation which we vainly seek in any collateral influences. The phænomenon of retention is, indeed, so natural, on the ground of the self-energy of mind, that we have no need to suppose any special faculty for memory; the conservation of the action of the mind being involved in the very conception of its power of self-activity.

These resemblances of use simply as metaphors.

The phænomenon of retention naturally arises from the self-energy of mind.

"Let us consider how knowledge is acquired by the mind. Knowledge is not acquired by a mere passive affection, but through the exertion of spontaneous activity on the part of the knowing subject; for though this activity be not exerted without some external excitation, still this excitation is only the occasion on which

---

1 *De Oratore*, i. 5. — ED.

2 Cf. Plato, *Theætetus*, p. 197. — ED.

3 Cf. Plato, *Theætetus*, p. 191. Arist., *De Anima*, iii 4. Boethius, *De Consol. Phil.*, lib. v. metr. 4. — ED.

4 *Physica*, sect. iii., membr. post., lib. viii. c. 8. *Opera*, Lugd. 1658, vol. ii. p. 406. — ED. [Cf. Descartes, *Œuvres*, t. ix. p. 167 (ed. Cousin).] [St. Hilaire, *Psychologie d' Aristotle*, Pref. p. 18 *et seq.* — ED.]

the mind develops its self-energy. But this energy being once determined, it is natural that it should persist, until again annihilated by other causes. This would in fact be the case, were the mind merely passive in the impression it receives; for it is a universal law of nature, that every effect endures as long as it is not modified or opposed by any other effect. But the mental activity, the act of knowledge, of which I now speak, is more than this; it is an energy of the self-active power of a subject one and indivisible: consequently, a part of the ego must be detached or annihilated, if a cognition once existent be again extinguished.

This specially shown. Knowledge acquired by the spontaneous activity of mind.

Hence it is, that the problem most difficult of solution is not, how a mental activity endures, but how it ever vanishes. For as we must here maintain not merely the possible continuance of certain energies, but the impossibility of the non-continuance of any one, we, consequently, stand in apparent contradiction to what experience shows us; showing us, as it does, our internal activities in a ceaseless vicissitude of manifestation and disappearance. This apparent contradiction, therefore, demands solution. If it be impossible, that an energy of mind which has once been should be abolished, without a laceration of the vital unity of the mind as a subject one and indivisible; — on this supposition, the question arises, How can the facts of our self-consciousness be brought to harmonize with this statement, seeing that consciousness proves to us, that cognitions once clear and vivid are forgotten; that feelings, wishes, desires, in a word, every act or modification, of which we are at one time aware, are at another vanished; and that our internal existence seems daily to assume a new and different aspect.

The problem most difficult of solution is not, how a mental activity endures, but how it ever vanishes.

"The solution of this problem is to be sought for in the theory of obscure or latent modifications, [that is, mental activities, real but beyond the sphere of consciousness, which I formerly explained.]¹ The disappearance of internal energies from the view of internal perception, does not warrant the conclusion, that they no longer exist; for we are not always conscious of all the mental energies whose existence cannot be disallowed. Only the more vivid changes sufficiently affect our consciousness to become objects of its apprehension: we, consequently, are only conscious of the more prominent series of changes

The difficulty removed by the principle of latent modifications. The obscuration of a mental activity arises from the weakening of the degree in which it affects self-consciousness.

---

1 See above, lect. xviii. p. 235 *et seq.* — ED.

in our internal state; the others remain for the most part latent. Thus we take note of our memory only in its influence on our consciousness; and, in general, do not consider that the immense proportion of our intellectual possessions consists of our delitescent cognitions. All the cognitions which we possess, or have possessed, still remain to us, — the whole complement of all our knowledge still lies in our memory; but as new acquisitions are continually pressing in upon the old, and continually taking place along with them among the modifications of the ego, the old cognitions, unless from time to time refreshed and brought forward, are driven back, and become gradually fainter and more obscure. This obscuration is not, however, to be conceived as an obliteration, or as a total annihilation. The obscuration, the delitescence of mental activities, is explained by the weakening of the degree in which they affect our self-consciousness or internal sense. An activity becomes obscure, because it is no longer able adequately to affect this. To explain, therefore, the disappearance of our mental activities, it is only requisite to explain their weakening or enfeeblement, — which may be attempted in the following way: — Every

The distribution of mental force explains the weakening of our activities, and the phænomenon of Forgetfulness.

mental activity belongs to the one vital activity of mind in general; it is, therefore, indivisibly bound up with it, and can neither be torn from, nor abolished in, it. But the mind is only capable, at any one moment, of exerting a certain quantity or degree of force. This quantity must, therefore, be divided among the different activities, so that each has only a part; and the sum of force belonging to all the several activities taken together, is equal to the quantity or degree of force belonging to the vital activity of mind in general. Thus, in proportion to the greater number of activities in the mind, the less will be the proportion of force which will accrue to each; the feebler, therefore, each will be, and the fainter the vivacity with which it can affect self-consciousness. This weakening of vivacity can, in consequence of the indefinite increase in the number of our mental activities, caused by the ceaseless excitation of the mind to new knowledge, be carried to an indefinite tenuity, without the activities, therefore, ceasing altogether to be. Thus it is quite natural, that the great proportion of our mental cognitions should have waxed too feeble to affect our internal perception with the competent intensity; it is quite natural that they should have become obscure or delitescent. In these circumstances it is to be supposed, that every new cognition, every newly-excited activity, should be in the greatest vivacity, and should draw to itself the greatest amount of force : this force will, in the same proportion, be withdrawn from the other earlier cognitions; and it is they, consequently, which must undergo the fate of obscuration. Thus is explained the phænomenon of Forgetfulness or Oblivion. And here, by the way, it should perhaps be noticed, that forgetfulness is not to be limited merely to our cognitions : it applies equally to the feelings and desires.

"The same principle illustrates, and is illustrated by, the phænomenon of Distraction and Attention. If a

And the phænomenon of Distraction and Attention.

great number of activities are equally excited at once, the disposable amount of mental force is equally distributed among this multitude, so that each activity only attains a low degree of vivacity; the state of mind which results from this is Distraction. Attention is the state the converse of this; that is, the state in which the vital activity of mind is, voluntarily or involuntarily, concentrated, say, in a single activity; in consequence of which concentration this activity waxes stronger, and, therefore, clearer. On this theory, the proposition with which I started, — that all mental activities, all acts of knowledge, which have been once excited, persist, — becomes intelligible; we never wholly lose them, but they become obscure. This obscuration can be conceived in every infinite degree, between incipient latescence and irrecoverable latency. The obscure cognition may exist simply out of consciousness, so that it can be recalled by a common act of reminiscence. Again, it may be impossible to recover it by an act of voluntary recollection; but some association may revivify it enough to make it flash after a long oblivion into consciousness. Further, it may be obscured so far that it can only be resuscitated by some morbid affection of the system; or, finally, it may be absolutely lost for us in this life, and destined only for our reminiscence in the life to come.

"That this doctrine admits of an immediate application to the faculty of Retention, or Memory Proper, has

Two observations regarding Memory, that arise out of the preceding theory.

1. The law of retention extends over all the phænomena of mind alike.

been already signified. And in further explanation of this faculty, I would annex two observations, which arise out of the preceding theory. The first is, that retention, that memory, does not belong alone to the cognitive faculties, but that the same law extends, in like manner, over all the three primary classes of the mental phænomena. It is not ideas, notions, cognitions only, but feelings and conations, which are held fast, and which can, therefore, be again awakened.[1] This fact of the conservation of our practical modifica-

[1] [Cf. Tetens, *Versuche über die menschliche Natur*, i. p. 66.]

tions is not indeed denied; but psychologists usually so represent the matter, as if, when feelings or conations are retained in the mind, that this takes place only through the medium of the memory; meaning by this, that we must, first of all, have had notions of these affections, which notions being preserved, they, when recalled to mind, do again awaken the modification they represent. From the theory I have detailed to you, it must be seen that there is no need of this intermediation of notions, but that we immediately retain feelings, volitions, and desires, no less than notions and cognitions; inasmuch as all the three classes of fundamental phænomena arise equally out of the vital manifestations of the same one and indivisible subject.

"The second result of this theory is, that the various attempts to explain memory by physiological hypotheses are as unnecessary as they are untenable. This is

2. The various attempts to explain memory by physiological hypotheses are unnecessary.

not the place to discuss the general problem touching the relation of mind and body. But in proximate reference to memory, it may be satisfactory to show, that this faculty does not stand in need of such crude modes of explanation. It must be allowed, that no faculty affords a more tempting

Memory greatly dependent on corporeal conditions.

subject for materialistic conjecture. No other mental power betrays a greater dependence on corporeal conditions than memory. Not only in general does its vigorous or feeble activity essentially depend on the health and indisposition of the body, more especially of the nervous systems; but there is manifested a connection between certain functions of memory and certain parts of the cerebral apparatus."[1] This connection, however, is such, as affords no countenance to any particular hypotheses at present in vogue. For example, after certain diseases, or certain affections of the brain, some partial loss of memory takes place. Perhaps the patient loses the whole of his stock of knowledge previous to the disease; the faculty of acquiring and retaining new information remaining entire. Perhaps he loses the memory of words, and preserves that of things. Perhaps he may retain the memory of nouns, and lose that of verbs, or *vice versa;* nay, what is still more marvellous, though it is not a very unfrequent occurrence, one language may be taken neatly out of his retention, without affecting his memory of others. "By such observations, the older psychologists were led to the various physiological hypotheses by which they hoped to

1 H. Schmid, *Versuch einer Metaphysik der inneren Natur* [p. 231—235; translated with occasional brief interpolations. — ED.]

account for the phænomena of retention, — as, for example, the hypothesis of permanent material impressions on the brain, or of permanent dispositions in the nervous fibres to repeat the same oscillatory movements, — of particular organs for the different functions of memory, — of particular parts of the brain as the repositories of the various classes of ideas, — or even of a particular fibre, as the instrument of every several notion. But all these hypotheses betray only an ignorance of the proper object of philosophy, and of the true nature of the thinking principle. They are at best but useless; for if the unity and self-activity of mind be not denied, it is manifest, that the mental activities, which have been once determined, must persist, and these corporeal explanations are superfluous. Nor can it be argued, that the limitations to which the Retentive, or rather the Reproductive, Faculty is subjected in its energies, in consequence of its bodily relations, prove the absolute dependence of memory on organization, and legitimate the explanation of this faculty by corporeal agencies; for the incompetency of this inference can be shown from the contradiction in which it stands to the general laws of mind, which, howbeit conditioned by bodily relations, still ever preserves its self-activity and independence."[1]

Physiological hypothesis of the older psychologists regarding memory.

There is perhaps no mental power in which such extreme differences appear, in different individuals, as in memory. To a good memory there are certainly two qualities requisite, — 1,° The capacity of Retention, and 2°, The faculty of Reproduction. But the former quality appears to be that by which these marvellous contrasts are principally determined. I should only fatigue you, were I to enumerate the prodigious feats of retention, which are proved to have been actually performed. Of these, I shall only select the one which, upon the whole, appears to me the most extraordinary, both by reason of its own singularity, and because I am able to afford it some testimony, in confirmation of the veracity of the illustrious scholar by whom it is narrated, and which has most groundlessly been suspected by his learned editor. The story I am about to detail to you is told by Muretus, in the first chapter of the third book of his incomparable work, the *Variæ Lectiones.*[2]

Two qualities requisite to a good memory — viz., Retention and Reproduction.

---

1 H. Schmid, *Versuch einer Metaphysik,* [p. 285, 286. — ED.]

2 *Opera,* edit. Ruhnken., tom. ii. p. 55. — ED. Muretus is one of the most distinguished philologers and critics of modern times; and from himself to Cicero, a period of sixteen centuries, there is to be found no one who equalled him in Latin eloquence. Besides

After noticing the boast of Hippias, in Plato, that he could repeat, upon hearing once, to the amount of five hundred words, he observes that this was nothing as compared with the power of retention possessed by Seneca the rhetorician. In his *Declamations*, Seneca, complaining of the inroads of old age upon his faculties of mind and body, mentions, in regard to the tenacity of his now failing memory, that he had been able to repeat two thousand names read to him, in the order in which they had been spoken; and that, on one occasion, when at his studies, two hundred unconnected verses having been pronounced by the different pupils of his preceptor, he repeated them in a reversed order, that is, proceeded from the last to the first uttered. After quoting the passage from Seneca, of which I have given you the substance, Muretus remarks, that this statement had always appeared to him marvellous, and almost incredible, until he himself had been witness of a fact to which he never could otherwise have afforded credit. The sum of this statement is, that at Padua there dwelt, in his neighborhood, a young man, a Corsican by birth, and of a good family in that island, who had come thither for the cultivation of civil law, in which he was a diligent and distinguished student. He was a frequent visitor at the house and gardens of Muretus, who, having heard that he possessed a remarkable art, or faculty of memory, took occasion, though incredulous in regard to reports, of requesting from him a specimen of his power. He at once agreed; and having adjourned with a considerable party of distinguished auditors into a saloon, Muretus began to dictate words, Latin, Greek, barbarous, significant and non-significant, disjoined and connected, until he wearied himself, the young man who wrote them down, and the audience who were present;—"we were all," he says, "marvellously tired." The Corsican alone was the one of the whole company alert and fresh, and continually desired Muretus for more words; who declared he would be more than satisfied, if he could repeat the half of what had been taken down, and at length he ceased. The young man, with his gaze fixed upon the ground, stood silent for a brief season, and then, says Muretus, "vidi facinus mirificissimum. Having begun to speak, he absolutely repeated the whole words, in the same order in which they had been delivered, without the slightest hesitation;

The remarkable case of retention narrated by Muretus.

<hr>

numerous editions of his several treatises, his works have been republished in a collected form six several times; and the editor of the edition before the one at present [1837] in the course of publication, by Professor Frotscher of Leipzig, was Ruhnkenius, perhaps the greatest scholar of the eighteenth century.

then, commencing from the last, he repeated them backwards till he came to the first. Then again, so that he spoke the first, the third, the fifth, and so on; did this in any order that was asked, and all without the smallest error. Having subsequently become familiarly acquainted with him, I have had other and frequent experience of his power. He assured me (and he had nothing of the boaster in him) that he could recite, in the manner I have mentioned, to the amount of thirty-six thousand words. And what is more wonderful, they all so adhered to the mind that, after a year's interval, he could repeat them without trouble. I know, from having tried him, he could do so after a considerable time (post multos dies). Nor was this all. Franciscus Molinus, a patrician of Venice, was resident with me, a young man ardently devoted to literature, who, as he had but a wretched memory, besought the Corsican to instruct him in the art. The hint of his desire was enough, and a daily course of instruction commenced, and with such success that the pupil could, in about a week or ten days, easily repeat to the extent of five hundred words or more in any order that was prescribed." "This," adds Muretus, "I should hardly venture to record, fearing the suspicion of falsehood, had not the matter been very recent (for a year has not elapsed), and had I not as fellow-witnesses, Nicolaus the son of Petrus Lippomanus, Lazarus the son of Francis Mocenicus, Joannes the son of Nicolaus Malipetrus, George the son of Laurence Contarenus — all Venetian nobles, worthy and distinguished young men, besides other innumerable witnesses. The Corsican stated that he received the art from a Frenchman, who was his domestic tutor." Muretus terminates the narrative by alleging sundry examples of a similar faculty, possessed in antiquity by Cyrus, Simonides, and Apollonius Tyanæus.

Now, on this history, Ruhnkenius has the following note, in reference to the silence of Muretus in regard

Ruhnkenius unduly skeptical in regard to this case.

to the name of the Corsican: "Ego nomen hominis tam mirabilis, citius quam patriam requisiissem. Idque pertinebat ad fidem narrationi faciendam." This skepticism is, I think, out of place. It would, perhaps, have been warranted, had Muretus not done far more than was necessary to establish the authenticity of the story; and, after the testimonies to whom he appeals, the omission of the Corsican's name is a matter of little import. But I am surprised that one confirmatory circumstance has escaped so learned a scholar as Ruhnkenius, seeing that it occurs in the works of a man with whose writings no one was more familiar. Muretus and Paulus

Manutius were correspondents, and Manutius, you must know, was a Venetian. Now, in the letters of Manutius to Muretus, at the date of the occurrence in question, there is frequent mention made of Molino, in whom Manutius seems to have felt much interest; and, on one occasion, there is an allusion (which I cannot at the moment recover so as to give you the precise' expressions) to Molino's cultivation of the Art of Memory, and to his instructor.[1] This, if it were wanted, corroborates the narrative of Muretus whose trustworthiness, I admit, was not quite as transcendent as his genius.[2]

---

[1] See *Pauli Manutii Epistolæ*, vol. i. l. iii. ep. xiii. p. 154 (edit. Krause, 1720): "Molino, parum abest, quin vehementer, invideam; quid ni? *artem Memoriæ* tenenti. Verumtamen impedit amor, a quo abesse solet invidia: etiam ea spes, quod ille, quo eum bono *alienus homo* impertivit, civi suo, homini amantissimo, certe numquam denegabit." Cf. vol. iii. *Notæ ad Epistolas*, p. 1138. — ED.

[2] "As Sophocles says that memory is the queen of things, and because the nurse of poetry herself is a daughter of Mnemosyne, I shall mention here another once world-renowned Corsican of Calvi — Giulio Guidi, in the year 1581, the wonder of Padua, on account of his unfortunate memory. He could repeat thirty-six thousand names after once hearing them. People called him *Guidi della gran memoria*. But he produced nothing; his memory had killed all his creative faculty. Pico von Mirandola, who lived before him, produced; but he died young. It is with the precious gift of memory, as with all other gifts — they are a curse of the gods when they give too much." — Gregorovius, *Wanderings in Corsica*, vol. ii. book vi. chap. vi. p. 84 (Constable's edition). [A case similar to that narrated by Muretus is given by Joseph Scaliger in the *Secunda Scaligerana*, v. *Memoire*, t. ii. p. 450, 451, edit. 1740. — ED.]

LECTURE XXXI.

THE REPRODUCTIVE FACULTY.— LAWS OF ASSOCIATION.

IN my last Lecture, I entered on the consideration of that faculty

Recapitulation.

of mind by which we keep possession of the knowledge acquired by the two faculties of External Perception, and Self-consciousness; and I endeavored to explain to you a theory of the manner in which the fact of retention may be accounted for, in conformity to the nature of mind, considered as a self-active and indivisible subject. At the conclusion of the Lecture, I gave you, *instar omnium*, one memorable example of the prodigious differences which exist between mind and mind in the capacity of retention. Before passing from the

Two opposite doc-
trines maintained in
regard to the relations
of Memory to the
higher powers of
mind.

faculty of Memory, considered simply as the power of conservation, I may notice two opposite doctrines, that have been maintained, in regard to the relation of this faculty to the higher powers of mind. One of these doctrines holds, that a great development of memory is incompatible with a high degree of intelligence; the other, that a high degree of intelligence supposes such a development of memory as its condition.

The former of these opinions is one very extensively prevalent,

1. That a great
power of memory is
incompatible with a
high degree of intelli-
gence.

not only among philosophers, but among mankind in general, and the words — *Beati memoria, expectantes judicium* — have been applied to express the supposed incompatibility of great memory and sound judgment.[1] There seems, however, no valid ground for this belief. If an extraordinary power of retention is frequently not accompanied with a corresponding power of intelligence, it is a natural, but not a very logical procedure, to jump to the conclusion, that a great memory

1 [Niethammer, *Der Streit des Philanthropinismus und Humanismus*, p. 294.] [Ausserdem sey es eine selbst Sprichwörtlich gewordene Erfahrung (beati memoria exspectant judicium), dass vorherrschende *Gedächtnissfertigkeit* der *Urtheilshraft* Abbruch thue. — ED.]

is inconsistent with a sound judgment. The opinion is refuted by the slightest induction; for we immediately

This opinion refuted by facts. Examples of high intelligence and great memory. find, that many of the individuals who towered above their fellows in intellectual superiority, were almost equally distinguished for the capacity of their memory. I recently quoted to you a passage from the *Scaligerana*, in which Joseph Scaliger is made

Joseph Scaliger. to say that he had not a good memory, but a good reminiscence; and he immediately adds, "never, or rarely, are judgment and a great memory found in conjunction." Of this opinion Scaliger himself affords the most illustrious refutation. During his lifetime, he was hailed as the Dictator of the Republic of Letters, and posterity has ratified the decision of his contemporaries, in crowning him as the prince of philologers and critics. But to elevate a man to such an eminence, it is evident, that the most consummate genius and ability were conditions. And what were the powers of Scali-

His great powers of memory testified to by Casaubon. ger, let Isaac Casaubon,[1] among a hundred other witnesses, inform us; and Casaubon was a scholar second only to Scaliger himself in erudition. "Nihil est quod discere quisquam vellet, quod ille (Scaliger) docere non posset: Nihil legerat (quid autem ille non legerat?), quod non statim meminisset; nihil tam obscurum aut abolitum in ullo vetere scriptore Græco, Latino, vel Hebræo, de quo interrogatus non statim responderet. Historias omnium populorum, omnium ætatum, successiones imperiorum, res ecclesiæ, veteris in numerato habebat: animalium, plantarum, metallorum, omniumque rerum naturalium, proprietates, differentias, et appellationes, qua veteres, qua recentes, tenebat accurate. Locorum situs, provinciarum fines et varias pro temporibus illarum divisiones ad unguem callebat; nullam disciplinarum, scientiarumve graviorum reliquerat intactam; linguas tam multas tam exacte sciebat, ut vel si hoc unum per totum vitæ spatium egisset digna res miraculo potuerit videri."

For intellectual power of the highest order, none were distinguished above Grotius and Pascal; and Grotius[2]

Grotius. Pascal. Leibnitz. Euler. and Pascal[3] forgot nothing they had ever read or thought. Leibnitz[4] and Euler[5] were not less celebrated for their intelligence than for their memory, and both

1 [*Prefatio in Opuscula Jos. Justi Scaligeri.*]
2 *Grotii Manes Vindicati* (1727), pars post. p. 585. — ED.
3 *Pensées*, Pref. (ed. Renouard). — ED.
4 Fontenelle, *Eloge de M. Leibnitz.—Leib. Op.* p. xx. (edit. Dutens). — ED.
5 [Biunde, *Versuch einer Systematischen Behandlung der empirischen Psychologie,* i. 856.]

could repeat the whole of the *Æneid*. Donellus[1] knew the *Corpus Juris* by heart, and yet he was one of the pro-

Donellus.

foundest and most original speculators in juris-

Muratori.

prudence. Muratori,[2] though not a genius of the very highest order, was still a man of great ability and judgment; and so powerful was his retention, that in making quotations, he had only to read his passages, put the books in their place, and then to write out from mem-

Ben Jonson.

ory the words. Ben Jonson[3] tells us that he could repeat all he had ever written, and whole books that he had read. Themistocles[4] could call by their names

Themistocles.
Cyrus.
Hortensius.

the twenty thousand citizens of Athens; Cyrus[5] is reported to have known the name of every soldier in his army. Hortensius, after Cicero, the greatest orator of Rome, after sitting a whole day at a public sale, correctly enunciated from memory all the things sold, their

Niebuhr.

prices, and the names of the purchasers.[6] Niebuhr,[7] the historian of Rome, was not less distinguished for his memory than for his acuteness. In his youth he was employed in one of the public offices of Denmark; part

Sir James Mackintosh.

of a book of accounts having been destroyed, he restored it from his recollection. Sir James Mackintosh was, likewise, remarkable for his power of memory. An instance I can give you which I witnessed myself. In a conversation I had with him, we happened to touch upon an author whom I mentioned in my last Lecture, — Muretus; and Sir James recited from his oration in praise of the massacre of St. Bartholomew some considerable passages. Mr. Dugald Stewart, and

Dugald Stewart.
Dr. Gregory.

the late Dr. Gregory, are, likewise, examples of great talent, united with great memory.

But if there be no ground for the vulgar opinion, that a strong faculty of retention is incompatible with intel-

2. That a high degree of intelligence supposes great power of memory.

lectual capacity in general, the converse opinion is not better founded, which has been maintained, among others, by Hoffbauer.[8] This doctrine does not, however, deserve an articulate refutation; for the common experience of every one sufficiently

---

1 Teissier, *Eloges des Hommes Savans*, t. iv. p. 146. — ED.

2 [Biunde, *Versuch*, etc., as above.] [*Vita di Muratori*, c. xi. p. 236. — ED.]

3 *Timber; or, Discoveries made upon Men and Matter* (*Works*, ed. Gifford, vol. ix. p. 169.)—ED.

4 Cicero, *De Senectute*, c. vii. Val. Maximus, viii. 7. — ED.

5 Pliny, *Nat. Hist.* vii. 24. Quintilian, *Orat.* xi. 2. — ED.

6 Seneca (M.) *Controv.* Pref. — ED.

7 See *Life of Niebuhr*, vol. ii. p. 412, 413, where a similar anecdote is mentioned, but not exactly as stated in the text. See also vol. i. c. vii. p. 298. — ED.

8 [See Biunde, *Versuch einer systematischen*

proves that intelligence and memory hold no necessary proportion to each other. On this subject I may refer you to Mr. Stewart's excellent chapter on Memory in the first volume of his *Elements*.[1]

I now pass to the next faculty in order — the faculty which I have called the Reproductive. I am not satis-

The Reproductive Faculty. This name inappropriate; the limitation in which it is here employed.

fied with this name; for it does not precisely of itself mark what I wish to be expressed, — viz., the process by which what is lying dormant in memory is awakened, as contradistinguished from the representation in consciousness of it as awakened. The two processes certainly suppose each other; for we cannot awaken a cognition without its being represented, — the representation being, in fact, only its state of waking; nor can a latent thought or affection be represented, unless certain conditions be fulfilled, by which it is called out of obscurity into the light of consciousness. The two processes are relative and correlative, but not more identical than hill and valley. I am not satisfied, I say, with the term *reproduction* for the process by which the dormant thought or affection is aroused; for it does not clearly denote what it is intended to express. Perhaps the *Resuscitative Faculty* would have been better; and the term *reproduction* might have been employed to comprehend the whole process, made up of the correlative acts of retention, resuscitation, and representation. Be this, however, as it may, I shall at present continue to employ the term, in the limited meaning I have already assigned.

The phænomenon of Reproduction is one of the most wonderful in the whole compass of psychology; and it is

Interest excited by the phænomenon of Reproduction. The Schoolmen.

one in the explanation of which philosophy has been more successful than in almost any other. The scholastic psychologists seem to have regarded the succession in the train of thought, or, as they called it, the excitation of the species, with peculiar wonder, as one of the most inscrutable mysteries of nature; and yet, what is curious, Aristotle has left almost as complete an

Aristotle's analysis of the phænomenon, nearly perfect.

analysis of the laws by which this phænomenon is regulated, as has yet been accomplished. It required, however, a considerable progress in the inductive philosophy of mind, before this analysis of Aristotle could be appreciated at its proper value; and in fact, it was only after modern philosophers had rediscovered the principal laws of

Behandlung der empirischen Psychologie, i. 357, where Hoffbauer is referred to.] [See Hoff-　bauer, *Naturlehre der Seele in Briefen*, p. 181– 183. — ED.]

1 Chap. vi. *Works*, ii. 348. — ED.

Association, that it was found that these laws had been more completely given two thousand years before. Joseph Scaliger, speaking of his father, whose philosophical acuteness I have more than once had occasion to commemorate, says, "My father declared, that of the causes of three things in particular he was wholly ignorant, — of the interval of fevers, of the ebb and flow of the sea, and of reminiscence."[1]

Julius Cæsar Scaliger.

Poncius. Oviedo.

The excitation of the species is declared by Poncius[2] to be "one of the most difficult secrets of nature" (ex difficilioribus naturæ arcanis); and Oviedo,[3] a Jesuit schoolman, says, "therein lies the very greatest mystery of all philosophy (maximum totius philosophiæ sacramentum), never to be competently explained by human ingenuity;" "and this because we can neither discover the cause which, for example, in the recitation of an oration, excites the species in the order in which they are excited, nor the reason why often, when wishing to recollect a matter, we do not, whereas when not wishing to recollect it, we sometimes do. Hence the same Poncius says, that for the excitation of the species we must either recur at once to God, or to some sufficient cause, which, however, he does not specify."[4]

Reproduction, what.

The faculty of Reproduction is governed by the laws which regulate the Association of the mental train; or, to speak more correctly, reproduction is nothing but the result of these laws. Every one is conscious of a ceaseless succession or train of thoughts, one thought suggesting another, which again is the cause of exciting a third, and so on. In what manner, it may be asked, does the presence of any thought determine the introduction of another? Is the train subject to laws, and if so, by what laws is it regulated?

The train of thought subject to laws. This illustrated by Hobbes.

That the elements of the mental train are not isolated, but that each thought forms a link of a continuous and uninterrupted chain, is well illustrated by Hobbes. "In a company," he says, "in which the conversation turned upon the late civil war, what could be conceived more impertinent than for a person to ask abruptly, what was the value of a Roman denarius? On a little reflection, however, I was easily able to trace the train of thought which suggested the question; for the original subject of discourse

---

1 [*Prima Scaligerana, v.* "Causa,"] [t. ii. p. 46, edit. 1740. — ED]

2 [Poncius, *Cursus Philosophicus, De Anima,* Disp. lxiii. qu. iii. concl. 3.]

3 [*Francisci de Oviedo Cursus Philosophicus,* De Anima, Cont. v. punct. iv. n. 13.] [Cf. *Reid's Works,* Note D * *, p. 889. — ED.]

4 [Fr. Bonæ Spei, *Physica,* p. iv. *In de Anima,* disp. x. p. 94. Cf. Ancillon, *Essais Philos.* (*Nouv. Mel.*) v. ii. c. iii. p. 139.]

naturally introduced the history of the king, and of the treachery of those who surrendered his person to his enemies; this again introduced the treachery of Judas Iscariot, and the sum of money which he received for his reward.[1]

But if thoughts, and feelings, and conations (for you must observe, that the train is not limited to the phænomena of cognition only),[2] do not arise of themselves, but only in causal connection with preceding and subsequent modifications of mind, it remains to be asked and answered, — Do the links of this chain follow each other under any other condition than that of simple connection, — in other words, may any thought, feeling, or desire, be connected with any other?

The expression train of thought includes the phænomena of Cognition, Feeling and Conation.

Is there any law besides that of simple connection which regulates this train?

Or, is the succession regulated by other and special laws, according to which certain kinds of modification exclusively precede, and exclusively follow, each other? The slightest observation of the phænomenon shows, that the latter alternative is the case; and on this all philosophers are agreed. Nor do philosophers differ in regard to what kind of thoughts (and under that term, you will remark, I at present include also *feelings* and *conations*) are associated together. They differ almost exclusively in regard to the subordinate question, of how these thoughts ought to be classified, and carried up into system. This, therefore, is the question to which I shall address myself, referring you for illustrations and examples of the fact and effects of Association, to the chapter on the subject in the first volume of Mr. Stewart's *Elements*,[3] in which you will find its details treated with great elegance and ability.

The point on which philosophers differ; and question to be considered.

In my last Lecture, I explained to you how thoughts, once experienced, remain, though out of consciousness, still in possession of the mind; and I have now to show you, how these thoughts retained in memory, may, without any excitation from without, be again retrieved by an excitation or awakening from other thoughts within. Philosophers having observed, that one thought determined another to arise, and that

Conditions of Reproduction, as generalized by philosophers; in all seven.

1 *Leviathan*, part i. chap. iii. — ED.

2 [Cf. Fries, *Anthropologie*, vol. i. § 8, p. 29, edit. 1820. *Kritik*, i. § 33. H. Schmid, *Versuch einer Metaphysik der inneren Natur*, pp. 236, 242. Carus, *Psychologie*, i. p. 183. Stewart,

Elements, i. c. v. *Works*, vol. ii. p. 257. Brown, *Philosophy of the Human Mind*, lect. xliv. p. 282 (edit 1830).] [For Aristotle, see *Reid's Works*, p. 892, 893. — ED.]

3 Chap. v. *Works*, ii. 252. — ED.

this determination only took place between thoughts which stood in certain relations to each other, set themselves to ascertain and classify the kinds of correlation under which this occurred, in order to generalize the laws by which the phænomenon of Reproduction was governed.   Accordingly, it has been established, that thoughts are associated, that is, are able to excite each other; — 1°, If coëxistent, or immediately successive, in time; 2°, If their objects are conterminous or adjoining in space; 3°, If they hold the dependence to each other of cause and effect, or of mean and end, or of whole and part; 4°, If they stand in a relation either of contrast or of similarity; 5°, If they are the operations of the same power, or of different powers conversant about the same object; 6°, If their objects are the sign and the signified; or, 7°, Even if their objects are accidentally denoted by the same sound.   These, as far as I

recollect, are all the classes to which philoso-

Aristotle reduces the laws of association to three; and implicitly to one canon.

phers have attempted to reduce the principles of Mental Association.   Aristotle recalled the laws of this connection to four, or rather to three, — Contiguity in time and space, Resemblance, and

Contrariety.[1] He even seems to have thought they might all be carried up into the one law of Coëxistence.

St. Augustin explicitly reduces these laws to one, — which the author calls the law of Redintegration.

Aristotle implicitly, St. Augustin[2] explicitly, — what has never been observed, — reduces association to a single canon, — viz., Thoughts that have once coëxisted in the mind are afterwards

Malebranche.
Wolf.
Bilfinger.
Hume.

associated.   This law, which I would call the law of Redintegration, was afterwards enounced by Malebranche,[3] Wolf,[4] and Bilfinger;[5] but without any reference to St. Austin.   Hume,

who thinks himself the first philosopher who had ever attempted to generalize the laws of association, makes them three, — Resemblance,

Gerard.   Beattie.

Contiguity in time and place, and Cause and Effect.[6]   Gerard[7] and Beattie[8] adopt, with little

modification, the Aristotelic classification.   Omitting a hundred others, whose opinions would be curious in a his-

Stewart. Brown.
Stewart quoted.

tory of the doctrine, I shall notice only Stewart and Brown.   Stewart,[9] after disclaiming any at-

---

1 *De Memoria et Reminiscentia*, c. ii. § viii.- ED.

2 *Confessiones*, lib. x. chap. xix. — ED.

3 *Recherche de la Vérité*, l. ii. c. v. — ED.

4 *Psychologia Empirica*, § 230. — ED.

5 See *Reid's Works*, p. 899. — ED.

6 *Enquiry concerning Human Understanding*, sect. iii. — ED.

7 *Essay on Taste*, part iii. § 1. pp. 167, 168, edit. 1759. — ED

8 *Dissertations, Moral and Critical.* — Of Imagination, c. ii. § 1 *et seq.*, p 78. Cf. pp. 9, 145. — ED.

9 *Elements*, vol. ii. c. v. part i. sect. ii Works, vol. iii. p. 263. — ED.

tempt at a complete enumeration, mentions two classes of circumstances as useful to be observed. "The relations," he says, "upon which some of them are founded, are perfectly obvious to the mind; those which are the foundation of others, are discovered only in consequence of particular efforts of attention. Of the former kind are the relations of Resemblance and Analogy, of Contrariety, of Vicinity in time and place, and those which arise from accidental coincidences in the sound of different words. These, in general, connect our thoughts together, when they are suffered to take their natural course, and when we are conscious of little or no active exertion. Of the latter kind are the relations of Cause and Effect, of Means and End, of Premises and Conclusion; and those others which regulate the train of thought in the mind of the philosopher, when he is engaged in a particular investigation."

Brown[1] divides the circumstances affecting association into primary and secondary. Under the primary laws of Suggestion, he includes Resemblance, Contrast, Contiguity in time and place, — a classification identical with Aristotle's. By the secondary, he means the vivacity, the recentness, and the frequent repetition of our thoughts; circumstances which, though they exert an influence on the recurrence of our thoughts, belong to a different order of causes from those we are at present considering.[2]

Brown's classification.

Now all the laws which I have hitherto enumerated may be easily reduced to two, — the law of the Simultaneity, and the law of the Resemblance or Affinity, of Thought.[3] Under Simultaneity I include Immediate Consecution in time; to the other category of Affinity every other circumstance may be reduced. I shall take the several cases I have above enumerated, and having exemplified their influence as associating principles, I shall show how they are all only special modifications of the two laws of Simultaneity and Affinity; which two laws, I shall finally prove to you, are themselves only modifications of one supreme law, — the law of Redintegration.

The laws enumerated admit of reduction to two; and these two again to one grand law.

The first law, — that of Simultaneity, or of Coëxistence and Immediate Succession in time, — is too evident to require any illustration. "In passing along a road," as Mr. Stewart[4] observes,

---

1 *Philosophy of the Human Mind*, lects. xxxiv. xxxvii. — ED.

2 See *Reid's Works*, p. 910. — ED.

3 See H. Schmid, *Versuch einer Metaphysik*

der inneren Natur, p. 241. [Cf. Fries, *Anthropologie*, i. § 8, p. 29 (edit. 1820)].

4 *Elements*, vol. i. c. v. p. i, § 1. *Works*, ii. 252, 253. — ED.

"which we have formerly travelled in the company of a friend, the particulars of the conversation in which we were then engaged, are frequently suggested to us by the objects we meet with. In such a scene, we recollect that a particular subject was started; and in passing the different houses, and plantations, and rivers, the arguments we were discussing when we last saw them, recur spontaneously to the memory. The connection which is formed in the mind between the words of a language and the ideas they denote; the connection which is formed between the different words of a discourse we have committed to memory; the connection between the different notes of a piece of music in the mind of the musician, are all obvious instances of the same general law of our nature."

The influence of the special laws, as associating principles, illustrated.

I. The law of Simultaneity.

The second law, — that of the Affinity of thoughts, — will be best illustrated by the cases of which it is the more general expression. In the first place, in the case of resembling, or analogous, or partially identical objects, it will not be denied that these virtually suggest each other. The imagination of Alexander carries me to the imagination of Cæsar, Cæsar to Charlemagne, Charlemagne to Napoleon. The vision of a portrait suggests the image of the person portrayed. In a company one anecdote suggests another analogous. This principle is admirably illustrated from the mouth of Shakspeare's Merchant of Venice:

II. The law of Affinity.

1. The case of resembling, analogous, or partially identical objects.

> " My wind, cooling my broth,
> Would blow me to an ague, when I thought,
> What harm a wind too great might do at sea.
> I should not see the sandy hour-glass run,
> But I should think of shallows and of flats,
> And see my wealthy Andrew dock'd in sand,
> Vailing her high top lower than her ribs,
> To kiss her burial. Should I go to church,
> And see the holy edifice of stone,
> And not bethink me strait of dang'rous rocks?
> Which, touching but my gentle vessel's side,
> Would scatter all the spices on the stream,
> Enrobe the roaring waters with my silks;
> And in a word,— but even now worth this,
> And now worth nothing." [1]

1 *Merchant of Venice*, act i. scene i.

That resembling, analogous, or partially identical objects stand in reciprocal affinity, is apparent; they are its strongest exemplifications. So far there is no difficulty.

In the second place, thoughts standing to each other in the relation of contrariety or contrast, are mutually suggestive. Thus the thought of vice suggests the thought of virtue; and, in the mental world, the prince and the peasant, kings and beggars, are inseparable concomitants. On this principle are dependent those associations which constitute the charms of antithesis and wit. Thus the whole pathos of Milton's apostrophe to light, lies in the contrast of his own darkness to the resplendent object he addresses:

2. The case of contrary or contrasted thoughts.

> "Hail, holy light, offspring of heaven first-born,
> .   .   .   .   Thee I revisit safe,
> And feel thy sovran vital lamp; but thou
> Revisit'st not these eyes, that roll in vain
> To find thy piercing ray, and find no dawn."[1]

It is contrast that animates the Ode of Horace to Archytas:

> "Te maris et terræ, numeroque carentis arenæ
>   Mensorem cohibent, Archyta,
>   Pulveris exigui prope littus parva Matinum
>   Munera: nec quidquam tibi prodest
>   Aërias tentasse domos, animoque rotundum
>   Percurrisse polum, morituro."[2]

The same contrast illuminates the stanza of Gray:

> "The boast of heraldry, the pomp of power,
>   And all that beauty, all that wealth ere gave,
>   Awaits alike the inevitable hour; —
>   The paths of glory lead but to the grave."

And in what else does the beauty of the following line consist, but in the contrast and connection of life and death; life being represented as but a wayfaring from grave to grave?

> Τίς βίος; — ἐκ τύμβοιο θορὼν, ἐπὶ τύμβον ὀδεύω.[3]

Who can think of Marius sitting amid the ruins of Carthage, without thinking of the resemblance of the consul and the city, —

---

1 *Paradise Lost*, book iii. — Ed.   2 *Carm.* i. xxviii. — Ed.   3 [Gregor. Nazianz. *Carm.* xiv.]

without thinking of the difference between their past and present fortunes? And in the incomparable epigram of Molsa on the great Pompey, the effect is produced by the contrast of the life and death of the hero, and in the conversion of the very fact of his post-humous dishonor into a theme of the noblest panegyric.

> "Dux, Pharia quamvis jaceas inhumatus arena,
>   Non ideo fati est sævior ira tui:
> Indignum fuerat tellus tibi victa sepulcrum;
>   Non decuit cœlo, te, nisi, Magne, tegi."[1]

Thus that objects, though contrasted, are still akin, — still stand to each other in a relation of affinity, depends on their logical analogy. The axiom, that the knowledge of contraries is one, proves that the thought of the one involves the thought of the other.[2]

Depends on the logical principle, — that the knowledge of contraries is one.

In the third place, objects contiguous in place are associated. You recollect the famous passage of Cicero in the first chapter of the fifth book *De Finibus*, of which the following is the conclusion:—

8. The law of contiguity.

"Tanta vis admonitionis est in locis, ut, non sine causa, ex his memoriæ deducta sit disciplina. . . . Id quidem infinitum in hac urbe; quocumque enim ingredimur, in aliquam historiam vestigium ponimus." But how do objects adjacent in place stand in affinity to each other? Simply because local contiguity binds up objects, otherwise unconnected, into a single object of perceptive thought.

In the fourth place, thoughts of the whole and the parts, of the thing and its properties, of the sign and the thing signified, — of these it is superfluous to illustrate either the reality of the influence, or to show that they are only so many forms of affinity; both are equally manifest. But in this case affinity is not the only principle of association; here simultaneity also occurs. One observation I may make to show, that what Mr. Stewart promulgates as a distinct principle of association, is only a subordinate modification of the two great laws I have laid down, — I mean his association of objects, arising from accidental coincidences in the sound of the words by which they are denoted. Here the association between

4. The law of whole and parts, etc.

---

1 [*Carmina Illustrium Poetarum Italorum*, t. vi. 369. Florentiæ, 1719.]

2 [Alex. Aphrodisiensis (*In Top.* i. 18) makes Contrariety equivalent to Simultaneity, inasmuch as contraries, etc., have common attributes.]

the objects or ideas is not immediate. One object or idea signified suggests its term signifying. But a complete or partial identity in sound suggests another word, and that word suggests the thing or thought it signifies. The two things or thoughts are thus associated, only mediately, through the association of their signs, and the several immediate associations are very simple examples of the general laws.

In the fifth place, thoughts of causes and effects reciprocally suggest each other. Thus the falling snow

5. The law of cause and effect.

excites the imagination of an inundation; a shower of hail a thought of the destruction of the fruit; the sight of wine carries us back to the grapes, or the sight of the grapes carries us forward to the wine; and so forth. But cause and effect not only naturally but necessarily suggest each other; they stand in the closest affinity, and, therefore, whatever phænomena are subsumed under this relation, as indeed under all relations, are, consequently, also in affinity.

I have now, I think, gone through all the circumstances which philosophers have constituted into separate laws

All these separate laws thus resolved into two: — Simultaneity and Affinity: and these again are resolvable into the one grand law of Redintegration.

of Association; and shown that they easily resolve themselves into the two laws of Simultaneity and Affinity. I now proceed to show you that these two laws themselves are reducible to that one law, which I would call the law of Redintegration or Totality, which, as I already stated, I have found incidentally expressed by St. Augustin.[1] This law may be thus enounced, — Those thoughts suggest each other which had previously constituted parts of the same entire or total act of cognition. Now to the same entire or total act belong, as integral or constituent parts, in the first place, those thoughts which arose at the same time, or in immediate consecution; and in the second, those thoughts which are bound up into one by their mutual affinity. Thus, therefore, the two laws of Simultaneity and Affinity are carried up into unity, in the higher law of Redintegration or Totality; and by this one law the whole phænomena of Association may be easily explained.[2]

---

1 *Confessiones*, x. 19. — ED.
2 For historical notices of the law of

Redintegration, see *Reid's Works*, Note D**, p. 889. — ED.

LECTURE XXXII.

THE REPRODUCTIVE FACULTY. — LAWS OF ASSOCIATION. SUGGESTION AND REMINISCENCE.

In our last Lecture we were occupied with the phænomena of

Recapitulation. Reproduction, as the result of the laws which govern the succession of our mental train. These laws, as they have been called, of the Association of our Thoughts, comprehend equally the whole phænomena of mind, — the Cognitions, the Feelings, the Desires. I enumerated to you the principal heads under which philosophers had classed the circumstances which constitute between thoughts a bond of association, — a principle of mutual suggestion; and showed you that these could all easily be reduced to two laws, — the law of Simultaneity, and the law of Affinity. By the former of these, objects coëxistent or immediately consequent in time are associated; by the latter, things which stand in a mutual affinity to each other, either objectively and in themselves, or subjectively, through the modes under which the mind conceives them, are in like manner reciprocally suggestive. These two laws, I further showed you, might themselves be carried up into one supreme principle of Association, which I called the law of Redintegration or of Totality; and according to which thoughts or mental activities, having once formed parts of the same total thought or mental activity, tend ever after immediately to suggest each other. Out of this universal law every special law of Association may easily be evolved, as they are all only so many modified expressions of this common principle — so many applications of it to cases more or less particular.

But this law being established by induction

No legitimate presumption against the truth of the law of Redintegration, if found inexplicable. and generalization, and affording an explanation of the various phænomena of Association, it may be asked, How is this law itself explained? On what principle of our intellectual nature is it founded? To this no answer can be legitimately demanded. It is enough for the natural philosopher to reduce the special laws of the attraction of distant bodies to the one principle of gravitation; and his theory is not invalidated, because he can give no account of how gravitation is itself determined. In all our explanations of the phænomena of mind and matter, we must always arrive at an ultimate fact or law, of which we are wholly unable to afford an ulterior explanation. We are, therefore, entitled to decline attempting any illustration of the ground on which the supreme fact or law of Association reposes; and if we do attempt such illustration, and fail in the endeavor, no presumption is, therefore, justly to be raised against the truth of the fact or principle itself.

But an illustration of this great law is involved in the principle of the unity of the mental energies, as the activities of the subject one and indivisible, to which I have had occasion to refer.[1] "The various acts of mind must not be viewed as single, — as isolated, manifestations; they all belong to the one activity of the ego: and, consequently, if our various mental energies are only partial modifications of the same general activity, they must all be associated among themselves. Every mental energy, — every thought, feeling, desire that is excited, excites at the same time all other previously existent activities, in a certain degree; it spreads its excitation over the whole activities of the mind, as the agitation of one place of a sheet of water expands itself, in wider and wider circles, over the whole surface of the fluid,[2] although, in proportion to its eccentricity, it is always becoming fainter, until it is at last not to be perceived. The force of every internal activity exists only in a certain limited degree; consequently, the excitation it determines has only likewise a certain limited power of expansion, and is continually losing in vigor in proportion to its eccentricity. Thus there are formed particular centres, particular spheres, of internal unity, within which the activities stand to each other in a closer relation of action and reäction; and this, in proportion as they more or less belong already to a single energy, — in proportion as they gravitate more or less proximately to the same centre of action. A plurality, a complement, of several activities forms, in a stricter sense, one whole activity for itself; an invigoration of any of its several activities is, therefore, an invigoration of the part of a whole activity; and as a part cannot be active for itself alone, there, consequently, results an invigoration of the whole, that is, of all the other parts

Attempted illustration of the ground on which this law reposes, from the unity of the subject of the mental energies.

---

1 See above, lect. xxx. p. 415. — ED.   2 Cf. Pope, *Essay on Man*, iv. 363. — ED.

of which it is composed. Thus the supreme law of association, — that activities excite each other in proportion as they have previously belonged, as parts, to one whole activity, — is explained from the still more universal principle of the unity of all our mental energies in general.[1]

"But, on the same principle, we can also explain the two subaltern laws of Simultaneity and Affinity. The

The laws of Simultaneity and Affinity, explicable on the same principle.

phænomena of mind are manifested under a twofold condition or form; for they are only revealed, 1°, As occurrences in time; and, 2°, As the energies or modifications of the ego, as their cause and subject. Time and Self are thus the two forms of the internal world. By these two forms, therefore, every particular, every limited, unity of operation, must be controlled; — on them it must depend. And it is precisely these two forms that lie at the root of the two laws of Simultaneity and Affinity. Thus acts which are exerted at the same time, belong, by that very circumstance, to the same particular unity, — to the same definite sphere of mental energy; in other words, constitute through their simultaneity a single activity. Thus energies, however heterogeneous in themselves, if developed at once, belong to the same activity, — constitute a particular unity; and they will operate with a greater suggestive influence on each other, in proportion as they are more closely connected by the bond of time. On the other hand, the affinity of mental acts or modifications will be determined by their particular relations to the ego, as their cause or subject. As all the activities of mind obtain a unity in being all the energies of the same soul or active principle in general, so they are bound up into particular unities, inasmuch as they belong to some particular faculty, — resemble each other in the common ground of their manifestation. Thus cognitions, feelings, and volitions, severally awaken cognitions, feelings, and volitions; for they severally belong to the same faculty, and, through that identity, are themselves constituted into distinct unities: or again, a thought of the cause suggests a thought of the effect, a thought of the mean suggests a thought of the end, a thought of the part suggests a thought of the whole; for cause and effect, end and mean, whole and parts, have subjectively an indissoluble affinity, as they are all so many forms or organizations of thought. In like manner, the notions of all resembling objects suggest each other, for they possess some common quality, through which they are in thought bound up in a single act of thought. Even the notions of opposite and contrasted objects

---

[1] (Cf. Fries, *Anthropologie*, i. 29, § 8. *Kritik*, i. § 83.)

mutually excite each other upon the same principle; for these are logically associated, inasmuch as, by the laws of thought, the notion of one opposite necessarily involves the notions of the other; and it is also a psychological law, that contrasted objects relieve each other. *Opposita, juxta posita, se invicem collustrant.* When the operations of different faculties are mutually suggestive, they are, likewise, internally connected by the nature of their action; for they are either conversant with the same object, and have thus been originally determined by the same affection from without, or they have originally been associated through some form of the mind itself; thus moral cognitions, moral feelings, and moral volitions, may suggest each other, through the common bond of morality; the moral principle in this case uniting the operations of the three fundamental powers into one general activity."[1]

Before leaving this subject, I must call your attention to a circumstance which I formerly incidentally noticed.[2]

Thoughts, apparently unassociated, seem to follow each other immediately.

It sometimes happens that thoughts seem to follow each other immediately, between which it is impossible to detect any bond of association. If this anomaly be insoluble, the whole theory of association is overthrown. Philosophers have accordingly set themselves to account for this phænomenon. To deny the fact of the phænomenon is impossible; it must, therefore, be explained on the hypothesis of association. Now, in their attempts at such an explanation, all philosophers agree in regard to the first step of the solution, but they differ in regard to the second. They agree in this, — that, admitting the apparent, the phænomenal, immediacy of the consecution of the two unassociated thoughts, they deny its reality. They all affirm, that there have actually intervened one or more thoughts, through the mediation of which, the suggestion in question has been effected, and on the assumption of which intermediation the theory of association remains intact. For example, let us suppose that A and C are thoughts, not on any law of association suggestive of each other, and that A and C appear to our consciousness as following each other immediately. In this case, I say, philosophers agree in supposing, that a thought B, associated with A and with C, and which consequently could be awakened by A, and could awaken C, has intervened. So far they are at one. But now comes their separation. It is asked, how can a thought be supposed to intervene, of which consciousness gives us no indi-

---

1 H. Schmid, *Versuch einer Metaph.* p. 242-4; [translated with occasional brief interpola-   tions. — ED.]   Cf. *Reid's Works*, Notes D** and D***. — ED.

2 See above, lect. xviii. p 244 — ED.

cation? In reply to this, two answers have been made. By one set of philosophers, among whom I may particularly specify Mr. Stewart, it is said, that the immediate thought B, having been awakened by A, did rise into consciousness, suggested C, and was instantly forgotten. This solution is apparently that exclusively known in Britain. Other philosophers, following the indication of Leibnitz, by whom the theory of obscure or latent activities was first explicitly promulgated, maintain that the intermediate thought never did rise into consciousness. They hold that A excited B, but that the excitement was not strong enough to rouse B from its state of latency, though strong enough to enable it obscurely to excite C, whose latency was less, and to afford it vivacity sufficient to rise into consciousness.

Two modes of explication adopted by philosophers.

Of these opinions, I have no hesitation in declaring for the latter. I formerly showed you an analysis of some of the most palpable and familiar phænomena of mind, which made the supposition of mental modifications latent, but not inert, one of absolute necessity. In particular, I proved this in regard to the phænomena of Perception.[1] But the fact of such latencies being established in one faculty, they afford an easy and philosophical explanation of the phænomena in all. In the present instance, if we admit, as admit we must, that activities can endure, and consequently can operate, out of consciousness, the question is at once solved. On this doctrine, the whole theory of association obtains an easy and natural completion; as no definite line can be drawn between clear and obscure activities, which melt insensibly into each; and both, being of the same nature, must be supposed to operate under the same laws. In illustration of the mediatory agency of latent thoughts in the process of suggestion, I formerly alluded to an analogous phænomenon under the laws of physical motion, which I may again call to your remembrance. If a series of elastic balls, say of ivory, are placed in a straight line, and in mutual contact, and if the first be sharply struck, what happens? The intermediate balls remain at rest; the last alone is moved.

To be explained on the principle of latent modifications of mind.

The other doctrine, which proceeds upon the hypothesis that we can be conscious of a thought and that thought be instantly forgotten, has everything against it, and nothing in its favor. In the first place, it does not, like the counter hypothesis of latent agencies, only apply

The counter solution untenable.

1 See above, lect. xviii. p. 242. — ED.

a principle which is already proved to exist; it on the contrary lays its foundation in a fact which is not shown to be real. But in the second place, this fact is not only not shown to be real: it is improbable, — nay impossible; for it contradicts the whole analogy of the intellectual phænomena. The memory or retention of a thought is in proportion to its vivacity in consciousness; but that all trace of its existence so completely perished with its presence, that reproduction became impossible, even the instant after, — this assumption violates every probability, in gratuitously disallowing the established law of the proportion between consciousness and memory. But on this subject, having formerly spoken, it is needless now again to dwell.[1]

So much for the laws of association, — the laws to which the faculty of Reproduction is subjected.

This faculty, I formerly mentioned, might be considered as operating, either spontaneously, without any interference of the will, or as modified in its action by the intervention of volition. In the one case, as in the other, the Reproductive Faculty acts in subservience to its own laws. In the former case, one thought is allowed to suggest another according to the greater general connec-

The Reproductive Faculty divided into two: — Spontaneous Suggestion and Reminiscence.

tion subsisting between them; in the latter, the act of volition, by concentrating attention upon a certain determinate class of associating circumstances, bestows on these circumstances an extraordinary vivacity, and, consequently, enables them to obtain the preponderance, and exclusively to determine the succession of the intellectual train. The former of these cases, where the Reproductive Faculty is left wholly to itself, may not improperly be called Spontaneous Suggestion, or Suggestion simply; the latter ought to obtain the name of Reminiscence or Recollection, (in Greek ἀνάμνησις). The employment of these terms in these significations, corresponds with the meaning they obtain in common usage. Philosophers have not, however, always so applied them. But as I have not entered on a criticism of the analyses attempted by philosophers of the faculties, so I shall say nothing in illustration of their perversion of the terms by which they have denoted them.

Recollection or Reminiscence supposes two things. "First, it is necessary that the mind recognize the identity

What Reminiscence involves.

of two representations, and then it is necessary that the mind be conscious of something different from the first impression, in consequence of which it affirms to

---

1 See above, lect. xviii. p. 245. — ED.

itself that it had formerly experienced this modification. It is passing marvellous, this conviction that we have of the identity of two representations; for they are only similar, not the same. Were they the same, it would be impossible to discriminate the thought reproduced from the thought originally experienced."[1] This cir-

St. Augustin's analysis of this power,— detailed.

cumstance justly excited the admiration of St. Augustin, and he asks how, if we had actually forgotten a thing, we could so categorically affirm, — it is not that, when some one named to us another; or, it is that, when it is itself presented. The question was worthy of his subtlety, and the answer does honor to his penetration. His principle is, that we cannot seek in our own memory for that of which we have no sort of recollection, "Quod omnino obliti fueramus amissum quærere non possumus."[2] We do not seek what has been our first reflective thought in infancy, the first reasoning we have performed, the first free act which raised us above the rank of automata. We are conscious that the attempt would be fruitless; and even if modifications thus lost should chance to recur to our mind, we should not be able to say with truth that we had recollected them, for we should have no criterion by which to recognize them, "Cujus nisi memor essem, si offeretur mihi, non invenirem, quia non agnoscerem." And what is the consequence he deduces? It is worthy of your attention.

From the moment, then, that we seek aught in our memory, we

Its condition, — the law of totality.

declare, by that very act, that we have not altogether forgotten it; we still hold of it, as it were, a part, and by this part, which we hold, we seek that which we do not hold, "Ergo non totum exciderat; sed ex parte qua tenebatur, alia quærebatur." And what is the secret motive which determines us to this research? It is that our memory feels, that it does not see together all that it was accustomed to see together, "Quia sentiebat se memoria non simul volvere quæ simul solebat." It feels with regret that it still only discovers a part of itself, and hence its disquietude to seek out what is missing, in order to reännex it to the whole ; like to those reptiles, if the comparison may be permitted, whose members when cut asunder seek again to reünite, "Et quasi detruncata consuetudine claudicans, reddi quod deerat flagitabat." But when this detached portion of our memory at length presents itself, — the name, for example, of a person, which had escaped us; how shall we proceed

---

[1] Ancillon, *Essais Philosophiques*, ii. pp. 141, 142. — ED. Cf. André, *Traité de l'Homme*, i, 277.
[2] *Confessions*, lib. x. caps. 18, 19.

to reännex it to the other? We have only to allow nature to do her work. For if the name, being pronounced, goes of itself to reünite itself to the thought of the person, and to place itself, so to speak, upon his face, as upon its ordinary seat, we will say, without hesitation,—there it is. And if, on the contrary, it obstinately refuses to go there to place itself, in order to rejoin the thought to which we had else attached it, we will say peremptorily and at once,— no, it does not suit, "Non connectitur, quia non simul cum illo cogitari consuevit." But when it suits, where do we discover this luminous accordance which consummates our research? And where can we discover it, except in our memory itself,—in some back chamber I mean, of that labyrinth where what we considered as lost had only gone astray, "Et unde adest, nisi ex ipsa memoria." And the proof of this is manifest. When the name presents itself to our mind, it appears neither novel nor strange, but old and familiar, like an ancient property of which we have recovered the title-deeds, "Non enim quasi novum credimus, sed recordantes approbamus."

Such is the doctrine of one of the profoundest thinkers of antiquity, and whose philosophical opinions, were they collected, arranged, and illustrated, would raise him to as high a rank among metaphysicians, as he already holds among theologians.

"Among psychologists, those who have written on Memory and Reproduction with the greatest detail and precision, have still failed in giving more than a meagre outline of these operations. They have taken account only of the notions which suggest each other, with a distinct and palpable notoriety. They have viewed the associations only in the order in which language is competent to express them; and as language, which renders them still more palpable and distinct, can only express them in a consecutive order,— can only express them one after another, they have been led to suppose that thoughts only awaken in succession. Thus, a series of ideas mutually associated, resembles, on the doctrine of philosophers, a chain in which every link draws up that which follows; and it is by means of these links that intelligence labors through, in the act of reminiscence, to the end which it proposes to attain.[1]

"There are some, indeed, among them, who are ready to acknowledge, that every actual circumstance is associated to several fundamental notions, and, consequently, to several chains, between which

Defect in the analysis of Memory and Reproduction by psychologists,—in recognizing only a consecutive order of association.

---

1 Cf. *Reid's Works*, p 906, note †. — ED.

the mind may choose; they admit even that every link is attached to several others, so that the whole forms a kind of trellis, — a kind of net-work, which the mind may traverse in every direction, but still always in a single direction at once, — always in a succession similar to that of speech. This manner of explaining reminiscence is founded solely on this, — that, content to have observed all that is distinctly manifest in the phænomenon, they have paid no attention to the under play of the latescent activities, — paid no attention to all that custom conceals, and conceals the more effectually in proportion as it is more completely blended with the natural agencies of mind.

"Thus their theory, true in itself, and departing from a well-established principle, — the Association of Ideas, explains in a satisfactory manner a portion of the phænomena of Reminiscence; but it is incomplete, for it is unable to account for the prompt, easy, and varied operation of this faculty, or for all the marvels it performs.

Element in the phænomena, which the common theory fails to explain,—the movement of thought from one order of subjects to another.

On the doctrine of the philosophers, we can explain how a scholar repeats, without hesitation, a lesson he has learned, for all the words are associated in his mind according to the order in which he has studied them; how he demonstrates a geometrical theorem, the parts of which are connected together in the same manner; these and similar reminiscences of simple successions present no difficulties which the common doctrine cannot resolve. But it is impossible, on this doctrine, to explain the rapid and certain movement of thought, which, with a marvellous facility, passes from one order of subjects to another, only to return again to the first; which advances, retrogades, deviates, and reverts, sometimes marking all the points on its route, again clearing, as if in play, immense intervals; which runs over now in a manifest order, now in a seeming irregularity, all the notions relative to an object, often relative to several, between which no connection could be suspected; and this without hesitation, without uncertainty, without error, as the hand of a skilful musician expatiates over the keys of the most complex organ. All this is inexplicable on the meagre and contracted theory on which the phænomena of reproduction have been thought explained."[1]

"To form a correct notion of the phænomena of Reminiscence, it is requisite, that we consider under what conditions it is determined to exertion. In the first place, it is to be noted that, at every crisis

---

[1] Cardaillac, [*Etudes Elémentaires de Philosophie*, t. ii. c v. p. 124 *et seq.* — Ed.]

of our existence, momentary circumstances are the causes which awaken our activity, and set our recollection at work to supply the necessaries of thought.[1] In the second place, it is as constituting a want (and by *want* I mean the result either of an act of desire or of volition), that the determining circumstance tends principally to awaken the thoughts with which it is associated. This being the case, we should expect that each circumstance which constitutes a want should suggest, likewise, the notion of an object, or objects, proper to satisfy it; and this is what actually happens. It is, however, further to be observed, that it is not enough that the want suggests the idea of the object; for if that idea were alone, it would remain without effect, since it could not guide me in the procedure I should follow. It is necessary, at the same time, that to the idea of this object there should be associated the notion of the relation of this object to the want, of the place where I may find it, of the means by which I may procure it, and turn it to account, etc. For instance, I wish to make a quotation:—This want awakens in me the idea of the author in whom the passage is to be found, which I am desirous of citing; but this idea would be fruitless, unless there were conjoined, at the same time, the representation of the volume, of the place where I may obtain it, of the means I must employ, etc.

> *Conditions under which Reminiscence is determined to exertion.*
> 1. Momentary circumstances the causes of our mental activity.
> 2. The determining circumstance must constitute a want.

Hence I infer, in the first place, that a want does not awaken an idea of its object alone, but that it awakens it accompanied with a number, more or less considerable, of accessory notions, which form, as it were, its train or attendance. This train may vary according to the nature of the want which suggests the notion of an object; but the train can never fall wholly off, and it becomes more indissolubly attached to the object, in proportion as it has been more frequently called up in attendance.

> *Conditions under which a want is effective to determine reminiscence.*
> 1. Awakens the idea of its object along with certain accessory notions.

"I infer, in the second place, that this accompaniment of accessory notions, simultaneously suggested with the prinpal idea, is far from being as vividly and distinctly represented in consciousness as that idea itself; and when these accessories have once been completely blended with the habits of the mind, and its reproductive agency, they at length finally dis-

> *2. These accessory notions less vividly represented in consciousness than the idea itself.*

---

[1] [Sæpe jam spatio obrutam
Levis exoletam memoriam renovat nota.
Seneca, *Œdipus*, v. 820.]

appear, becoming fused, as it were, in the consciousness of the idea to which they are attached. Experience proves this double effect of the habits of reminiscence. If we observe our operations relative to the gratification of a want, we shall perceive that we are far from having a clear consciousness of the accessory notions; the consciousness of them is, as it were, obscured, and yet we cannot doubt that they are present to the mind, for it is they that direct our procedure in all its details.

"We must, therefore, I think, admit that the thought of an object immediately suggested by a desire, is always accompanied by an escort more or less numerous of accessory thoughts, equally present to the mind, though, in general, unknown in themselves to consciousness; that these accessories are not without their influence in guiding the operations elicited by the principal notion; and, it may even be added, that they are so much the more calculated to exert an effect in the conduct of our procedure, in proportion as, having become more part and parcel of our habits of reproduction, the influences they exert are further withdrawn, in ordinary, from the ken of consciousness."[1] The same thing may be illustrated by what happens to us in the case of reading. Originally each word, each letter, was a separate object of consciousness. At length, the knowledge of letters and words and lines being, as it were, fused into our habits, we no longer have any distinct consciousness of them, as severally concurring to the result, of which alone we are conscious. But that each word and letter has its effect, — an effect which can at any moment become an object of consciousness, is shown by the following experiment. If we look over a book for the occurrence of a particular name or word, we glance our eye over a page from top to bottom, and ascertain, almost in a moment, that it is or is not to be found therein. Here the mind is hardly conscious of a single word, but that of which it is in quest; but yet it is evident, that each other word and letter must have produced an obscure effect, and which effect the mind was ready to discriminate and strengthen, so as to call it into clear consciousness, whenever the effect was found to be that which the letters of the word sought for could determine. But, if the mind be not unaffected by the multitude of letters and words which it surveys, if it be able to ascertain whether the combination of letters constituting the

The accessory notions, the more influential on our conduct, as they are further withdrawn from consciousness.

Illustrated by the case of reading.

---

1 Cardaillac, [*Etudes Elément. de Philos.* t. ii. c. v. p. 128 *et seq.* — ED.]

word it seeks, be or be not actually among them, and all this without any distinct consciousness of all it tries and finds defective; — why may we not suppose, — why are we not bound to suppose, that the mind may, in like manner, overlook its book of memory, and search among its magazines of latescent cognitions for the notions of which it is in want, awakening these into consciousness, and allowing the others to remain in their obscurity?

   "A more attentive consideration of the subject will show, that we have not yet divined the faculty of Reminiscence in its whole extent. Let us make a single reflection. Continually struck by relations of every kind, continually assailed by a crowd of perceptions and sensations of every variety, and, at the same time, occupied with a complement of thoughts; we experience at once, and we are more or less distinctly conscious of, a considerable number of wants, — wants sometimes real, sometimes factitious or imaginary, — phænomena, however, all stamped with the same characters, and all stimulating us to act with more or less of energy. And as we choose among the different wants which we would satisfy, as well as among the different means of satisfying that want which we determine to prefer; and as the motives of this preference are taken either from among the principal ideas relative to each of these several wants, or from among the accessory ideas which habit has established into their necessary escorts; — in all these cases it is requisite, that all the circumstances should at once, and from the moment they have taken the character of wants, produce an effect, correspondent to that which, we have seen, is caused by each in particular. Hence we are compelled to conclude, that the complement of the circumstances by which we are thus affected, has the effect of rendering always present to us, and, consequently, of placing at our disposal, an immense number of thoughts; some of which certainly are distinctly recognized, being accompanied by a vivid consciousness, but the greater number of which, although remaining latent, are not the less effective in continually exercising their peculiar influence on our modes of judging and acting.[1]

Grounds for inferring that we have not yet compassed the faculty of Reminiscence in its whole extent.

   "We might say, that each of these momentary circumstances is a kind of electric shock which is communicated to a certain portion, — to a certain limited sphere, of intelligence; and the sum of all these circumstances is equal to so many shocks which, given at once

---

1 [Cf. Wolf, *Psychologia Rationalis*, §§ 96, 97. Maynettus Maynetius, *In Arist. De Sensu et*   *Sensili*, partic. 78, pp. 155, 156 (Florence, 1555), and Simon Simonius, *Ibid.* p. 257.]

at so many different points, produce a general agitation. We may form some rude conception of this phænomenon by an analogy. We may compare it, in the former case, to those concentric circles which are presented to our observation on a smooth sheet of water, when its surface is agitated by throwing in a pebble; and, in the latter case, to the same surface when agitated by a number of pebbles thrown simultaneously at different points.

"To obtain a clearer notion of this phænomenon, I may add some observations on the relation of our thoughts among themselves, and with the determining circumstances of the moment.

This further shown from the relations of our thoughts among themselves, and with the determining circumstances of the moment.

"1°, Among the thoughts, notions, or ideas which belong to the different groups, attached to the principal representations simultaneously awakened, there are some reciprocally connected by relations proper to themselves; so that, in this whole complement of coëxistent activities, these tend to excite each other to higher vigor, and, consequently, to obtain for themselves a kind of preëminence in the group or particular circle of activity to which they belong.

"2°, There are thoughts associated, whether as principals or accessories, to a greater number of determining circumstances, or to circumstances which recur more frequently. Hence they present themselves oftener than the others, they enter more completely into our habits, and take, in a more absolute manner, the character of customary or habitual notions. It hence results, that they are less obtrusive, though more energetic, in their influence, enacting, as they do, a principal part in almost all our deliberations; and exercising a stronger influence on our determinations.

"3°, Among this great crowd of thoughts, simultaneously excited, those which are connected with circumstances which more vividly affect us, assume not only the ascendant over others of the same description with themselves, but likewise predominate over all those which are dependent on circumstances of a feebler determining influence.

"From these three considerations we ought, therefore, to infer, that the thoughts connected with circumstances on which our attention is more specially concentrated, are those which prevail over the others; for the effect of attention is to render dominant and exclusive the object on which it is directed, and during the moment of attention, it is the circumstance to which we attend that necessarily obtains the ascendant.

"Thus if we appreciate correctly the phænomena of Reproduction or Reminiscence, we shall recognize, as an incontestable fact, that our thoughts suggest each other, not one by one successively, as the order to which language is astricted might lead us to infer; but that the complement of circumstances under which we at every moment exist, awakens simultaneously a great number of thoughts; these it calls into the presence of the mind, either to place them at our disposal, if we find it requisite to employ them, or to make them coöperate in our deliberations by giving them, according to their nature and our habits, an influence, more or less active, on our judgments and consequent acts.

General conclusions. Thoughts awakened not only in succession, but simultaneously.

"It is also to be observed, that in this great crowd of thoughts always present to the mind, there is only a small number of which we are distinctly conscious: and that in this small number we ought to distinguish those which, being clothed in language, oral or mental, become the objects of a more fixed attention; those which hold a closer relation to circumstances more impressive than others; or which receive a predominant character by the more vigorous attention we bestow on them. As to the others, although not the objects of clear consciousness, they are nevertheless present to the mind, there to perform a very important part as motive principles of determination; and the influence which they exert in this capacity is even the more powerful in proportion as it is less apparent, being more disguised by habit."[1]

Of these some only become objects of clear consciousness.

1 Cardaillac, [*Etudes Elément. de Philos.*, t. ii. c. v. p. 134 *et seq.*—Ed.]

57

LECTURE XXXIII.

THE REPRESENTATIVE FACULTY.—IMAGINATION.

In my last Lecture, I concluded the special consideration of the

Recapitulation. elementary process of calling up or resuscitating out of unconsciousness the mental modifications which the mind, by its Retentive Faculty, preserves from absolute extinction; the process to which I gave the not unexceptionable name of the Reproductive, and which, as left to its spontaneous action, or as modified by the will, obtains the several denominations of Suggestion, or of Reminiscence. In the latter part of the Lecture, I was engaged in showing that the common doctrine in regard to Reproduction is altogether inadequate to the phænomena,—that it allows to the mind only the power of reproducing the minima of thought in succession, as in speech it can only enunciate these one after another; whereas, in the process of Suggestion and Reminiscence, thoughts are awakened simultaneously in multitudes, in so far as to be brought into the immediate presence of the mind; in other words, they all, like the letters of a writing which we glance over, produce their effect, but those only upon which the mind concentrates its attention are drawn out into the light and foreground of consciousness.

Having thus terminated the separate consideration of the two first of the three correlative processes of Retention, Reproduction, and Representation, I proceed to the special discussion of the last, —the Representative Faculty.

By the faculty of Representation, as I formerly mentioned, I

The Faculty of Representation,—what. mean strictly the power the mind has of holding up vividly before itself the thoughts which, by the act of Reproduction, it has recalled into consciousness. Though the processes of Representation and Reproduction cannot exist independently of each other, they are nevertheless not more to be confounded into one than those of Reproduction and Conservation. They are, indeed, discriminated by differences sufficiently decisive. Reproduction, as we have seen, operates, in part at least, out of consciousness. Representation, on the contrary, is only realized as it is realized in consciousness; the degree or vivacity of the representation being always in proportion to the degree or vivacity of our consciousness of its reality. Nor

Representation and Reproduction not always exerted by the same individual in equal intensity; but all strong or weak in the same individuals in reference to the same classes of objects.

are the energies of Representation and Reproduction always exerted by the same individual in equal intensity, any more than the energies of Reproduction and Retention. Some minds are distinguished for a higher power of manifesting one of these phænomena; others, for manifesting another; and as it is not always the person who forgets nothing, who can most promptly recall what he retains, so neither is it always the person who recollects most easily and correctly, who can exhibit what he remembers in the most vivid colors. It is to be recollected, however, that Retention, Reproduction, and Representation, though not in different persons of the same relative vigor, are, however, in the same individuals, all strong or weak in reference to the same classes of objects. For example, if a man's memory be more peculiarly retentive of words, his verbal reminiscence and imagination will, in like manner, be more particularly energetic.

I formerly observed, that philosophers not having carried their psychological analysis so far as the constituent or elementary processes, the faculties in their systems are only precarious unions of these processes, in binary or even trinary combination,—unions, consequently, in which hardly any two philosophers are at one. In common language, it is not of course to be expected that there should be found terms to express the result of an analysis, which had not even been performed by philosophers; and, accordingly, the term *Imagination* or *Phantasy*, which denotes most nearly the representative process, does this, however, not without an admixture of other processes, which it is of consequence for scientific precision that we should consider apart.

Philosophers have divided Imagination into Reproductive (Conception,) and Productive.

Philosophers have divided Imagination into two,—what they call the Reproductive and the Productive. By the former, they mean imagination considered as simply reëxhibiting, representing the objects presented by perception, that is, exhibiting them without addition, or retrenchment, or any change in the relations which they reciprocally held, when first made known to us through sense. This operation Mr.

Stewart[1] has discriminated as a separate faculty, and bestowed on
it the name of Conception. This discrimina-

This discrimination unfortunate in itself and in its nomenclature.

tion and nomenclature, I think unfortunate.
The discrimination is unfortunate, because it is
unphilosophical to distinguish, as a separate
faculty, what is evidently only a special application of a common power. The nomenclature is unfortunate, for
the term *Conception*, which means a taking up in bundles, or
grasping into unity, — this term, I say, ought to have been left to
denote, what it previously was, and only properly could be, applied
to express, — the notions we have of classes of objects, in other
words, what have been called our *general ideas.* Be this, however,
as it may, it is evident, that the Reproductive Imagination (or Conception, in the abusive language of the Scottish philosophers) is
not a simple faculty. It comprises two processes : — first, an act of
representation strictly so called ; and, secondly, an act of reproduction, arbitrarily limited by certain contingent circumstances ; and it
is from the arbitrary limitation of this second constituent, that the
faculty obtains the only title it can exhibit to an independent existence. Nor can the Productive Imagination establish a better claim
to the distinction of a separate faculty than the Reproductive. The
Productive or Creative Imagination is that which is usually signified by the term *Imagination* or *Fancy*, in ordinary language.
Now, in the first place, it is to be observed, that the terms *productive* or *creative* are very improperly applied to Imagination, or the
Representative Faculty of mind. It is admitted on all hands, that
Imagination creates nothing, that is, produces nothing new ; and
the terms in question are, therefore, by the acknowledgment of those
who employ them, only abusively applied to denote the operations
of Fancy, in the new arrangement it makes of the old objects
furnished to it by the senses. We have now,

Imagination, as a plastic energy, is a complex operation.

therefore, only to consider, whether, in this corrected meaning, Imagination, as a plastic energy,
be a simple or a complex operation. And that
it is a complex operation, I do not think it will be at all difficult to
prove.

In the view I take of the fundamental processes, the act of
representation is merely the energy of the mind

The act of Repre-sentation, — what.

in holding up to its own contemplation what it
is determined to represent. I distinguish, as
essentially different, the representation, and the determination to

---

1 *Elements*, vol. i. part i. c. 3　*Works*, vol. tion, see Sir W. Hamilton's Edition of his
ii. p. 144　On Reid's use of the term Concep-　*Works*, p 360, note †, and p 407, note ‡. — ED.

represent. I exclude from the faculty of Representation all power of preference among the objects it holds up to view. This is the function of faculties wholly different from that of Representation, which, though active in representing, is wholly passive as to what it represents.

What, then, it may be asked, are the powers by which the Representative Faculty is determined to represent, and to represent this particular object, or this particular complement of objects, and not any other? These are two. The first of these is the Reproductive Faculty. This faculty is the great immediate source from which the Representative receives both the materials and the determination to represent; and the laws by which the Reproductive Faculty is governed, govern also the Representative. Accordingly, if there were no other laws in the arrangement and combination of thought than those of association, the Representative Faculty would be determined in its manifestations, and in the character of its manifestations, by the Reproductive Faculty alone; and, on this supposition, representation could no more be distinguished from reproduction than reproduction from association.

Two powers by which the Representative Faculty is determined to energy.

1. The Reproductive Faculty.

But there is another elementary process which we have not yet considered, — Comparison, or the Faculty of relations, to which the representative act is likewise subject, and which plays a conspicuous part in determining in what combinations objects are represented. By the process of Comparison, the complex objects, — the congeries of phænomena called up by the Reproductive Faculty, undergo various operations. They are separated into parts, they are analyzed into elements; and these parts and elements are again compounded in every various fashion. In all this the Representative Faculty coöperates. It, first of all, exhibits the phænomena so called up by the laws of ordinary association. In this it acts as handmaid to the Reproductive Faculty. It then exhibits the phænomena as variously elaborated by the analysis and synthesis of the Comparative Faculty, to which, in like manner, it performs the part of a subsidiary.

2. The Faculty of Relations.

This being understood, you will easily perceive, that the Imagination of common language, — the Productive Imagination of philosophers, — is nothing but the Representative process *plus* the process to which I would give the name of the *Comparative*. In this compound operation, it is true that the representative act is the most conspicuous, perhaps the most essential, element. For, in the first place, it is a condition of the possibility of the act of comparison, — of the act of analytic synthesis,

The Imagination of common language is equivalent to the processes of Representation and Comparison.

that the material on which it operates (that is, the objects reproduced in their natural connections) should be held up to its observation in a clear light, in order that it may take note of their various circumstances of relation; and, in the second, that the result of its own elaboration, that is, the new arrangements which it proposes, should be realized in a vivid act of representation. Thus it is, that, in the view both of the vulgar and of philosophers, the more obtrusive, though really the more subordinate, element in this compound process has been elevated into the principal constituent; whereas, the act of comparison, — the act of separation and reconstruction, has been regarded as identical with the act of representation.

Thus Imagination, in the common acceptation of the term, is not a simple but a compound faculty, — a faculty,

The process of Representation the principal constituent of Imagination, as commonly understood.

however, in which representation, — the vivid exhibition of an object, — forms the principal constituent. If, therefore, we were obliged to find a common word for every elementary process of our analysis, — *Imagination* would be the term, which, with the least violence to its meaning, could be accommodated to express the Representative Faculty.

By Imagination, thus limited, you are not to suppose that the faculty of representing mere objects of sense

Imagination not limited to objects of sense.

alone is meant. On the contrary, a vigorous power of representation is as indispensable a condition of success in the abstract sciences, as in the poetical and plastic arts; and it may, accordingly, be reasonably doubted whether Aristotle or Homer were possessed of the more powerful imagination. "We may, indeed, affirm, that there are as many different kinds of imagination as there are different kinds of intellectual activity. There is the imagination of abstraction, which represents to us certain phases of an object to the exclusion of others, and, at the same time, the sign by which the phases are united; the imagination of wit, which represents differences and contrasts, and the resemblances by which these are again combined; the imagination of judgment, which represents the various qualities of an object, and binds them together under the relations of substance, of attribute, of mode; the imagination of reason, which represents a principle in connection with its consequences, the effect in dependence on its cause; the imagination of feeling, which represents the accessory images, kindred to some particular, and which therefore confer on it greater compass, depth, and intensity; the imagination of volition, which represents all the circumstances which concur to persuade or dissuade from a certain act of will; the imagination of the passions, which, according to the nature of the affection, represents all that is homogeneous or analogous; finally, the imagination of the poet, which represents whatever is new, or beautiful, or sublime,—whatever, in a word, it is determined to represent by any interest of art."[1] The term *imagination*, however, is less generally applied to the representations of the Comparative Faculty considered in the abstract, than to the representations of sensible objects, concretely modified by comparison. The two kinds of imagination are in fact not frequently combined. Accordingly, using the term in this its ordinary extent, that is, in its limitation to objects of sense, it is finely said by Mr. Hume: "Nothing is more dangerous to reason than the flights of imagination, and nothing has been the occasion of more mistakes among philosophers. Men of bright fancies may, in this respect, be compared to those angels whom the Scriptures represent as covering their eyes with their wings."[2]

Considering the Representative Faculty in subordination to its two determinants, the faculty of Reproduction and the faculty of Comparison or Elaboration, we may distinguish three principal orders in which Imagination represents ideas:—"1°, The Natural order; 2°, The Logical order; 3°, The Poetical order. The natural order is that in which we receive the impression of external objects, or the order according to which our thoughts spontaneously group themselves. The logical order consists in presenting what is universal, prior to what is contained under it as particular, or in presenting the particulars first, and then ascending to the universal which they constitute. The former is the order of deduction, the latter that of induction. These two orders have this in common, that they deliver to us notions in the dependence in which the antecedent explains the subsequent. The poetical order consists in seizing individual circumstances, and in grouping them in such a manner that the imagination shall represent them so as they might be offered by the sense. The natural order is involuntary; it is established independently of our concurrence. The

Marginal notes:

Three principal orders in which Imagination represents ideas.

Poetical order.

1. The natural order.

2. The logical order.

8. The poetical order.

---

1 Ancillon, *Essais Philosophiques*, ii. 151.   2 *Treatise of Human Nature*, book i. part iv. § 7.—ED.

logical order is a child of art, it is the result of our will; but it is conformed to the laws of intelligence, which tend always to recall the particular to the general, or the general to the particular. The poetical order is exclusively calculated on effect. Pindar would not be a lyric poet, if his thoughts and images followed each other in the common order, or in the logical order. The state of mind in which thought and feeling clothe themselves in lyric forms, is a state in which thoughts and feelings are associated in an extraordinary manner, — in which they have, in fact, no other relation than that which groups and moves them around the dominant thought or feeling which forms the subject of the ode."

"Thoughts which follow each other only in the natural order, or as they are associated in the minds of men in general, form tedious conversations and tiresome books. Thoughts, on the other hand, whose connection is singular, capricious, extraordinary, are unpleasing; whether it be that they strike us as improbable, or that the effort which has been required to produce, supposes a corresponding effort to comprehend. Thoughts whose association is at once simple and new, and which, though not previously witnessed in conjunction, are yet approximated without a violent exertion, — such thoughts please universally, by affording the mind the pleasures of novelty and exercise at once."

Associations tedious, unpleasing, and agreeable.

"A peculiar kind of imagination, determined by a peculiar order of association, is usually found in every period of life, in every sex, in every country, in every religion. A knowledge of men principally consists in a knowledge of the principles by which their thoughts are linked and represented. The study of this is of importance to the instructor, in order to direct the character and intellect of his pupils; to the statesman, that he may exert his influence on the public opinion and manners of a people; to the poet, that he may give truth and reality to his dramatic situations; to the orator, in order to convince and persuade; to the man of the world, if he would give interest to his conversation."

Peculiar kinds of Imagination determined by peculiar orders of association.

"Authors who have made a successful study of this subject, skim over a multitude of circumstances under which an occurrence has taken place; because they are aware that it is proper to reject what is only accessory to the object which they would present in prominence. A vulgar mind forgets and spares nothing; he is ignorant that conversation is always but a selection; that every story

Difference between a cultivated and a vulgar mind.

is subject to the laws of dramatic poetry, — *festinat ad eventum :* and that all which does not concur to the effect, destroys or weakens it. The involuntary associations of their thoughts are imperative on minds of this description; they are held in thraldom to the order and circumstances in which their perceptions were originally obtained."[1] This has not, of course, escaped the notice of the greatest observer of human nature. Mrs. Quickly, in reminding Falstaff of his promise of marriage, supplies a good example of this peculiarity. "Thou didst swear to me upon a parcel-gilt goblet, sitting in my Dolphin chamber, at the round table, by a sea-coal fire, upon Wednesday in Whitsun week, when the prince broke thy head for likening his father to a singing man of Windsor," — and so forth. In Martinus Scriblerus, the coachman thus describes a scene in the Bear Garden: "He saw two men fight a prize; one was a fair man, a sergeant in the guards; the other black, a butcher; the sergeant had red breeches, the butcher blue; they fought upon a stage, about four o'clock, and the sergeant wounded the butcher in the leg."

"Dreaming, Somnambulism, Reverie, are so many effects of imagination, determined by association, — at least states of mind in which these have a decisive influence. If an impression on the sense often commences a dream, it is by imagination and suggestion that it is developed and accomplished. Dreams have frequently a degree of vivacity which enables them to compete with the reality; and if the events which they represent to us were in accordance with the circumstances of time and place in which we stand, it would be almost impossible to distinguish a vivid dream from a sensible perception."[2] "If," says Pascal,[3] "we dreamt every night the same thing, it would perhaps affect us as powerfully as the objects which we perceive every day. And if an artisan were certain of dreaming every night for twelve hours that he was king, I am convinced that he would be almost as happy as a king, who dreamt for twelve hours that he was an artisan. If we dreamt every night that we were pursued by enemies and harassed by horrible phantoms, we should suffer almost as much as if that were true, and we should stand in as great dread of sleep, as we should of waking, had we real cause to apprehend these misfortunes. . . . . It is only because dreams are different and inconsistent, that we can say, when we awake, that we have dreamt; for life is a dream a little less inconstant." Now the case which Pascal here hypotheti-

Dreaming an effect of imagination, determined by association.

---

[1] Ancillon, *Essais Philos.* ii. 152—156. — ED.
[2] Ancillon, *Ess. Phil.* ii. 159. — ED.
[3] *Pensées*, partie i. art. vi. § 20. Vol. ii. p. 102, (edit. Faugère.) — ED.

cally supposes, has actually happened. In a very curious German work, by Abel, entitled *A Collection of*
Remarkable Phœnomena from Human Life,
I find the following case, which I abridge : — A
young man had a cataleptic attack, in consequence of which a
singular effect was operated ,in his mental constitution. Some six
minutes after falling asleep, he began to speak distinctly, and almost
always of the same objects and concatenated events, so that he
carried on from night to night the same history, or rather continued
to play the same part. On wakening, he had no reminiscence
whatever of his dreaming thoughts, — a circumstance, by the way,
which distinguishes this as rather a case of somnambulism than of
common dreaming. Be this, however, as it may, he played a double
part in his existence. By day he was the poor apprentice of a merchant; by night he was a married man, the father of a family, a
senator, and in affluent circumstances. If during his vision anything was said in regard to his waking state, he declared it unreal
and a dream. This case, which is established on the best evidence,
is, as far as I am aware, unique.

Case of dreaming mentioned by Abel.

The influence of dreams upon our character is not without its
interest. A particular tendency may be strengthened in a man
solely by the repeated action of dreams. Dreams do not, however,
as is commonly supposed, afford any appreciable indication of the
character of individuals. It is not always the subjects that occupy
us most, when awake, that form the matter of our dreams; and it is
curious that the persons the dearest to us are precisely those about
whom we dream most rarely.

Somnambulism is a phænomenon still more astonishing. In this
singular state, a person performs a regular series
of rational actions, and those frequently of the
most difficult and delicate nature, and, what is still more marvellous,
with a talent to which he could make no pretension when awake.[1]
His memory and reminiscence supply him with recollections of
words and things, which perhaps were never at his disposal in the
ordinary state; he speaks more fluently a more refined language;
and, if we are to credit what the evidence on which it rests hardly
allows us to disbelieve, he has not only perceptions through other
channels than the common organs of sense, but the sphere of his
cognitions is amplified to an extent far beyond the limits to which
sensible perception is confined. This subject is one of the most
perplexing in the whole compass of philosophy; for, on the one

Somnambulism.

---

1 Cf. Ancillon, *Essais Philos.* ii. 161. — ED.

hand, the phænomena are so marvellous that they cannot be believed, and yet, on the other, they are of so unambiguous and palpable a character, and the witnesses to their reality are so numerous, so intelligent, and so high above every suspicion of deceit, that it is equally impossible to deny credit to what is attested by such ample and unexceptionable evidence.

"The third state, that of Reverie or Castle-building, is a kind of waking dream, and does not differ from dreaming, except by the consciousness which accompanies it. In this state, the mind abandons itself without a choice of subject, without control over the mental train, to the involuntary associations of imagination. The mind is thus occupied without being properly active; it is active, at least, without effort. Young persons, women, the old, the unemployed, and the idle, are all disposed to reverie. There is a pleasure attached to its illusions, which render it as seductive as it is dangerous. The mind, by indulgence in this dissipation, becomes enervated, it acquires the habit of a pleasing idleness, loses its activity, and at length even the power and the desire of action."[1]

Reverie.

"The happiness and misery of every individual of mankind depends almost exclusively on the particular character of his habitual associations, and the relative kind and intensity of his imagination. It is much less what we actually are, and what we actually possess, than what we imagine ourselves to be and have, that is decisive of our existence and fortune."[2] Apicius committed suicide to avoid starvation, when his fortune was reduced to somewhere, in English money, about £100,000. The Roman epicure imagined that he could not subsist on what, to men in general, would seem more than affluence.

The happiness and misery of the individual dependent on the character of his habitual associations.

"Imagination, by the attractive or repulsive pictures with which, according to our habits and associations, it fills the frame of our life, lends to reality a magical charm, or despoils it of all its pleasantness. The imaginary happy and the imaginary miserable are common in the world, but their happiness and misery are not the less real; everything depends on the mode in which they feel and estimate their condition. Fear, hope, the recollection of past pleasures, the torments of absence and of desire, the secret and almost resistless tendency of the mind towards certain objects, are

The influence of imagination on human life.

1 Ancillon, *Essais Philos.* ii. 162. — ED.   2 Ancillon, *Essais Philos.* ii. 163, 164. — ED.

the effects of association and imagination. At a distance, things seem to us radiant with a celestial beauty, or in the lurid aspect of deformity. Of a truth, in either case we are equally wrong. When the event which we dread, or which we desire, takes place, when we obtain, or when there is forced upon us, an object environed with a thousand hopes, or with a thousand fears, we soon discover that we have expected too much or too little; we thought it by anticipation infinite in good or evil, and we find it in reality not only finite, but contracted. 'With the exception,' says Rousseau, 'of the self-existent Being, there is nothing beautiful, but that which is not.' In the crisis whether of enjoyment or suffering, happiness is not so much happiness, nor misery so much misery, as we had anticipated. In the past, thanks to a beneficent Creator, our joys reäppear as purer and more brilliant than they had been actually experienced; and sorrow loses not only its bitterness, but is changed even into a source of pleasing recollection."[1] "Suavis laborum est præteritorum memoria," says Cicero;[2] while "hæc olim meminisse juvabit,"[3] is, in the words of Virgil, the consolation of a present infliction. "In early youth, the present and the future are displayed in a factitious magnificence; for at this period of life imagination is in its spring and freshness, and a cruel experience has not yet exorcised its brilliant enchantments. Hence the fair picture of a golden age, which all nations concur in placing in the past; it is the dream of the youth of mankind."[4] In old age, again, where the future is dark and short, imagination carries us back to the reënjoyment of a past existence. "The young," says Aristotle,[5] "live forwards in hope, the old live backwards in memory;" as Martial has well expressed it,

Hoc est
Vivere bis, vita posse priore frui.

From all this, however, it appears that the present is the only time in which we never actually live; we live either in the future, or in the past. So long as we have a future to anticipate, we contemn the present; and when we can no longer look forward to a future, we revert and spend our existence in the past. In the words of Manilius:

"Victuros agimus semper, nec vivimus unquam."[7]

1 Ancillon, *Ess. Phil.* ii. 164–5.—Ed.
2 *De Finibus*, ii. 32, translated from Euripides, (quoted by Macrobius, *Sat.* vii. 2):—
Ὡς ἡδύ τοι σωθέντα μεμνῆσθαι πόνων. —Ed.

3 *Æneid*, i. 203.—Ed.
4 Ancillon, *Essais Philos.* ii. 166.—Ed.
5 *Rhet.* ii. 12 and 13.—Ed.
6 Lib. x. epigr. 23.—Ed.
7 *Astronomicon*, iv. 4.—Ed.

In the words of Pope:

"Man never is, but always to be blest."[1]

I shall terminate the consideration of Imagination Proper by a speculation concerning the organ which it employs in the representations of sensible objects. The organ which it thus employs seems to be no other than the organs themselves of Sense, on which the original impressions were made, and through which they were originally perceived. Experience has shown, that Imagination depends on no one part of the cerebral apparatus exclusively. There is no portion of the brain which has not been destroyed by mollification, or induration, or external lesion, without the general faculty of Representation being injured. But experience equally proves, that the intracranial portion of any external organ of sense cannot be destroyed, without a certain partial abolition of the Imagination Proper. For example, there are many cases recorded by medical observers, of persons losing their sight, who have also lost the faculty of representing the images of visible objects. They no longer call up such objects by reminiscence, they no longer dream of them. Now in these cases, it is found that not merely the external instrument of sight, — the eye, — has been disorganized, but that the disorganization has extended to those parts of the brain which constitute the internal instrument of this sense, that is, the optic nerves and thalami. If the latter, — the real organ of vision, — remain sound, the eye alone being destroyed, the imagination of colors and forms remains as vigorous as when vision was entire. Similar cases are recorded in regard to the deaf. These facts, added to the observation of the internal phænomena which take place during our acts of representation, make it, I think, more than probable that there are as many organs of Imagination as there are organs of Sense. Thus I have a distinct consciousness, that, in the internal representation of visible objects, the same organs are at work which operate in the external perception of these; and the same holds good in an imagination of the objects of Hearing, Touch, Taste, and Smell.

Imagination employs the organs of sense in the representations of sensible objects.

But not only sensible perceptions, voluntary motions likewise are imitated in and by the imagination. I can, in imagination, represent the action of speech, the play of the muscles of the countenance, the movement of the limbs; and, when I do this, I feel clearly that I awaken a kind of tension in the same nerves through

Voluntary motions imitated in and by the imagination.

---

[1] *Essay on Man*, i. 95. — Ed.

which, by an act of will, I can determine an overt and voluntary motion of the muscles; nay, when the play of imagination is very lively, this external movement is actually determined. Thus we frequently see the countenances of persons under the influence of imagination undergo various changes; they gesticulate with their hands, they talk to themselves, and all this is in consequence only of the imagined activity going out into real activity. I should, therefore, be disposed to conclude, that, as in Perception the living organs of sense are from without determined to energy, so in Imagination they are determined to a similar energy by an influence from within.

LECTURE XXXIV.

THE ELABORATIVE FACULTY. — CLASSIFICATION. ABSTRACTION.

THE faculties with which we have been hitherto engaged, may be regarded as subsidiary to that which we are now about to consider. This, to which I gave the name of the Elaborative Faculty, — the Faculty of Relations, — or Comparison, — constitutes what is properly denominated Thought. It supposes always at least two terms, and its act results in a judgment, that is, an affirmation or negation of one of these terms of the other. You will recollect that, when treating of Consciousness in general, I stated to you, that consciousness necessarily involves a judgment; and as every act of mind is an act of consciousness, every act of mind, consequently, involves a judgment.[1] A consciousness is necessarily the consciousness of a determinate something; and we cannot be conscious of anything without virtually affirming its existence, that is, judging it to be. Consciousness is thus primarily a judgment or affirmation of existence. Again, consciousness is not merely the affirmation of naked existence, but the affirmation of a certain qualified or determinate existence. We are conscious that we exist only in and through our consciousness that we exist in this or that particular state, — that we are so or so affected, — so or so active; and we are only conscious of this or that particular state of existence, inasmuch as we discriminate it as different from some other state of existence, of which we have been previously conscious and are now reminiscent; but such a discrimination supposes, in consciousness, the affirmation of the existence of one state of a specific character, and the negation of another. On this ground it was that I maintained, that consciousness necessarily involves, besides recol-

The Elaborative Faculty, — what and how designated.

Every act of mind involves a judgment.

---

1 See above, p. 410. — ED. [Cf. Aristotle, *De Motione Animal.* c. vi. [Ἡ φαντασία καὶ ἡ αἴσθησις . . . κριτικά. — ED.] *Post An.*, ii. c. ult. Gatien-Arnoult, *Programme*, pp. 31, 103, 105. Reid, *Int. Powers*, Ess. vi. [c. i. *Works*, p. 414. — ED.]

lection, or rather a certain continuity of representation, also judgment or comparison; and, consequently, that, so far from comparison or judgment being a process always subsequent to the acquisition of knowledge, through perception and self-consciousness, it is involved as a condition of the acquisitive process itself. In point of fact, the various processes of Acquisition (Apprehension), Representation, and Comparison, are all mutually dependent. Comparison cannot judge without something to compare; we cannot originally acquire,—apprehend, we cannot subsequently represent our knowledge, without in either act attributing existence, and a certain kind of existence, both to the object known and to the subject knowing, that is, without enouncing certain judgments and performing certain acts of comparison; I say without performing certain acts of comparison, for taking the mere affirmation that a thing is,—this is tantamount to a negation that it is not, and necessarily supposes a comparison,—a collation, between existence and non-existence.

What I have now said may perhaps contribute to prepare you for what I am hereafter to say of the faculty or elementary process of Comparison,—a faculty which, in the analysis of philosophers, is exhibited only in part; and even that part is not preserved in its integrity. They take into account only a fragment of the process, and that fragment they again break down into a plurality of faculties. In opposition to the views hitherto promulgated in regard to Comparison, I will show that this faculty is at work in every, the simplest, act of mind; and that, from the primary affirmation of existence in an original act of consciousness to the judgment contained in the conclusion of an act of reasoning, every operation is only an evolution of the same elementary process,—that there is a difference in the complexity, none in the nature, of the act; in short, that the various products of Analysis and Synthesis, of Abstraction and Generalization, are all merely the results of Comparison, and that the operations of Conception or Simple Apprehenison, of Judgment, and of Reasoning, are all only acts of Comparison, in various applications and degrees.

Defect in the analysis of this faculty by philosophers.

What I have, therefore, to prove is, in the first place, that Comparison is supposed in every, the simplest, act of knowledge; in the second, that our factitiously simple, our factitiously complex, our abstract, and our generalized notions, are all merely so many products of Comparison; in the third, that Judgment, and, in the fourth, that Reasoning, is identical with Comparison. In doing

Positions to be established.

this, I shall not formally distribute the discussion into these heads, but shall include the proof of what I have now advanced, while tracing Comparison from its simplest to its most complex operations.

The first or most elementary act of Comparison, or of that mental process in which the relation of two terms is recognized and affirmed, is the judgment virtually pronounced, in an act of Perception, of the non-ego, or, in an act of Self-consciousness, of the ego. This is the primary affirmation of existence. The notion of existence is one native to the mind. It is the primary condition of thought. The first act of experience awoke it, and the first act of consciousness was a subsumption of that of which we were conscious under this notion; in other words, the first act of consciousness was an affirmation of the existence of something. The first or simplest act of comparison is thus the discrimination of existence from non-existence; and the first or simplest judgment is the affirmation of existence, in other words, the denial of non-existence.[1]

Comparison as determined by objective conditions.

The first act.

But the something of which we are conscious, and of which we predicate existence, in the primary judgment, is twofold, — the ego and the non-ego. We are conscious of both, and affirm existence of both. But we do more; we do not merely affirm the existence of each out of relation to the other, but, in affirming their existence, we affirm their existence in duality, in difference, in mutual contrast; that is, we not only affirm the ego to exist, but deny it existing as the non-ego; we not only affirm the non-ego to exist, but deny it existing as the ego. The second act of comparison is thus the discrimination of the ego and the non-ego; and the second judgment is the affirmation, that each is not the other.

Second.

The third gradation in the act of comparison, is in the recognition of the multiplicity of the coëxistent or successive phænomena, presented either to Perception or Self-consciousness, and the judgment in regard to their resemblance or dissimilarity.

Third.

The fourth is the comparison of the phænomena with the native notion of Substance, and the judgment is the grouping of these phænomena into different bundles, as the attributes of different subjects. In the external

Fourth.

1 [Cf. Troxler, *Logik*, ii. 20 *et seq.* Reinhold, *Theorie des Men. Erkennt.* 1. 290. Beneke, *Psych. Skizzen*, i. 227 *et seq.* Cousin, *Cours de* *l'Histoire de la Philosophie*, (xviii. Siécle) 1. xxiii., xxiv. Garnier, *Cours de Psychologie*, p. 87.]

world, this relation constitutes the distinction of things; in the internal, the distinction of powers.

The fifth act of comparison is the collation of successive phæ-

Fifth.

nomena under the native notion of Causality, and the affirmation or negation of their mutual relation as cause and effect.

So far the process of comparison is determined merely by objec-

Comparison viewed as determined by the necessities of the thinking subject.

Classification shown to be an act of Comparison.

tive conditions; hitherto it has followed only in the footsteps of nature. In those, again, we are now to consider, the procedure is, in a certain sort, artificial, and determined by the necessities of the thinking subject itself. The mind is finite in its powers of comprehension; the objects, on the contrary, which are presented to it are, in proportion to its limited capacities, infinite in number. How then is this disproportion to be equalized? How can the infinity of nature be brought down to the finitude of man? This is done by means of Classification. Objects, though infinite in number, are not infinite in variety; they are all, in a certain sort, repetitions of the same common qualities, and the mind, though lost in the multitude of particulars, — individuals, can easily grasp the classes into which their resembling attributes enable us to assort these. This whole process of Classification is a mere act of Comparison, as the following deduction will show.

In the first place, this may be shown in regard to the formation

1. In regard to Complex or Collective notions.

of Complex notions, with which, as the simplest species of classification, we may commence. By Complex or Collective notions, I mean merely the notion of a class formed by the repetition of the same constituent notion.[1] Such are the notions of *an army, a forest, a town, a number*. These are names of classes, formed by the repetition of the notion of *a soldier*, of *a tree*, of *a house*, of *a unit*. You are not to confound, as has sometimes been done, the notion of *an army, a forest, a town, a number*, with the notions of *army, forest, town,* and *number;* the former, as I have said, are complex or collective, the latter are general or universal notions.

It is evident that a collective notion is the result of comparison. The repetition of the same constituent notion supposes that these notions were compared, their identity or absolute similarity affirmed.

In the whole process of classification, the mind is in a great

---

[1] Cf. Locke, *Essay on the Human Understanding*, b. ii. c. xii. § 5. — ED. Degerando, *Des Signes*, vol. i. c. vii. p. 170. — ED.

measure dependent upon language for its success; and in this, the simplest of the acts of classification, it may be proper to show how language affords to mind the assistance it requires. Our complex notions being formed by the repetition of the same notion, it is evident that the difficulty we can experience in forming an adequate conception of a class of identical constituents, will be determined by the difficulty we have in conceiving a multitude. "But the comprehension of the mind is feeble and limited; it can embrace at once but a small number of objects. It would thus seem that an obstacle is raised to the extension of our complex ideas at the very outset of our combinations. But here language interposes, and supplies the mind with the force of which it is naturally destitute."[1] We have formerly seen that the mind cannot in one act embrace more than five or six, at the utmost seven, several units.[2] How then does it proceed? "When, by a first combination, we have obtained a complement of notions as complex as the mind can embrace, we give this complement a name. This being done, we regard the assemblage of units thus bound up under a collective name as itself a unit, and proceed, by a second combination, to accumulate these into a new complement of the same extent. To this new complement we give another name; and then again proceed to perform, on this more complex unit, the same operation we had performed on the first; and so we may go on rising from complement to complement to an indefinite extent. Thus, a merchant, having received a large unknown sum of money in crowns, counts out the pieces by fives, and having done this till he has reached twenty, he lays them together in a heap; around these, he assembles similar piles of coin, till they amount, let us say, to twenty; and he then puts the whole four hundred into a bag. In this manner he proceeds until he fills a number of bags, and placing the whole in his coffers, he will have a complex or collective notion of the quantity of crowns which he has received."[3] It is on this principle that arithmetic proceeds, — tens, hundreds, thousands, myriads, hundreds of thousands, millions, etc., are all so many factitious units which enable us to form notions, vague indeed, of what otherwise we could have obtained no conception at all. So much for complex or collective notions, formed without decomposition, — a process which I now go on to consider.

Our thought, — that is, the sum total of the perceptions and representations which occupy us at any given moment, is always, as

In this, the simplest act of Classification, the mind is dependent on language.

---

1 Degerando, *Des Signes*, vol. i. c. vii. p. 165.
2 See above, lect. xiv. p. 173. — ED.
3 Degerando, *Des Signes*, vol. i. c. vii, p. 165, 165, [slightly abridged. — ED.]

I have frequently observed, compound. The composite objects of thoughts may be decomposed in two ways, and

Decomposition two-fold.
1. In the interest of the Fine Arts.

for the sake of two different interests. In the first place, we may decompose in order that we may recombine, influenced by the mere pleasure which this plastic operation affords us. This is poetical analysis and synthesis. On this process it is needless to dwell. It is evidently the work of comparison. For example, the minotaur, or chimæra, or centaur, or gryphon (hippogryph), or any other poetical combination of different animals, could only have been effected by an act in which the representations of these animals were compared, and in which certain parts of one were affirmed, compatible with certain parts of another. How, again, is the imagination of all ideal beauty or perfection formed? Simply by comparing the various beauties or excellencies of which we have had actual experience, and thus being enabled to pronounce in regard to their common and essential quality.

In the second place, we may decompose in the interest of science;

2. In the interest of Science.

and as the poetical decomposition was principally accomplished by a separation of integral parts, so this is principally accomplished by an abstraction of constituent qualities. On this process it is necessary to be more particular.

Suppose an unknown body is presented to my senses, and that it

Abstraction of the senses.

is capable of affecting each of these in a certain manner. "As furnished with five different organs, each of which serves to introduce a certain class of perceptions and representations into the mind, we naturally distribute all sensible objects into five species of qualities. The human body, if we may so speak, is thus itself a kind of abstractive machine. The senses cannot but abstract. If the eye did not abstract colors, it would see them confounded with odors and with tastes, and odors and tastes would necessarily become objects of sight."

"The abstraction of the senses is thus an operation the most natural; it is even impossible for us not to perform it. Let us now see whether abstraction by the mind be more arduous than that of the senses."[1] We have formerly found that the comprehension of the mind is extremely limited; that it can only take cognizance of one object at a time, if that be known with full intensity; and

---

[1] Laromiguière, [*Leçons Philosophie*, t. ii. p. ii. l. xi. p. 340. Ed.] Condillac, [*L'Art de Penser*, p. i. c. viii. *Cours*, t. iii. p. 295. Ed.] [Cf. Fonseca, *Isagoge Philosophica*], [c. iv. p. 742, appended to his *Institut. Dialect.* (edit. 1604).] Ed.]

that it can accord a simultaneous attention to a very small plurality of objects, and even that imperfectly.   Thus it is that attention fixed on one object is tantamount to a withdrawal, — to an abstrac-

Abstraction,—what.

tion, of consciousness from every other.   Abstraction is thus not a positive act of mind, as it is often erroneously described in philosophical treatises, — it is merely a negation to one or more objects, in consequence of its concentration on another.

This being the case, Abstraction is not only an easy and natural,

Abstraction, — a natural and necessary process.

but a necessary result.   "In studying an object, we neither exert all our faculties at once, nor at once apply them to all the qualities of an object. We know from experience that the effect of such a mode of procedure is confusion.   On the contrary, we converge our attention on one alone of its qualities, — nay, contemplate this quality only in a single point of view, and retain it in that aspect until we have obtained a full and accurate conception of it. The human mind proceeds from the confused and complex to the distinct and constituent, always separating, always dividing, always simplifying; and this is the only mode in which, from the weakness of our faculties, we are able to apprehend and to represent with correctness."[1]

"It is true, indeed, that after having decomposed everything, we

Synthesis necessary after analysis.

must, as it were, return on our steps by recomposing everything anew; for unless we do so, our knowledge would not be conformable to the reality and relations of nature.   The simple qualities of body have not each a proper and independent existence; the ultimate faculties of mind are not so many distinct and independent existences.   On either side, there is a being one and the same; on that side, at once extended, solid, colored, etc.; on this, at once capable of thought, feeling, desire, etc."

"But although all, or the greater number of, our cognitions comprehend different fasciculi of notions, it is necessary to commence by the acquisition of these notions one by one, through a successive application of our attention to the different attributes of objects. The abstraction of the intellect is thus as natural as that of the senses.   It is even imposed upon us by the very constitution of our mind."[2]

"I am aware that the expression, *abstraction of the senses*, is incorrect; for it is the mind always which acts, be it through the

1 Laromiguière, *Leçons*, t. ii. p. 341. — ED.   2 Laromiguière, *Leçons*, t. ii. p. 342. — ED.

medium of the senses. The impropriety of the expression is not,
however, one which is in danger of leading into
error; and it serves to point out the important
fact, that abstraction is not always performed in
the same manner. In Perception, — in the presence of physical
objects, the intellect abstracts colors by the eyes, sounds by the ear,
etc. In Representation, and when the external object is absent, the
mind operates on its reproduced cognitions, and looks at them successively in their different points of view."[1]

The expression, ab-
straction of the senses.

"However abstraction be performed, the result is notions which
are simple, or which approximate to simplicity; and if we apply it
with consistency and order to the different qualities of objects, we
shall attain at length to a knowledge of these qualities and of their
mutual dependencies; that is, to a knowledge of objects as they
really are. In this case, abstraction becomes analysis, which is the
method to which we owe all our cognitions."[2]

The process of abstraction is familiar to the most uncultivated
minds; and its uses are shown equally in the mechanical arts as in
the philosophical sciences. "A carpenter," says Kames,[3] speaking
of the great utility of abstraction, "considers a log of wood with
regard to hardness, firmness, color, and texture; a philosopher,
neglecting these properties, makes the log undergo a chemical
analysis, and examines its taste, its smell, and component principles;
the geometrician confines his reasoning to the figure, the length,
breadth, and thickness; in general, every artist, abstracting from
all other properties, confines his observations to those which have a
more immediate connection with his profession."

But is Abstraction, or rather, is exclusive attention, the work of
Comparison? This is evident. The application
of attention to a particular object, or quality of
an object, supposes an act of will, — a choice or
preference, and this again supposes comparison and judgment. But
this may be made more manifest from a view of the act of Generalization, on which we are about to enter.

Abstraction the work
of comparison.

The notion of the figure of the desk before me is an abstract
idea, — an idea that makes part of the total
notion of that body, and on which I have concentrated my attention, in order to consider it
exclusively. This idea is abstract, but it is at
the same time individual; it represents the figure of this particular

Generalization. Idea
abstract and individ-
ual.

---

[1] Laromiguière, *Leçons*, t. ii. p. 344, slightly
abridged. — Ed.

[2] Laromiguière, *Leçons*, t. ii. p. 345. — Ed.

[3] *Elements of Criticism*, Appendix, § 40; vol.
ii. p. 533, ed. 1788. — Ed.

desk, and not the figure of any other body. But had we only individual abstract notions, what would be our knowledge? We should be cognizant only of qualities viewed apart from their subjects; (and of separate phænomena there exists none in nature); and as these qualities are also separate from each other, we should have no knowledge of their mutual relations.[1]

It is necessary, therefore, that we should form Abstract General notions. This is done when, comparing a number of objects, we seize on their resemblances; when we concentrate our attention on these points of similarity, thus abstracting the mind from a consideration of their differences; and when we give a name to our notion of that circumstance in which they all agree. The general notion is thus one which makes us know a quality, property, power, action, relation; in short, any point of view, under which we recognize a plurality of objects as a unity. It makes us aware of a quality, a point of view, common to many things. It is a notion of resemblance; hence the reason why general names or terms, the signs of general notions, have been called *terms of resemblance* (*termini similitudinis*). In this process of generalization, we do not stop short at a first generalization. By a first generalization we have obtained a number of classes of resembling individuals. But these classes we can compare together, observe their similarities, abstract from their differences, and bestow on their common circumstance a common name. On these second classes we can again perform the same operation, and thus ascending the scale of general notions, throwing out of view always a greater number of differences, and seizing always on fewer similarities in the formation of our classes, we arrive at length at the limit of our ascent in the notion of *being* or *existence*. Thus placed on the summit of the scale of classes, we descend by a process the reverse of that by which we have ascended; we divide and subdivide the classes, by introducing always more and more characters, and laying always fewer differences aside; the notions become more and more composite, until we at length arrive at the individual.

I may here notice that there is a twofold kind of quantity to be considered in notions. It is evident, that in proportion as the class is high, it will, in the first place, contain under it a greater number of classes, and, in the second, will include the smallest complement of attributes. Thus *being* or *existence*

Abstract General notions,—what and how formed.

Twofold quantity in notions,—Extension and Comprehension.

---

1 We should also be overwhelmed with their number.—*Jotting.*

contains under it every class; and yet when we say that a thing exists, we say the very least of it that is possible. On the other hand, an individual, though it contain nothing but itself, involves the largest amount of predication. For example, when I say,— this is Richard, I not only affirm of the subject every class from existence down to man, but likewise a number of circumstances proper to Richard as an individual. Now, the former of these

Their designations.

quantities, the external, is called the *Extension* of a notion (*quantitas ambitus*); the latter, the internal quantity, is called its *Comprehension* or *Intension* (*quantitas complexus*). The extension of a notion is, likewise, styled its *circuit, region, domain,* or *sphere* (*sphœra*), also its *breadth* (πλάτος). On the other hand, the comprehension of a notion is, likewise, called its *depth* (βάθος). These names we owe to the Greek logi-

Their law.

cians.[1] The internal and external quantities are in the inverse ratio of each other. The greater the extension, the less the comprehension; the greater the comprehension, the less the extension.[2]

---

1 [See Ammonius, *In Categ.*, f. 88. Gr. f. 29. Lat. Brandis, *Scholia in Arist.*, p. 45.] ('Αι κατηγορίαι καὶ πλάτος ἔχουσι καὶ βάθος, βάθος μὲν τὴν εἰς τὰ μερικώτερα αὐτῶν πρόοδον, πλάτος δὲ τὴν εἰς τὰ πλάγια μετάστασιν, οἷον ἵνα βάθος μὲν λάβῃς οὕτω τὴν

οὐσίαν καὶ τὸ σῶμα καὶ τὸ ἔμψυχον καὶ τὸ ζῷον καὶ οὕτως ἐφεξῆς, πλάτος δέ, ὅταν διέλῃς τὴν οὐσίαν εἰς σῶμα καὶ ἀσώματον.—

2 [Cf. *Port Royal Logic*, p. i. c. vi. p. 74. Eugenios (Λογικὴ), b. i. c. iv. p. 194 *et seq.*— Ed.]

LECTURE XXXV.

THE ELABORATIVE FACULTY. — GENERALIZATION. — NOMINALISM AND CONCEPTUALISM.

I ENTERED, in my last Lecture, on the discussion of that great cognitive power which I called the Elaborative Faculty, — the Faculty of Relations, — the Discursive Faculty, — Comparison, or Judgment; and which corresponds to what the Greek philosophers understood by διάνοια, when opposed, as a special faculty, to νοῦς. I showed you, that, though a comparison, — a judgment, involved the supposition of two relative terms, still it was an original operation, in fact involved in consciousness, and a condition of every energy of thought. But, besides the primary judgments of existence, — of the existence of the ego and non-ego, and of their existence in contrast to, and in exclusion of, each other, — I showed that this process is involved in perception, external and internal; inasmuch as the recognitions, — that the objects presented to us by the Acquisitive Faculty are many and complex, that one quality is different from another, and that different bundles of qualities are the properties of different things or subjects, — are all so many acts of Comparison or Judgment.

Recapitulation.

This being done, I pointed out that a series of operations were to be referred to this faculty, which, by philosophers, had been made the functions of specific powers. Of these operations I enumerated: — 1°, Composition or Synthesis; 2°, Abstraction, Decomposition or Analysis; 3°, Generalization; 4°, Judgment; and 5°, Reasoning.

The first of these, — Composition or Synthesis, — which is shown in the formation of Complex or Collective notions, I stated to you was the result of an act of comparison. For a complex notion (I gave you as examples *an army, a forest, a town*) being only the repetition of notions absolutely similar, this similarity could be ascertained only by comparison. In speaking of this process, I

60

explained the support afforded in it to the mind by language. I then recalled to you what was meant by abstraction. Abstraction is no positive act; it is merely the negation of attention. We can fully attend only to a single thing at a time; and attention, therefore, concentrated on one object or one quality of an object, necessarily more or less abstracts our consciousness from others. Abstraction from, and attention to, are thus correlative terms, the one being merely the negation of the other. I noticed the improper use of the term *abstraction* by many philosophers, in applying it to that on which attention is converged.[1] This we may indeed be said to *prescind*,[2] but not to *abstract*. Thus let A, B, C, be three qualities of an object. We prescind A, in abstracting it from B and C; but we cannot, without impropriety, simply say that we abstract A. Thus by attending to one object to the abstraction from all others, we, in a certain sort, decompose or analyze the complex materials presented to us by Perception and Self-consciousness. This analysis or decomposition is of two kinds. In the first place, by concentrating attention on one integrant part of an object, we, as it were, withdraw or abstract it from the others. For example, we can consider the head of an animal to the exclusion of the other members. This may be called Partial or Concrete Abstraction. The process here noticed has, however, been overlooked by philosophers, insomuch that they have opposed the terms *concrete* and *abstract* as exclusive contraries. In the second place, we can rivet our attention on some particular mode of a thing, as its smell, its color, its figure, its motion, its size, etc., and abstract it from the others. This may be called Modal Abstraction.

The abstraction we have been now speaking of is performed on individual objects, and is consequently particular. There is nothing necessarily connected with Generalization in Abstraction. Generalization is indeed dependent on abstraction, which it supposes; but abstraction does not involve generalization. I remark this, because you will frequently find the terms *abstract* and *general* applied to notions, used as convertible. Nothing, however, can be more incorrect. "A person," says Mr. Stewart, "who had never seen but one rose, might yet have been able to consider its *color* apart from its other qualities; and, therefore, there may be such

---

1 [Cf. Kant, *De Mundi Sensibilis Forma* [§ 6. *Vermischte Schriften*, ii. 449: "Proprie dicendum esset *ab aliquibus abstrahere*, non *aliquid abstrahere*. . . . . Conceptus intellectualis *abstrahit* ab omni sensitivo, non *abstrahitur* a sensitivis, et forsitan rectius diceretur *abstrahens*, quam *abstractus*." — ED.] Maine de Biran. [*Examen des Leçons de M. Laromiguière*, § 3, *Nouvelles Considerat.* p. 194. — ED.] Bilfinger, *Dilucidationes*, § 262.]

2 [On *Precision*, and its various kinds, see Derodon, *Logica*, pars ii. c. vi. § 11. *Opera*, p. 233, ed. 1668; and Chauvin, *Lex. v. Præcisio* (*Præscisio*).]

a thing as an idea which is at once abstract and particular. After having perceived this quality as belonging to a variety of individuals, we can consider it without reference to any of them, and thus form the notion of redness or whiteness in general, which may be called a *general abstract idea*. The words *abstract* and *general*, therefore, when applied to ideas, are as completely distinct from each other as any two words to be found in the language."[1]

I showed that abstraction implied comparison and judgment; for attention supposes preference, preference is a judgment, and a judgment is the issue of comparison.

I then proceeded to the process of Generalization, which is still more obtrusively comparison, and nothing but comparison. Generalization is the process through which we obtain what are called *general* or *universal* notions. A general notion is nothing but the abstract notion of a circumstance in which a number of individual objects are found to agree, that is, to resemble each other. In so far as two objects resemble each other, the notion we have of them is identical, and, therefore, to us the objects may be considered as the same. Accordingly, having discovered the circumstance in which objects agree, we arrange them by this common circumstance into classes, to which we also usually give a common name.

I explained how, in the prosecution of this operation, commencing with individual objects, we generalized these into a lowest class. Having found a number of such lowest classes, we then compare these again together, as we had originally compared individuals; we abstract their points of resemblance, and by these points generalize them into a higher class. The same process we perform upon these higher classes; and thus proceed, generalizing class from classes, until we are at last arrested in the one highest class, that of *being*. Thus we find Peter, Paul, Timothy, etc., all agree in certain common attributes, and which distinguish them from other animated beings. We accordingly collect them into a class, which we call *man*. In like manner, out of the other animated beings which we exclude from *man*, we form the classes, *horse, dog, ox*, etc. These and *man* form so many lowest classes or species. But these species, though differing in certain respects, all agree in others. Abstracting from their diversities, we attend only to their resemblances; and as all manifesting life, sense, feeling, etc.—this resemblance gives us a class, on which we bestow the name *animal*. Animal, or living sentient existences, we then compare with lifeless existences, and thus going on

---

1 *Elements*, vol. i. c. iv. § 1.	*Works*, vol. ii. p. 165.—ED.]	So Whately, [*Logic*, b. i. § 6, p. 49; b. ii. c. v. § 1, p. 122 (8th edit).—ED.]

abstracting from differences, and attending to resemblances, we arrive at naked or undifferenced existence. Having reached the pinnacle of generalization, we may redescend the ladder; and this is done by reversing the process through which we ascended. Instead of attending to the similarities, and abstracting from the differences, we now attend to the differences, and abstract from the similarities. And as the ascending process is called Generalization, this is called Division or Determination; — division, because the higher or wider classes are cut down into lower or narrower; — determination, because every quality added on to a class limits or determines its extent, that is, approximates it more to some individual, real, or determinate, existence.

Having given you this necessary information in regard to the nature of Generalization, I proceed to consider one of the most simple, and, at the same time, one of the most perplexed problems in philosophy, — in regard to the object of the mind, — the object of consciousness, when we employ a general term. In the explanation of the process of generalization all philosophers are at one; the only differences that arise among them relate to the point, — whether we can form an adequate idea of that which is denoted by an abstract, or abstract and general term. In the discussion of this question, I shall pursue the following order: first of all, I shall state to you the arguments of the Nominalists, — of those who hold, that we are unable to form an idea corresponding to the abstract and general term; in the second place, I shall state to you the arguments of the Conceptualists, — of those who maintain that we are so competent; and, in the last, I shall show you that the opposing parties are really at one, and that the whole controversy has originated in the imperfection and ambiguity of our philosophical nomenclature. In this discussion I avoid all mention of the ancient doctrine of Realism. This is curious only in an historical point of view; and is wholly irrelevant to the question at issue among modern philosophers.

This controversy has been principally agitated in this country, and in France, for a reason that I shall hereafter explain; and, to limit ourselves to Great Britain, the Doctrine of Nominalism has, among others, been embraced by Hobbes, Berkeley, Hume, Principal Campbell, and Mr. Stewart; while Conceptualism has found favor with Locke, Reid, and Brown.[1]

Generalization. — Can we form an adequate idea of what is denoted by an abstract general term?

Order of discussion.

This controversy principally agitated in Britain and France.

_____

[1] See below, pp. 477, 301. — ED.

Throwing out of view the antiquities of the question (and this question is perhaps more memorable than any other in the history of philosophy), — laying, I say, out of account opinions which have been long exploded, there are two which still divide

Two opinions which still divide philosophers.

philosophers. Some maintain that every act and every object of mind is necessarily singular, and that the name is that alone which can pretend to generality. Others again hold that the mind is capable of forming notions representations, correspondent in universality to the classes contained under, or expressed by, the general term.

The former of these opinions, — the doctrine as it is called of Nominalism, — maintains that every notion, con-

Nominalism.

sidered in itself, is singular, but becomes, as it were, general, through the intention of the mind to make it represent every resembling notion, or notion of the same class. Take, for example, the term *man*. Here we can call up no notion, no idea, corresponding to the universality of the class or term. This is manifestly impossible. For as *man* involves contradictory attributes, and as contradictions cannot coëxist in one representation, an idea or notion adequate to *man* cannot be realized in thought. The class *man* includes individuals, male and female, white and black and copper-colored, tall and short, fat and thin, straight and crooked, whole and mutilated, etc., etc.; and the notion of the class must, therefore, at once represent all and none of these. It is, therefore, evident, though the absurdity was maintained by Locke,[1] that we cannot accomplish this; and, this being impossible, we cannot represent to ourselves the class *man* by any equivalent notion or idea. All that we can do is to call up some individual image, and consider it as representing, though inadequately representing, the generality. This we easily do, for as we can call into imagination any individual, so we can make that individual image stand for any or for every other which it resembles, in those essential points which constitute the identity of the class. This opinion, which, after Hobbes, has been in this country maintained, among others, by Berkeley,[2] Hume,[3] Adam Smith,[4] Campbell,[5] and Stewart,[6] appears to me not only true but self-evident.

1 *Essay on Human Understanding*, i. b. iv. c. c. vii. § 9. — ED.

2 *Principles of Human Knowledge*, Introd. § 10. — ED.

3 *Treatise of Human Nature*, part i. sect. vii. *Works*, i. p. 34. *Essay on the Academical Philosophy*, *Works*, iv. p. 184. — ED.

4 *Dissertation concerning the first Formation of Languages.* — ED.

5 *Philosophy of Rhetoric*, book ii. c. 7. — ED.

6 *Elements*, part ii. c. iv. *Works*, vol. ii. p. 173. — ED.

No one has stated the case of the nominalists more clearly than Bishop Berkeley, and as his whole argument is, as far as it goes, irrefragable, I beg your attention to the following extract from his Introduction to the *Principles of Human Knowledge*.[1]

The doctrine of Nominalism as stated by Berkeley.

"It is agreed, on all hands, that the qualities or modes of things do never really exist each of them apart by itself, and separated from all others, but are

Berkeley quoted.

mixed, as it were, and blended together, several in the same object. But we are told, the mind, being able to consider each quality singly, or abstracted from those other qualities with which it is united, does by that means frame to itself abstract ideas. For example, there is perceived by sight an object extended, colored, and moved: this mixed or compound idea the mind resolving into its simple, constituent parts, and viewing each by itself, exclusive of the rest, does frame the abstract ideas of extension, color, and motion. Not that it is possible for color or motion to exist without extension; but only that the mind can frame to itself by *abstraction* the idea of color exclusive of extension, and of motion exclusive of both color and extension.

"Again, the mind having observed that in the particular extensions perceived by sense, there is something common and alike in all, and some other things peculiar, as this or that figure or magnitude, which distinguish them one from another; it considers apart or singles out by itself that which is common, making thereof a most abstract idea of extension, which is neither line, surface, nor solid, nor has any figure or magnitude, but is an idea entirely prescinded from all these. So likewise the mind, by leaving out of the particular colors perceived by sense, that which distinguishes them one from another, and retaining that only which is common to all, makes an idea of color in abstract which is neither red, nor blue, nor white, nor any other determinate color. And in like manner, by considering motion abstractedly not only from the body moved, but likewise from the figure it describes, and all particular directions and velocities, the abstract idea of motion is framed; which equally corresponds to all particular motions whatsoever that may be perceived by sense.

"Whether others have this wonderful faculty of *abstracting their ideas*, they best can tell: for myself I find, indeed, I have a faculty of imagining, or representing to myself the ideas of those particular things I have perceived, and of variously compounding

---

[1] Sections vii. viii. x.　*Works*, i. 5 *et seq.*, 4to edit.　Cf. *Encyclopædia Britannica*, art. *Metaphysics*, vol. xiv. p. 622, 7th edit. — Ed.

and dividing them. I can imagine a man with two heads, or the upper parts of a man joined to the body of a horse. I can consider the hand, the eye, the nose, each by itself abstracted or separated from the rest of the body. But then whatever hand or eye I imagine, it must have some particular shape and color. Likewise the idea of man that I frame to myself, must be either of a white, or a black, or a tawny, a straight or a crooked, a tall, or a low, or a middle-sized man. I cannot by any effort of thought conceive the abstract idea above described. And it is equally impossible for me to form the abstract idea of motion distinct from the body moving, and which is neither swift nor slow, curvilinear nor rectilinear; and the like may be said of all other abstract general ideas whatsoever.[1] To be plain, I own myself able to abstract in one sense, as when I consider some particular parts or qualities separated from others, with which though they are united in some object, yet it is possible they may really exist without them. But I deny that I can abstract one from another, or conceive separately, those qualities which it is impossible should exist so separated: or that I can frame a general notion by abstracting from particulars in the manner aforesaid. Which two last are the proper acceptations of *abstraction*. And there are grounds to think most men will acknowledge themselves to be in my case. The generality of men, which are simple and illiterate, never pretend to *abstract notions*. It is said they are difficult, and not to be attained without pains and study. We may therefore reasonably conclude that, if such there be, they are confined only to the learned."

Such is the doctrine of Nominalism, as asserted by Berkeley, and as subsequently acquiesced in by the principal philosophers of this country. Reid himself is, indeed, hardly an exception, for his opinion on this point is, to say the least of it, extremely vague.[2]

The counter-opinion, that of Conceptualism, as it is called, has, however, been supported by several philosophers of distinguished ability. Locke maintains the doctrine in its most revolting absurdity, boldly admitting that the general notion must be realized, in spite of the principle of Contradiction. "Does it not require," he says, "some pains and skill to form the *general idea* of a triangle (which is yet none of the most abstract, comprehensive, and difficult), for it must be neither oblique or rectangle, neither equilateral, equicrural, nor scalenon; but all and none of these at once.

Conceptualism.
Locke.

---

1 This argumentation is employed by Derodon, *Logica* [pars ii. c. vi. § 16. *Opera*, p 236. — Ed.], and others.

2 For Reid's opinion, see *Intellectual Powers*, essay v., chap. ii. and vi. — Ed.

In effect, it is something imperfect, that cannot exist; an idea wherein some parts of several different and inconsistent ideas are put together."[1]

This doctrine was, however, too palpably absurd to obtain any advocates; and conceptualism, could it not find a firmer basis, behoved to be abandoned. Passing over Dr. Reid's speculations on the question, which are, as I have said, wavering and ambiguous, I solicit your attention to the principal statement and defence of conceptualism by Dr. Brown, in whom the doctrine has obtained a strenuous advocate. "If, then, the generalizing process be, first,

Brown quoted.

the perception or conception of two or more objects; secondly, the relative feeling of their resemblance in certain respects; thirdly, the designation of these circumstances of resemblance, by an appropriate name,—the doctrine of the Nominalists, which includes only two of these stages, — the perception of particular objects, and the invention of general terms, must be false, as excluding that relative suggestion of resemblance in certain respects, which is the second and most important step of the process; since it is this intermediate feeling alone that leads to the use of the term, which otherwise it would be impossible to limit to any set of objects. Accordingly, we found that, in their impossibility of accounting, on their own principles, for this limitation, which it is yet absolutely necessary to explain in some manner or other,—the Nominalists, to explain it, uniformly take for granted the existence of those very general notions, which they at the same time profess to deny,—that, while they affirm that we have no notion of a kind, species, or sort, independently of the general terms which denote them, they speak of our application of such terms only to objects of the same kind, species, or sort; as if we truly had some notions of these general circumstances of agreement to direct us,—and that they are thus very far from being Nominalists in the spirit of their argument, at the very moment when they are Nominalists in assertion,—strenuous opposers of those very general feelings, of the truth of which they avail themselves, in their very endeavor to disprove them.

"If, indeed, it were the name which formed the class, and not that previous relative feeling, or general notion of resemblance of some sort, which the name denotes, then might anything be classed with anything, and classed with equal propriety. All which would be necessary, would be merely to apply the same name uniformly to the same objects; and, if we were careful to do this, John and a triangle might as well be classed together, under the name man,

---

1 See above, p. 477, note 1.—ED.

as John and William. Why does the one of those arrangements appear to us more philosophic than the other? It is because something more is felt by us to be necessary in classification, than the mere giving of a name at random. There is, in the relative suggestion that arises on our very perception or conception of objects, when we consider them together, a reason for giving the generic name to one set of objects rather than to another,— the name of man, for instance, to John and William, rather than to John and a triangle. This reason is the feeling of the resemblance of the objects which we class,— that general notion of the relation of similarity in certain respects, which is signified by the general term,— and without which relative suggestion, as a previous state of the mind, the general term would as little have been invented, as the names of John and William would have been invented, if there had been no perception of any individual being whatever to be denoted by them."[1]

This part of Dr. Brown's philosophy has obtained the most unmeasured encomium; it has been lauded as the most important step ever made in the philosophy of mind; and as far as I am aware, no one has as yet made any attempt at refutation. I regret that in this, as in many other principal points of his doctrine, I find it impossible not to dissent from Dr. Brown. An adequate refutation of his views would, indeed, require a more elaborate criticism than I am at present able to afford them; but I trust that the following hasty observations will be sufficient to evince, that the doctrine of Nominalism is not yet overthrown.

Dr. Brown has taken especial care that his theory of generalization should not be misunderstood; for the

Brown's doctrine criticized.

following is the seventh, out of nine recapitulations, he has given us of it in his forty-sixth and forty-seventh Lectures. "If then the generalizing process be, first, the perception or conception of two or more objects; secondly, the relative feeling of their resemblance in certain respects; thirdly, the designation of these circumstances of resemblance by an appropriate name, the doctrine of the Nominalists, which includes only two of these stages,— the perception of particular objects, and the invention of general terms,— must be false, as excluding that relative suggestion of resemblance in certain respects, which is the second and most important step of the process; since it is this intermediate feeling alone that leads to the use of the term, which, otherwise, it would be impossible to limit to any set of objects."

[1] *Philosophy of the Human Mind*, lecture xlvii. p. 803.— ED.

This contains, in fact, both the whole of his own doctrine, and the whole ground of his rejection of that of the Nominalists. Now, upon this, I would, first of all, say, in general, that what in it is true is not new. But I hold it idle to prove, that his doctrine is old and common, and to trace it to authors with whom Brown has shown his acquaintance, by repeatedly quoting them in his Lectures; it is enough to show that it is erroneous.

The first point I shall consider is his confutation of the Nominalists. In the passage I have just adduced,

His confutation of Nominalism.

and in ten others, he charges the Nominalists with excluding "the relative suggestion of resemblance in certain respects, which is the second and most important step in the process." This, I admit, is a weighty accusation, and I admit at once that if it do not prove that his own doctrine is right, it would at least demonstrate theirs to be sublimely wrong. But is the charge well founded? Dr. Brown, in a passage which I once read to you,[1] and with which he concludes his supposed exposition of what he calls "the series of Reid's wonderful misconceptions," wisely warns his pupils against according credit to all second-hand statements. "I trust," he says, "it will impress you with one important lesson, which could not be taught more forcibly than by the errors of so great a mind, that it will always be necessary for you to consult the opinions of authors, when their opinions are of sufficient importance to deserve to be accurately studied, in their own works, and not in the works of those who profess to give a faithful account of them. From my own experience, I can most truly assure you, that there is scarcely an instance in which, on examining the works of those authors whom it is the custom more to cite than to read, I have found the view which I had received of them faithful." No advice assuredly can be more sound, and I shall accordingly follow it now, as I have heretofore done, in application to his own reports. Let

I. That the Nominalists allow the apprehension of resemblance, proved against Brown by reference to Hobbes.

us see whether the nominalists, as he assures us, do really exclude the apprehension of resemblance in certain respects, as one step in their doctrine of generalization. I turn first to Hobbes as the real father of this opinion,—to him, as Leibnitz truly says, "*nominalibus ipsis nominaliorem*." The classical place of this philosopher on the subject is the fourth chapter of the *Leviathan*; and there we have the following passage—"One universal name is imposed on many things for their *similitude in some quality or*

[1] See above, lect. xxiii. p. 312.—Ed.

other accident ; and whereas a proper name bringeth to mind one thing only, universals recall *any one* of those many." There are other passages to the same effect in Hobbes, but I look no further.

The second great nominalist is Berkeley; and to him the doctrine chiefly owes the acceptation it latterly obtained. His doctrine on the subject is chiefly contained in the Introduction to the *Principles of Human Knowledge*, sect. 7, etc., and in the seventh Dialogue of the *Minute Philosopher*, sect. 5, etc. Out of many similar passages, I select the two following. In both he is stating his own doctrine of nominalism. In the Introduction, sect. 22 : "To discern *the agreements or disagreements* that are between my ideas, to see what ideas are included in any compound idea, etc." In the *Minute Philosopher*, sect. 7 : "But may not words become general by being made to stand indiscriminately for all particular ideas, which, from a *mutual resemblance*, belong to the same kind, without the intervention of any abstract general idea?"

Berkeley.

I next take down Hume. His doctrine on the point at issue is found in book i. part i. sect. 7 of the *Treatise of Human Nature*, entitled, *On Abstract Ideas*. This section opens with the following sentence : "A great philosopher has disputed the received opinion in this particular, and has asserted that all general ideas are nothing but particular ones annexed to a certain term, which gives them a more extensive signification, and makes them recall upon occasion other individuals which are similar to them. As I look upon this to be one of the greatest and most valuable discoveries that has been made of late years in the republic of letters, I shall here endeavor to confirm it by some arguments, which I hope will put it beyond all doubt and controversy." In glancing over the subsequent exposition of the doctrine, I see the following :— "When we have found a *resemblance* among several objects, we apply the same name to all of them," etc. Again :— "As individuals are collected together and placed under a general term, with a view to that *resemblance* which they bear to each other," etc. In the last page and a half of the section, it is stated, no less than four times that *perceived resemblance* is the foundation of classification.

Hume.

Adam Smith's doctrine is to the same effect as his predecessor's. It is contained in his *Dissertation concerning the First Formation of Languages* (appended to his *Theory of Moral Sentiments*), which literally is full of statements to the purport of the following, which alone I adduce : "It is this application of the name of an individual to a great num-

Adam Smith.

ber of objects, whose *resemblance* naturally recalls the idea of that individual, and of the name which expresses it, that seems originally to have given occasion to the formation of these classes and assortments, which in the schools are called *genera* and *species*, and of which the ingenious and eloquent Rousseau finds himself so much at a loss to account for the origin. What constitutes a species is merely a number of objects, bearing *a certain degree of resemblance* to one another, and on that account denominated by a single appellation, which may be applied to express any one of them."

The assertion, that perceived resemblance is the principle of classification, is repeated *ad nauseam* by Principal

Campbell. Stewart.

Campbell and Mr. Stewart. I shall quote only from the latter, and I take the first passage that strikes my eye: "According to this view of the process of the mind, in carrying on general speculations, that idea which the ancient philosophers considered as the essence of an individual, is nothing more than the particular quality or qualities in which it *resembles* other individuals of the same class; and in consequence of which a generic name is applied to it." [1]

From the evidence I have already quoted, you will see how marvellously wrong is Brown's assertion, that the nominalists not only took no account of, but absolutely excluded from their statement of the process of generalization, the apprehension of the mutual similarity of objects. You will, therefore, not be surprised when I assure you, that not only no nominalist ever overlooked, ever excluded, the manifested resemblance of objects to each other, but that every nominalist explicitly founded his doctrine of classification on this resemblance, and on this resemblance alone. [2] No nominalist ever dreamt of disallowing the notion of relativity,—the conception of similarity between things,—this they maintain not less strenuously than the conceptionalist; they only deny that this could ever constitute a general notion.

But perhaps it may be admitted, that Brown is wrong in asserting

II. That Brown wrong in holding that the feeling (notion) of similitude is general, and constitutes the general notion,— proved by the following axioms.

that the nominalist excludes resemblance as an element of generalization, and yet maintained, that he is right in holding, against the nominalists, that the notion, or, as he has it, the feeling of the similitude of objects in certain respects, is general, and constitutes what is called the general notion. I am afraid, however, that the misconception in regard to this point will be found not inferior to that in regard to the other.

---

[1] *Elements*, vol. i. c. iv. sect. ii. *Works*, vol. ii. p. 175.

[2] [See Tellez, *Summa Phil. Universæ*, [vol. i. p. i. disp. iv. sect. i. subs. 8—16, p. 49, *et seq.*,

In the first place, then, resemblance is a relation ; and a relation necessarily supposes certain objects as related

1. Notion of similarity supposes notion of certain similar objects.

terms. There can thus be no relation of resemblance conceived, apart from certain resembling objects. This is so manifest, that a formal enumeration of the principle seems almost puerile. Let it, however, be laid down as a first axiom, that the notion of similarity supposes the notion of certain similar objects.

In the second place, objects cannot be similar without being similar in some particular mode or accident, —

2 Similar objects are similar in some particular mode.

say in color, in figure, in size, in weight, in smell, in fluidity, in life, etc., etc. This is equally evident, and this I lay down as a second axiom.

In the third place, I assume, as a third axiom, that a resemblance is not necessarily and of itself universal. On the

3. A resemblance not necessarily universal.

contrary, a resemblance between two individual objects in a determinate quality, is as individual and determinate as the objects and their resembling qualities themselves. Who, for example, will maintain that my actual notion of the likeness of a particular snowball and a particular egg, is more general than the representations of the several objects and their resembling accidents of color?

Now let us try Dr. Brown's theory on these grounds. In reference to the first, he does not pretend that what

Brown's theory tested by these axioms.

he calls the general feeling of resemblance, can exist except between individual objects and individual representations. The universality, which he arrogates to this feeling, cannot accrue to it from any universality in the relative or resembling ideas. This neither he nor any other philosopher ever did or could pretend. They are supposed, *ex hypothesi*, to be individual, — singular.

Neither, in reference to the second axiom, does he pretend to derive the universality which he asserts to his feeling of resemblance from the universality of the notion of the common quality, in which this resemblance is realized. He does not, with Locke and others, maintain this; on the contrary, it is on the admitted absurdity of such a foundation that he attempts to establish the doctrine of conceptualism on another ground.

But if the universality, assumed by Dr. Brown for his " feeling of

(edit. 1644). Cf. sect. ii. subs. i. *et seq.*, p. 65. —Ed.] Derodon, *Logica,* [p. ii. c. v. art. 2, § 5, p. 211. Cf. art. 4, p. 224 *et seq.*—Ed.] Arriaga, *Logica,* (disp. vi. sect. i. subs. i. *et seq., Cursus Philosophicus,* p. 110 (edit. 1632). —

Ed.] Mendoza, *Disp. Log.* [d. iii. § 1, *Disp. a Summulis ad Metaphysicam,* vol. i. p. 248.] Fran. Bonæ Spei, *Logica,* [*De Porphyrianis Universalibus,* disp. i., *Commentarii in Arist. Phil.* p. 53, (edit. 1652.) —Ed.]

resemblance," be found neither in the resembling objects, nor in the qualities through which they are similar, we must look for it in the feeling of resemblance itself, apart from its actual realization; and this in opposition to the third axiom we laid down as self-evident. In these circumstances, we have certainly a right to expect that Dr. Brown should have brought us cogent proof for an assertion so contrary to all apparent evidence, that although this be the question which perhaps has been more ably, keenly, and universally agitated than any other, still no philosopher before himself was found even to imagine such a possibility. But in proof of this new paradox, Dr. Brown has not only brought no evidence; he does not even attempt to bring any. He assumes and he asserts, but he hazards no argument. In this state of matters, it is perhaps superfluous to do more than to rebut assertion by assertion; and as Dr. Brown is not *in possessorio*, and as his opinion is even opposed to the universal consent of philosophers, the counter assertion, if not overturned by reasoning, must prevail.

But let us endeavor to conceive on what grounds it could possibly be supposed by Dr. Brown, that the feeling of

Possible grounds of Brown's supposition that the feeling of resemblance is universal.

resemblance between certain objects, through certain resembling qualities, has in it anything of universal, or can, as he says, constitute the general notion. This to me is indeed not easy; and every hypothesis I can make is so absurd, that it appears almost a libel to attribute it, even by conjecture, to so ingenious and acute a thinker.

In the first place, can it be supposed that Dr. Brown believed that

First.

a feeling of resemblance between objects in a certain quality or respect was general because it was a relation? Then must every notion of a relation be a general notion; which neither he nor any other philosopher ever asserts.

In the second place, does he suppose that there is anything in the

Second.

feeling or notion of the particular relation called *similarity*, which is more general than the feeling or notion of any other relation? This can hardly be conceived. What is a feeling or notion of resemblance? Merely this; two objects affect us in a certain manner, and we are conscious that they affect us in the same way that a single object does, when presented at different times to our perception. In either case, we judge that the affections of which we are conscious are similar or the same. There is nothing general in this consciousness, or in this judgment. At all events, the relation recognized between the consciousness of similarity produced on us by two different eggs, is not more general than the feeling of similarity produced on us by the successive presentation of the same egg. If the one is to be called general, so is the other. Again, if the feeling or notion of resemblance be made general, so must the feeling or notion of difference. They are absolutely the same notion, only in different applications. You know the logical axiom, — the science of contraries is one. We know the like only as we know the unlike. Every affirmation of similarity is virtually an affirmation that difference does not exist; every affirmation of difference is virtually an affirmation that similarity is not to be found. But neither Brown nor any other philosopher has pretended, that the apprehension of difference is either general, or a ground of generalization. On the contrary, the apprehension of difference is the negation of generalization, and a descent from the universal to the particular. But if the notion or feeling of the dissimilarity is not general, neither is the feeling or notion of the similarity.

In the third place, can it be that Dr. Brown supposes the particular feeling or consciousness of similarity between certain objects in certain respects to be

Third.

general, because we have, in general, a capacity of feeling or being conscious of similarity? This conjecture is equally improbable. On this ground every act of every power would be general; and we should not be obliged to leave Imagination, in order to seek for the universality which we cannot discover in the light and definitude of that faculty, in the obscurity and vagueness of another.

In the fourth place, only one other supposition remains; and this may perhaps enable us to explain the possibility of Dr. Brown's hallucination. A relation cannot

Fourth.

be represented in Imagination. The two terms, the two relative objects, can be severally imaged in the sensible phantasy, but not the relation itself. This is the object of the Comparative Faculty, or of Intelligence Proper. To objects so different as the images of sense and the unpicturable notions of intelligence, different names ought to be given; and accordingly this has been done wherever a philosophical nomenclature of the slightest pretensions to perfection has been formed. In the German language, which is now the richest in metaphysical expressions of any living tongue, the two kinds of objects are carefully distinguished.[1] In our language, on the contrary, the *idea, conception, notion*, are used almost as convertible for either; and the vagueness and confusion which is thus produced, even within the narrow sphere of speculation to which the want of

---

1 See *Reid's Works*, p. 407, note ‡, and 412, note. — ED.

the distinction also confines us, can be best appreciated by those who are conversant with the philosophy of the different countries.

Dr. Brown seems to have had some faint perception of the difference between intellectual notions and sensible representations; and if he had endeavored to signalize their contrast by a distinction of terms, he would have deserved well of English philosophy. But he mistook the nature of the intellectual notion, which connects two particular qualities by the bond of similarity, and imagined that there lurked under this intangible relation the universality which, he clearly saw, could not be found in a representation of the related objects, or of their resembling qualities. At least, if this do not assist us in accounting for his misconception, I do not know in what way we otherwise can.

What I have now said is, I think, sufficient in regard to the nature of Generalization. It is notoriously a mere act of Comparison. We compare objects; we find them similar in certain respects, that is, in certain respects they affect us in the same manner; we consider the qualities in them, that thus affect us in the same manner, as the same; and to this common quality we give a name; and as we can predicate this name of all and each of the resembling objects, it constitutes them into a class. Aristotle has truly said that general names are only abbreviated definitions,[1] and definitions, you know, are judgments. For example, *animal* is only a compendious expression for *organized and animated body; man*, only a summary of *rational animal*, etc.

Summary of the Author's doctrine of Generalization.

---

1 *Rhet.* iii. 6. — ED.

LECTURE XXXVI.

THE ELABORATIVE FACULTY. — GENERALIZATION. — THE PRIMUM COGNITUM.

WE were principally employed, in our last Lecture, in considering Dr. Brown's doctrine of Generalization; and, in doing this, I first discussed his refutation of Nominalism, and, secondly, his own theory of Conceptualism. In reference to the former, I showed you that the ground on which he attempts to refute the Nominalists, is only an inconceivable mistake of his own. He rejects their doctrine as incomplete, because, he says, they take no account of the mutual resemblance of the classified objects. But so far are the nominalists from taking no account of the mutual resemblance of the classified objects, that their doctrine is notoriously founded on the apprehension of this similarity, and on the apprehension of this similarity alone. How Dr. Brown could have run into this radical misrepresentation of so celebrated an opinion, is, I repeat, wholly inconceivable. Having proved to you by the authentic testimony of the British nominalists of principal celebrity, that Dr. Brown had in his statement of their doctrine simply reversed it, I proceeded, in the second place, to test the accuracy of his own. Dr. Brown repudiates the doctrine of Conceptualism as held by Locke and others. He admits that we can represent to ourselves no general notion of the common attribute or attributes which constitute a class; but he asserts that the generality, which cannot be realized in a notion of the resembling attribute, is realized in a notion of the resemblance itself. This theory, I endeavored to make it evident, was altogether groundless. In the first place, the doctrine supposes that the notion, or, as he calls it, the feeling, of the mutual resemblance of particular objects in particular respects, is general. This, the very foundation of his theory, is not self-evidently true; — on the contrary, it stands obtrusively, self-evidently, false. It was primarily incumbent on Dr. Brown to prove the reality of this basis. But he makes not even an attempt at this. He assumes all that is in question. To the

62

noun-substantive, "feeling of resemblance," he prefixes the adjective, "general;" but he does not condescend to evince that the verbal collocations have any real connection.

But, in the second place, as it is not proved by Dr. Brown, that our notion of the similarity of certain things in certain respects is general, so it can easily be shown against him that it is not.

The generality cannot be found in the relation of resemblance, apart from all resembling objects, and all circumstances of resemblance; for a resemblance only exists, and is only conceived, as between determinate objects, and in determinate attributes.[1] This is not denied by Dr. Brown. On the contrary, he arrogates generality to what he calls the "feeling of similarity of certain objects in certain respects." These are the expressions he usually employs. So far, therefore, all is manifest, all is admitted; a resemblance is only conceived, is only conceivable, as between particular objects, in particular qualities. Apart from these, resemblance is not asserted to be thinkable. This being understood, it is apparent, that the notion of the resemblance of certain objects in a certain attribute, is just the notion of that attribute itself; and if it be impossible, as Brown admits, to conceive that attribute generally, in other words, to have a general notion of it, it is impossible to have a general notion of the resemblance which it constitutes. For example, we have a perception or imagination of two figures resembling each other, in having three angles. Now here it is admitted, that if either the figures themselves be removed, or the attribute belonging to each (of three angles) be thrown out of account, the notion of any resemblance is annihilated. It is also admitted, that the notion of resemblance is realized through the notion of triangularity. In this all philosophers are at one. All likewise agree that the notion of similarity, and the notion of generality, are the same; though Brown, as we have seen, has misrepresented the doctrine of Nominalism on this point. But though all maintain that things are conceived similar only as conceived similar in some quality, and that their similarity in this quality alone constitutes them into a class, they differ in regard to their ulterior explanation. Let us suppose that, of our two figures, the one is a rectangled, and the other an equilateral, triangle; and let us hear, on this simple example, how the different theorists explain themselves. The nominalists say, — you can imagine a rectangular triangle alone, and an equilateral triangle alone, or you can imagine both at once; and, in this case, in the consciousness of their similarity, you may view

[1] If generality in relation of resemblance apart from particular objects and qualities, then only one general notion at all. — *Marginal Jotting.*

either as the inadequate representative of both. But you cannot imagine a figure which shall adequately represent both *qua* triangle; that is, you cannot imagine a triangle which is neither an equilateral nor a rectangled triangle, and yet both at once. And as on our (the nominalist) doctrine, the similarity is only embodied in an individual notion, having relation to another, there is no general notion properly speaking at all.

The older Conceptualists, on the other hand, assert that it is possible to conceive a triangle neither equilateral nor rectangular, —but both at once. Dr. Brown differs from nominalists and older conceptualists; he coincides with the nominalists in rejecting as absurd the hypothesis of the conceptualists, but he coincides with the conceptualists in holding, that there is a general notion adequate to the term triangle. This general notion he does not, however, place, with the conceptualist, in any general representation of the attribute triangle, but in the notion or feeling of resemblance between the individual representations of an equilateral and of a rectangled triangle. This opinion is, however, untenable. In the first place, there is here no generalization; for what is called the common notion can only be realized in thought through notions of all the several objects which are to be classified. Thus, in our example, the notion of the similarity of the two figures, in being each triangular, supposes the actual perception or imagination of both together. Take out of actual perception, or actual representation, one or both of the triangles, and no similarity, that is, no general notion remains. Thus, upon Dr. Brown's doctrine, the general notion only exists in so far as the individual notions, from which it is generalized, are present, that is, in so far as there is no generalization at all. This is because resemblance is a relation; but a relation supposes two particular objects; and a relation between particular objects is just as particular as the objects themselves.

But let us consider his doctrine in another point of view. In the example we have taken of the equilateral and rectangular triangles, triangularity is an attribute of each, and in each the conceived triangularity is a particular, not a general, notion. Now the resemblance between these figures lies in their triangularity, and the notion or feeling of resemblance in which Dr. Brown places the generality, must be a notion or feeling of triangularity, — triangularity must constitute their resemblance. This is manifest. For if it be not a notion of triangularity, it must be a notion of something else, and if a notion of something else, it cannot be a general notion of two figures as triangles. The

Brown's doctrine of general notions, — further considered.

notion of resemblance between the figures in question must, therefore, be a notion of triangularity. Now the triangularity thus conceived must be one notion, — one triangularity; for otherwise it could not be (what is supposed) one common or general notion, but a plurality of notions. Again, this one triangularity must not be the triangularity, either of the equilateral triangle, or of the rectangular triangle alone; for, in that case, it would not be a general notion, — a notion common to both. But if it cannot be the triangularity of either, it must be the triangularity of both. Of such a triangularity, however, it is impossible to form a notion, as Dr. Brown admits; for triangularity must be either rectangular or not rectangular; but as these are contradictory or exclusive attributes, we cannot conceive them together in the same notion, nor can we form a notion of triangularity except as the one or the other.

This being the case, the notion or feeling of similarity between the two triangles cannot be a notion or feeling of triangularity at all. But if it be not this, what can it otherwise possibly be? There is only one conceivable alternative. As a general notion, containing under it particular notions, it must be given up, but it may be regarded as a particular relation between the particular figures, and which supposes them to be represented, as the condition of being itself not represented, but conceived. And thus, by a different route, we arrive again at the same conclusion, — that Dr. Brown has mistaken a particular, an individual, relation for a general notion. He clearly saw that all that is picturable in imagination, is determinate and individual; he, therefore, avoided the absurdity involved in the doctrine of the old conceptualists; but he was not warranted (if this were, indeed, the ground of his assumption) in assuming, that because a notion cannot be pictured in imagination, it is, therefore, general.

Instead of recapitulating what I stated in opposition to Dr. Brown's views in my last Lecture, I have been led into a new line of argument; for, in fact, his doctrine is open to so many objections that, on what side soever we regard it, argument will not be wanting for its refutation. So far, therefore, from Nominalism being confuted by Brown, it is plain that, apart from the misconception he has committed, he is himself a nominalist.

The question, — Does Language originate in General Appellatives or by Proper Names, — considered.

I proceed now to a very curious question, which has likewise divided philosophers. It is this, — Does Language originate in General Appellatives, or by Proper Names? Did mankind in the formation of language, and do children in their first applications of it, commence with the one kind of words, or with the other? The determination of this question, — the question of the *Primum Cognitum*, as it was called in the schools, is not involved in the doctrine of Nominalism. Many illustrious philosophers have maintained that all terms, as at first employed, are expressive of individual objects, and that these only subsequently obtain a general acceptation.

This opinion I find maintained by Vives,[1] Locke,[2] Rousseau,[3] Condillac,[4] Adam Smith,[5] Strinbart,[6] Tittel,[7] Brown,[8] and others.[9] "The order of learning" (I translate from Vives) "is from the senses to the imagination, and from this to the intellect, — such is the order of life and of nature. We thus proceed from the simple to the complex, from the singular to the universal. This is to be observed in children who first of all express the several parts of different things, and then conjoin them. Things general they call by a singular name; for instance, they call all smiths by the name of that individual *smith* whom they have first known, and all meats, *beef* or *pork*, as they have happened to have heard the one or the other first, when they begin to speak. Thereafter the mind collects universals from particulars, and then again reverts to particulars from universals." The same doctrine, without probably any knowledge of Vives, is

[margin note: 1. That all terms, as first employed, expressive of individual objects, — maintained by Vives and others.]

[margin note: Locke.]

maintained by Locke.[10] "There is nothing more evident than that the ideas of the persons children converse with (to instance in them alone), are like the persons themselves, only particular. The ideas of the nurse and the mother are well framed in their minds; and, like pictures of them there, represent only those individuals. The names they first gave to them are confined to these individuals; and the names of *nurse* and *mamma*, the child uses, determine themselves to those persons. Afterwards, when time and a larger acquaintance have made them observe that there are a great many other things in the world, that in some common agreements of shape, and several other qualities, resemble their father and mother, and those persons they have been used to, they frame an idea which they find those many particulars do partake in; and to that they give, with others, the name *man*,

1 *De Anima*, lib. ii. *De Discendi Ratione, Opera*, vol. ii. p. 530, Basileæ, 1555. — ED.

2 See below, p. 494. — ED.

3 [See Toussaint, *De la Pensée*, c. x. p. 278—79.] *Discours sur l' Origine de l' Inegalité parmi les Hommes, Œuvres*, t. i. p. 268, ed. 1826. — ED.

4 See below, p. 494. — ED.

5 See below, p. 494. — ED

6 [*Anleitung des Verstandes*, § 45. Cf. § 83–89.]

7 [*Erläuterungen der Philosophie.*] [*Logik*, p. 214, *et seq.* (edit. 1793). — ED.]

8 See below, p. 494. — ED.

9 Cf. Toletus, *In Phys. Arist.* lib. i. c. i. t. 5, q. 5, f. 10b. Conimbricenses, *Ibid.* lib. i. c. i. q. 3, art. 2, p. 79; and q. 4, art. 2, p. 89. — ED.

10 *Essay*, iii. 3, 7. — ED.

for example. And thus they come to have a general name, and a general idea."

The same doctrine is advanced in many places of his works by

Condillac.
Adam Smith.

Condillac.[1] Adam Smith has, however, the merit of having applied this theory to the formation of language; and his doctrine, which Dr. Brown,[2] absolutely, and Mr. Stewart,[3] with some qualification,

Brown.   Stewart.

adopts, is too important not to be fully stated, and in his own powerful language: — "The assignation," says Smith,[4] "of particular names, to denote particular

Smith quoted.

objects, — that is, the institution of nouns substantive, would probably be one of the first steps towards the formation of language. Two savages, who had never been taught to speak, but had been bred up remote from the societies of men, would naturally begin to form that language by which they would endeavor to make their mutual wants intelligible to each other, by uttering certain sounds whenever they meant to denote certain objects. Those objects only which were most familiar to them, and which they had most frequent occasion to mention, would have particular names assigned to them. The particular cave whose covering sheltered them from the weather, the particular tree whose fruit relieved their hunger, the particular fountain whose water allayed their thirst, would first be denominated by the words, *cave, tree, fountain,* or by whatever other appellations they might think proper, in that primitive jargon, to mark them. Afterwards, when the more enlarged experience of these savages had led them to observe, and their necessary occasions obliged them to make mention of other caves, and other trees, and other fountains, they would naturally bestow upon each of those new objects the same name by which they had been accustomed to express the similar object they were first acquainted with. The new objects had none of them any name of its own, but each of them exactly resembled another object, which had such an appellation. It was impossible that those savages could behold the new objects, without recollecting the old ones; and the name of the old ones, to which the new bore so close a resemblance. When they had occasion, therefore, to mention or to point out to each other any of the new objects, they would naturally utter the name of the correspondent old one, of which the idea could not fail, at that instant, to present

[1] See *Origine des Connoissances Humaines,* part i. sect. iv. c. i. sect. v.; part ii. sect. ii. c. ix. — ED.

[2] Lecture xlvii. p. 306 (edit. 1830).

[3] *Elements,* vol. i. part ii. c. iv. *Works,* vol. ii. p. 159. Cf. *Elements,* vol. ii. part. ii. c. ii. § 4. *Works,* p. 173. — ED.

[4] *Considerations concerning the First Formation of Languages,* appended to *Theory of Moral Sentiments.* — ED.

itself to their memory in the strongest and liveliest manner. And thus those words, which were originally the proper names of individuals, would each of them insensibly become the common name of a multitude. A child that is just learning to speak, calls every person who comes to the house its papa, or its mamma; and thus bestows upon the whole species those names which it had been taught to apply to two individuals. I have known a clown who did not know the proper name of the river which ran by his own door. It was *the river*, he said, and he never heard any other name for it. His experience, it seems, had not led him to observe any other river. The general word *river*, therefore, was, it is evident, in his acceptance of it, a proper name signifying an individual object. If this person had been carried to another river, would he not readily have called it a river? Could we suppose a person living on the banks of the Thames so ignorant as not to know the general word *river*, but to be acquainted only with the particular word *Thames*, if he was brought to any other river, would he not readily call it *a Thames?* This, in reality, is no more than what they who are well acquainted with the general word are very apt to do. An Englishman, describing any great river which he may have seen in some foreign country, naturally says, that it is another Thames. The Spaniards, when they first arrived upon the coast of Mexico, and observed the wealth, populousness, and habitations of that fine country, so much superior to the savage nations which they had been visiting for some time before, cried out that it was another Spain. Hence, it was called New Spain; and this name has stuck to that unfortunate country ever since. We say, in the same manner, of a hero, that he is an Alexander; of an orator, that he is a Cicero; of a philosopher, that he is a Newton. This way of speaking, which the grammarians call an Antonomasia, and which is still extremely common, though now not at all necessary, demonstrates how much all mankind are naturally disposed to give to one object the name of any other which nearly resembles it; and thus, to denominate a multitude by what originally was intended to express an individual.

" It is this application of the name of an individual to a great multitude of objects, whose resemblance naturally recalls the idea of that individual, and of the name which expresses it, that seems originally to have given occasion to the formation of those classes and assortments which, in the schools, are called *genera* and *species*."

On the other hand, an opposite doctrine is maintained by many profound philosophers. A large section of the schoolmen [1] embraced

---

1 Cf. Conimbricenses, *In Phys. Arist.* l. 1. c.   Toletus, *Ibid.*, l. 1, c. 1, text 8 *et seq.* f. 10a.— ·i. q. 3, art. 1, p. 78; and q. 4, art. 1, p. 37.   ED.

it, and, among more modern thinkers, it is adopted by Campanella.[1] Campanella was an author profoundly studied by Leibnitz, who even places him on a line with, if not above, Bacon; and from him it is not improbable that Leibnitz may have taken a hint of his own doctrine on the subject. In his great work, the *Nouveaux Essais*, of which Stewart was not till very latterly aware, he says,[2] that, "general terms serve not only for the perfection of languages, but are even necessary for their essential constitution. For if by *particulars* be understood things individual, it would be impossible to speak, if there were only proper names, and no appellatives, that is to say, if there were only names for things individual, since, at every moment we are met by new ones, when we treat of persons, of accidents, and especially of actions, which are those that we describe the most; but if by particulars be meant the lowest species (*species infimas*), besides that it is frequently very difficult to determine them, it is manifest that these are already universals, founded on similarity. Now, as the only difference of *species* and *genera* lies in a similarity of greater or less extent, it is natural to note every kind of similarity or agreement, and, consequently, to employ general terms of every degree; nay, the most general being less complex with regard to the essences which they comprehend, although more extensive in relation to the things individual to which they apply, are frequently the easiest to form, and are the most useful. It is likewise seen that children, and those who know but little of the language which they attempt to speak, or little of the subject on which they would employ it, make use of general terms, as *thing, plant, animal*, instead of using proper names, of which they are destitute. And it is certain that all *proper* or individual names have been originally *appellative* or general." In illustration of this latter most important doctrine, he, in a subsequent part of the work, says:[3] "I would add, in conformity to what I have previously observed, that proper names have been originally appellative, that is to say, general in their origin, as Brutus, Cæsar, Augustus, Capito, Lentulus, Piso, Cicero, Elbe, Rhine, Rhur, Leine, Ocker, Bucephalus, Alps, Pyrenees, etc.," and, after illustrating this in detail, he concludes: — "Thus I would make bold to affirm that almost all words have been originally general terms, because it would happen very rarely that men would invent a name, expressly and without a reason, to denote this or

2. An opposite doctrine maintained by many of the Schoolmen.

Campanella.
Leibnitz.

Leibnitz quoted.

---

[1] [See Tennemann, *Geschichte der Philosophie*, vol. ix. p. 334.]

[2] Lib. iii. c. i. p. 297 (Erdmann). — ED.

[3] Lib. iii. c. iii. p. 303 (Erdmann). — ED.

that individual. We may, therefore, assert that the names of individual things were names of species, which were given *par excellence,*
or otherwise, to some individual, as the name *Great Head* to him
of the whole town who had the largest, or who was the man of
most consideration, of the Great Heads known. It is thus likewise
that men give the names of genera to species, that is to say, that
they content themselves with a term more general or vague to
denote more particular classes, when they do not care about the
differences. As, for example, we content ourselves with the general name *absinthium* (wormwood), although there are so many
species of the plant that one of the Bauhins has filled a whole book
with them."

That this was likewise the opinion of the great Turgot, we learn
from his biographer. "M. Turgot," says Con-
dorcet,[1] "believed that the opinion was wrong,
which held that in general the mind only acquired general or abstract ideas by the comparison of more particular ideas. On the
contrary, our first ideas are very general, for, seeing at first only a
small number of qualities, our idea includes all the existences to
which these qualities are common. As we acquire knowledge, our
ideas become more particular, without ever reaching the last limit;
and, what might have deceived the metaphysicians, it is precisely
by this process that we learn that these ideas are more general than
we had at first supposed."

Here are two opposite opinions, each having nearly equal authority in its favor, maintained on both sides with equal ability and
apparent evidence. Either doctrine would be held established were
we unacquainted with the arguments in favor of the other.

But I have now to state to you a third opinion, intermediate between these, which conciliates both, and seems,
moreover, to carry a superior probability in its
statement. This opinion maintains, that as our
knowledge proceeds from the confused to the
distinct, — from the vague to the determinate,
— so, in the mouths of children, language at first
expresses neither the precisely general nor the
determinately individual, but the vague and confused; and that,
out of this the universal is elaborated by generification, the particular and singular by specification and individualization.

I formerly explained why I view the doctrine held by Mr. Stewart
and others in regard to perception in general and vision in partic-

Turgot.

3. A third or inter-
mediate opinion main-
tained,—that language
at first expresses only
the vague and con-
fused.

---

1 [*Vie de M. Turgot,* Londres, 1786, p. 214.]

ular, as erroneous; inasmuch as they conceive that our sensible cognitions are formed by the addition of an almost

*That perception com-
mences with masses,
already shown.*

infinite number of separate and consecutive
acts of attentive perception, each act being cognizant of a certain *minimum sensibile.*[1] On the
contrary, I showed that, instead of commencing with minima, perception commences with masses; that, though our capacity of attention be very limited in regard to the number of objects on which a
faculty can be simultaneously directed, yet that these objects may
be large or small. We may make, for example, a single object of
attention either of a whole man, or of his face, or of his eye, or of
the pupil of his eye, or of a speck upon the pupil. To each of
these objects there can only be a certain amount of attentive
perception applied, and we can concentrate it all on any one. In
proportion as the object is larger and more complex, our attention
can of course be less applied to any part of it, and consequently,
our knowledge of it in detail will be vaguer and more imperfect.
But having first acquired a comprehensive knowledge of it as a
whole, we can descend to its several parts, consider these both in
themselves, and in relation to each other, and to the whole of which
they are constituents, and thus attain to a complete and articulate
knowledge of the object. We decompose, and then we recompose.
   But in this we always proceed first by decomposition or analysis.

*The mind in elabo-
rating its knowledge,
proceeds by analysis,
from the whole to the
parts.*

All analysis indeed supposes a foregone composition or synthesis, because we cannot decompose
what is not already composite. But in our acquisition of knowledge, the objects are presented
to us compounded; and they obtain a unity only
in the unity of our consciousness. The unity
of consciousness is, as it were, the frame in which objects are seen.
I say, then, that the first procedure of mind in the elaboration of
its knowledge is always analytical. It descends from the whole to
the parts, — from the vague to the definite. Definitude, that is,
a knowledge of minute differences, is not, as the opposite theory

Illustrated.

supposes, the first, but the last, term of our cognitions. Between two sheep an ordinary spec-
tator can probably apprehend no difference, and if they were twice
presented to him, he would be unable to discriminate the one from
the other. But a shepherd can distinguish every individual sheep;
and why? Because he has descended from the vague knowledge
which we all have of sheep, — from the vague knowledge which

---

1 See above, lect. xiii. p. 168. — ED.

makes every sheep, as it were, only a repetition of the same undifferenced unit, — to a definite knowledge of qualities by which each is contrasted from its neighbor. Now, in this example, we apprehend the sheep by marks not less individual than those by which the shepherd discriminates them; but the whole of each sheep being made an object, the marks by which we know it are the same in each and all, and cannot, therefore, afford the principle by which we can discriminate them from each other. Now this is what appears to me to take place with children. They first know, — they first cognize, the things and persons presented to them as wholes. But wholes of the same kind, if we do not descend to their parts, afford us no difference, — no mark by which we can discriminate the one from the other. Children, thus, originally perceiving similar objects, — persons, for example, — only as wholes, do at first hardly distinguish them. They apprehend first the more obtrusive marks that separate species from species, and, in consequence of the notorious contrast, of dress, men from women; but they do not as yet recognize the finer traits that discriminate individual from individual. But, though thus apprehending individuals only by what we now call their specific or their generic qualities, it is not to be supposed that children know them by any abstract general attributes, that is, by attributes formed by comparison and attention. On the other hand, because their knowledge is not general, it is not to be supposed to be particular or individual, if by particular be meant a separation of species from species, and by individual the separation of individual from individual; for children are at first apt to confound individuals together, not only in name but in reality. "A child who has been taught to say *papa*, in pointing to his father, will give at first, as Locke [and Aristotle before him] had remarked, the name of *papa* to all the men whom he sees.[1] As he only at first seizes on the more striking appearances of objects, they would appear to him all similar, and he denotes them by the same names. But when it has been pointed out to him that he is mistaken, or when he has discovered this by the consequences of his language, he studies to discriminate the objects which he had confounded, and he takes hold of their differences. The child commences, like the savage, by employing only isolated words in place of phrases; he commences by taking verbs and nouns only in their absolute state. But as these imperfect attempts at speech express at once many and very different things, and produce,

---

1 Aristotle, *Phys. Ausc.* i. 1. Cf. Locke, who adduces the same instance, but not quite *Essay on the Human Understanding*, iii. 8, 7, for the same purpose. — ED.

in consequence, manifold ambiguities, he soon discovers the necessity of determining them with greater exactitude; he endeavors to make it understood in what respects the thing which he wishes to denote, is distinguished from those with which it is confounded; and, to succeed in this endeavor, he tries to distinguish them himself. Thus when, at this age, the child seems to us as yet unoccupied, he is in reality very busy; he is devoted to a study which differs not in its nature from that to which the philosopher applies himself; the child, like the philosopher, observes, compares, and analyzes."[1]

In support of this doctrine I can appeal to high authority; it is

This doctrine main-
tained by Aristotle.

that maintained by Aristotle. Speaking of the order of procedure in physical science, he says, "We ought to proceed from the better known to the less known, and from what is clearer to us to that which is clearer in nature. But those things are first known and clearer, which are more complex and confused; for it is only by subsequent analysis that we attain to a knowledge of the parts and elements of which they are composed. We ought, therefore, to proceed from universals to singulars; for the whole is better known to sense than its parts; and the universal is a kind of whole, as the universal comprehends many things as its parts. Thus it is that names are at first better known to us than definitions; for the name denotes a whole, and that indeterminately; whereas the definition divides and explicates its parts. Children, likewise, at first call all men fathers and all women mothers; but thereafter they learn to discriminate each individual from another."[2]

The subtle Scaliger teaches the same doctrine; and he states

J. C. Scaliger.

it better perhaps than any other philosopher:

"Universalia magis, ac prius esse nota nobis. Sic enim patres a pueris omnes homines appellari. Quia æquivocationibus nomina communicantur ab ignaris etiam rebus differentibus definitione. Sic enim chirothecam meam, puerulus quidam manum appellabat. An ei pro chirothecæ specie manus species sese representabat? Nequaquam. Sed judicium aberat, quod distingueret differentias. An vero summa genera nobis notiora? Non. Composita enim notiora nobis. Genera vero partes sunt specierum: quas in partes ipsæ species multa resolvuntur arte. Itaque eandem ob rationem ipsa genera, sub notione comprehensionis et prædicabilitatis, sunt notiora quam ipsæ species. Cognoscitur animal. Animalium species quot ignorantur? Sunt enim species partes

1 Degerando, *Des Signes*, i. 156.
2 *Phys. Ausc.* i. 1.—Ed. [Cf. in *loc. cit.*   Philoponus, Themistius, Averroes, Simplicius, Pacius, Conimbricenses, Tolet.]

prædicabiles. Sic totum integrum nobis notius, quam partes e quibus constat. Omne igitur quodcunque sub totius notione sese offert, prius cognoscitur, quam ejus partes. Sic species constituta, prius quam constituentia: ut equus, prius quam animal domabile ad trahendum, et vehendum. Hoc enim postea scimus per resolutionem. Sic genus prædicabile, prius quam suæ species. Sic totum integrum, prius quam partes. Contrarius huic ordo Naturæ est."[1]

1 *De Subtilitate*, Ex. cccvii. § 21. [Cf. Zabarella, *De Ordine Intelligendi*, c. i. (*De Rebus Naturalibus*, p. 1042), and *In Phys. Arist.* i. 1, text. 5. Andreæ Cæsalpiui, *Peripateticæ Quæstiones*, lib. i. q. 1, p. 1 (edit. 1571). Herbart, *Lehrbuch zur Psychologie*, § 194. Crousaz, *Logique*, t. iii. p. 1, § iii. c. iv. p. 141.]

LECTURE XXXVII.

THE ELABORATIVE FACULTY. — JUDGMENT AND REASONING.

In our last Lecture, I terminated the consideration of the faculty of Comparison in its process of Generalization. I am to-day to consider it in those of its operations, which have obtained the special names of Judgment and Reasoning.

Judgment and Reasoning.

In these processes the act of Comparison is a judgment of something more than a mere affirmation of the existence of a phænomenon, — something more than a mere discrimination of one phænomenon from another; and, accordingly, while it has happened, that the intervention of judgment in every, even the simplest, act of primary cognition, as monotonous and rapid, has been overlooked, the name has been exclusively limited to the more varied and elaborate comparison of one notion with another, and the enouncement of their agreement or disagreement. It is in the discharge of this, its more obtrusive, function, that we are now about to consider the Elaborative Faculty.

Acts of Comparison.

Considering the Elaborative Faculty as a mean of discovering truth, by a comparison of the notions we have obtained from the Acquisitive Powers, it is evident that, though this faculty be the attribute by which a man is distinguished as a creation higher than the animals, it is equally the quality which marks his inferiority to superior intelligences. Judgment and Reasoning are rendered necessary by the imperfection of our nature. Were we capable of a knowledge of things and their relations at a single view, by an intuitive glance, discursive thought would be a superfluous act. It is by such an intuition that we must suppose that the Supreme Intelligence knows all things at once.

Judgment and Reasoning, necessary from the limitation of the human mind.

I have already noticed that our knowledge does not commence with the individual and the most particular, objects of knowledge,

— that we do not rise in any regular progress from the less to the more general, first considering the qualities

Our knowledge commences with the vague and confused.

which characterize individuals, then those which belong to species and genera, in regular ascent. On the contrary, our knowledge commences with the vague and confused, in the way which Aristotle has so well illustrated in the passage alleged to you.[1] This I may further

Illustrated.

explain by another analogy. We perceive an object approaching from a distance. At first we do not know whether it be a living or an inanimate thing. By degrees we become aware that it is an animal, but of what kind, — whether man or beast, — we are not as yet able to determine. It continues to advance, we discover it to be a quadruped, but of what species we cannot yet say. At length, we perceive that it is a horse, and again, after a season, we find that it is Bucephalus. Thus, as I formerly observed, children, first of all, take note of the generic differences, and they can distinguish species long before they are able to discriminate individuals. In all this, however, I must again remark, that our knowledge does not properly commence with the general, but with the vague and confused. Out of this the general and the individual are both equally evolved.

"In consequence of this genealogy of our knowledge we usually commence by bestowing a name upon a whole

Act of judgment, — what.

object, or congeries of objects, of which, however, we possess only a partial and indefinite conception. In the sequel, this vague notion becomes somewhat more determinate; the partial idea which we had becomes enlarged by new accessions; by degrees, our conception waxes fuller, and represents a greater number of attributes. With this conception, thus amplified and improved, we compare the last notion which has been acquired, that is to say, we compare a part with its whole, or with the other parts of this whole, and finding that it is harmonious, — that it dovetails and naturally assorts with other parts, we acquiesce in this union; and this we denominate an act of Judgment.

"In learning Arithmetic, I form the notion of the number *six*, as surpassing *five* by a single unit, and as sur-

Illustrated.

passed in the same proportion by *seven*. Then I find that it can be divided into two equal halves, of which each contains three units. By this procedure, the notion of the number six becomes more complex; the notion of an even number is one

---

[1] See above, p. 500. — ED.

of its parts. Comparing this new notion with that of the number, six becomes fuller by its addition. I recognize that the two notions suit, — in other words, I judge that six is an even number.

"I have the conception of a triangle, and this conception is composed in my mind of several others. Among these partial notions, I select that of two sides greater than the third, and this notion, which I had at first, as it were, taken apart, I reünite with the others from which it had been separated, saying the triangle contains always two sides, which together are greater than the third.

"When I say, body is divisible; among the notions which concur in forming my conception of body, I particularly attend to that of divisible, and finding that it really agrees with the others, I judge accordingly that body is divisible.

"Every time we judge, we compare a total conception with a partial, and we recognize that the latter really constitutes a part of the former. One of these conceptions has received the name of *subject*, the other that of *attribute* or *predicate*."[1] The verb which connects these two parts is called the *copula*. *The quadrangle is a double triangle; nine is an odd number; body is divisible.* Here *quadrangle*, *nine*, *body*, are subjects; *a double triangle, an odd number, divisible*, are predicates. The whole mental judgment, formed by the subject, predicate, and copula, is called, when enounced in words, *proposition*.

Subject. Predicate. Copula.

Proposition.

"In discourse, the parts of a proposition are not always found placed in logical order; but to discover and discriminate them, it is only requisite to ask — What is the thing of which something else is affirmed or denied ? The answer to this question will point out the subject; and we shall find the predicate if we inquire, — What is affirmed or denied of the matter of which we speak ?

How the parts of a proposition are to be discriminated.

"A proposition is sometimes so enounced that each of its terms may be considered as subject and as predicate. Thus, when we say, — *Death is the wages of sin ;* we may regard *sin* as the subject of which we predicate *death*, as one of its consequences, and we may likewise view *death* as the subject of which we predicate *sin*, as the origin. In these cases, we must consider the general tenor of the discourse, and determine from the context what is the matter of which it principally treats."

"In fine, when we judge we must have, in the first place, at least

---

[1] Crousaz, [*Logique*, tom. iii. part ii. c. i. pp. 178, 181. — ED.]

two notions; in the second place, we compare these; in the third,
we recognize that the one contains or excludes
the other; and, in the fourth, we acquiesce in
this recognition."[1]

What Judgment involves.

Simple Comparison or Judgment is conversant with two notions,
the one of which is contained in the other. But
it often happens that one notion is contained in
another not immediately, but mediately, and we may be able to
recognize the relation of these to each other only through a third,
which, as it immediately contains the one, is immediately contained
in the other. Take the notions, A, B, C. — A
contains B; B contains C; — A, therefore, also
contains C. But as, *ex hypothesi,* we do not at once and directly
know C as contained in A, we cannot immediately compare them
together, and judge of their relation. We, therefore, perform a
double or complex process of comparison; we compare B with A,
and C with B, and then C with A, through B. We say B is a part
of A; C is a part of B; therefore, C is a part of A. This double
act of comparison has obtained the name of *Reasoning ;* the term
Judgment being left to express the simple act of comparison, or
rather its result.

Reasoning, — what.

Illustrated.

If this distinction between Judgment and Reasoning were merely
a verbal difference to discriminate the simpler and more complex
act of comparison, no objection could be raised to it on the score
of propriety, and its convenience would fully warrant its establishment. But this distinction has not always been meant to express
nothing more. It has, in fact, been generally supposed to mark out
two distinct faculties.

Reasoning is either from the whole to its parts; or from all the
parts, discretively, to the whole they constitute,
collectively. The former of these is Deductive;
the latter is Inductive Reasoning. The state-
ment you will find, in all logical books, of reasonings from certain
parts to the whole, or from certain parts to cer-
tain parts, is erroneous. I shall first speak of the
reasoning from the whole to its parts, — or of the
Deductive Inference.

*Reasoning, — Deduc-
tive and Inductive.*

1°, It is self-evident, that whatever is the part
of a part, is a part of the whole. This one axiom is the foundation of all reasoning from the
whole to the parts. There are, however, two kinds of whole and

*Deductive Reason-
ing, — its axiom. Two
phases of Deductive
Reasoning, determin-
ed by two kinds of
whole and parts.*

1 Crousaz, [*Logique.* t. iii. p. ii. c. i. pp. 181, 186. — ED.]

parts; and these constitute two varieties, or rather two phases, of deductive reasoning. This distinction, which is of the most important kind, has nevertheless been wholly overlooked by logicians, in consequence of which the utmost perplexity and confusion have been introduced into the science.

I have formerly stated that a proposition consists of two terms, — the one called subject, the other predicate; the subject being that of which some attribute is said, the predicate being the attribute so said. Now, in different relations, we may regard the subject as the whole, and the predicate as its part, or the predicate as the whole and the subject as its part.

Subject or predicate may be considered severally as whole and as part.

Let us take the proposition, — *milk is white*. Now, here we may either consider the predicate *white* as one of a number of attributes, the whole complement of which constitutes the subject *milk*. In this point of view, the predicate is a part of the subject. Or, again, we may consider the predicate *white* as the name of a class of objects, of which the subject is one. In this point of view, the subject is a part of the predicate.

Illustrated.

You will remember the distinction, which I formerly stated, of the twofold quantity of notions or terms. The Breadth or Extension of a notion or term corresponds to the greater number of subjects contained under a predicate; the Depth, Intension, or Comprehension of a notion or term, to the greater number of predicates contained in a subject. These quantities or wholes are always in the inverse ratio of each other. Now, it is singular, that logicians should have taken this distinction between notions, and yet not have thought of applying it to reasoning. But so it is, and this is not the only oversight they have committed in the application of the very primary principles of their science. The great distinction we have established between the subject and predicate considered severally, as, in different relations, whole and as part, constitutes the primary and principal division of Syllogisms, both Deductive and Inductive; and its introduction wipes off a complex mass of rules and qualifications, which the want of it rendered necessary. I can of course, at present, only explain in general the nature of this distinction; its details belong to the science of the Laws of Thought, or Logic, of which we are not here to treat.

Comprehension. Extension of notions, as applied to Reasoning.

I shall first consider the process of that Deductive Inference in which the subject is viewed as the whole, the predicate as the part.

In this reasoning, the whole is determined by the Comprehension, and is, again, either a Physical or Essential whole, or an Integral or Mathematical whole.[1] A Physical or Essential whole is that which consists of not really separable parts, of or pertaining to its substance. Thus, man is made up of two substantial parts, — a mind and a body; and each of these has again various qualities, which, though separable only by mental abstraction, are considered as so many parts of an essential whole. Thus the attributes of respiration, of digestion, of locomotion, of color, are so many parts of the whole notion we have of the human body; cognition, feeling, desire, virtue, vice, etc., so many parts of the whole notion we have of the human mind; and all these together, so many parts of the whole notion we have of man. A Mathematical, or Integral, or Quantitative whole, is that which has part out of part, and which, therefore, can be really partitioned. The Integral or, as it ought to be called, Integrate whole (*totum integratum*), is composed of integrant parts (*partes integrantes*), which are either homogeneous, or heterogeneous. An example of the former is given in the division of a square into two triangles; of the latter, of the animal body into head, trunk, extremities, etc.

marginal note: 1. Deductive Reasoning in the whole of Comprehension, — in which the subject is viewed as the whole, the predicate as the part. This whole either Physical or Mathematical.

These wholes (and there are others of less importance which I omit) are varieties of that whole which we may call a Comprehensive, or Metaphysical; it might be called a Natural whole.

This being understood, let us consider how we proceed when we reason from the relation between a comprehensive whole and its parts. Here, as I have said, the subject is the whole, the predicate its part; in other words, the predicate belongs to the subject. Now, here it is evident, that all the parts of the predicate must also be parts of the subject; in other terms, all that belongs to the predicate must also belong to the subject. In the words of the scholastic adage, — *Nota notæ est nota rei ipsius; Predicatum predicati est predicatum subjecti.* An example of this reasoning:

marginal note: Canon of Deductive reasoning in the whole of comprehension.

Europe contains England;

England contains Middlesex;

Therefore, Europe contains Middlesex.

---

1 See Eugenios, [Λογικὴ, c. iv. pp. 196, 203 (1746).—Ed.] [Cf. Burgersdyck, In- *stitut. Logicæ*, l. i. c. xiv. p. 52 *et seq.* edit. 1660.]

In other words, England is an integrant part of Europe; Middlesex is an integrant part of England; therefore, Middlesex is an integrant part of Europe. This is an example from a mathematical whole and parts. Again:

Socrates is just (that is, Socrates contains justice as a quality);

Justice is a virtue (that is, justice contains virtue as a constituent part);

Therefore, Socrates is virtuous.

In other words;—justice is an attribute or essential part of Socrates; virtue is an attribute or essential part of justice; therefore, virtue is an attribute or essential part of Socrates. This is an example from a physical or essential whole and parts.

What I have now said will be enough to show, in general, what I mean by a deductive reasoning, in which the subject is the whole, the predicate the part.

I proceed, in the second place, to the other kind of Deductive Reasoning,— that in which the subject is the part, the predicate is the whole. This reasoning proceeds under that species of whole which has been called the Logical or Potential or Universal. This whole is determined by the Extension of a notion; the genera having species, and the species individuals, as their parts. Thus *animal* is a universal whole, of which *bird* and *beast*, are immediate, *eagle* and *sparrow*, *dog* and *horse*, mediate, parts; while *man*, which, in relation to animal, is a part, is a whole in relation to Peter, Paul, Socrates, etc. The parts of a logical or universal whole, I should notice, are called the *subject parts*.

2. Deductive Reasoning in the whole of Extension,— in which the subject is viewed as the part, the predicate as the whole.

From what you now know of the nature of generalization, you are aware that general terms are terms expressive of attributes which may be predicated of many different objects; and inasmuch as these objects resemble each other in the common attribute, they are considered by us as constituting a class. Thus, when I say, that a horse is a quadruped; Bucephalus is a horse; therefore, Bucephalus is a quadruped;— I virtually say,— *horse* the subject is a part of the predicate *quadruped*, *Bucephalus* the subject is part of the predicate *horse;* therefore, *Bucephalus* the subject, is part of the predicate *quadruped*. In the reasoning under this whole, you will observe that the same word, as it is whole or part, changes from predicate to subject; *horse*, when viewed as a part of *quadruped*, being the subject of the proposition; whereas when viewed as a whole, containing *Bucephalus*, it becomes the predicate.

Such is a general view of the process of Deductive Reasoning,

under the two great varieties determined by the two different kinds
of whole and parts.　I now proceed to the coun-
Inductive Reasoning,　ter-process,—that of Inductive Reasoning.　The
—its axiom.　deductive is founded on the axiom, that what is
part of the part, is also part of the containing whole; the inductive
on the principle, that what is true of every constituent part belongs,
or does not belong, to the constituted whole.

Induction, like deduction, may be divided into two kinds, according as the whole and parts about which it is
Of two kinds, as it　conversant, are a Comprehensive or Physical or
proceeds in the whole　Natural, or an Extensive or Logical, whole.
of Comprehension or　Thus, in the former:
of Extension.

Gold is a metal, yellow, ductile, fusible in
aqua regia, of a certain specific gravity, and so on;

These qualities constitute this body (are all its parts);

Therefore, this body is gold.

In the latter;—Ox, horse, dog, etc., are animals,—that is, are
contained under the class animal;

Ox, horse, dog, etc., constitute (are all the constituents of) the
class quadruped;

Therefore, quadruped is contained under animal.

Both in the deductive and inductive processes the inference must
be of an absolute necessity, in so far as the men-
Deductive and In-　tal illation is concerned; that is, every conse-
ductive illation must　quent proposition must be evolved out of every
be of an absolute ne-　antecedent proposition with intuitive evidence.
cessity.

I do not mean by this, that the antecedent
should be necessarily true, or that the consequent be really contained
in it; it is sufficient that the antecedent be assumed as true, and that
the consequent be, in conformity to the laws of thought, evolved
out of it as its part or its equation.　This last is called Logical or
Formal or Subjective truth; and an inference may be subjectively
or formally true, which is objectively or really false.

The account given of induction in all works
Account of Induc-　of Logic is utterly erroneous.　Sometimes we
tion by Logicians, er-　find this inference described as a precarious, not
roneous.　　a necessary reasoning.　It is called an illation
from some to all.　But here *the some*, as it neither contains nor
constitutes *the all*, determines no necessary movement, and a conclusion drawn under these circumstances is logically vicious.　Others
again describe the inductive process thus:

What belongs to some objects of a class belongs to the whole
class;

This property belongs to some objects of the class;

Therefore, it belongs to the whole class.

This account of induction, which is the one you will find in all the English works on Logic, is not an inductive reasoning at all. It is, logically considered, a deductive syllogism; and, logically considered, a syllogism radically vicious. It is logically vicious to say, that, because some individuals of a class have certain common qualities apart from that property which constitutes the class itself, therefore the whole individuals of the class should partake in these qualities. For this there is no logical reason,—no necessity of thought. The probability of this inference, and it is only probable, is founded on the observation of the analogy of nature, and, therefore, not upon the laws of thought, by which alone reasoning, considered as a logical process, is exclusively governed. To become a formally legitimate induction, the objective probability must be clothed with a subjective necessity, and *the some* must be translated into *the all* which it is supposed to represent.

In the deductive syllogism we proceed by analysis,—that is, by decomposing a whole into its parts; but as the two wholes with which reasoning is conversant are in the inverse ratio of each other, so our analysis in the one will correspond to our synthesis in the other. For example, when I divide a whole of extension into its parts,—when I divide a genus into the species, a species into the individuals, it contains,—I do so by adding new differences, and thus go on accumulating in the parts a complement of qualities which did not belong to the wholes. This, therefore, which, in point of extension, is an analysis, is, in point of comprehension, a synthesis. In like manner, when I decompose a whole of comprehension, that is, decompose a complex predicate into its constituent attributes, I obtain by this process a simpler and more general quality, and thus this, which, in relation to a comprehensive whole, is an analysis, is, in relation to an extensive whole, a synthesis.

In Extension and Comprehension, the analysis of the one corresponds to the synthesis of the other.

As the deductive inference is Analytic, the inductive is Synthetic. But as induction, equally as deduction, is conversant with both wholes, so the Synthesis of induction on the comprehensive whole is a reversed process to its synthesis on the extensive whole.

Confusion among philosophers from not having observed this.

From what I have now stated, you will, therefore, be aware, that the terms *analysis* and *synthesis*, when used without qualification, may be employed, at cross purposes, to denote operations precisely the converse of each other. And so it has happened.

Analysis, in the mouth of one set of philosophers, means precisely what synthesis-denotes in the mouth of another; nay, what is even still more frequent, these words are perpetually converted with each other by the same philosopher. I may notice, what has rarely, if ever, been remarked, that *synthesis* in the writings of the Greek logicians is equivalent to the *analysis* of modern philosophers: the former, regarding the extensive whole as the principal, applied analysis, κατ' ἐξοχὴν, to its division;[1] the latter, viewing the comprehensive whole as the principal, in general limit analysis to its decomposition. This, however, has been overlooked, and a confusion the most inextricable prevails in regard to the use of these words, if the thread to the labyrinth is not obtained.

---

1 Thus the Platonic method of Division is called Analytical. See Laertius, ii. 24. Compare *Discussions*, p. 178. — Ed. [Cf. Zabarella, *In Post Analyt.* l. ii. c. xii. t. 70, *Opera Logica,* p. 1190, and t. 81, p. 1212.]

LECTURE XXXVIII.

THE REGULATIVE FACULTY.

I NOW enter upon the last of the Cognitive Faculties, — the faculty which I denominated the Regulative.

The Regulative Faculty. Peculiarity of sense in which the term Faculty is here employed. Here the term *faculty*, you will observe, is employed in a somewhat peculiar signification, for it is employed not to denote the proximate cause of any definite energy, but the power the mind has of being the native source of certain necessary or *a priori* cognitions; which cognitions, as they are the conditions, the forms, under which our knowledge in general is possible, constitute so many fundamental laws of intellectual nature. It is in this sense that I call the power which the mind possesses of modifying the knowledge it receives, in conformity to its proper nature, its Regulative Faculty. The Regulative Faculty is, however, in fact, nothing more than the complement of such laws, — it is the *locus principiorum.* It thus corresponds to what was known in the Greek philosophy under the name of *νοῦς*, when that term was rigorously used. To *Designations of the Regulative Faculty. — Νοῦς, Reason. Common Sense, — its various meanings.* this faculty has been latterly applied the name *Reason;* but this term is so vague and ambiguous, that it is almost unfitted to convey any definite meaning. The term *Common Sense* has likewise been applied to designate the place of principles. This word is also ambiguous. In the first place, it was the expression used in the Aristotelic philosophy to denote the Central or Common Sensory, in which the different external senses met and were united.[1] In the second place, it was employed to signify a sound understanding applied to vulgar objects, in contrast to a scientific or speculative intelligence, and it is in this signification that it has been taken by those who have derided the principle on which the philosophy, which has been distinctively denominated the Scottish,

---

[1] See *De Anima*, iii. 2, 7. Cf. *in loc. cit.* Conimbricenses, pp. 373, 407. — ED.

professes to be established. This is not, however, the meaning
which has always or even principally been attached to it; and an
incomparably stronger case might be made out in defence of this
expression than has been done by Reid, or even

Authorities for the
use of the term Com-
mon Sense as equiva-
lent to Noûs.

by Mr. Stewart. It is in fact a term of high
antiquity, and very general acceptation. We
find it in Cicero,[1] in several passages not hitherto observed. It is found in the meaning in
question in Phædrus,[2] and not in the signification of community of
sentiment, which it expresses in Horace[3] and Juvenal.[4] "Natura,"
says Tertullian,[5] speaking of the universal consent of mankind to
the immortality of the soul, — "Natura pleraque suggeruntur quasi
de *publico sensu*, quo animam Deus dotare dignatus est." And
in the same meaning the term *Sensus Communis* is employed by
St. Augustin.[6] In modern times it is to be found in the philosophical writings of every country of Europe. In Latin it is used by
the German Melanchthon,[7] Victorinus,[8] Keckermannus,[9] Christian
Thomasius,[10] Leibnitz,[11] Wolf,[12] and the Dutch De Raei,[13] — by the
Gallo-Portuguese Antonius Goveanus,[14] the Spanish Nunnesius,[15]
the Italian Genovesi,[16] and Vico,[17] and by the Scottish Abercromby;[18] in French by Balzac,[19] Chanet,[20] Pascal,[21] Malebranche,[22]
Bouhours, Barbeyrac;[23] in English by Sir Thomas Browne,[24] To-
land,[25] Charleton.[26] These are only a few of the testimonies I could
adduce in support of the term Common Sense for the faculty in
question; in fact, so far as use and wont may be allowed to weigh,
there is perhaps no philosophical expression in support of which
a more numerous array of authorities may be alleged. The expres-

2 L. i. f. 7. — ED.

3 *Sat.* i. 3, 66. But see *Reid's Works*, p. 774.
— ED.

4 *Sat.* viii. 73. — ED.

5 See *Reid's Works*, p. 776. — ED.

6 *Ibid.*, p. 776. — ED.

7 *Ibid.*, p. 778. — ED.

8 [Victorini Strigelii, *Hypomnemata in Dialect. Melanchthonis*, pp. 798, 1040, ed. 1566.]

9 See *Reid's Works*, p. 780. — ED.

10 *Ibid.*, p. 785. — ED.

11 See *Reid's Works*, p. 785. — ED.

12 *Ibid.*, p. 790. — ED.

13 See *Clavis Philosophiæ Naturalis Aristotelico-
Cartesiana*, Dissert. i. *De Cognitione Vulgari et
Philosophica*, p. 7. "Communis facultas om-
nium hominum." Dissert. ii. *De Præcogni-
tis in Genere*, §§ iv. v. pp. 34, 35. "Communes
Notiones;" § x. p. 41. "Communis Sensus."
— ED.

14 See *Reid's Works*, p. 779.

15 *Ibid.* — ED.

16 *Ibid.*, p 790. — ED.

17 *Ibid.* — ED.

18 *Ibid.*, p. 785. — ED.

19 *Ibid.*, p. 782. — ED.

20 *Ibid.* — ED.

21 *Ibid.*, p. 783. — ED.

22 *Ibid.*, p 784. — ED.

23 *Des Droits de la Puissance Souveraine, Recueil de Discours*, t. i. pp. 36, 37. A translation
from the Latin of Noodt, in which *mens sana*
and *sensus communis* are both rendered by *le
sens commun*. — ED.

24 See *Reid's Works*, p. 782. — ED.

25 *Ibid.*, p. 745. — ED.

26 Charleton uses the term in its Aristotelian signification, as denoting the central or
common sensory and its function. See his
*Immortality of the Human Soul demonstrated by
the Light of Nature* (1657), pp. 92, 98, 158. — ED.

sion, however, is certainly exceptionable, and it can only claim toleration in the absence of a better.

I may notice that Pascal and Hemsterhuis[1] have applied *Intuition* and *Sentiment* in this sense; and Jacobi[2] originally employed *Glaube* (*Belief* or *Faith*), in the same way, though he latterly superseded this expression by that of *Vernunft* (*Reason*).

Were it allowed in metaphysical philosophy, as in physical, to discriminate scientific differences by scientific terms, I would employ the word *noetic*, as derived from νοῦς, to express all those cognitions that originate in the mind itself, *dianoetic* to denote the operations of the Discursive, Elaborative, or Comparative Faculty. So much for the nomenclature of the faculty itself.

Noetic and Dianoetic,—how to be employed.

Nomenclature of the cognitions due to the Regulative Faculty.

On the other hand, the cognitions themselves, of which it is the source, have obtained various appellations. They have been denominated κοιναὶ προλήψεις, κοιναὶ ἔννοιαι, φυσικαὶ ἔννοιαι, πρῶται ἔννοιαι, πρῶτα νοήματα; *naturæ judicia, judicia communibus hominum sensibus infixa, notiones* or *notitiæ connatæ* or *innatæ, semina scientiæ, semina omnium cognitionum, semina æternitatis, zopyra* (*living sparks*), *præcognita necessaria, anticipationes; first principles, common anticipations, principles of common sense, self-evident* or *intuitive truths, primitive notions, native notions, innate cognitions, natural knowledges* (*cognitions*), *fundamental reasons, metaphysical* or *transcendental truths, ultimate* or *elemental laws of thought, primary* or *fundamental laws of human belief*, or *primary laws of human reason, pure* or *transcendental* or *a priori cognitions, categories of thought, natural beliefs, rational instincts*, etc., etc.[3]

The history of opinions touching the acceptation, or rejection, of such native notions, is, in a manner, the history of philosophy: for as the one alternative, or the other, is adopted in this question, the character of a system is determined. At present I content myself with stating that, though from the earliest period of philosophy, the doctrine was always common, if not always predominant, that our knowledge originated, in part at least, in the mind, yet it was only at a very recent date that the criterion was explicitly enounced, by which the native may be discriminated from the adventitious elements of knowledge. Without touching on some ambiguous expressions in more ancient philoso-

Importance of the distinction of native and adventitious knowledge.

---

1 See *Reid's Works*, p. 792.—Ed.
2 *Ibid.*, p. 793.—Ed.
3 See *Reid's Works*, note A, § v. p. 755 *et seq.* —Ed.

phers, it is sufficient to say that the character of universality and necessity, as the quality by which the two classes of knowledge are distinguished, was first explicitly proclaimed by Leibnitz. It is true, indeed, that, previously to him, Descartes all but enounced it. In the notes of Descartes on the *Programma* of 1647 (which you will find under Letter XCIX. of the First Part of his *Epistolæ*), in arguing against the author who would derive all our knowledge from observation or tradition, he has the following sentence: "I wish that our author would inform me what is that corporeal motion which is able to form in our intellect any common notion, — for example, things that are equal to the same thing are equal to each other, or any other of the same kind; for all those motions are particular, but these notions are universal, having no affinity with motions, and holding no relation to them." Now, had he only added the term *necessary* to universal, he would have completely anticipated Leibnitz. I have already frequently had occasion incidentally to notice, that we should carefully distinguish between those notions or cognitions which are primitive facts, and those notions or cognitions which are generalized or derivative facts. The former are given us; they are not, indeed, obtrusive, — they are not even cognizable of themselves. They lie hid in the profundities of the mind, until drawn from their obscurity by the mental activity itself employed upon the materials of experience. Hence it is, that our knowledge has its commencement in sense, external or internal, but its origin in intellect. "Cognitio omnis a sensibus exordium, a mente originem habet primum."[1] The latter, the derivative cognitions, are of our own fabrication; we form them after certain rules; they are the tardy result of Perception and Memory, of Attention, Reflection, Abstraction. The primitive cognitions, on the contrary, seem to leap ready armed from the womb of reason, like Pallas from the head of Jupiter; sometimes the mind places them at the commencement of its operations, in order to have a point of support and a fixed basis, without which the operations would be impossible; sometimes they form, in a certain sort, the crowning, — the consummation, of all the intellectual operations. The derivative or generalized notions are an artifice of intellect, — an ingenious mean of giving order and compactness to the materials of our knowledge. The primitive and general notions are the root of all principles, — the foundation of the whole edifice of human science. But how different soever be the two classes of our cognitions, and however

Criterion of necessity first enounced by Leibnitz.

Partially anticipated by Descartes.

1 See above, lect. xxi. p. 285. — ED.

distinctly separated they may be by the circumstance, — that we cannot but think the one, and can easily annihilate the other in thought, — this discriminative quality was not explicitly signalized till done by Leibnitz. The older philosophers are at best undeveloped. Descartes made the first step towards a more perspicuous and definite discrimination. He frequently enounces that our primitive notions (besides being clear and distinct) are universal. But this universality is only a derived circumstance ; — a notion is universal (meaning thereby that a notion is common to all mankind), because it is necessary to the thinking mind, — because the

And by Spinoza.   mind cannot but think it. Spinoza, in one passage of his treatise *De Emendatione Intellectus,*[1] says: "The ideas which we form clear and distinct, appear so to follow from the sole necessity of our nature, that they seem absolutely to depend from our sole power [of thought]; the confused ideas on the contrary," etc. This is anything but explicit; and, as I said, Leibnitz is the first by whom the criterion of necessity, — of the impossibility not to think so and so, — was established as a discriminative type of our native notions, in contrast to those which we educe from experience, and build up through generalization.

The enouncement of this criterion was, in fact, a great discovery in the science of mind; and the fact that a truth

The enouncement of this criterion, a great step in the science of mind.

so manifest, when once proclaimed, could have lain so long unnoticed by philosophers, may warrant us in hoping that other discoveries of equal importance may still be awaiting the advent of another Leibnitz. Leibnitz has, in several parts of his works, laid down the distinction in question; and, what is curious, almost always in relation to Locke. In the fifth volume of his works by Dutens,[2] in an Epistle to Bierling of 1710, he says, (I translate from the Latin) : — "In Locke there are some particu-

Leibnitz quoted.

lars not ill expounded, but upon the whole he has wandered far from the gate,[3] nor has he understood the nature of the intellect (natura mentis). Had he sufficiently considered the difference between necessary truths or those apprehended by demonstration, and those which become known to us by induction alone, — he would have seen that those which are necessary, could only be approved to us by principles native to the mind (menti insitis) ; seeing that the senses indeed inform us what may take place, but not what necessarily takes place. Locke has not observed, that the notions of being, of sub-

---

[1] *Opera Posthuma,* p. 391.
[2] P. 858.

[3] This refers to Aristotle's *Metaphysics* [A minor, c. i. — Ed.]

stance, of one and the same, of the true, of the good, and many others, are innate to our mind, because our mind is innate to itself, and finds all these in its own furniture. It is true, indeed, that there is nothing in the intellect which was not previously in the sense, — except the intellect itself." He makes a similar observation in reference to Locke, in Letter XI., to his friend Mr. Burnet of Kemnay.[1] And in his *Nouveaux Essais* (a detailed refutation of Locke's Essay, and not contained in the collected edition of his works by Dutens), he repeatedly enforces the same doctrine. In one

Leibnitz further quoted. place he says,[2] — "Hence there arises another question, viz. :   Are all truths dependent on experience, that is to say, on induction and examples? Or are there some which have another foundation? For if some events can be foreseen before all trial has been made, it is manifest that we contribute something on our part. The senses, although necessary for all our actual cognitions, are not, however, competent to afford us all that cognitions involve; for the senses never give us more than examples, that is to say, particular or individual truths. Now all the examples, which confirm a general truth, how numerous soever they may be, are insufficient to establish the universal necessity of this same truth; for it does not follow, that what has happened will happen always in like manner. For example: the Greeks and Romans and other nations have always observed that during the course of twenty-four hours, day is changed into night, and night into day. But we should be wrong, were we to believe that the same rule holds everywhere, as the contrary has been observed during a residence in Nova Zembla. And he again would deceive himself, who should believe that, in our latitudes at least, this was a truth necessary and eternal; for we ought to consider, that the earth and the sun themselves have no necessary existence, and that there will perhaps a time arrive when this fair star will, with its whole system, have no longer a place in creation, — at least under its present form. Hence it appears, that the necessary truths, such as we find them in Pure Mathematics, and particularly in Arithmetic and Geometry, behoove to have principles the proof of which does not depend upon examples, and, consequently, not on the evidence of sense; howbeit, that without the senses, we should never have found occasion to call them into consciousness. This is what it is necessary to distinguish accurately, and it is what Euclid has so well understood, in demonstrating by reason what is sufficiently apparent by experience and sensible

1 *Opera*, vol. vi. p. 274 (edit. Dutens).   2 *Avant-propos*, p. 5 (edit. Raspe).

images. Logic, likewise, with Metaphysics and Morals, the one of which constitutes Natural Theology, the other Natural Jurisprudence, are full of such truths; and, consequently, their proof can only be derived from internal principles, which we call innate. It is true, that we ought not to imagine that we can read in the soul, these eternal laws of reason, *ad aperturam libri*, as we can read the edict of the Prætor without trouble or research; but it is enough, that we can discover them in ourselves by dint of attention, when the occasions are presented to us by the senses. The success of the observation serves to confirm reason, in the same way as proofs serve in Arithmetic to obviate erroneous calculations, when the computation is long. It is hereby, also, that the cognitions of men differ from those of beasts. The beasts are purely empirical, and only regulate themselves by examples; for as far as we can judge, they never attain to the formation of necessary judgments, whereas, men are capable of demonstrative sciences, and herein the faculty which brutes possess of drawing inferences is inferior to the reason which is in men." And, after some other observations, he proceeds: "Perhaps our able author" (he refers to Locke) "will not be wholly alien from my opinion. For after having employed the whole of his first book to refute innate cognitions, taken in a certain sense, he, however, avows at the commencement of the second and afterwards, that ideas which have not their origin in Sensation, come from Reflection. Now reflection is nothing else than an attention to what is in use, and the senses do not inform us of what we already carry with us. This being the case, can it be denied that there is much that is innate in our mind, seeing that we are as it were innate to ourselves, and that there are in us existence, unity, substance, duration, change, action, perception, pleasure, and a thousand other objects of our intellectual notions? These same objects being immediate, and always present to our understanding (although they are not always perceived by reason of our distractions and our wants), why should it be a matter of wonder, if we say that these ideas are innate in us, with all that is dependent on them? In illustration of this, let me make use likewise of the simile of a block of marble which has veins, rather than of a block of marble wholly uniform, or of blank tablets, that is to say, what is called a *tabula rasa* by philosophers; for if the mind resembled these blank tablets, truths would be in us, as the figure of Hercules is in a piece of marble, when the marble is altogether indifferent to the reception of this figure or of any other. But if we suppose that there are veins in the stone, which would mark out the figure of Hercules by preference to other figures, this stone would be more determined thereunto, and Hercules would exist there, innately in a certain sort; although it would require labor to discover the veins, and to clear them by polishing and the removal of all that prevents their manifestation. It is thus that ideas and truths are innate in us; like our inclinations, dispositions, natural habitudes or virtualities, and not as actions; although these virtualities be always accompanied by some corresponding actions, frequently however unperceived.

"It seems that our able author [Locke] maintains, that there is nothing virtual in us, and even nothing of which we are [not] always actually conscious. But this cannot be strictly intended, for in that case his opinion would be paradoxical, since even our acquired habits and the stores of our memory are not always in actual consciousness, nay, do not always come to our aid when wanted; while again, we often call them to mind on any trifling occasion which suggests them to our remembrance, like as it only requires us to be given the commencement of a song to help us to the recollection of the rest. He, therefore, limits his thesis in other places, saying that there is at least nothing in us which we have not, at some time or other, acquired by experience and perception." And in another remarkable passage,[1] Leibnitz says, "The mind is not only capable of knowing pure and necessary truths, but likewise of discovering them in itself; and if it possessed only the simple capacity of receiving cognitions, or the passive power of knowledge, as indetermined as that of the wax to receive figures, or a blank tablet to receive letters, it would not be the source of necessary truths, as I am about to demonstrate that it is: for it is incontestable, that the senses could not suffice to make their necessity apparent, and that the intellect has, therefore, a disposition, as well active as passive, to draw them from its own bosom, although the senses be requisite to furnish the occasion, and the attention to determine it upon some in preference to others. You see, therefore, these very able philosophers, who are of a different opinion, have not sufficiently reflected on the consequence of the difference that subsists between necessary or eternal truths and the truths of experience, as I have already observed, and as all our contestation shows. The original proof of necessary truths comes from the intellect alone, while other truths are derived from experience or the observations of sense. Our mind is competent to both kinds of knowledge, but it is itself the source of the former; and how great soever may be the number of particular experiences in support of a universal truth, we should never be able to assure ourselves forever of its universality by induc-

1 *Nouveaux Essais*, p. 36 (edit. Raspe). [L. i. § 5. — ED.]

tion, unless we knew its necessity by reason. . . . . . The senses may register, justify, and confirm these truths, but not demonstrate their infallibility and eternal certainty."

And in speaking of the faculty of such truths, he says: "It is not a naked faculty, which consists in the mere possibility of understanding them; it is a disposition, an aptitude, a preformation, which determines our mind to elicit, and which causes that they can be elicited; precisely as there is a difference between the figures which are bestowed indifferently on stone or marble, and those which veins mark out or are disposed to mark out, if the sculptor avail himself of the indications."[1]　I have quoted these passages from Leibnitz, not only for their own great importance, as the first full and explicit enouncement, and certainly not the least able illustrations, of one of the most momentous principles in philosophy; but, likewise, because the *Nouveaux Essais*, from which they are principally extracted, though of all others the most important psychological work of Leibnitz, was wholly unknown, not only to the other philosophers of this country, but even to Mr. Stewart, prior to the last years of his life.[2]

We have thus seen that Leibnitz was the first philosopher who explicitly established the quality of necessity as the criterion of distinction between empirical and *a priori* cognitions. I may, however, remark, what is creditable to Dr. Reid's sagacity, that he founded the same discrimination on the same difference: and I am disposed to think, that he did this without being aware of his coincidence with Leibnitz; for he does not seem to have studied the system of that philosopher in his own works; and it was not till Kant had shown the importance of the criterion, by its application in his hands, that the attention of the learned was called to the scattered notices of it in the writings of Leibnitz. In speaking of the principle of causality, Dr. Reid says: "We are next to consider whether we may not learn this truth from experience, — That effects which have all the marks and tokens of design, must proceed from a designing cause."

Reid discriminated native from adventitious knowledge by the same difference, independently of Leibnitz.

Reid quoted.　"I apprehend that we cannot learn this truth from experience, for two reasons.

"*First*, Because it is a necessary truth, not a contingent one. It

---

[1] *Nouv. Essais*, l. i. § 11. See above, lect. xxix. p. 404. — ED.

[2] The reason of this was, that it was not published till long after the death of its author, and it is not included in the collected edition of the works of Leibnitz by Dutens. In consequence of its republication in *Leibnitzii Opera Philosophica*, by Erdmann, it is now easily procured.

agrees with the experience of mankind since the beginning of the world, that the area of a triangle is equal to half the rectangle under its base and perpendicular. It agrees no less with experience, that the sun rises in the east and sets in the west. So far as experience goes, these truths are upon an equal footing. But every man perceives this distinction between them, — that the first is a necessary truth, and that it is impossible that it should not be true; but the last is not necessary, but contingent, depending upon the will of Him who made the world. As we cannot learn from experience that twice three must necessarily make six, so neither can we learn from experience that certain effects must proceed from a designing and intelligent cause. Experience informs us only of what has been, but never of what must be."[1]

And in speaking of our belief in the principle that an effect manifesting design must have had an intelligent cause, he says, — "It has been thought, that, although this principle does not admit of proof from abstract reasoning, it may be proved from experience, and may be justly drawn by induction, from instances that fall within our observation.

"I conceive this method of proof will leave us in great uncertainty, for these three reasons:

1st, Because the proposition to be proved is not a contingent but a *necessary* proposition. It is not that things which begin to exist commonly have a cause, or even that they always in fact have a cause; but that they must have a cause, and cannot begin to exist without a cause.

"Propositions of this kind, from their nature, are incapable of proof by induction. Experience informs us only of what *is* or *has been*, not of what *must be;* and the conclusion must be of the same nature with the premises.

"For this reason, no mathematical proposition can be proved by induction. Though it should be found by experience in a thousand cases, that the area of a plain triangle is equal to the rectangle under the altitude and half the base, this would not prove that it must be so in all cases, and cannot be otherwise; which is what the mathematician affirms.

"In like manner, though we had the most ample experimental proof, that things which had begun to exist had a cause, this would not prove that they must have a cause. Experience may show us what is the established course of nature, but can never show what connections of things are in their nature necessary.

---

1 *Int. Powers*, Essay vi. chap. vi.   *Coll. Works*, p. 459.

2dly, General maxims, grounded on experience, have only a degree of probability proportioned to the extent of our experience, and ought always to be understood so as to leave room for exceptions, if future experience shall discover any such.

"The law of gravitation has as full a proof from experience and induction as any principle can be supposed to have. Yet, if any philosopher should, by clear experiment, show that there is a kind of matter in some bodies which does not gravitate, the law of gravitation ought to be limited by that exception.

"Now, it is evident that men have never considered the principle of the necessity of causes, as a truth of this kind which may admit of limitation or exception; and therefore it has not been received upon this kind of evidence.

"*3dly*, I do not see that experience could satisfy us that every change in nature actually has a cause.

"In the far greatest part of the changes in nature that fall within our observation, the causes are unknown; and, therefore, from experience, we cannot know whether they have causes or not.

"Causation is not an object of sense. The only experience we can have of it, is in the consciousness we have of exerting some power in ordering our thoughts and actions. But this experience is surely too narrow a foundation for a general conclusion, that all things that have had or shall have a beginning, must have a cause.

"For these reasons, this principle cannot be drawn from experience, any more than from abstract reasoning."[1]

It ought, however to be noticed that Mr. Hume's acuteness had arrived at the same conclusion. "As to past experience," he observes, "it can be allowed to give direct and certain information of those precise objects only, and that precise period of time, which fell under its cognizance; but why this experience should be extended to future times and to other objects, — this is the main question on which I would insist."[2]

Hume arrived at the same conclusion.

The philosopher, however, who has best known how to turn the criterion to account, is Kant; and the general success with which he has applied it, must be admitted even by those who demur to many of the particular conclusions which his philosophy would establish.

1 *Intellectual Powers*, Essay vi. chap. vi. *Coll. Works*, pp. 455, 456. Reid has several other passages to the same effect in the same chapter of this Essay.

2 *Inquiry concerning the Human Understanding*, § iv. *Philosophical Works*, vol. iv. p. 42. — ED.

But though it be now generally acknowledged, by the profoundest thinkers, that it is impossible to analyze all our knowledge into the produce of experience, external or internal, and that a certain complement of cognitions must be allowed as having their origin in the nature of the thinking principle itself; they are not at one in regard to those which ought to be recognized as ultimate and elemental, and those which ought to be regarded as modifications or combinations of these. Reid and Stewart, (the former in particular), have been considered as too easy in their admission of primary laws; and it must be allowed that the censure, in some instances, is not altogether unmerited. But it ought to be recollected, that those who thus agree in reprehension are not in unison in regard to the grounds of censure; and they wholly forget that our Scottish philosophers made no pretension to a final analysis of the primary laws of human reason, — that they thought it enough to classify a certain number of cognitions as native to the mind, leaving it to their successors to resolve these into simpler elements. "The most general phænomena," says Dr. Reid,[1] "we can reach, are what we call Laws of Nature. So that the laws of nature are nothing else but the most general facts relating to the operations of nature, which include a great many particular facts under them. And if, in any case, we should give the name of a law of nature to a general phænomenon, which human industry shall afterwards trace to one more general, there is no great harm done. The most general assumes the name of a law of nature when it is discovered; and the less general is contained and comprehended in it." In another part of his work, he has introduced the same remark. "The labyrinth may be too intricate, and the thread too fine, to be traced through all its windings; but, if we stop where we can trace it no farther, and secure the ground we have gained, there is no harm done; a quicker eye may in time trace it farther."[2] The same view has been likewise well stated by Mr. Stewart.[3] "In all the other sciences, the progress of discovery has been gradual, from the less general to the more general laws of nature; and it would be singular indeed, if, in this science, which but a few

Philosophers divided in regard to what cognitions ought to be classed as ultimate; and what as modifications of the ultimate.

Reid and Stewart have been censured for their too easy admission of first principles.

Reid quoted in self-vindication.

Stewart quoted to the same effect.

---

1 *Inquiry*, chap. vi. § 13, *Works*, p. 163. — Ed.
2 *Inquiry into the Human Mind*, c. i. § 2. *Works*, p. 99. — Ed.

3 *Philosophical Essays*, Prel. Diss. o. i. *Works.* vol. v. p. 13. Cf. *Elements*, vol. i. o. v. p. 2, § 4. *Works*, vol. ii. pp. 342, 343. — Ed.

years ago was confessedly in its infancy, and which certainly labors under many disadvantages peculiar to itself, a step should all at once be made to a single principle, comprehending all the particular phænomena which we know. As the order established in the intellectual world seems to be regulated by laws analogous to those which we trace among the phænomena of the material system; and as in all our philosophical inquiries (to whatever subject they may relate) the progress of the mind is liable to be affected by the same tendency to a premature generalization, the following extract from an eminent chemical writer may contribute to illustrate the scope and to confirm the justness of some of the foregoing reflections. 'Within the last fifteen or twenty years, several new metals and new earths have been made known to the world. The names that support these discoveries are respectable, and the experiments decisive. If we do not give our assent to them, no single proposition in chemistry can for a moment stand. But whether all these are really simple substances, or compounds not yet resolved into their elements, is what the authors themselves cannot possibly assert; nor would it, in the least, diminish the merit of their observations, if future experiments should prove them to have been mistaken, as to the simplicity of these substances. This remark should not be confined to later discoveries; it may as justly be applied to those earths and metals with which we have been long acquainted.' 'In the dark ages of chemistry, the object was to rival nature; and the substance which the adepts of those days were busied to create, was universally allowed to be simple. In a more enlightened period, we have extended our inquiries and multiplied the number of the elements. The last task will be to simplify; and by a closer observation of nature, to learn from what a small store of primitive materials, all that we behold and wonder at was created.'"

That the list of the primary elements of human reason, which our two philosophers have given, has no pretence to order; and that the principles which its contains are not systematically deduced by any ambitious process of metaphysical ingenuity, is no valid ground of disparagement. In fact, which of the vaunted classifications of these primitive truths can stand the test of criticism? The most celebrated, and by far the most ingenious, of these,—the scheme of Kant,—though the truth of its details may be admitted, is no longer regarded as affording either a necessary deduction or a natural arrangement of our native cognitions; and the reduction of these to system still remains a problem to be resolved.

That Reid and Stewart offer no systematic deduction of the primary elements of human reason, is no valid ground for disparaging their labors.

In point of fact, philosophers have not yet purified the antecedent conditions of the problem,—have not yet established the principles on which its solution ought to be undertaken. And here I would solicit your attention to a circumstance, which shows how far philosophers are still removed from the prospect of an ultimate decision. It is agreed, that the quality of necessity is that which discriminates a native from an adventitious element of knowledge. When we find, therefore, a cognition which contains this discriminative quality, we are entitled to lay it down as one which could not have been obtained as a generalization from experience. This I admit. But when philosophers lay it down not only as native to the mind, but as a positive and immediate datum of an intellectual power, I demur.

Philosophers have not yet established the principle on which our ultimate cognitions are to be classified, and reduced to system.

It is evident that the quality of necessity in a cognition may depend on two different and opposite principles, inasmuch as it may either be the result of a power, or of a powerlessness, of the thinking principle. In the one case, it will be a Positive, in the other a Negative, necessity. Let us take examples of these opposite cases. In an act of perceptive consciousness, I think, and cannot but think, that I and that something different from me exist,—in other words, that my perception, as a modification of the ego, exists, and that the object of my perception, as a modification of the non-ego, exists. In these circumstances, I pronounce Existence to be a native cognition, because I find that I cannot think except under the condition of thinking all that I am conscious of to exist. Existence is thus a form, a category of thought. But here, though I cannot but think existence, I am conscious of this thought as an act of power,—an act of intellectual force. It is the result of strength, and not of weakness.

Necessity,—either Positive, or Negative, as it results from a power, or from a powerlessness of mind.

The first order of Necessity,—the Positive,—illustrated, by the act of Perception.

In like manner, when I think $2 \times 2 = 4$, the thought, though inevitable, is not felt as an imbecility; we know it as true, and, in the perception of the truth, though the act be necessary, the mind is conscious that the necessity does not arise from impotence. On the contrary, we attribute the same necessity to God. Here, therefore, there is a class of natural cognitions, which we may properly view as so many positive exertions of the mental vigor, and the cognitions of this class we consider as Positive. To this class will belong the notion of Existence and its modifications, the principles of Identity,

By an arithmetical example.

and Contradiction, and Excluded Middle, the intuitions of Space and Time, etc.

But besides these, there are other necessary forms of thought, which, by all philosophers, have been regarded as standing precisely on the same footing, which to me seem to be of a totally different kind. In place of being the result of a power, the necessity which belongs to them is merely a consequence of the impotence of our faculties. But if this be the case, nothing could be more unphilosophical than to arrogate to these negative inabilities, the dignity of positive energies. Every rule of philosophizing would be violated. The law of Parcimony prescribes, that principles are not to be multiplied without necessity, and that an hypothetical force be not postulated to explain a phænomenon which can be better accounted for by an admitted impotence. The phænomenon of a heavy body rising from the earth, may warrant us in the assumption of a special power; but it would surely be absurd to devise a special power (that is, a power besides gravitation) to explain the phænomenon of its descent.

The second order of necessity, — the Negative. This not recognized by philosophers.

Illustrated.

Now, that the imbecility of the human mind constitutes a great negative principle, to which sundry of the most important phænomena of intelligence may be referred, appears to me incontestable; and though the discussion is one somewhat abstract, I shall endeavor to give you an insight into the nature and application of this principle.

I begin by the statement of certain principles, to which it is necessary in the sequel to refer.

Principles referred to in the discussion.

The highest of all logical laws, in other words the supreme law of thought, is what is called the principle of Contradiction, or more correctly the principle of Non-Contradiction.[1] It is this: A thing cannot be and not be at the same time, — *Alpha est, Alpha non est,* are propositions which cannot both be true at once. A second fundamental law of thought, or rather the principle of Contradiction viewed in a certain aspect, is called the principle of Excluded Middle, or, more fully, the principle of Excluded Middle between two Contradictories. A thing either is or it is not, — *Aut est Alpha aut non est;* there is no medium; one must be true, both cannot. These principles require, indeed admit of, no proof. They prove everything, but are proved by nothing. When

1. The Law of Non-Contradiction.

2. The Law of excluded Middle.

1 See Appendix, II. — ED.

I, therefore, have occasion to speak of these laws by name, you will know to what principle I refer.

Now, then, I lay it down as a law which, though not generalized

Grand law of thought,—That the conceivable lies between two contradictory extremes.

by philosophers, can be easily proved to be true by its application to the phænomena: That all that is conceivable in thought, lies between two extremes, which, as contradictory of each other, cannot both be true, but of which, as mutual contradictories, one must. For example, we conceive space,—we cannot but conceive space. I admit, therefore, that Space, indefinitely, is a positive and necessary form of thought.

Established and illustrated, by reference to Space,—1°, as a Maximum.

But when philosophers convert the fact, that we cannot but think space, or, to express it differently, that we are unable to imagine anything out of space,—when philosophers, I say, convert this fact with the assertion, that we have a notion,—a positive notion, of absolute or of infinite space, they assume, not only what is not contained in the phænomenon, nay, they assume what is the very reverse of what the phænomenon manifests. It is

Space either bounded or not bounded.

plain, that space must either be bounded or not bounded. These are contradictory alternatives; on the principle of Contradiction, they cannot both be true, and, on the principle of Excluded Middle, one must be true. This cannot be denied, without denying the primary laws of intelligence. But though space must be admitted to be necessarily either finite or infinite, we are able to conceive the possibility neither of its finitude, nor of its infinity.

We are altogether unable to conceive space as bounded,—as finite;

Space as absolutely bounded inconceivable.

that is, as a whole beyond which there is no further space. Every one is conscious that this is impossible. It contradicts also the supposition of space as a necessary notion; for if we could imagine space as a terminated sphere, and that sphere not itself enclosed in a surrounding space, we should not be obliged to think everything in space; and, on the contrary, if we did imagine this terminated sphere as itself in space, in that case we should not have actually conceived all space as a bounded whole. The one contradictory is thus found inconceivable; we cannot conceive space as positively limited.

On the other hand, we are equally powerless to realize in thought the possibility of the opposite contradictory; we cannot conceive space as infinite, as without limits. You may launch out in thought beyond the solar walk, you may transcend in fancy even the universe of matter, and rise from sphere to sphere in the region of empty space, until imagination sinks exhausted; — with all this what have you done? You have never gone beyond the finite, you have attained at best only to the indefinite, and the indefinite, however expanded, is still always the finite. As Pascal energetically says, "Inflate our conceptions as we may, with all the finite possible we cannot make one atom of the infinite."[1] "The infinite is infinitely incomprehensible."[2] Now, then, both contradictories are equally inconceivable, and could we limit our attention to one alone, we should deem it at once impossible and absurd, and suppose its unknown opposite as necessarily true. But as we not only can, but are constrained to consider both, we find that both are equally incomprehensible; and yet, though unable to view either as possible, we are forced by a higher law to admit that one, but one only, is necessary.

That the conceivable lies always between two inconceivable extremes, is illustrated by every other relation of thought. We have found the maximum of space incomprehensible, can we comprehend its minimum? This is equally impossible. Here, likewise, we recoil from one inconceivable contradictory only to infringe upon another. Let us take a portion of space however small, we can never conceive it as the smallest. It is necessarily extended, and may, consequently, be divided into a half or quarters, and each of these halves or quarters may again be divided into other halves or quarters, and this *ad infinitum*. But if we are unable to construe to our mind the possibility of an absolute minimum of space, we can as little represent to ourselves the possibility of an infinite divisibility of any extended entity.

In like manner Time; — this is a notion even more universal than space, for while we exempt from occupying space the energies of mind, we are unable to conceive these as not occupying time. Thus, we think everything, mental and material, as in time, and out of time we can think nothing. But, if we attempt to comprehend time, either in whole or in part, we find that thought

Space as infinitely unbounded inconceivable.

Though both these contradictory alternatives are inconceivable, one or other is yet necessary.

Space, 2°, as a Minimum.

An absolute minimum of space, and its infinite divisibility, alike inconceivable.

Further illustration by reference to Time; — 1°, as a Maximum.

---

[1] *Pensées*, Première Partie, art. iv. 1, (vol. ii. p. 64 Faugère.) Pascal's words are: — "Nous avons beau enfler nos conceptions au delà des espaces imaginables; nous n'enfantons que des atomes, au prix de la réalité des choses." — Ed.

[2] *Ibid*. Sec. Part., art. iii. 1. — Ed.

is hedged in between two incomprehensibles. Let us try the whole. And here let us look back,—let us consider time *a parte ante.*

I. Time, *a parte ante,* as an absolute whole, inconceivable.

And here we may surely flatter ourselves that we shall be able to conceive time as a whole, for here we have the past period bounded by the present; the past cannot, therefore, be infinite or eternal, for a bounded infinite is a contradiction. But we shall deceive ourselves. We are altogether unable to conceive time as commencing; we can easily represent to ourselves time under any relative limitation of commencement and termination, but we are conscious to ourselves of nothing more clearly, than that it would be equally possible to think without thought, as to construe to the mind an absolute commencement, or an absolute termination, of time, that is, a beginning and an end beyond which, time is conceived as non-existent. Goad imagination to the utmost, it still sinks paralyzed within the bounds of time, and time survives as the condition of the thought itself in which we annihilate the universe.

2. Time, as an infinite regress, inconceivable.

On the other hand, the concept of past time as without limit,—without commencement, is equally impossible. We cannot conceive the infinite regress of time; for such a notion could only be realized by the infinite addition in thought of finite times, and such an addition would itself require an eternity for its accomplishment. If we dream of effecting this, we only deceive ourselves by substituting the indefinite for the infinite, than which no two notions can be more opposed. The negation of a commencement of time involves, likewise, the affirmation, that an infinite time has, at every moment, already run; that is, it implies the contradiction, that an infinite has been completed.

3. Time, as an infinite progress, inconceivable.

For the same reasons, we are unable to conceive an infinite progress of time; while the infinite regress and the infinite progress taken together, involve the triple contradiction of an infinite concluded, of an infinite commencing, and of two infinities, not exclusive of each other.

Time, 2°, as a Minimum. The moment of time either divisible to infinity, or composed of certain absolutely smallest parts. Both alternatives inconceivable.

Now take the parts of time,—a moment, for instance; this we must conceive, as either divisible to infinity, or that it is made up of certain absolutely smallest parts. One or other of these contradictories must be the case. But each is, to us, equally inconceivable. Time is a protensive quantity, and, consequently, any part of it, however small, cannot, without a contradiction, be imagined as not divisible into parts, and these parts into others *ad infinitum.* But the opposite alternative is equally impossible; we cannot think this infinite division. One is necessarily true; but neither can be conceived possible. It is on the inability of the mind to conceive either the ultimate indivisibility, or the endless divisibility of space and time, that the arguments of the Eleatic Zeno against the possibility of motion are founded, — arguments which at least show, that motion, however certain as a fact, cannot be conceived possible, as it involves a contradiction.

The same principle could be shown in various other relations, but what I have now said is, I presume, sufficient to make you understand its import. Now the law of mind, that the conceivable is in every relation bounded by the inconceivable, I call the Law of the Conditioned. You will find many philosophers who hold an opinion the reverse of this, — maintaining that the absolute is a native or necessary notion of intelligence. This, I conceive, is an opinion founded on vagueness and confusion. They tell us we have a notion of absolute or infinite space, of absolute or infinite time. But they do not tell us in which of the opposite contradictories this notion is realized. Though these are exclusive of each other, and though both are only negations of the conceivable on its opposite poles, they confound together these exclusive inconceivables into a single notion; suppose it positive, and baptize it with the name of absolute. The sum, therefore, of what I have now stated is, that the Conditioned is that which is alone conceivable or cogitable; the Unconditioned, that which is inconceivable or incogitable. The conditioned or the thinkable lies between two extremes or poles; and these extremes or poles are each of them unconditioned, each of them inconceivable, each of them exclusive or contradictory of the other. Of these two repugnant opposites, the one is that of Unconditional or Absolute Limitation; the other that of Unconditional or Infinite Illimitation. The one we may, therefore, in general call the Absolutely Unconditioned, the other, the Infinitely Unconditioned; or, more simply, the Absolute and the Infinite; the term *absolute* expressing that which is finished or complete, the term *infinite* that which cannot be terminated or concluded. These terms, which, like the Absolute and Infinite themselves, philosophers have confounded, ought not only to be distinguished, but opposed as contradictory. The notion of either unconditioned is negative: — the absolute and the infinite can each only be conceived as a negation of the thinkable. In other words, of the absolute and

This grand principle called the Law of the Conditioned.

The counter opinion founded on vagueness and confusion.

Sum of the author's doctrine.

infinite we have no conception at all. On the subject of the unconditioned, — the absolute and infinite, it is not necessary for me at present further to dilate.

I shall only add in conclusion, that, as this is the one true, it is

The author's doctrine both the one true and the only orthodox inference.

the only orthodox, inference. We must believe in the infinity of God; but the infinite God cannot by us, in the present limitation of our faculties, be comprehended or conceived. A Deity understood, would be no Deity at all; and it is blasphemy to say that God only is as we are able to think Him to be. We know God, according to the finitude of our faculties; but we believe much that we are incompetent properly to know. The Infinite, the infinite God, is what, to use the words of Pascal, is infinitely inconceivable. Faith, — Belief, — is the organ by which we apprehend what is beyond our knowledge. In this all Divines and Philosophers, worthy of the name, are found to coincide; and the few who assert to man a knowledge of the infinite, do this on the daring, the extravagant, the paradoxical supposition, either that Human Reason is identical with the Divine, or that Man and the Absolute are one.

The assertion has, however, sometimes been hazarded, through a

To assert that the infinite can be thought, but only inadequately thought, is contradictory.

mere mistake of the object of knowledge or conception; as if that could be an object of knowledge, which was not known; as if that could be an object of conception which was not conceived. It has been held, that the infinite is known or conceived, though only a part of it (and every part, be it observed, is *ipso facto* finite) can be apprehended; and Aristotle's definition of the infinite has been adopted by those who disregard his declaration, that the infinite, *qua* infinite, is beyond the reach of human understanding.[1] To say that the infinite can be thought, but only inadequately thought, is a contradiction *in adjecto ;* it is the same as saying, that the infinite can be known, but only known as finite.

The Scriptures explicitly declare that the infinite is for us now incognizable ; — they declare that the finite, and the finite alone, is within our reach. It is said (to cite one text out of many), that "*now* I know *in part*" (*i. e.* the finite); "but *then*" (*i. e.* in the life to come) "shall I know even as I am known"[2] (*i. e* .without limitation).[3]

---

1 *Phys.* i. 4, 6 (Bekker): Τὸ μὲν ἄπειρον ἦ ἄπειρον ἄγνωστον. The definition occurs, *Phys.* iii. 6, 11: Ἄπειρον μὲν οὖν ἐστὶν οὗ κατὰ ποσὸν λαμβάνουσιν αἰεί τι λαβεῖν ἐστιν ἔξω. To the ἄπειρον is opposed the ὅλον and τέλειον; for it is added ;—Οὐ δὲ μηδὲν ἔξω, τοῦτ' ἐστὶ τέλειον καὶ ὅλον. See *Discussions*, p. 27. — ED.

2 1 *Corinthians*, xiii. 12.

3 See Appendix, III. — ED.

LECTURE XXXIX.

THE REGULATIVE FACULTY.—LAW OF THE CONDITIONED, IN ITS APPLICATIONS.—CAUSALITY.

I HAVE been desirous to explain to you the principle of the
Conditioned, as out of it we are able not only
to explain the hallucination of the Absolute, but
to solve some of the most momentous, and hitherto
most puzzling, problems of mind. In particular,
this principle affords us, I think, a solution of the two great
intellectual principles of Cause and Effect, and of Substance and
Phænomenon or Accident. Both are only applications of the principle
of the Conditioned, in different relations.

Law of the Conditioned in its applications.

Of all questions in the history of philosophy, that concerning the
nature and genealogy of the notion of Causality,
is, perhaps, the most famous; and I shall endeavor
to give you a comprehensive, though
necessarily a very summary, view of the problem,
and of the attempts which have been made at its solution.
This, however imperfect in detail, may not be without advantage;
for there is not, as far as I am aware, in any work a generalized
survey of the various actual and possible opinions on the subject.

Causality — the problem, and attempts at solution.

But before proceeding to consider the different attempts to
explain the phænomenon, it is proper to state
and to determine what the phænomenon to be
explained really is. Nor is this superfluous, for
we shall find that some philosophers, instead of accommodating
their solutions to the problem, have accommodated the problem to
their solutions.

The phænomenon of Causality, — what.

[1] When we are aware of something which begins to be, we are,
by the necessity of our intelligence, constrained to believe that it
has a Cause. But what does the expression, *that it has a cause,*
signify? If we analyze our thought, we shall find that it simply

---

[1] Cf. *Discussions*, p. 609. — ED.

means, that as we cannot conceive any new existence to commence, therefore, all that now is seen to arise under a new appearance had previously an existence under a prior form. We are utterly unable to realize in thought the possibility of the complement of existence being either increased or diminished. We are unable, on the one hand, to conceive nothing becoming something, — or, on the other, something becoming nothing. When God is said to create out of nothing, we construe this to thought by supposing that He evolves existence out of Himself; we view the Creator as the cause of the universe. "Ex nihilo nihil, in nihilum nil posse reverti,"[1] expresses, in its purest form, the whole intellectual phænomenon of causality.

What appears to us to begin to be, is necessarily thought by us as having previously existed under another form.

There is thus conceived an absolute tautology between the effect and its causes. We think the causes to contain all that is contained in the effect; the effect to contain nothing which was not contained in the causes. Take an example. A neutral salt is an effect of the conjunction of an acid and alkali. Here we do not, and here we cannot, conceive that, in effect, any new existence has been added, nor can we conceive that any has been taken away. But another example:—Gunpowder is the effect of a mixture of sulphur, charcoal, and nitre, and these three substances are again the effect, — result, of simpler constituents, and these constituents again of simpler elements, either known or conceived to exist. Now, in all this series of compositions, we cannot conceive that aught begins to exist. The gunpowder, the last compound, we are compelled to think, contains precisely the same quantum of existence that its ultimate elements contained, prior to their combination. Well, we explode the powder. Can we conceive that existence has been diminished by the annihilation of a single element previously in being, or increased by the addition of a single element which was not heretofore in nature? "Omnia mutantur; nihil interit,"[2] — is what we think, what we must think. This then is the mental phænomenon of causality, — that we necessarily deny in thought that the object which appears to begin to be, really so begins; and that we necessarily identify its present with its past existence. Here it is not requisite that we should know, under what form, under what combinations, this existence was

Hence an absolute tautology between the effect and its causes. This illustrated.

1 Persius, iii. 84. [Cf. Rixner, *Geschichte der Philosophie,* v. i. p. 83, § 62.]
2 Ovid, *Met.* xv. 165. — ED.

previously realized, in other words, it is not requisite that we should know what are the particular causes of the par-

Not necessary to the notion of Causality, that we should know the particular causes of the particular effect. ticular effect. The discovery of the connection of determinate causes and determinate effects is merely contingent and individual, — merely the datum of experience; but the principle that every event should have its causes, is necessary and universal, and is imposed on us as a condition of our human intelligence itself. This last is the only phænomenon to be explained. Nor are philosophers, in general, really at variance in their statement of the problem. However divergent in their mode of explanation, they are at one in regard to the matter to be explained.[1] But there is one exception. Dr. Brown has given a very different account of the phænomenon in question. To

Brown's account of the phænomenon of Causality. this statement of it, I beg to solicit your attention; for as his theory is solely accommodated to his view of the phænomenon, so his theory is refuted by showing that his view of the phænomenon is erroneous. To prevent misconception, I shall exhibit to you his doctrine In his own words:[2]

"Why is it, then, we believe that continual similarity of the future

Brown quoted. to the past, which constitutes, or at least is implied in, our notion of power? A stone tends to the earth, — a stone will always tend to the earth, — are not the same proposition; nor can the first be said to involve the second. It is not to experience, then, alone that we must have recourse for the origin of the belief, but to some other principle which converts the simple facts of experience into a general expectation or confidence, that is afterwards to be physically the guide of all our plans and actions.

"This principle, since it cannot be derived from experience itself, which relates only to the past, must be an original principle of our nature. There is a tendency in the very constitution of the mind from which the experience arises, — a tendency, that, in everything which it adds to the mere facts of experience, may truly be termed instinctive; for though that term is commonly supposed to imply something peculiarly mysterious, there is no more real mystery in it than in any of the simplest successions of thought, which are all, in like manner, the results of a natural tendency of the mind to exist in certain states, after existing in certain other states. The

---

1 On the nature and origin of the notion　　2 *Phil. of the Human Mind*, Lect. vi. p. 34,
Causality, see Platner, *Phil. Aph.* i. § 845 *et seq.*　edit. 1880.
— ED.

belief is, a state or feeling of the mind as easily conceivable as any other state of it, — a new feeling, arising in certain circumstances, as uniformly as, in certain other circumstances, there arise other states or feelings of the mind, which we never consider as mysterious; those, for example, which we term the sensations of sweetness or of sound. To have our nerves of taste or hearing affected in a certain manner, is not, indeed, to taste or hear, but it is immediately afterwards to have those particular sensations; and this merely because the mind was originally so constituted, as to exist directly in the one state after existing in the other. To observe, in like manner, a series of antecedents and consequents, is not, in the very feeling of the moment, to believe in the future similarity, but, in consequence of a similar original tendency, it is immediately afterwards to believe that the same antecedents will invariably be followed by the same consequents. That this belief of the future is a state of mind very different from the mere perception or memory of the past, from which it flows, is indeed true; but what resemblance has sweetness, as a sensation of the mind, to the solution of a few particles of sugar on the tongue; or the harmonies of music, to the vibration of particles of air? All which we know, in both cases, is, that these successions regularly take place; and in the regular successions of nature, which could not, in one instance more than in another, have been predicted without experience, nothing is mysterious, or everything is mysterious. . . . .

"It is more immediately our present purpose to consider, What it truly is which is the object of inquiry, when we examine the physical successions of events, in whatever manner the belief of their similarity of sequence may have arisen? Is it the mere series of regular antecedents and consequents themselves? or, Is it anything more mysterious, which must be supposed to intervene and connect them by some invisible bondage?

"We see in nature one event followed by another. The fall of a spark on gunpowder, for example, followed by the deflagration of the gunpowder; and, by a peculiar tendency of our constitution, which we must take for granted, whatever be our theory of power, we believe, that, as long as all the circumstances continue the same, the sequence of events will continue the same; that the deflagration of gunpowder, for example, will be the invariable consequence of the fall of a spark on it: in other words, we believe the gunpowder to be susceptible of deflagration on the application of a spark, and a spark to have the power of deflagrating gunpowder.

"There is nothing more, then, understood in the train of events, however regular, than the regular order of antecedents and consequents which compose the train; and between which, if anything else existed, it would itself be a part of the train. All that we mean, when we ascribe to one substance a susceptibility of being affected by another substance, is that a certain change will uniformly take place in it when that other is present;—all that we mean, in like manner, when we ascribe to one substance a power of affecting another substance, is, that, where it is present, a certain change will uniformly take place in that other substance. Power, in short, is significant not of anything different from the invariable antecedent itself, but of the mere invariableness of the order of its appearance in reference to some invariable consequent, — the invariable antecedent being denominated a *cause*, the invariable consequent an *effect*. To say, that water has the power of dissolving salt, and to say that salt will always melt when water is poured upon it, are to say precisely the same thing;—there is nothing in the one proposition, which is not exactly and to the same extent enunciated in the other."

Now, in explaining to you the doctrine of Dr. Brown, I am happy to avail myself of the assistance of my late lamented friend, Dr. Brown's successor, whose metaphysical acuteness was not the least remarkable of his many brilliant qualities.

"Now, the distinct and full purport of Dr. Brown's doctrine, it will be observed, is this,—that when we apply in this way the words *cause* and *power*, we attach no other meaning to the terms than what he has explained. By the word *cause*, we mean no more than that in this instance the spark falling is the event immediately prior to the explosion: including the belief that in all cases hitherto, when a spark has fallen on gunpowder (of course, supposing other circumstances the same), the gunpowder has kindled; and that whenever a spark shall again so fall, the grains will again take fire. The present immediate priority, and the past and future invariable sequence of the one event upon the other, are all the ideas that the mind can have in view in speaking of the event in that instance as a cause; and in speaking of the power in the spark to produce this effect, we mean merely to express the invariableness with which this has happened and will happen.

Wilson quoted on Brown's doctrine of Causality.

"This is the doctrine; and the author submits it to this test:— 'Let any one,' he says, 'ask himself what it is which he means by the term 'power,' and without contenting himself with a few phrases that signify nothing, reflect before he give his answer, — and he will find that he means nothing more than that, in all similar circumstances, the explosion of gunpowder will be the immediate and uniform consequence of the application of a spark.

"This test, indeed, is the only one to which the question can be brought. For the question does not regard causes themselves, but solely the ideas of cause, in the human mind. If, therefore, every one to whom this analysis of the idea that is in his mind when he speaks of a cause, is proposed, finds, on comparing it with what passed in his mind, that this is a complete and full account of his conception, there is nothing more to be said, and the point is made good. By that sole possible test the analysis is, in such a case, established. If, on the contrary, when this analysis is proposed, as containing all the ideas which we annex to the words cause and power, the minds of most men cannot satisfy themselves that it is complete, but are still possessed with a strong suspicion that there is something more, which is not here accounted for, — then the analysis is not yet established, and it becomes necessary to inquire, by additional examination of the subject, what that more may be.

"Let us then apply the test by which Dr. Brown proposes that the truth of his views shall be tried. Let us ask ourselves what we mean when we say, that the spark has power to kindle the gunpowder, — that the powder is susceptible of being kindled by the spark. Do we mean only that whenever they come together this will happen? Do we merely predict this simple and certain futurity?

"We do not fear to say, that when we speak of a power in one substance to produce a change in another, and of a susceptibility of such change in that other, we express more than our belief that the change has taken and will take place. There is more in our mind than a conviction of the past and a foresight of the future. There is, besides this, the conception included of a fixed constitution of their nature, which determines the event, — a constitution, which, while it lasts, makes the event a necessary consequence of the situation in which the objects are placed. We should say then, that there are included in these terms, 'power,' and 'susceptibility of change,' two ideas which are not expressed in Dr. Brown's analysis, — one of necessity, and the other of a constitution of things, in which that necessity is established. That these two ideas are not expressed in the terms of Dr. Brown's analysis, is seen by quoting again his words : — 'He will find that he means nothing more than that, in all similar circumstances, the explosion of gunpowder will be the immediate and uniform consequence of the application of a spark.'

"It is certain, from the whole tenor of his work, that Dr. Brown has designed to exclude the idea of necessity from his analysis."[1]

---

1 Prof. Wilson, in *Blackwood's Magazine*, vol. xl. p. 122 *et seq.*

68

Now this admirably expresses what I have always felt is the grand and fundamental defect in Dr. Brown's theory, — a defect which renders that theory *ab initio* worthless. Brown professes to explain the phænomenon of causality, but, previously to explanation, he evacuates the phænomenon of all that desiderates explanation. What remains in the phænomenon, after the quality of necessity is thrown, or rather silently allowed to drop out, is only accidental, — only a consequence of the essential circumstance.

Fundamental defect in Brown's theory.

The opinions in regard to the nature and origin of the principle of Causality, in so far as that principle is viewed as a subjective phænomenon, — as a judgment of the human mind, — fall into two great categories. The first category (A) comprehends those theories which consider this principle as Empirical, or *a posteriori*, that is, as derived from experience; the other (B) comprehends those which view it as Pure or *a priori*, that is, as a condition of intelligence itself. These two primary genera are, however, severally subdivided into various subordinate classes.

Classification of opinions on the nature and origin of the Principle of Causality.

The former category (A), under which this principle is regarded as the result of experience, contains two classes, inasmuch as the causal judgment may be supposed founded either (a) on an Original, or (b) on a Derivative, cognition. Each of these again is divided into two, according as the principle is supposed to have an objective, or a subjective, origin. In the former case, that is, where the cognition is supposed to be original and underived, it is Objective, or rather Objectivo-Objective, when held to consist in an immediate perception of the power or efficacy of causes in the external and internal worlds (1); and Subjective, or rather Objectivo-Subjective, when viewed as given in a self-consciousness alone of the power or efficacy of our own volitions (2). In the latter case, that is, where the cognition is supposed to be derivative, if objective, it is viewed as a product of Induction and Generalization (3); if subjective, of Association and Custom (4).

In like manner, the latter category (B), under which the causal principle is considered not as a result, but as a condition, of experience, is variously divided and subdivided. In the first place, the opinions under this category fall into two classes, inasmuch as some regard the causal judgment (c) as an Ultimate or Primary law of mind, while others regard it (d) as a Secondary or Derived. Those who hold the former doctrine, in viewing it as a simple original principle, hold likewise that it is a positive act, — an affirmative datum, of intelligence. This class is finally subdivided into two opinions. For some hold that the causal judgment, as necessary, is given in what they call "the principle of Causality," that is, the principle which declares that everything which begins to be, must have its cause (5); whilst at least one philosopher, without explicitly denying that the causal judgment is necessary, would identify it with the principle of our "Expectation of the Constancy of nature" (6).

Those who hold that it can be analyzed into a higher principle, also hold that it is not of a positive but of a negative character. These, however, are divided into two classes. By some it has been maintained, that the principle of Causality can be resolved into the principle of Contradiction (7), which, as I formerly stated to you, ought in propriety to be called the principle of Non-Contradiction. On the other hand, it may be (though it never has been) argued, that the judgment of Causality can be analyzed into what I called the principle of the Conditioned, — the principle of Relativity (8). To one or the other of these eight heads, all the doctrines that have been actually maintained in regard to the origin of the principle in question, may be referred; and the classification is the better worthy of your attention, as in no work will you find any attempt at even an enumeration of the various theories, actual and possible, on this subject.[1]

An adequate discussion of these several heads, and a special consideration of the differences of the individual opinions which they comprehend, would far exceed our limits. I shall, therefore, confine myself to a few observations on the value of these eight doctrines in general, without descending to the particular modifications under which they have been maintained by particular philosophers.

These eight doctrines considered in general.

Of these, the first, — that which asserts that we have a perception of the causal agency, as we have a perception of the existence of external objects, — this opinion has been always held in combination with the second, — that which maintains that we are self-conscious of efficiency; though the second has been frequently held by philosophers who have abandoned the first as untenable.

I. Objectivo-Objective and Objectivo-Subjective.

Perception of causal efficiency, external and internal.

Considering them together, that is, as forming the opinion that we directly and immediately apprehend the efficiency of causes, both

1 A Tabular View of the Theories in regard to the Principle of Causality will be found on the next page.

A TABULAR VIEW

OF THE

THEORIES IN REGARD TO THE PRINCIPLES OF CAUSALITY.

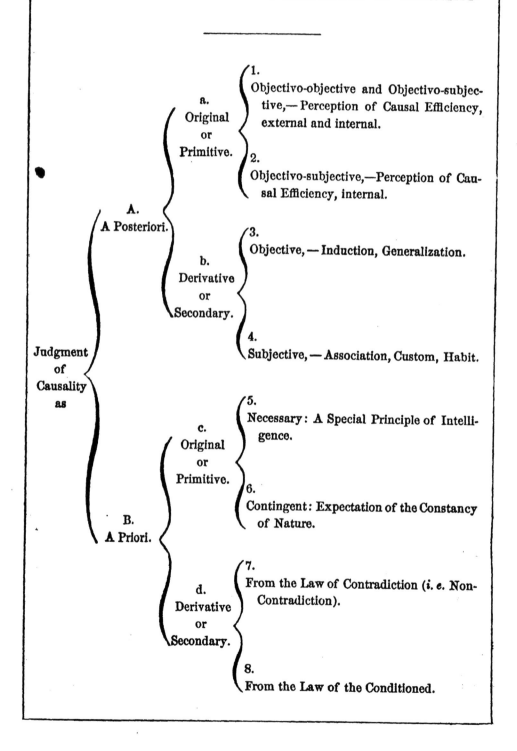

Judgment of Causality as

A. A Posteriori.

a. Original or Primitive.

1. Objectivo-objective and Objectivo-subjective,—Perception of Causal Efficiency, external and internal.

2. Objectivo-subjective,—Perception of Causal Efficiency, internal.

b. Derivative or Secondary.

3. Objective,—Induction, Generalization.

4. Subjective,—Association, Custom, Habit.

B. A Priori.

c. Original or Primitive.

5. Necessary: A Special Principle of Intelligence.

6. Contingent: Expectation of the Constancy of Nature.

d. Derivative or Secondary.

7. From the Law of Contradiction (*i. e.* Non-Contradiction).

8. From the Law of the Conditioned.

external and internal, — this opinion is refuted by two objections.

The first is, that we have no such apprehen-

Refuted on two grounds.

sion, — no such knowledge; the second, that if we had, this being merely empirical, — merely conversant with individual instances, could never account for the quality of necessity and universality which accompanies the judgment of causality. In regard to the first of these objections, it is now universally admitted that we have no perception of the connection of cause and effect in the external world. For example, when one billiard-ball is seen to strike another, we perceive only that the impulse of the one is followed by the motion of the other, but have no perception of any force or efficiency in the first, by

That we have no perception of the connection of cause and effect in the external world, — maintained by Hume.

which it is connected with the second, in the relation of causality. Hume was the philosopher who decided the opinion of the world on this point. He was not, however, the first who stated the fact, or even the reasoner who stated it most clearly. He, however, believed himself, or would induce us to believe that in this he was original. Speaking of this point, "I am sensible," he says, "that of all the paradoxes, which I have had, or shall hereafter have, occasion to advance, in the course of this treatise, the present one is the most violent, and that it is merely by dint of solid proof and reasoning I can ever hope it will have admission, and overcome the inveterate prejudices of mankind. Before we are reconciled to this doctrine, how often must we repeat to ourselves, that the simple view of any two objects or actions, however related, can never give us any idea of power, or of a connection betwixt them; that this idea arises from the repetition of their union: that the repetition neither discovers nor causes anything in the objects, but has an influence only on the mind, by that customary transition it produces: that this customary transition is, therefore, the same with the power and necessity; which are consequently qualities of perceptions, not of objects, and are internally felt by the soul, and not perceived externally in bodies?"[1]

I could adduce to you a whole army of philosophers previous to Hume, who had announced and illustrated the fact.[2] As far as I

[1] *Treatise of Human Nature*, v. i. b. i. p. iii. § 14, p. 291, orig. edit.

[2] Cf. Sturm, *Physica Electiva*, c. iv. p. 168 (edit. 1697). Stewart, *Elements*, i. *Works*, ii. note C, p. 476, *Elements*. ii. *Works*, iii. note O, p. 319. — ED. [See Le Clerc, *Ontologia*, c. x. § 8, 4. *Opera. Phil.*, i. p. 318. Chev. Ramsay, *Philos. Prin. of Natural and Revealed Religion*, p. 109; Glasgow, 1748. That Aristotle did not acknowledge that sense had any perception of the causal connection, is shown by his denying sense as principle of science, i. 4.

have been able to trace it, this doctrine was first promulgated towards the commencement of the twelfth century,
And, before him, by many philosophers.
at Bagdad, by Algazel (El Gazeli), a pious Mohammedan philosopher, who not undeservedly obtained the title of Imaum of the World. Algazel did not deny the reality of causation, but he maintained that
Algazel, — probably the first.
God was the only efficient cause in nature;[1] and that second causes were not properly causes but only occasions, of the effect. That we have no perception of any real agency of one body on another, is a truth which has not more clearly been stated or illustrated by any subsequent philosopher than by him who first proclaimed it. The doctrine of Algazel
Mussulman doctors.
was adopted by that great sect among the Mussulman doctors, who were styled *those speaking in the law* (*loquentes in lege*), that is, the law of Mohammed. From
The Schoolmen.
the Eastern Schools the opinion passed to those of the West; and we find it a problem which divided the scholastic philosophers, whether God were the only efficient, or whether causation could be attributed to created existences.[2] After the revival of letters, the opinion of Algazel was maintained by many individual thinkers, though it no longer retained the same prominence in the schools. It was held, for example,
Malebranche.
ple, by Malebranche,[3] and his illustration from the collision of two billiard-balls is likewise that of Hume, who probably borrowed from Malebranche both the opinion and the example.

II. Objectivo-Subjective. Perception of causal efficiency, internal.
Locke.
M. de Biran.
But there are many philosophers who surrender the external perception, and maintain our internal consciousness, of causation or power. This opinion was, in one chapter of his *Essay*,[4] advanced by Locke, and, at a very recent date, it has been amplified and enforced with distinguished ability by the late M. Maine de Biran,[5] — one of the acutest

---

ὅτι, (see *Post. An.*, i. p. 81; and *ibi*, Zabarella), and by his denying that sense is principle of wisdom, as ignorant of cause (see *Met.*, i. p. 50, and *ibi*, Fonseca. See also Conimbricenses, *In Org.* ii. 486.)]

1 See Averroes, *Destructio Destructionis. Aristotelis Opera*, Venet. 1550, vol. ix. p 56. Quoted by Tennemann, *Gesch. der Phil.* vol. viii. p. 405. — Ed.

2 [See Biel, *In Sent.* l. iv. dist. 50. q. 1. D'Ailly, *Ibid.* dist. 2. q. 23; referred to by Scheibler, *Opera Metaphysica*, l. ii. c. iii. tit. 19, p. 124 (edit. 1665). See also Sturm, *Physica*

Electiva, c. iv. p. 128 *et seq.* Poiret *Œconomia Divina*, i. vi. § 6, p. 66 *et seq.* (edit. 1705).]

3 [*Recherche de la Vérité*, l. vi. p. c. iii.]

4 Book ii. c. xxi. § 5 — Ed.

5 See *Examen des Leçons de Philosophie*, § viii., *Nouvelles Considérations*, p. 241; and *Réponses aux Arguments contre l' Apperception Immediate d'une Liaison Causale entre le Vouloir et la Motion*, etc., *Nouv. Con.* p. 363 (edit 1634). Cf. Prèface, by M. Cousin, p. 84; and *Cours de l' Histoire de la Philosophie* (xviii⁰ Siècle) t. ii. l. xix. p. 231 (edit. 1829). — Ed.

metaphysicians of France. On this doctrine, the notion of cause is not given to us by the observations of external phænomena, which, as considered only by the senses, manifest no causal efficiency, and appear to us only as successive; it is given to us within, in reflection, in the consciousness of our operations and of the power which exerts them, — viz., the will. I make an effort to move my arm, and I move it. When we analyze attentively the phænomenon of effort, which M. de Biran considers as the type of the phænomena of volition, the following are the results : — 1°, the consciousness of an act of will; 2°, The consciousness of a motion produced; 3°, A relation of the motion to the volition. And what is this relation? Not a simple relation of succession. The will is not for us a pure act without efficiency, — it is a productive energy; so that in a volition there is given to us the notion of cause, and this notion we subsequently transport, — project out from our internal activities, into the changes of the external world.

[1]This reasoning, in so far as regards the mere empirical fact of our consciousness of causality, in the relation of our will as moving, and of our limbs as moved, is refuted by the consideration, that between the overt fact of corporeal movement of which we are cognizant, and the internal act of mental determination of which we are also cognizant,

Shown to be untenable.

1. No consciousness of causal connection between volition and motion.

there intervenes a numerous series of intermediate agencies of which we have no knowledge; and, consequently, that we can have no consciousness of any causal connection between the extreme links of this chain, — the volition to move and the limb moving, as this hypothesis asserts. No one is immediately conscious, for example, of moving his arm through his volition. Previously to this ultimate movement, muscles, nerves, a multitude of solid and fluid parts, must be set in motion by the will, but of this motion we know, from consciousness, absolutely nothing. A person struck with paralysis is conscious of no inability in his limb to fulfil the determinations of his will; and it is only after having willed and finding that his limbs do not obey his volition, that he learns by his experience, that the external movement does not follow the internal act. But as the paralytic learns after the volition, that his limbs do not obey his mind; so it is only after volition that the man in health learns, that his limbs do obey the mandates of his will.

But, independently of all this, the second objection above mentioned is fatal to the theory which would found the judgment of

1 See *Reid's Works*, p. 866. *Discuss.*, p. 612. — ED.

causality on any empirical cognition, whether of the phænomena of mind or of the phænomena of matter. Ad-

2. And even if this admitted, fails to account for the judgment of Causality.

mitting that causation were cognizable, and that perception and self-consciousness were competent to its apprehension, still as these faculties could only take note of individual causations, we should be wholly unable, out of such empirical acts, to evolve the quality of necessity and universality, by which this notion is distinguished. Admitting that we had really observed the agency of any number of causes, still this would not explain to us, how we are unable to think a manifestation of existence without thinking it as an effect. Our internal experience, especially in the relation of our volitions to their effects, may be useful in giving us a clearer notion of causality; but it is altogether incompetent to account for what in it there is of the quality of necessity. So much for the two theories at the head of the Table.

As the first and second opinions have been usually associated, so also have the third and fourth, — that is, the doctrine that our notion of causality is the offspring of the objective principle of Induction or Generalization, and the doctrine, that it is the offspring of the subjective principle of Association or Custom.

In regard to the former, — the third, it is plain that the observa-

III. Objective — Induction. Generalization.

tion, that certain phænomena are found to succeed certain other phænomena, and the generalization consequent thereon, that these are reciprocally causes and effects, could never of itself have engendered not only the strong but the irresistible belief, that every event must have its cause. Each of these observations is contingent; and any number of observed contingencies will never impose upon us the feeling of necessity, — of our inability to think the opposite. Nay more; this theory evolves the absolute notion of causality out of the observation of a certain number of uniform consecutions among phænomena. But we find no difficulty whatever in conceiving the reverse of all or any of the consecutions we have observed; and yet the general notion of causality, which, *ex hypothesi*, is their result, we cannot possibly think as possibly unreal. We have always seen a stone fall to the ground, when thrown into the air, but we find no difficulty in representing to ourselves the possibility of one or all stones gravitating from the earth; only we cannot conceive the possibility of this, or any other event, happening without a cause.

Nor does the latter, — the fourth theory, — that of Custom or Association, — afford a better solution. The attribute of necessity cannot be derived from custom. Allow the force of custom to

IV. Subjective — Association. be great as may be, still it is always limited to the customary, and the customary has nothing whatever in it of the necessary. But we have

here to account not for a strong, but for an absolutely irresistible, belief. On this theory, also, the causal judgment, when association is recent, should be weak, and should only gradually acquire its full force in proportion as custom becomes inveterate. But do we find that the causal judgment is weaker in the young, stronger in the old? There is no difference. In either case there is no less and no more; the necessity in both is absolute. Mr. Hume patronized the opinion, that the notion of causality is the offspring of experience engendered upon custom.[1] But those have a sorry insight into the philosophy of that great thinker, who suppose that this was a dogmatic theory of his own. On the contrary, in his hands, it was a mere reduction of dogmatism to absurdity by showing the inconsistency of its results. To the Lockian sensualism, Hume proposed the problem, — to account for the phænomenon of necessity in our notion of the causal nexus. That philosophy afforded no other principle through which even the attempt at a solution could be made; — and the principle of custom, Hume shows, could not furnish a real necessity. The alternative was plain. Either the doctrine of sensualism is false, or our nature is a delusion. Shallow thinkers adopted the latter alternative, and were lost; profound thinkers, on the contrary, were determined to lay a deeper foundation of philosophy than that of the superficial edifice of Locke; and thus it is that Hume became the cause or the occasion of all that is of principal value in our more recent metaphysics. Hume is the parent of the philosophy of Kant, and, through Kant, of the whole philosophy of Germany; he is the parent of the philosophy of Reid and Stewart in Scotland, and of all that is of preëminent note in the metaphysics of France and Italy. — But to return.

I now come to the second category (B), and to the first of the four particular heads which it likewise contains,

V. A special principle of intelligence. — the opinion, namely, that the judgment, that everything that begins to be must have a cause, is a simple primary datum, a positive revelation of intelligence. To this head are to be referred the theories on causality of Descartes, Leibnitz, Reid, Stewart, Kant, Fichte, Cousin, and the majority of recent philosophers. This is the fifth theory in order.

1 [On Hume's theory, See Platner, *Phil. Aph.* q. 1. § 850, p. 485-6; edit. 1793.]

Dr. Brown has promulgated a doctrine of Causality, which may be numbered as the sixth; though perhaps it is hardly deserving of distinct enumeration. He actually identifies the causal judgment, which to us is necessary, with the principle by which we are merely inclined to believe in the uniformity of nature's operations.

VI. Expectation of the constancy of nature.

Superseding any articulate consideration of this opinion, and reverting to the fifth, much might be said in relation to the several modifications of this opinion, as held by different philosophers; but I must content myself with a brief criticism of the doctrine in reference to its most general features.

Now it is manifest, that, against the assumption of a special principle, which this doctrine makes, there exists a primary presumption of philosophy. This is the law of Parcimony, which forbids, without necessity, the multiplication of entities, powers, principles, or causes; above all the postulation of an unknown force, where a known impotence can account for the effect. We are, therefore, entitled to apply Occam's razor to this theory of causality, unless it be proved impossible to explain the causal judgment at a cheaper rate, by deriving it from a higher and that a negative origin. On a doctrine like the present is thrown the onus of vindicating its necessity, by showing that unless a special and positive principle be assumed, there exists no competent mode to save the phænomena. It can only, therefore, be admitted provisorily; and it falls of course, if the phænomenon it would explain can be explained on less onerous conditions.

Fifth opinion criticised.

Primary presumption of philosophy against assumption of special principle of causality.

Leaving, therefore, the theory to stand or fall according as the two remaining opinions are or are not found insufficient, I proceed to the consideration of these. The first, — the seventh, is a doctrine that has long been exploded. It attempts to establish the principle of Causality upon the principle of Contradiction. Leibnitz was too acute a metaphysician to attempt to prove the principle of Sufficient Reason or Causality, which is an ampliative or synthetic principle, by the principle of contradiction, which is merely explicative or analytic. But his followers were not so wise. Wolf,[1] Baumgarten,[2] and many other Leibnitzians, paraded demonstrations of the law of the Sufficient Reason on the ground of the law of Contradiction;

VII. The principle of Non-Contradiction.

---

1 [*Ontologia*, § 70.]

2 [*Metaphysik*, § 18.] [Cf. Walch, *Lexikon v.*

Zureichender Grund. Zedler, *Lexikon, v. Causalität.*]

but the reasoning always proceeds on the covert assumption of the very point in question. The same argument is, however, at an earlier date, to be found in Locke,[1] and modifications of it in Hobbes[2] and Clarke.[3] Hume,[4] who was only aware of the argument as in the hands of the English metaphysicians, has given it a refutation, which has earned the approbation of Reid; and by foreign philosophers its emptiness, in the hands of the Wolfian metaphysicians, has frequently been exposed.[5] Listen to the pretended demonstration: — Whatever is produced without a cause, is produced by nothing; in other words, has nothing for its cause. But nothing

Fallacy of the supposed demonstration. can no more be a cause than it can be something. The same intuition that makes us aware, that

nothing is not something, shows us that everything must have a real cause of its existence. To this it is sufficient to say, that the existence of causes being the point in question, the existence of causes must not be taken for granted, in the very reasoning which attempts to prove their reality. In excluding causes we exclude all causes; and consequently exclude nothing considered as a cause; it is not, therefore, allowable, contrary to that exclusion, to suppose nothing as a cause, and then from the absurdity of that supposition to infer the absurdity of the exclusion itself. If everything must have a cause, it follows that, upon the exclusion of other causes, we must accept of nothing as a cause. But it is the very point at issue, whether everything must have a cause or not; and, therefore, it violates the first principles of reasoning to take this quæsitum itself as granted. This opinion is now universally abandoned.

The eighth and last opinion is that which regards the judgment of causality as derived; and derives it not from

VIII. The Law of the Conditioned. a power, but from an impotence, of mind; in a word, from the principle of the Conditioned. I

do not think it possible, without a detailed exposition of the various categories of thought, to make you fully understand the grounds and bearings of this opinion. In attempting to explain, you must, therefore, allow me to take for granted certain laws of thought, to which I have only been able incidentally to allude. Those, how-

---

1 [*Essay*, book iv. c. 10, § 3. *Works*, i. p. 294.] [This is doubtless the passage of Locke which is criticized by Hume (*Treat. of Hum. Nat.*, b. i. p. 1. § 3); but it will hardly bear the interpretation put upon it by Hume and Sir W. Hamilton. — ED.]

2 *Of Liberty and Necessity, Works*, edit. Molesworth, vol. iv. p. 276. — ED.

3 [*Demonstration*, p. 9, *alibi*. See also S. Gravesande, *Introd. ad Phil.* § 80.]

4 *Treat. of Hum. Nature*, b. i. p. iii. § 3, Cf. Reid, *Works*, p. 455. Stewart, *Dissert. Works*, i. p. 441. — ED.

5 [See Walch, *Lex v. Zureichender Grund.* Biedermanni *Acta Scholastica*, t. vii. p. 120, Schwab, *Preisschriften über die Metaphysik*, p. 149. Lossius, *Lexikon, v. Caussalität*, i. p. 669.]

ever, which I postulate, are such as are now generally admitted by all philosophers who allow the mind itself to be a source of cogni-tions; and the only one which has not been recognized by them, but which, as I endeavored briefly to prove to you in my last Lec-ture, must likewise be taken into account, is the Law of the Condi-tioned, — the law that the conceivable has always two opposite extremes, and that the extremes are equally inconceivable. That the Conditioned is to be viewed, not as a power, but as a powerless-ness, of mind, is evinced by this, — that the two extremes are con-tradictories, and, as contradictories, though neither alternative can be conceived, — thought as possible, one or other must be admitted to be necessary.

Philosophers, who allow a native principle to the mind at all, allow that Existence is such a principle. I shall, therefore, take for granted Existence as the highest category or condition of thought. As I noticed to you in my last Lecture,[1] no thought is possible

Judgment of Caus-ality, how deduced from this law.

Categories of thought.

Existence.

except under this category. All that we per-ceive or imagine as different from us, we perceive or imagine as objectively existent. All that we are conscious of as an act or modification of self, we are conscious of only as subjectively exist-ent. All thought, therefore, implies the thought of existence; and this is the veritable exposition of the enthymeme of Descartes, — *Cogito ergo sum.* I cannot think that I think, without thinking that I exist, — I cannot be conscious, without being conscious that I am. Let existence, then, be laid down as a necessary form of thought. As a second category or subjective con-

Time.

dition of thought, I postulate that of Time. This, likewise, cannot be denied me. It is the necessary condition of every conscious act; thought is only realized to us as in succession, and succession is only conceived by us under the concept of time. Existence and existence in Time is thus an elementary form of our intelligence.

But we do not conceive existence in time absolutely or infinitely,

The Conditioned.

— we conceive it only as conditioned in time; and Existence Conditioned in Time expresses, at once and in relation, the three categories of thought, which afford us in combination the principle of Causality. This requires some explanation.

When we perceive or imagine an object, we perceive or imagine it — 1°, As existent, and, 2°, As in Time; Existence and Time be-

ing categories of all thought. But what is meant by saying, I perceive, or imagine, or, in general, think, an ob-
Existence Condi- ject only as I perceive, or imagine, or, in general,
tioned in Time affords think it to exist? Simply this;—that, as think-
the principle of Caus- ing it, I cannot but think it to exist, in other
ality. words, that I cannot annihilate it in thought. I
may think away from it, I may turn to other things; and I can thus
exclude it from my consciousness; but, actually thinking it, I cannot think it as non-existent, for as it is thought, so it is thought
existent.

But a thing is thought to exist, only as it is thought to exist in
time. Time is present, past, and future. We cannot think an
object of thought as non-existent *de presenti,* — as actually an object
of thought. But can we think that quantum of existence of which
an object, real or ideal, is the complement, as non-existent, either in
time past, or in time future? Make the experiment. Try to think
the object of your thought as non-existent in the moment before
the present. — You cannot. Try it in the moment before that. —
You cannot. Nor can you annihilate it by carrying it back to any
moment, however distant in the past. You may conceive the parts
of which this complement of existence is composed, as separated;
if a material object, you can think it as shivered to atoms, subli-
mated into æther; but not one iota of existence can you conceive
as annihilated, which subsequently you thought to exist. In like
manner try the future, — try to conceive the prospective annihilation of any present object, — of any atom of any present object. —
You cannot. All this may be possible, but of it we cannot think
the possibility. But if you can thus conceive neither the absolute
commencement nor the absolute termination of anything that is
once thought to exist, try, on the other hand, if you can conceive
the opposite alternative of infinite non-commencement, of infinite
non-termination. To this you are equally impotent. This is the
category of the Conditioned, as applied to the category of Existence under the category of Time.

But in this application is the principle of Causality not given?
Why, what is the law of Causality? Simply this, — that when an
object is presented phænomenally as commencing, we cannot but
suppose that the complement of existence, which it now contains,
has previously been; — in other words, that all that we at present
come to know as an effect must previously have existed in its
causes; though what these causes are we may perhaps be altogether
unable even to surmise.

LECTURE XL.

THE REGULATIVE FACULTY.—LAW OF THE CONDITIONED, IN ITS APPLICATIONS.—CAUSALITY.

OUR last Lecture was principally occupied in giving a systematic view and a summary criticism of the various opinions of philosophers, regarding the origin of that inevitable necessity of our nature, which compels us to refuse any real commencement of existence to the phænomena which arise in and around us; in other words, that necessity of our nature, under which we cannot but conceive everything that occurs, to be an effect, that is, to be something consequent, which, as wholly derived from, may be wholly refunded into, something antecedent. The opinions of philosophers with regard to the genealogy of this claim of thought, may be divided into two *summa genera* or categories; as all opinions on this point view the Causal Judgment either, 1°, As resting immediately or mediately on experience, or 2°, As resting immediately or mediately on a native principle of the mind itself; — in short, all theories of causality make it either *a posteriori* or Empirical, or make it *a priori* or Pure.

I shall not again enumerate the various subordinate doctrines into which the former category is subdivided; and, in relation to all of these, it is enough to say that they are one and all wholly worthless, as wholly incapable of accounting for the quality of necessity, by which we are conscious that the causal judgment is characterized.

The opinions which fall under the second category are not obnoxious to this sweeping objection (except Brown's), as they are all equally competent to save the phænomenon of a subjective necessity. Of the three opinions (I discount Brown's) under this head, one supposes that the law of Causality is a positive affirmation, and a primary fact of thought, incapable of all further analysis. The other two, on the contrary, view it as a negative principle, and as capable of resolution into a higher law.

Recapitulation.

Of these, the first opinion (the sixth) is opposed *in limine*, by the presumption of philosophy against the multiplication of special principles. By the law of Parcimony, the assumption of a special principle can only be legitimated by its necessity; and that necessity only emerges if the phænomenon to be explained can be explained by no known and ordinary causes. The possible validity of this theory, therefore, depends on the two others being actually found incompetent. As postulating no special, no new, no positive principle, and professing to account for the phænomenon upon a common and a negative ground, they possess a primary presumption in their favor; and if one or other be found to afford us a possible solution of the problem, we need not, nay, we are not entitled to, look beyond.

Of these two theories, the one (the seventh) attempts to analyze the principle of Causality into the principle of Contradiction; the other (the eighth), into the principle of the Conditioned. The former has been long exploded, and is now universally abandoned. The attempt to demonstrate that a negation of causes involves an affirmation of two contradictory propositions, has been shown to be delusive, as the demonstration only proceeds on a virtual assumption of the point in question. The field, therefore, is left open for the last (the eighth), which endeavors to analyze the mental law of Causality into the mental law of the Conditioned. This theory, which has not hitherto been proposed, is recommended by its extreme simplicity. It postulates no new, no special, no positive principle. It only supposes that the mind is limited; and the law of limitation, the law of the Conditioned, in one of its applications, constitutes the law of Causality. The mind is necessitated to think certain forms; and, under these forms, thought is only possible in the interval between two contradictory extremes, both of which are absolutely inconceivable, but one of which, on the principle of Excluded Middle, is necessarily true. In reference to the present subject, it is only requisite to specify two of these forms, — Existence and Time. I showed you that thought is only possible under the native conceptions, — the *a priori* forms, — of existence and time; in other words, the notions of existence and time are essential elements of every act of intelligence. But while the mind is thus astricted to certain necessary modes or forms of thought, in these forms it can only think under certain conditions. Thus, while obliged to think under the thought of time, it cannot conceive, on the one hand, the absolute commencement of time, and it cannot conceive, on the other, the infinite non-commencement of time; in like manner, on the one hand, it cannot conceive

The law of Causality constituted by the law of the Conditioned.

The law of the Conditioned.

an absolute minimum of time, nor yet, on the other, can it conceive
the infinite divisibility of time.   Yet these form two pairs of contradictories, that is, of counter-propositions, which, if our intelligence
be not all a lie, cannot both be true, but of which, on the same
authority, one necessarily must be true.   This proves : 1°, That it is
not competent to argue, that what cannot be comprehended as possible by us, is impossible in reality ; and 2°, That the necessities of
thought are not always positive powers of cognition, but often
negative inabilities to know.   The law of mind, that all that is positively conceivable, lies in the interval between two inconceivable
extremes, and which, however palpable when stated, has never been
generalized, as far as I know, by any philosopher, I call the Law or
Principle of the Conditioned.

Thus, the whole phænomenon of causality seems to me to be nothing more than the law of the Conditioned, in its
application to a thing thought under the form or
mental category of Existence, and under the
form or mental category of Time.   We cannot
know, we cannot think a thing, except as existing, that is, under the category of existence ; and
we cannot know or think a thing as existing, ex-
cept in time.   Now the application of the law of the conditioned to
any object, thought as existent, and thought as in time, will give us
at once the phænomenon of causality.   And thus : — An object is
given us, either by sense or suggestion, — imagination.   As known,
we cannot but think it existent, and in time.   But to say that
we cannot but think it to exist, is to say, that we are unable
to think it non-existent, that is, that we are unable to annihilate
it in thought.   And this we cannot do.   We may turn aside from
it ; we may occupy our attention with other objects ; and we
may thus exclude it from our thoughts.   This is certain : we need
not think it ; but it is equally certain, that thinking it, we cannot
think it not to exist.   This will be at once admitted of the present ;
but it may possibly be denied of the past and future.   But if we
make the experiment, we shall find the mental annihilation of an
object equally impossible under time past, present, or future.   To
obviate misapprehension, however, I must make
a very simple observation.   When I say that it
is impossible to annihilate an object in thought —
in other words, to conceive it as non-existent, —
it is of course not meant that it is impossible to imagine the object
wholly changed in form.   We can figure to ourselves the elements
of which it is composed, distributed and arranged and modified

*This law in its ap-
plication to a thing
thought under Exist-
ence and Time, affords
the phænomenon of
Causality.*

*Annihilation and
Creation, — as con-
ceived by us.*

in ten thousand forms, — we can imagine anything of it, short of annihilation. But the complement, the quantum, of existence, which is realized in any object, — that we can represent to ourselves, either as increased, without abstraction from other bodies, or as diminished, without addition to them. In short, we are unable to construe it in thought, that there can be an atom absolutely added to, or an atom absolutely taken away from, existence in general. Make the experiment. Form to yourselves a notion of the universe; now can you conceive that the quantity of existence, of which the universe is the sum, is either amplified or diminished? You can conceive the creation of a world as lightly as you conceive the creation of an atom. But what is a creation? It is not the springing of nothing into something. Far from it: — it is conceived, and is by us conceivable, merely as the evolution of a new form of existence, by the fiat of the Deity. Let us suppose the very crisis of creation. Can we realize it to ourselves, in thought, that, the moment after the universe came into manifested being, there was a larger complement of existence in the universe and its Author together, than there was the moment before, in the Deity himself alone? This we cannot imagine. What I have now said of our conceptions of creation, holds true of our conceptions of annihilation. We can conceive no real annihilation, — no absolute sinking of something into nothing. But, as creation is cogitable by us only as an exertion of divine power, so annihilation is only to be conceived by us as a withdrawal of the divine support. All that there is now actually of existence in the universe, we conceive as having virtually existed, prior to creation, in the Creator; and in imagining the universe to be annihilated by its Author, we can only imagine this, as the retractation of an outward energy into power. All this shows how impossible it is for the human mind to think aught that it thinks, as non-existent either in time past or in time future.

[[1] Our inability to think, what we have once conceived existent in Time, as in time becoming non-existent, corresponds with our inability to think, what we have conceived existent in Space, as in space becoming non-existent. We cannot realize it to thought, that a thing should be extruded, either from the one quantity or the other. Hence, under extension, the law of Ultimate Incompressibility; under protension, the law of Cause and Effect.]

Our inability to think aught as extruded from Space gives the law of Ultimate Incompressibility.

We have been hitherto speaking only of one inconceivable extreme of the conditioned, in its application to the category of existence in the category of time, — the extreme of absolute com-

The infinite regress of Time no less inconceivable than its absolute commencement.

mencement; the other is equally incomprehensible, that is, the extreme of infinite regress or non-commencement. With this latter we have, however, at present nothing to do. [[1] Indeed, as not obtrusive, the Infinite figures far less in the theatre of mind, and exerts a far inferior influence in the modification of thought, than the Absolute. It is, in fact, both distant and delitescent; and in place of meeting us at every turn, it requires some exertion on our part to seek it out.] It is the former alone, — it is the inability we experience of annihilating in thought an exist-

Our inability to conceive existence as absolutely beginning in time, constitutes the phænomenon of causality.

ence in time past, in other words, our utter impotence of conceiving its absolute commencement, that constitutes and explains the whole phænomenon of causality. An object is presented to our observation which has phænomenally begun to be. Well, we cannot realize it in thought that the object, that is, this determinate complement of existence, had really no being at any past moment; because this supposes that, once thinking it as existent, we could again think it as non-existent, which is for us impossible. What, then, can we do? That the phænomenon presented to us began, as a phænomenon, to be, — this we know by experience; but that the elements of its existence only began, when the phænomenon they constitute came into being, — this we are wholly unable to represent in thought. In these circumstances, how do we proceed? — How must we proceed? There is only one possible mode. We are compelled to believe that the object (that is, a certain *quale* and *quantum* of being) whose phænomenal rise into existence we have witnessed, did really exist, prior to this rise, under other forms;[2] [and by *form*, be it observed, I mean any mode of existence, conceivable by us or not]. But to say that a thing previously existed under different forms, is only in other words to say, that a thing had causes. I have already noticed to you the error of philosophers in supposing,

Of Second Causes there must be at least a concurrence of two, to constitute an effect.

that anything can have a single cause. Of course, I speak only of Second Causes. Of the causation of the Deity we can form no possible conception. Of second causes, I say, there must almost always be at least a concurrence of two to constitute an effect. Take the example of vapor. Here to say that heat is the cause of evaporation, is a very inaccurate, — at least a very inadequate ex-

---

[1] Supplied from *Discussions*, p. 621. — Ed.   [2] Supplied from *Discussions*, p. 621. — Ed.

pression. Water is as much the cause of evaporation as heat. But heat and water together are the causes of the phænomenon. Nay, there is a third concause which we have forgot, — the atmosphere. Now, a cloud is the result of these three concurrent causes or constituents; and, knowing this, we find no difficulty in carrying back the complement of existence, which it contains prior to its appearance. But on the hypothesis, that we are not aware what are the real constituents or causes of the cloud, the human mind must still perforce suppose some unknown, some hypothetical, antecedents, into which it mentally refunds all the existence which the cloud is thought to contain.

Nothing can be a greater error in itself, or a more fertile cause of delusion, than the common doctrine, that the causal judgment is elicited only when we apprehend objects in consecution, and uniform consecution. Of course, the observation of such succession prompts and enables us to assign particular causes to particular effects. But this consideration ought to be carefully distinguished from the law of Causality, absolutely, which consists not in the empirical attribution of this phænomenon, as cause, to that phænomenon as effect, but in the universal necessity of which we are conscious, to think causes for every event, whether that event stand isolated by itself, and be by us referable to no other, or whether it be one in a series of successive phænomena, which, as it were, spontaneously arrange themselves under the relation of effect and cause. [[1]Of no phænomenon, as observed, need we think *the* cause; but of every phænomenon, must we think *a* cause. The former we may learn through a process of induction and generalization; the latter we must always and at once admit, constrained by the condition of Relativity. On this, not sunken rock, Dr. Brown and others have been shipwrecked.]

To suppose that the causal judgment is elicited only by objects in uniform consecution, is erroneous.

This doctrine of Causality seems to me preferable to any other, for the following, among other, reasons:

In the first place, to explain the phænomenon of the Causal Judgment, it postulates no new, no extraordinary, no express principle. It does not even found upon a positive power; for, while it shows that the phænomenon in question is only one of a class, it assigns, as their common cause, only a negative impotence. In this, it stands advantageously contrasted with the one other theory which saves the

The author's doctrine of Causality, to be preferred.
1°. From its simplicity.

phænomenon, but which saves it only by the hypothesis of a special principle, expressly devised to account for this phænomenon alone. Nature never works by more, and more complex instruments than are necessary;— μηδὲν περιττῶς; and to assume a particular force, to perform what can be better explained by a general imbecility, is contrary to every rule of philosophizing.

But, in the second place, if there be postulated an express and positive affirmation of intelligence to account for the fact, that existence cannot absolutely commence, we must equally postulate a counter affirmation of intelligence, positive and express, to explain the counter fact, that existence cannot infinitely not commence. The one necessity of mind is equally strong as the other; and if the one be a positive doctrine, an express testimony of intelligence, so also must be the other. But they are contradictories; and, as contradictories, they cannot both be true. On this theory, therefore, the root of our nature is a lie! By the doctrine, on the contrary, which I propose, these contradictory phænomena are carried up into the common principle of a limitation of our faculties. Intelligence is shown to be feeble, but not false; our nature is, thus, not a lie, nor the Author of our nature a deceiver.

2°. Averting skepticism.

In the third place, this simpler and easier doctrine avoids a serious inconvenience, which attaches to the more difficult and complex. It is this:— To suppose a positive and special principle of causality, is to suppose, that there is expressly revealed to us, through intelligence, the fact that there is no free causation, that is, that there is no cause which is not itself merely an effect; existence being only a series of determined antecedents and determined consequents. But this is an assertion of Fatalism. Such, however, most of the patrons of that doctrine will not admit. The assertion of absolute necessity, they are aware, is virtually the negation of a moral universe, consequently of the Moral Governor of a moral universe; in a word, Atheism. Fatalism and Atheism are, indeed, convertible terms. The only valid arguments for the existence of a God, and for the immortality of the soul, rest on the ground of man's moral nature;[1] consequently, if that moral nature be annihilated, which in any scheme of necessity it is, every conclusion, established on such a nature, is annihilated also. Aware of this, some of those who make the judgment of causality a special principle,—a positive dictate of intelligence,—find themselves compelled, in order to escape from the consequences of their doctrine,

3°. Avoiding the alternatives of fatalism or inconsistency.

---

1 See above, lect. ii. p. 18 *et seq.* — ED.

to deny that this dictate, though universal in its deliverance, should be allowed to hold universally true; and, accordingly, they would exempt from it the facts of volition. Will, they hold to be a free cause, that is, a cause which is not an effect; in other words, they attribute to will the power of absolute origination. But here their own principle of causality is too strong for them. They say, that it is unconditionally given, as a special and positive law of intelligence, that every origination is only an apparent, not a real, commencement. Now to exempt certain phænomena from this law, for the sake of our moral consciousness, cannot validly be done. For, in the first place, this would be to admit that the mind is a complement of contradictory revelations. If mendacity be admitted of some of our mental dictates, we cannot vindicate veracity to any. "Falsus in uno, falsus in omnibus." Absolute skepticism is hence the legitimate conclusion. But, in the second place, waiving this conclusion, what right have we, on this doctrine, to subordinate the positive affirmation of causality to our consciousness of moral liberty,—what right have we, for the interest of the latter, to derogate from the universality of the former? We have none. If both are equally positive, we have no right to sacrifice to the other the alternative, which our wishes prompt us to abandon.

But the doctrine which I propose is not exposed to these difficulties. It does not suppose that the judgment of *Advantages of the Author's doctrine further shown.* Causality is founded on a power of the mind to recognize as necessary in thought what is necessary in the universe of existence; it, on the contrary, founds this judgment merely on the impotence of the mind to conceive either of two contradictories, and, as one or other of two contradictories must be true, though both cannot, it shows that there is no ground for inferring from the inability of the mind to conceive an alternative as possible, that such alternative is really impossible. At the same time, if the causal judgment be not an affirmation of mind, but merely an incapacity of positively thinking the contrary, it follows that such a negative judgment cannot stand in opposition to the positive consciousness,—the affirmative deliverance, that we are truly the authors,—the responsible originators, of our actions, and not merely links in the adamantine series of effects and causes. It appears to me that it is only on this doctrine that we can philosophically vindicate the liberty of the will,—that we can rationally assert to man a "fatis avolsa voluntas." How the will can possibly be free must remain to us, under the present limitation of our faculties, wholly incomprehensible. We cannot conceive absolute commencement; we cannot, therefore, conceive a free volition. But as little can we conceive the alternative on which liberty is denied, on which necessity is affirmed. And in favor of our moral nature, the fact that we are free, is given us in the consciousness of an uncompromising law of Duty, in the consciousness of our moral accountability; and this fact of liberty cannot be redargued on the ground, that it is incomprehensible, for the doctrine of the Conditioned proves, against the necessitarian, that something may, nay must, be true, of which the mind is wholly unable to construe to itself the possibility; whilst it shows that the objection of incomprehensibility applies no less to the doctrine of fatalism than to the doctrine of moral freedom. If the deduction, therefore, of the Causal Judgment, which I have attempted, should speculatively prove correct, it will, I think, afford a securer and more satisfactory foundation for our practical interests, than any other which has ever yet been promulgated.[1]

---

1 Here, in the manuscript, occurs the following sentence, with mark of deletion:— "But of this we shall have to speak, when we consider the question of the Liberty or Necessity of our Volitions, under the Third Great Class of the Mental Phænomena, — the Conative." The author does not, however, resume the consideration of this question in these Lectures. It will also be observed that Sir. W. Hamilton does not pursue the application of the Law of the Conditioned to the principle of Substance and Phænomenon, as proposed at the outset of the discussion. See above, p. 532. On Causality, and on Liberty and Necessity, see further in *Discussions*, p. 625 *et seq.*, and Appendix vi. — ED.

LECTURE XLI.

SECOND GREAT CLASS OF MENTAL PHÆNOMENA — THE FEEL-
INGS; THEIR CHARACTER, AND RELATION TO THE COGNI-
TIONS AND CONATIONS.

HAVING concluded our consideration of the First Great Class of the Phænomena revealed to us by conscious-

Second Great Class of mental phænomena, — the Feelings.

ness, — the phænomena of knowledge, — we are now to enter on the Second of these Classes, — the class which comprehends the phænomena of Pleasure and Pain, or, in a single word, the phænomena of Feeling.[1] Before, however, proceeding to a discussion of this class of mental appearances, considered in themselves, there are several questions of a preliminary character, which it is proper to dispose of. Of these, two naturally present themselves in the

Two preliminary questions regarding the Feelings.

very threshold of our inquiry. The first is, — Do the phænomena of Pleasure and Pain con- stitute a distinct order of internal states, so that we are warranted in establishing the capacity of Feeling as one of the fundamental powers of the human mind?

The second is, — In what position do the Feelings stand by refer- ence to the Cognitions and the Conations; and, in particular, whether ought the Feelings or the Conations to be considered first, in the order of science?

Of these questions, the former is by no means one that can be either superseded or lightly dismissed. This is

1. Do the phænomena of Pleasure and Pain constitute a distinct or- der of internal states?

shown, both by the very modern date at which the analysis of the Feelings into a separate class of phænomena was proposed, and by the contro- versy to which this analysis has given birth.

Until a very recent epoch, the feelings were not recognized by any philosopher as the manifestations of any fundamental power. The distinction taken in the Peripatetic School, by which the

---

1 See above, lect. xi. p. 126. — ED.

mental modifications were divided into Gnostic or Cognitive, and Orectic or Appetent, and the consequent reduc-

The Feelings were not recognized as the manifestations of any fundamental power, until a very recent period.

Peripatetic division of the mental phænomena.

tion of all the faculties to the *Facultas cognoscendi* and the *Facultas appetendi*, was the distinction which was long most universally prevalent, though under various, but usually less appropriate, denominations. For example, the modern distribution of the mental powers into those of the Understanding and those of the Will, or into Powers Speculative and Powers Active,—these are only very inadequate, and very incorrect, versions of the Peripatetic analysis, which, as far as it went, was laudable for its conception, and still more laudable for its expression. But this Aristotelic division of the internal states, into the two categories of Cognitions and of Appetencies, is exclusive of the Feelings, as a class coördinate with the two other genera; nor was there, in antiquity, any other philosophy which accorded to the feelings the rank denied to them in the analysis of the Peripatetic school. An attempt has, indeed, been made to show that, by Plato, the capacity of Feeling was regarded as one of the three fundamental powers; but it is only by a total perversion of Plato's language, by a total reversion of the whole analogy of his psychology, that any color can be given to this opinion. Kant, as I have

formerly observed, was the philosopher to whom we owe this tri-logical classification. But it ought to be stated, that Kant only placed the keystone in the arch, which had been raised by previous philosophers among his countrymen. The phænomena of Feeling had, for thirty years prior to the reduction of Kant, attracted

the attention of the German psychologists, and had by them been considered as a separate class of mental states. This had been done by Sulzer[1] in 1751, by Mendelssohn[2] in 1763, by Kæstner[3] in 1763 (?), by Meiners[4] in 1773, by Eberhard[5] in 1776, and by

---

[1] See *Untersuchung über den Ursprung der angenehmen und unangenehmen Empfindungen;* first published in the Memoirs of the Berlin Academy, in 1751 and 1752. See *Verm. philos. Schriften*, v. i. p. 1. Leipsic, 1800. Cf. his *Allgemeine Theorie der schönen Künste*, 1771. — Ed. [For a summary and criticism of the former work, see Reinhold, *Über die bisherigen Begriffe vom Vergnügen. Vermischte Schriften*, i. p. 296. Jena, 1796.]

[2] *Briefe über die Empfindungen*, 1755. — Ed.

[3] See *Nouvelle Theorie des Plaisirs*, par M.

Sulzer; *avec des Réflexions sur l'Origine du Plaisir*, par M. Kæstner, de l'Académie Royale de Berlin, 1767, first published in the Memoirs of the Academy in 1749. See below, p. 591. — Ed.

[4] See *Abriss der Psychologie*, 1773. — Ed.

[5] See *Allgemeine Theorie des Denkens und Empfindens*, read before the Royal Society of Berlin in 1776; new edit. 1786. Cf. *Theorie der schönen Wissenchaften*, 2d edit. Halle, 1786. — Ed.

Platner[1] in 1780 (?). It remained, however, for Kant to establish, by his authority, the decisive trichotomy of the mental powers. In his *Critique of Judgment* (*Kritik der Urtheilskraft*), and, likewise, in his *Anthropology*, he treats of the capacities of Feeling, apart from, and along with, the faculties of Cognition and Conation.[2] At the same time, he called attention to their great importance in the philosophy of mind, and more precisely and more explicitly than any of his predecessors did he refer them to a particular power,—a power which constituted one of the three fundamental phænomena of mind.

Kant,—the first to establish the trichotomy of the mental powers.

This important innovation necessarily gave rise to controversy. It is true that the Kantian reduction was admitted, not only by the great majority of those who followed the impulsion which Kant had given to philosophy, but, likewise, by the great majority of the psychologists of Germany, who ranged themselves in hostile opposition to the principles of the Critical School. A reäction was, however, inevitable; and while, on the one hand, the greater number were disposed to recognize the Feelings in their new rank, as one of the three grand classes of the mental phænomena; a smaller number,—but among them some philosophers of no mean account,—endeavored, however violent the procedure, to reännex them, as secondary manifestations, to one or other of the two coördinate classes,—the Cognitions and the Conations.

Kant's doctrine controverted by some philosophers of note.

Before proceeding to consider the objections to the classification in question, it is proper to premise a word in reference to the meaning of the term by which the phænomena of Pleasure and Pain are designated, —the term *Feeling;* for this is an ambiguous expression, and on the accident of its ambiguity have been founded some of the reasons against the establishment of the class of phænomena, which it is employed to denote.

Meaning of the term Feeling.

It is easy to convey a clear and distinct knowledge of what is meant by a word, when that word denotes some object which has an existence external to the mind. I have only to point out the object, and to say, that such or such a thing is signified by such or such a

---

1 The threefold division of the mental phænomena forms the basis of the psychological part of Platner's *Neue Anthropologie*, 1790; see book ii. The first edition (*Anthropologie*) appeared in 1772-4. Cf. *Phil. Aphorismen*, vol. i.

b. i. §§ 27—43, edit. 1793. Kant's *Kr. d. Urtheilskraft* was first published in 1790; the *Anthropologie*, though written before it, was only first published in 1798. — ED.

2 See above, lect. xi. p. 129. — ED.

name; for example, this is called a *house*, that a *rainbow*, this a *horse*, that an *ox*, and so forth. In these cases, the exhibition of

the reality is tantamount to a definition; or, as an old logician expresses it, "Cognitio omnis intuitiva est definitiva."[1] The same, however, does not hold in regard to an object which lies within the mind itself. What was easy in the one case becomes difficult in the other. For although he to whom I would explain the mean-

ing of a term, by pointing out the object which it is intended to express, has, at least may have, that very object

present in his mind, still I c. not lay my finger on it, — I cannot give it to e amine by the eye, — to smell, to taste, to hanc . Thus it is that misunderstandings frequently occur in reference to this class of objects, inasmuch as one attaches a different meaning to the word from that in which another uses it ; and we ought not to be surprised that, in the nomenclature of our mental phænomena, it has come to pass, that, in all languages, one term has become the sign of a plurality of notions, while at the same time a single notion is designated by a plurality of terms. This vacillation in the applica- tion and employment of language, as it originates in the impossi- bility, anterior to its institution, of approximating different minds to a common cognition of the same internal object; so this ambiguity, when once established, reäcts powerfully in perpetuating the same difficulty; insomuch that a principal, if not the very greatest, im- pediment in the progress of the philosopher of mind, is the vague- ness and uncertainty of the instrument of thought itself. A remark- able example of this, and one extending to all languages, is seen in

the words most nearly correspondent to the very indeterminate expression *feeling*. In English, this, like all others of a psychological application, was primarily of a purely physical relation, being originally employed to denote the sensations we experience through the sense of Touch, and in this meaning it still continues to be em- ployed. From this, its original relation to matter and the corporeal sensibility, it came, by a very natural analogy, to express our con- scious states of mind in general, but particularly in relation to the qualities of pleasure and pain, by which they are characterized. Such is the fortune of the term in English ; and precisely similar is

---

[1] Cf. Melanchthon, *Erotemata Dialectica, De Definitione*, who quotes it as an old saying: "Vetus enim dictum est, et dignum memoria: Omnis intuitiva notitia est definitio."—Ed. [Cf. Keckermann, *Opera*, t. i. p. 198.]

that of the cognate term *Gefühl* in German. The same, at least a similar, history might be given of the Greek term αἴσθησις, and of the Latin *sensus, sensatio*, with their immediate and mediate deriva-, tives in the different Romanic dialects of modern Europe, — the Italian, Spanish, French, and English dialects. In applying the term *feeling* to the mental states, strictly in so far as these manifest the phænomena of pleasure and pain, it is, therefore, hardly necessary to observe, that the word is used, not in all the meanings in which it can be employed, but in a certain definite relation, were it not that a very unfair advantage has been taken of this ambiguity of the expression. *Feeling*, in one meaning, is manifestly a cognition ; but this affords no ground for the argument, that *feeling*, in every signification, is also a cognition. This reasoning has however, been proposed, and that by a philosopher from whom so paltry a sophism was assuredly not to be expected.

It being, therefore, understood that the word is ambiguous, and that it is only used because no preferable can be found, the question must be determined by the proof or disproof of the affirmation, — that I am able to discriminate in consciousness certain states, certain qualities of mind, which cannot be reduced to those either of Cognition or Conation ; and that I can enable others, in like manner, to place themselves in a similar position, and observe for themselves these states or qualities, which I call *Feelings*. Let us take an example. In reading the story of Leonidas and his three hundred Spartans at Thermopylæ, what do we experience? Is there nothing in the state of mind, which the narrative occasions, other than such as can be referred either to the cognition or to will and desire ? Our faculties of knowledge are called certainly into exercise ; for this is, indeed, a condition of every other state. But is the exultation which we feel at this spectacle of human virtue, the joy which we experience at the temporary success, and the sorrow at the final destruction of this glorious band, — are these affections to be reduced to states either of cognition or of conation in either form ? Are they not feelings, — feelings partly of pleasure, partly of pain ?

Take another, and a very familiar, instance. You are all probably acquainted with the old ballad of *Chevy Chase*, and you probably recollect the fine verse of the original edition, so lamentably spoiled in the more modern versions :

Can we discriminate in consciousness certain states which cannot be reduced to those of Cognition or Conation ?

This question decided in the affirmative by an appeal to experience.

" For Widdrington my soul is sad,
That ever he slain should be,
For when his legs were stricken off,
He kneeled and fought on his knee." [1]

Now, I ask you, again, is it possible, by any process of legitimate analysis, to carry up the mingled feelings, some pleasurable, some painful, which are called up by this simple picture, into anything bearing the character of a knowledge, or a volition, or a desire? If we cannot do this, and if we cannot deny the reality of such feelings, we are compelled to recognize them as belonging to an order of phænomena, which, as they cannot be resolved into either of the other classes, must be allowed to constitute a third class by themselves.

But it is idle to multiply examples, and I shall now proceed to consider the grounds on which some philosophers,

Grounds on which objection has been taken to the Kantian classification of the mental phænomena. and among these, what is remarkable, a distinguished champion of the Kantian system, have endeavored to discredit the validity of the classification.

Passing over the arguments which have been urged against the power of Feeling as a fundamental capacity of mind, in so far as these proceed merely on the ambiguities of language, I shall consider only the principal objections from the nature of the phænomena themselves, which have been urged by the three principal opponents of the classification in question, — Carus, Weiss, and Krug. The last of these is the philosopher by whom these objections have been urged most explicitly, and with greatest force. I shall, therefore, chiefly confine myself to a consideration of the difficulties which he proposes for solution.

I may premise that this philosopher (Krug), admitting only two fundamental classes of psychological phænomena, — the Cognitions and the Conations, — goes so far as not only to maintain, that what have obtained, from other psychologists, the name of *Feelings*, constitute no distinct and separate class of mental functions; but

Krug quoted. that the very supposition is absurd and even impossible. "That such a power of feeling," he argues, [2] "is not even conceivable, if by such is understood a power

[1] " For Wetharryngton my harte was wo,
That ever he slayne shulde be;
For when both his leggis wear hewyne
in to,
He knyled and fought on hys kne."
— *Original Version,* in Percy's *Reliques.* —
ED.

[2] This objection is given in substance, though not exactly in language, in Krug's *Philosophisches Lexikon,* art. *Seelenkräfte.* The author, in the same work, art. *Gefühl,* refers to his *Grundlage zu einer neuen Theorie der Gefühle, und des sogenannten Gefühlsvermögens,* Königsberg, 1823, for a fuller discussion of the question. See also above, lect. xi. p. 130. — ED.

essentially different from the powers of Cognition and Conation," (thus I translate *Vorstellungund Bestrebungsvermögen*), " is manifest from the following consideration. . . . . The powers of cognition and the powers of conation are, in propriety, to be regarded as two different fundamental powers, only because the operation of our mind exhibits a twofold direction of its whole activity, — one inwards, another outwards; in consequence of which we are constrained to distinguish, on the one hand, an Immanent, ideal or theoretical, and, on the other a Transeunt, real or practical, activity. Now, should it become necessary to interpolate between these two powers, a third; consequently, to convert the original duplicity of our activity into a triplicity; in this case, it would be requisite to attribute to the third power a third species of activity, the product of which would be, in fact, the Feelings. Now this activity of feeling must necessarily have either a direction inwards, or a direction outwards, or both directions at once, or finally neither of the two, that is, no direction at all; for apart from the directions inwards and outwards, there is no direction conceivable. But, in the first case, the activity of feeling would not be different from the cognitive activity, at least not essentially; in the second case, there is nothing but a certain appetency manifested under the form of a feeling; in the third, the activity of feeling would be only a combination of theoretical and practical activity; consequently, there remains only the supposition that it has no direction. We confess, however, that an hypothetical activity of such a kind we cannot imagine to ourselves as a real activity. An activity without any determinate direction, would be in fact directed upon nothing, and a power conceived as the source of an activity, directed upon nothing, appears nothing better than a powerless power, — a wholly inoperative force, in a word, a nothing." — So far our objectionist.

In answer to this reasoning, I would observe, that its cogency depends on this, — that the suppositions which it makes, and afterwards excludes, are exhaustive and complete. But this is not the case. "For, in place of two energies, an immanent and a transeunt, we may competently suppose three, — an ineunt, an immanent, and a transeunt. 1°, The Ineunt energy might be considered as an act of mind, directed upon objects in order to know them, — to bring them within the sphere of consciousness, — mentally to appropriate them; 2°, The Immanent energy might be considered as a kind of internal fluctuation about the objects, which had been brought to representation and thought, — a

Criticized. 1. The suppositions on which the reasoning proceeds, are not exhaustive.

We may suppose three kinds of energy, Ineunt, Immanent, and Transeunt.

pleasurable or a painful affection caused by them, in a word, a feeling; and 3°, The Transeunt energy might be considered as an act tending towards the object in order to reach it, or to escape from it. This hypothesis is quite as allowable as that in opposition to which it is devised, and were it not merely in relation to an hypothesis, which rests on no valid foundation, it would be better to consider the feelings not as immanent activities, but as immanent passivities.

" But, in point of fact, we are not warranted, by any analogy of our spiritual nature, to ascribe to the mental powers a direction either outwards or inwards; on the contrary, they are rather the principles of our internal states, of which we can only improperly predicate a direction, and this only by relation to the objects of the states themselves. For directions are relations and situations of external things; but of such there are none to be met with in the internal world, except by analogy to outer objects. In our Senses, which have reference to the external world, there is an outward direction when we perceive, or when we act on external things; whereas, we may be said to turn inwards, when we occupy ourselves with what is contained within the mind itself, be this in order to compass a knowledge of our proper nature, or to elevate ourselves to other objects still more worthy of a moral intelligence. Rigorously considered, the feelings are in this meaning so many directions, — so many turnings towards those objects which determine the feelings, and which please or displease us. Take, for example, the respect, the reverence, we feel in the contemplation of the higher virtues of human nature; this feeling is an immanent conversion on its object.

2. But we are not warranted to ascribe to the mental powers a direction either outwards or inwards.

" The argument of the objectors is founded on the hypothesis, that as in the external world, all is action and reäction, — all is working and counterworking, — all is attraction and repulsion; so in the internal world, there is only one operation of objects on the mind, and one operation of the mind on objects; the former must consist in cognition, the latter in conation. But when this hypothesis is subjected to a scrutiny, it is at once apparent how treacherous is the reasoning which infers of animated, what is true of inanimate, nature; for, to say nothing of aught else that militates against it, this analogy would in truth leave no will or desire in the universe at all; for action and reäction are already compensated in cognition, or to speak more correctly, in sensitive Perception itself."[1]

3. The argument founded on the hypothesis, that what is true of inanimate, is true of animated nature; and would leave no will or desire in the universe.

1 Biunde, *Versuch d. empirischen Psychologie,* ii. § 207, p. 54—56. — ED.

Such is a specimen of the only argument of any moment, against the establishment of the Feelings as an ultimate class of mental phænomena.

I pass on to the second question;—What is the position of the Feelings by reference to the two other classes;

II. What is the position of the Feelings by reference to the two other classes of mental phænomena?

—and, in particular, should the consideration of the Feelings precede, or follow, that of the Conations?

The answer to the second part of this question, will be given in the determination of the first part; for Psychology proposes to exhibit the mental phænomena in their natural consecution, that is, as they condition and suppose each other. A system which did not accomplish this, could make no pretension to be a veritable exposition of our internal life.

"To resolve this problem, let us take an example. A person is fond of cards. In a company where he beholds

Resolved by an example.

a game in progress, there arises a desire to join in it. Now the desire is here manifestly kindled by the pleasure, which the person had, and has, in the play. The feeling thus connects the cognition of the play with the desire to join in it; it forms the bridge, and contains the motive, by which we are roused from mere knowledge to appetency,—to conation, by reference to which we move ourselves so as to attain the end in view.

"Thus we find, in actual life, the Feelings intermediate between the Cognitions and the Conations. And this

The Feelings intermediate between the Cognitions and Conations.

relative position of these several powers is necessary; without the previous cognition, there could be neither feeling nor conation; and without the previous feeling there could be no conation. Without some kind or another of complacency with an object, there could be no tendency, no pretension of the mind to attain this object as an end; and we could, therefore, determine ourselves to no overt action. The mere cognition leaves us cold and unexcited; the awakened feeling infuses warmth and life into us and our action; it supplies action with an interest, and, without an interest, there is for us no voluntary action possible. Without the intervention of feeling, the cognition stands divorced from the conation, and, apart from feeling, all conscious endeavor after anything would be altogether incomprehensible.

"That the manifestations of the Conative Powers are determined by the Feelings, is also apparent from the following reflection. The volition or desire tends towards a something, and this something is only given us in and through some faculty or other of cognition. Now, were the mere cognition of a thing sufficient of itself to rouse our conation, in that case, all that was known in the same manner and in the same degree, would become an equal object of desire or will. But we covet one thing; we eschew another. On the supposition, likewise, that our conation was only regulated by our cognition, it behooved that every other individual besides should be desirous of the object which I desire, and be desirous of it also so long as the cognition of the object remained the same. But one person pursues what another person flies; the same person now yearns after something which anon he loathes. And why? It is manifest that here there lies hid some very variable quantity, which, when united with the cognition, is capable of rousing the powers of conation into activity. But such a quantity is given, and only given, in the feelings, that is, in our consciousness of the agreeable and disagreeable. If we take this element, — this influence, — this quantity, — into account, the whole anomalies are solved. We are able at once to understand why all that is thought or cognized with equal intensity, does not, with equal intensity, affect the desires or the will; why different individuals, with the same knowledge of the same objects, are not similarly attracted or repelled; and why the same individual does not always pursue or fly the same object. This is all explained by the fact, that a thing may please one person and displease another; and may now be pleasurable, now painful, and now indifferent, to the same person.

That the Conative Powers are determined by the Feelings further shown.

Mere cognition not sufficient to rouse Conation.

1. Because all objects known in the same manner and degree, are not equal objects of desire or will.

2. Because different individuals are desirous of different objects.

"From these interests for different objects, and from these opposite interests which the same object determines in our different powers, are we alone enabled to render comprehensible the change and confliction of our desires, the vacillations of our volitions, the warfare of the sensual principle with the rational, — of the flesh with the spirit; so that, if the nature and influence of the feelings be misunderstood, the problems most important for man are reduced to insoluble riddles.

Importance of a correct understanding of the nature and influence of the Feelings.

"According to this doctrine, the Feelings, placed in the midst between the powers of Cognition and the powers of Conation, perform the functions of connecting principles to these two extremes; and thus the objection that has been urged against the feelings as a class coördinate with the cognitions and the conations, — on the ground that they afford no principle of mediation, is of all objections the most futile and erroneous. Our conclusion, therefore, is, that as, in our actual existence, the feelings find their place after the cognitions, and before the conations, — so, in the science of mind, the theory of the Feelings ought to follow that of our faculties of Knowledge, and to precede that of our faculties of Will and Desire."[1] Notwithstanding this, various even of those psychologists who have adopted the Kantian trichotomy, have departed from the order which Kant had correctly indicated, and have averted it in every possible manner, — some treating of the feelings in the last place, while others have considered them in the first.

Place of the theory of the Feelings in the science of mind.

The last preliminary question which presents itself is — Into what subdivisions are the Feelings themselves to be distributed? In considering this question, I shall first state some of the divisions which have been proposed by those philosophers who have recognized the capacity of feeling as an ultimate, a fundamental, phænomenon of mind. This statement will be necessarily limited to the distributions adopted by the psychologists of Germany; for, strange to say, the Kantian reduction, though prevalent in the Empire, has remained either unknown to, or disregarded by, those who have speculated on the mind in France, Italy, and Great Britain.

III. Into what subdivisions are the Feelings to be distributed?

To commence with Kant himself. In the *Critique of Judgment*,[2] he enumerates three specifically different kinds of complacency, the objects of which are severally the Agreeable (*das Angenehm*), the Beautiful, and the Good. In his treatise of *Anthropology*,[3] subsequently published, he divides the feelings of pleasure and pain into two great classes; — 1°, The Sensuous; 2°, The Intellectual. The former of these classes is again subdivided into two subordinate kinds, inasmuch as the feeling arises either through the Senses (Sensual Pleasures), or through the Imagination (Pleasures of Taste). The latter of these classes is also subdivided into subordinate kinds; for our Intellectual Feelings are connected either with the notions of the Understanding, or with the ideas of Reason. I may notice that in his published manual of *Anthropology*, the Intellectual Feelings of the first subdivision, — the feelings of the Understanding, are not treated of in detail.

Kant.

---

1 Biunde, *Versuch d. empirischen Psychologie*, ii. § 208, p. 60—64. — ED.

2 § 5. *Werke*, iv. p. 53. — ED.
3 B. ii. *Werke*, vii. p. 143. — ED.

Gottlob Schulze, though a decided antagonist of the Kantian
philosophy in general, adopts the threefold clas-

Schulze.

sification into the Cognitions, the Feelings, and
the Conations; but he has preferred a division of the Feelings different from that of the philosopher of Königsberg. These he distributes into two classes, — the Corporeal and the Spiritual; to
which he annexes a third class made up of these in combination, —
the Mixed Feelings.

Hillebrand[2] divides the Feelings, in a threefold manner, into
those of States, those of Cognitions, and those

Hillebrand.

of Appetency (will and desire); and again into
Real, Sympathetic, and Ideal.

Herbart[3] distributes them into three classes; — 1°, Feelings which
are determined by the character of the thing

Herbart.

felt; 2°, Feelings which depend on the disposi-
tion of the feeling mind; 3°, Feelings which are intermediate and
mixed.

Carus[4] (of Leipzig, — the late Carus) thus distributes them.
"Pure feeling," he says, "has relation either to

Carus.

Reason, and in this case we obtain the Intellect-
ual Feelings; or it has relation to Desire and Will, and in this case
we have the moral feelings." Between these two classes, the Intellectual and the Moral Feelings, there are placed the Æsthetic Feelings, or feelings of Taste, to which he also adds a fourth class, that
of the Religious Feelings.

Such are a few of the more illustrious divisions of the Feelings
into their primary classes. It is needless to enter at present into
any discussion of the merits and demerits of these distributions. I
shall hereafter endeavor to show you, that they may be divided, in
the first place, into two great classes, — the Higher and the Lower,
— the Mental and the Corporeal, in a word, into Sentiments and
Sensations.

---

1 *Anthropologie*, § 144-146, p. 295 *et seq.*, 3d
edit. 1626. — ED.

2 *Anthropologie*, ii. 283. — ED.

3 *Lehrbuch zur Psychologie*, § 98. *Werke*, vol.
v. p. 72. On the divisions of the Feelings
mentioned in the text, see Biunde, *Versuch*

*einer systematischen Behandlung der empirischen
Psychologie*, ii. § 210, p. 74, edit. 1831. Cf.
Scheidler, *Psychologie*, § 64, p. 443, edit. 1833.
— ED.

4 *Psychologie*, *Werke*, i. 428, edit. Leipsic,
1808. — ED.

LECTURE XLII.

THE FEELINGS. — THEORY OF PLEASURE AND PAIN.

In our last Lecture, we commenced the consideration of the Sec-

The Feelings.

ond Great Class of the Mental Phænomena, — the phænomena of Feeling, — the phænomena of Pleasure and Pain.

Though manifestations of the same indivisible subject, and them-

Cognitions, Feelings and Conation, — their essential peculiarities.

selves only possible through each other, the three classes of mental phænomena still admit of a valid discrimination in theory, and require severally a separate consideration in the philosophy of mind. I formerly stated to you, that though knowledge, though consciousness, be the necessary condition not only of the phænomena of Cognition, but of the phænomena of Feeling, and of Conation, yet the attempts of philosophers to reduce the two latter classes to the first, and thus to constitute the faculty of Cognition into the one fundamental power of mind, had been necessarily unsuccessful; because, though the phænomena of Feeling and of Conation appear only as they appear in consciousness, and, therefore, in cognition; yet consciousness shows us in these phænomena certain qualities, which are not contained, either explicitly or implicitly, in the phænomena of Cognition itself. The characters by which these three classes are reciprocally discriminated are the following. — In the

Cognition.

phænomena of Cognition, consciousness distinguishes an object known from the subject knowing. This subject may be of two kinds: — it may either be the quality of something different from the ego; or it may be a modification of the ego or subject itself. In the former case, the object, which may be called for the sake of discrimination the *object-object*, is given as something different from the percipient subject. In the latter case, the object, which may be called the *subject-object*, is given as really identical with the conscious ego, but still consciousness distinguishes it, as an accident, from the ego; — as the subject of that accident, it projects, as it were, this subjective phænomenon from itself, — views it at a distance, — in a word, objectifies it. This discrimination of self from self, — this objectification, — is the quality which constitutes the essential peculiarity of Cognition.

In the phænomena of Feeling, — the phænomena of Pleasure and

Feeling, — how discriminated from Cognition.

Pain, — on the contrary, consciousness does not place the mental modification or state before itself; it does not contemplate it apart, — as separate from itself, — but is, as it were, fused into one. The peculiarity of Feeling, therefore, is that there is nothing but what is subjectively subjective; there is no object different from self, — no objectification of any mode of self. We are, indeed, able to constitute our states of pain and pleasure into objects of reflection, but in so far as they are objects of reflection, they are not feelings, but only reflex cognitions of feelings.

In the phænomena of Conation, — the phænomena of Desire and

Conation, — how discriminated from Cognition.

Will, — there is, as in those of Cognition, an object, and this object is also an object of knowledge. Will and desire are only possible through knowledge, — "Ignoti nulla cupido." But though both cognition and conation bear relation to an object, they are discriminated by the difference of this relation itself. In cognition, there exists no want; and the object, whether objective or subjective, is not sought for, nor avoided; whereas in conation, there is a want, and a tendency supposed, which results in an endeavor, either to obtain the object, when the cognitive faculties represent it as fitted to afford the fruition of the want; or to ward off the object, if these faculties represent it as calculated to frustrate the tendency, of its accomplishment.

The feelings Pleasure and Pain and the Conations are, thus, though

Conation, — how discriminated from Feeling.

so frequently confounded by psychologists, easily distinguished. It is, for example, altogether different to feel hunger and thirst, as states of pain, and to desire or will their appeasement; and still more different is it to desire or will their appeasement, and to enjoy the pleasure afforded in the act of this appeasement itself. Pain and pleasure, as feelings, belong exclusively to the present; whereas conation has reference only to the future, for conation is a longing, — a striving, either to maintain the continuance of the present state, or to exchange it for another. Thus, conation is not the feeling of pleasure and pain, but the power of overt activity, which pain and pleasure set in motion.

But although, in theory, the Feelings are thus to be discriminated from the Desires and Volitions, they are, as I have frequently observed, not to be considered as really divided. Both are conditions of perhaps all our mental states; and while the Cognitions go principally to determine our speculative sphere of existence, the Feelings and the Conations more especially concur in regulating our practical.

In my last Lecture, I stated the grounds on which it is expedient to consider the phænomena of Feeling prior to discussing those of Conation; — but before entering on the consideration of the several feelings, and before stating under what heads, and in what order, these are to be arranged, I think it proper, in the first place, to take up the general question, — What are the general conditions which determine the existence of Pleasure and Pain; for pleasure and pain are the phænomena which constitute the essential attribute of feeling, under all its modifications?

What are the general conditions which determine the existence of Pleasure and Pain?

In the consideration of this question, I shall pursue the following order : — I shall, first of all, state the abstract Theory of Pleasure and Pain, in other words, enounce the fundamental law by which these phænomena are governed, in all their manifestations. I shall, then, take an historical retrospect of the opinions of philosophers in regard to this subject, in order to show in what relation the doctrine I would support stands to previous speculations. This being accomplished, we shall then be prepared to inquire, how far the theory in question is borne out by the special modifications of Feeling, and how far it affords us a common principle on which to account for the phænomena of Pleasure and Pain, under every accidental form they may assume.

Order of discussion.

I proceed, therefore, to deliver in somewhat abstruse formulæ, the theory of pleasure. The meaning of these formulæ I cannot expect should be fully apprehended, in the first instance, — far less can I expect that the validity of the theory should be recognized, before the universality of its application shall be illustrated in examples.

1. The theory of Pleasure and Pain, — stated in the abstract.

1. Man exists only as he lives; as an intelligent and sensible being, he consciously lives, but this only as he consciously energizes. Human existence is only a more general expression for human life, and human life only a more general expression for the sum of energies, in which that life is realized, and through which it is manifested in consciousness. In a word, life is energy, and conscious energy is conscious life.[1]

First momentum.

---

1 Cf Aristotle, *Eth. Nic.* ix. 9; x. 4. — ED. Lossius, *Lexikon v. Vergnügen* ; theory of cessation and activity; makes partly active, partly passive; partly tending to rest, partly to action. — *Memorandum.*

In explanation of this paragraph, and of those which are to follow, I may observe, that the term *energy*, which is equivalent to *act*, *activity*, or *operation*, is here used to comprehend also all the mixed states of action and passion, of which we are conscious; for, inasmuch

Comprehension of the term energy.

as we are conscious of any modification of mind, there is necessarily more than a mere passivity of the subject; consciousness itself implying at least a reäction. Be this, however, as it may, the nouns *energy*, *act*, *activity*, *operation*, with the correspondent verbs, are to be understood to denote, indifferently and in general, all the processes of our higher and our lower life, of which we are conscious.[1] This being premised, I proceed to the second proposition.

II. Human existence, human life, human energy, is not unlimited,

Second.

but on the contrary, determined to a certain number of modes, through which alone it can possibly be exerted. These different modes of action are called, in different relations, *powers*, *faculties*, *capacities*, *dispositions*, *habits*.

In reference to this paragraph, it is only necessary to recall to your attention, that *power* denotes either a faculty or

Explanation of terms, — power, faculty, etc.

a capacity; *faculty* denotes a power of acting, *capacity* a power of being acted upon or suffering; *disposition*, a natural, and *habit*, an acquired, tendency to act or suffer.[2] In reference to habit, it ought however to be observed, that an acquired necessarily supposes a natural tendency. Habit, therefore, comprehends a disposition and something supervening on a disposition. The disposition, which at first was a feebler tendency, becomes, in the end, by custom, that is, by a frequent repetition of exerted energy, a stronger tendency. Disposition is the rude original, habit is the perfect consummation.

III. Man, as he consciously exists, is the subject of pleasure and

Third.

pain; and these of various kinds: but as man only consciously exists in and through the exertion of certain determinate powers, so it is only through the exertion of these powers that he becomes the subject of pleasure and pain; each power being in itself at once the faculty of a specific energy, and a capacity of an appropriate pleasure or pain, as the concomitant of that energy.

Fourth.

IV. The energy of each power of conscious existence having, as its reflex or concomitant, an appropriate pleasure or pain, and no pain or pleasure being competent

1 Here a written interpolation — *Occupation*, *exercise*, perhaps better [expressions than energy, as applying equally to all mental processes, whether active or passive.] See below, p. 595. — ED.

2 See above, lect. x. p. 123. — ED.

to man, except as the concomitant of some determinate energy of life, the all-important question arises, — What is the general law under which these counter-phænomena arise, in all their special manifestations?

In reference to this proposition, I would observe that pleasure and pain are opposed to each other as contraries, not

Pleasure and Pain opposed as contraries, not as contradictories.

as contradictories, that is, the affirmation of the one implies the negation of the other, but the negation of the one does not infer the affirmation of the other; for there may be a third or intermediate state, which is neither one of pleasure nor one of pain, but one of indifference. Whether such a state of indifference do ever actually exist; or whether, if it do, it be not a complex state in which are blended an equal complement of pains and pleasures, it is not necessary, at this stage of our progress, to inquire. It is sufficient, in considering the quality of pleasure as one opposed to the quality of pain, to inquire, what are the proximate causes which determine them: or, if this cannot be answered, what is the general fact or law which regulates their counter-manifestation; and if such a law can be discovered for the one, it is evident that it will enable us also to explain the other, for the science of contraries is one. I now proceed to the fifth proposition.

V. The answer to the question proposed is: — the more perfect, the more pleasurable, the energy; the more

Fifth.

imperfect, the more painful.

In reference to this proposition, it is to be observed that the answer here given is precise, but inexplicit; it is the enouncement of the law in its most abstract form, and requires at once development and explanation. This I shall endeavor to give in the following propositions.

VI. The perfection of an energy is twofold; 1°, By relation to the power of which it is the exertion, and 2°, By

Sixth.

relation to the object about which it is conversant. The former relation affords what may be called its *subjective*, the latter what may be called its *objective*, condition.

The explanation and development of the preceding proposition is given in the following.

VII. By relation to its power: — An energy is perfect, when it is tantamount to the full, and not to more than the

Seventh.

full, complement of free or spontaneous energy, which the power is capable of exerting; an energy is imperfect, either 1°, When the power is restrained from putting forth the whole amount of energy it would otherwise tend to do, or, 2°, When it is stimulated to put forth a larger amount than that to which it is spontaneously disposed. The amount or quantum of energy in the case of a single power is of two kinds, — 1°, An intensive, and 2°, A protensive; the former expressing the higher degree, the latter the longer duration, of the exertion. A perfect energy is, therefore, that which is evolved by a power, both in the degree and for the continuance to which it is competent without straining; an imperfect energy, that which is evolved by a power in a lower or in a higher degree, for a shorter or for a longer continuance, than, if left to itself, it would freely exert. There are, thus, two elements of the perfection, and, consequently, two elements of the pleasure, of a simple energy : — its adequate degree and its adequate duration ; and four ways in which such an energy may be imperfect, and, consequently, painful ; inasmuch as its degree may be either too high, or too low ; its duration either too long, or too short.

When we do not limit our consideration to the simple energies of individual powers, but look to complex states, in which a plurality of powers may be called simultaneously into action, we have, besides the intensive and protensive quantities of energy, a third kind, to wit, the extensive quantity. A state is said to contain a greater amount of extensive energy, in proportion as it forms the complement of a greater number of simultaneously coöperating powers. This complement, it is evident, may be conceived as made up either of energies all intensively and protensively perfect and pleasurable, or of energies all intensively and protensively imperfect and painful, or of energies partly perfect, partly imperfect, and this in every combination afforded by the various perfections and imperfections of the intensive and protensive quantities. It may be here noticed, that the intensive and the two other quantities stand always in an inverse ratio to each other; that is, the higher the degree of any energy, the shorter is its continuance, and, during its continuance, the more completely does it constitute the whole mental state, — does it engross the whole disposable consciousness of the mind. The maximum of intensity is thus the minimum of continuance and of extension. So much for the perfection, and proportional pleasure, of an energy or state of energies, by relation to the power out of which it is elicited. This paragraph requires, I think, no commentary.

VIII. By relation to the object (and by the term *object*, be it observed, is here denoted every objective cause by which a power is determined to activity), about which it is conversant, an energy is perfect, when this object is of such a character as to afford to its power the condition requi-

Eighth.

site to let it spring to full spontaneous activity; imperfect, when the object is of such a character as either, on the one hand, to stimulate the power to a degree, or to a continuance, of activity beyond its maximum of free exertion; or, on the other hand, to thwart it in its tendency towards this its natural limit. An object is, consequently, pleasurable or painful, inasmuch as it thus determines a power to perfect or to imperfect energy.

But an object, or complement of objects simultaneously presented, may not only determine one but a plurality of powers into coäctivity. The complex state, which thus arises, is pleasurable, in proportion as its constitutive energies are severally more perfect; painful, in proportion as these are more imperfect; and in proportion as an object, or a complement of objects, occasions the average perfection or the average imperfection of the complex state, is it, in like manner, pleasurable or painful.

IX. Pleasure is, thus, the result of certain harmonious relations, — of certain agreements; pain, on the contrary, the effect of certain unharmonious relations — of certain disagreements. The pleasurable is, therefore, not inappropriately called *the agreeable,* the painful *the disagreeable;* and, in conformity to this doctrine, pleasure and pain may be thus defined:

Ninth.

Definitions of Pleasure and Pain.

Pleasure is a reflex of the spontaneous and unimpeded exertion of a power, of whose energy we are conscious.[1] Pain, a reflex of the overstrained or repressed exertion of such a power.

I shall say a word in illustration of these definitions. Taking pleasure, — pleasure is defined to be the reflex of energy, and of perfect energy, and not to be either energy or the perfection of energy itself, — and why? It is not simply defined an energy, exertion, or act, because some energies are not pleasurable, — being either painful or indifferent. It is not simply defined the perfection of an energy, because we can easily separate in thought the perfection of an act, a conscious act, from any feeling of pleasure in its performance. The same holds true, *mutatis mutandis,* of the definition of pain, as a reflex of imperfect energy.

The definition of Pleasure illustrated.

1. Pleasure the reflex of energy.

Again, pleasure is defined the reflex of the spontaneous and unimpeded, — of free and unimpeded, exertion of a power, of whose

---

1 This is substantially the definition of Aristotle, whose doctrine, as expounded in the 10th book of the *Nicomachean Ethics,* is more fully stated below, p. 584. In the less accurate dissertation, which occurs in the 7th book of the same treatise, and which perhaps properly belongs to the *Endemian Ethics,* the pleasure is identified with the energy itself. — ED.

energy we are conscious. Here the term *spontaneous* refers to the

2. Spontaneous and unimpeded.

subjective, the term *unimpeded* to the objective, perfection. Touching the term *spontaneous*, every power, all conditions being supplied, and all impediments being removed, tends, of its proper nature and without effort, to put forth a certain determinate maximum, intensive and protensive, of free energy. This determinate maximum of free energy, it, therefore, exerts spontaneously: if a less amount than this be actually put forth, a certain quantity of tendency has been forcibly repressed; whereas, if a greater than this has been actually exerted, a certain amount of nisus has been forcibly stimulated in the power. The term *spontaneously*, therefore, provides that the exertion of the power has not been constrained beyond the proper limit, — the natural maximum, to which, if left to itself, it freely springs.

Again, in regard to the term *unimpeded*, — this stipulates that the power should not be checked in the spring it would thus spontaneously make to its maximum of energy, that is, it is supposed that the conditions requisite to allow this spring have been supplied, and that all impediments to it have been removed. This postulates of course the presence of an object. The definition further states, that the exertion must be that of a power of whose energy we are

3. Of which we are conscious.

conscious. This requires no illustration. There are powers in man, the activities of which lie beyond the sphere of consciousness. But it is of the very essence of pleasure and pain to be felt, and there is no feeling out of consciousness. What has now been said of the terms used in the definition of pleasure, renders all comment superfluous on the parallel expressions employed in that of pain.

On this doctrine it is to be observed, that there are given differ-

Pleasure, — Positive and Negative.

ent kinds of pleasure, and different kinds of pain. In the first place, these are twofold, inasmuch as each is either Positive and Absolute, or Negative and Relative. In regard to the former, the mere negation of pain does, by relation to pain, constitute a state of pleasure. Thus, the removal of the toothache replaces us in a state which, though one really of indifference, is, by contrast to our previous agony, felt as pleasurable. This is negative or relative pleasure. Positive or absolute pleasure, on the contrary, is all that pleasure which we feel above a state of indifference, and which is, therefore, prized as a good in itself, and not simply as the removal of an evil.

On the same principle, pain is also divided into Positive or Absolute, and into Negative or Relative. But, in the second place, there is, moreover, a subdivision of positive pain into that which accompanies a repression of the spontaneous energy of a power, and that which is conjoined with its effort, when stimulated to over-activity.[1]

Pain, — Positive and Negative.

Positive pain, subdivided.

I proceed now to state certain corollaries, which flow immediately from the preceding doctrine.

In the first place, as the powers which, in an individual, are either preponderantly strong by nature, or have become preponderantly strong by habit, have comparatively more perfect energies; so the pleasures which accompany these will be proportionally intense and enduring. But this being the case, the individual will be disposed principally, if not exclusively, to exercise these more vigorous powers, for their energies afford him the largest complement of purest pleasure. " Trahit sua quemque voluptas,"[2] each has his ruling passion.

Corollaries from preceding doctrine.

1. The individual will be disposed to exercise his more vigorous powers.

But, in the second place, as the exercise of a power is the only means by which it is invigorated, but as, at the same time, this exercise, until the development be accomplished, elicits imperfect, and, therefore, painful, or at least less pleasurable, energy, — it follows that those faculties which stand the most in need of cultivation, are precisely those which the least secure it; while, on the contrary, those which are already more fully developed, are precisely those which present the strongest inducements for their still higher invigoration.

2. Those faculties which most need cultivation, the least secure it.

---

1 [With the foregoing theory compare Hutcheson, *System of Moral Philosophy*, i. p. 21 *et seq.* Lüders, *Kritik d. Statistik*, p. 457-9. Tiedemann, *Psychologie*, p. 151. edit. 1804.]

[Bonnet, *Essai Analytique sur l'Ame*, caps. xvii. xx. Ferguson, *Prin. of Moral and Political Science*, Part ii. c. 1, § 2. — Ed.]

2 Virgil, *Ecl.* ii. 65. — Ed.

LECTURE XLIII.

THE FEELINGS. — HISTORICAL ACCOUNT OF THEORIES OF PLEASURE AND PAIN.

IN my last Lecture, I gave an abstract statement of that Theory of Pleasure and Pain, which, I think, is compe-

Recapitulation.

tent, and exclusively competent, to explain the whole multiform phænomena of our Feelings, — a theory, consequently, which those whole phænomena concur in establishing. It is, in truth, nothing but a generalization of what is essential in the concrete facts themselves. Before, however, proceeding to show, by its application to particular cases, that this theory affords us a simple principle, on which to account for the most complicated and perplexing phænomena of Feeling, I shall attempt to give you a

General historical notices of Theories of the Pleasurable.

slight survey of the most remarkable opinions on this point. To do this, however imperfectly, is of the more importance, as there is no work in which any such historical deduction is attempted; but principally, because the various theories of philosophers on the doctrine of the pleasurable, are found, when viewed in connection, all to concur in manifesting the truth of that one which I have proposed to you, — a theory, in fact, which is the resumption and complement of them all. In attempting this survey, I by no means propose to furnish even an indication of all the opinions that have been held in regard to the pleasurable in general, nor even of all the doctrines on this subject that have been advanced by the authors to whom I specially refer. I can only afford to speak of the more remarkable theories, and, in these, only of the more essential particulars. But, in point of fact, though there is no end of what has been written upon pleasure and pain, considered in their moral relations and effects, the speculations in regard to their psychological causes and conditions are comparatively few. In general, I may also premise that there is apparent a remarkable gravitation in the various doctrines promulgated on this point, towards a common centre; and, however one-sided and insufficient the several opinions may appear, they are all substantially grounded upon truth, being usually right in what they affirm, and wrong only in what they deny; all are reflections, but only partial reflections, of the truth.

These opinions, I may further remark, fall into two great classes; and at the head of each there is found one of the two great philosophers of antiquity, — Plato being the founder of the one general theory, Aristotle of the other. But though the distinction of these classes pervades the whole history of the doctrines, I do not deem it necessary to follow this classification in the following observations, but shall content myself with a chronological arrangement.

These theories fall into two grand classes, — the Platonic and Aristotelic.

Plato is the first philosopher who can be said to have attempted the generalization of a law which regulates the manifestation of pleasure and pain; and it is but scanty justice to acknowledge that no subsequent philosopher has handled the subject with greater ingenuity and acuteness. For though the theory of Aristotle be more fully developed, and, as I am convinced, upon the whole the most complete and accurate which we possess, it is but fair to add, that he borrowed a considerable portion of it from Plato, whose doctrine he corrected and enlarged.

Plato the first to attempt the generalization of a law of Pleasure and Pain.

The opinion of Plato regarding the source of pleasure is contained in the *Philebus*, and in the ninth book of the *Republic*, with incidental allusions to his theory in other dialogues. Thus, in the opening of the *Phædo*,[1] we have the following statement of its distinguishing principle, — that a state of pleasure is always preceded by a state of pain. Phædo, in describing the conduct of Socrates in the prison and on the eve of death, narrates, that "sitting upright on the bed he (Socrates) drew up his leg, and stroking it with his hand, said at the same time, — 'What a wonderful thing is this, my friends, which men call the pleasant and agreeable! and how wonderful a relation does it bear by nature to that which seems to be its contrary, the painful! For they are unwilling to be present with us both together; and yet, if any person pursues and obtains the one, he is most always under a necessity of accepting also the other, as if both of them depended from a single summit. And it seems to me' (he continues), 'that if Æsop had perceived this, he would have written a fable upon it, and have told us that the Deity, being willing to reconcile the conflictive natures, but at the same time unable to accomplish this design, con-

Plato's theory, — that a state of pleasure is always preceded by a state of pain.

joined their summits in an existence one and the same; and that hence it comes to pass that whoever partakes of the one, is soon after compelled to participate in the other. And this, as it appears, is the case with myself at present; for the pain which was before in my leg, through the stricture of the fetter, is now succeeded by a pleasant sensation.'"

The following extract from the *Philebus*[1] will, however, show more fully the purport and grounds of his opinion:

Quotation from the Philebus.

"*Socrates.* I say then, that whenever the harmony in the frame of any animal is broken, a breach is then made in its constitution, and, at the same time, rise is given to pains.

"*Protarchus.* You say what is highly probable.

"*Soc.* But when the harmony is restored, and the breach is healed, we should say that then pleasure is produced; if points of so great importance may be despatched at once in so few words.

"*Prot.* In my opinion, O Socrates, you say what is very true; but let us try if we can show these truths in a light still clearer.

"*Soc.* Are not such things as ordinarily happen, and are manifest to us all, the most easy to be understood?

"*Prot.* What things do you mean?

"*Soc.* Want of food makes a breach in the animal system, and, at the same time, gives the pain of hunger.

"*Prot.* True.

"*Soc.* And food, in filling up the breach again, gives a pleasure.

"*Prot.* Right.

"*Soc.* Want of drink also, interrupting the circulation of the blood and humors, brings on us corruption together with the pain of thirst; but the virtue of a liquid in moistening and replenishing the parts dried up, yields a pleasure. In like manner, unnatural suffocating heat, in dissolving the texture of the parts, gives a painful sensation; but a cooling again, a refreshment agreeable to nature, affects us with a sense of pleasure.

"*Prot.* Most certainly.

"*Soc.* And the concretion of the animal humors through cold, contrary to their nature, occasions pain; but a return to their pristine state of fluidity, and a restoring of the natural circulation, produce pleasure. See, then, whether you think this general account of the matter not amiss, concerning that sort of being which I said was composed of indefinite and definite, — that, when by nature any beings of that sort become animated with soul, their passage into corruption, or a total dissolution, is accompanied with pain;

1 P. 31. — ED.

and their entrance into existence, the assembling of all those particles which compose the nature of such a being, is attended with a sense of pleasure.

"*Prot.* I admit your account of this whole matter; for, as it appears to me, it bears on it the stamp of truth."

And, in a subsequent part of the dialogue, Socrates is made to approve of the doctrine of the Eleatic School, in regard to the unreality of pleasure, as a thing always in generation, that is, always in progress towards existence, but never absolutely existent.

"*Soc.* But what think you now of this? Have we not heard it said concerning pleasure, that it is a thing always in generation, always produced anew, and which, having no stability of being, cannot properly be said to be at all? For some ingenious persons there are, who endeavor to show us that such is the nature of pleasure; and we are much obliged to them for this their account of it."[1]

Then, after an expository discourse on the Eleatic doctrine, Socrates proceeds:[2]—"Therefore, as I said in the beginning of this argumentation, we are much obliged to the persons who have given us this account of pleasure, — that the essence of it consists in being always generated anew, but that never has it any kind of being. For it is plain that these persons would laugh at a man who asserted, that pleasure and good were the same thing.

"*Prot.* Certainly they would.

"*Soc.* And these very persons would undoubtedly laugh at those men, wherever they met with them, who place their chief good and end in a becoming, — an approximation to existence?

"*Prot.* How? what sort of men do you mean?

"*Soc.* Such as, in freeing themselves from hunger or thirst, or any of the uneasinesses from which they are freed by generation, — by tending towards being, are so highly delighted with the action of removing those uneasinesses, as to declare they would not choose to live without suffering thirst and hunger, nor without feeling all those other sensations which may be said to follow from such kinds of uneasiness."

The sum of Plato's doctrine on this subject is this, — that pleasure is nothing absolute, nothing positive, but a mere relation to, a mere negation of, pain. Pain is the root, the condition, the antecedent of pleasure, and the latter is only a restoration of the feeling subject, from a state contrary to nature to a state conformable with nature. Pleasure is the mere replenishing of a vacuum, —

Sum of Plato's doctrine of the Pleasurable.

the mere satisfying of a want. With this principal doctrine, — that pleasure is only the negation of pain, Plato connects sundry collateral opinions in conformity to his general system. That pleasure, for example, is not a good, and that it is nothing real or existent, but something only in the progress towards existence, — never being, ever becoming (ἀεὶ γιγνόμενον, οὐδέποτε ὄν).

Aristotle saw the partiality and imperfection of this theory, and himself proposed another, which should supply its deficiencies. His speculations concerning the pleasurable are to be found in his Ethical Treatises, and, to say nothing of the two lesser works, the *Magna Moralia* and the *Eudemian Ethics*,[1] you will find the subject fully discussed in the seventh and tenth Books of the *Nicomachean Ethics*. I shall say nothing of Aristotle's arguments against Eudoxus, as to whether pleasure be the chief good, and against Plato, as to whether it be a good at all, — these are only ethical questions; I shall confine my observations to the psychological problem touching the law which governs its manifestation. Aristotle, in the first place, refutes the Platonic theory, that pleasure is only the removal of a pain. "Since it is asserted," he says,[2] "that pain is a want, an indigence (ἔνδεια) contrary to nature, pleasure will be a repletion, a filling up (ἀναπλήρωσις) of that want in conformity to nature. But want and its repletion are corporeal affections. Now if pleasure be the repletion of a want contrary to nature, that which contains the repletion will contain the pleasure, and the faculty of being pleased. But the want and its repletion are in the body; the body, therefore, will be pleased, — the body will be the subject of this feeling. But the feeling of pleasure is an affection of the soul. Pleasure, therefore, cannot be merely a repletion. True it is, that pleasure is consequent on the repletion of a want, as pain is consequent on the want itself. For we are pleased when our wants are satisfied; pained when this is prevented.

"It appears," proceeds the Stagirite, "that this opinion has originated in an exclusive consideration of our bodily pains and pleasures, and more especially those relative to food. For when inanition has taken place, and we have felt the pains of hunger, we experience pleasure in its repletion. But the same does not hold good

The doctrine of Aristotle proposed to correct and supplement the Platonic.

Aristotle refutes the Platonic doctrine, — that pleasure is only the removal of a pain.

---

1 The genuineness of these two works is questionable. The chapters on pleasure in *Eudemian Ethics* are identical with those in the 7th book of the *Nicomachean*, being part of the three books which are common to both treatises. — Ed.

2 *Eth. Nic.* x. 3. — Ed.

in reference to all our pleasures. For the pleasure we find, for example, in mathematical contemplations, and even in some of the senses, is wholly unaccompanied with pain. Thus the gratification we derive from the energies of hearing, smell, and sight, is not consequent on any foregone pain, and in them there is, therefore, no repletion of a want. Moreover, hope, and the recollection of past good, are pleasing; but are the pleasures from these a repletion? This cannot be maintained; for in them there is no want preceding, which could admit of repletion. Hence it is manifest, that pleasure is not the negation of a pain."

Having disposed of Plato's theory, Aristotle proposes his own; and his doctrine, in as far as it goes, is altogether conformable to that I have given to you, as the one that appears to me the true.

The theory of Aristotle.

Pleasure is maintained by Aristotle to be the concomitant of energy,—of perfect energy, whether of the functions of Sense or Intellect; and perfect energy he describes as that which proceeds from a power in health and vigor, and exercised upon an object relatively excellent, that is, suited to call forth the power into unimpeded activity. Pleasure, though the result, — the concomitant of perfect action, he distinguishes from the perfect action itself. It is not the action, it is not the perfection, though it be consequent on action, and a necessary efflorescence of its perfection. Pleasure is thus defined by Aristotle to be the concomitant of the unimpeded energy of a natural power, faculty, or acquired habit.[1] "Thus when a sense, for example, is in perfect health, and it is presented with a suitable object of the most perfect kind, there is elicited the most perfect energy, which, at every instant of its continuance, is accompanied with pleasure. The same holds good with the function of Imagination, Thought, etc. Pleasure is the concomitant in every case where powers and objects are in themselves perfect, and between which there subsists a suitable relation. Hence arises the pleasure of novelty. For on the first presentation of a new object, the energy of cognition is intensely directed upon it, and the pleasure high; whereas when the object is again and again presented, the energy relaxes, and the pleasure declines. But pleasure is not merely the consequent of the most perfect exertion of power; for it reäcts upon the power itself, by raising, invigorating, and perfecting its development. For we make no progress in a study, except we feel a pleasure in its pursuit.

Pleasure, according to Aristotle, is the concomitant of the unimpeded energy of a power.

Aristotle quoted.

---

1 See above, p. 577. — ED.

"Every different power has its peculiar pleasure and its peculiar pain; and each power is as much corrupted by its appropriate pain as it is perfected by its appropriate pleasure. Pleasure is not something that arises, — that comes into existence, part after part; it is, on the contrary, complete at every indivisible instant of its continuance. It is not, therefore, as Plato holds, a change, a motion, a generation (γένεσις, κίνησις), which exists piecemeal as it were, and successively in time, and only complete after a certain term of endurance; but on the contrary something instantaneous, and, from moment to moment, perfect."[1]

Such were the two theories touching the law of pleasure and pain, propounded by the two principal thinkers of antiquity. To their doctrines on this point we find nothing added, worthy of commemoration, by the succeeding philosophers of Greece and Rome; nay, we do not find that in antiquity these doctrines received any farther development or confirmation. Among the ancients, however, the Aristotelic theory seems to have soon superseded the Platonic; for, even among the lower Platonists themselves, there is no attempt to vindicate the doctrine of their master, in so far as to assert that all pleasure is only a relief from pain. Their sole endeavor is to reconcile Plato's opinion with that of Aristotle, by showing that the former did not mean to extend the principle in question to pleasure in general, but applied it only to the pleasures of certain of the senses. And, in truth, various passages in the *Philebus* and in the ninth book of the *Republic*, afford countenance to this interpretation.[2] Be this, however, as it may, it was only in more recent times that the Platonic doctrine, in all its exclusive rigor, was again revived; and that too by philosophers who seem not to have been aware of the venerable authority in favor of the paradox which they proposed as new. I may add that the philosophers, who in modern times have speculated upon the conditions of the pleasurable, seem, in general, unaware of what had been attempted on this problem by the ancients; and it is indeed this circumstance alone that enables us to explain, why the modern theories on this subject, in principle the same with that of Aristotle, have remained so inferior to his in the great virtues of a theory, — comprehension and simplicity.

Marginal note: Nothing added in antiquity to the two theories of Plato and Aristotle.

---

[1] See *Eth. Nic.* x. 4, 5. — ED. [On Aristotle's doctrine of the Pleasurable; see Tennemann, *Gesh. der Philosophie*, iii. 200.]

[2] [Plato, as well as Aristotle, seems to have made pleasure consist in a harmonious, pain in a disharmonious, energy. Every energy, both of Sense and Intellect, is, according to Plato, accompanied with a sensation of pleasure and pain. *Republic*, ix. 557. *Philebus*, p. 211, edit. Bip. See Tennemann, *Geschichte der Philosophie*, ii. p. 290.]

Before, however, proceeding to the consideration of subsequent opinions, it may be proper to observe that the theories of Plato and Aristotle, however opposite in appearance, may easily be reduced to unity, and the theory of which I have given you the general expression, will be found to be the consummated complement of both. The two doctrines differ only essentially in this: — that the one makes a previous pain the universal condition of pleasure; while the other denies this condition as a general law, and holds that pleasure is a positive reality, and more than the mere alternative of pain. Now, in regard to this difference, it must be admitted, on the one hand, that in so far as the instances are concerned, on which Plato attempts to establish his principle, Aristotle is successful in showing, that these are only special cases, and do not warrant the unlimited conclusion in support of which they are adduced.

The theories of Plato and Aristotle reduced to unity.

But, on the other hand, it must be confessed that Aristotle has not shown the principle to be false, — that all pleasure is an escape from pain. He shows, indeed, that the analogy of hunger, thirst, and other bodily affections, cannot be extended to the gratification we experience from the energies of intellect, — cannot be extended even to that which we experience in the exercise of the higher senses. It is true, that the pleasure I experience in this particular act of vision, cannot be explained from the pain I had felt in another particular act of vision, immediately preceding; and if this example were enough, it would certainly be made out that pleasure is not merely the negation of a foregoing pain. But let us ascend a step higher and inquire, — would it not be painful if the faculty of vision (to take the same example) were wholly restrained from operation? Now it will not be denied, that the repression of any power in its natural *nisus*, — *conatus*, to action, is positively painful; and, therefore, that the exertion of a power, if it afforded only a negation of that positive pain, and were, in its own nature, absolutely indifferent, would, by relation to the pain from which it yields us a relief, appear to us a real pleasure. We may, therefore, I think, maintain, with perfect truth, that as the holding back of any power from exercise is positively painful, so its passing into energy is, were it only the removal of that painful repression, negatively pleasurable; on this ground, consequently, and to this extent, we may rightly hold with Plato, — that every state of pleasure and free energy is, in fact, the escape from an alternative state of pain and compulsory inaction.

In what sense the Platonic dogma is true.

So far we are warranted in going. But we should be wrong were we to constitute this partial truth into an unlimited, — an exclusive principle; that is, were we to maintain that the whole pleasure we

The doctrine that the whole pleasure of activity arises from the negation of the pain of forced iner- tion, — erroneous.

derive from the exercise of our powers, is noth- ing more than a negation of the pain we expe- rience from their forced inertion. This I say would be an erroneous, because an absolute, con- clusion. For the pleasure we find in the free play of our faculties is, as we are most fully con- scious, far more than simply a superseding of pain. That philoso- phy, indeed, would only provoke a smile which would maintain, that all pleasure is in itself only a zero, — a nothing, which becomes a something only by relation to the reality of pain which it annuls.

After compulsory in- ertion, pleasure high- er than in ordinary circumstances, — ex- plained.

It is true, indeed, that after a compulsory iner- tion, our pleasure, in the first exertion of our faculties, is frequently far higher than that which we experience in their ordinary exercise, when left at liberty. But this does not, at least does not exclusively, arise from the contrast of the previous and subse- quent states of pain and pleasure, but principally because the powers are in excessive vigor, — at least in excessive erethism or excitation, and have thus a greater complement of intenser energy suddenly to expend. On the principle, therefore, that the degree of pleasure is always in the ratio of the degree of spontaneous activity, the pleas- ure immediately consequent on the emancipation of a power from thraldom, would, if the power remain uninjured by the constraint, be naturally greater, because the energy would in that case be, for a season, more intense. At the same time, the state of pleasure would in this case appear to be higher than what it absolutely is; because it would be set off by proximate contrast with a previous state of pain. Thus it is that a basin of water of ordinary blood heat, ap- pears hot, if we plunge in it a hand which had previously been dipped in snow; and cold, if we immerse in it another which had previously been placed in water of a still higher temperature. But it is unfair to apply this magnifying effect of contrast to the one

Unfair to apply the magnifying effect of contrast to disprove the positive reality of pleasure more than of pain.

relative and not to the other; and any argument drawn from it against the positive reality of pleasure, applies equally to disprove the positive reality of pain. The true doctrine I hold to be this : — that pain and pleasure are, as I have said, each to be considered both as Absolute and as Relative; — absolute, that is, each is something real, and would exist were the other taken out of being; relative, that is, each is felt as greater or less by immediate contrast to the other. I may illustrate this by the analogy of a scale. Let the state of indifference, — that is, the negation of both pain and pleasure, be marked as zero, let the degrees of pain be denoted by a descending series of numbers below zero, and the degrees of pleasure by an ascending series of numbers above zero. Now, suppose the degree of pain we feel from a certain state of hunger, to be six below zero; in this case our feeling, in the act of eating, will not merely rise to zero, that is, to the mere negation of pain, as the Platonic theory holds, but to some degree of positive pleasure, say six. And here I may observe, that, were the insufficiency of the Platonic theory shown by nothing else, this would be done by the absurd consequences it implies, in relation to the function of nutrition alone; for if its principles be true, then would our gratification from the appeasement of hunger, be equally great by one kind of viand as by another.

Pleasure and pain both Absolute and Relative.

Thus, then, the counter theories of Plato and Aristotle are, as I have said, right in what they affirm, wrong in what they deny; each contains the truth, but not the whole truth. By supplying, therefore, to either that in which it was defective, we reduce their apparent discord to real harmony, and show that they are severally the partial expressions of a theory which comprehends and consummates them both. But to proceed in our historical survey.

The counter theories of Plato and Aristotle the partial expressions of the true.

Passing over a host of commentators in the Lower Empire, and during the middle ages, who were content to repeat the doctrines of Aristotle and Plato; in modern times, the first original philosopher I am aware of, who seems to have turned his attention upon the phænomena of pain and pleasure, is the celebrated Cardan; and the result of his observation was a theory identical with Plato's, though of Plato's speculation he does not seem to have been aware. In the sixth chapter of his very curious autobiography, *De Vita Propria Liber*, he tells us, that it was his wont to anticipate the causes of disease, because he was of opinion that pleasure consisted in the appeasement of a preëxistent pain, (quod arbitrarer, voluptatem consistere in dolore præcedenti, sedato). But in the thirteenth book of his great work, *De Subtilitate*, this theory is formally propounded. This, however, was not done in the earlier editions of the work; and, the theory was, therefore, not canvassed by the ingenuity of his critic, the elder Scaliger,

Historical notices of the theories of the Pleasurable, resumed.

Cardan, — held a theory identical with Plato's.

whose *Exercitationes contra Cardanum* are totally silent on the subject. It is only in the editions of the *De Subtilitate* of Cardan, subsequent to the year 1560, that a statement of the theory in question is to be found. The following is a summary of his reasoning:

Summary of his doctrine.

— "All pleasure has its root in a preceding pain. Thus it is that we find pleasure in rest after hard labor; in meat and drink after hunger and thirst; in the sweet after the bitter; in light after darkness; in harmony after discord. Such are the facts in confirmation of this doctrine, which simple experience affords. But philosophy supplies, likewise, a reason from the nature of things themselves. Pleasure and pain exist only as they are states of feeling; but feeling is a change, and change always proceeds from one contrary to another; consequently, either from the good to the bad, or from the bad to the good. The former of these alternatives is painful, and, therefore, the other, when it takes its place, is pleasing; a state of pain must thus always precede a state of pleasure." Such are the grounds on which Cardan thinks himself entitled to reject the Aristotelic theory of pleasure, and to substitute in its place the Platonic. It does not, however, appear from anything he says, that he was aware of the relative speculations of these two philosophers.

But the reasoning of Cardan is incompetent: for if it proves anything, it proves too much, seeing that it would follow from his premises, that a pleasurable feeling cannot gradually, continually, uninterruptedly, rise in intensity; for it behooves that every new degree of pleasure should be separated from the preceding by an intermediate state of higher pain; a conclusion which is contradicted by the most ordinary and manifest experience. This theory remained, therefore, in Cardan's as in Plato's hands, destitute of the necessary proof.

His theory criticized.

The same doctrine — that pleasure is only the alternation and consequent of pain — was adopted, likewise, by Montaigne. In the famous twelfth chapter of the second book of his *Essays*, he says: — "Our states of pleasure are only the privation of our states of pain;" but this universal inference he, like his predecessors, deduces only from the special phænomena given in certain of the senses.

Montaigne, — held a similar doctrine.

The philosopher next in order is Descartes;[1] and his opinion is

---

[1] Before Descartes, Vives held a positive theory of the pleasurable. His definition of pleasure and its illustration, are worthy of a passing notice:" Delectatio sita est in congruentia, quam invenire non est sine propor- tionis ratione aliqua inter facultatem et objectum, ut quædam sit quasi similitudo inter illa; tum ne notabiliter sit majus, quod adfert delectationem; nec notabiliter minus, quam ea vis quæ recipit voluptatem, ea utique parte

deserving of attention, not so much from its intrinsic value, as

Descartes.

from the influence it has exerted upon those who have subsequently speculated upon the causes of pleasure. These philosophers seem to have been totally ignorant of the far profounder theories of the ancients; and while the regular discussions of the subject by Aristotle and Plato were, for our modern psychologists, as if they had never been, the incidental allusion to the matter by Descartes, originated a series of speculations which is still in progress.

Descartes' philosophy of the pleasurable is promulgated in one

His doctrine of the pleasurable.

short sentence of the sixth letter of the First Part of his *Epistles*, which is addressed to the Princess Elizabeth. It is as follows: — "All our pleasure is nothing more than the consciousness of some one or other of our perfections." — ("Tota nostra voluptas posita est tantum in perfectionis alicujus nostræ conscientia.") It is curious to hear the praises that have been lavished upon this definition of the

Groundlessly lauded for its novelty and importance.

pleasurable. It has been lauded for its novelty; it has been lauded for its importance. "Descartes," says Mendelssohn in his *Letters on the Sensations (Briefe über die Empfindungen)*,
" was the first who made the attempt to give a real explanation of the pleasurable."[1] The celebrated Kaestner thus opens his *Réflexions sur l'Origine du Plaisir*.[2] — "I shall not pretend decidedly to assert that no one before Descartes has said, that pleasure consisted in the feeling of some one of our perfections. I confess, however, that I have not found this definition in any of the dissertations, sometimes tiresome, and frequently uninstructive, of the ancient philosophers on the nature and effects of pleasure. I am, therefore, disposed to attribute a discovery which has occasioned so many controversies, to that felicitous genius, which has disencumbered metaphysics of the confused chaos of disputes, as unintelligible as vain, in order to render it the solid and instructive science of God and of the human soul." And M. Bertrand, another very intelligent philosopher, in his *Essai sur le Plaisir*[3] says, "Descartes is probably the first who has enounced, that all pleasure consists in the inward feeling we

---

qua recipitur. Ideo mediocris lux gratior est oculis, quam ingens: et subobscura gratiora sunt hebeti visui; eundem in modum de sonis." *De Anima*, l. iii. p. 202, edit. 1555. — ED.

 1 Anmerkung, 6. — ED.

 2 The *Reflexions sur l'Origine du Plaisir*, is

appended to the *Nouvelle Théorie des Plaisirs, par M. Sulzer* (1767). The *Nouvelle Théorie* is a French version of Sulzer's treatise, *Untersuchung über den Ursprung der angenehmen und unangenehmen Empfindungen*. See above, p. 416 — ED.

 3 Sect. i. ch. i. p. 3. Neuchatel. 1777. — ED.

have of some of our perfections, and, in these few words, he has unfolded a series of great truths."

Now what is the originality, what is the importance, of this cele-

The doctrine of Descartes, a vague version of that of Aristotle.

brated definition? This is easily answered, — in so far as it has any meaning, it is only a statement, in vague and general terms, of the truth which Aristotle had promulgated, in precise and proximate expressions. Descartes says, that pleasure is the consciousness of one or other of our perfections. This is not false; but it is not instructive. 'We are not conscious of any perfection of our nature, except in so far as this is the perfection of one or other of our powers; and we are not conscious of a power at all, far less of its perfection, except in so far as we are conscious of its operation. It, therefore, behooved Descartes to have brought down his definition of pleasure from the vague generality of a consciousness of perfection, to the precise and proximate declaration, that pleasure is a consciousness of the perfect energy of a power. But this improvement of his definition would have stripped it of all novelty. It would then have appeared to be, what it truly is, only a version, and an inadequate version, of Aristotle's. These are not the only objections that could be taken to the Cartesian definition; but for our present purpose it would be idle to advance them.

Leibnitz is the next philosopher to whose opinion I shall refer;

Leibnitz, — adopted both the counter theories.

and this you will find stated in his *Nouveaux Essais*,[1] and other works latterly published. Like Descartes, he defines pleasure the feeling of a perfection, pain the feeling of an imperfection; and, in another part of the work,[2] he adopts the Platonic theory, that all pleasure is grounded in pain, which he ingeniously connects with his own doctrine of latent modifications, or, as he calls them, obscure perceptions. As this work, however, was not published till long after not only his own death, but that of his great disciple Wolf, the indication (for it is nothing more) of his opinion on this point had little influence on subsequent speculations; indeed I do not remember to have seen the doctrine of Leibnitz upon pleasure ever alluded to by any of his countrymen.

Wolf, with whose doctrine that of Baumgarten[3] nearly coincides,

Wolf.

defines pleasure, the intuitive cognition (that is, in our language, the perception or imagination) of any perfection whatever, either true or apparent. — "Voluptas

---

[1] Lib. ii. ch. xxi. § 41. *Opera*, ed. Erdmann, p. 261. — ED.

[2] Lib. ii. ch. xx. § 6. *Opera*, ed. Erdmann, p. 248. — ED.

[3] See his *Metaphysik*, § 482 *et seq.*, p. 233, edit. 1783. Cf. Platner, *Phil. Aphorismen*, ii. § 865, p. 218. — ED.

est intuitus, seu cognitio intuitiva, perfectionis cujuscunque, sive
veræ sive apparentis."[1]　His doctrine you will find detailed in his
Psychologia Empirica, and in his *Horæ Subse-*
civæ.　It was manifestly the offspring, but the
degenerate offspring, of the doctrine of Descar-
tes, which, as we have seen, was itself only a corruption of that of
Aristotle.　Descartes rightly considered pleasure as a quality of the
subject, in defining it a consciousness of some perfection in ourselves.

His doctrine criti-
cized.

Wolf, on the contrary, wrongly considers pleasure more as an attribute of the object, in defining it a cognition of any perfection whatever.
Now in their definitions of pleasure, as Descar-
tes was inferior to Aristotle, so Wolf falls far below Descartes, and
in the same quality, — in want of precision and proximity.

1. Wrongly considers
pleasure as an attri-
bute of the object.

Pleasure is a feeling, and a feeling is a merely subjective state,
that is, a state which has no reference to anything beyond itself, —
which exists only as we are conscious of its existence.　Now, then,
the perfection or imperfection of an object, considered in itself, and
as out of relation to our subjective states, is thought — is judged,
but is not felt; and this judgment is not pleasure or pain, but approbation or disapprobation, that is, an act of the cognitive faculties,
but not an affection of the capacities of feeling.　In this point of
view, therefore, the definition of pleasure, as the cognition of any
sort of perfection, is erroneous.　It may, indeed, be true that the
perfection of an object can determine the cognitive faculty to a perfect energy; and the concomitant of this perfect energy will be a
feeling of pleasure.　But, in this case, the objective perfection, as
cognized, is not itself the pleasure; but the pleasure is the feeling
which we have of the perfection, that is, of the state of vigorous
and unimpeded energy of the cognitive faculty, as exercised on that
perfection.　Wolf ought, therefore, to have limited his definition,
like Descartes, to the consciousness of subjective perfection; as
Descartes should have explicated his consciousness of subjective
perfection into the consciousness of full, spontaneous and unimpeded activity.

But there is another defect in the Wolfian definition: — it limits
the pleasures from the cognition of perfection to the Intuitive Faculties, that is, to Sense and Imagination, denying it to the Understanding, — the faculty of relations, — Thought Proper.　This part
of his theory was, accordingly, assailed by Moses Mendelssohn, —
one of the best writers and most ingenious philosophers of the last

---

1 *Psychologia Empirica*, § 511, where he expressly refers to Descartes as the author of the
definition. — ED.

century, — who, in other respects, however, remained faithful to the

2. Limits pleasure to the cognition of perfection by the Intuitive Faculties.

This part of Wolf's doctrine assailed by Mendelssohn.

objective point of view, from whence Wolf had contemplated the phænomenon of pleasure. This was done in his *Briefe über die Empfindungen*, 1755.[1] A reäction was, however, inevitable ; and other German philosophers were soon found who returned to the subjective point of view from which Wolf, Baumgarten, and Mendelssohn had departed.

But before passing to these, it would be improper to overlook the

Du Bos and Pouilly, — considered pleasure in its subjective aspect.

doctrine of two French philosophers, who had already explained pleasure in its subjective aspect, and who prepared the way for the profounder theories of the German speculators, — I mean Du Bos and Pouilly. As their doctrines nearly coincide, I shall consider them as one. The former treats of this subject in his *Réflexions Critiques sur la Peinture*,[2] etc.; the latter in his *Théorie des Sentimens Agréables*.[3] The following are the principal momenta of their inquiries :

" 1. Considering pleasure only in relation to the subject, the ques-

Their theory stated.

tion they propose to answer is, What takes place in the state which we call pleasurable?

" 2. The gratification of a want causes pleasure. If the want be natural, the result is a natural pleasure, and an unnatural pleasure if the want be unnatural.

" 3. The fundamental want — the want to which all others may be reduced — is the occupation of the mind. All that we know of the mind is that it is a thinking, a knowing power. We desire objects only for the sake of intellectual occupation.

" The activity of mind is either occupied or occupies itself. The matters which afford the objects of our faculties of knowledge are either sensible impressions, which are delivered over to the understanding — this is the case in perception of sense; or this matter

---

1 See Anmerkung, 6; and Reinhold, *Über die bisherigen Begriffe vom Vergnügen*, § 2. *Vermischte Schriften* i. p. 281 *et seq.* — ED.

2 See tom. p. i. §§ 1, 2. First published in 1719, Paris. — ED.

3 See chaps. i. iii. iv. v. First published in 1743 To these should be added the valuable treatise of the Père André, — the *Essai sur le Beau*, which was first published in 1741. There is also, previously to Sulzer, another French æsthetical writer of merit, — Batteux, whose treatise, *Les Beaux Arts reduits d un même Prin-* cipe, first appeared in 1746. This work, along with two relative treatises, was republished in 1774, under the title of *Principes de la Littérature*. All these authors consider pleasure, more or less, from the subjective point of view, and are, in principle, Aristotelic. For a collection of treatises, in whole and part, on pleasure in its psychological and moral aspects, see *Le Temple du Bonheur ou Recueil des plus Excellens Traités sur le Bonheur;* in 4 vols. New edition, 1770. — ED.

is furnished by the cognitive faculty itself — as is the case in thinking.

"5. If this activity meets with impediments in its prosecution, — be this in the functions either of thought or sense, — there results a feeling of restraint; and this of two kinds, positive and negative.

"6. When the activity, whether in perception or thinking, is prevented from being brought to its conclusion, there emerges the feeling of straining, — of effort, — the feeling of positive limitation of our powers. This is painful.

"7. If the mind be occupied less than usual in all its functions, there arises a feeling of unsatisfied want; this constitutes that state of negative restraint, — the state of ennui, of tedium. This is painful.

"8. The stronger and at the same time the easier the activity of mind in any of its functions, the more agreeable."[1]

This theory is evidently only that of Aristotle; to whom, however, the French philosophers make no allusion. What they call *occupation* or *exercise*, he calls *energy*. The former expressions are, perhaps, preferable on this account, that they apply equally well to the mental processes, whether active or passive, whereas the terms *energy, act, activity, operation*, etc., only properly denote these processes as they are considered in the former character.

Subsequently to the French philosophers, and as a reäction against the partial views of the school of Wolf, there appeared the theory of Sulzer, the Academician of Berlin, — a theory which was first promulgated in his *Enquiry into the Origin of our Agreeable and Disagreeable Feelings*,[2] in 1752. This is one of the ablest discussions upon the question, and though partial, like the others, it concurs in establishing the truth of that doctrine of which Aristotle has left, in a short compass, the most complete and satisfactory exposition. The following are the leading principles of Sulzer's theory:

Sulzer, — his theory a reäction against the views of Wolf.

"1. We must penetrate to the essence of the soul, if we would discover the primary source of pleasure.

"2. The essence of the soul consists in its natural activity, and this activity again consists in the production of ideas." [By that he means the faculty in general of Cognition or Thought. I may

1 Abridged from Reinhold, *Über die bisherigen Begriffe vom Vergnügen*, § 1. *Verm. Schrift.* p. 275. — ED.

2 *Untersuchung über den Ursprung der angenehmen und unangenehmen Empfindungen.* Published in the Memoirs of the Royal Academy of Berlin for the years 1751, 1752. See *Verm. Phil. Schriften*, vol. i. p. i., 1773. See above, p. 560. — ED.

here observe, by the way, that he adopts the opinion that the

His theory stated. faculty of thought or cognition is the one fundamental power of mind; and in this he coincides
with Wolf, whose theory of pleasure, however, he rejects.]

"3. In this essential tendency to activity are grounded all our pleasurable and painful feelings.

"4. If this natural activity of the soul, or this ceaseless tendency to think, encounters an impediment, pain is the result; whereas if it be excited to a lively activity, the result is pleasure.

"5. There are two conditions which regulate the degree of capacity and incapacity in the soul for pleasurable and painful feelings, the habitude of reflection, and the natural vivacity of thought; and both together constitute the perfect activity of mind.

"6. Pleasurable feelings, consequently, can only be excited by objects which at once comprise a variety of constituent qualities or characters, and in which these characters are so connected that the mind recognizes in them materials for its essential activity. An object which presents to the mental activity no exercise, remains altogether indifferent.

"7. No object which moves the mind in a pleasurable or in a painful manner is simple;[1] it is necessarily composite or multiplex. The difference between agreeable and disagreeable objects can only lie in the connection of the parts of this multiplicity. Is there order in this connection, the object is agreeable; is there disorder, it is painful.

"8. Beauty is the manifold, the various, recalled to unity. The mere multitude of parts does not constitute an object beautiful; for there is required that an object should have at once such multiplicity and connection as to form a whole.

"9. This is the case in intellectual beauty; that is, in the beauty of those objects which the understanding contemplates in distinct notions. The beauty of geometrical theorems, of algebraic formulæ, of scientific principles, of comprehensive systems, consists, no less than the beauty of objects of Imagination and Sense, in the unity of the manifold, and rises in proportion to the quantity of the multiplicity and the unity.

"10. All these objects present a multitude of constituent characters, — of elementary ideas, at once; and these are so connected, so bound together by a principle of unity, that the mind is, in consequence thereof, enabled to unfold and then to bring back the different parts to a common centre, that is, reduce them to unity, — to totality, — to system.

---

[1] [But see Tiedemann's *Psychologie*, p. 152.]

"11. From this it is evident, that the Beautiful only causes pleasure through the principle of activity. Unity, multiplicity, correspondence of parts, render an object agreeable to us, only inasmuch as they stand in a favorable relation to the active power of the mind.

"12. The relation in which beauty stands to the mind is thus necessary, and, consequently, immutable. A single condition is alone required in order that what is in itself beautiful should operate on us; it is necessary that we should know it; and to know, it is necessary that, to a certain extent, we be conversant with the kind to which it belongs; for otherwise we should not be competent to apprehend the beauty of an object. (!)

"13. A difference of taste is found only among the ignorant or the half-learned; and taste is a necessary consequence of knowledge."[1]

I shall not pursue this theory to the explanation it attempts of the pleasures of the Senses and of the Moral Powers, in which it is far less successful than in those of the Intellect. This was to be expected in consequence of the one-sided view Sulzer had taken of the mental phænomena, in assuming the Cognitive Faculty as the elementary power out of which the Feelings and Conations are evolved.[2]

The theory of Sulzer is manifestly only a one-sided modification of the Aristotelic; but it does not appear that he was himself aware how completely he had been anticipated by the Stagirite. "On the contrary, he once and again denominates his explanation of the pleasurable a discovery. This can, however, hardly be allowed him, even were the Aristotelic theory out of the question; for it required no mighty ingenuity for a philosopher who was well acquainted with the works of his immediate predecessors, in France and Germany, by whom pleasure had been explained as the vigorous and easy exercise of the faculties, — as the feeling of perfection in ourselves, and as the apprehension of perfection in other things, that is, their unity in variety : — I say, after these opinions of his precursors, it required no such uncommon effort of invention to hit upon the thought, — that pleasure is determined when the variety in the object calls forth the activity of the subject, and when this activity is rendered easy by the unity in which the variety is contained. His explanation is more explicit, but, except a change of expression,

The theory of Sulzer criticized.

1 See Reinhold [Über die bisherigen Begriffe vom Vergnügen, § 8. Verm. Schrift. p. 296 et seq. — ED.

2 For Sulzer's doctrines on these points see Reinhold, as above, p. 801 et seq. — ED.

it is not easy to see what Sulzer added to Du Bos and Pouilly, to say nothing of Wolf and Mendelssohn."

"The theory of Sulzer is summed up in the following result:—

Summary of the theory.
Every variety of pleasure may, subjectively considered, be carried into the prompt and vigorous activity of the cognitive faculty; and, objectively considered, be explained as the product of objects which, in consequence of their variety in unity, intensely occupy the mind without fatiguing it. The peculiar merit of the theory of Sulzer, in

Its merit.
contrast to those of his immediate predecessors, is that it combines both the subjective and objective points of view. In this respect, it is favorably contrasted with the opinion of Wolf and Mendelssohn. But it takes a one-

Its defect.
sided view of the character of the subject. In the first place, the essence of the mind in general, and the essence of the cognitive faculty in particular, does not consist of activity exclusively, but of activity and receptivity in correlation. But receptivity is a passive power, not an active, and thus the theory in its fundamental position is only half true. This one-sided view by Sulzer, in which regard is had to the active or intellectual element of our constitution to the exclusion of the passive or sensual, is precisely the opposite to that other, and equally one-sided, view which was taken by Helvetius[1] and the modern Epicureans and Materialists; but their theory of the pleasurable may be passed over as altogether without philosophical importance. In the second place, it is erroneous to assert that pleasure is nothing else than the consciousness of the unimpeded activity of mind. The activity of mind is manifested principally in thinking, whereas the state of pleasure consists wholly of a consciousness of feeling. In the enjoyment of pleasure we do not think, but feel; and in an intenser enjoyment there is almost a suspension of thought."[2]

It is not necessary to say much of the speculations upon pleasure

Genovesi and Verri adopted the Platonic theory.
subsequent to Sulzer, and prior to Kant. In Italy, I find that two philosophers of the last century had adopted the Platonic opinion,—of pleasure being always an escape from pain,
—Genovesi and Verri; the former in a chapter of his *Metaphysics*,[3] the latter in a chapter of his *Dissertation on the Nature of Pleasure and Pain*.[4] This opinion, however, reäcquires importance from

[1] *De l'Esprit*, disc. i. ch. i. Cf. *De l'Homme*, sect. ii. ch. x. — ED.

[2] See Reinhold, as above, pp. 308, 315, 317. — ED.

[3] Cap. vi. t. ii. p. 213, edit. 1753. — ED.

[4] *Discorso sull' Indole del Piacere, e del Dolore*, §§ iii. iv. *Opere Filosofiche*, i. p. 20 *et seq.*, edit. 1784. This treatise is translated into German by Meiners, — *Gedanken über die Natur des Vergnügens*. Leipsic, 1777. — ED.

having been adopted from Verri by the philosopher of Könisberg.

Kant adopted the Platonic theory. In his *Manual of Anthropology*, Kant briefly and generally states his doctrine on this point; but in the notes which have been recently printed of his Lectures on this subject, we have a more detailed view of the character and grounds of his opinion. The Kantian doctrine is as follows:

His doctrine stated. "Pleasure is the feeling of the furtherance (*Beförderung*), pain of the hindrance of life. Under pleasure is not to be understood the feeling of life; for in pain we feel life no less than in pleasure, nay, even perhaps more strongly. In a state of pain, life appears long, in a state of pleasure, it seems brief; it is only, therefore, the feeling of promotion,— the furtherance, of life, which constitutes pleasure. On the other hand, it is not the mere hindrance of life which constitutes pain; the hindrance must not only exist, it must be felt to exist." (Before proceeding further, I may observe, that these definitions of pleasure and pain are virtually identical with those of Aristotle, only far less clear and explicit.)

But to proceed: "If pleasure be a feeling of the promotion of life, this presupposes a hindrance of life; for there can be no promotion, if there be no foregoing hindrance to overcome. Since, therefore, the hindrance of life is pain, pleasure must presuppose pain. . . . .

"If we intend our vital powers above their ordinary degree, in order to go out of the state of indifference or equality, we induce an opposite state; and when we intend the vital powers above the suitable degree we occasion a hindrance, a pain. The vital force has a degree along with which a state exists, which is one neither of pleasure nor of pain, but of content, of comfort (*das Wohlbefinden*). When this state is reduced to a lower pitch by any hindrance, then, a promotion, a furtherance of life is useful in order to overcome this impediment. Pleasure is thus always a consequent of pain. When we cast our eyes on the progress of things, we discover in ourselves a ceaseless tendency to escape from our present state. To this we are compelled by a physical stimulus, which sets animals, and man, as an animal, into activity. But in the intellectual nature of man, there is also a stimulus, which operates to the same end. In thought, man is always dissatisfied with the actual; he is ever looking forward from the present to the future; he is incessantly in a state of transition from one state to another, and is unable to continue in the same. But what is it that thus constrains us to be always passing from one state to another, but pain? And that it is not a pleasure which entices us to this, but a kind of discontent with present suffering, is shown by the fact that we are always seeking for some object of pleasure, without knowing what that object is, merely as an aid against the disquiet, — against the complement of petty pains, which in the moment irritate and annoy us. It is thus apparent that man is urged on by a necessity of his nature to go out of the present as a state of pain, in order to find in the future one less irksome. Man thus finds himself in a never-ceasing pain; and this is the spur for the activity of human nature. Our lot is so cast that there is nothing enduring for us but pain; some indeed have less, others more, but all, at all times, have their share; and our enjoyments at best are only slight alleviations of pain. Pleasure is nothing positive; it is only a liberation of pain, and, therefore, only something negative. Hence it follows, that we never begin with pleasure but always with pain; for while pleasure is only an emancipation from pain, it cannot precede that of which it is only a negation. Moreover, pleasure cannot endure in an unbroken continuity, but must be associated with pain, in order to be always suddenly breaking through this pain, — in order to realize itself. Pain, on the contrary, may subsist without interruption in one pain, and be only removed through a gradual remission; in this case, we have no consciousness of pleasure. It is the sudden, the instantaneous removal of pain, which determines all that we can call a veritable pleasure. We find ourselves constantly immersed, as it were, in an ocean of nameless pains, which we style disquietudes or desires, and the greater the vigor of life an individual is endowed with, the more keenly is he sensible to the pain. Without being in a state of determinate corporeal suffering, the mind is harassed by a multitude of obscure uneasinesses, and it acts, without being compelled to act, for the mere sake of changing its condition. Thus men run from solitude to society, and from society to solitude, without having much preference for either, in order merely, by the change of impressions, to obtain a suspension of their pain. It is from this cause that so many have become tired of their existence, and the greater number of such melancholic subjects have been urged to the act of suicide in consequence of the continual goading of pain, — of pain from which they found no other means of escape.[1]

"It is certainly the intention of Providence that, by the alternation of pain, we should be urged on to activity. No one can find pleasure in the continual enjoyment of delights; these soon pall upon us, — pall upon us in fact the sooner, the more intense was

---

[1] Cf. *Anthropologie*, § 60. — ED.

their enjoyment. There is no permanent pleasure to be reaped except in labor alone. The pleasure of toil consists in a reäction against the pain to which we should be a victim, did we not exert a force to resist it. Labor is irksome, labor has its annoyances, but these are fewer than those we should experience were we without labor. As man, therefore, must seek even his recreation in toil itself, his life is at best one of vexation and sorrow; and as all his means of dissipation afford no alleviation, he is left always in a state of disquietude, which incessantly urges him to escape from the state in which he actually is." [This is the doom of man, — to be born to sorrow as the sparks fly upwards, and to eat his bread in the sweat of his brow.]

"Men think that it is ungrateful to the Creator to say, that it is the design of Providence to keep us in a state of constant pain; but this is a wise provision in order to urge human nature on to exertion. Were our joys permanent, we should never leave the state in which we are, we should never undertake aught new. That life we may call happy, which is furnished with all the means by which pain can be overcome; we have in fact no other conception of human happiness. Contentment is when a man thinks of continuing in the state in which he is, and renounces all means of pleasure; but this disposition we find in no man."[1]

1 *Menschenkunde*, p. 248 *et seq.*; published by Starke, 1831. This is not included in Kant's collected works by Rosenkranz and Schubert. Cf. *Anthropologie*, § 59. *Werke*, vii. part ii. p. 144. — ED. [For further historical notices of theories of the Pleasurable, see Lossius, *Lexikon*, v. *Vergnügen*.]

LECTURE XLIV.

THE FEELINGS. — APPLICATION OF THE THEORY OF PLEASURE AND PAIN TO THE PHÆNOMENA.

THE Feelings being mere subjective states, involving no cognition or thought, and, consequently, no reference to any object, it follows, that they cannot be classified by relation to aught beyond themselves. The differences in which we must found all divisions of the Feelings into genera and species, must be wholly internal, and must be sought for and found exclusively in the states of Feeling themselves. Now, in considering these states, it appears to me, that they admit of a classification in two different points of view; — we may consider these states either as Causes or as Effects. As causes, they are viewed in relation to their product, — their product either of pleasure or of pain. As effects, they are viewed as themselves products, — products of the action of our different constitutive functions. In the former of these points of view, our states of Feeling will be divided simply into the three classes — 1°, The Pleasurable; 2°, The Painful; and, 3°, The partly Pleasurable partly Painful, — without considering what kind of pleasure and what kind of pain it is which they involve; and here, it only behooves us to inquire, — what are the general conditions which determine in a feeling one or other of these counter-qualities. In the latter of these points of view, our states of Feeling will be divided according as the energy, of which they are concomitant, be that of a power of one kind or of another, — a distinction, which affords a division of our pleasures and pains, taken together, into various sorts. I shall take these points of view in their order.

In the former point of view, these feelings are distributed simply into the Pleasurable and the Painful; and it remains, on the theory I have proposed, to explain, in general, the causes of these opposite affections, without descending to their special kinds. Now,

Margin notes:

Feelings,—their principle of classification internal.

Admit of a two-fold classification,—as Causes and Effects.

it has been stated, that a feeling of pleasure is experienced, when
any power is consciously exerted in a suitable
manner; that is, when we are neither on the
one hand, conscious of any restraint upon the
energy which it is disposed spontaneously to put
forth, nor, on the other, conscious of any effort
in it, to put forth an amount of energy greater,
either in degree or in continuance, than what it
is disposed freely to exert.   In other words, we
feel positive pleasure, in proportion as our pow-
ers are exercised, but not over-exercised; we feel positive pain, in
proportion as they are compelled either not to operate, or to operate too much.   All pleasure, thus, arises from the free play of our
faculties and capacities; all pain from their compulsory repression
or compulsory activity.

The Feelings as Causes,—divided into Pleasurable and Painful.

Application of foregoing theory to explain in general the causes of Pleasurable and Painful feeling.

The doctrine meets with no contradiction from the facts of actual
life; for the contradictions which, at first sight,
these seem to offer, prove, when examined, to be
real confirmations.   Thus it might be thought,
that the aversion from exercise,—the love of
idleness,—in a word, the *dolce far niente*,—is
a proof that the inactivity, rather than the exertion, of our powers, is the condition of our pleasurable feelings.
This objection, from a natural proneness to inertion in man, is
superficial; and the very examples on which it proceeds, refute it,
and, in refuting it, concur in establishing our theory of pleasure and
pain.   Now, is the *far niente*,—is that doing
nothing, in which so many find so sincere a
gratification, in reality a negation of activity,
and not in truth itself an activity intense and
varied?   To do nothing in this sense, is simply to do nothing irksome,—nothing difficult,—nothing fatiguing,—especially to do no
outward work.   But is the mind internally, the while, unoccupied
and inert?   This, on the contrary, may be vividly alive,—may be
intently engaged in the spontaneous play of imagination; and so
far, therefore, in this case, from pleasure being the concomitant of
inactivity, the activity is, on the contrary, at once vigorous and
unimpeded; and such, accordingly, as, on our theory, would be
accompanied by a high degree of pleasure.
Ennui is the state in which we find nothing on
which to exercise our powers; but ennui is a
state of pain.   We must recollect, that all energy,
all occupation, is either play or labor.   In the former, the energy ap-

Apparent contradictions of the doctrine prove real confirmations.

The dolce far niente.

This is not the negation of activity, but the opposite.

Ennui—what.

All occupation either play or labor.

pears as free or spontaneous; in the latter, as either compulsorily put forth, or its exertion so impeded by difficulties, that it is only continued by a forced and painful effort, in order to accomplish certain ulterior ends. Under certain circumstances, indeed, play may become a labor, and labor may become a play. A play is, in fact, a labor, until we have acquired the dexterity requisite to allow the faculties exerted to operate with ease; and, on the other hand, a labor is said to become a play, when a person has by nature, or has acquired by custom, such a facility in the relative operations, as to energize at once vigorously and freely. In point of fact, as man by his nature is determined to pursue happiness (happiness is only another name for a complement of pleasures), he is determined to that spontaneous activity of his faculties, in which pleasure consists.

The love of action signalized as a fact in human nature by all observers.

Samuel Johnson.

The love of action is, indeed, signalized, as a fact in human nature, by all who have made man an object of observation, though few of them have been able to explain its true rationale. "The necessity of action," says Samuel Johnson,[1] "is not only demonstrable from the fabric of the body, but evident from observation of the universal practice of mankind, who, for the preservation of health" (he should have said for pleasure), "in those whose rank or wealth exempts them from the necessity of lucrative labor, have invented sports and diversions, which, though not of equal use to the world with manual trades, are yet of equal fatigue to those who practise them."

Adam Ferguson.

It is finely observed by another eloquent philosopher,[2] in accounting, on natural principles, for man's love of war: — "Every animal is made to delight in the exercise of his natural talents and forces: the lion and the tiger sport with the paw; the horse delights to commit his mane to the wind, and forgets his pasture to try his speed in the field; the bull, even before his brow is armed, and the lamb, while yet an emblem of innocence, have a disposition to strike with the forehead, and anticipate in play the conflicts they are doomed to sustain. Man, too, is disposed to opposition, and to employ the forces of his nature against an equal antagonist; he loves to bring his reason, his eloquence, his courage, even his bodily strength, to the proof. His sports are frequently an image of war; sweat and blood are freely expended in play; and fractures or death are often made to terminate the pastime of idleness and festivity. He was not made to live for ever, and even his love of amusement has opened a way to the grave."

[1] *Rambler*, No. 85. — ED.
[2] Adam Ferguson, *Essay on the History of Civil Society.* Part
I. section iv. — ED.

"The young of all animals," says Paley,[1] "appear to me to receive pleasure simply from the exercise of their limbs and bodily faculties, without reference to any end to be attained, or any use to be answered by the exertion. A child, without knowing anything of the use of language, is in a high degree delighted with being able to speak. Its incessant repetition of a few articulate sounds, or, perhaps, of the single word which it has learnt to pronounce, proves this point clearly. Nor is it less pleased with its first successful endeavors to walk, or rather to run, (which precedes walking), although entirely ignorant of the importance of the attainment to its future life, and even without applying it to any present purpose. A child is delighted with speaking, without having anything to say, and with walking, without knowing where to go. And prior to both these, I am disposed to believe, that the waking hours of infancy are agreeably taken up with the exercise of vision, or perhaps, more properly speaking, with learning to see.

"But it is not for youth alone that the great Parent of creation hath provided. Happiness is found with the purring cat, no less than with the playful kitten; in the arm-chair of dozing age, as well as in either the sprightliness of the dance, or the animation of the chase. To novelty, to acuteness of sensation, to hope, to ardor of pursuit, succeeds, what is, in no inconsiderable degree, an equivalent for them all, 'perception of ease.' Herein is the exact difference between the young and the old. The young are not happy, but when enjoying pleasure; the old are happy, when free from pain. And this constitution suits with the degrees of animal power which they respectively possess. The vigor of youth was to be stimulated to action by impatience of rest; whilst to the imbecility of age, quietness and repose become positive gratifications. In one important respect, the advantage is with the old. A state of ease is, generally speaking, more attainable than a state of pleasure. A constitution, therefore, which can enjoy ease, is preferable to that which can taste only pleasure. This same perception of ease oftentimes renders old age a condition of great comfort, especially when riding at its anchor after a busy or tempestuous life."

The theory confirmed by the phænomena presented by the Painful Affections. A strong confirmation of the doctrine, that all pleasure is a reflex of activity, and that the free energy of every power is pleasurable, is derived from the phænomena presented by those affections which we emphatically denominate the Painful. This fact is too striking, from its apparent inconsistency, not to have soon attracted attention:

---

[1] *Natural Theology. Works*, vol. iv. chap. xxvi. p. 359.

> " Non tantum sanctis instructæ legibus urbes,
>   Tectaque divitiis luxuriosa suis
> Mortalem alliciunt pulcra ad spectacula visum,
>   Sed placet annoso squalida terra situ.
> Oblectat pavor ipse animum; sunt gaudia curis,
>   Et stupuisse juvat, quem doluisse piget." [1]

Take, for example, in the first place, the affection of Grief, — the sorrow we feel in the loss of a beloved object. Is this affection unaccompanied with pleasure? So far is this from being the case, that the pleasure so greatly predominates over the pain as to produce a mixed emotion, which is far more pleasurable than any other of which the wounded heart is susceptible. It is expressly stated by the younger Pliny, in a passage which commences with these words:—"Est quædam etiam dolendi voluptas," etc.[2] This has also been frequently signalized by the poets: Thus Ovid:[3]

Grief accompanied with pleasure.

Noticed by Pliny.

Ovid.

> "Fleque meos casus: est quædam flere voluptas;
>   Expletur lacrymis egeriturque dolor."

Lucan.

Thus Lucan:[4] of Cornelia after the murder of Pompey:

> "Caput ferali obduxit amictu,
> Decrevitque pati tenebras, puppisque cavernis
> Delituit: sævumque arcte complexa dolorem,
> Perfruitur lachrymis, et amat pro conjuge luctum."

Statius.

Thus Statius:[5]

> "Nemo vetat, satiare malis; ægrumque dolorem
> Libertate doma, jam flendi expleta voluptas."

Seneca.

Thus Seneca, the tragedian:[6]

> "Mœror lacrymas amat assuetas,
> Flendi miseris dira cupido est."

Petrarch.

Thus Petrarch:[7]

---

1 Virginius Cæsarinus [*Poemata Virginii Cæsarini, Urbani* viii. *Pont. Opt. Max. Cubicula Præfecti.* Printed in *Septem Illustrium Virorum Poemata.* Amstelodami, apud Dan. zevirium, 1672, p. 465.—ED.

2 Lib. viii. Ep. 16: "Est quædam etiam dolendi voluptas; præsertim si in amici sinu defleas, apud quem lacrymis tuis vel laus sit parata, vel venia.—ED.

3 *Tristia,* iv. iii. 37.—ED.

4 *Pharsalia,* ix. 108.—ED.

5 II. *Sylv.* i. 14.—ED.

6 *Thyestes,* l. 952.—ED.

7 *Epist.* L. I. *Barbato Sulmonensi.*—ED.

"Non omnia terræ

Obruta; vivit amor, vivit dolor; ora negatur

Regia conspicere, at flere et meminisse relictum est."

Shenstone.   Thus Shenstone:[1]

"Heu quanto minus est cum reliquis versari, quam tui meminisse."

Pembroke.   Finally, Lord Pembroke:[2]

"I would not give my dead son for the best living son in Christendom.

In like manner, Fear is not simply painful. It is a natural disposition; has a tendency to act; and there is, consequently, along with its essential pain, a certain
pleasure, as the reflex of its energy. This is
finely expressed by Akenside:[3]

*Fear, not simply
painful.
Akenside quoted.*

"Hence, finally, by might

The village matron round the blazing hearth

Suspends the infant audience with her tales,

Breathing astonishment! of witching rhymes

And evil spirits of the deathbed call

Of him who robb'd the widow, and devour'd

The orphan's portion, of unquiet souls

Ris'n from the grave to ease the heavy guilt

Of deeds in life conceal'd, of shapes that walk

At dead of night and clank their chains, and wave

The torch of hell around the murd'rer's bed.

At every solemn pause, the crowd recoil,

Gazing each other speechless, and congeal'd

With shivering sighs till, eager for th' event,

Around the beldame all erect they hang,

Each trembling heart with grateful terrors quell'd."

In like manner, Pity, which, being a sympathetic passion, implies
a participation in sorrow, is yet confessedly
agreeable. The poet even accords to the energy
of this benevolent affection a preference over the enjoyments of an
exclusive selfishness:

Pity.

"The broadest mirth unfeeling folly wears,

Is not so sweet as virtue's very tears."

1 Inscription on an urn. See Dodsley's
Description of the Leasowes, in Shenstone's
Works (1777), vol. ii. p. 307. — Ed.

2 The anecdote is told in a somewhat different form of the Duke of Ormond. See

Carte's *Life*, b. viii. Anno 1680. Hume, chap.
lxix., tells the story of the Duke of Ormond,
but as in the text. — Ed.

3 *Pleasures of Imagination*, b. i. 255. — Ed.

On the same principle is to be explained the enjoyment which men have in spectacles of suffering, — in the combats of animals and men, in executions, tragedies, etc., — a disposition which not unfrequently becomes an irresistible habit, not only for individuals, but for nations. The excitation of energetic emotions painful in themselves is, however, also pleasurable. St. Austin affords curious examples of this in his own case, and in that of his friend Alypius. Speaking of himself in his *Confessions*,[1] he says: " Theatrical exhibitions were to me irresistible, replete as they were with the images of my own miseries, and the fuel of my own fire. What is the cause why a man chooses to grieve at scenes of tragic suffering, which he would have the utmost aversion himself to endure ? And yet the spectator wishes to derive grief from these; in fact, the grief itself constitutes his pleasure. For he is attracted to the theatre, not to succour, but only to condole."

Energetic emotions painful in themselves still pleasurable.

Illustrated in the case of St. Augustine.

In another part of the same work,[2] he gives the following account of his friend Alypius, who had been carried by his fellow-students, much against his inclination, to the amphitheatre, where there was to be a combat of gladiators. At first, unable to regard the atrocious spectacle, he closed his eyes, but, to give you the result of the story in the words of St. Austin, "Abstulit inde secum insaniam qua stimularetur redire, non tantum cum illis a quibus prius abstractus est, sed etiam præ illis, et alios trahens."

Also in the case of his friend Alypius.

I now proceed to consider the General Causes which contribute to raise or to lower the intensity of our energies, and, consequently, to determine the corresponding degree of pleasure or pain. These may be reduced to Four; for an object rouses the activity of our powers, 1°, In proportion as it is New or Unexpected; 2°, In proportion as it stands in a relation of Contrast; 3°, In proportion as it stands in a relation of Harmony; and, 4°, In proportion as it is Associated with more, or more interesting, objects.

General Causes which contribute to raise or lower the intensity of our energies.

I. The principle on which Novelty determines higher energy, and, consequently, a higher feeling of pleasure, is twofold; and of these the one may be called the Subjective, the other the Objective.

I. Novelty.

---

1 Lib. iii. cap. 2. — Ed.

2 *Conf.*, lib. vi. cap. 8. — Ed. See Purchot, *Physica*, p. iii. ; iii. c. v. *Institut. Phil.* iii. p. 416.

In a subjective relation, — the new is pleasurable, inasmuch as
this supposes that the mind is determined to a
Twofold, — subjec-   mode of action, either from inactivity or from
tive and objective.   another state of energy.   In the former case,
energy (the condition of pleasure), is caused ; in the latter, a change
of energy is afforded, which is also pleasurable ; for powers energize
less vigorously in proportion to the continuance of the same exertion, consequently, a new activity being determined, this replaces a
strained or expiring exercise, that is, it replaces a painful, indifferent, or unpleasurable feeling, by one of comparatively vivid enjoyment.   Hence all that the poets, from Homer downward, have said
of the satiety consequent on our enjoyments, and of the charms of
variety and change ; but if I began to give quotations on these
heads there would be no end.   In an objective relation, — a novel
object is pleasing, because it affords a gratification to our desire of
knowledge ; for to learn, as Aristotle has observed,[1] is to man naturally pleasing.   But the old is already known, — it has been learned
— has been referred to its place, and, therefore, no longer occupies
the cognitive faculties ; whereas, the new, as new, is still unknown,
and rouses to energy the powers by which it is to be brought within
the system of our knowledge.

II. The second general principle is Contrast.   Contrast operates
in two ways ; for it has the effect both of en-
II Contrast.   hancing the real or absolute intensity of a feeling, and of enhancing the apparent or relative.   As an instance of
the former, the unkindness of a person from
Subordinate appli-   whom we expect kindness, rouses to a far higher
cations of this prin-   pitch the emotions consequent on injury.   As
ciple.   an instance of the latter, the pleasure of eating
appears proportionally great, when it is immediately connected and
contrasted with the removal of the pangs of
1. Recollection of   hunger.   It is on this principle, that the recol-
past suffering.   lection of our past suffering is agreeable, — " hæc
olim meminisse juvabit." [2]   To the same purport Seneca,[3] the tragedian :

> " Quæ furit durum pati
> Meminisse dulce est."

Cowley.   And Cowley :[4]

> " Things which offend, when present, and affright,
> In memory, well painted, move delight."

---

1 *Rhet.* i. 11, 21 ; iii. 10, 2. — ED.   3 *Hercules Furens,* act. iii. 656. — ED.
2 Virgil *Æneid,* i. 203. — ED.   4 *Ode upon his Majesty's Restoration.* — ED..

Southern.

Whereas the remembrance of a former happiness only augments the feeling of a present misery.

> "Could I forget
> What I have been, I might the better bear
> What I am destin'd to. I'm not the first
> That have been wretched: but to think how much
> I have been happier."[1]

2. Consciousness of our own felicity as contrasted with the wretchedness of others.

Lucretius quoted.

It is, likewise, on this principle, that whatever recalls us to a vivid consciousness of our own felicity, by contrasting it with the wretchedness of others, is, though not unaccompanied with sympathetic pain, still predominantly pleasurable. Hence, in part, but in part only, the enjoyment we feel from all representations of ideal suffering. Hence, also, in part, even the pleasure we have in witnessing real suffering:

> "Suave, mari magno turbantibus æquora ventis,
> E terra magnum alterius spectare laborem:
> Non quia vexari quemquam est jucunda voluptas,
> Sed quibus ipse malis careas, quia cernere suave est.
> Suave etiam belli certamina magna tueri
> Per campos instructa, tua sine parte pericli."[2]

But on this, and other subjects, I can only touch.

III. The third general principle on which our powers are roused

III. Harmony and Discord.

to a perfect and pleasurable, or to an imperfect and painful energy, is the relation of Harmony, or Discord, in which one coëxistent activity stands to another.

It is sufficient merely to indicate this principle, for its influence is

Illustrated.

manifest. At different times, we exist in different complex states of feeling, and these states are made up of a number of constituent thoughts and affections. At one time,—say during a sacred solemnity,—we are in a very different frame of mind from what we are at another,—say during the representation of a comedy. Now, then, in such a state of mind, if anything occurs to waken to activity a power previously unoccupied, or to occupy a power previously in energy in a different manner, this new mode of activity is either of the same general character and tendency with the other constituent elements of the complex state, or it is not. In the former case, the new energy chimes in with the old; each operates without impediment from the

---

[1] Southern, *Innocent Adultery*, act ii.   [2] Lucretius, ii. 2. — ED

other, and the general harmony of feeling is not violated: in the latter case, the new energy jars with the old, and each severally counteracts and impedes the other. Thus, in the sacred solemnity, and when our minds are brought to a state of serious contemplation, everything that operates in unison with that state, — say a pious discourse, or a strain of solemn music, — will have a greater effect, because all the powers which are thus determined to exertion, go to constitute one total complement of harmonious energy. But suppose that, instead of the pious discourse or the strain of solemn music, we are treated to a merry tune or a witty address;— these, though at another season they might afford us considerable pleasure, would, under the circumstances, cause only pain; because the energies they elicited, would be impeded by those others with which the mind was already engrossed, while those others would, in like manner, be impeded by them. But, as we have seen, pleasure is the concomitant of unimpeded energy.

IV. The fourth and last general principle by which the activity of our powers is determined to pleasurable or painful activity, is Association. With the nature and influence of association you are familiar, and are aware that, a determinate object being present in consciousness with its proper thought, feeling, or desire, it is not present, isolated and alone, but may draw after it the representation of other objects, with their respective feelings and desires.

IV. Association. Its nature.

Now it is evident, in the first place, that one object, considered simply and in itself, will be more pleasing than another, in proportion as it, of its proper nature, determines the exertion of a greater amount of free energy. But, in the second place, the amount of free energy which an object may itself elicit, is small, when compared to the amount that may be elicited by its train of associated representations. Thus, it is evident, that the object which in itself would otherwise be pleasing, may, through the accident of association, be the occasion of pain; and, on the contrary, that an object naturally indifferent or even painful may, by the same contingency, be productive of pleasure.

And influence.

This principle of Association accounts for a great many of the phænomena of our intellectual pleasures and pains; but it is far from accounting for everything. In fact, it supposes, as its condition, that there are pains and pleasures not founded on Association. Association is a principle of pleasure and pain, only as it is a principle of energy of one character or another; and the attempts that have been made to resolve all

Association supposes as its condition pains and pleasures not founded on itself.

our mental pleasures and pains into Association, are guilty of a twofold vice. For, in the first place, they con-

The attempt to resolve all our pleasures and pains into Association, vicious in a twofold way.

vert a partial into an exclusive law; and, in the second, they elevate a subordinate into a supreme principle. The influence of Association, by which Mr. Alison[1] and Lord Jeffrey,[2] among others, have attempted to explain the whole phænomena of our intellectual pleasures, was more properly, I think, appreciated by Hutcheson, — a philoso-

Hutcheson more properly appreciated the influence of Association.

pher whose works are deserving of more attention than has latterly been paid to them. "We shall see hereafter," he says, and Aristotle said the same thing, "that associations of ideas make objects pleasant and delightful, which are not naturally apt to give any such pleasures; and the same way, the casual conjunction of ideas may give a disgust where there is nothing disagreeable in the form itself. And this is the occasion of many fantastic aversions to figures of some animals, and to some other forms. Thus swine, serpents of all kinds, and some insects really beautiful enough, are beheld with aversion, by many people who have got some accidental ideas associated with them. And for distastes of this kind no other account can be given."[3]

---

1 See his *Essays on Taste.* 6th edit. Edinburgh, 1825. — ED.

2 See *Encyclopædia Britannica*, art. *Beauty*, 7th edit. p. 487. — ED.

3 *Inquiry into the Origin of our Ideas of Beauty and Virtue*, treatise i. sect. vi., 4th edition, p. 78. — ED.

LECTURE XLV.

THE FEELINGS. — THEIR CLASSES.

HAVING thus terminated the consideration of the Feelings considered as Causes,— causes of Pleasure and Pain,— I proceed to consider them as Effects, — as products of the action of our different powers. Now, it is evident, that, since all Feeling is the state in which we are conscious of some of the energies or processes of life, as these energies or processes differ, so will the correlative feelings. In a word, there will be as many different Feelings as there are distinct modes of mental activity. In the Lecture in which I commenced the discussion of the Feelings, I stated to you various distributions of these states by different philosophers.[1] To these I do not think it necessary again to recur, and shall simply state to you the grounds of the division I shall adopt.

The Feelings,—considered as Effects.

As many different feelings as there are distinct modes of mental activity.

As the Feelings, then, are not primitive and independent states, but merely states which accompany the exertion of our faculties, or the excitation of our capacities, they must, as I have said, take their differences from the differences of the powers which they attend. Now, though all consciousness and all feeling be only mental, and, consequently, to say that any feeling is corporeal, would, in one point of view, be inaccurate, still it is manifest that there is a considerable number of mental functions, cognitive as well as appetent, clearly marked out as in proximate relation to the body; and to these functions we give the name of *Sensitive, Sensible, Sensuous,* or *Sensual.* Now, the feelings which accompany the exertion of these Sensitive or Corporeal Powers, whether cognitive or appetent, will constitute a distinct class, and to these we may, with great propriety, give the name of *Sensations;* whereas, on the Feelings which accompany the energies of all our higher powers of

Two grand classes of Feelings.

I. Sensations.

1 See above, lect. xli. p. 570. — ED.

mind, we may, with equal propriety, bestow the name of *Sentiments*.

II. Sentiments. The first grand distribution of our feelings will, therefore, be into the Sensations, — that is, the Sensitive or External Feelings ; and into the Sentiments, — that is, the Mental or Internal Feelings. Of these in their order.

I. Of the Sensations. — The Sensations may be divided into two classes. The first class will contain those which **Sensations. Two classes.** accompany .our perceptions through the five determinate Senses, — of Touch, Taste, Smell, Hearing, and Sight, — the *Sensus Fixus.* The second class will **1. Of the Five Senses.** comprise those sensations which are included under what has been called the *Cœnæsthesis,* or *Sensus Communis,* — *the Common Sense,* — *Vital Sense,* — *Sensus Vagus,* — such as the feelings of Heat and Cold, of Shuddering, the feeling of Health, of **2. Of the Sensus Vagus.** Muscular Tension and Lassitude, of Hunger and Thirst, the Visceral Sensations, etc., etc.[1]

In regard to the determinate senses, each of these organs has its specific action, and its appropriate pleasure and **The first class considered.** pain ; for there is a pleasure experienced in each of these, when an object is presented which determines it to suitable activity ; and a pain or dissatisfaction experienced, when the energy elicited is either inordinately vehement or too remiss. This pleasure and pain, which is that alone belonging to the action of the living organ, and which, therefore, may be styled *organic,* we must distinguish from that higher **Organic pleasure and pain discriminated and illustrated.** feeling, which, perhaps, results from the exercise of Imagination and Intellect upon the phænomena delivered by the senses. Thus, I would call *organic* the pleasure we feel in the perception of green or blue, and the pain we feel in the perception of a dazzling white ; but I would be, perhaps, disposed to refer to some other power than the External Sense, the enjoyment we experience in the harmony of colors, and certainly that which we find in the proportions of figure. The same observation applies to Hearing. I would call *organic* the pleasure we have in single sounds ; whereas the satisfaction we receive from the harmony, and, still more, from the melody of tones, seems to require a higher faculty. This, however, is a very obscure and difficult problem ; but, in whatever manner it be determined, the Aristotelic theory of pleasure and pain is the only one that can account for the phænomena. Limiting, however, the organic pleasure, of which a sense is capable, to that from the activity de-

---

[1] See above, lect. **xxvii.** p. 377. — **Ed.**

termined in it by its elementary objects, — this will be competent to every sense, but in very different degrees. In treating of the Cognitive Powers, I formerly noticed that in all the senses we could discriminate two phænomena, —the phænomenon of Perception Proper, and the phænomenon of Sensation Proper.[1] By *perception* is understood the objective relation of the sense, that is, the information obtained through it of the qualities of external existences in their action on the organ ; by *sensation* is understood the subjective relation of the sense, that is, our consciousness of the affection of the organ itself, as acted on, — as affected by an object. I stated that these phænomena were in an inverse ratio to each other, that is, the greater the perception the less always the sensation, the greater the sensation the less always the perception. I further observed, that, of the senses, some were more objective, others more subjective ; — that in some the phænomenon of perception predominated, in others the phænomenon of sensation ; that is, some gave us much information in regard to the qualities of their object and little in regard to their own affection in the act ; whereas the information we received from others, was almost limited exclusively to their own modification, when at work. Thus the two higher senses of Sight and Hearing might be considered as preëminently objective, the two lower senses of Taste and Smell might be considered as preëminently subjective ; while the sense of Touch might be viewed as that in which the two phænomena are, as it were, *in æquilibrio.*

The degree of organic pleasure determined by the objectivity and subjectivity of the Sense.

Sight and Hearing objective; Taste and Smell subjective ; hence in the two former, organic pleasure and pain feeble, in two latter strong.

Now, according to this doctrine, we ought to find the organic pleasure and pain in the two higher senses comparatively feeble, in the two lower, comparatively strong. And so it is. The satisfaction or dissatisfaction we receive from certain single colors and certain single sounds, in determining the organs of Sight and Hearing to perfect or imperfect activity, is small in proportion to the pleasure or the displeasure we are conscious of from the application of certain single objects to the organs of Taste or Smell.

How far the theory of pleasure and pain affords an explanation of the phænomena.

So far we may safely go. But when it is required of us to explain, particularly and in detail, why the rose, for example, produces this sensation of smell, assafœtida that other, and so forth, and to say in what peculiar action does the perfect or pleasurable, and the imperfect or painful, activity of an organ

---

1 See above, lect. xxiv. p. 335. — ED.

consist, we must at once profess our ignorance. But it is the same with all our attempts at explaining any of the ultimate phænomena of creation. In general, we may account for much; in detail, we can rarely account for anything; for we soon remount to facts which lie beyond our powers of analysis and observation.

All that we can say in explanation of the agreeable in sensation, is, that, on the general analogy of our being, when the impression of an object on a sense is in harmony with its amount of power, and thus allows it the condition of springing to full spontaneous energy, the result is pleasure; whereas, when the impression is out of harmony with the amount of power, and thus either represses it or stimulates it to over-activity, the result is pain.

The theory applicable to the Vital Sense.
The same explanation, drawn from the observation of the phænomena within our reach, must be applied to the sensations which belong to the Vital Sense, but in regard to these it is not necessary to say anything in detail.

II. The Mental or Internal Feelings, — the Sentiments, — may be divided into Contemplative and Practical.
II. Sentiments,—divided into Contemplative and Practical.
The former are the concomitants of our Cognitive Powers, the latter of our Powers of Conation. Of these in their order.

The Contemplative Feelings are again distributed into two classes, — into those of the Subsidiary Faculties and those of the Elaborative; and the Feelings
Contemplative Feelings divided into those of the Subsidiary Faculties; and of the Elaborative. The first class divided into those of Self-Consciousness and of Imagination.
accompanying the subsidiary faculties may be again subdivided into those of Self-Consciousness or Internal Perception, and into those of Imagination, — *Imagination* being here employed to comprehend its relative faculty, the faculty of Reproduction. Of these in their order; and first of the Feelings or Sentiments attending the faculty of Reflex Perception or Self-Consciousness.

By this faculty we become aware of our internal states; that is, in other words, that we live. Now we are conscious of our life only as we are conscious of our
a. Sentiments attending Self-Consciousness.
activity, and we are conscious of our activity only as we are conscious of a change of state, — for all activity is the going out of one state into another; while, at the same time, we are only conscious of one state by contrast to, or as discriminated from, a preceding. Now pleas-
Tedium or Ennui.
ure, we have also seen, is the consciousness of a vigorous and unimpeded energy; pain, the consciousness of re-

pressed or impeded tendency to action. This being the case, if there be nothing which presents to our faculties the objects on which they may exert their activity, in other words, if there be no cause whereby our actual state may be made to pass into another, there results a peculiar irksome feeling for a want of excitement, which we denominate *tedium* or *ennui*. This feeling is like that of being unable to die, and not being allowed to live; and sometimes becomes so oppressive that it leads to suicide or madness.

The pain we experience in the feeling of Tedium, arises from the feeling of a repressed tendency to action; and it is intense in proportion as this feeling is lively and vigorous. An inability to thought is a security against this feeling, and, therefore, tedium is far less felt by the uncultivated than by the educated. The more varied the objects presented to our thought,—the more varied and vivacious our activity, the intenser will be our consciousness of living, and the more rapidly will the time appear to fly. But when we look back upon the series of thoughts, with which our mind was occupied the while, we marvel at the apparent length of its duration. Thus it is that, in travelling, a month seems to pass more rapidly than a week; but cast a retrospect upon what has occurred, and occupied our attention during the interval, and the month appears to lengthen to a year. Hence we explain why we call our easy occupations *pastimes;* and why play is so engaging when it is at all deep. Games of hazard determine a continual change,—now we hope, and now we fear; while in games of skill, we experience also the pleasure which arises from the activity of the understanding, in carrying through our own, and in frustrating the plan of our antagonist.

All that relieves tedium, by affording a change and an easy exercise for our thoughts, causes pleasure. The best cure of tedium is some occupation which, by concentrating our attention on external objects, shall divert it from a retortion on ourselves. All occupation is either labor or play; labor when there is some end ulterior to the activity, play when the activity is for its own sake alone. In both, however, there must be ever and anon a change of object, or both will soon grow tiresome. Labor is thus the best preventive of tedium, for it has an external motive which holds us steadfast to the work; while after the completion of our task, the feeling of repose, as the change from the

Sidenotes:
Arises from a repressed tendency to action.

The more varied and vivacious our activity, the intenser our consciousness of life, and the more rapidly does time appear to fly.

Pastimes.
Games of chance and skill.

Tedium, how cured.

feeling of a constrained to that of a spontaneous state, affords a vivid and peculiar pleasure. Labor must alternate with repose, or we shall never know what is the true enjoyment of life.

Thus it appears that a uniform continuity in our internal states is painful, and that pleasure is the result of their commutation. It is, however, to be observed, that the change of our perceptions and thoughts to be pleasing must not be too rapid; for as the intervals, when too long, produce the feeling of Tedium, so, when too short, they cause that of Giddiness or Vertigo. The too rapid passing, for example, of visible objects or of tones before the Senses, of images before the Phantasy, of thoughts before the Understanding, occasions the disagreeable feeling of confusion or stupefaction, which, in individuals of very sensitive temperament, results in Nausea, — Sickness.[1]

The change of our perceptions and thoughts to be pleasing must not be too rapid.

Giddiness.

Nausea.

I proceed now to the Speculative Feelings which accompany the energies of Imagination. It has already been frequently stated, that whatever affords to a power the mean of full spontaneous energy is a cause of pleasure; and that whatever either represses the free exertion of a power, or stimulates it into strained activity, is the cause of pain.

b. Sentiments concomitant of Imagination.

I shall now apply this law to the Imagination. Whatever, in general, facilitates the play of the Imagination, is felt as pleasing; whatever renders it more difficult is felt as displeasing. And this applies equally to Imagination considered as merely reproductive of the objects presented by sense, or as combining these in the phantastic forms of its own productive, or rather plastic, activity. Considering the Phantasy merely as reproductive, we are pleased with the portrait of a person whose face we know, if like, because it enables us to recall the features into consciousness easily and freely; and we are displeased with it if unlike, because it not only does not assist, but thwarts us in our endeavor to recall them; while after this has been accomplished, we are still farther pained by the disharmony we experience between the portrait on the canvas and the representation in our own imagination. A short and characteristic description of things which we have seen, pleases us, because, without exacting a protracted effort of attention, and through a few striking traits, it enables the imagina-

Condition of the pleasurable applicable to Imagination, both as Reproductive and as Plastic.

As Reproductive.

[1] See Marcus Herz, *Über den Schwindel*, 1791.

tion to place the objects vividly before it. On the same principle, whatever facilitates the reproduction of the objects which have been consigned to memory, is pleasurable; as for example, resemblances, contrasts, other associations with the passing thought, metre, rhyme, symmetry, appropriate designations, etc. To realize an act of imagination, it is necessary that we grasp up, — that we comprehend, — the manifold as a single whole: an object, therefore, which does not allow itself, without difficulty, to be thus represented in unity, occasions pain; whereas an object which can easily be recalled to system, is the cause of pleasure. The former is the case when the object is too large or too complex to be perceived at once; when the parts are not prominent enough to be distinctly impressed upon the memory. Order and symmetry facilitate the acts of Reproduction and Representation, and, consequently, afford us a proportional gratification. But, on the other hand, as pleasure is in proportion to the amount of free energy, an object which gives no impediment to the comprehensive energy of Imagination, may not be pleasurable, if it be so simple as not to afford to this faculty a sufficient exercise. Hence it is, that not variety alone, and not unity alone, but variety combined with unity, is that quality in objects, which we emphatically denominate *beautiful*.

An act of Imagination involves the comprehension of the manifold as a single whole.

The Beautiful in objects constituted by variety in unity.

As to what is called the Productive or Creative Imagination, — this is dependent for its materials on the Senses and on the Reproductive Imagination. The Imagination produces, the Imagination creates, nothing; it only reärranges parts, — it only builds up old materials into new forms; and in reference to this act, it ought, therefore, to be called, not the *productive* or *creative*, but the *plastic*.[1] Now this reconstruction of materials by the Plastic Imagination is twofold; for it either arranges them in one representation, or in a series of representations. Of the pleasure we receive from single representations, I have already spoken; it, therefore, only remains to consider the enjoyment we find in the activity of imagination, in so far as this is excited in concatenating a series of representations. I do not at present speak of any pleasure or pain which the contents of these concatenated representations may produce; these are not feelings of imagination, but of appetency or conation; I have here exclusively in view the

Office of the Plastic Imagination to reconstruct and reärrange.

This reconstruction twofold.

---

1 See above, lect. xxxiii. p. 452. — ED.

feelings which accompany the facilitated, or impeded, energy of this function of the phantasy. Now it is manifest that a series of representations are pleasing:—1°, In proportion as they severally call up in us a more varied and harmonious image; and, 2°, In proportion as they stand to each other in a logical dependence.

Conditions of the pleasurable, as regards the Understanding.

This latter is, however, a condition not of the Imagination, but of the Understanding or Elaborative Faculty; and, therefore, before speaking of those feelings which accompany the joint energies of these faculties, it will be proper to consider those which arise from the operations of the Understanding by itself. To these, therefore, I now pass on.

The function of the Understanding may, in general, be said to bestow on the cognitions which it elaborates, the greatest possible compass (comprehension and extension), the greatest possible clearness

Function of the Understanding.

and distinctness, the greatest possible certainty, and systematic order; and in as much as we approximate to the accomplishment of these ends, we experience pleasure, in as much as we meet with hindrances in our attempts, we experience pain. The tendency, the desire we have, to amplify the limits of our knowledge, is one of the strongest principles of human nature. To learn is thus pleasurable; to be frustrated in our attempted knowledge, painful.

Obscurity and confusion in our cognitions we feel as disagreeable; whereas their clearness and distinctness affords us sincere gratification. We are pained by a hazy and perplexed discourse; but rejoice in one perspicuous and profound. Hence the

Obscure and confused cognitions,— how disagreeable.

pleasure we experience in having the cognitions we possessed, but darkling and confused, explicated into life and order; and, on this account, there is hardly a more pleasing object than a tabular conspectus of any complex whole. We are soothed by a solution of a riddle; and the wit which, like a flash of light-

Wit,—how pleasing.

ning, discovers similarities between objects which seemed contradictory, affords a still intenser enjoyment.

Our cognitions may be divided into two classes,—the Empirical or Historical, and the Rational. In the former we only apprehend the fact that they are; in the latter, we comprehend the reason why they are. The Understanding, therefore, does not

Cognitions divided into two classes,— Empirical and Rational.

for each demand the same kind or degree of knowledge; but in each, if its demand be successful, we are pleased; if unsuccessful, we are chagrined.

From the tendency of men towards knowledge and certainty, there arises a peculiar feeling which is commonly called the Feeling or Sentiment of Truth, but might be more correctly styled the Feeling or Sentiment of Conviction. For we must not mistake this feeling for the faculty by which we discriminate truth from error; this feeling, as merely subjective, can determine nothing in regard to truth and error, which are, on the contrary, of an objective relation; and there are found as many examples of men who have died the confessors of an error they mistook for truth, as of men who have laid down their lives in testimony of the real truth. "Every opinion," says Montaigne,[1] "is strong enough to have had its martyrs." Be this, however, as it may, the feeling of conviction is a pleasurable sentiment, because it accompanies the consciousness of an unimpeded energy; whereas the counter-feeling, — that of doubt or uncertainty, is a painful sentiment, because it attends a consciousness of a thwarted activity. The uneasy feeling which is thus the concomitant of doubt, is a powerful stimulus to the extension and perfecting of our knowledge.

Sentiment of Truth, — what, and how pleasurable.

The multitude, — the multifarious character, — of the objects presented to our observation, stands in signal contrast with the very limited capacity of the human intellect. This disproportion constrains us to classify; that is, by a comparison of the objects of sense to reduce these to notions; on these primary notions we repeat the comparison, and thus carry them up into higher, and these higher into highest, notions. This process is performed by that function of the Understanding, which apprehends resemblances; and hence originate *species* and *genera* in all their gradations. In this detection of the similarities between different objects, an energy of the understanding is fully and freely exerted; and hence results a pleasure. But as in these classes, — these general notions, — the knowledge of individual existences loses in precision and completeness, we again endeavor to find out differences in the things which stand under a notion, to the end that we may be able to specify and individualize them. This counter-process is performed by that function of the Understanding, which apprehends dissimilarities between resembling objects, and in the full and free exertion of this energy there is a feeling of pleasure.

Generalization and Specification, — how pleasurable.

The Intellect further tends to reduce the piecemeal and fragmentary cognitions it possesses, to a systematic whole, in other

1 *Essais,* i. ch. xl. — ED.

words, to elevate them to a Science; hence the pleasure we derive from all that enables us with ease and rapidity to survey the relation of complex parts, as constituting the members of one organic whole.

The Intellect, from the necessity it has of thinking of everything as the result of some higher reason, is thus determined to attempt the deduction of every object of cognition from a simple principle. When, therefore, we succeed or seem to succeed in the discovery of such a principle, we feel a pleasure; as we feel a pain, when the intellect is frustrated in this endeavor.

To the feelings of pleasure which are afforded by the unimpeded energies of the Understanding, belongs, likewise, the gratification we find in the apprehension of external or internal adaptation of Means to Ends. Human intelligence is naturally determined to propose to itself an end: and, in the consideration of objects, it thus necessarily thinks them under this relation. If an object, viewed as a mean, be fitted to effect its end, this end is either an external, that is, one which lies beyond the thing itself, in some other existence; or an internal, that is, one which lies within the thing itself, and consummates its own existence. If the end be external, an object suited to accomplish it is said to be *useful*. If, again, the end be internal, and all the parts of the object be viewed in relation to their whole as to their end, an object, as suited to effect this end, is said to be *perfect*. If, therefore, we consider an object in reference either to an external or to an internal end, and if this object be recognized to fulfil the conditions which this relation implies, the act of thought in which this is accomplished is an unimpeded, and, consequently, pleasurable energy; whereas the act of cognizing that these conditions are awanting, and the object therefore ill adapted to its end, is a thwarted, and therefore a painful, energy of thought.

LECTURE XLVI.

THE FEELINGS. — THEIR CLASSES. — THE BEAUTIFUL AND SUBLIME.

AFTER terminating the consideration of the Feelings viewed as Causes, — causes of Pleasure and Pain, we entered, in our last Lecture, on their discussion regarded as Effects, — effects of the various processes of conscious life. In this latter relation, I divided them into two great classes, — the Sensations and Sentiments. The Sensations are those feelings which accompany the vital processes more immediately connected with the corporeal organism. The Sentiments are those feelings which accompany the mental processes, which, if not wholly inorganic, are at least less immediately dependent on the conditions of the nervous system. The Sensations I again subdivided into two orders, — into those which accompany the action of the five Determinate Senses, and into those which accompany, or, in fact, constitute the manifestations of the Indeterminate or Vital Sense. After a slight consideration of the Sensations, I passed on to the Sentiments. These I also subdivided into orders, according as they accompany the energies of the Cognitive, or the energies of the Conative, Powers. The former of these I called the Contemplative, — the latter, the Practical Feelings or Sentiments. Taking the former, — the Contemplative, — into discussion, I further subdivided these into two classes, according as they are the concomitants of the lower or Subsidiary, or of the higher or Elaborative Faculty of Cognition. The sentiments which accompany the lower or Subsidiary Faculties, by a final Subdivision, I distributed into those of the Faculty of Self-consciousness and into those of the Imagination, — referring to the Imagination the relative faculty of Reproduction. I ought also to have observed, that, as the Imagination always coöperates in every act of complex perception, and, in fact, bestows on such a cognition its whole unity, under the Feelings of Imagination (or of Imagination and the Understanding in conjunction), would fall to be considered those sentiments of pleasure which, in the perceptions of sense, we receive from the relations of the objects presented. Under the Feelings connected with the energies of the Elaborative Faculty or Understanding, I comprehended those which arise from the gratification of the Regulative Faculty,— Reason or Intelligence,—because it is only through the operations of the former that the laws of the latter are carried into effect. In relation to Feelings, the two faculties may, therefore, be regarded as one. I then proceeded to treat of the several kinds of Contemplative Feeling in detail; and, before the conclusion of the Lecture, had run rapidly through those of Self-consciousness, those of Imagination, considered apart from the Understanding, and those of the Understanding, considered apart from Imagination. We have now, therefore, in the first place, to consider the feelings which arise from the acts of Imagination and Understanding in conjunction.

Feelings that arise from the Imagination and Understanding in conjunction.

The feelings of satisfaction which result from the joint energy of the Understanding and Phantasy, are principally those of Beauty and Sublimity; and the judgments which pronounce an object to be *sublime, beautiful,* etc., are called, by a metaphorical expression, *Judgments of Taste.* These have been also styled *Æsthetical Judgments;* and the term *æsthetical* has now, especially among the philosophers of Germany, nearly superseded the term *taste.* Both terms are unsatisfactory.

Beauty and Sublimity.

The gratification we feel in the beautiful, the sublime, the picturesque, etc., is purely contemplative, that is, the feeling of pleasure which we then experience, arises solely from the consideration of the object, and altogether apart from any desire of, or satisfaction in, its possession. In the following observations, it is almost needless to observe, that I can make no attempt at more than a simple indication of the origin of the pleasure we derive from the contemplation of those objects, which, from the character of the feelings they determine, are called *beautiful, sublime,* etc.

In relation to the Beautiful, this has been distinguished into the Free or Absolute, and into the Dependent or Relative.[1] In the former case, it is not necessary to have a notion of what the object ought to be, before we pronounce it beautiful or not; in the latter case, such a previous notion is required. Flowers,

Beauty distinguished as Absolute and Relative.

---

[1] See Hutcheson, *Inquiry,* treatise i. sects. 2, 4. — ED.

shells, arabesques, etc., are freely or absolutely beautiful. We judge, for example, a flower to be beautiful, though unaware of its destination, and that it contains a complex apparatus of organs all admirably adapted to the propagation of the plant. When we are made cognizant of this, we obtain, indeed, an additional gratification, but one wholly different from that which we experience in the contemplation of the flower itself, apart from all consideration of its adaptations. A house, a pillar, a piece of furniture, are dependently or relatively beautiful; for here the object is judged beautiful by reference to a certain end, for the sake of which it exists. This distinction, which is taken by Kant[1] and others,

This distinction unsound.

appears to me unsound. For Relative Beauty is only the confusion of two elements, which ought to have been kept distinct. There is no doubt, I think, that certain objects please us directly and of themselves, that is, no reference being had to aught beyond the form itself which they exhibit. These are things of themselves beautiful. Other things, again, please us not directly and of themselves, that is, their form presents nothing, the cognition of which results in an agreeable feeling. But these same things may please indirectly and by relation; that is, when we are informed that they have a purpose, and are made aware of their adaptation to its accomplishment, we may derive a pleasure from the admirable relation which here subsists between the end and means. These are things Useful. But the

The Useful and the Beautiful distinct.

pleasure which results from the contemplation of the useful, is wholly different from that which results from the contemplation of the beautiful, and, therefore, they ought not to be confounded. It may, indeed, happen that the same object is such as affords us both kinds of pleasure, and it may at once be beautiful and useful. But why, on such a ground, establish a second series of beauty? In this respect,

St. Augustin's doctrine on this point superior to the modern.

St. Augustin shows himself superior to our great modern analyst. In his *Confessions*, he informs us that he had written a book (unfortunately lost), addressed to Hierius, the Roman rhetorician, under the title *De Apto et Pulcro*, in which he maintained, that the beautiful is that which pleases absolutely and of itself, the well-adapted that which pleases from its accommodation to something else. " Pulcrum esse, quod per se ipsum; aptum, autem, quod ad aliquid accommodatum deceret." [2]

---

1 Partially, perhaps; see *Kritik der Urtheilskraft,* §§ 6, 10. But Kant distinguishes Beauty from Adaptation to an End, though he refers both to the faculty of Judgment — Ed.

2 Lib. iv. cap. xv. — Ed.

Now what has been distinguished as Dependent or Relative Beauty, is nothing more than a beautified utility, or a utilized beauty. For example, a pillar taken by itself and apart from all consideration of any purpose it has to serve, is a beautiful object; and a person of good taste, and ignorant of its relations, would at once pronounce it so. But when he is informed that it is also a mean towards an end, he will then find an additional satisfaction in the observation of its perfect adaptation to its purpose; and he will no longer consider the pillar as something beautiful and useless; his taste will desiderate its application, and will be shocked at seeing, as we so often see, a set of columns stuck on upon a building, and supporting nothing. Be this, however, as it may, our pleasure, in both cases, arises from a free and full play being allowed to our cognitive faculties. In the case of Beauty,—Free Beauty,—both the Imagination and the Understanding find occupation; and the pleasure we experience from such an object, is in proportion as it affords to these faculties the opportunity of exerting fully and freely their respective energies. Now, it is the principal function of the Understanding, out of the multifarious presented to it, to form a whole. Its entire activity is, in fact, a tendency towards unity; and it is only satisfied when this object is so constituted as to afford the opportunity of an easy and perfect performance of this its function. In this case, the object is judged beautiful or pleasing.

Relative Beauty is only a beautified utility, or utilized beauty.

The theory of Free or Absolute Beauty.

The greater the number of the parts of any object given by the Imagination, which the Understanding has to bind up into a whole, and the shorter the time in which it is able to bring this process to its issue, the more fully and the more easily does the understanding energize, and, consequently, the greater will be the pleasure afforded as the reflex of its energy.[1]

This not only affords us the rationale of what the Beautiful is, but it also enables us to explain the differences of different individuals in the apprehension of the beautiful. The function of the Understanding is in all men the same; and the understanding of every man binds up what is given as plural and multifarious into the unity of a whole. But as it is only the full and facile accomplishment of this function,

The theory explains the differences of individuals in the apprehension of the Beautiful.

---

[1] [Cf Mendelssohn, *Philosophische Schriften,* ii. p. 74. Hemsterhuis, *Lettre sur la Sculpture Œuvres Philosophiques* I, p. 2.]

which has pleasure for its concomitant, it depends wholly on the capacity of the individual understanding, whether this condition shall be fulfilled. If an understanding, by natural constitution, by cultivation and exercise, be vigorous enough to think up rapidly into a whole what is presented in complexity, — multiplicity, — the individual has an enjoyment in the exertion, and he regards the object as beautiful; whereas, if an intellect perform this function slowly and with effort, if it succeed in accomplishing the end at all, the individual can feel no pleasure (if he does not experience pain), and the object must to him appear as one destitute of beauty, if not positively ugly. Hence it is that children, boors, in a word, persons of a weak or uncultivated mind, may find the parts of a building beautiful, while unable to comprehend the beauty of it as a whole. On the other hand, we may also explain why the pleasure we have in the contemplation of an object is lessened, if not wholly annihilated, if we mentally analyze it into its parts. The fairest human head would lose its beauty were we to sunder it in thought, and consider how it is made up of integuments, of cellular tissue, of muscular fibres, of bones, of brain, of blood-vessels, etc. It is no longer a whole; it is the multifarious without unity. In reference to Taste, it is quite a different thing to sunder a whole into its parts, and a whole into its lesser wholes. In the one case, we separate only to separate, and not again to connect. In the other, we look to the parts, in order to be able in a shorter time more perfectly to survey the whole. This must enhance the gratification, and it is a process always requisite when the whole comprises a more multiplex plurality than our understanding is competent to embrace at the first attempt. When a whole head is found too complex to be judged at once, out of the brow, eyes, nose, cheeks, mouth, etc., we make so many lesser wholes, in order, in the first place, to comprehend them by the intellect as wholes together; we then bind up these petty wholes into one great whole, which, in a shorter or longer time, we overlook, and award to it accordingly, a greater or a less amount of beauty.

In the case of Relative or Dependent Beauty, we must distinguish the pleasure we receive into two, combined indeed, but not identical. The one of these pleasures is that from the beauty which the object contains, and the principle of which

And affords the reason why our pleasure in the contemplation of an object is lessened, when we analyze it into its parts.

Difference between sundering a whole into its parts, and into its lesser wholes.

Relative Beauty, from the conformity of Mean to End.

we have been just considering. The other of these pleasures is that which, in our last Lecture, we showed was attached to a perfect energy of the Understanding, in thinking an object under the notion of conformity as a mean adapted to an end.

A judgment of Taste may be called *pure*, when the pleasure it enounces is one exclusively derived from the Beautiful, and *mixed*, when with this pleasure there are conjoined feelings of pain or pleasure from other sources. Such, for example, are the organic excitations of particular colors, tones, etc., emotions, the moral feeling, the feeling of pleasure from the sublime, etc. It requires a high cultivation of the taste in order to find gratification in a pure beauty, and also to separate from our judgment of an object, in this respect, all that is foreign to this source of pleasure. The uncultivated man at first finds gratification only in those qualities which stimulate his organs; and it is only gradually that he can be educated to pay attention to the form of objects, and to find pleasure in what lightly exercises his faculties of Imagination and Thought, — the Beautiful. The result, then, of what has now been said is, that a thing beautiful is one whose form occupies the Imagination and Understanding in a free and full, and, consequently, in an agreeable, activity: and to this definition of the Beautiful all others may without difficulty be reduced; for these, like the definitions of the pleasurable, are never absolutely false, but, in general, only partial expressions of the truth. On these it is, however, at present impossible to touch.

Judgments of Taste either Pure or Mixed.

The Beautiful defined.

The feeling of pleasure in the Sublime is essentially different from our feeling of pleasure in the Beautiful. The beautiful awakens the mind to a soothing contemplation; the sublime rouses it to strong emotion. The beautiful attracts without repelling; whereas the sublime at once does both; the beautiful affords us a feeling of unmingled pleasure, in the full and unimpeded activity of our cognitive powers; whereas our feeling of sublimity is a mingled one of pleasure and pain, — of pleasure in the consciousness of the strong energy, of pain in the consciousness that this energy is vain.

The Sublime, — the feeling partly pleasurable.

But as the amount of pleasure in the sublime is greater than the amount of pain, it follows, that the free energy it elicits must be greater than the free energy it repels. The beautiful has reference to the form of an object, and the facility with which it is comprehended.

Theory of the Sublime.

For beauty, magnitude is thus an impediment. Sublimity, on the contrary, requires magnitude as its condition; and the formless is not unfrequently sublime. That we are at once attracted and repelled by sublimity, arises from the circumstance that the object which we call *sublime*, is proportioned to one of our faculties, and disproportioned to another; but as the degree of pleasure transcends the degree of pain, the power whose energy is promoted must be superior to that power whose energy is repressed.

The sublime has been divided into two kinds, the Theoretical and the Practical, or as they are also called, the Mathematical and the Dynamical.[1] A preferable division would be according to the three quantities, — into the sublime of Extension, the sublime of Protension, and the sublime of Intension; or, what comes to the same thing, — the sublime of Space, the sublime of Time, and the sublime of Power. In the two former the cognitive, in the last the conative, powers come into play. An object is extensively, or protensively sublime, when it comprises so great a multitude of parts that the Imagination sinks under the attempt to represent it in an image, and the Understanding to measure it by reference to other quantities. Baffled in the attempt to reduce the object within the limits of the faculties by which it must be comprehended, the mind at once desists from the ineffectual effort, and conceives the object not by a positive, but by a negative, notion; it conceives it as inconceivable, and falls back into repose, which is felt as pleasing by contrast to the continuance of a forced and impeded energy. Examples of the sublime, — of this sudden effort, and of this instantaneous desisting from the attempt, are manifested in the extensive sublime of Space, and in the protensive sublime of Eternity.

The Sublime, — divided into that of Extension, Protension, and Intension.

These divisions illustrated.

The Sublime of Extension and Protension.

An object is intensively sublime, when it involves such a degree of force or power that the Imagination cannot at once represent, and the Understanding cannot bring under measure, the quantum of this force; and when, from the nature of the object, the inability of the mind is made at once apparent, so that it does not proceed in the ineffectual effort, but at once calls back its energies from the attempt. It is thus manifest that the feeling of the sublime will be one of mingled pain and pleasure; pleasure from the vigorous exertion and

The sublime of Intension.

---

1 Kant, *Kritik der Urtheilskraft*, § 24 *et seq.* — ED.

from the instantaneous repose; pain, from the consciousness of limited and frustrated activity. This mixed feeling in the contemplation of a sublime object is finely expressed by Lucretius when he says:

"Me quædam divina voluptas,
Percipit atque horror."[1]

I do not know a better example of the sublime, in all its three forms, than in the following passage of Kant:[2]

"Two things there are, which, the oftener and the more stead-fastly we consider, fill the mind with an ever new, an ever rising admiration and reverence; — *the* Starry Heaven *above, the* Moral Law *within.* Of neither am I compelled to seek out the reality, as veiled in darkness, or only to conjecture the possibility, as beyond the hemisphere of my knowledge. Both I contemplate lying clear before me, and connect both immediately with my consciousness of existence. The one departs from the place I occupy in the outer world of sense; expands, beyond the bounds of imagination, this connection of my body with worlds lying beyond worlds, and systems blending into systems; and protends it also into the illimitable times of their periodic movement, — to its commencement and continuance. The other departs from my invisible self, from my personality; and represents me in a world, truly infinite indeed, but whose infinity can be tracked out only by the intellect, with which also my connection, unlike the fortuitous relation I stand in to all worlds of sense, I am compelled to recognize as universal and necessary. In the former the first view of a countless multitude of worlds annihilates, as it were, my importance as an *animal product,* which, after a brief and that incomprehensible endowment with the powers of life, is compelled to refund its constituent matter to the planet — itself an atom in the universe — on which it grew. The aspect of the other, on the contrary, elevates my worth as an *intelligence* even without limit; and this through my personality, in which the moral law reveals a faculty of life independent of my animal nature, nay, of the whole material world: — at least, if it be permitted to infer as much from the regulation of my being, which a conformity with that law exacts; proposing, as it does, my moral worth for the absolute end of my activity, conceding no compromise of its imperative to a necessitation of nature, and spurning, in its infinity, the conditions and boundaries of my present transitory life."

The Sublime, in its three forms, exemplified in a passage from Kant.

1 iii. 28. — Ed.　　　2 *Kritik der practischen Vernunft,* Beschluss. — Ed.

" Spirat enim majora animus seque altius effert

Sideribus, transitque vias et nubila fati,

Et momenta premit pedibus quæcunque putantur

Figere propositam natali tempore sortem." [1]

Here we have the extensive sublime in the heavens and their interminable space, the protensive sublime in their illimitable duration, and the intensive sublime in the omnipotence of the human will, as manifested in the unconditional imperative of the moral law.

The Picturesque, however, opposite to the Sublime, seems, in my opinion, to stand to the Beautiful in a somewhat similar relation. An object is positively ugly, when it is of such a form that the Imagination and Understanding cannot help attempting to think it up into unity, and yet their energies are still so impeded that they either fail in the endeavor, or accomplish it only imperfectly, after time and toil. The cause of this continuance of effort is, that the object does not present such an appearance of incongruous variety as at once to compel the mind to desist from the attempt of reducing it to unity; but, on the contrary, leads it on to attempt what it is yet unable to perform, — its reduction to a whole. But variety, — variety even apart from unity,—is pleasing; and if the mind be made content to expatiate freely and easily in this variety, without attempting painfully to reduce it to unity, it will derive no inconsiderable pleasure from this exertion of its powers. Now a picturesque object is precisely of such a character. It is so determinately varied and so abrupt in its variety, it presents so complete a negation of all rounded contour, and so regular an irregularity of broken lines and angles, that every attempt at reducing it to an harmonious whole is at once found to be impossible. The mind, therefore, which must forego the energy of representing and thinking the object as a unity, surrenders itself at once to the energies which deal with it only in detail.

The Picturesque,— wherein it consists, and how it differs from the Sublime and Beautiful.

I proceed now to those feelings which I denominated Practical, — those, namely, which have their root in the powers of Conation, and thus have reference to overt action.

The Practical Feelings.

The Conative, like the Cognitive, powers are divided into a higher and a lower order, as they either are, or are not, immediately relative to our bodily condition. The former may be called the Pathological, the latter the Moral.

Their divisions.

<hr/>

1 Prudentius, *Contra Sym.* ii. 479. Quoted in *Discussions*, p. 311. — ED.

Neglecting this distribution, the Practical Feelings are relative either — 1°, To our Self-preservation; or, 2°, To the Enjoyment of our Existence; or, 3°, To the Preservation of the Species; or, 4°, To our Tendency towards Development and Perfection; or, 5°, To the Moral Law. Of these in their order.

In the first place, of the feelings relative to Self-preservation: —

Those relative — 1. To Self-preservation. these are the feelings of Hunger and Thirst, of Loathing, of Sorrow, of Bodily Pain, of Repose, of Fear at danger, of Anxiety, of Shuddering, of Alarm, of Composure, of Security, and the nameless feeling at the Representation of Death. Several of these feelings are corporeal, and may be considered, with equal propriety, as modifications of the Vital Sense.

In the second place, man is determined not only to exist, but to

2. Enjoyment of existence. exist well; he is, therefore, determined also to desire whatever tends to render life agreeable, and to eschew whatever tends to render it disagreeable. All, therefore, that appears to contribute to the former, causes in him the feeling of Joy; whereas, all that seems to threaten the latter, excites in him the repressed feelings of Fear, Anxiety, Sorrow, etc., which we have already mentioned.

In the third place, man is determined, not only to preserve himself, but to preserve the species to which he be-

3. Preservation of the species. longs, and with this tendency various feelings are associated. To this head belong the feelings of Sexual Love; and the Sentiment of Parental Affection. But the human affections are not limited to family connections. "Man," says Aristotle, "is the sweetest thing to man."[1] Man is more political than any bee or ant."[2] We have thus a tendency to social intercourse, and society is at once the necessary condition of our happiness and our perfection. "The solitary," says Aristotle again, "is either above or below humanity; he is either a god or a beast."[3]

In conformity with his tendency to social existence, man is en-

Sympathy. dowed with a Sympathetic Feeling, that is, he rejoices with those that rejoice, and grieves with those that grieve. Compassion, — Pity, — is the name given to the latter modification of sympathy; the former is without a definite name. Besides sympathetic sorrow and sympathetic joy, there are

Vanity. Shame. a variety of feelings which have reference to our existence in a social relation. Of these there is that connected with Vanity, or the wish to please others from the desire of being respected by them; with Shame,

1 *Eth. Eud.* vii. 2, 26. — ED.   2 *Polit.* i. 2, 10. — ED.   3 *Polit.* i. 2, 9, 14. — ED.

or the fear and sorrow at incurring their disrespect; with Pride, or the overweening sentiment of our own worth.

Pride.

To the same class we may refer the feelings connected with Indignation, Resentment, Anger, Scorn, etc.

In the fourth place, there is in man implanted a desire of developing his powers, — there is a tendency towards perfection. In virtue of this, the consciousness of all comparative inability causes pain; the consciousness of all comparative power causes pleasure. To this class belong the feelings which accompany Emulation, — the desire of rising superior to others; and Envy, — the desire of reducing others beneath ourselves.

4. Tendency to development.

In the fifth place, we are conscious that there is in man a Moral Law, — a Law of Duty, which unconditionally commands the fulfilment of its behests. This supposes, that we are able to fulfil them, or our nature is a lie; and the liberty of human action is thus, independently of all direct consciousness, involved in the datum of the Law of Duty. Inasmuch also as Moral Intelligence unconditionally commands us to perform what we are conscious to be our duty, there is attributed to man an absolute worth, — an absolute dignity. The feeling which the manifestation of this worth excites, is called Respect. With the consciousness of the lofty nature of our moral tendencies, and our ability to fulfil what the law of duty prescribes, there is connected the feeling of Self-respect; whereas, from a consciousness of the contrast between what we ought to do and what we actually perform, there arises the feeling of Self-abasement. The sentiment of respect for the law of duty is the Moral Feeling, which has by some been improperly denominated the Moral Sense; for through this feeling we do not take cognizance whether anything be morally good or morally evil, but when, by our intelligence, we recognize aught to be of such a character, there is herewith associated a feeling of pain or pleasure, which is nothing more than our state in reference to the fulfilment or violation of the law.

5. The Moral Law.

Man, as conscious of his liberty to act, and of the law by which his actions ought to be regulated, recognizes his personal accountability, and calls himself before the internal tribunal which we denominate Conscience. Here he is either acquitted or condemned. The acquittal is connected with a peculiar feeling of pleasurable exultation, as the condemnation with a peculiar feeling of painful humiliation, — Remorse.

APPENDIX.

I. A.—FRAGMENT ON ACADEMICAL HONORS.—(1836.)

(See p. 13.)

BEFORE commencing the Lecture of to-day, I would occupy a few minutes with a matter in which I am confident you generally feel an interest;—I refer to the Academical Honors to be awarded to those who approve their zeal and ability in the business of the Class. After what I formerly had occasion to say, I conceive it wholly unnecessary now to attempt any proof of the fact,—that it is not by anything done by others for you, but by what alone you do for yourselves, that your intellectual improvement must be determined. Reading and listening to lectures are only profitable, inasmuch as they afford you the means and the occasions of exerting your faculties;—for these faculties are only developed in proportion as they are exercised. This is a principle I take for granted.

A second fact, I am assured you will also allow me to assume, is, that although strenuous energy is the one condition of all improvement,—yet this energy is, at first and for a long time, comparatively painful. It is painful, because it is imperfect. But as it is gradually perfected, it becomes gradually more pleasing, and when finally perfect, that is, when its power is fully developed, it is purely pleasurable; for pleasure is nothing but the concomitant or reflex of the unforced and unimpeded energy of a faculty or habit,—the degree of pleasure being always in proportion to the degree of such energy. The great problem in education is, therefore, how to induce the pupil to undertake and go through with a course of exertion, in its result good and even agreeable, but immediately and in itself, irksome. There is no royal road to learning. "The gods," says Epicharmus,[1] "sell us everything for toil;" and the curse inherited from Adam,—that in the sweat of his face man should eat his bread,—is true of every human acquisition. Hesiod, not less beautifully than philosophically, sings of the painful commencement, and the pleasant consummation, of virtue, in the passage of which the following is the commencement:

Τῆς δ' Ἀρετῆς ἱδρῶτα θεοὶ προπάροιθεν ἔθηκαν
Ἀθάνατοι:[2]

---

1 Xenophon, *Memorabilia*, ii. 1, 20.—ED.   2 *Opera et Dies*, 287.—ED.

(a passage which, it will be recollected, Milton has not less beautifully imitated) ;[1] and the Latin poet has, likewise, well expressed the principle, touching literary excellence in particular:

———— " Gaudent sudoribus artes
Et sua difficilem reddunt ad limina cursum." [2]

But as the pain is immediate, while the profit and the pleasure are remote, you will grant, I presume, without difficulty, a third fact, that the requisite degree and continuance of effort can only be insured, by applying a stimulus to counteract and overcome the repressive effect of the feeling with which the exertion is for a season accompanied. A fourth fact will not be denied, that emulation and the love of honor constitute the appropriate stimulus in education. These affections are of course implanted in man for the wisest purposes; and, though they may be misdirected, the inference from the possibility of their abuse to the absolute inexpediency of their employment, is invalid. However disguised, their influence is universal:

" Ad has se
Romanus, Graiusque, et Barbarus induperator
Erexit: causas discriminis atque laboris
Inde habuit; "[3]

and Cicero shrewdly remarks, that the philosophers themselves prefix their names to the very books they write on the contempt of glory.[4] These passions actuate most powerfully the noblest minds. " Optimos mortalium," [5] says the father of the Senate to Tiberius, — " Optimos mortalium altissima cupere : contemptu famæ contemni virtutes." " Naturâ," says Seneca,[6] " gloriosa est virtus, et anteire priores cupit; " and Cicero,[7] in more proximate reference to our immediate object, — " Honor alit artes omnesque incenduntur ad studia gloriâ." But, though their influence be universal, it is most powerfully conspicuous in the young, of whom Aristotle has noted it as one of the most discriminating characteristics, that they are lovers of honor, but still more lovers of victory.[8] If, therefore, it could be but too justly proclaimed of man in general:

———— " Quis enim virtutem amplectitur ipsam,
Præmia si tollas? "[9]

it was least of all to be expected that youth should do so. " In learning," says the wisdom of Bacon, " the flight will be [low and] slow without some feathers of ostentation." [10] Nothing, therefore, could betray a greater ignorance of human nature, or a greater negligence in employing the most efficient mean

---

1 Sir W. Hamilton here probably refers to the lines in *Lycidas*, —
" Fame is the spur that the clear spirit doth raise," etc. — ED.

2 B. Mantuanus, *Carmen de suscepto Theologico Magisterio, Opera,* Antverpiæ, 1576, tom. i. p. 174. — ED.

3 Juvenal, *Sat.* x. 138. — ED.

4 *Pro Archia,* c. 11. — ED.

5 Tacitus, *Ann.* iv. 38. — ED.

6 *De Beneficiis,* iii. 36. — ED.

7 *Tusc. Quæst.* i. 2. — ED.

8 *Rhet.* ii. 12. — ED.

9 Juvenal, *Sat.* x. 141. — ED.

10 *Essay* liv. *Of Vain Glory.* — ED.

within its grasp, than for any seminary of education to leave unapplied these great promoting principles of activity, and to take for granted that its pupils would act precisely as they ought, though left with every inducement strong against, and without any sufficient motive in favor of, exertion.

Now, I express, I believe, the universal sentiment, both within and without these walls, in saying, that this University has been unhappily all too remiss, in leaving the most powerful mean of academical education nearly, if not altogether, unemployed. You will observe I use the term *University* in contradiction to individual Professors, for many of these have done much in this respect, and all of them, I believe, are satisfied that a great deal more ought to be done. But it is not in the power of individual instructors to accomplish what can be only accomplished by the public institution. The rewards proposed to meritorious effort are not sufficiently honorable; and the efforts to which they are frequently accorded, not of the kind or degree to be of any great or general advantage. I shall explain myself.

A distinction is sought after with a zeal proportioned to its value; and its value is measured by the estimation which it holds in public opinion. Now, though there are prizes given in many of our classes, nothing has been done to give them proper value by raising them in public estimation. They are not conferred as matters of importance by any external solemnity; they are not conferred in any general meeting of the University; far less under circumstances which make their distribution a matter of public curiosity and interest. Compared to the publicity that might easily have been secured, they are left, so to speak, to be given in holes and corners; and while little thought of today, are wholly forgotten to-morrow; so that the wonder only is, that what the University has thus treated with such apparent contempt, should have awakened even the inadequate emulation that has been so laudably displayed. Of this great defect in our discipline, I may safely say that every Professor is aware, and it is now actually under the consideration of the Senatus, what are the most expedient measures to obtain a system of means of full efficiency for the encouragement and reward of academical merit. It will, of course, form the foundation of any such improvement, that the distribution of prizes be made an act of the University at large; and one of the most public and imposing character. By this means a far more powerful emulation will be roused; a spirit which will not be limited to a certain proportion of the students, but will more or less pervade the whole; nay, not merely the students themselves, but their families; so that when this system is brought to its adequate perfection, it will be next to impossible for a young man of generous disposition not to put forth every energy to raise himself as high as possible in the scale of so honorable a competition.

But, besides those who can only be affected by an act of the whole University, important improvement may, I think, be accomplished in this respect in the several classes. In what I now say, I would not be supposed to express any opinion in regard to other classes; but confine my observations to one under the circumstances of our own.

In the first place, then, I am convinced that excitement and rewards are principally required to promote a general and continued diligence in the ordinary business of the class. I mean, therefore, that the prizes should with us be awarded for general eminence, as shown in the Examinations and Exercises; and I am averse on principle from proposing any premium during the course of the sessional labors for single and detached efforts. The effect of this would naturally be to distract attention from what ought to be the principal and constant object of occupation; and if honor is to be gained by an irregular and transient spirit of activity, less encouragement will necessarily be afforded to regular and sedulous application. Prizes for individual Essays, for Written Analyses of important books, and for Oral Examination on their contents, may, however, with great advantage, be proposed as occupation during the summer vacation; and this I shall do. But the honors of the Winter Session must belong to those who have regularly gone through its toils.

In the second place, the value of the prizes may be greatly enhanced by giving them greater and more permanent publicity. A very simple mode, and one which I mean to adopt, is to record upon a tablet each year, the names of the successful competitors; this tablet to be permanently affixed to the walls of the class-room, while a duplicate may, in like manner, be placed in the Common Reading-Room of the Library.

In the third place, the importance of the prizes for general eminence in the business of the class may be considerably raised, by making the competitors the judges of merit among themselves. This I am persuaded is a measure of the very highest efficiency. On theory I would argue this, and in practice it has been fully verified. On this head, I shall quote to you the experience of my venerated preceptor, the late Professor Jardine of Glasgow, — a man, I will make bold to say, who, in the chair of Logic of that University, did more for the intellectual improvement of his pupils than any other public instructor in this country within the memory of man. This he did not accomplish either by great erudition or great philosophical talent, — though he was both a learned and an able thinker, — but by the application of that primary principle of education, which, wherever employed, has been employed with success, — I mean the determination of the pupil to self-activity, — doing nothing for him which he is able to do for himself. This principle, which has been always inculcated by theorists on education, has, however, by few been carried fully into effect.

"One difficult and very important part," says Mr. Jardine,[1] "in administering the system of prizes, still remains to be stated; and this is the method by which the different degrees of merit are determined; a point in which any error with regard to principle, or suspicion of practical mistake, would completely destroy all the good effects aimed at by the establishment in question. It has been already mentioned, that the qualifications which form the ground of competition for the class prizes, as they are sometimes called, and which are to be distinguished from the university prizes, are diligence, regularity of attendance, general eminence at the daily examinations, and in the execution of themes, propriety of academical conduct, and habitual good manners; and, on these heads, it is very obvious, a judgment must be pronounced either by the professor, or by the students themselves, as no others have access to the requisite information.

"It may be imagined, at first view, that the office of judge would be best performed by the professor; but after long experience, and much attention to the subject in all its bearings, I am inclined to give a decided preference to the exercise of this right as vested in the students. Were the professor to take this duty upon himself, it would be impos-

1 *Outlines of Philosophical Education*, etc., pp. 384, 385; 387, 389.

sible, even with the most perfect conviction, on the part of the students, that his judgment and candor were unimpeachable, to give satisfaction to all parties; while, on the other hand, were there the slightest reason to suspect his impartiality, in either of these points, or the remotest ground for insinuation that he gave undue advantage to any individuals, in bringing forward their claims to the prejudice of others, the charm of emulation would be dissolved at once, and every future effort among his pupils would be enfeebled.

* * * * * * * *

" The indispensable qualities of good judges, then, are a competent knowledge of the grounds upon which their judgment is to rest, and a firm resolution to determine on the matter before them with strict impartiality. It is presumed that the students, in these respects, are sufficiently qualified. They are every day witnesses of the manner in which the business of the class goes on, and have, accordingly, the best opportunities of judging as to the merits of their fellow-students; they have it in their power to observe the regularity of their attendance, and the general propriety of their conduct; they hear the questions which are put, with the answers which are given; their various themes are read aloud, and observations are made on them from the chair. They have, likewise, an opportunity of comparing the respective merits of all the competitors, in the extemporaneous exercises of the class; and they, no doubt, hear the performances of one another canvassed in conversation, and made the subject of a comparative estimate. Besides, as every individual is, himself, deeply interested, it is not possible but that he should pay the closest attention to what is going on around him; whilst he cannot fail to be aware that he, in like manner, is constantly observed by others, and subjected to the ordeal of daily criticism. In truth, the character, the abilities, the diligence, and progress of students, are as well known to one another, before the close of the session, as their faces. There cannot, therefore, be any deficiency as to means of information to enable them to act the part of enlightened and upright judges.

" But they likewise possess the other requisite for an equitable decision; for the great majority have really a desire to judge honorably and fairly on the merit of their fellows. The natural candor and generosity of youth, the sense of right and obligations of justice, are not yet so perverted, by bad example and the ways of the world, as, to permit any deliberate intention of violating the integrity on which they profess to act, or any wish to conspire in supporting an unrighteous judgment. There is greater danger, perhaps, that young persons, in their circumstances, may allow themselves to be influenced by friendship or personal dislike, rather than by the pure and unbiassed sense of meritorious exertion, or good abilities; but, on the other hand, when an individual considers of how little consequence his single vote will be among so many, it is not at all likely that he will be induced to sacrifice it either to friendship or to enmity. There are, however, no perfect judges in any department of human life. Prejudices and unperceived biasses make their way into the minds even of the most upright of our fellow-creatures; and there can be no doubt that votes are sometimes thrown away, or injudiciously given, by young students in the Logic class. Still, these little aberrations are never found to disturb the operation of the general principle on which the scale of merit is determined, and the list of honors filled up."

Now, Gentlemen, from what I know of you, I think it almost needless to say, that, in confiding to you a function on the intelligent and upright discharge of which the value and significance of the prizes will wholly depend, I do this without any anxiety for the result. I am sure at least that if aught be wanting, the defect will be found neither in your incompetency nor want of will.

And here I would conclude what I propose to say to you on this subject; (this has extended to a far greater length than I anticipated); I would conclude with a most earnest exhortation to those who may be discouraged from coming forward as competitors for academical honors, from a feeling or a fancy of inferiority. In the first place, I would dissuade them from this, because they may be deceived in the estimate of their own powers. Many individuals do not become aware of their own talents, till placed in circumstances which compel them to make strenuous exertion. Then they and those around them discover the mistake. In the second place, even though some of you may now find yourselves somewhat inferior to others, do not for a moment despair of the future. The most powerful minds are frequently of a tardy development, and you may rest assured, that the sooner and more vigorously you exercise your faculties, the speedier and more complete will be their evolution. In the third place, I exhort you to remember that the distinctions now to be gained, are on their own account principally valuable as means towards an end, — as motives to induce you to cultivate your powers by exercise. All of you, even though nearly equal, cannot obtain equal honors in the struggle, but all of you will obtain advantage equally substantial, if you all, what is wholly in your own power, equally put forth your energies to strive. And though you should all endeavor to be first, let me remind you, in the words of Cicero, that — "Prima sequentem, pulchrum est in secundis, tertiisque consistere."[1]

B. — FRAGMENTS ON THE SCOTTISH PHILOSOPHY.

(a) Portion of Introductory Lecture (1836).

Before entering on the proposed subjects of consideration, I must be allowed a brief preliminary digression. In entering on a course of the Philosophy of Mind, — of Philosophy Proper, — we ought not, as Scotsmen, to forget that on this is, and always has been, principally founded the scientific reputation of Scotland; and, therefore, that independently of the higher claims of this philosophy to attention, it would argue almost a want of patriotism in us, were we to neglect a study with the successful cultivation of which our country, and in particular this University, have been so honorably associated.

Whether it be that the characteristic genius of our nation — the *præfervidum Scotorum ingenium* — was more capable of powerful effort than of persevering industry, and, therefore, carried us more to studies of principle than studies of detail; or (what is more probable), that institutions and circumstances have been here less favorable, than in other countries, for the promotion of erudition and research; certain it is that the reputation for intellectual capacity which Scotland has always sustained among the nations of Europe, is founded far less on the achievements of her sons in learning and scholarship, than on what they have done, or shown themselves capable of doing, in Philosophy Proper and its dependent sciences.

In former ages, Scotland presented but few objects for scientific and literary ambition; and Scotsmen of intellectual enterprise usually sought in other coun-

1 *Orator,* c. i.

tries, that education, patronage, and applause, which were denied them in their own. It is, indeed, an honorable testimony to the natural vigor of Scottish talent, that, while Scotland afforded so little encouragement for its production, a complement so large in amount, and of so high a quality, should have been, as it were, spontaneously supplied. During the sixteenth and seventeenth centuries, there was hardly to be found a Continental University without a Scottish professor. It was, indeed, a common saying, that a Scottish pedlar and a Scottish professor were everywhere to be met with. France, however, was long the great nursery of Scottish talent; and this even after the political and religious estrangement of Scotland from her ancient ally, by the establishment of the Reformation, and the accession of the Scottish monarch to the English crown; and the extent of this foreign patronage may be estimated from the fact, that a single prelate — the illustrious Cardinal Du Perron — is recorded to have found places in the seminaries of France for a greater number of literary Scotsmen than all the schools and universities of Scotland maintained at home.[1]

But this favor to our countrymen was not without its reasons; and the ground of partiality was not their superior erudition. What principally obtained for them reputation and patronage abroad, was their dialectical and metaphysical acuteness; and this they were found so generally to possess, that philosophical talent became almost a proverbial attribute of the nation.[2]

During the ascendant of the Aristotelic philosophy, and so long as dexterity in disputation was considered the highest academical accomplishment, the logical subtlety of our countrymen was in high and general demand. But they were remarkable less as writers than as instructors; for were we to consider them only in the former capacity, the works that now remain to us of these expatriated philosophers, — these *Scoti extra Scotiam agentes*, — though neither few nor unimportant, would still never enable us to account for the high and peculiar reputation which the Scottish dialecticians so long enjoyed throughout Europe.

Such was the literary character of Scotland, before the establishment of her intellectual independence, and such has it continued to the present day. In illustration of this, I cannot now attempt a comparative survey of the contributions made by this country and others to the different departments of knowledge, nor is it necessary; for no one, I am assured, will deny that it is only in the Philosophy of Mind that a Scotsman has established an epoch, or that Scotland, by the consent of Europe, has bestowed her name upon a School.

The man who gave the whole philosophy of Europe a new impulse and direction, and to whom, mediately or immediately, must be referred every subsequent advance in philosophical speculation, was our countryman, — David Hume. In speaking of this illustrious thinker, I feel anxious to be distinctly understood. I would, therefore, earnestly request of you to bear in mind, that religious disbelief and philosophical skepticism are not merely not the same, but have no natural connection; and that while the one must ever be a matter of reprobation and regret, the other is in itself deserving of applause. Both were united in Hume; and this union has unfortunately contributed to associate them together in popular opinion, and to involve them equally in one vague condemnation. They must, therefore, I repeat, be accurately distinguished;

1 See *Discussions*, p. 120. — ED.   2 See *Discussions*, p. 119. — ED.

81

661

and thus, though decidedly opposed to one and all of Hume's theological conclusions, I have no hesitation in asserting of his philosophical skepticism, that
this was not only beneficial in its results, but, in the circumstances of the period, even a necessary step in the progress of Philosophy towards truth. In the
first place, it was requisite in order to arouse thought from its lethargy. Men
had fallen asleep over their dogmatic systems. In Germany, the Rationalism
of Leibnitz and Wolf; in England, the Sensualism of Locke, with all its melancholy results, had subsided almost into established faiths. The Skepticism of
Hume, like an electric spark, sent life through the paralyzed opinions; philosophy awoke to renovated vigor, and its problems were again to be considered
in other aspects, and subjected to a more searching analysis.

In the second place, it was necessary, in order to manifest the inadequacy of
the prevailing system. In this respect, skepticism is always highly advanta-
geous; for skepticism is only the carrying out of erroneous philosophy to the
absurdity which it always virtually involved. The skeptic, *qua* skeptic, cannot
himself lay down his premises; he can only accept them from the dogmatist; if
true, they can afford no foundation for the skeptical inference; if false, the
sooner they are exposed in their real character, the better. Accepting his principles from the dominant philosophies of Locke and Leibnitz, and deducing
with irresistible evidence these principles to their legitimate results, Hume
showed, by the extreme absurdity of these results themselves, either that Philosophy altogether was a delusion, or that the individual systems which afforded
the premises, were erroneous or incomplete. He thus constrained philosophers
to the alternative, — either of surrendering philosophy as null, or of ascending
to higher principles, in order to reëstablish it against the skeptical reduction.
The dilemma of Hume constitutes, perhaps, the most memorable crisis in the
history of philosophy; for out of it the whole subsequent Metaphysic of Europe
has taken its rise.

To Hume we owe the philosophy of Kant, and, therefore, also, in general,
the latter philosophy of Germany. Kant explicitly acknowledges that it was
by Hume's *reductio ad absurdum* of the previous doctrine of Causality, he was
first roused from his dogmatic slumber. He saw the necessity that had arisen,
of placing philosophy on a foundation beyond the reach of skepticism, or of
surrendering it altogether; and this it was that led him to those researches into
the conditions of thought, which considered, whether in themselves or in their
consequences, whether in what they established or in what they subverted, are,
perhaps, the most remarkable in the annals of speculation.

To Hume, in like manner, we owe the philosophy of Reid, and, consequently, what is now distinctively known in Europe as the Philosophy of the
Scottish School.

Unable to controvert the reasoning of Berkeley, as founded on the philosophy of Descartes and Locke, Reid had quietly resigned himself to Idealism,
and he confesses that he would never have been led to question the legitimacy
of the common doctrine of Perception, involving though it did the negation of
an external world, had Hume not startled him into hesitation and inquiry, by
showing that the same reasoning which disproved the Existence of Matter, disproved, when fairly carried out, also the Substantiality of Mind. Such was the
origin of the philosophy founded by Reid, — illustrated and adorned by Stewart;

and it is to this philosophy, and to the writings of these two illustrious thinkers, that Scotland is mainly indebted for the distinguished reputation which she at present enjoys, in every country where the study of the Mind has not, as in England, been neglected for the study of Matter.

The Philosophy of Reid is at once our pride and our reproach. At home, mistaken and undervalued; abroad, understood and honored. The assertion may be startling, yet is literally true, that the doctrines of the Scottish School have been nowhere less fairly appreciated than in Scotland itself. To explain how they have been misinterpreted, and, consequently neglected, in the country of their birth, is more than I can now attempt; but as I believe an equal ignorance prevails in regard to the high favor accorded to these speculations by those nations who are now in advance, as the most enlightened cultivators of philosophy, I shall endeavor, as briefly as possible, to show that it may be for our credit not rashly to disparage what other countries view as our chief national claim to scientific celebrity. In illustration of this, I shall only allude to the account in which our Scottish Philosophy is held in Germany and in France.

There is a strong general analogy between the philosophies of Reid and Kant; and Kant, I may observe by the way, was a Scotsman by proximate descent. Both originate in a recoil against the skepticism of Hume; both are equally opposed to the Sensualism of Locke; both vindicate with equal zeal the moral dignity of man; and both attempt to mete out and to define the legitimate sphere of our intellectual activity. There are however, important differences between the doctrines, as might be anticipated from the very different characters of the men; and while Kant surpassed Reid in systematic power and comprehension, Reid excelled Kant in the caution and security of his procedure. There is, however, one point of difference in which it is now acknowledged, even by the representatives of the Kantian philosophy, that Kant was wrong. I allude to the doctrine of Perception, — the doctrine which constitutes the very cornerstone of the philosophy of Reid. Though both philosophies were, in their origin, reäctions against the skepticism of Hume, this reäction was not equally determined in each by the same obnoxious conclusion. For, as it was primarily to reconnect Effect and Cause that Kant was roused to speculation, so it was primarily to regain the worlds of Mind and Matter, that Reid was awakened to activity. Accordingly Kant, admitting, without question, the previous doctrine of philosophers, that the mind has no immediate knowledge of any existence external to itself, adopted it without hesitation as a principle, — that the mind is cognizant of nothing beyond its own modifications, and that what our natural consciousness mistakes for an external world, is only an internal phænomenon, only a mental representation of the unknown and inconceivable. Reid, on the contrary, was fortunately led to question the grounds on which philosophers had given the lie to the natural beliefs of mankind; and his inquiry terminated in the conclusion, that there exists no valid ground for the hypothesis, universally admitted by the learned, that an immediate knowledge of material objects is impossible. The attempt of Kant, if the attempt were serious, to demonstrate the existence of an external and unknown world, was, as is universally admitted, a signal failure; and his Hypothetical Realism was soon analyzed by an illustrious disciple — Fichte — into an Absolute Idealism, with a logical rigor that did not admit of refutation.[1]   In the meanwhile Reid's doctrine of Perception had attracted the attention of an acute opponent of the Critical Philosophy in Germany;[2] and that doctrine, divested of those superficial errors which have led some ingenious reasoners in this country to view and represent Reid as holding an opinion on this point identical with Kant's, was, in Kant's own country, placed in opposition against his opinion, fortified as that was by the authority of all modern philosophers.   And with what result? Simply this: — that the most distinguished representatives of the Kantian school now acknowledge Kant's doctrine of Perception to be erroneous, and one analogous to that of Reid they have adopted in its stead.   Thus, while, in Scotland, the fundamental position of Reid's philosophy has been misunderstood, his criticism of the ideal theory treated as a blunder, and his peculiar doctrine of perception represented as essentially the same with that of the philosophers whom he assailed; in Germany, and by his own disciples, Kant's theory of perception is admitted to be false, and the doctrine of Reid, on this point, appreciated at its just value, and recognized as one of the most important and original contributions ever made to philosophy.

But in France, I may add Italy, the triumph of the Scottish school has been even more signal than in Germany.   The philosophy of Locke, first recommended to his countrymen by the brilliant fancy of Voltaire, was, by the lucid subtlety of Condillac, reduced to a simplicity which not only obtained an ascendant over the philosophy of Descartes, but rendered it in France the object of all but universal admiration.   Locke had deduced all knowledge from Experience, but Condillac analyzed every faculty into Sense.   Though its author was no materialist, the system of transformed sensation is only a disguised materialism; and the import of the doctrine soon became but too apparent in its effects.   Melancholy, however, as it was, this theory obtained an authority in France unparalleled for its universality and continuance.   For seventy years, not a single work of an opposite tendency made the smallest impression on the public mind; all discussion of principles had ceased; it remained only to develop the remoter consequences of the system; philosophy seemed accomplished.

Such was the state of opinion in France until the downfall of the Empire. In the period of tranquillity that followed the Restoration, the minds of men were again turned with interest to metaphysical speculation; and it was then that the doctrines of the Scottish Philosophy were, for the first time, heard in the public schools of France.   Recommended by the powerful talent and high authority of Royer-Collard, these doctrines made converts of some of the loftiest intellects of France.   A vigorous assault, in which the prowess of Cousin was remarkable, was made against the prevalent opinions, and with a success so decisive, that, after a controversy of twenty years, the school of Condillac is now, in its own country, considered as extinct; while our Scottish philosophy not only obtained an ascendant in public opinion, but, through the influence of my illustrious friend M. Cousin, forms the basis of philosophical instruction

---

[1] Some fragmentary criticisms of the Kantian philosophy in this respect, will be found appended to this dissertation. See below, p. 646. — ED.

[2] Schulze, in his *Ænesidemus*, published in 1792; and again in his *Kritik der theoretischen Philosophie*, 1801. See *Reid's Works*, p. 797. — ED.

in the various Colleges connected with the University of France. It must not, however, be supposed, that the French have servilely adopted the opinions of our countrymen. On the contrary, what they have borrowed they have so ably amplified, strengthened, simplified, and improved, that the common doctrines of Reid and Stewart, of Royer-Collard and Jouffroy (for Cousin falls under another category), ought in justice to be denominated the *Scoto-Gallican Philosophy*, — a name, indeed, already bestowed upon them by recent historians of philosophy in Germany.

* * * * * * *

(b.) M. Jouffroy's Criticism of the Scottish School.

(Probably 1837, or a little later. See *Œuvres de Reid*, vol. 1. Preface, p. clxxxvi.- cxcix. — Ed.)

* * * * I must be allowed to make an observation in reference to the criticism of M. Jouffroy.

Dr. Reid and Mr. Stewart not only denounce as absurd the attempt to demonstrate, that the original data of Consciousness are for us the rule of what *we* ought to believe, that is, the criteria of a relative, — human, — subjective, truth; but interdict as unphilosophical all question in regard to their validity, as the vehicles of an absolute or objective truth.

M. Jouffroy, of course, coincides with the Scottish philosophers in regard to the former; but as to the latter, he maintains, with Kant, that the doubt is legitimate, and, though he admits it to be insoluble, he thinks it ought to be entertained. Nor, on the ground on which they and he consider the question, am I disposed to dissent from his conclusion. But on that on which I have now placed it,[1] I cannot but view the inquiry as incompetent. For what is the question in plain terms? Simply, — Whether what our nature compels us to believe as true and real, be true and real, or only a consistent illusion? Now this question cannot be philosophically entertained, for two reasons. 1°, Because there exists a presumption in favor of the veracity of our nature, which either precludes or peremptorily repels a gratuitous supposition of its mendacity. 2°, Because we have no mean out of Consciousness of testing Consciousness. If its data are found concordant, they must be trustworthy; if repugnant, they are already proved unworthy of credit. Unless, therefore, the mutual collation of the primary data of Consciousness be held such an inquiry, this is, I think, manifestly incompetent. It is only in the case of one or more of these original facts being rejected as false, that the question can emerge in regard to the truth of the others. But, in reality, on this hypothesis, the problem is already decided; their character for truth is gone; and all subsequent canvassing of their probability is profitless speculation.

Kant started, like the philosophers in general, with the non-acceptance of the deliverance of Consciousness, — that we are immediately cognizant of extended objects. This first step decided the destiny of his philosophy. The external world, as known, was, therefore, only a phænomenon of the internal; and our knowledge in general only of self, the objective only subjective; and

---

1 See *Reid's Works*, p. 746. — Ed.

truth only the harmony of thought with thought, not of thought with things; — reality only a necessary illusion.

It was quite in order, that Kant should canvass the veracity of all our primary beliefs, having founded his philosophy on the presumed falsehood of one; and an inquiry followed out with such consistency and talent could not, from such a commencement, terminate in a different result.

(c.) General Characteristics of the Scottish School.

(Written in connection with proposed Memoir of Mr. Dugald Stewart. On Desk, May 1856; written Autumn 1855. — Ed.)

The Scottish School of Philosophy is distinctively characterized by its opposition to all the destructive schemes of speculation; — in particular, to Skepticism, or the uncertainty of Knowledge; to Idealism, or the non-existence of the material world; to Fatalism, or the denial of a moral universe. Reid has the merit of originating this movement, and Stewart the honor of continuing, and promoting, and extending it.

In the philosophy which prevailed before Descartes, in whose doctrines it may be affirmed that modern speculation took its rise, we find all these schemes, indeed, but all marked and modified in a peculiar manner. In antiquity, we have the skepticism of Pyrrho and Ænesidemus; but this, however ingenious its object, never became popular or dangerous, and without a formal or decisive refutation, gradually died out.

In the scholastic ages, Idealism was [countenanced] by the dominant psychology, and would perhaps have taken root, but for the check it encountered from the Church, to the dogmas of which all philosophy was then voluntarily subjected. The doctrine of Representative Perception, in its cruder form, was generally accepted, and the question often mooted, " Could not God maintain the species in the sensory, the object (external reality) being annihilated?" This problem, as philosophy affirmed, theology denied. It was possible, nay probable, according to the former; impossible, because heretical, according to the latter. [1]

Finally, on the other hand, the Absolute decrees of God might, at the first view, be thought, not only to favor, but to establish, a doctrine of unconditioned Fatalism. But this inference was disavowed by the most strenuous advocates of Prescience and Predestination; and the Freewill of man asserted no less vehemently than the Free Grace of God.

(d) Kant and Reid.

(Written in connection with proposed Memoir of Mr. Stewart. On Desk, May, 1856; written Autumn 1855. — Ed.)

*　　*　　*　　*　　*　　*　　*

In like manner, Kant assailed Skepticism, and the skepticism of Hume; but with a very different result. For, if in one conclusion he controverted skep-

---

1 See *Discussions*, p. 198, second edition, — why Idealism and the doctrine of Transubstantiation were incompatible.

ticism, he himself introduced and patronized the most unexclusive doubt. He showed, indeed, that Hume's rejection of the notion of Causality was groundless. He proved that, although this notion was not, and could not be, constructed from experience, still causality was a real and efficient principle, native and necessary in human intelligence; and that although experience did not explain its genesis, experience always supposes its operation. So far so good. But Kant did not stop here. He endeavored to evince that pure Reason, that Intelligence is naturally, is necessarily, repugnant with itself, and that speculation ends in a series of insoluble antilogies. In its highest potence, in its very essence, thought is thus infected with contradiction; and the worst and most pervading skepticism is the melancholy result. If I have done anything meritorious in philosophy, it is in the attempt to explain the phænomena of these contradictions; in showing that they arise only when intelligence transcends the limits to which its legitimate exercise is restricted; and that within these bounds (the Conditioned), natural thought is neither fallible nor mendacious—

"Neque decipitur, nec decipit umquam."

If this view be correct, Kant's antinomies, with their consequent skepticism, are solved; and the human mind, however weak, is shown not to be the work of a treacherous Creator.

Reid, on the contrary, did not subvert the trustworthiness of the one witness, on whose absolute veracity he relied. In his hands natural (and, therefore, necessary) thought, — Consciousness, — Common Sense, — are always held out as entitled to our implicit and thorough-going confidence. The fact of the testimony sufficiently guarantees the truth of what the testimony avouches. The testimony, if delivered, is to be believed *pro tanto* impeccable.

* * * * * *

(e) KANT'S DOCTRINE OF SPACE AND TIME.

(Fragments from early Papers. Probably before 1836. — ED.)

Kant, 1°, Made our actual world one merely of illusion. Time and Space, under which we must perceive and think, he reduced to mere subjective spectral forms, which have no real archetype in the noumenal or real universe. We can infer nothing from this to that. Cause and Effect govern thing and thought in the world of Space and Time; the relation will not subsist where Time and Space have no reality. (Lines from Fracastorius.)[1] Corresponds with the Platonic, but more thorough-going. Kant, 2°, Made Reason, Intelligence, contradict itself in its legitimate exercise. Antilogy, — antinomy, part and parcel of its nature; not only "reasoning, but to err," but reason itself.

Thus, the conviction that we live in a world of unreality and illusion, and that our very faculty of knowledge is only given us to mislead, is the result of our criticism, — Skepticism.

On the contrary, my doctrine holds, 1°, That Space and Time, as given, are real forms of thought and conditions of things; 2°, That Intelligence, — Reason,

1 See lect. xxi. p. 290. — ED.

—within its legitimate limits, is legitimate; within this sphere it never deceives; and it is only when transcending that sphere, when founding on its illegitimate as on its legitimate exercise, that it affords a contradictory result; "Ne sapiamus ultra facultates." The dogmatic assertion of necessity,—of Fatalism, and the dogmatic assertion of Liberty, are the counter and equally inconceivable conclusions from reliance on the illegitimate and one-sided.

*　　*　　*　　*　　*　　*　　*

Kant holds the subjectivity of Space (and Time), and, if he does not deny, will not affirm the existence of a real space, external to our minds; because it is a mere form of our perceptive faculty. He holds that we have no knowledge of any external thing as really existing, and that all our perceptions are merely appearances, i. e. subjective representations,—subjective modifications,—which the mind is determined to exhibit, as an apparently objective opposition to itself,—its pure and real subjective modifications. Yet, while he gives up the external existence of space, as beyond the sphere of consciousness, he holds the reality of external material existences (things in themselves), which are equally beyond the sphere of consciousness. It was incumbent on him to render a reason for this seeming inconsistency, and to explain how his system was not, in its legitimate conclusions, an universal Idealism; and he has accordingly attempted to establish, by necessary inference, what his philosophy could not accept as an immediate fact of consciousness.

In the second edition of his *Kritik der Reinen Vernunft*, he has accordingly given what he calls a "*strict, and, as he is convinced, the only possible*, demonstration for the objective reality of our external perceptions;" and, at the same time, he declares that it would be the eternal scandal of Philosophy, and the general reason of mankind, if we were compelled to yield our assent to the existence of an external world, only as an article of Faith, and were unable to oppose a satisfactory refutation to any skeptical objections that might be suggested touching their reality (Vorrede, p. xxxix). The demonstration which is thus exclusively and confidently proposed, attempts to prove, that the existence of an external world is involved in the very consciousness of self,—that without a *Thou*, there can be no *I*, and that the *Cogito ergo sum* is not more certain than the *Cogito ergo es*.

*　　*　　*　　*　　*　　*　　*

II.—PHYSIOLOGICAL. (See p. 183.)

(a.) PHRENOLOGY.

Such is a very general view of that system [the Nervous] and its relations, which physiologists and philosophers in general have held to be the proximate organ of the thinking principle, and many to be even the thinking principle itself.

That the mind, in its lower energies and affections, is immediately dependent on the conditions of the nervous system, and that, in general, the development of the brain in the different species of animals is correspondent to their intelligence,—these are conclusions established upon an induction too extensive and too certain to admit of doubt. But when we attempt to proceed a step farther, and to connect the mind or its faculties with particular parts of the nervous system, we find ourselves at once checked. Observation and experiment seem to fail; they afford only obscure and varying reports; and if, in this uncertainty, we hazard a conclusion, this is only a theory established upon some arbitrary hypotheses, in which fictions stand in place of facts. The uncertainty of such conclusions is shown by the unexampled diversity of opinion that has always reigned among those who, discontented with a prudent ignorance, have attempted to explain the phænomena of mind by the phænomena of organization.

In the first place, some (and their opinion is not, certainly, the least philosophical) hold that, in relation to the body, the soul is less contained than containing,—that it is all in the whole, and all in every part. This is the common doctrine of many of the Fathers, and of the scholastic Aristotelians.[1]

In the second place, others have attempted to connect the conscious principle in general with a particular part of the organism, but by very different relations. Some place it there, as in a local seat; others make it dependent on that part, as on its organ; while others hold that the mind stands in a more immediate relation to this part, only because it is the point of convergence where all the bodily sensations meet. I shall not attempt to enumerate the hundred and one conjectures in regard to the point in the corporeal organism, in proximate connection with the mind. It would occupy more than our hour to give you even a summary account of the hypotheses on this subject.

In the third place, no opinion has been more generally prevalent than that different faculties and dispositions of the mind are dependent on different parts of the bodily organism, and more especially on different parts of the nervous system. Under this head, I shall state to you one or two of the more famous opinions. The most celebrated doctrine—that which was more universally adopted, and for a longer period, than any other—was that which, with certain modifications, assigned different places in the Encephalos to Memory, Imagination, Sense, and the Locomotive Faculty,—Reason or Intelligence being left inorganic. This opinion we trace upward, through the Latin and Arabian schools,[2] to St. Austin,[3] Nemesius,[4] the Greek physician Aetius, and even to the anatomists Rufus and Posidonius. Memory, on this hypothesis, was placed in the substance of the cerebellum, or in the subjacent ventricle; and as the phrenologists now attempt to prove that the seat of this faculty lies above the eyebrows, by the alleged fact that, when a man wishes to stimulate his recollection, he rubs the lower part of his forehead,—so, of old, the same conclusion was established on the more plausible assertion, that a man in such

---

1 See lect. xx. p. 271.—ED.

2 [See Gassendi, *Physica*, § iii. memb. post. l. viii. *Opera*, t. ii. pp. 400, 401. Averroes, *Destruct. Destructionum. Arist. Opera*, t. x. p. 340. Venice, 1560.]

3 *De Genesi ad Literam*, l. vii. caps. xvii. xviii.—ED. [See Tenneman, t. x. p. 241.]

4 *De Natura Hominis*, c. xiii. p. 204. edit. Matthæi.—ED.

circumstances naturally scratches the back of his head. The one indication is at least as good as the other.

Among modern physiologists, Willis was the first who attempted a new attribution of mental functions to different parts of the nervous system. He placed Perception and Sensation in the *corpus callosum*, Imagination and Appetite in the *corpora striata*, Memory in the cerebral convolutions, Involuntary Motion in the cerebellum, etc.; and to Willis is to be traced the determination, so conspicuous among subsequent physiologists, of attributing different mental uses to different parts of the brain.

It would be bootless to state to you the many various and contradictory conjectures in regard to these uses. To psychologists they are, with one exception, all comparatively uninteresting, as, were they even ascertained to be something better than conjectures, still, as the physical condition is in all of them occult, it could not be applied as an instrument of psychological discovery. The exception which I make is, the celebrated doctrine of Gall. If true, that doctrine would not only afford us a new instrument, but would in a great measure supersede the old. In fact, the psychology of consciousness, and the psychology founded on Gall's organology, are mere foolishness to each other. They arrive at conclusions the most contradictory; insomuch that the establishment of the one necessarily supposes the subversion of the other.

In these circumstances, no one interested in the philosophy of man can be indifferent to an inquiry into the truth or falsehood of the new doctrine. This doctrine cannot be passed over with contempt. It is maintained not only by too many, but by too able advocates, to be summarily rejected. That its results are repugnant to those previously admitted, is but a sorry reason for not inquiring into their foundation. This doctrine professes to have discovered new principles, and to arrive at new conclusions; and the truth or falsehood of these cannot, therefore, be estimated merely by their conformity or disconformity with those old results which the new professedly refute. To do so would be mere prejudice, — a mere assumption of the point at issue. At the same time, this doctrine professes to be founded on sensible facts. Sensible facts must be shown to be false, not by reasoning, but by experiment; for, as old Fernelius has well expressed it, — "Insipientis arrogantiæ est argumentationis necessitatem sensuum testimonio anteponere." To oppose such a doctrine in such a manner is not to refute, but to recommend; and yet, unfortunately, this has been the usual mode in which the organology of Gall and his followers has been assailed. Such an opinion must be taken on its own ground. We must join issue with it upon the facts and inferences it embraces. If the facts are true, and if the inferences necessarily follow, the opinion must be admitted; the sooner, therefore, that we candidly inquire into these the better, for it is only thus that we shall be enabled to form a correct estimate of the evidence on which such a doctrine rests.

With these views I many years ago undertook an investigation of the fundamental facts on which the phrenological doctrine, as it is unfortunately called, is established. By a fundamental fact I mean a fact, by the truth of which the hypothesis could be proved, and, consequently, by the falsehood of which it could be disproved. Now, what are such facts? The one condition of such a fact is, that it should be general. The phrenological theory is, that there is a correspondence between the volume of certain parts of the brain, and the intensity of certain qualities of mind and character; — the former they call development, the latter manifestation. Now, individual cases of alleged conformity of development and manifestation could prove little in favor of the doctrine, as individual cases of alleged disconformity could prove little against it; because, 1°, The phrenologists had no standard by which the proportion of cerebral development could be measured by themselves or their opponents; 2°, Because the mental manifestation was vague and indeterminate; 3°, Because they had introduced, as subsidiary hypotheses, the occult qualities of temperament and activity, so that, in individual cases, any given head could always be explained in harmony with any given character. Individual cases were thus ambiguous; they were worthless either to establish or to refute the theory. But where the phrenologist had proclaimed a general fact, by that fact their doctrine could be tried. For example, when they asserted as the most illustrious discovery of Gall, and as the surest inference of their doctrine, that the cerebellum is the organ of the sexual appetite, and established this inference as the basis of certain general facts which, as common to the whole animal kingdom, could easily be made matter of precise experiment; — by these facts the truth of their doctrine could be brought to the test, and this on ground the most favorable for them. For the general probability of their doctrine was thus estimated by the truth of its best-established element. But, on the other hand, if such general facts were found false, their disproval afforded the most satisfactory refutation of the whole system. For the phrenologists themselves readily admit, that their theory is exploded, if their doctrine of the function of the cerebellum is disproved. Because, therefore, an examination of the general facts of Phrenology was at once decisive and comparatively easy, I determined, on this ground, to try the truth of the opinion. I shall state to you very generally a few results of the investigation, of which I may, without boasting, affirm that no inquiry of the kind was ever conducted with greater care or more scrupulous accuracy.

I shall commence with the phrenological doctrine of the cerebellum, on which you will see the propriety of dwelling as briefly as I can. I may mention that the extent of my experiments on this organ is wholly unconnected with Phrenology. My attention was, indeed, originally turned to the relation of the after-brain to the other parts of the nervous system, when testing the accuracy of the phrenological doctrine on this point; but that end was very soon accomplished, and it was certain discoveries which I made in regard to the laws of development and the function of this organ, and the desire of establishing these by an induction from as many of the species as possible of the animal kingdom, that led me into a more extensive inquiry than has hitherto been instituted by any professional physiologist. When I publish its results, they will disprove a hundred times over all the phrenological assertions in regard to the cerebellum; but this will be only an accidental circumstance, and of comparatively little importance. I may add, that my tables extend to above one thousand brains of above fifty species of animals, accurately weighed by a delicate balance; and you will remark that the phrenologists have not a single observation of any accuracy to which they can appeal. The only evidence in the shape of precise experiment on which they can found, is a table of Serres, who is no phrenologist, affording the general averages of certain weighings, said to have been made by him, of the brain and cerebellum, in the human subject. I shall prove that table an imaginary fabrication in support of a now exploded hypothesis of the author.

The alleged facts on which Gall and his followers establish their conclusion in regard to the function of the cerebellum, are the following:

The first is, that in all animals, females have this organ, on an average, greatly smaller, in proportion to the brain proper, than males. Now, so far is this assertion from being correct, it is the very reverse of truth; and I have ascertained, by an immense induction, that in no species of animal has the female a proportionally smaller cerebellum than the male, but that in most species, and this according to a certain law, she has a considerably larger. In no animal is this difference more determinate than in man. Women have on an average a cerebellum to the brain proper, as 1 : 7; men as 1 : 8. This is a general fact which I have completely established.[1]

The second alleged fact is, that in impuberal animals the cerebellum is in proportion to the brain proper greatly less than in adults. This is equally erroneous. In all animals, long previous to puberty, has the cerebellum attained its maximum proportion. And here also I am indebted to the phrenologists for having led me to make the discovery of another curious law, and to establish the real function of the cerebellum. Physiologists have hitherto believed that the cerebella of all animals, indifferently, were, for a certain period subsequent to birth, greatly less, in proportion to the brain proper, than in adults; and have taken no note of the differences in this respect between different classes. Thus, completely wrong in regard to the fact, they have necessarily overlooked the law by which it is governed. In those animals that have from the first the full power of voluntary motion, and which depend immediately on their own exertions, and on their own power of assimilation for nutriment, the proportion of the cerebellum is as large, nay, larger, than in the adult. In the chicken of the common fowl, pheasant, partridge, etc., this is the case; and most remarkably after the first week or ten days, when the yolk (corresponding in a certain sort to the milk in quadrupeds) has been absorbed. In the calf, kid, lamb, and probably in the colt, the proportion of the cerebellum at birth is very little less than in the adult. In those birds that do not possess at once the full power of voluntary motion, but which are in a rapid state of growth, the cerebellum, within a few days at least after being hatched, and by the time the yolk is absorbed, is not less or larger than in the adult; the pigeon, sparrow, etc., etc., are examples. In the young of those quadrupeds that for some time wholly depend for support on the milk of the mother, as on half-assimilated food, and which have at first feeble powers of regulated motion, the proportion of the cerebellum to the brain proper is at birth very small; but, by the end of the full period of lactation, it has with them as with other animals (nor is man properly an exception), reached the full proportion of the adult. This, for example, is seen in the young rabbit, kitten, whelp, etc.; in them the cerebellum is to the brain proper at birth about as 1 to 14; at six and eight weeks old, about as 1 to 6. Pigs, etc., as

---

[1] See below (b) *On Weight of Brain*, p. 658. — ED.

possessing immediately the power of regulated motion, but wholly dependent on the milk of the mother during at least the first month after birth, exhibit a medium between the two classes. At birth the proportion is in them as 1 to 9, in the adult as 1 to 6. This analogy, at which I now only hint, has never been suspected; it points at the new and important conclusion (corroborated by many other facts), that the cerebellum is the intracranial organ of the nutritive faculty, that term being taken in its broadest signification; and it confirms also an old opinion, recently revived, that it is the condition of voluntary or systematic motion.[1]

The third alleged fact is, that the proportion of the cerebellum to the brain proper in different species, is in proportion to the *energy* of the phrenological function attributed to it. This assertion is groundless as the others. There are many other fictions in regard to this organ; but these, I think, are a sufficient specimen of the truth of the doctrine in regard to the function of the cerebellum; and the cerebellum, you will recollect, is the citadel of Phrenology.

I shall, however, give you the sample of another general fact. The organ of Veneration rises in the middle on the coronal surface of the head. Women, it is universally admitted, manifest religious feeling more strongly and generally than men; and the phrenologists accordingly assert, that the female cranium is higher in proportion in that region than the male. This I found to be the very reverse of truth, by a comparative average of nearly two hundred skulls of either sex. In man, the female encephalos is considerably smaller than that of the male, and in shape the crania of the sexes are different. By what dimension is the female skull less than the male? The female skull is longer, it is nearly as broad, but it is much lower than the male. This is only one of several curious sexual differences of the head.

I do not know whether it be worth while mentioning, that, by a comparison of all the crania of murderers preserved in the Anatomical Museum of this University, with about nearly two hundred ordinary skulls indifferently taken, I found that these criminals exhibited a development of the phrenological organs of Destructiveness and other evil propensities smaller, and a development of the higher moral and intellectual qualities larger, than the average. Nay, more, the same result was obtained when the murderers' skulls were compared, not merely with a common average, but with the individual crania of Robert Bruce, George Buchanan, and Dr. David Gregory.

I omit all notice of many other decisive facts subversive of the hypothesis in question; but I cannot leave the subject without alluding to one which disproves, at one blow, a multitude of organs, affords a significant example of their accuracy of statement, and shows how easily manifestation can, by the phrenologists, be accommodated to any development, real or supposed. I refer to the Frontal Sinuses. These are cavities between the tables of the frontal bone, in consequence of a divergence from each other. They are found in all puberal crania, and are of variable and [from without] wholly inappreciable extent and depth. Where they exist, they of course interpose an insuperable bar to any estimate of the cerebral development; and their extent being undiscoverable, they completely baffle all certain observation. Now, the phrenologists have,

1 From a communication by the Author, printed in Dr. Munro's *Anatomy of the Brain*, pp. 6, 7. See below (b) *On Weight of Brain.* — ED.

fortunately or unfortunately, concentrated the whole of their very smallest organs over the region of the sinus; which thus, independently of other impediments, renders all phrenological observation more or less uncertain in regard to sixteen of their organs. Of these cavities the anatomists in general seem to have known not much, and the phrenologists absolutely nothing. At least, the former are wrong in many of their positions, the latter wrong in all. I shall give you a sample of the knowledge and consistency of the phrenologists on this point.

Gall first of all answered the objection of the sinus by asserting, that even when it existed, the plates of the frontal bone were still parallel. The truth is, that the cavity is only formed by their divergence from parallelism, and thus it is now described by the phrenologists themselves. In his latest works, Gall asserted that the sinus is frequently absent in men, and seldom or never found in women. But Spurzheim carried the negation to its highest climax, for he avers (I quote his words), "that children and young adult persons have no holes between the two tables of the skull at the forehead, and that they occur only in old persons, or after chronic insanity." He did not always, indeed, assert as much, and in some of his works he allows that they throw some uncertainty over the organs of Individuality and Size, but not much over that of Locality.

Now the fact is, as I have established by an inspection of several hundred crania, that *no skull is without a sinus.* This is, indeed, the common doctrine of the anatomists. But I have also proved that the vulgar doctrine of their increasing in extent in proportion as the subject advances in life, is wholly erroneous. The smallest sinus I ever saw was in the cranium of a woman of a hundred years of age.

The two facts — the fact of the universal existence of the sinus, and its great and various and inappreciable extent, and the fact of the ignorance of the phrenologists in regard to every circumstance connected with it — these two facts prove that these observers have been going on finding always manifestation and development in exact conformity; when, lo! it turns out, that in nearly half their organs, the protuberance or depression apparent on the external bone has no connection with any correspondent protuberance or depression in the brain. Now, what does this evince? Not merely that they were wrong in regard to these particular observations and the particular organs established upon the mistake. Of course, the whole organs lying over the sinuses are swept away. But this is not all; for the theory supposes, as its condition, that the amount of the two qualities of mental manifestation and cerebral development can be first accurately measured apart, and then compared together, and found to be either conformable or disconformable; and the doctrine, assuming this possibility, proves its truth only by showing that the two qualities thus severally estimated, are, in all cases, in proportion to each other. Now, if the possibility thus assumed by Phrenology were true, it would at once have discovered that the apparent amount of development over the sinus was not in harmony with the mental manifestation. But this it never did; it always found the apparent or cranial development over the sinus conformable to the mental manifestation, though this bony development bore no more a proportion to the cerebral brain, than if it had been looked for on the great toe;

and thus it is at once evident, that manifestation and development in general are, in their hands, such factitious, such arbitrary quantities, that they can always, under any circumstances, be easily brought into unison. Phrenology is thus shown to be a mere leaden rule, which bends to whatever it is applied; and, therefore, all phrenological observation is poisoned, in regard even to those organs where a similar obstacle did not prevent the discovery of the cerebral development. Suppose a mathematician to propose a new method for the solution of algebraical equations. If we applied it and found it gave a false result, would the inventor be listened to if he said, — "True, my method is wrong in these cases in which it has been tried, but it is not, therefore, proved false in those in which it has not been put to the test?" Now, this is precisely the plea I have heard from the phrenologists in relation to the sinus. "Well!" they say, "we admit that Gall and Spurzheim have been all wrong about the sinus, and we give up the organs above the eyes; but our system is untouched in the others which are situate beyond the reach of that obnoxious cavity." To such reasoning there was no answer.

I should have noticed, that, even supposing there had been no intervening caverns in the forehead, the small organs arranged, like peas in a pod, along the eyebrows could not have severally manifested any difference of development. If we suppose (what I make bold to say was never yet observed in the brain) that a portion of it so small in extent as any one of the six phrenological organs of Form, Size, Weight, Color, Order, and Number, which lie side by side upon the eyebrows, was ever prominent beyond the surrounding surface, — I say, supposing the protuberance of so small a spot upon the cerebral convolutions, it could never determine a corresponding eminence on the external table of the skull. What would be the effect of such a protrusion of brain upon the cranium? It would only make room for itself in the thickness of the bone which it would attenuate. This is shown by two examples. The first is taken from the convolutions themselves. I should, however, state, that convolution, and anfractuosity or furrow, are correlative terms, like hill and valley, — the former (convolutions) being applied to the windings of the cerebral surface as rising up, — the latter (anfractuosity, or furrow) being applied to them as sinking in. Convolutions are the winding eminences between the furrows; anfractuosities the winding depressions between the convolutions. This being understood, we find, on looking to the internal surface of the cranium, that the convolutions attenuate the bone, which is sometimes quite transparent — diaphanous — over them, whereas it remains quite thick over the anfractuosities; but they cause no inequality on the outer surface. Yet the convolutions, which thus make room for themselves in the bone without elevating it externally, are often broader, and of course always longer, than the little organs which the phrenologists have placed along the eyebrows. A fortiori, therefore, we must suppose that an organ like Size, or Weight, or Color, if it did not project beyond the surrounding brain, would only render the superincumbent bone thinner, without causing it to rise, unless we admit that nature complaisantly changes her laws in accommodation to the new doctrine.

But we have another parallel instance still more precisely in point. In many heads there are certain rounded eminences (called *Glandulæ Pacchioni*), on the coronal surface of the brain, which nearly correspond in size with the little organs in question. Now, if the phrenological supposition were correct, that an elevation on the brain, of so limited an extent, would cause an elevation on the external table of the bone, — these eminences would do so far more certainly than any similar projection over the eyebrows. For the frontal bone in the frontal region is under the continual action of muscles, and this action would tend powerfully to prevent any partial elevation; whereas, on the upper part of the head, the bone is almost wholly exempt from such an agency. But do the glands, as they are called, of Pacchioni (though they are no glands), — do they determine an elevation on the external surface of the skull corresponding to the elevation they form on the cerebral surface? Not in the very least; the cranium is there outwardly quite equable — level — uniform — though probably attenuated to the thinness of paper to accommodate the internal rising.

The other facts which I have stated as subversive of what the phrenologists regard as the best-established constituents of their system, — I could only state to you on my own authority. But they are founded on observations made with the greatest accuracy, and on phænomena, which every one is capable of verifying. If the general facts I gave you in regard to the cerebellum, etc., are false, then am I a deliberate deceiver; for these are of such a nature that no one with the ordinary discourse of reason could commit an error in regard to them, if he actually made the observations. The maxim, however, which I have myself always followed, and which I would earnestly impress upon you, is to take nothing upon trust that can possibly admit of doubt, and which you are able to verify for yourselves; and had I not been obliged to hurry on to more important subjects, I might have been tempted to show you by experiment what I have now been compelled to state to you upon authority alone.[1]

I am here reminded of a fact, of which I believe none of our present phrenologists are aware, — at least all their books confidently assert the very reverse. It is this, — that the new system is the result, not of experience but of conjecture, — and that Gall, instead of deducing the faculties from the organs, and generalizing both from particular observations, first of all cogitated a faculty *a priori*, and then looked about for an organ with which to connect it. In short, Phrenology was not discovered, but invented.

You must know, then, that there are two faculties, or rather two modifications of various faculties, which cut a conspicuous figure in the psychologies of Wolf and other philosophers of the Empire; — these are called in German *Tiefsinn* and *Scharfsinn*, — literally *deep sense* and *sharp sense*, but are now known in English phrenological language by the terms *Causality* and *Comparison*. Now what I wish you to observe is, that Gall found these two clumsy modifications of mind, ready shaped out in the previous theories of philosophy prevalent in his own country, and then in the language itself. Now, this being understood, you must also know that, in 1798, Gall published a letter to Retzer, of Vienna, wherein he, for the first time, promulgates the nature of his doctrine, and we here catch him — *reum confitentem* — in the very act of conjecturing. In this letter he says: " I am not yet so far advanced in my researches as to have discovered special organs for Scharfsinn and Tiefsinn (Comparison

---

[1] See below (d) *On Frontal Sinus*, p. 662. — ED.

and Causality), for the principle of the Representative Faculty (*Vorstellungs-vermögen*, — another faculty in German philosophy), and for the different varieties of judgment, etc." In this sentence we see exhibited the real source and veritable derivation of the system.

In the *Darstellung* of Froriep, a favorite pupil of Gall, under whose eye the work was published in the year 1800, twenty-two organs are given, of which the greater proportion are now either translated to new localities, or altogether thrown out. We find also that the sought-for organs had, in the interval, been found for Scharfsinn (Comparison), and Tiefsinn (Causality); and what further exhibits the hypothetical genealogy of the doctrine, is, that a great number of organs are assumed, which lie wholly beyond the possible sphere of observation, at the base and towards the centre of the brain; as those of the External Senses, those of Desire, Jealousy, Envy, love of Power, love of Pleasure, love of Life, etc.

An organ of Sensibility is placed above that of Amativeness, between and below two organs of Philoprogenitiveness, — an organ of Liberality (its deficiency standing instead of an organ of Avarice or Acquisitiveness), is situated above the eyebrows, in the position now occupied by that of Time. An organ of Imagination is intimately connected with that of Theosophy or Veneration, towards the vertex of the head; and Veracity is problematically established above an organ of Parental Love. An organ of Vitality is not to be forgotten, situated in the *medulla oblongata*, the development of which is measured by the size of the *foramen magnum* and the thickness of the neck. These faculties and organs are all now cashiered; and who does not perceive that, like those of Causality and Comparison, which are still suffered to remain, they were first devised, and then quartered on some department of the brain?

We thus see that, in the first edition of the craniological hypothesis, there were several tiers or stories of organs, — some at the base, some about the centre, and others on the surface of the brain. Gall went to lecture through Germany, and among other places he lectured at Göttingen. Here an objection was stated to his system by the learned Meiners. Gall measured the development of an external organ by its prominence. "How," said Meiners, "do you know that this prominence of the outer organ indicates its real size? May it not merely be pressed out, though itself of inferior volume, by the large development of a subjacent organ?" This objection it was easily seen was checkmate. A new game must be commenced, the pieces arranged again. Accordingly, all the organs at the base and about the centre of the brain were withdrawn, and the whole organs were made to run very conveniently upwards and outwards from the lower part of the brain to its outer periphery.

It would be tiresome to follow the history of phrenological variation through the works of Leune and Villars to those of Bischoff and Blöde, — which last represent the doctrine as it flourished in 1805. In these, the whole complement of organs which Gall ever admitted is detailed, with the exception of Ideality. But their position was still vacillating. For example, in Froriep, Bischoff and Blöde, the organ of Destructiveness is exhibited as lying principally on the parietal bone, above and a little anterior to the organ of Combativeness; while the region of the temporal bone, above and before the opening of the ear, in other words, its present situation, is marked as *terra adhuc incognita.*

No circumstance, however, is more remarkable than the successive changes of shape in the organs. Nothing can be more opposite than the present form of these as compared with those which the great work of Gall exhibits. In Gall's plates they are round or oval; in the modern casts and plates they are of every variety of angular configuration; and I have been told that almost every new edition of these varies from the preceding. We may, therefore, well apply to the phrenologist and his organology the line of Horace [1]—

" Diruit, ædificat, mutat quadrata rotundis, "

with this modification, that we must read in the latter part, *mutat rotunda quadratis.*

So much for Phrenology, — for the doctrine which would substitute the callipers for consciousness in the philosophy of man; and the result of my observation — the result at which I would wish you also to arrive — I cannot better express than in the language of the Roman poet [2]—

" Materiæ ne quære modum, sed perspice vires
Quas ratio, non pondus habet "

In what I have said in opposition to the phrenological doctrine, I should, however, regret if it could be ever supposed that I entertain any feelings of disrespect for those who are converted to this opinion. On the contrary, I am prompt to acknowledge that the sect comprises a large proportion of individuals of great talent; and I am happy to count among these some of my most valued and respected friends. To the question, how comes it that so many able individuals can be believers in a groundless opinion? — I answer, that the opinion is not wholly groundless; it contains much of truth, — of old truth it must be allowed; but it is assuredly no disparagement to any one that he should not refuse to admit facts so strenuously asserted, and which, if true, so necessarily infer the whole conclusions of the system. But as to the mere circumstance of numbers, that is of comparatively little weight, — *argumentum pessimi turba,* — and the phrenological doctrines are of such a nature that they are secure of finding ready converts among the many. There have been also, and there are now, opinions far more universally prevalent than the one in question, which nevertheless we do not consider on that account to be undeniable.

(*b.*) An Account of Experiments on the Weight and Relative Proportions of the Brain, Cerebellum, and Tuber Annulare in Man and Animals, under the various circumstances of Age, Sex, Country, etc.

(Published in Dr. Monro's *Anatomy of the Brain,* p. 4—8.
Edinburgh, 1831. — Ed.)

The following, among other conclusions, are founded on an induction drawn from above sixty human brains, from nearly three hundred human skulls, of

---

1 *Epist.* L. i. ep. i. 100. — Ed.   2 Manilius, iv. 929. — Ed.

determined sex, — the capacity of which, by a method I devised, was taken in sand, and the original weight of the brain thus recovered, — and from more than seven hundred brains of different animals.

1. In man, the adult male Encephalos is heavier than the female; the former nearly averaging, in the Scot's head, 3 lb. 8 oz. troy, the latter, 3 lb. 4 oz.; the difference, 4 oz. In males of this country, about one brain in seven is found above 4 lb. troy; in females, hardly one in one hundred.

2. In man, the Encephalos reaches its full size about seven years of age. This was never before proved. It is commonly believed that the brain and the body attain their full development together. The Wenzels rashly generalized from two cases the conclusion, that the brain reaches its full size about seven years of age; as Sœmmering had, in like manner, on a single case, erroneously assumed that it attains its last growth by three. Gall and Spurzheim, on the other hand, assert that the increase of the encephalos is only terminated about forty. The result of my induction is deduced from an average of thirty-six brains and skulls of children, compared with an average of several hundred brains and skulls of adults. It is perhaps superfluous to observe, that it is the greater development of the bones, muscles, and hair, which renders the adult head considerably larger than that of the child of seven.

3. It is extremely doubtful whether the cranial contents usually diminish in old age. The vulgar opinion that they do, rests on no adequate evidence, and my induction would rather prove the negative.

4. The common doctrine, that the African brain, and in particular that of the Negro, is greatly smaller than the European, is false. By a comparison of the capacity of two Caffre skulls, male and female, and of thirteen negro crania (six male, five female, and two of doubtful sex), the encephalos of the African was found not inferior to the average size of the European.

5. In man, the Cerebellum, in relation to the brain proper, comes to its full proportion about three years. This anti-phrenological fact is proved by a great induction.

6. It is extremely doubtful whether the Cerebellum usually diminishes in old age; probably only in cases of *atrophia senilis*.

7. The female Cerebellum is, in general, considerably larger in proportion to the brain proper, than the male. In the human subject (the tuber excluded), the former is nearly as 1 to 7.6; the latter nearly as 1 to 8.4; and this sexual difference appears to be more determinate in man than in most other animals. Almost the whole difference of weight between the male and female encephali lies in the brain proper; the cerebella of the two sexes, absolutely, are nearly equal, — the preponderance rather in favor of the women. This observation is new; and the truth of the phrenological hypothesis implies the reverse. It confirms the theory of the function of the cerebellum noticed in the following paragraph.

8. The proportion of the Cerebellum to the Brain proper at birth, varies greatly in different animals.[1]

9. Castration has no effect in diminishing the cerebellum, either absolutely

---

[1] For the remainder of this section, see above, Appendix II. (a) p. 652, " Physiologists," etc., to p. 653, " motion." — ED.

or in relation to the brain proper.[2] The opposite doctrine is an idle fancy: though asserted by the phrenologists as their most incontrovertible fact. Proved by a large induction.

10. The universal opinion is false, that man, of all or almost all animals, has the smallest cerebellum in proportion to the brain proper. Many of the commonest quadrupeds and birds have a cerebellum, in this relation, proportionally smaller than man.

11. What has not been observed, the proportion of the Tuber Annulare to the Cerebellum (and, *a majore*, to the brain proper) is greatly less in children than in adults. In a girl of one year (in my table of human brains) it is as 1 to 16.1; in another of two, as 1 to 14.8; in a boy of three, as 1 to 15.5; and the average of children under seven, exhibits the pores, in proportion to the cerebellum, much smaller than in the average of adults, in whom it is only as 1 to 8, or 1 to 9.

12. In specific gravity, contrary to the current doctrine, the encephalos and its parts vary very little, if at all, from one age to another. A child of two, and a woman of a hundred years, are, in this respect, nearly equal, and the intermediate ages show hardly more than individual differences.

13. The specific gravity of the brain does not vary in madness (if one case of chronic insanity is to be depended on), contrary to what has been alleged. In fever it often does, and remarkably.

14. The cerebellum (the converse of the received opinion) has a greater specific gravity than the brain proper; and this difference is considerably more marked in birds than in man and quadrupeds. The opinion also of the ancients is probably true, that the cerebellum is harder than the brain proper.

15. The human brain does not, as asserted, possess a greater specific gravity than that of other animals.

(c.) REMARKS ON DR. MORTON'S TABLES ON THE SIZE OF THE BRAIN.

(Communicated to the *Edinburgh New Philosophical Journal,* conducted by Professor JAMESON. See Vol. XLVIII., p. 330 (1850). For Dr. MORTON'S Tables, see the same Journal, Vol. XLVIII., p. 262. — ED.)

What first strikes me in Dr. Morton's Tables, completely invalidates his conclusions, — he has not distinguished male from female crania. Now, as the female encephalos is, on an average, some four ounces troy less than the male, it is impossible to compare national skulls with national skulls, in respect of their capacity, unless we compare male with male, female with female heads, or, at least, know how many of either sex go to make up the national complement.

A blunder of this kind is made by Mr. Sims, in his paper and valuable correlative table of the weight of two hundred and fifty-three brains (*Medico Chirurgical Transactions*, vol. xix.). He there attacks the result of my observation (published by Dr. Monro, *Anatomy of the Brain*, etc., 1831), *that the human encephalos (brain proper and after-brain) reaches its full size by seven*

---

[1] The effect is, in fact, to increase the cerebellum. See the experiments recorded by M. Leuret, cited by Sir Benjamin Brodie, *Psychological Inquiries*, note H. — ED.

years of age, perhaps somewhat earlier. In refutation of this paradox, he slumps the male and female brains together; and then, because he finds that the average weight of his adults, among whom the males are greatly the more numerous, is larger than the average weight of his impuberals, among whom the females preponderate, he jumps at once to the conclusion, that I am wrong, and that the encephalos continues to grow, to diminish, and to grow again (!), for, I forget how long, after the period of maturity. Fortunately, along with his crotchets, he has given the detail of his weighings; and his table, when properly arranged, confutes himself, and superfluously confirms me. That is, comparing the girls with the women, and the boys with the men, it appears, from his own induction, that the cranial contents do reach the average amount, even before the age of seven.

Tiedemann (*Das Hirn des Negers, etc.*, 1837, p. 4) notes the contradiction of Sims's result and mine; but he does not solve it. The same is done and not done, by Dr. Bostock, in his *Physiology*. Tiedemann, however, remarks, that his own observations coincide with mine (p. 10); as is, indeed, evident from his Table (p. 11) " Of the cranial capacity from birth to adolescence," though, unfortunately, in that table, but in that alone, he has not discriminated the sex.

Dr. Morton's conclusion as to the comparative size of the Negro brain, is contrary to Tiedemann's larger, and to my smaller, induction, which concur in proving, that the Negro encephalos is not less than the European, and greatly larger than the Hindoo, the Ceylonese, and sundry other Asiatic brains. But the vice, already noticed, of Dr. Morton's induction, renders it, however extensive, of no cogency in the question.

Dr. Morton's method of measuring the capacity of the cranium, is, certainly, no "invention" of his friend Mr. Phillips, being, in either form, only a clumsy and unsatisfactory modification of mine. Tiedemann's millet-seed affords, likewise, only an inaccurate approximation to the truth; for seeds, as found by me, vary in weight according to the drought and moisture of the atmosphere, and are otherwise ill adapted to recover the size of the brain in the smaller animals. The physiologists who have latterly followed the method of filling the cranium, to ascertain the amount of the cranial contents, have adopted, not without perversion, one-half of my process, and altogether omitted the other. After rejecting mustard seed, which I first thought of employing, and for the reason specified, I found that pure silicious sand was the best mean of accomplishing the purpose, from its suitable ponderosity, incompressibility, equality of weight in all weathers, and tenuity. Tiedemann (p. 21) says, that he did not employ sand, " because, by its greater specific gravity, it might easily burst the cranial bones at the sutures." He would, by trial, have found that this objection is futile. The thinnest skull of the youngest infant can resist the pressure of sand, were it many times greater than it is; even Morton's lead shot proved harmless in this respect. But, while nothing could answer the purpose better than sand, still this afforded only one, and that an inadequate, mean towards an end. Another was requisite. By weighing the brain of a young and healthy convict, who was hanged, and afterwards weighing the sand which his prepared cranium contained, I determined the proportion of the specific gravity of cerebral substance (which in all ages and animals is nearly equal) to the specific gravity of the sand which was employed. I thus obtained a formula by which to recover the original weight of the encephalos in all the crania which were filled; and hereby brought brains weighed and skulls gauged into a universal relation. On the contrary, the comparisons of Tiedemann and Morton, as they stand, are limited to their own Tables. I have once and again tested the accuracy of this process, by experiment, in the lower animals, and have thus perfect confidence in the certainty of its result, be the problem to recover the weight of the encephalos from the cranium of a sparrow, or from the cranium of an elephant.

I may conclude by saying, that I have now established, apart from the proof by averages, *that the human encephalos does not increase after the age of seven, at highest.* This has been done, by measuring the heads of the same young persons from infancy to adolescence and maturity; for the slight increase in the size of the head, after seven (or six) is exhausted by the development to be allowed in the bones, muscles, integuments and hair.

(The following is an unpublished Memorandum in reference to preceding.—ED.)

March 23, 1850.

Found that the specific weight of the sand I had employed for measuring the capacity of crania, was that the sand filling 32 cubic inches, weighed 12,160 grains.

Found at the same time that the millet-seed occupying the same number of cubic inches, weighed 5665 grains.

Thus the proportion of millet-seed to sand, in specific gravity is as 1 : 2.147.

One cubic inch thus contains 380 grains sand; and 177 grains millet-seed.

(d.) ORIGINAL RESEARCHES ON THE FRONTAL SINUSES, WITH OBSERVATIONS ON THEIR BEARINGS ON THE DOGMAS OF PHRENOLOGY.

(From *The Medical Times*, May, 1845, Vol. XII., p. 159; June 7, 1845, Vol. XII., p. 177; August, 1845, Vol. XII., p. 371.—ED.)

Before proceeding to state in detail the various facts and fictions relative to the Frontal Sinus,[1] it will be proper to premise some necessary information touching the nature and relations of the sinuses themselves.

The *cruces phrenologorum* are two cavities, separated from each other by a perpendicular osseous partition, and formed between the tables of the frontal bone, in consequence of a divergence of these tables from their parallelism, as they descend to join the bones of the nose, and to build the orbits of the eye.

---

[1] It is proper to observe, that the notes, of which the following is an abstract, were written above sixteen years ago, and have not since been added to, or even looked at. They were intended for part of a treatise to be entiled, " *The Fictions of Phrenology and the Facts of Nature.*" My researches, however, particularly into the relations of the cerebellum, and the general growth of the brain, convinced me that the phrenological doctrine was wholly unworthy of a serious refutation; and should the detail of my observations on these points be ever published, it will not be done in a polemical form. My notes on the frontal sinuses having, however, been cast in relation to the phrenological hypothesis, I have not thought it necessary to take the labor of altering them, — especially as the phrenological fiction is, in truth, a complement of all possible errors on the subject of these cavities.

They are not, however, mere inorganic vacuities, arising from the recession of the bony plates; they constitute a part of the olfactory apparatus; they are lined with a membrane, a continuation of the pituitary, and this, copiously supplied with blood, secretes a lubricating mucus which is discharged by an aperture into the nose.

Various theories have been proposed to explain the mode of their formation; but it is only the fact of their existence, frequency, and degree, with which we are at present interested. In the fœtus, manifested only in rudiment, they are gradually, but in different subjects variously developed, until the age of puberty; they appear to obtain their ultimate expansion towards the age of twenty-five. They are exclusively occasioned by the elevation of the external table, which determines, in fact, the rise of the nose at the period of adolescence, by affording to the nasal bones their formation and support.

Sundry hypotheses have likewise been advanced to explain their uses, but it will be enough for us, from the universality of their appearance, to refute the singular fancy of the phrenologists, that these cavities are abnormal varieties, the product of old age or disease.

But though the sinuses are rarely if ever absent, their size in every dimension varies to infinity. Laying aside all rarer enormities, and speaking, of course, only of subjects healthy and in the prime of life, in superficial extent the sinus sometimes reaches hardly above the root of the nose, sometimes it covers nearly the whole forehead, penetrates to the bottom of the orbit, and, turning the external angle of the eyebrow, is terminated only at the junction of the frontal and parietal bones. Now, a sinus is small, or almost null upon one side, — on the other it is, perhaps, unusually large; while in no dimension are the two cavities, in general strictly correspondent, even although the outer forehead presents the most symmetrical appearance. In depth (or transverse distance between the tables) the sinus is equally inconstant, varying indeterminably in different heads, from a line or less to half an inch and more. Now, a sinus gradually disappears by a gradual convergence of its walls; now these walls, after running nearly parallel, suddenly unite. Now, the depth of the cavity decreases from centre to circumference; now the plates approximate in the middle, and recede farther from each other immediately before they ultimately unite. In one cranium, a sinus, collected within itself, is fairly rounded off; in another, it runs into meandering bays, or is subdivided into separate chambers, these varying without end in their relative capacity and extent. In depth, as well as in extent, the capacity of the sinus is thus wholly indeterminable; and no one can predict, from external observation, whether the cavity shall be a lodging scanty for a fly or roomy for a mouse.

It is an error of the grossest, that the extent of the sinus is indicated by a ridge, or crest, or blister, in the external bony plate. Such a protuberance has no certain or even probable relation to the extent, depth, or even existence, of any vacuity beneath. Over the largest cavities there is frequently no bony elevation; and women, in whose crania these protuberances are in general absent or very small, exhibit the sinuses as universally existent, and not, perhaps, proportionably less extensive than those of men. The external ridge, however prominent, is often merely a sudden outward thickening of the bony wall, which sometimes has a small, sometimes no cavity at all, beneath. Apart also from the vacuity, though over the region of the sinus, no quarter of the cranium presents greater differences in thickness, whether in different subjects or in the same head, than the plates and diploe of the frontal bone; and I have found that the bony walls themselves presented an impediment which varied inappreciably from three to thirteen lines : — "*fronti nulla fides.*"

But the "*fronti nulla fides,*" in a phrenological relation, is further illustrated by the accidents of its sinus, which all concur in manifesting the universality and possibly capacious size of that cavity.   That cavity is sometimes occupied by stony concretions, and is the seat of ulcers, cancer, polypus, and sarcoma. When acutely inflamed the sensibility of its membrane becomes painfully intense; and every one has experienced its irritation when simply affected with catarrh.   The mucosity of this membrane, the great extent and security of the caverns, joined with their patent openings into the nose, render the sinuses a convenient harbor for the nidulation, hatching, and nourishment of many parasitic animals; indeed, the motley multitude of its guests might almost tempt us to regard it as

> ———— "The cistern for all creeping things
> To knot and gender in."1

"Chacun a son Vercoquin dans la teste " — " Quemque suus vellicat Vermis " — are adages which, from the vulgarity of the literal occurrence, would seem more than metaphorically true.2   With a frequency sometimes epidemic,3 flies and insects here ascend to spawn their eggs, and maggots (other than phrenological) are bred and fostered in these genial labyrinths.   Worms, in every loathsome diversity of slime and hair, — reptiles armed with fangs, — crawlers of a hundred feet, — ejected by the score, and varying from an inch to half an ell in length, cause by their suction, burrowing, and erosion, excruciating headache, convulsions, delirium, and phrensy.   With many a nameless or nondescript visitor, the leech, the lumbricus, the ascaris, the ascarius lumbricoides, the fasciola, the eruca, the oniscus, the gordius, the forficula, the scolopendra, the scorpiodes, and even the scorpion,4 are by a hundred observers recorded as finding in these "antres vast" — these "spelunci ferarum," — a birthplace or an asylum.5   And the fact, sufficiently striking in itself, is not without signifi-

---

1 " Or keep it as a cistern for *foul toads*
   To knot and gender in."
             Othello, act. iv. sc. 8. — ED.

2 In the frontal sinuses worms and insects are *not unfrequently* found. Voigtel, *Handb. d. Pathol. Anat.* 1804, vol. i. p. 292. I quote him, *instar omnium*, as one of the best and one of the most recent authorities.

3 Forestus, *Obs. Med.*, lib. xxi. schol., 28.

4 Hollerius, *De Morb. Int.* lib. i. c. 1; Gesner, *Hist. Anat.* lib. v.; Boneti, *Sepul. Obs.*, 121; Ferretti. I here refer to the scorpion alone.

5 Long before the sinus was anatomically described by Carpi, this pathological fact had been well known to physicians. The prescription of the Delphic oracle to Demosthenes of Athens for his epilepsy shows that the Greeks were aware of the existence of worms in the frontal sinuses of the goat. (Alex. Trallian, lib. i. c. 15.) Among the Arabians, Avicenna (Fenestella lib. iii. tr. 2. c. 3) tells us it was well known to the Indian physicians, that worms were generated in the forehead immediately above the root of the nose, were frequently the cause of headaches; and Rhazes (Continet, lib. i. c. 10) observes that this was the opinion of Schare and others.   Among the moderns, my medical ignorance suggests more authorities than I can almost summon patience simply to name. The curious reader may consult, among others. Valescus de Taranta, Nicolaus de Nicolis, Vega, Marcellus Donatus, Trincavelli, Benedetti, Hollerius, Duretus, Fabricius

cance in relation to the present inquiry, that these intruders principally infest the sinuses of women, and more especially before the period of full puberty.

Such is the great and inappreciable variation of the frontal sinus and its walls, that we may well laugh at every attempt to estimate, in that quarter, the development of any part of the subjacent hemispheres, were that part larger than the largest even of the pretended phrenological organs. But this is nothing. Behind these spacious caverns, in utter ignorance of the extent, frequency, and even existence of this impediment, the phrenologists have placed, not one large, but seventeen of their very smallest organs; and have thus enabled an always insurmountable obstacle to operate in disproof of their system in its highest intensity.

By concentrating all their organs of the smallest size within the limits of the sinus, they have, in the first place, carried all those organs whose range of development was least, behind the obstacle whose range of development was greatest. Where the cranium is thinner and comparatively more equal in thickness, they have placed all the organs (those of the propensities and sentiments) which present the broadest surface, and, as they themselves assure us, varying in their development from the centre to circumference by an inch and upwards; while all the organs (those of the intellect) which have the narrowest expansion, and whose varying range of development from the centre is stated to be only a quarter of an inch (less even than the fourth of the variation of the others),[1] these have been accumulated behind an impediment whose ordinary differences are far more than sufficient to explain every gradation of the pretended development of the pretended organs from their smallest to their largest size.

In the second place, they have thus at once thrown one half of their whole organology beyond the verge of possible discovery and possible proof.

In the third place, by thus evincing that their observations on that one half had been only illusive fancies, they have afforded a criterion of the credit to be fairly accorded to their observations in relation to the other; they have shown in this, as in other parts of their doctrine, that *manifestation* and *development*

Hildanus, Zacuta Lusitanus, Hercules de Saxonia, Petrus Paulus Magnus, Angellinus, Alsarius, Cornelius Gemma, Gesner, Benevenius, Fernelius, Riolanus, Forestus, Bartholinus, Ferretti, Rolfinck, Olaus Wormius (who himself ejected a worm from the nose — was it a family affection?) Smetius (who also relates his own case), Tulpius, Heurnius, Roussæus, Monardis, Schenk, Senertus, Montuus, Borelli, Bonetus, Hertodius, Kerkringius, Joubert, Volkammer, Wohlfarth, Nannoni, Stalpert, Vander Wiel, Morgagni, Clericus, De Blegny, Salzmann, Honold, Hill, Kilgour, Littré, Maloet, Sandifort, Henkel, Harder, Stocket, Slabber, Nil Rosen, Razoux, Schaarschmidt, Quelmatz, Wolf, Blumenbach, Ploucquet, Baur, Riedlin, Zacharides, Lange, Boettcher, Welge, Wrisberg, Troia, Voigtel, Rudolphi, Bremser, etc., etc.; and of journals — *Ephem. Misc.*; *Acta et Nova Acta Cursos. Nat.*; *Commerc. Liter.*, Nov. 2; *Breslauer Sammlung*; *Duncan's Med. Journ.*; *Edinb. Med. Essays*; *London Chronicle*; *Philadelphia Transactions*; *Blumenbach's Med. Bibl.*, etc., etc.

I may here mention, that the nidulation of the œstrus ovinus (which occasionally infects the human sinus) forms a frequent epidemic among sheep and goats. The horse, the dog (and probably most other animals) are similarly afflicted.

1 Combe's *System*, etc., p. 31. "The difference in development between a large and a small organ of the propensities and some of the sentiments, amounts to an inch and upwards; and to a quarter of an inch in the organs of intellect, which are naturally smaller than the others."

are quantities which, be they what they may, can on their doctrine always be brought to an equation.

Nay, in the fourth place, as if determined to transcend themselves — to find "a lower deep beneath the lowest deep," they have even placed the least of their least organs at the very point where this, the greatest obstacle, was in its highest potency, by placing the organs of configuration, size, weight, and resistance, etc., towards the internal angle of the eyebrow, the situation where the sinus is almost uniformly deepest.[1]

Nor, in the fifth place, were they less unfortunate in the location of the rest of their minutest organs. These they arranged in a series along the upper edge of the orbit, where, independently even of the sinus, the bone varies more in thickness, from one individual and from one nation to another, than in any other part of the skull; and where these organs, hardly larger, are packed together more closely than peas 'in a pod. These pretended organs, if they even severally protruded from the brain, as they never do — if no sinus intervened — and if, instead of lying under the thickest, they were situate under the thinnest bone of the cranium; these petty organs could not, even in these circumstances, reveal their development by determining any elevation, far less any sudden elevation, of the incumbent bone. That bone they could only attenuate at the point of contact, by causing an indentation on its inner surface. This is shown by what are called the glands of Pacchioni, though erroneously. These bodies, which are often found as large as, or larger than, the organs in question, and which arise on the coronal surface of the encephalos, attenuate to the thinnest, but never elevate in the slightest, the external bony plate, though there the action of the muscles presents a smaller impediment to a partial elevation than in the superciliary region. This I have frequently taken note of.

As it is, these minute organs are expected to betray their distinct and relative developments through the obstacle of two thick bony walls, and a large intervening chamber; the varying difference of the impediment being often considerably greater than the whole diameter even of the organs themselves. The fact, however, is, that those organs are commonly, if not always, developed only in the bone, and may be cut out of the cranium, even in an impuberal skull destitute of the sinus, without trenching on the confines of the brain itself. At the external angle of the eyebrow at the organ of slumber, the bone, exclusive of any sinus, is sometimes found to exceed an inch in thickness.

How then have the phrenologists attempted to obviate the objection of the sinus?

The first organs which Gall excogitated, he placed in the region of the sinus; and it is manifest he was then in happy unacquaintance with everything connected with that obnoxious cavity. In ignorance, however, Gall was totally eclipsed by Spurzheim; who, while he seems even for a time unaware of its

---

[1] Every one who has ever examined the sinus knows that what Schulze has observed is true — "in illo angulo qui ad nares est, cavitatis fundus est, et hoc in loco fere ossium laminæ a *se invicem maxime distant.*" — (*De Cav. Cranii, Acta Phys. Med. Acad. Cæs.,* i. p. 508.)

existence as a normal occurrence, has multiplied the number and diminished the size of the organs which the sinus regularly covers. By both the founders, their organology was published before they had discovered the formidable nature of the impediment, and then it was too late to retract. They have attempted, indeed, to elude the objection; but the manner in which they have floundered on from blunder to blunder, — blunders not more inconsistent with each other, than contrary to the fact, — shows that they have never dared to open their eyes on the reality, or never dared to acknowledge their conviction of its effect. The series of fictions in relation to the frontal sinus, is, out of Phrenology, in truth, unparalleled in the history of science. These fictions are substituted for facts the simplest and most palpable in nature; they are substituted for facts contradicted by none, and proclaimed by every anatomical authority; and they are substituted for facts which, as determining the competency of phrenological proof, ought not to have been rejected without a critical refutation by the founders of that theory themselves. But while it seemed possible for the phrenologists to find only truth, they have yet continued to find nothing but error — error always at the greatest possible distance from the truth. But if they were thus so curiously wrong in matters so easy, notorious, and fundamental, how far may we not presume them to have gone astray where they were not, as it were, preserved from wandering?

The fictions by which phrenologists would obviate the objection of the frontal sinus, may, with the opposing facts, be divided into four classes; — as they relate 1°, to its *nature* and *effect;* 2°, to its *indication;* 3°, to its *frequency;* and 4°, to its *size.*

I. — NATURE AND EFFECT OF THE SINUS.

Fact. — The frontal sinus only exists in consequence of the recession of the two cranial tables from their parallelism; and as this recession is inappreciable, consequently, no indication is afforded by the external plate of the eminence or depression of the brain, in contact with the internal.

To this fact, Gall opposed the following

Fiction. — The frontal sinus interposes no impediment to the observation of cerebral development; for as the walls of this cavity are exactly parallel, the effect of the brain upon the inner table must consequently be expressed by the outer.

Authorities for the Fiction. — This fiction was originally advanced by Gall, in his Lectures, and, though never formally retracted, has not been repeated by him or Spurzheim in their works subsequently published. I therefore adduce it, not as an opinion now actually held by the phrenologists, but as a part only of that cycle of vacillation and absurdity which, in their attempts to elude the objection of the sinus, they have fruitlessly accomplished. That it was so originally advanced, is shown by the following authorities; which, as beyond the reach of readers in general, I shall not merely refer to, but translate.

The first is Froriep; and I quote from the third edition of his *Darstellung,* etc., which appeared in 1802. This author was a pupil and friend of Gall, on whose doctrine he delivered lectures, and his work is referred to by Gall, in his *Apologetic Memorial* to the Austrian Government, in that very year, as containing an authentic exposition of his opinions. — " Although at this place the frontal sinuses are found, and here constitute the vaulting of the forehead, nevertheless, Gall maintains that the brain, in consequence of the walls of the sinuses lying quite parallel (? !), is able to affect likewise the outer plate, and to determine its protuberance."— P. 61. The doubt and wonder are by the disciple himself.

The second authority is Bartels, whose *Anthropologische Bemerkungen* appeared in 1806. " In regard to the important objection drawn from the frontal sinuses, Gall's oral reply is very conformable to nature. ' Here, notwithstanding the intervening cavity in the bones, there is found a parallelism between the external and internal plates of the cranium.' "— P. 125.

Proof of the Fact.—In refutation of a fiction so ridiculous, it is unnecessary to say a single word; even the phrenologists now define the sinus by " a divergence from parallelism between the two tables of the bone."[1]

It was only in abandoning this one fiction, and from the conviction that the sinus, when it existed, did present an insuperable obstacle to observation, that the phrenologists were obliged to resort to a plurality of fictions of far inferior efficacy; for what mattered it to them, whether these cavities were indiscoverable, frequent, and capacious, if, in effect, they interposed no obstacle to an observation of the brain ?

II.—INDICATION OF THE SINUS.

Fact. — There is no correlation between the extent and existence of a sinus, and the existence and extent of any elevation, whether superciliary or glabellar; either may be present without the other, and when both are coëxistent they hold no reciprocal proportion in dimension or figure. Neither is there any form whatever of cranial development which guarantees either the absence or the presence of a subjacent cavity.

To this fact the phrenologists are unanimous in opposing the following

Fiction. — The sinus, when present, betrays its existence and extent by an irregular elevation of a peculiar character, under the appearance of a bony ridge, or crest, or blister, and is distinguished from the regular forms under which the phrenological organs are developed.

Authorities for the Fiction. — It is sufficient to adduce Gall[2] and Spurzheim,[3] followed by Combe,[4] and the phrenologists in general. In support of their position, they adduce no testimony by anatomists, — no evidence from nature.

Proof of the Fact. — All anatomical authority, as will be seen in the sequel, is opposed to the fiction, for every anatomist concurs in holding that the sinuses are rarely, if ever, absent; whereas the crests or blisters which the phrenologists regard as an index of these cavities, are comparatively of rare occurrence. It must be admitted, however, that some anatomists have rashly connected the extent of the internal sinus with the extent of the external elevation. The

1 Combe, *System*, p. 32.

2 *Anat et Phys.*, t. iv. p. 43, *et seq.;* and, in the same terms, *Sur les Fonct.*

3 *Phys. Sysi.*, p. 236; *Exam. of Object.* p. 79; *Phren.*, p. 115.

4 *Syst*, pp. 21, 35, 308.

statement of the *fact* is the result of my own observation of above three hundred crania; and any person who would in like manner interrogate nature, will find that the largest sinuses are frequently in those foreheads which present no superciliary or glabellar elevations. I may notice, that of the fifty skulls whose phrenological development was marked under the direction of Spurzheim, and of which a table is appended, the only one head where the frontal sinuses are noted, from the ridge, as present, is the male cranium No. 19; and that cranium, it will be seen, has sinuses considerably beneath even the average extent.

III.—FREQUENCY OF THE SINUS.

Fact. — The sinuses are rarely, if ever, wanting in any healthy adult head of either sex.

To this fact, the phrenologists oppose the three following inconsistent fictions:

Fiction I. — The sinuses are only to be found in some male heads, being frequently absent in men until a pretty advanced age.

Fiction II. — In women the sinuses are rarely found.

Fiction III. — The presence of the sinus is abnormal; young and adult persons have no cavities between the tables of the frontal bone — the real frontal sinuses occurring only in old persons, or after chronic insanity.

Authorities for Fiction I. — This fiction is held in terms by Gall.[1] The other phrenologists, as we shall see, are much further in the wrong. But even for this fiction they have adduced no testimony of other observers, and detailed no observations of their own.

Proof of the Fact in opposition to this Fiction. — All anatomists — there is not a single exception — concur in maintaining a doctrine diametrically opposed to the figment of the phrenologists, that the sinuses are, even in men, frequently or generally absent. Some, however, assert that the sinus in a state of health is *never* wanting; while others insist that, though *very rarely*, cases do occur in which it is actually deficient.

Of the latter opinion, Fallopius[2] holds that they are present "in all adults," except occasionally in the case of simous foreheads, an exception which Riolanus[3] and others have shown to be false. Schulze,[4] Winslow,[5] Buddeus,[6] " that they are *sometimes* absolutely wanting in cases where the cranium is *spongy* and *honeycombed*." Palfyn,[7] " that they are sometimes, though *rarely*, absent." Wittich,[8] "that they are *almost always* present, though it may be admitted that in *some very rare cases* they are wanting;" and Stalpart Van der Weil[9] relates, that " he had seen in Nuck's Museum, preserved as a *special rarity*, a cranium without a frontal sinus." Of more recent authorities, Hippolite Cloquet[10] observes, " that they are *seldom wanting;*" and the present Dr. Monro[11] found, in

1 As quoted above.
2 *Opera.*
3 *Comm. de Oss* p. 468.
4 *De Sin. Oss. Cap. Acta Phys. Med. Leop. Cæs.*, vol i. obs. 288.
5 *Expos. Anat. tr. des Oss. Secs.*, sec. 30.
6 *Obs. Anat. Sel.*, obs. 1.
7 *Ost.*, p. 105.
8 *De Olfactu*, p. 17.
9 *Obs. Rar. Cent. Post.* pars prior, obs. 4.
10 *Anat. Descr.*, seq. 153, ed. 1824.
11 *Elem. of Anat.* i. p. 134.

forty-five skulls, that while three only were without the sinus, in two of them (as observed by Schulze, Winslow and Buddeus) the cavity had merely been filled up by the deposition of a spongy bone.

Of the former opinion, which holds that the sinus is always present, I need only quote, *instar omnium*, the authority of Blumenbach,[1] whose illustrious reputation is in a peculiar manner associated with the anatomy of the human cranium, and who even celebrated his professional inauguration by a dissertation, in some respects the most elaborate we possess, on the Frontal Sinuses themselves. This anatomist cannot be persuaded, even on the observation of Highmore, Albinus, Haller, and the first Monro, that normal cases ever occur of so improbable a defect; "for," he says, "independently of the diseases afterwards to be considered, I can with difficulty admit, that healthy individuals are ever wholly destitute of the frontal sinus; on the contrary, I am convinced that these distinguished men have not applied the greatest diligence and research." In this opinion, as observed by the present Dr. Monro,[2] Blumenbach is supported by the concurrence of Bertin, Portal, Sömmering, Caldani, etc. Nor does the fiction obtain any countenance from the authors whom Blumenbach opposes. I have consulted them, and find that they are all of that class of anatomists who regard the absence of the sinus, though a possible, as a rare and memorable phenomenon. Highmore[3] founds his assertion on the single case of a female. Albinus,[4] on his own observation, and on that of other anatomists, declares that "the sinuses are *very rarely* absent." The first Monro,[5] speaking of the infinite variety in size and figure, notices as a remarkable occurrence that he had "*even seen cases* in which they were absolutely wanting." And Haller[6] is only able to establish the exception on the case of a solitary cranium.

My own experience is soon stated. Having examined above three hundred crania for the purpose of determining this point, I have been unable to find a single skull wholly destitute of a sinus. In crania, which were said to be examples of their absence, I found that the sinus still existed. In some, indeed, I found it only on one side, and in many not ascending to the point of the glabellar region, through which crania are generally cut round. The only instances of its total deficiency are, I believe, those abnormal cases in which, as observed by anatomists, the original cavity has been subsequently occupied by a pumicose deposit. Of this deposit the only examples I met with occurred in males.

Authorities for Fiction II. — This fiction also is in terms maintained by Gall.[7] Neither he nor any other phrenologist has adduced any proof of this paradox; nor is there, I believe, to be found a single authority for its support; while its refutation is involved in the refutation already given to fiction I. Nannoni,[8] indeed, says — "the opinion of Fallopius that the frontal sinuses are often wanting in women, is refuted by observation;" but Fallopius says nothing of the sort. It is also a curious circumstance, that the great majority of cases in

1 *De Sin. Front.*, p. 5.

2 *Elem.*, vol. i. p. 133.

3 *Disq. Anat.* lib iii. c. 4.

4 *Annot. Acad.*, lib. i. c. 11, et Tab. Oss.

5 *Osteol. par Sue*, p. 54.

6 *Elem. Phys.* v. p. 138.

7 As above.

8 *Trattato de Anatomia*, 1788, p. 55.

which worms, etc., have been found in the sinus, have occurred in females. This is noticed by Salzmann and Honold.[1]

My own observations, extending, as I have remarked, to above three hundred crania, confirm the doctrine of all anatomists, that in either sex, the absence of this cavity is a rare and abnormal phænomenon, if not an erroneous assertion. I may notice, by the way, the opinion of some anatomists,[2] that the sinuses are smaller in women than in men, seems to be the result of too hasty an induction; and I am inclined to think, from all I have observed, that proportionally to the less size of the female cranium, they will be found equally extensive with the male.

Authorities for Fiction III.— This fiction was maintained by Spurzheim while in this country, from one of whose publications[3] it is extracted. It is, perhaps, one of the highest flights of phrenological fancy. Nor has it failed of exciting emulation in the sect. " While a man," says Sir George Mackenzie,[4] " is in the prime of life, and healthy, and manifests the faculties of the frontal organs, such a cavity *very seldom* exists " (!) * * * * * " We have examined a GREAT MANY skulls, and *we have not yet seen* ONE having the sinus, that could be proved to have belonged to a person in the vigor of life and mind." (!!) Did Sir George ever see any skull which belonged to any " person in the vigor of life and mind" without a sinus? Did he ever see any adult skull of any person whatever in which such a cavity was not to be found?

Proof of the Fact, in opposition to this Fiction. — This fiction deserves no special answer. It is already more than sufficiently refuted under the first.

It is true, indeed, the doctrine that the frontal sinuses wax large in old age is stated in many anatomical works. I find it as far back as those of Vidus Vidius and Fallopius, but I find no ground for such a statement in nature. This I assert on a comparative examination of some thirty aged skulls. In fact, about the smallest frontal sinus that I ever saw, was in the head of a woman who was accidentally killed in her hundred and first year. (See also the appended Table.) I take this indeed for one of the instances in which anatomical authors have blindly copied each other; so that what originates in a blunder or a rash induction, ends in having, to appearance, almost catholic authority in its favor. A curious instance of this sequacity occurs to me. The common fowl has an encephalos, in proportion to its body, about as one to five hundred; that is, it has a brain less, by relation to its body, than almost any other bird or beast. Pozzi (Puetos), in a small table which he published, gave the proportion of the encephalos of the cock to its body, by a blunder, at about half its amount; that is, as one to two hundred and fifty. Haller, copying Pozzi's observation, dropt the cipher, and records in his table, the brain of the common fowl as bearing a proportion to the body of one to twenty-five. This double error was shortly copied by Cuvier, Tiedemann, and, as I have myself noticed, by some twenty other physiologists; so that, at the present moment, to dispute the fact of the common fowl having a brain more than double the size of the human, in proportion to its body, would be to maintain a paradox coun-

1 *De Verm. e. Nar Excuss.* (Haller, *Disp. Med. Pract.* i. n. 25.)

2 *Instar omnium*, v. Sömmering, *De F. C. H.* i. sec. 62.

3 *Answer to Objections against the Doctrines of Gall,* etc , p. 79.

4 *Illustrations,* p. 228.

ter to the whole stream of scientific authority. The doctrine of the larger the sinus the older the skull, stands, I believe, on no better footing. Indeed, the general opinion, that the brain contracts in the decline of life, is, to say the least of it, very doubtful, as I may take another opportunity of showing.

As to the effect of chronic insanity in amplifying the sinuses, I am a skeptic; for I have seen no such effect in the crania of madmen which I have inspected. At all events, admitting the phrenological fancy, it could have no influence on the question, for the statistics of insanity show, that there could not be above one cranium in four hundred where madness could have exerted any effect.

IV.—Extent of the Sinus.

Fact.—While the sinus is always regularly present, it, however, varies appreciably in its extent. For whilst, on the average, it affects six or seven organs, it is, however, impossible to determine whether it be confined to one or extended to some seventeen of these.

This fact is counter to three phrenological fictions:

Fiction I.—The frontal sinus is a small cavity.

Fiction II.—The frontal sinus, when present, affects only the organ of locality.

Fiction III.—When the sinus does exist, it only extends an obstacle over two organs (Size and Lower Individuality), or at most, partially affects a third (Locality).

Authorities for Fiction I.—Mr. Combe[1] maintains this fiction, that the frontal sinus "is a small cavity."

Authorities for Fiction II.—Gall[2] contemplates and speaks of the sinus as only affecting locality; and the same may be said of Spurzheim, in his earlier English works.[3]

Authorities for Fiction III.—This fiction is that into which Spurzheim modified his previous paradoxes, when, in 1825, he published his "Phrenology."[4] Mr. Combe allows that the sinus, in ordinary cases, extends over locality, as well as over size and lower individuality.

All these fictions are, however, sufficiently disproved at once by the following

Proof of the Fact.—The phrenologists term the sinus (when they allow it being) "*a small cavity.*" Compare this with the description given by impartial anatomists of these caverns. Vidus Vidius[5] characterizes them by "spatium *non parvum;*" Banhinus[6] styles them "cavitates *insignes;*" Spigelius,[7] "cavernæ satis *amplæ;*" Laurentius,[8] "sinus *amplissimi;*" Bartholinus,[9] "cavitates *amplissimæ;*" Petit,[10] "*grands* cavités irregulières;" Sabatier,[11] "cavités *larges*

---

1 *System*, p. 32.
2 As quoted above.
3 *Phys. Syst.*, p. 236, and *Exam. of Obj.* p. 79.
4 P. 115.
5 *Anat.* lib. ii. c. 2.

6 *Anat.* lib. iii. c. 5.
7 *De Fabr.* lib. ii. c. 5.
8 *Hist. Anat.* lib. ii. c. 9.
9 *Anat.* lib. iv., c. 6.
10 *Palfyn An.* ch. 1 p. 52.
11 *Anat.*

et *profondes;*" Sömmering,[1] "*cava ampla;*" Monro, *primus,*[2] "*great* cavities ;*" and his grandson,[3] "*large* cavities."

The phrenologists further assert, that in ordinary cases the frontal sinus covers only two petty organs and a half; that is, extends only a few lines beyond the root of the nose. But what teach the anatomists? "The frontal sinuses," says Portal,[4] "are much more extensive than is generally believed." "*In general,*" says Professor Walther,[5] "the sinuses ascend in height nearly to the *middle of the frontal bone.*" Patissier[6] observes, that "their extent varies to infinity, is sometimes stretched upwards to the frontal protuberances, and to the sides, as far as the external orbitar apophyses, as is seen in many crania in the cabinet of the Paris Faculty of Medicine." Bichat[7] delivers the same doctrine nearly in the same words; which, contradicted by none, is maintained by Albinus,[8] Haller,[9] Buddeus,[10] Monro *primus,*[11] and *tertius,*[12] Blumenbach,[13] Sömmering,[14] Fife,[15] Cloquet,[16] Velpeau,[17] — and, in a word, by every osteologist; for all represent these cavities as endless in their varieties, and extending not unfrequently to the outer angles of the eyebrow, and even to the parietal bones. To finish by a quotation from one of the last and best observers: "In relation," says Voigtel,[18] "to their abnormal greatness or smallness, the differences, in this respect, whether in one subject as compared with another, or in one sinus in relation to the opposite of the same skull, are of so frequent occurrence that they vary almost in every cranium. They are found so small, that their depth, measured from before backwards, is hardly more than a line; in others, on the contrary, a space of from four, five, to six lines (*i. e.* half an inch), is found between the anterior and posterior wall. Still more remarkable are the variations of these cavities, in relation to their height, as they frequently rise from the trifling height of four lines to an inch at the glabella." M. Velpeau, speaking of this great and indeterminable extent of the sinus, adds: "this disposition must prevent us from being able to judge of the volume of the anterior parts of the brain by the exterior of the cranium;"—an observation sufficiently obvious in relation to Phrenology, and previously made by the present Dr. Monro.[19]

On the sinus and its extent, two anatomists only, as far as I am aware, have given an articulate account of their inductions — Schulze, and the present Dr. Monro.

The former,[20] who wrote a distinct treatise *On the Cavities or Sinuses of the Cranial Bones,* examined only ten skulls, and does not detail the dimensions of each several sinus. After describing these cavities, which he says "plerisque hominibus formantur," he adds, that "when of a middling size they hardly extend towards the temples beyond the centre of the eye, where the orbital

1 *De Fab.* i. sec. 35.
2 *Osteol. par Sue,* p. 54.
3 *Elements.*
4 *Anat. Med.* i. pp. 102, 238.
5 *Abh. v. trokn. Kn.,* p. 133.
6 *Dict. des Sc. Med.,* t. 51, p. 372.
7 *Anat. Desc.,* c. p. 102.
8 *Annot. Acad.,* lib. i. c. ii. (?)
9 *Elem.* v. p. 138.
10 *Obs. Anat.,* sec. 8.

11 *Osteol. par. Sue,* p. 54.
12 *Elements.*
13 *Anat.*
14 *Anat. Descr.* t. 1, sec. 153, edit. 3.
15 *Traitté d'Anat. Chir.*
16 *De Sin. Fr.,* p. 3.
17 *De Fab.* c. ii. t. sec. 94.
18 *Path. anat.* i. p. 289.
19 *Elem.* p. 133.
20 *Loc. cit.*

vault is highest; and if you measure their height, from the insertion of the nasal bones, you will find it equal to an inch. Such is the condition of this cavity when moderate. That there are sinuses far greater, was taught me by another inspection of a cranium. In this case, the vacuity on the right did not pass the middle of the orbit, but that on the left stretched so far that it only ended over the external angle of the eyebrow, forming a cavity of at least two inches in breadth. Its depth was such as easily to admit the least joint of the middle finger. Its height, measured from the root of the nose on the left side, exceeded two inches, on the right it was a little less; the left sinus was, however, shallower than the right. On the left side I have said the cavity terminated over the external angle of the orbit. From this place, a bony wall ran towards the middle of the *crista Galli*, and thus separated the sinus into a posterior and an anterior cavity. The posterior extended so far towards the temples, that it reached the place where the frontal and sincipetal bones and the processes of the sphenoidal meet. It covered the whole arch of the orbit, so that all was here seen hollow," etc.

After describing sundry appearances which the sinuses exhibited in another skull, he observes: "It was my fortune to see and to obtain possession of *one* cranium in which of neither of the frontal nor the sphenoidal cavities was there any vestige whatsoever. In this specimen the bones in which these vacuities are situated were thicker than usual, and more cavernous;" an observation, as we have seen, made by other anatomists. However subversive of the phrenological statement, it will soon be seen that Schulze has understated the usual extent of the impediment.

Dr. Monro,[1] after mentioning that there "were forty-five crania of adults in the Anatomical Museum, cut with a view to exhibit the different sizes and forms of the frontal sinuses," says: "I measured the breadth or distance across the forehead; the height or distance upwards from the transverse suture, where it divides the frontal bones and bones of the nose; and also the depth of the frontal sinuses; in nine different skulls in which these sinuses were large." Omitting the table, it is sufficient to say, that in these crania the average is as follows:— *Breadth*, within a trifle of *three inches; height, one inch and five-tenths; depth*, above *one inch*. Here the depth seems not merely the distance between the external and internal tables, but the horizontal distance from the glabella to the posterior wall of the sinus. These nine crania thus yield an average, little larger than an indifferent induction; and though the sinuses are stated to have been large, the skulls appear to have been selected by Dr. Monro, not so much in consequence of that circumstance, as because they were so cut as to afford the means of measuring the cavity in its three dimensions.

By the kindness of Dr. Monro and Mr. Mackenzie, I was permitted to examine all the crania in the public anatomical museum, and in the private collection of the Professor; many were, for the first time, laid open for my inspection. I was thus enabled to institute an impartial induction. A random measurement of above thirty perfect crania (laying aside three skulls of old persons, in which the cavity of the sinus was almost entirely occupied by a pumicose deposit) gave the following average result: breadth, two inches four-tenths;

1 *Elements*, i., p. 134.

height, one inch and nearly five-tenths; depth (taken like Dr. Monro), rather more than eight-tenths of an inch. What in this induction was probably accidental, the sinuses of the female crania exhibited an average, in all the three dimensions, almost absolutely equal to that of the male. The relative size was consequently greater.

Before the sinuses of the fifty crania of Dr. Spurzheim's collection (of which I am immediately to speak) were, with the sanction of Professor Jameson, laid open upon one side, I had measured their three dimensions by the probe. This certainly could not ascertain their full extent, as, among other impediments, the probe is arrested by the septa, which so frequently subdivide each sinus into lesser chambers; but the labor was not to be undergone a second time, especially as the proportional extent of these cavities is by relation to the phrenological organs articulately exhibited in the table. As it was, the average obtained by the probe is as follows:—In the thirty-six male crania (one could not be measured by the probe), the breadth was two inches and nearly four-tenths; the height, one inch and nearly three-tenths; the depth, rather more than one inch. In the twelve female crania (here, also, one could not be measured by the probe), the breadth was one inch, and rather more than nine-tenths; the height, nearly one inch; the depth, within a trifle of nine-tenths.

I should notice that in all these measurements, the thickness of the external plate is included in the depth.

So true is the observation of Portal, that the "*frontal sinuses are much more extensive than is generally believed.*"

The collection of fifty crania, of which the average size of the frontal sinuses has been given above, and of which a detailed table of the impediment interposed by these cavities to phrenological observation now follows, was sent by M. Royer, of the Jardin des Plantes (probably by mistake) to the Royal Museum of Natural History in Edinburgh; the skulls, taken from the catacombs of Paris, having, under Dr. Spurzheim's inspection, been selected to illustrate the development of the various phrenological organs, which development is diligently marked on the several crania.

Thus, though I have it in my power to afford a greatly more extensive table, the table of these fifty crania is, for the present purpose, sufficient. For—

1°, They constitute a complete and definite collection;

2°, A collection authoritative in all points against the phrenologists;

3°, One to which it can be objected by none, that it affords only a selected or partial induction in a question touching the frontal sinus;

4°, It is a collection patent to the examination of the whole world;

5°, In all the skulls a sinus has on one side been laid open to its full extent; the capacity of both is thus easily ascertained; and, at the same time with the size of the cavity, the thickness and salience of the external frontal table remains apparent.

Table exhibiting the variable extent and unappreciable impediment, in a phrenological relation, of the Frontal Sinuses; in a collection of fifty crania, selected, and their development marked, under the direction of Dr. Spurzheim:

Number of Skull, as here arranged, according to sex and age.	Number of Skull, according to Spurzheim's fortuitous order.	Sex, as marked by Spurzheim.	Age, as inferred from teeth and other criteria.	Extent of the Sinuses, as entirely or nearly *covering* (†), or as more or less *affecting* (*), the pretended phrenological organs, according to the late and latest numeration (1).																
				20	21	22	2 19	24	1 19	23	25	L. 29	26	W. 29	27	30	31	28	32	7
				xxiii	xxiv	xxv	xxii	xxvii	xxx	xxvi	xxix	L. xxxiii	xxxi	W. xxxiii	xxviii	xxxiv	xxxv	xxxii	xx	ix
1	viii	Male.	Young.	†	†	†	†													
2	xii			†	†	†	†	*												
3	xiii			†	†	†	†													
4	xvi			†	†	†	†													
5	xxvi			†	†	†	†	†	†	†	†	†	†	†			*	*		
6	xxxiv			†	†	†	†	†	†			†								
7	xxxvi			†	†	†	†	†	*	*	*	†	*							
8	xxxvii			†	†	†	†	†	*			†								
9	xli			†	†	†	†	†												
10	xxxv			†	†	†	†		†	†	†	†	†	†	†	*	*	*		*?
11	xxxix	Young or Middle-aged.		†	†	†	†	*		*		*								
12	ii	Middle-aged.		†	†	†	†	†		†	*	*								
13	iv			†	†	†	†	†		†				*?						
14	v			†	†	†	†	*	*?	†		*								
15	vi			†	†	†	†	*	*?	†		*								
16	vii			†	†	†	†	†				*								
17	ix			†	†	†	†	†	*	*		*								
18	x			†	†	†	†	*	*	†		*								
19	xiv			†	†	†	†	†		†		*								
20	xvii			†	†	†	†	†	*	*		*								
21	xxi			†	†	†	†	*	*	†		*								
22	xxiii			†	†	†	†		*			*								
23	xxv			†	†	†	†	†	†	†	*	*	*							
24	xxvii			†	†	†	†		†	†	*	*	*							
25	xxviii			†	†	†	†			†		*								
26	xxix			†	†	†	†	*		†	*	*								
27	xxx			†	†	†	†	*			*	*	†							
28	xlii			†	†	†	†	*	*			*								
29	xliii			†	†	†	†	*		*		*		*			*?			
30	xliv			†	†	†	†	*		*		*		*						
31	xlv			†	†	†	†	*		†		*								
32	xlvii			†	†	†	†	*	*	*		*	†							
33	xlviii														*	*	*			
34	xxii	Middle-aged, or Old.		†	†	†	†	*												
35	xlix			*	*	†	†	*												
36	xxxiii			†	†	*	†	*												
37	l	Male.	Old.	†	†	†	*	*												
38	xv	Female.	{ Young. }	†	†	†	†	†		*										
39	xxxii									†	*	*								
40	xxxviii		Young, or Middle-aged.	†	†	†	*													
41	xl	Male?	Middle-aged.	†	†	†	†													
42	xviii			†	†	†	†													
43	xix			†	†	†	†	†	†											
44	xxiv			†	†	†	†	*	†	†										
45	xxxi			†	†	†	†	*	†	†	*	*	*							
46	xl			†	†	†	†	*	*			*	†							
47	xlvi			†	†	†	†	*	*	†			†			*				
48	l	Female.	Middle-aged, or Old.	†	†	†	*													
49	xx			†	†	†	*	*		†										
50	iii		Old.	†	†	†														

(1) The organs denoted by these numbers:—ix. 7, Constructiveness; xx. 32, Mirthfulness or Wit; xxii. 19 (2), Individuality, Lower Individuality; xxiii. 20, Configuration, Figure; xxiv. 21, Size; xxv. 22, Weight, Resistance; xxvi. 23, Color; xxvii. 24, Locality; xxviii. 26, Calculation, Number; xxix. 25, Order; xxx. 19, (1) Eventuality, Upper Individuality; xxxi. 26, Time; xxxii. 28, Melody, Tune; xxxviii. 29, Language — this organ Gall divides in two, to wit, into the organ of Language and the organ of Words; xxxiv. 30, Comparison; xxxv. 31, Causality. The order of the numbers in this table was taken from that of a more extensive and general table: so that whilst here xx. 32, has not been affected at all, there it was affected more frequently than ix. 7.

In these circumstances it is to be observed —

In the first place, that, as already noticed, while the developments of all the crania have been carefully marked, the presence of the frontal sinuses has been signalized only in one skull (the male No. 19, xiv.), in which they are, however, greatly below even the average.

In the second place, that the extent of the sinus varies indeterminably from an affection of one to an affection of sixteen organs.

In the third place, in this induction of thirty-seven male and thirteen female crania, the average proportional extent of the sinuses is somewhat less in the female than in the male skulls; the sinus in the former covering 4.4, and affecting 1.2 organs; in the latter covering 5, and affecting 2.1 organs. This induction is, however, too limited, more especially in the female crania, to afford a determination of the point, even were it not at variance with other and more extensive observations.

In the fourth place, the male crania exhibit at once the largest and the smallest sinuses. The largest male sinus covers 12, and affects 4; while the largest female sinus covers 7, and affects 3 organs; whereas, while the smallest male sinus affects only 1, the smallest female sinus covers 2 organs.

In the fifth place, so far from supporting the phrenological assertion that the sinuses are only found, or only found in size, in the crania of the old, this their collection tends to prove the very reverse; for here we find about the smallest sinuses in the oldest heads.

III. PERCEPTION. — FRAGMENTS. — (See p. 286.)

(Written in connection with proposed MEMOIR OF MR. STEWART. On Desk, May 1856; written Autumn 1855.—ED.)

There are three considerations which seem to have been principally effective in promoting the theory of a Mediate or Representative Perception, and by *perception* is meant the apprehension, through sense, of external things. These might operate severally or together.

The first is, that such a hypothesis is necessary to render possible the perception of distant objects. It was taken as granted that certain material realities, (as a sun, stars, etc.), not immediately present to sense, were cognized in a perceptive act. These realities could not be known immediately, or in themselves, unless known as they existed; and they existed only as they existed in their place in space. If, therefore, the perceptive mind did not sally out to them, (which, with the exception of one or two theorists, was scouted as an impossible hypothesis), an immediate perception behooved to be abandoned, and the sensitive cognition we have of them must be vicarious; that is, not of the realities themselves, as present to our organs, and presented to apprehension, but of something different from the realities eternally existing, through which, however, they are mediately represented. Various theories in regard to the nature of this mediate or vicarious object may be entertained; but these may be overpassed. This first consideration alone was principally effectual among materialists: on them the second had no influence.

A second consideration was the opposite and apparently inconsistent nature of the object and subject of cognition; for here the reality to be known is material, whereas the mind knowing is immaterial; while it was long generally believed, that what is known must be of an analogous essence (the same or similar) to what knows. In consequence of this persuasion, it was deemed impossible that the immaterial, unextended mind could apprehend in itself, as extended, a material reality. To explain the fact of sensitive perception, it was therefore supposed requisite to attenuate — to immaterialize the immediate object of perception, by dividing the object known from the reality existing. Perception thus became a vicarious or mediate cognition, in which the corporeal was said to be represented by the incorporeal.

PERCEPTION — POSITIVE RESULT.

1. We perceive only through the senses.
2. The senses are corporeal instruments, — parts of our bodily organism.
3. We are, therefore, percipient only through, or by means of, the body. In other words, material and external things are to us only not as zero, inasmuch as they are apprehended by the mind in their relation with the material organ which it animates, and with which it is united.
4. An external existence, and an organ of sense, as both material, can stand in relation only according to the laws of matter. According to these laws, things related, — connected, must act and be acted on; but a thing can act only where it is. Therefore the thing perceived, and the percipient organ, must meet in place, — must be contiguous. The consequence of this doctrine is a complete simplification of the theory of perception, and a return to the most ancient speculation on the point. All sensible cognition is, in a certain acceptation, reduced to Touch, and this is the very conclusion maintained by the venerable authority of Democritus.

According to this doctrine, it is erroneous, in the first place, to affirm that we are percipient of distant, etc., objects.

It is erroneous, in the second place, to say that we perceive external things in themselves, in the signification that we perceive them as existing in their own nature, and not in relation to the living organ. The real, the total, the only object perceived has, as a relative, two phases. It may be described either as the idiopathic affection of the sense (i. e. the sense in relation to an external reality), or as the quality of a thing actually determining such or such an affection of the sentient organ (i. e. an external reality in correlation to the sense).

A corollary of the same doctrine is, that what have been denominated the Primary Qualities of body, are only perceived through the Secondary; in fact, Perception Proper cannot be realized except through Sensation Proper. But synchronous.

The object of perception is an affection, not of the mind as apart from body, not of the body as apart from mind, but of the composite formed by union of the two; that is, of the animated or living organism (Aristotle).

In the process of perception there is required both an act of the conscious mind and a passion of the affected body; the one without the other is null. Galen has, therefore, well said, "Sensitive perception is not a mere passive or affective change, but the discrimination of an affective change."[1] (Aristotle,—judgment.)

Perception supposes Consciousness, and Consciousness supposes Memory and Judgment; for, abstract Consciousness, and there is no Perception; abstract Memory, or Judgment, and Consciousness is abolished. (Hobbes,—Memory; Aristotle,—Judgment of Sense.) Memory, Recollection; for change is necessary to Consciousness, and change is only to be apprehended through the faculty of Remembrance. Hobbes has, therefore, truly said of Perception,—"Sentire semper idem, et non sentire, ad idem recident."[2] But there could be no discriminative apprehension, supposing always memory without an act whereby difference was affirmed, or sameness denied; that is, without an act of Judgment. Aristotle[3] is, therefore, right in making Perception a Judgment.

IV. LAWS OF THOUGHT.—(See p. 527.)

(Written in connection with proposed MEMOIR OF MR. STEWART. On Desk, May 1856; written Autumn, 1855.—ED.)

The doctrine of Contradiction, or of Contradictories (ἀξίωμα τῆς ἀντιφάσεως), that Affirmation or Negation is a necessity of thought, whilst Affirmation and Negation are incompatible, is developed into three sides or phases, each of which implies both the others,—phases which may obtain, and actually have received, severally, the name of *Law*, *Principle*, or *Axiom*. Neglecting the historical order in which these were scientifically named and articulately developed, they are:

1°, The Law, Principle, or Axiom, of *Identity*, which, in regard to the same thing, immediately or directly enjoins the affirmation of it with itself, and mediately or indirectly prohibits its negation: (*A is A*.)

2°, The Law, etc., of *Contradiction* (properly *Non-contradiction*), which, in regard to contradictories, explicitly enjoining their reciprocal negation, implicitly prohibits their reciprocal affirmation: (*A is not Not-A*.) In other words, contradictories are thought as existences incompatible at the same time,—as at once mutually exclusive.

3°, The Law, etc., of *Excluded Middle* or *Third*, which declares that, whilst contradictories are only two, everything, if explicitly thought, must be thought as of these either the one or the other: (*A is either B or Not-B*.) In different terms:— Affirmation and negation of the same thing, in the same respect, have no conceivable medium; whilst anything actually may, and virtually must, be

---

[1] See *Reid's Works*, p. 878.—ED.   [2] See *Ibid*.—ED.   [3] See *Ibid*.—ED.

either affirmed or denied of anything. In other words: — Every predicate is true or false of every subject; or, contradictories are thought as incompossible, but, at the same time, the one or the other as necessary. The argument from Contradiction is omnipotent within its sphere, but that sphere is narrow. It has the following limitations:

1°, It is negative, not positive; it may refute, but it is incompetent to establish. It may show what is not, but never of itself, what is. It is exclusively Logical or Formal, not Metaphysical or real; it proceeds on a necessity of thought, but never issues in an Ontology or knowledge of existence.

2°, It is dependent; to act it presupposes a counter-proposition to act from.

3°, It is explicative, not ampliative; it analyzes what is given, but does not originate information, or add anything, through itself, to our stock of knowledge.

4°, But, what is its principal defect, it is partial, not thorough-going. It leaves many of the most important problems of our knowledge out of its determination; and is, therefore, all too narrow in its application as a universal criterion or instrument of judgment. For were we left, in our reasonings, to a dependence on the principle of Contradiction, we should be unable competently to attempt any argument with regard to some of the most interesting and important questions. For there are many problems in the philosophy of mind where the solution necessarily lies between what are, to us, the one or the other of two counter, and, therefore, incompatible alternatives, neither of which are we able to conceive as possible, but of which, by the very conditions of thought, we are compelled to acknowledge that the one or the other cannot but be; and it is as supplying this deficiency, that what has been called the argument from Common Sense becomes principally useful.

The principle of Contradiction, or rather of Non-contradiction, appears in two forms, and each of these has a different application.

In the first place (what may be called the *Logical* application), it declares that, of Contradictories, two only are possible in thought; and that of these alternatives the one or the other, exclusively, is thought as necessarily true. This phasis of the law is unilateral; for it is with a consciousness or cognition that the one contradictory is necessarily true, and the other contradictory necessarily false. This one logical phasis of the law is well known, and has been fully developed.

In the second place (what may be called the *Psychological* application), while it necessarily declares that, of Contradictories, both cannot, but one must, be, still bilaterally admits that we may be unable positively to think the possibility of either alternative. This, the psychological phasis of the law, is comparatively unknown, and has been generally neglected. Thus, *Existence* we cannot but think, — cannot but attribute in thought; nevertheless we can actually conceive neither of these contradictory alternatives, — the absolute commencement, the infinite non-commencement, of being. As it is with Existence, so is it with *Time*. We cannot think time beginning; we cannot think time not beginning. So also with *Space*. We are unable to conceive an existence out of space; yet we are equally unable to compass the notion of illimitable or infinite space. Our capacity of thought is thus peremptorily proved incompetent to what we necessarily think about; for, whilst what we think about must be thought to Exist, — to exist in Time, — to exist in Space, — we are unable to realize the counter-notions of Existence commencing or not commencing, whether in Time or in Space. And thus, whilst Existence, Time, and Space, are the indispensable conditions, forms, or categories of actual thought, still are we unable to conceive either of the counter-alternatives, in one or other of which we cannot but admit that they exist. These and such like impotencies of positive thought have, however, as I have stated, been strangely overlooked.

V. THE CONDITIONED.

(a.) KANT'S ANALYSIS OF JUDGMENTS. — (See page 532.)

(Fragment from Early Papers, probably before 1836. — ED.)

Kant analyzed judgments (*a priori*) into *analytic* or *identical* [or *explicative*], and *synthetical*, or [*ampliative, non-identical*]. Great fame from this. But he omitted a third kind, — those that the mind is compelled to form by a law of its nature, but which can neither be reduced to analytic judgments, because they cannot be subordinated to the law of Contradiction, nor to synthetical, because they do not seem to spring from a positive power of mind, but only arise from the inability of the mind to conceive the contrary.

In Analytic judgments — (principle of contradiction) — we conceive the one alternative as necessary, and the other as impossible. In Synthetic judgments, we conceive the affirmative as necessary, but not [its negation as self-contradictory].

Would it not be better to make the synthetic of two kinds — a positive and negative? Had Kant tried whether his synthetic judgments *a priori* were positive or negative, he would have reached the law of the Conditioned, which would have given a totally new aspect to his Critique, — simplified, abolished the distinction of *Verstand* and *Vernunft*, which only positive and negative, (at least as a faculty conceiving the Unconditioned, and left it only, as with Jacobi, the Noῦς, the *locus principiorum*, — the faculty, — revelation, of the primitive facts or faiths of consciousness, — the Common Sense of Reid), the distinction of *Begriffe* and *Ideen*, and have reduced his whole Categories and Ideas to the category of the Conditioned and its subordinates.

* * * * * * * * *

(1853, November). — There are three degrees or epochs which we must distinguish in philosophical speculation touching the Necessary.

In the first, which we may call the Aristotelic or Platonico-Aristotelic, the Necessary was regarded, if not exclusively, principally and primarily, in an objective relation; — at least the objective and subjective were not discriminated; and it was defined that of which the existence of the opposite, — contrary, — is impossible — what could not but be.

In the second, which we may call the Leibnitzian or Leibnitzio-Kantian, the Necessary was regarded primarily in a subjective respect, and it was defined that of which the thought of the opposite, — contrary, — is impossible — what we cannot but think. It was taken for granted, that what we cannot think cannot be, and what we must think, must be; and from hence there was also inferred, without qualification, that this subjective necessity affords the discriminating criterion of our native or *a priori* cognitions, — notions and judgments.

But a third discrimination was requisite; for the necessity of thought behooved *to* be again distinguished into two kinds. — (See *Discussions*, 2d edit. Addenda.)

(*b*) CONTRADICTIONS PROVING THE PSYCHOLOGICAL THEORY OF THE CONDITIONED. — (July 1852.)

1. Finite cannot comprehend, contain the Infinite. — Yet an inch or minute, say, are finites, and are divisible *ad infinitum*, that is, their terminated division incogitable.

2. Infinite cannot be terminated or begun. — Yet eternity *ab ante* ends *now;* and eternity *a post* begins *now.* — So apply to Space.

3. There cannot be two infinite maxima. — Yet eternity *ab ante* and *a post* are two infinite maxima of time.

4. Infinite maximum if cut into two, the halves cannot be each infinite, for nothing can be greater than infinite, and thus they could not be parts; nor finite, for thus two finite halves would make an infinite whole.

5. What contains infinite extensions, protensions, intensions, [*quantities*] cannot be passed through, — come to an end. An inch, a minute, a degree contains these; *ergo*, etc. Take a minute. This contains an infinitude of protended quantities, which must follow one after another; but an infinite series of successive protensions can, *ex termino*, never be ended; *ergo*, etc.

6. An infinite maximum cannot but be all inclusive. Time *ab ante* and *a post* infinite and exclusive of each other; *ergo*.

7. An infinite number of quantities must make up either an infinite or a finite whole. I. The former. — But an inch, a minute, a degree, contain each an infinite number of quantities; therefore, an inch, a minute, a degree, are each infinite wholes; which is absurd. II. The latter. — An infinite number of quantities would thus make up a finite quantity; which is equally absurd.

8. If we take a finite quantity (as an inch, a minute, a degree), it would appear equally that there are, and that there are not, an equal number of quantities between these and a greatest, and between these and a least.[1]

9. An absolutely quickest motion is that which passes from one point to another in space in a minimum of time. But a quickest motion from one point to another, say a mile distance, and from one to another, say a million million of miles, is thought the same; which is absurd.

10. A wheel turned with quickest motion; if a spoke be prolonged, it will

[1] See Boscovich on Stay, *Philosophia Recentior*, i. p. 284, edit. 1755.

therefore be moved by a motion quicker than the quickest. The same may be shown using the rim and the nave.

11. Contradictory are Boscovich Points, which occupy space, and are inextended.[1] Dynamism, therefore, inconceivable. *E contra,*

12. Atomism also inconceivable; for this supposes atoms, — minima extended but indivisible.

13. A quantity, say a foot, has an infinity of parts. Any part of this quantity, say an inch, has also an infinity. But one infinity is not larger than another. Therefore, an inch is equal to a foot.[2]

14. If two divaricating lines are produced *ad infinitum* from a point where they form an acute angle, like a pyramid, the base will be infinite and, at the same time, not infinite; 1°, Because terminated by two points; and, 2°, Because shorter than the sides;[3] 3°, Base could not be drawn, because sides infinitely long.[4]

15. An atom, as existent, must be able to be turned round. But if turned round, it must have a right and left hand, etc., and these its signs must change their place; therefore, be extended.[5]

(c.) PHILOSOPHY OF ABSOLUTE — DISTINCTIONS OF MODE OF REACHING IT.

I. Some carry the Absolute by assault, — by a single leap, — place themselves at once in the absolute, — take it as a datum; others climb to it by degrees, — mount to the absolute from the conditioned, — as a result.

Former — Plotinus, Schelling; latter — Hegel, Cousin, are examples.

II. Some place cognition of Absolute above, and in opposition to consciousness, — conception, — reflection, the conditions of which are difference, plurality, and, in a word, condition, limitation. (Plotinus, Schelling.) Others do not, but reach it through consciousness, etc. — the consciousness of difference, contrast, etc.; giving, when sifted, a cognition of identity (absolute). (Hegel, Cousin.)

III. Some, to realize a cognition of Absolute, abolish the logical laws of Contradiction and Excluded Middle (as Cusa, Schelling, Hegel. Plotinus is not explicit.). Others do not (as Cousin).

IV. Some explicitly hold, that, as the Absolute is absolutely one, cognition and existence must coincide; — to know the absolute is to be the absolute, — to know the absolute is to be God. Others do not explicitly assert this, but only hold the impersonality of reason, — a certain union with God; in holding that we are conscious of eternal truths as in the divine mind. (Augustin, Malebranche, Price, Cousin.)

---

1 See Boscovich, i. p. 304.

2 See Tellez, quoted by F. Bonæ Spei, [*Physica*, pars i. tract. iii. disp. i. dub. 4, p. 154, edit. 1652. — ED.]

3 See Bonæ Spei, *Physica*, [pars. i. tract. iii. disp. i. dub. 2, p. 139. — ED.]

4 See Carleton, [*Philosophia Universa, Auctore Thoma Comptono Carleton, Antverpiæ*, p. 392, 1649. — ED.]

5 See Kant in Krug's *Metaphysik*, p. 193.

V. Some carry up man into the Deity (as Schelling). Others bring down the Deity to man; in whose philosophy the latter is the highest manifestation of the former, — man apex of Deity.

I*. Some think Absolute can be known as an object of knowledge, — a notion of absolute competent; others that to know the absolute we must *be* the absolute (Schelling, Plotinus?).

* Some [hold] that unconditioned is to be believed, not known; others that it can be known.[1]

(d.) Sir W. Hamilton to Mr. Henry Calderwood.

Cordale, 26th Sept., 1854.

My Dear Sir: I received a few days ago your *Philosophy of the Infinite*, and beg leave to return you my best thanks, both for the present of the book itself, and for the courteous manner in which my opinions are therein controverted. The ingenuity with which your views are maintained, does great credit to your metaphysical ability; and, however I may differ from them, it gives me great satisfaction to recognize the independence of thought by which they are distinguished, and to acknowledge the candid spirit in which you have written.

At the same time, I regret that my doctrines (briefly as they are promulgated on this abstract subject) have been, now again, so much mistaken, more especially in their theological relations. In fact, it seems to me, that your admissions would, if adequately developed, result in establishing the very opinions which I maintain, and which you so earnestly set yourself to controvert.

In general, I do not think that you have taken sufficiently into account the following circumstances:

1°, That the Infinite which I contemplate is considered only as *in thought;* the Infinite beyond thought being, it may be, an object of belief, but not of knowledge. This consideration obviates many of your objections.

2°, That the sphere of our belief is much more extensive than the sphere of our knowledge; and, therefore, when I deny that the Infinite can by us be *known*, I am far from denying that by us it is, must, and ought to be, *believed.* This I have indeed anxiously evinced, both by reasoning and authority. When, therefore, you maintain, that in denying to man any positive cognizance of the Infinite, I virtually extenuate his belief in the infinitude of Deity, I must hold you to be wholly wrong, in respect both of my opinion, and of the theological dogma itself.

Assuredly, I maintain that an infinite God cannot be by us (positively) comprehended. But the Scriptures, and all theologians worthy of the name, assert the same. Some indeed of the latter, and, among them, some of the most illustrious Fathers, go the length of asserting, that "an understood God is no God at all," and that, "if we maintain God to be as we can think that he is, we blaspheme." Hence the assertion of Augustin; "Deum potius ignorantia quam scientia attingi."

---

[1] Cf. *Discussions*, p. 12 *et seq.* — Ed.

3°, That there is a fundamental difference between *The Infinite* (τὸ"Ἐν καὶ Πᾶν,) and a relation to which we may apply the term *infinite*. Thus, Time and Space must be excluded from the supposed notion of *The Infinite;* for The Infinite, if postively thought it could be, must be thought as under neither Space nor Time.

But I would remark specially on some essential points of your doctrine; · and these I shall take up without order, as they present themselves to my recollection.

You maintain (*passim*) that thought, conception, knowledge, is and must be finite, whilst the *object of thought*, etc., may be infinite. This appears to me to be erroneous, and even contradictory. An existence can only be an object of thought, conception, knowledge, inasmuch as it is an object thought, conceived, known; as such only does it form a constituent of the circle of thought, conception, knowledge. A thing may be partly known, conceived, thought, partly unknown, etc. But that part of it only which is thought, can be an object of thought, etc.; whereas the part of it not thought, etc., is, as far as thought, etc., is concerned, only tantamount to zero. The infinite, therefore, in this point of view, can be *no object* of thought, etc.; for nothing can be more self-repugnant than the assertion, that we know the infinite through a finite notion, or have a finite knowledge of an infinite object of knowledge.

But you assert (*passim*) that we have a knowledge, a notion of the infinite; at the same time asserting (*passim*) that this knowledge or notion is " inadequate,"— " partial,"— " imperfect,"— " limited,"— " not in all its extent,"— " incomplete,"— " only to some extent,"— " in a certain sense,"— " indistinct," etc., etc.

Now, in the first place, this assertion is in contradiction of what you also maintain, that " the infinite is one and indivisible " (pp. 25, 26, 226); that is that having *no parts*, it cannot be *partially* known. But, in the second place, this also subverts the possibility of conceiving, of knowing, the Infinite; for as partial, inadequate, not in all its extent, etc., our conception includes *some part* only of the object supposed infinite, and *does not include* the rest. Our knowledge is, therefore, by your own account, limited and finite; consequently, you implicitly admit that we have no knowledge, at least no positive knowledge, of the infinite.

Neither can I surmise how we should ever come to know that the object thus partially conceived *is* in itself infinite; seeing that we are denied the power of knowing it *as* infinite, that is, not partially, not inadequately, not in some parts only of its extent, etc., but totally, adequately, in its whole extent, etc.; in other words, under the criteria compatible with the supposition of infinitude. For, as you truly observe, " everything *short* of the infinite is limited" (p. 223).

Again, as stated, you describe the infinite to be " one and indivisible." But, to conceive as inseparable into *parts*, an entity which, not excluding, in fact includes, the worlds of mind and matter, is for the human intellect utterly improbable. And does not the infinite contain the finite? If it does, then it contains what has parts, and is divisible; if it does not, then is it exclusive: the finite is out of the infinite: and the infinite is conditioned, limited, restricted,—*finite*.

You controvert (p. 233, *alibi*) my assertion, that to conceive a thing *in relation*, is, *ipso facto*, to conceive it as finite, and you maintain that the relative is not incompatible with infinity, unless it be also restrictive. But restrictive I hold the relative always to be, and, therefore, incompatible with *The Infinite* in the more proper signification of the term, though infinity, in a looser signification, may be applied to it. My reasons for this are the following: A relation is always a *particular* point of view; consequently, the things thought as relative and correlative are always thought restrictively, in so far as the thought of the one discriminates and excludes the other, and likewise all things not conceived in the same special or relative point of view. Thus, if we think of Socrates and Xanthippe under the matrimonial relation, not only do the thoughts of Socrates and Xanthippe exclude each other as separate existences, and, *pro tanto*, therefore are restrictive; but thinking of Socrates *as husband*, this excludes our conception of him as citizen, etc., etc. Or, to take an example from higher relatives: what is thought as the *object* excludes what is viewed as the *subject*, of thought; and hence the necessity which compelled Schelling and other absolutists to place *The Absolute* in the indifference of subject and object, of knowledge and existence. Again: we conceive God in the relation of Creator, and in so far as we merely conceive Him as Creator, we do not conceive him as unconditioned, as infinite; for there are many other relations of the Deity under which we may conceive Him, but which are not included in the relation of Creator. In so far, therefore, as we conceive God only in this relation, our conception of Him is manifestly restrictive. Further, the created universe is, and you assert it to be (pp. 175, 180, 229), finite. The creation is, therefore, an act, of however great, of finite power; and the Creator is thus thought only in a finite capacity. God, in his own nature, is infinite; but we do not positively think Him as infinite, in thinking Him under the relation of the Creator of a finite creation. Finally, let us suppose the created universe (which you do not) to be infinite; in that case we should be reduced to the dilemma of asserting *two* infinities, which is contradictory, or of asserting the supernal absurdity, that God the Creator is finite, and the universe created by Him is infinite.

In connection with this, you expressly deny Space and Time to be restrictions, whilst you admit them to be necessary conditions of thought (p. 103—117). I hold them both to be restrictive.

In the first place, take *Space*, or Extension. Now what is conceived as extended, does it not exclude the unextended? Does it not include body, to the exclusion of mind? *Pro tanto*, therefore, space is a limitation, a restriction.

In the same way *Time*,—is it not restrictive in excluding the Deity, who must be held to exist above or beyond the condition of time or succession? This, His existence, we must believe as real, though we cannot positively think, conceive, understand its possibility. Time, like Space, thus involving limitation, both must be excluded, as has been done by Schelling, from the sphere,—from the supposed notion of the infinito-absolute,—

"Whose kingdom is where Time and Space are not."

You ask, if we had not a positive notion of the thing, how such a name as

Infinite could be introduced into language (p. 58). The answer to this is easy. In the first place, the word Infinite (*infinitum,* ἄπειρον) is negative, expressing the negation of limits; and I believe that this its negative character holds good in all languages. In the second place, the question is idle; for we have many words which, more directly and obtrusively expressing a negation of thought, are extant in every language, as *incogitable, unthinkable, incomprehensible, inconceivable, unimaginable, nonsense,* etc., etc.; whilst the term *infinite* directly denotes only the negation of limits, and only indirectly a negation of thought.

I may here notice what you animadvert on (p. 60, 76), the application of the term *notion,* etc., to what cannot be positively conceived. At best this is merely a verbal objection against an abuse of language; but I hardly think it valid. The term *notion* can, I think, be not improperly applied to what we are unable positively to construe in thought, and which we understand only by a problematic supposition. *A round square* cannot certainly be represented; but, understanding what is hypothetically required, the union of the attribute *round* with the attribute *square,* I may surely say, " the notion round-square is a representative impossibility."

You misrepresent, in truth reverse, my doctrine, in saying (p. 169) that I hold " God *cannot* act as a cause, for the unconditioned cannot exist in relation." I never denied, or dreamed of denying, that the Deity, though infinite, though unconditioned, *could* act in a finite relation. I only denied, in opposition to Cousin, that so He *must.* True it is, indeed, that in thinking God under relation, we do not *then* think Him, even negatively, as infinite; and in general, whilst always believing Him to be infinite, we are ever unable to construe to our minds, — positively to conceive, — His attribute itself of infinity. This is " unsearchable.". This is " past finding out." What I have said as to the infinite being (subjectively) inconceivable, does not at all derogate from our belief of its (objective) reality. In fact, the main scope of my speculation is to show articulately that we *must believe,* as actual, much that we are unable (positively) *to conceive,* as even possible.

I should have wished to make some special observations on your seventh chapter, in relation to Causality; for I think your objections to my theory of causation might be easily obviated. Assuredly that theory applies equally to mind and matter. These, however, I must omit. But what can be more contradictory than your assertion " that creation is conceived, and is by us conceivable, only as *the origin of existence,* by the fiat of the Deity ? " (p. 156.) Was the *Deity not existent before the creation ?* or did the *non-existent Deity at the creation originate existence ?* I do not dream of imputing to you such absurdities. But you must excuse me in saying, that there is infinitely less ground to wrest my language (as you seem to do) to the assertion of a material Pantheism, than to suppose you guilty of them.

Before concluding, I may notice your denial (p. 108) of my statement, that time present is conceivable only as a line in which the past and future limit each other. As a position of time (time is a protensive quantity), the present, if positively conceived, must have a certain duration, and that duration can be measured and stated. Now, does the present endure for an hour, a minute, a second, or for any part of a second ? If you state what length of duration it contains, you are lost. So true is the observation of St. Augustin.

These are but a few specimens of the mode in which I think your objections to my theory of the infinite may be met. But, however scanty and imperfect, I have tired myself in their dictation, and must, therefore, now leave them, without addition or improvement, to your candid consideration.—Believe me, my dear sir, very truly yours,

(Signed)   W. HAMILTON.

(e.) Doctrine of Relation.

(Written in connection with proposed Memoir of Mr. Stewart. On Desk, May 1856; written Autumn 1855. — Ed.)

I. Every Relation (*Quod esse habet ad aliud,—unius accidens,— σχέσις,— respectivum,—ad aliquid,—ad aliud,—relatum,—comparatum,—sociale*) supposes at least two things, or, as they are called, terms thought as relative; that is, thought to exist only as thought to exist in reference to each other: in other words, Relatives (*τὰ πρός τι σχέσιν ἔχοντα,—relativa sunt, quorum esse est ad aliud*) are, from the very notion of relativity, necessarily plural. Hence Aristotle's definition is not of Relation, but of things relative. Indeed, a relation of one term,—a relative not referred,—not related (*πρός τι οὐ πρός τι*), is an overt contradiction,—a proclaimed absurdity. The Absolute (the one, the not-relative,—not-plural) is diametrically opposed to the relative,—these mutual negatives.

II. A relation is a unifying act,—a synthesis; but it is likewise an antithesis. For even when it results in denoting agreement, it necessarily proceeds through a thought of difference; and thus relatives, however they may in reality coincide, are always mentally contrasted. If it be allowed, even the relation of identity,—of the sameness of a thing to itself, in the formula $A = A$, involves the discrimination and opposition of the two terms. Accordingly, in the process of a relation, there is no conjunction of a plurality in the unity of a single notion, as in a process of generalization; for in the relation there is always a division, always an antithesis of the several connected and constituent notions.

III. Thus relatives are severally discriminated; inasmuch as the one is specially *what is referred*, the other specially *what is referred to*. The former, opening the relation, retains the generic name of *the Relative* (and is sometimes called exclusively *the Subject*); whilst the latter, closing it, is denominated *the Correlative* (and to this the word *Term* is not unfrequently restricted). Accordingly, even the relation of the thing to itself in the affirmation of identity, distinguishes a Relative and a Correlative. Thus in the judgment, "God is just," God is first posited as subject and Relative, and then enounced as predicate and Correlative.

IV. The Relative and the Correlative are mutually referred, and can always be reciprocated or converted (*πρὸς ἀντιστρέφοντα λέγεσθαι, reciproce, ad convertentiam dici*); that is, we can view in thought the Relative as the Correlative, and the Correlative as the Relative. Thus, if we think the Father as the Relative of the Son as Correlative, we can also think the Son as Relative of the Father as Correlative. But, in point of fact, there are here always, more or less obtrusive, two different, though not independent, relations: for the relation, in which the Father is relative and the Son correlative, is that of Paternity; while the relation, in which the Son is relative and the Father correlative, is that of Filiation; relations, however, which mutually imply each other. Thus, also, Cause and Effect may be either Relative or Correlative. But where Cause is made the Relative, the relation is properly styled *Causation;* whereas we ought to denominate it *Effectuation,* when the Effect becomes the relative term. To speak of the relation of Knowledge; we have here Subject and Object, either of which we may consider as the Relative or as the Correlative. But, in rigid accuracy, under Knowledge, we ought to distinguish two reciprocal relations, — the relation of *knowing,* and the relation of *being known.* In the former, the Subject (that *known as knowing*) is the Relative, the Object (that *known as being known*) is the Correlative; in the latter, the terms are just reversed.

V. The Relatives (the things relative and correlative), as relative, always coëxist in nature (ἅμα τῇ φύσει), and coëxist in thought (ἅμα τῇ γνώσει). To speak now only of the latter simultaneity; — we cannot conceive, we cannot know, we cannot define the one relative, without, *pro tanto,* conceiving, knowing, defining also the other. Relative and Correlative are each thought through the other; so that in enouncing Relativity as a condition of the thinkable, in other words, that thought is only of the Relative; this is tantamount to saying that we think one thing only as we think two things mutually and at once; which again is equivalent to a declaration that the Absolute (the non-Relative) is for us incogitable, and even incognizable.

In these conditions of Relativity, all philosophers are at one; so far there is among them no difference or dispute.

Note.—No part of philosophy has been more fully and more accurately developed, or rather no part of philosophy is more determinately certain than the doctrine of Relation; insomuch that in this, so far as we are concerned, there is no discrepancy of opinion among philosophers. The only variation among them is merely verbal; some giving a more or less extensive meaning to the words employed in the nomenclature. For whilst all agree in calling by the generic name of *relative* both what are specially denominated the *Relative* and the *Correlative;* some limit the expression *Term* (*terminus*), to the latter, and others the expression, *Subject* (*subjectum*) to the former; whilst the greater number of recent philosophers (and these I follow) apply these expressions indifferently to both Relative and Correlative.

VI. CAUSATION.—LIBERTY AND NECESSITY.

(See p. 558.)

(a.) CAUSATION.

/Written in connection with proposed MEMOIR OF MR. STEWART. On Desk, May 1856; written Autumn 1855. — ED.)

My doctrine of Causality is accused of neglecting the phenomenon of *change,* and of ignoring the attribute of *power.* This objection precisely reverses the fact. Causation is by me proclaimed to be identical with change, — change of power into act ("omnia mutantur"); change, however, only of appearance, — we being unable to realize in thought either existence (substance) apart from phænomena, or existence absolutely commencing, or absolutely terminating. And specially as to power; power is the property of an existent something (for it is thought only as the essential attribute of what is able so or so to exist); power is, consequently, the correlative of existence, and a necessary supposition, in this theory, of causation. Here the cause, or rather the complement of causes, is nothing but powers capable of producing the effect; and the effect is only that now existing actually, which previously existed potentially, or in the causes. We must, in truth, define: — a cause, the power of effectuating a change; and an effect, a change actually caused. Let us make the experiment.

And, first, of Causation at its highest extremity: Try to think creation. Now, all that we can here do is to think the existence of a creative power, — a Fiat; which creation (unextended or mental, extended or material) must be thought by us as the evolution, the incomprehensible evolution, by the exertion or putting forth of God's attribute of productive power, into energy. This Divine power must always be supposed as preëxistent. Creation excludes the commencement of being: for it implies creative God as prior; and the existence of God is the negation of nonentity.[1] We cannot, indeed, compass the thought of what has no commencement; we cannot, therefore, positively conceive (what, however, we firmly believe) the eternity of a Self-existent, — of God: but still less can we think, or tolerate the supposition, of something springing out of nothing, — of an absolute commencement of being.

Again, to think Causation at its lowest extremity: As it is with Creation, so is it with Annihilation. The thought of both supposes a Deity and Divine power; for as the one is only the creative power of God exerted or put forth into act, so the other is only the withdrawal of that exerted energy into power. We are able to think no complete annihilation, — no absolute ending of existence ("omnia mutantur, nihil interit"); as we cannot think a creation from nothing, in the sense of an origination of being without a previously existing Creator, — a prior creative power. Causation is, therefore, necessarily *within* existence; for we cannot think of a change either from non-existence to existence, or from existence to non-existence. The thought of power, therefore, always precedes that of creation, and follows that of annihilation; and as the thought of power always involves the thought of existence, therefore, in so far as the thoughts of creation and annihilation go, the necessity of thinking a cause for these changes exemplifies the facts, — that change is only from one form of existence to another, and that causation is simply our inability to think an absolute commencement or an absolute termination of being. The sum of being (actual and potential) now extant in the mental and material worlds, together with that in their Creator, and the sum of being (actual and potential) in the Creator alone, before and after these worlds existed, is necessarily

---

[1] I have seen an attempt at the correction of my theory of creation, in which the Deity is made to originate or create existence. That is, either existence is created by an existent God, on which alternative the definition is stultified by self-contradiction; or existence is created by a non-existent God, — an alternative, if deliberately held, at once absurd and impious.

thought as precisely the same. Take the instance of a neutral salt. This is an effect, the product of various causes, — and all are necessarily powers. We have here, 1°, An acid involving its power (active or passive) of combining with the alkali; 2°, An alkali, involving its power (active or passive) of combining with the acid; 3° (Since, as the chemical brocard has it, "corpora non agunt nisi soluta"), a fluid, say water, with its power of dissolving and holding in solution the acid and alkali; 4°, a translative power, say the human hand, capable of bringing the acid, the alkali, and the water, into correlation, or within the sphere of mutual affinity. These (and they might be subdivided) are all causes of the effect; for, abstract any one, and the salt is not produced. It wants a coëfficient cause, and the concurrence of every cause is requisite for an effect.[1]

But all the causes or coëfficient powers being brought into reciprocal relation, the salt is the result; for an effect is nothing but the actual union of its constituent entities, — concauses or coëfficient powers. In thought, causes and effects are thus, *pro tanto*, tautological: an effect always preëxisted potentially in its causes; and causes always continue actually to exist in their effects. There is a change of form, but we are compelled to think an identity in the elements of existence:

"Omnia mutantur; nihil interit."

And we might add, — "Nihil incipit;" for a creative power must always be conceived as preëxistent.

Mutation, Causation, Effectuation, are only the same thought in different respects; they may, therefore, be regarded as virtually terms convertible. Every change is an effect; every effect is a change. An effect is in truth just a change of power into act; every effect being an actualization of the potential.

But what is now considered as the cause may at another time be viewed as the effect; and *vice versâ*. Thus, we can extract the acid or the alkali, as effect, out of the salt, as principal concause; and the square which, as effect, is made up of two triangles in conjunction, may be viewed as cause when cut into these figures. In opposite views, Addition and Multiplication, Subtraction and Division, may be regarded as causes, or as effects.

Power is an attribute or property of existence, but not coëxtensive with it: for we may suppose (negatively think) things to exist which have no capacity of change, no capacity of appearing.

Creation is the existing subsequently in act of what previously existed in power; annihilation, on the contrary, is the subsequent existence in power of what previously existed in act.

Except the first and last causal agencies (and these, as Divine operations, are by us incomprehensible), every other is conceived also as an effect; therefore, every event is, in different relations, a power and an act. Considered as

---

[1] See above, lect. iii. p. 42. — ED.

a cause, it is a power,—a power to coöperate an effect. Considered as an effect, it is an act,—an act coöperated by causes.

Change (cause and effect) must be *within existence;* it must be merely of phænomenal existence. Since change can be for us only as it appears to us, —only as it is known by us; and we cannot know, we cannot even think a change either from non-existence to existence, or from existence to non-existence. The change must be from substance to substance; but substances, apart from phænomena, are (positively) inconceivable, as phænomena are (positively) inconceivable apart from substances. For thought requires as its condition the correlatives both of an appearing and of something that appears.

And here I must observe that we are unable to think the Divine Attributes as in themselves they are, we cannot think God without impiety, unless we also implicity confess our impotence to think Him worthily; and if we should assert that God is as we think or can affirm Him to be, we actually blaspheme. For the Deity is adequately inconceivable, is adequately ineffable; since human thought and human language are equally incompetent to His Infinities.

(*b.*) THE QUESTION OF LIBERTY AND NECESSITY AS VIEWED BY THE SCOTTISH SCHOOL.

(Written in connection with proposed MEMOIR OF MR. STEWART. On Desk, May 1856; written Autumn 1855.—ED.)

The Scottish School of Philosophy has much merit in regard to the problem of the Morality of human actions; but its success in the polemic which it has waged in this respect, consists rather in having intrenched the position maintained behind the common sense or natural convictions of mankind, than in having rendered the problem and the thesis adopted intelligible to the philosopher. This, indeed, could not be accomplished. It would, therefore, have been better to show articulately that Liberty and Necessity are both incomprehensible, as both beyond the limits of legitimate thought; but that though the Free-agency of Man cannot be speculatively proved, so neither can it be speculatively disproved; while we may claim for it as a *fact* of real actuality though of inconceivable possibility, the testimony of consciousness,—that we are morally free, as we are morally accountable for our actions. In this manner, the whole question of free and bond-will is in theory abolished, leaving, however, practically our Liberty, and all the moral interests of man entire.

Mr. Stewart seems, indeed, disposed to acknowledge, against Reid, that, in certain respects, the problem is beyond the capacity of human thought, and to admit that all reasoning for, as all reasoning against, our liberty, is on that account invalid. Thus in reference to the arguments against human free-agency, drawn from the prescience of the Deity, he says, "In reviewing the arguments that have been advanced on the opposite sides of this question, I have hitherto taken no notice of those which the Necessitarians have founded on the prescience of the Deity, because I do not think these fairly applicable to the subject; inasmuch as they draw an inference from what is altogether *placed beyond the reach of our faculties,* against a fact for which every man *has the evidence of his own consciousness.*"[1]

(c.) LIBERTY AND NECESSITY.

(Written in connection with proposed MEMOIR OF MR. STEWART. On Desk, May 1856; written Autumn 1855. — ED.)

The question of Liberty and Necessity may be dealt with in two ways.

I. The opposing parties may endeavor to show each that his thesis is distinct, intelligible, and consistent, whereas that the anti-thesis of his opponent is indistinct, unintelligible, and contradictory.

II. An opposing party may endeavor to show that the thesis of either side is unthinkable, and thus abolish logically the whole problem, as, on both alternatives, beyond the limits of human thought; it being, however, open to him to argue that, though unthinkable, his thesis is not annihilated, there being contradictory opposites, one of which must consequently be held as true, though we be unable to think the possibility of either opposite; whilst he may be able to appeal to a direct or indirect declaration of our conscious nature in favor of the alternative which he maintains.

The former of these modes of arguing has been the one exclusively employed in this controversy. The Libertarian, indeed, has often endeavored to strengthen his position by calling in a deliverance of consciousness; the Necessitarian, on the contrary, has no such deliverance to appeal to, and he has only attempted, at best, to deprive his adversary of this ground of argumentation by denying the fact or extenuating the authority of the deliverance.

The latter of these lines of argumentation, I may also observe, was, I believe, for the first time employed, or, at least, for the first time legitimately employed, by myself: for Kant could not consistently defer to the authority of Reason in its practical relations, after having shown that Reason in its speculative operations resulted only in a complexus of antilogies. On the contrary, I have endeavored to show that Reason, — that Consciousness within its legitimate limits, is always veracious, — that in generating its antinomies, Kant's Reason transcended its limits, violated its laws, — that Consciousness, in fact, is never spontaneously false, and that Reason is only self-contradictory when driven beyond its legitimate bounds. We are, therefore, warranted to rely on a deliverance of Consciousness, when that deliverance is *that* a thing is, though we may be unable to think *how* it can be.

[1] *Active and Moral Powers,* vol. i. *Works,* vol. vi. p. 396.

INDEX.

ABEL, case of dreaming mentioned by, 458.

ABERCROMBIE (Dr. John), referred to on somnambulism, 223; on cases of mental latency, 236.

ABERCROMBY, 513.

ABSOLUTE, distinctions of mode of reaching it, 683-4, 684-8. *See* Regulative Faculty.

ABSTRACTION, *see* Attention and Elaborative Faculty.

ABSTRACTIVE knowledge, *see* Knowledge.

ACADEMICAL honors, principles which should regulate, 635 *et seq.*

ACCIDENT, what, 106.

ACT, what, 124. *See* Energy.

ACTIVE, its defects as a philosophical term, 79, 128.

ACTIVITY, always conjoined with passivity in creation, 216. *See* Consciousness.

ACTUAL, distinctions of from potential, 124. *See* Existence.

ADDISON, quoted to the effect that the mental faculties are not independent existences, 268.

ÆSCHYLUS, quoted, 244.

ÆGIDIUS, 292; on Touch, 376.

AGRIPPA (Cornelius), 53.

Αἴσθησις, ambiguous, 562. *See* Feeling.

AKENSIDE, quoted on Fear, 607.

ALBERTUS Magnus, 176, 292; on Touch, 376.

ALCHINDUS, 291.

ALCMÆON, 352.

ALENSIS, or Alesius, Alex., 176, 292, 337.

ALEXANDRIA, school of, 75.

ALFARABI, 213.

ALGAZEL, first explicitly maintained the hypothesis of Assistance or Occasional Causes, 210, 542; his surname, 542. *See* Causality.

ALISON, Rev. A., noticed on Association, 612.

AMMONIUS Hermiæ, referred to on definition of philosophy, 36, 81; quoted on mental powers, 271; quoted on Breadth and Depth of notions, 472.

ANALYSIS, what, 69; the necessary condition of philosophy, *ib.*; *see* Philosophy; relations of analysis and synthesis, 69, 70; nature of

scientific, 70 *et seq.*; three rules of psychological, 282; critical, its sphere, 403, *see* Critical Method; in extension and comprehension, the analysis of the one corresponds to the synthesis of the other, 510; confusion among philosophers from not having observed this, 511; synthesis in Greek logicians is equivalent to analysis of modern philosophers, 511; Platonic doctrine of division called Analytical, 511.

ANALYTIC judgment, what, 681.

ANAMNESTIC, *see* Mnemonic.

ANAXAGORAS, 352.

ANCILLON (Frederick), 50, 177, 263; quoted on difficulty of psychological study, 265, 266, 428; quoted on Reminiscence, 442; quoted on Imagination, 455; on the same, 457; *see* Representative Faculty; 459-60, *see ibid.*

ANDRE, Père, 442; his treatise *Sur le Beau.* 594.

ANNIHILATION, as conceived by us, 552.

APHRODISIENSIS, Alex. 81, 176; quoted on mental powers, 271, 291; quoted on Aristotle's doctrine of species, 293; on Touch, 376; on contrariety and simultaneity, 434.

APOLLINARIS, on Touch, 376.

APPETENCY, term objectionable as common designation both of will and desire, 128.

AQUINAS, 9, 43; maintained that the mind can attend to only a single object at once, 176; his doctrine of mental powers, 272, 292, 316

ARBUTHNOT, quoted, 115.

ARCHIMEDES, 180.

ARGENTINAS, 292.

ARISTOTLE, 9, 14, 26, 32; quoted on definition of philosophy, 35, 37; referred to on the same, 36, 45; quoted on the *quæstiones scibiles*, 39; *see* Empirical, 40; quoted on the end of philosophy, 42, 45, 46, 48, 49, 50, 52; quoted on Wonder as a cause of philosophy, 55, 59, 63, 66, 75, 79, 83; *see* Art; made the consideration of the soul part of the philosophy of nature, 89, 95, 98, 106, 110; dis-

term *faculty* not properly applicable to, 277, 512; designations of, 512–14; nomenclature of the cognitions due to, 514; importance of the distinction of native and adventitious knowledge, *ib.*; criterion of necessity first enounced by Leibnitz, 405, 515; partially anticipated by Descartes, 515; and by Spinoza, 516; the enouncement of this criterion a great step in the science of mind, *ib.*; Leibnitz quoted on criterion of necessity, 516—20; Reid discriminated native from adventitious knowledge by the same criterion, independently of Leibnitz, 520; Reid quoted to this effect, 520–22; Hume apprehended the distinction 522; Kant, the first who fully applied the criterion, 405, 522; philosophers divided in regard to what cognitions ought to be classed as ultimate, and what as modifications of the ultimate, 523; Reid and Stewart have been censured for their too easy admission of first principles, *ib.*; Reid quoted in self-vindication, *ib.*; Stewart quoted to the same effect, *ib.*; that Reid and Stewart offer no systematic deduction of the primary elements of human reason, is no valid ground for disparaging their labors, 524; philosophers have not yet established the principle on which our ultimate cognitions are to be classified and reduced to system, 525; necessity, either Positive or Negative, as it results from a power or from a powerlessness of mind, 525 *et seq.*; positive necessity illustrated by the act of Perception, 525; by an arithmetical example, *ib.*; negative necessity not recognized by philosophers, 526; illustrated, *ib. et seq.*; principles referred to in the discussion, *ib. et seq.*;—1. The law of Non-Contradiction, *ib.*; 2. The law of Excluded Middle, *ib.*; grand law of thought,—That the Conceivable lies between two contradictory extremes, 527 *et seq.*; this called the law of the Conditioned, 530; established and illustrated by reference to Space, 1°, as a maximum, 527; space either bounded or not bounded, *ib.*; space as absolutely bounded inconceivable, *ib.*; space as infinitely unbounded inconceivable, 528; though both these contradictory alternatives are inconceivable, one or other is yet necessary, *ib.*; space, 2°. as a minimum, *ib., et seq.*, an absolute minimum of space, and its infinite divisibility, alike inconceivable, *ib.*; further illustration by reference to Time, 1° as a maximum, 529 *et seq.*; 1. time *a parte ante*, as an absolute whole, inconceivable, *ib.*; 2. time as an infinite regress, inconceivable, *ib.*; 3. time as an infinite progress, inconceivable, *ib.*; time, 2°, as a minimum, *ib., et seq.*; the moment of time either divisible to infinity, or composed of certain absolutely smallest parts,—both alternatives in-

conceivable, *ib*; the counter opinion to the principle of the Conditioned, founded on vagueness and confusion, 530; sum of the author's doctrine, *ib.*; the author's doctrine both the one true and the only orthodox inference, 531; to assert that the infinite can be thought, but only inadequately thought, is contradictory, *ib.*; law of the Conditioned in its applications, 532 *et seq.*, *see* Causality; contradictions proving the psychological theory of the Conditioned, 529.

REID, 51; defines mind *a posteriori*, 110; wrongly identifies hypothesis and theory, 120; wrong in his criticism of Locke on power, 122 *et seq.*; gives no special account of Consciousness, 131, 139; does not allow that all immediate knowledge is consciousness, 140; quoted on consciousness, 144–5; holds consciousness to be a special faculty, 145, *see* Consciousness; quoted on Imagination and Conception, 147-8; on Memory, 149–50; his doctrine, that memory is an immediate knowledge of the past, false and contradictory, 151—3; the same holds true of his doctrine of Conception as an immediate knowledge of the distant, 153; contradistinguished Consciousness from Perception, 154; principal merit accorded to, as a philosopher, 155; his doctrine of consciousness shown to be wrong 156 *et seq.*; from the principle that the knowledge of opposites is one, 156-7; it is suicidal of his doctrine of an immediate knowledge of the external world, 157 *et seq.*; it involves a general absurdity, 158; it destroys the distinction of consciousness itself, *ib.*; supposition on which some of the self-contradictions of Reid's doctrine may be avoided, 159; but untenable, 160; maintains that Attention and Reflection are acts not contained in consciousness, *ib.*; wrong in his censure of Locke's use of the term Reflection, 161; and in saying that Reflection is employed in relation to objects of sense, 162; quoted on Attention, 164; inclines to the doctrine that God is the only real agent in the universe, 210; his theory of habit, mechanical, 247, refuted by Stewart, 248; referred to on our Mental Identity, 260; his doctrine of Perception adopted by Schulze, and opposed by him to the Hypothetical Realism of Kant, 643; his fundamental doctrine compared with that of Kant, 647; did not distinguish the two forms of the Representative Hypothesis in Perception, 288—99; his historical view of the theories of Perception criticised, 289 *et seq.*, *see* Perception; place of the doctrine of Perception in his philosophy, 297; was Reid a Natural Realist? 312 *et seq.*; his view of the distinction of Intuitive and Representative knowledge obscure, 313; and hence his philosophy in-

THE END.

Printed in the United Kingdom
by Lightning Source UK Ltd.
117269UKS00001B/3